Environmental and Natural Resource Economics

Seventh Edition

TOM TIETENBERG

Colby College

PEARSON

Addison
Wesley

Boston San Francisco New York
London Toronto Sydney Tokyo Singapore Madrid
Mexico City Munich Paris Cape Town Hong Kong Montreal

To Florence M. and Harry H. Tietenberg,
who provided me with a healthy
environment conducive
to development.

Publisher: Daryl Fox
Editor-in-Chief: Denise Clinton
Acquisitions Editor: Roxanne Hoch
Editorial Assistant: Julia Boyles
Senior Production Supervisor: Katherine Watson
Executive Marketing Manager: Stephen Frail
Design Manager: Gina Hagen-Kolenda, Charles Spaulding
Associate Media Producer: Bridget Page
Production Coordination and Electronic Page Makeup: Elm Street Publishing
    Services, Inc.
Manufacturing Buyer: Carol Melville
Cover Image: John Warden/AlaskaStock.com.

Library of Congress Cataloging-in-Publication Data

Tietenberg, Thomas H.
    Environmental and natural resource economics / Tom Tietenberg.—7th ed.
        p. cm.
    Includes index.
    ISBN 0-321-30504-3 (alk. paper)
    1. Environmental economics. 2. Environmental policy. 3. Natural resources—Government policy. 4. Raw materials—Government policy. I. Title.

HC79.E5T525 2006
333.7—dc22   2005015019

1 2 3 4 5 6 7 8 9—CRW—09 08 07 06 05

Contents

CHAPTER 3   Valuing the Environment: Methods   33

CHAPTER 9   Recyclable Resources: Minerals, Paper, Glass, and More   181

CHAPTER 10 Replenishable but Depletable Resources: Water   206

CHAPTER 13   Renewable Common-Pool Resources: Fisheries and Other Species   286

CHAPTER 14   Generalized Resource Scarcity   316

CHAPTER 21 **Environmental Justice**   503

When I wrote the First Edition of *Environmental and Natural Resource Economics* in 1981, environmental and natural resource economics was a well-developed, but underutilized, field. Its impact on environmental policy could most generously be described as "emerging." That is no longer the case. Economics has become an indispensable part of the education of anyone dealing with environmental policy. As *Our Common Future* put it in 1987, "Economics and ecology bind us in ever-tightening networks. . . . Economics and ecology must be completely integrated in decision-making and law-making processes."[1]

Signs of maturation abound. A number of journals are now devoted either exclusively or mostly to the topics covered in this book. One, *Ecological Economics*, is a journal dedicated to bringing economists and ecologists closer together in a common search for appropriate solutions for environmental challenges. Interested readers can also find advanced work in the field in *Land Economics, Journal of Environmental Economics and Management, Environmental and Resource Economics, Environment and Development Economics Resource and Energy Economics*, and *Natural Resources Journal*, among others.

New resources for student research projects have been made available in response to the growing popularity of the field. Original research on topics related to international environmental and natural resource issues was formerly very difficult for students because of the paucity of data. A number of good sources now exist, including *World Resources* (Washington, DC: Oxford University Press, published annually), which has an extensive data appendix, and *OECD Environmental Data* (Paris: Organization for Economic Cooperation and Development, published periodically).

A few Internet sources will be mentioned because they are so closely related to the focus of environmental and natural resource economics. Two discussion lists that involve material covered by this book are RES-ECON and ECOL-ECON. The former is a more academically inclined list focusing on problems related to natural resource management, whereas the latter is a more wide-ranging discussion list dealing with sustainable development.

Services on the Internet are changing so rapidly that some of this information may become obsolete. One way to keep up to date on the various Web options is to visit my Web site at http://www.colby.edu/~thtieten/. That site has links to other sites, including the site sponsored by the Association of Environmental and Resource Economists, which has information on graduate programs in this field.

Environmental and Natural Resource Economics attempts to bring those who are beginning the study of environmental and natural resource economics close to the

---

[1]The World Commission on Environment and Development, *Our Common Future* (New York: Oxford University Press, 1987): 27, 37.

frontiers of knowledge. Although it is designed to be accessible to students who have completed only a two-semester introductory course in economics or a one-semester introductory microeconomics course, it has been successfully used in several institutions in lower-level and upper-level undergraduate courses as well as lower-level graduate courses.

Intertemporal optimization is handled within a discrete-time, mathematical programming framework, and all mathematics, other than simple algebra, are relegated to chapter appendixes. Graphs and numerical examples are used to provide an intuitive understanding of the principles suggested by the math and the reasons for their validity. In the Seventh Edition, I have tried to retain the strengths that seem particularly valued by users, while expanding the number of applications of economic principles, clarifying some of the more difficult arguments, and updating the material to include the very latest global developments.

The structure and topical coverage of this book facilitate its use in a variety of contexts. For a survey course in environmental and natural resource economics, all chapters are appropriate, though many of us have found that the book contains somewhat more material than can be covered adequately in a quarter or even a semester. This surplus of material provides flexibility for the instructor to choose those topics that best fit his or her course design. A one-term course in natural resource economics could be based on Chapters 1 to 14 and 22 to 24. A brief introduction to environmental economics could be added by including Chapter 15. A single-term course in environmental economics could be structured around Chapters 1 to 5 and 15 to 21. Chapter 7 could be added if a brief introduction to natural economics seems desirable.

New to This Edition

This edition contains a series of completely new debates on controversies in the field and many new application examples, all described below. In addition to containing a greatly expanded glossary (over 60 new terms), new art work, and completely updated data, the text references over 100 new studies, covers a host of new topics, and expands on several previously introduced topics.

Debate Boxes

Textbooks often ignore the controversies in the field, but they shouldn't. Debates about methods or interpretations are a vital source of information about the state of the art.

This edition has added a number of these debates:

1. Ecological Economics Versus Environmental Economics
2. Should Humans Place an Economic Value on the Environment?
3. Is Valuing Human Life Immoral?
4. How Should the United States Deal with the Vulnerability of Its Imported Oil?
5. What Is the Value of Water?

6. Should Water Systems Be Privatized?
7. Should Genetically Modified Organisms Be Banned?
8. Should Developing Countries Rely on Market-Based Instruments to Control Pollution?
9. Should the New Source Review Program Be Changed?
10. The Particulate and Smog Ambient Standard Controversy
11. Should Carbon Sequestration Be Credited?
12. Is Global Greenhouse Gas Trading Immoral?
13. CAFE Standards or Fuel Taxes?
14. Jobs Versus the Environment: Which Side Is Right?
15. Should an Importing Country Be Able to Use Trade Restrictions to Influence Harmful Fishing Practices in an Exporting Nation?

New Example Boxes

One of the keys to the success of this text has been its rich use of examples to demonstrate how economic principles are used in actual environmental policy situations. These examples serve to ground the relevant principles in a familiar and hopefully interesting context.

This edition adds many new examples:

1. Valuing Ecological Services from Preserved Tropical Forests
2. The Alaskan Permanent Fund
3. Hubbert's Peak
4. Tradable Energy Certificates: The Texas Experience
5. Do Mandatory Labels Correct Externalities?
6. Are Consumers Willing to Pay a Premium for GMO-Free Foods?
7. The Swedish Nitrogen Charge
8. The Irish Bag Levy
9. Controlling SO_2 Emissions by Command-and-Control in Germany
10. Technology Diffusion in the Chlorine Manufacturing Sector
11. The European Emissions Trading System (EU ETS)
12. Modifying Car Insurance as an Environmental Strategy
13. Effluent Trading and the Cost of Reducing Waste Treatment Discharges into Long Island Sound
14. Does Offering Compensation for Accepting an Environmental Risk Always Increase the Willingness to Accept the Risk?
15. Has NAFTA Improved the Environment in Mexico?

New Topics Covered

One of the consequences of the popularity of both ecological economics and environmental economics is the proliferation of research in the field. This research brings new subjects under investigation and uses new techniques to generate the insights.

This edition responds to these trends by incorporating several new topics:

- Conjoint Analysis
- Boserup Hypothesis
- Downward Spiral Hypothesis
- Human Rights and the Environment
- AIDS and the Demographic Transition
- The Emerging Role for LNG
- Tradable Energy Certificates
- Renewable Portfolio Standards
- Managing E-trash (computers, TVs, etc.)
- Recycling Surcharges
- Host Fees
- Water-Extraction Land Subsidence
- Conjunctive Use of Surface Water and Groundwater
- Water Banking
- Water Desalination as a Backstop Resource
- Privatization of Water Systems and Access
- The Economics of Wildlife Poaching
- Marine Reserves
- The Impact of Technological Change on the Fishery
- Rome Declaration on World Food Scarcity
- Role of Organic Foods
- Genetically Modified Organisms
- Land Conversion Incentives
- Sustainable Forestry
- Tiered, Area, and Input Pricing Systems for Water
- Conservation Easements and Land Trusts
- Royalty Agreements to Protect Biodiversity
- NAFTA's Chapter 11 and the Environment
- EPAs 33/50 Program
- Game Theory and Climate Change Coalition Formation
- Results from the Sulfur Allowance Program
- The European Emission Trading System
- Debt Relief and the Environment
- Abrupt Climate Change
- Product Charges to Control Air Emissions
- Safety Valves in Emission Trading
- Double Dividend Effects
- Climate Change Hedging Strategies
- Ecological Footprint
- Adjusted Net Savings (Formerly Genuine Savings)
- The MTBE Story
- Pay-As-You-Drive Automobile Insurance
- Automobile Feebates
- EPAs Water Quality Trading Policy
- Successful Canadian, Japanese, and European Strategies for Locating Hazardous Waste Facilities

Major Expansions

Three areas covered in the previous edition are discussed in more depth in this text. These include:

- Climate Change Science and Policy
- Trade and the Environment
- The Land Use Conversion Threat to Forests

Expansions and Updates

And finally, many discussions have been updated to make sure readers are exposed to the latest developments. These include:

- The Role of Deep Ecology
- Environment in Russia and the Former Soviet Republics
- Hydrogen-Based Fuels
- Expanded Producer Responsibility
- Conflicts over Instream Flows of Water
- Water Pricing Systems
- Agricultural Trends
- Labeling and Certification Strategies
- Debt-Nature Swaps
- Delaney Clause
- Multilateral Fund
- ZEV Auto Sales Quotas
- Alternative Fuels
- Toxic Release Inventory
- California's Proposition 65
- Genuine Progress Indicator
- Human Development Index
- Environmental Justice and the Location of Hazardous Waste Facilities

This edition retains a strong policy orientation. Though a great deal of theory and empirical evidence is discussed, their inclusion is motivated by the desire to increase understanding of intriguing policy problems, and these aspects are discussed in the context of those problems. This explicit integration of research and policy within each chapter avoids the problem frequently encountered in applied economics textbooks—that is, in such texts the theory developed in earlier chapters is often only loosely connected to the rest of the book.

This is an economics book, but it goes beyond economics. Insights from the natural and physical sciences, literature and political science, as well as other disciplines, are scattered liberally throughout the text. In some cases these references raise unresolved issues that economic analysis can help resolve, while in others they affect the structure of the economic analysis or provide a contrasting point of view. They have an important role to play in overcoming the tendency to accept the material uncritically at a superficial level by highlighting those characteristics that make the economics approach unique.

Supplements

For each chapter in the text, the online *Instructor's Manual*, written by Lynne Lewis of Bates College, provides an overview, learning objectives, a chapter outline with key terms, common student difficulties, and suggested classroom exercises. Professors can download the *Instructor's Manual* and the PowerPoint slides, which contain the text figures, from the catalog page for this book at www.aw-bc.com.

The book's Companion Web site, www.aw-bc.com/tietenberg, features chapter-by-chapter Web links to additional readings and economic data. If you wish to supplement your course with newspaper subscriptions or economic news sources, ask your local sales representative for details about Addison-Wesley's special offers.

For the first time with the Seventh Edition, the text is accompanied by Excel-based models that can be used to numerically solve common forest-harvest problems. These examples may be presented in lecture to accentuate the intuition provided in the textbook, or they may underlie specific questions on a homework assignment. The models, developed by Arthur Caplan and John Gilbert of Utah State University, are available via the open-access Companion Web site (www.aw-bc.com/tietenberg).

Acknowledgments

Perhaps the most rewarding part of writing this book has been that it has put me in touch with so many thoughtful people I had not previously met. I very much appreciate the faculty and students who pointed out areas of particular strength or areas where coverage could be expanded in this edition. The support this book has received from faculty and students has been gratifying and energizing. One can begin to understand the magnitude of my debt to my colleagues by glancing at the several hundred names in the lists of references contained in the name index. Because their research contributions make this an exciting field, full of insights worthy of being shared, my task was easier and a lot more fun than it might otherwise have been.

My strongest debt of gratitude is to Professor Lynne Lewis of Bates College. Lynne took primary responsibility for expanding and modifying Chapters 3, 10, 11, 19, and 21. The book is stronger for her contributions and I am grateful for her assistance.

I also owe a large debt of gratitude to Professors Elena Alvarez (State University of New York at Albany); Frank Egan (Trinity College); Joseph Herriges (Iowa State University); Janet Kohlhase (University of Houston); Patricia Norris (Michigan State University); Tesa Stegner (Idaho State University); David Terkla (University of Massachusetts at Boston); and Roger von Haefen (University of Arizona, but visiting at Stanford University at the time of his review). This group provided detailed, helpful reviews of the text and supplied many useful ideas for this revision.

And, finally, I want to acknowledge the valuable assistance I received during various stages of the writing of this text from:

Dan S. Alexio	U.S. Military Academy at West Point
Gregory S. Amacher	Virginia Polytechnic Institute and State University

Michael Balch	University of Iowa
Maurice Ballabon	Baruch College
Edward Barbier	University of Wyoming
A. Paul Baroutsis	Slippery Rock University of Pennsylvania
Kathleen P. Bell	University of Maine
Peter Berck	University of California, Berkeley
Fikret Berkes	Brock University
Trond Bjørndal	Norwegian School of Economics and Business Administration
Sidney M. Blumner	California State Polytechnic University, Pomona
Vic Brajer	California State University, Fullerton
Stacy Brook	University of Sioux Falls
Richard Bryant	University of Missouri, Rolla
David Burgess	University of Western Ontario
Mary A. Burke	Florida State University
Richard V. Butler	Trinity University
Trudy Cameron	University of Oregon
Jill Caviglia-Harris	Salisbury University
Duane Chapman	Cornell University
Charles J. Chicchetti	University of Wisconsin, Madison
Hal Cochrane	Colorado State University
Jon Conrad	Cornell University
John Coon	University of New Hampshire
William Corcoran	University of Nebraska, Omaha
Gregory B. Christiansen	California State University, East Bay
Maureen L. Cropper	University of Maryland
John H. Cumberland	University of Maryland
Herman E. Daly	University of Maryland
Diane P. Dupont	Brock University
Randall K. Filer	Hunter College/CUNY
Ann Fisher	Pennsylvania State University
Anthony C. Fisher	University of California, Berkeley
Marvin Frankel	University of Illinois, Urbana-Champaign
A. Myrick Freeman III	Bowdoin College
James Gale	Michigan Technological University
David E. Gallo	California State University, Chico
Haynes Goddard	University of Cincinnati
Nikolaus Gotsch	Institute of Agricultural Economics (Zurich)
Doug Greer	San José State University
Ronald Griffin	Texas A&M University
W. Eric Gustafson	University of California, Davis
A. R. Gutowsky	California State University, Sacramento
Jon D. Harford	Cleveland State University
Gloria E. Helfand	University of Michigan
Ann Helwege	Tufts University
John J. Hovis	University of Maryland

Paul Huszar	Colorado State University
Craig Infanger	University of Kentucky
Allan Jenkins	University of Nebraska at Kearney
Donn Johnson	Quinnipiac College
James R. Kahn	Washington and Lee University
Chris Kavalec	Sacramento State University
Derek Kellenberg	University of Colorado, Boulder
John O. S. Kennedy	LaTrobe University
Thomas Kinnaman	Bucknell University
Andrew Kleit	Pennsylvania State University
Richard F. Kosobud	University of Illinois, Chicago
Douglas M. Larson	University of California, Davis
Dwight Lee	University of Georgia
Joseph N. Lekakis	University of Crete
Ingemar Leksell	Göteborg University
Randolph M. Lyon	Executive Office of the President (U.S.)
Robert S. Main	Butler University
Giandomenico Majone	Harvard University
David Martin	Davidson College
Charles Mason	University of Wyoming
Ross McKitrick	University of Guelph
Nicholas Mercuro	Michigan State University
David E. Merrifield	Western Washington University
Frederic C. Menz	Clarkson University
Michael J. Mueller	Clarkson University
Kankana Mukherjee	Clarkson University
Thomas C. Noser	Western Kentucky University
Lloyd Orr	Indiana University
Peter J. Parks	Rutgers University
Alexander Pfaff	Columbia University
Raymond Prince	University of Colorado, Boulder
H. David Robison	La Salle University
J. Barkley Rosser, Jr.	James Madison University
Jonathan Rubin	University of Maine
Milton Russell	University of Tennessee
Frederic O. Sargent	University of Vermont
Salah El Serafy	World Bank
Aharon Shapiro	St. John's University
W. Douglass Shaw	University of Nevada
James S. Shortle	Pennsylvania State University
Leah J. Smith	Swarthmore College
V. Kerry Smith	North Carolina State University
Rob Stavins	Harvard University
Joe B. Stevens	Oregon State University
Gert T. Svendsen	The Aarhus School of Business
Kenneth N. Townsend	Hampden-Sydney College

Robert W. Turner	Colgate University
Wallace E. Tyner	Purdue University
Nora Underwood	Florida State University
Myles Wallace	Clemson University
Patrick Welle	Bemidji State University
Randy Wigle	Wilfred Laurier University
Richard T. Woodward	Texas A&M University
Anthony Yezer	The George Washington University

My most helpful research assistant for this edition was Emila Tjernström. Working with all of the fine young scholars who have assisted me with this text over the years has made it all the more obvious to me why teaching is the world's most satisfying profession.

Finally, I should like to express publicly my deep appreciation to my wife Gretchen, my daughter Heidi, and my son Eric for their love and support.

Tom Tietenberg
Sand Cove
Prospect Harbor, Maine

Visions of the Future

From the arch of the bridge to which his guide has carried him, Dante now sees the Diviners ... coming slowly along the bottom of the fourth Chasm. By help of their incantations and evil agents, they had endeavored to pry into the future which belongs to the almighty alone, and now their faces are painfully twisted the contrary way; and being unable to look before them, they are forced to walk backwards.

—Dante Alighieri, *Divine Comedy: The Inferno*, translated by Carlyle (1867)

Introduction

The Self-Extinction Premise

About the time the American colonies won independence, Edward Gibbon completed his monumental *The History of the Decline and Fall of the Roman Empire*. In a particularly poignant passage that opens the last chapter of his opus, he re-creates a scene in which the learned Poggius, a friend, and two servants ascend the Capitoline Hill after the fall of Rome. They are awed by the contrast between what Rome once was and what Rome has become:

> In the time of the poet it was crowned with the golden roofs of a temple; the temple is overthrown, the gold has been pillaged, the wheel of fortune has accomplished her revolution, and the sacred ground is again disfigured with thorns and brambles. . . . The forum of the Roman people, where they assembled to enact their laws and elect their magistrates is now enclosed for the cultivation of potherbs, or thrown open for the reception of swine and buffaloes. The public and private edifices, that were founded for eternity lie prostrate, naked, and broken, like the limbs of a mighty giant; and the ruin is the more visible, from the stupendous relics that have survived the injuries of time and fortune [Vol. 6, pp. 650–651].

What could cause the demise of such a grand and powerful society? Gibbon weaves a complex thesis to answer this question, suggesting ultimately that the seeds for Rome's destruction were sown by the Empire itself. Though Rome finally succumbed to such external forces as fires and invasions, its vulnerability was based upon internal weakness.

Some Historic Examples

The premise that societies could germinate the seeds of their own destruction has long fascinated scholars. In 1798 Thomas Malthus published his classic "An Essay on the Principle of Population," in which he foresaw a time when the urge to reproduce would cause population growth to exceed the land's potential to supply sufficient food and result in starvation and death. In his view, the adjustment mechanism would involve rising death rates caused by environmental constraints, rather than a recognition of impending scarcity followed by either innovation or self-restraint.

Actual historic examples suggest that the Malthus vision may have merit. Consider two specific cases: the Mayan civilization and Easter Island.

The Mayan civilization, a vibrant and highly cultured society that occupied parts of Central America, did not survive. One of the major settlements, Copán, has been studied in sufficient detail to reveal reasons for its collapse (Webster et al., 2000).

The Webster et al. study reports that the population growth began to bump into environmental constraints in the 5th century, specifically the agricultural carrying capacity of the land. The growing population depended heavily on a single, locally grown crop (maize) for food. By early in the 6th century, however, the carrying capacity of the most productive local lands was exceeded, and farmers began to depend upon more fragile parts of the ecosystem. The economic result was diminishing returns to agricultural labor, and the production of food failed to keep pace with the increasing population.

By the mid-8th century, when the population was reaching its historic apex, widespread deforestation and erosion had set in, thereby intensifying the declining productivity problems associated with moving onto marginal lands. By the 8th and 9th centuries, the evidence reveals high levels of infant and adolescent mortality, as well as widespread malnutrition. The royal dynasty, an important source of leadership in this society, collapsed rather abruptly around A.D. 820–822.

The second case study, Easter Island, shares some remarkable similarities with both the Mayan case and the Malthusian vision. Easter Island lies some 2,000 miles off the coast of Chile. Current visitors note that it is distinguished by two features: (1) its enormous statues carved from volcanic rock and (2) a surprisingly sparse vegetation given the island's favorable climate and volcanic conditions, which typically support fertile soil. Both the existence of the imposing statues and the fact that they were erected such a long way from the quarry suggest the presence of an advanced civilization, but to current observers it is nowhere in evidence. What happened to that society?

The short answer is that rising population, coupled with a heavy reliance on wood for housing, canoe building, and transporting the statues, decimated the forest

(Brander and Taylor, 1998). The loss of the forest contributed to soil erosion, declining soil productivity, and, ultimately, diminished food production. How did the community react to impending scarcity? Apparently the social response was war and, ultimately, cannibalism.

We would like to believe that in the face of impending scarcity, societies would react by changing behavior to adapt to the diminishing resource supplies and that this benign response would follow automatically from a recognition of the problem. We even have a cliché to capture this sentiment, "Necessity is the mother of invention." While these stories do *not* imply that the cliché is always wrong (it isn't), they do point out that there is nothing automatic about a problem-solving response. Sometimes societal reactions not only fail to solve the problem, but also make it worse.

Future Environmental Challenges

Future societies, like those just discussed will, be confronted by both resource scarcity and accumulating pollutants. Though many specific examples of these broad categories of problems are discussed in detail in the chapters that follow, this section will provide a flavor of what is to come by illustrating the challenges posed by one pollution problem (climate change) and one resource scarcity problem (water accessibility).

Climate Change

Energy from the sun drives the earth's weather and climate. Incoming rays heat the earth's surface, radiating energy back into space. Atmospheric "greenhouse" gases (water vapor, carbon dioxide, and other gases) trap some of the outgoing energy.

Without this natural "greenhouse effect," temperatures on Earth would be much lower than they are now, and life as we know it today would be impossible. It is possible, however, to have too much of a good thing. Problems arise when the concentration of greenhouse gases increases beyond normal levels, thus retaining excessive heat somewhat like a car with the windows closed in the summer.

Since the Industrial Revolution, greenhouse gas emissions have increased considerably. These increases have enhanced the heat-trapping capability of the earth's atmosphere. According to the Committee on the Science of Climate Change (2001), the earth's surface temperature has risen by about one degree Fahrenheit in the past century, with accelerated warming during the past two decades. That study concludes that most of the warming over the last 50 years is attributable to human activities.

As the earth warms, extreme heat conditions are expected to affect human health. Some damage is caused directly by the more extreme heat, as illustrated by the heat waves that resulted in thousands of deaths in Europe in the summer of 2003. Human health can also be affected by pollutants, such as smog, that are exacerbated by warmer temperatures. Rising sea levels (as warmer water expands and previous frozen sources such as glaciers melt), coupled with an increase in storm intensity, are expected to flood coastal communities. Ecosystems will be subjected to unaccustomed temperatures; some will adapt by migrating to new areas, but others may not be able to adapt in time. While these processes have already begun, they will intensify slowly throughout the century.

Climate change also has an important moral dimension. Developing countries, which contribute the least to excess greenhouse gas production, are expected to be the hardest hit due to their more limited adaptation capabilities.

Dealing with climate change will require a coordinated international response. That is a significant challenge to a world system where the nation-state reigns supreme and international organizations are relatively weak.

Water Accessibility

Another class of threats is posed by the interaction of a rising demand for resources in the face of a finite supply. Water provides a particularly interesting example because it is so vital to life.

According to the United Nations, about 40% of the world's population lives in areas with moderate-to-high water stress. ("Moderate stress" is defined in the U.N. Assessment of Freshwater Resources as "human consumption of more than 20 percent of all accessible renewable freshwater resources," whereas "severe stress" denotes consumption greater than 40 percent.) By 2025 it is estimated that about two-thirds of the world's population—about 5.5 billion people—will live in areas facing such water stress.

This stress is not uniformly distributed around the globe. For example, in the United States, China, and India, groundwater is being consumed faster than it is being replenished and groundwater levels are steadily falling. Some rivers, such as the Colorado in the western United States and the Yellow in China, often run dry before they reach the sea.

According to U.N. data, Africa and Asia suffer the most from the lack of water supply and sanitation in urban areas. Up to 50% of Africa's urban residents and 75% of Asians lack adequate access to a water supply.

The availability of potable water is further limited by human activities that contaminate the finite supplies. According to the United Nations, 90% of sewage and 70% of industrial wastes in developing countries are discharged without treatment.

Some arid areas have compensated for their lack of water by importing it via aqueducts from more richly endowed regions. In addition to promoting political conflict (regions from which the water is obtained may resist supplying it), the aqueducts may be geologically vulnerable. In California, for example, many of the aqueducts cross or lie on known earthquake-prone fault lines (Reisner, 2003).

Meeting the Challenges

If our ancestors had recognized that human activities could seriously impact environmental life-support systems and could deny our generation the quality of life to which we have become accustomed, they might have chosen a different, more sustainable path for improving human welfare. Because they did not have that knowledge and, therefore, did not make sustainable choices years ago means that current generations are now faced with making more difficult choices with even fewer options. These choices will test the creativity of our solutions and the resilience of our social institutions.

As the scale of economic activity has proceeded steadily upward, the scope of environmental problems triggered by that activity has transcended both geographic and generational boundaries. While the nation-state used to be a sufficient form of political organization for resolving environmental problems, that may no longer be the case. Whereas each generation used to have the luxury of being able to satisfy its own needs without worrying about the needs of generations to come, that is no longer the case either. Solving problems such as poverty, climate change, ozone depletion, and the loss of biodiversity requires international cooperation. Because future generations cannot speak for themselves, we must speak for them. Our policies must incorporate our obligation to future generations, however difficult or imperfect that incorporation might prove to be.

International cooperation is by no means a foregone conclusion. Global environmental problems can trigger very different effects on the countries that will sit around the negotiating table. While low-lying countries could be completely submerged by the sea level rise predicted by some climate change models, or while arid nations could see their marginal agricultural lands succumb to desertification, other nations may see agricultural productivity rise as warmer climates in traditionally intemperate regions support longer growing seasons.

Countries that unilaterally set out to improve the global environmental situation run the risk of making their businesses vulnerable to competition from less conscientious nations. Industrialized countries that undertake stringent environmental policies may not suffer greatly at the national level. (Offsetting employment and income increases will in the industries producing pollution control equipment.) Some individual industries facing stringent regulations, however, will face higher costs than their competitors, and can be expected to suffer accordingly. Declining market share and employment in industries confronted by especially stringent regulations are powerful political weapons that can be used by industrial polluters to derail efforts to implement an aggressive environmental policy. The search for solutions must accommodate these concerns.

Many individuals and institutions currently have a large stake in maintaining the status quo, even when it involves environmental destruction. Fishermen harvesting their catch from an overexploited fishery are loath to undertake any reduction in harvests, even if the reduction is necessary to conserve the stock and to return the population to a healthy level. Farmers who have come to depend on fertilizer and pesticide subsidies will give them up only reluctantly. The principle of inertia applies to politics as fully as to physical bodies; A body at rest will tend to stay at rest unless a significant outside force is introduced.

How Will Societies Respond?

The fundamental question is how societies will respond to these challenges. One way to think systematically about this question involves feedback loops.

Positive feedback loops are those in which secondary effects tend to reinforce the basic trend. An example of a positive feedback loop is the process of capital accumulation. New investment generates greater output, which, when sold, generates profits. These profits can be used to fund additional new investments. This example suggests a manner in which the growth process is self-reinforcing.

Positive feedback loops may also be seen in climate change. Scientists believe, for example, that the relationship between emissions of methane and climate change may be described as a positive feedback loop. Because methane is a greenhouse gas, increases in methane emissions contribute to climate change. The rise of the planetary temperature, however, could trigger the release of extremely large quantities of additional methane currently trapped in the permafrost layer of the earth; the larger quantities of methane would further increase temperature, resulting in the release of more methane, and so on.

Human responses can also intensify environmental problems through positive feedback loops. When shortages of a commodity are imminent, for example, consumers typically begin to hoard the commodity. Hoarding intensifies the shortage. Similarly, people faced with shortages of food may eat the seed that is the key to more plentiful food in the future. Situations giving rise to this kind of downward spiral are particularly troublesome.

In contrast, a negative feedback loop is self-limiting rather than self-reinforcing. Perhaps the best-known planetary-scale example of a negative feedback loop is provided in a theory advanced by the English scientist James Lovelock. Called the Gaia hypothesis after the Greek concept for Mother Earth, this view of the world suggests that the earth is a living organism with a complex feedback system that seeks an optimal physical and chemical environment. Deviations from this optimal environment trigger natural, nonhuman response mechanisms that restore the balance. In essence, according to the Gaia hypothesis the planetary environment is characterized by negative feedback loops and is, within limits, a self-limiting process. As we proceed with our investigation, the degree to which our economic and political institutions serve to intensify or to limit emerging environmental problems will be a key concern.

The Role of Economics

How societies respond to challenges will depend largely on the behavior of human beings acting individually or collectively. Economic analysis provides an incredibly useful set of tools for anyone interested in understanding and/or modifying human behavior, particularly in the face of scarcity. Both ecological economics and environmental economics (Debate 1.1) provide a basis not only for identifying the circumstances that degrade the environment, but also for making clear how and why that set of circumstances supports degradation. This understanding can then be used as the basis for designing new incentives that harmonize the relationship between the economy and the environment. Harnessing the power of market forces allows them to be used in the service of sustainable environmental outcomes. Ignoring them means having to live with consequences that not only can be much more expensive to correct after the fact, but may even be irreversible.

DEBATE
1.1

Ecological Economics Versus Environmental Economics

Over the last decade or so, the community of scholars dealing with the role of the economy and the environment has settled into two camps: ecological economics (http://www.ecoeco.org/) and environmental economics (http://www.aere.org/). Although they share many similarities, ecological economics is consciously more methodologically pluralist, while environmental economics is based solidly on the standard paradigm of neoclassical economics. While neoclassical economics emphasizes maximizing human welfare and using economic incentives to modify destructive human behavior, ecological economics uses a variety of methodologies, including neoclassical economics, depending upon the purpose of the investigation.

While some observers see the two approaches as competitive (presenting an "either-or" choice), others, including the author of this text, see them as complementary. Complementarity, of course, does not mean full acceptance. Significant differences exist not only between these two fields, but also within them over such topics as the valuation of environmental resources, the impact of trade on the environment, and the appropriate means for evaluating policy strategies for long-duration problems such as climate change. These differences arise not only over methodologies, but also over the values that are brought to bear on the analysis.

As the author of this book has published in both fields and has served on the editorial boards of the leading journals in both fields, it probably will not be surprising that this book draws from both fields. Though the basic foundation for the analysis is environmental economics, the chapters draw heavily from ecological economics to critique that view when it is controversial and to complement it with useful insights drawn from outside the neoclassical paradigm when appropriate. Pragmatism is the reigning criterion. If a particular approach or study helps us to understand environmental problems and their resolution, it has been included in the text.

The Use of Models

All of the topics covered in this book will be examined as part of the general focus on economic development in light of limited environmental and natural resources. Because this subject is so complex, it is better understood when broken into manageable portions. Once we master the components, we will be able to reassemble them to form a more complete picture. In economics, as in most other disciplines, we use models to investigate complex subjects such as relationships between the economy and the environment.

Models are simplified characterizations of reality. For example, although a road map by design leaves out much detail, it is a useful guide to reality. The map shows how various locations relate to each other and gives an overall perspective. It cannot, however, capture the unique details that characterize any particular location. The map highlights only those characteristics crucial for the purpose at hand. The models in this text are similar. Through simplification, less detail is shown so that the main concepts become clear.

Models allow us to study rigorously issues that are interrelated and global in scale, but through their selectivity, models may yield conclusions that are dead wrong. Details that are omitted may turn out, in retrospect, to be crucial in understanding a particular dimension. Models are therefore useful abstractions that should always be viewed with some skepticism. Most people's views of the world are based on models, though frequently the assumptions and relationships involved may be hidden, perhaps even subconscious. In economics the models are explicit; objectives, relationships, and assumptions are clearly specified so that the reader understands exactly how the conclusions were derived.

The Road Ahead

Debate 1.2 examines the controversial question of whether or not societies are on a self-destructive path. In part, the differences between these two very different views depend on how human behavior is perceived. If increasing scarcity results in a behavioral response that intensifies the pressure on the environment, pessimism is justified. If, on the other hand, the human responses are currently reducing those pressures or can be reformed so as to reduce those pressures, then optimism may be justified.

The field of environmental and natural resource economics has become an important source of ideas for coping with this dilemma. Not only does the field provide a firm basis for understanding the human sources of environmental problems, this understanding also provides a firm foundation for crafting specific solutions to these problems. In subsequent chapters, for example, you shall be exposed to how economic analysis can be (and has been) used to forge solutions to climate change (Chapter 17), biodiversity loss (Chapter 13), population growth (Chapter 6), and water scarcity (Chapter 10). Many of the solutions are quite novel.

The search for solutions must recognize that market forces are extremely powerful. Attempts to solve environmental problems that ignore these forces run a high risk of failure. Instead, harnessing these forces and channeling them into directions that protect the environment are possible and desirable. Environmental and natural resource economics provides a specific set of directions for how that can be accomplished.

The Issues

Obviously the two opposing visions of the future identified in Debate 1.2 present us with rather different conceptions of what the future holds as well as different views of what policy choices should be made. They also suggest that to act as if one vision is correct, when it is not, could prove to be a costly error. Thus it is important to determine if one of these two views or some third view is correct.

In order to assess any model or view, we must address the basic issues:

1. Is the problem correctly conceptualized as exponential growth with fixed, immutable resource limits? Does the earth have a finite carrying capacity?

DEBATE
1.2

What Does the Future Hold?

Is the economy on a collision course with the environment? Or has the process of reconciliation begun? One group, led most notably by Bjørn Lomborg, Director of Demark's Environmental Assessment Institute, concludes that societies have resourcefully confronted environmental problems in the past and that environmentalist concerns to the contrary are excessively alarmist. As he states in his book *The Skeptical Environmentalist*:

> The fact is, as we have seen, that this civilization over the last 400 years has brought us fantastic and continued progress. . . . And we ought to face the facts—that on the whole we have no reason to expect that this progress will not continue.

On the other end of the spectrum are the researchers at the Worldwatch Institute, who believe that current development paths and the attendant strain they place on the environment are unsustainable. As reported in *State of the World 2004*:

> This rising consumption in the U.S., other rich nations, and many developing ones is more than the planet can bear. Forests, wetlands, and other natural places are shrinking to make way for people and their homes, farms, malls, and factories. Despite the existence of alternative sources, more than 90 percent of paper still comes from trees—eating up about one fifth of the total wood harvest worldwide. An estimated 75 percent of global fish stocks are now fished at or beyond their sustainable limit. And even though technology allows for greater fuel efficiency than ever before, cars and other forms of transportation account for nearly 30 percent of world energy use and 95 percent of global oil consumption.

These views not only interpret the available historical evidence differently, but they also imply very different strategies for the future.

Sources: Bjørn Lomborg. *The Skeptical Environmentalist: Measuring the Real State of the World* (Cambridge, UK: Cambridge University Press, 2001). The Worldwatch Institute. *The State of the World 2004* (New York: W.W. Norton & Co., 2004).

If so, how can the carrying-capacity concept be operationalized? Do current levels of economic activity exceed the carrying capacity?

2. How does the economic system respond to scarcities? Does the process involve mainly positive feedback loops? Would the responses intensify or ameliorate any initial scarcities?

3. What is the role of the political system in controlling these problems? In what circumstances is government intervention necessary? Is this intervention uniformly benign, or can it make the situation worse? What is an appropriate role for the executive, legislative, and judicial branches?

4. Many environmental problems involve a considerable degree of uncertainty about the severity of the problem and the effectiveness of possible solutions.

Can our economic and political institutions respond to this uncertainty in reasonable ways?

5. Can the economic and political systems work together to eradicate poverty while respecting our obligations to future generations? Or does our obligation to future generations inevitably conflict with the desire to raise the living standards of those currently in absolute poverty? Can short-term and long-term goals be harmonized? How? What does the need to preserve the environment imply about the future of economic activity in the industrialized nations? in the less industrialized nations?

The rest of the book uses economic analysis to suggest answers to these complex questions.

An Overview of the Book

In the following chapters you will study the rich and rewarding field of environmental and natural resource economics. The menu of topics is broad and varied. Economics provides a powerful analytical framework for examining the relationships between the environment, on the one hand, and the economic and political systems, on the other. The study of economics can assist in identifying circumstances that give rise to environmental problems, in discovering causes of these problems, and in searching for solutions. Each chapter introduces a unique topic in environmental and natural resource economics, while our overarching focus on development in a finite environment weaves these topics into a single theme.

We begin by comparing perspectives being brought to bear on these problems by economists and noneconomists. The manner in which scholars in various disciplines view problems and potential solutions depends on how they organize the available facts, how they interpret those facts, and what kinds of values they apply in translating these interpretations into policy. Before going into a detailed look at environmental problems, we shall compare the ideology of conventional economics to other prevailing ideologies in the natural and social sciences. This comparison not only explains why reasonable people may, upon examining the same set of facts, reach different conclusions, but it also conveys some sense of the strengths and weaknesses of economic analysis as it is applied to environmental problems.

Chapters 3–5 delve more deeply into the conventional economics approach. Specific evaluation criteria are defined, and examples are developed to show how these criteria can be applied to specific environmental problems.

After examining the major perspectives shaping environmental policy, we turn in Chapters 6–14 to some of the resource scarcities and to the manner in which the economic and political institutions have dealt with the resulting problems. We begin our examination in Chapter 6 with an inquiry into the nature, causes, and consequences of population growth, a major factor in determining how rapidly scarcity could develop.

Chapters 7–14 deal with several topics traditionally falling within natural resource economics. Chapter 7 provides an overview of the models used to characterize the "optimal" allocation of resources over time. These models allow us to show not only how the optimal allocation depends on such factors as the cost of extraction, environmental costs, and the availability of substitutes, but also how the allocations produced by our political and economic institutions measure up against this standard of optimality. Chapter 8 discusses energy as an example of a depletable, nonrecyclable resource, and examines such topics as the role of OPEC, the balance between imports and domestic production, the role of nuclear power, and many aspects of past and present energy policy. Chapter 9 focuses on minerals to illustrate how depletable, recyclable resources are allocated over time, and to define the appropriate role for recycling. We assess the degree to which the current situation approximates this ideal, paying particular attention to aspects such as tax policy, disposal costs, and product durability.

Chapters 10–13 focus on renewable or replenishable resources. These chapters show that the effectiveness with which current institutions manage renewable resources depends on whether the resources are living or inanimate and whether they are treated as private or common property. In Chapter 10, the focus is on allocating water in arid regions. Water is an example of an inanimate but replenishable resource. Specific examples from the American Southwest illustrate how the political and economic institutions have coped with this form of impending scarcity. In Chapter 11, the focus is on cereal grain, an animate, private-property resource, which is the most important source of food in combating the world hunger problem. Chapter 12 deals with forestry as an example of a renewable and storable private-property resource. Managing this resource poses a somewhat unique problem in that the amount of time required to produce an efficient harvest is longer than for the other resources considered; forests are also a major source of biodiversity. In Chapter 13, fisheries are used to illustrate the problems associated with an animate, free-access resource and to explore possible means of solving these problems.

The final chapter concerned with natural resources, Chapter 14, confronts the fear that we are entering an era of generalized resource scarcity. It seeks answers to key questions: Are we in an era of increasing scarcity? How can we be certain? What indicators can be used and what do they reveal? What responses should be taken given this evidence?

We then move on to an area of public policy—pollution control—that is coming to rely much more heavily on the use of economic incentives to produce the desired response. Chapter 15, an overview chapter, emphasizes not only the nature of the problems but differences among policy approaches taken to resolve them. The unique aspects of local air pollution, regional and global air pollution, automobile air pollution, water pollution, and the control of toxic substances are dealt with in the 5 subsequent chapters. Special attention is paid in Chapter 21 to the impacts of those policies—not only on the problems they were designed to correct, but also on other important policy concerns, such as the distribution of the benefit and cost burdens among various socioeconomic groups and geographic areas.

Following this examination of the individual environmental and natural resource problems and the policies that can be, and have been, used to ameliorate these problems, we turn to the development process itself. Certain questions must be asked: What are the causes and consequences of economic development? What role do natural resources and environmental control play in the sustainable development process? What is the likely future for sustainable development?

In Chapter 24 we close by assembling the bits and pieces of evidence accumulated thus far and fusing them into an overall response to the questions posed in the chapter. The chapter also suggests some of the major unresolved issues in environmental policy that are likely to be among those commanding center stage over the next several years or decades.

Summary

Are our institutions so myopic that they have chosen a path that can only lead to the destruction of society as we now know it? We have examined briefly two studies that provide different answers to that question. The Worldwatch Institute responds in the affirmative, while Lomborg responds negatively. The pessimistic view is based upon the inevitability of exceeding the carrying capacity of the planet as the population and the level of economic activity grow. The optimistic view sees initial scarcity triggering sufficiently powerful reductions in population growth and increases in technological progress that abundance, not deepening scarcity, is what the future holds.

Our examination of these different visions has revealed questions that must be answered if we are to assess what the future holds. Seeking the answers requires that we accumulate a much better understanding about how choices are made in economic and political systems and how those choices affect, and are affected by, the natural environment. We begin that process in Chapter 2, where the economic approach is developed in broad terms and is contrasted with other conventional approaches.

Discussion Questions

1. In his book *The Ultimate Resource*, economist Julian Simon makes the point that calling the resource base "finite" is misleading. To illustrate this point he uses a yardstick, with its 1-inch markings, as an analogy. The distance between two markings is finite—1 inch—but an infinite number of points is contained within that finite space. Therefore, in one sense, what lies between the markings is finite, while in another, equally meaningful sense, it is infinite. Is the concept of a finite resource base useful or not? Why or why not?

2. This chapter contains two views of the future. Since the validity of these views cannot completely be tested until the time period covered by the forecast has passed (so that predictions can be matched against actual events), how can we ever hope to establish whether one is a better view than the other? What criteria might be proposed for evaluating predictions?

3. Positive and negative feedback loops lie at the core of systematic thinking about the future. As you examine the key forces shaping the future, what examples of positive and negative feedback loops can you uncover?

Further Reading

Lovins, A., L. H. Lovins, and P. Hawken. "A Road Map for Natural Capitalism," *Harvard Business Review* (1999): 145–158. A vision suggesting that business strategies built on a more productive use of natural resources can solve many environmental problems at a profit.

Meadows, Donella, Jorgen Randers, and Dennis Meadows. *The Limits to Growth: The 30 Year Global Update* (White River Junction, VT: Chelsea Green Publishing, 2004). Sequel to an earlier (1972) book that argued that the current path of human activity would inevitably lead the economy to overshoot the earth's carrying capacity, leading in turn to a collapse of society as we now know it; this sequel brings recent data to bear on the overshoot and global ecological collapse thesis.

Oates, W. E., ed. *The RFF Reader in Environmental and Resource Management* (Washington, DC: Resources for the Future, Inc., 1999). A collection of short, highly readable commentaries on subjects ranging from biodiversity and climate change to environmental justice.

Stavins, R., ed. *Economics of the Environment: Selected Readings*, 4th ed (New York: W. W. Norton & Company, Inc., 2000). An excellent set of complementary readings that captures both the power of the discipline and the controversy it provokes.

World Commission on Environment and Development. *Our Common Future* (Oxford: Oxford University Press, 1987). An enormously influential book that has set the tone for international discussions of sustainable development.

Additional References and Historically Significant References are available on this book's companion Web site www.aw-bc.com/tietenberg.

Chapter 2

Valuing the Environment: Concepts

When you have eliminated the impossible, whatever remains, however improbable, must be the truth.

—Sherlock Holmes, From Sir Arthur Conan Doyle's
The Sign of Four (1890)

Introduction

Before examining specific environmental problems and the policy responses to them, it is important that we develop and clarify the economics approach, so that we will have some sense of the forest before examining each of the trees. By having a feel for the conceptual framework, it becomes easier not only to deal with individual cases, but, perhaps more importantly, to see how they fit into a comprehensive approach.

In this chapter we develop the general conceptual framework used in economics to approach environmental problems. We begin by examining the relationship between human actions, as manifested through the economic system, and the environmental consequences of those actions. We can then establish criteria for judging the desirability of the outcomes of this relationship. These criteria provide a basis for identifying the nature and severity of environmental problems, and a foundation for designing effective policies to deal with them.

Throughout this chapter the economic point of view is contrasted with alternative points of view. These contrasts bring the economic approach into sharper focus and stimulate deeper and more critical thinking about all possible approaches.

The Human Environment Relationship

The Environment as an Asset

In economics the environment is viewed as a composite asset that provides a variety of services. It is a very special asset, to be sure, since it provides the life-support systems that sustain our very existence, but it is an asset

FIGURE 2.1

The Economic System and the Environment

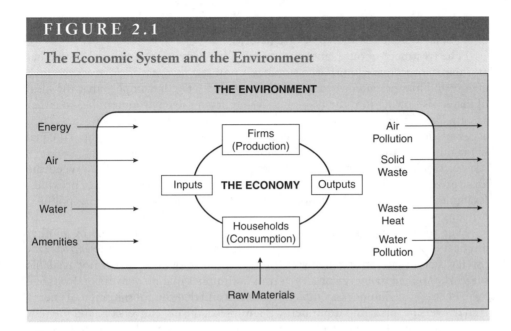

nonetheless. As with other assets, we wish to prevent undue depreciation of the value of this asset so that it may continue to provide aesthetic and life-sustaining services.

The environment provides the economy with raw materials, which are transformed into consumer products by the production process, and energy, which fuels this transformation. Ultimately these raw materials and energy return to the environment as waste products (see Figure 2.1).

The environment also provides services directly to consumers. The air we breathe, the nourishment we receive from food and drink, and the protection we derive from shelter and clothing are all benefits we receive either directly or indirectly from the environment. In addition, anyone who has experienced the exhilaration of white-water canoeing, the total serenity of a wilderness trek, or the breathtaking beauty of a sunset will readily recognize that the environment provides us with a variety of amenities for which no substitute exists.

If the environment is defined broadly enough, the relationship between the environment and the economic system can be considered a *closed system*. For our purposes, a closed system is one in which no inputs (energy, matter, and so on) are received from outside the system and no outputs are transferred outside the system. An *open system*, by contrast, is one in which the system imports or exports matter or energy.

If we restrict our conception of the relationship in Figure 2.1 to our planet and the atmosphere around it, then clearly we do not have a closed system. We derive most of our energy from the sun, either directly or indirectly. We have also sent spaceships well beyond the boundaries of our atmosphere. Nonetheless, historically speaking, for *material* inputs and outputs (not including energy), this system can be treated as a closed system because the amount of exports (such as abandoned space vehicles) and imports (moon rocks, for example) are negligible. Whether the system remains closed depends on the degree to which space exploration opens up the rest of our solar system as a source of raw materials.

The treatment of our planet and its immediate environs as a closed system has an important implication that is summed up in the *first law of thermodynamics—* energy and matter cannot be created or destroyed.[1] The law implies that the mass of materials flowing into the economic system from the environment has to either accumulate in the economic system or return to the environment as waste. When accumulation stops, the mass of materials flowing into the economic system is equal in magnitude to the mass of waste flowing into the environment.

Excessive wastes can, of course, depreciate the asset; when they exceed the absorptive capacity of nature, wastes reduce the services that the asset provides. Examples are easy to find: air pollution can cause respiratory problems; polluted drinking water can cause cancer; smog obliterates scenic vistas.

The relationship of people to the environment is also conditioned by another physical law, the *second law of thermodynamics*. Known popularly as the *entropy law*, this law states that entropy increases. *Entropy* is the amount of energy not available for work. Applied to energy processes, this law implies that no conversion from one form of energy to another is completely efficient and that the consumption of energy is an irreversible process. Some energy is always lost during conversion, and the rest, once used, is no longer available for further work. The second law also implies that in the absence of new energy inputs, any closed system must eventually use up its energy. Since energy is necessary for life, life ceases when energy ceases.

We should remember that our planet is not even approximately a closed system with respect to energy; we gain energy from the sun. The entropy law does suggest, however, that this flow of solar energy establishes an upper limit on the flow of energy that can be sustained. Once the stocks of stored energy (such as fossil fuels and nuclear energy) are gone, the amount of energy available for useful work will be determined solely by this flow and by the amount that can be stored (dams, trees, and so on). Thus, over the very long run, the growth process will be limited by the availability of solar energy and our ability to put it to work.

The Economic Approach

Two different types of economic analysis can be applied to increase our understanding of the relationship between the economic system and the environment: *Positive* economics attempts to describe *what is, what was.* or *what will be. Normative* economics, by contrast, deals with what *ought to be*. Disagreements within positive economics can usually be resolved by an appeal to the facts. Normative disagreements, however, involve value judgments.

Both branches are useful. Suppose, for example, we want to investigate the relationship between trade and the environment. Positive economics could be used to describe the kinds of impacts trade would have on the economy and the environment. It could not, however, provide any guidance on the question of whether trade was desirable. That judgment would have to come from normative economics.

---

[1]We know, however, from Einstein's famous equation ($E = mc^2$) that matter can be transformed into energy. This transformation is the source of energy in nuclear power.

Normative analysis can arise in several different contexts. It might be used, for example, to evaluate the desirability of either a proposed new pollution control regulation or a proposal to preserve an area currently scheduled for development. In these cases the analysis helps to provide guidance on the desirability of a program before that program is put into place. In other contexts it might be used to evaluate how an already-implemented program has worked out. Both of these types of situations share the characteristic that the alternatives being evaluated are well defined in advance. Here the relevant question is: Should we do it (or have done it) or not?

A rather different context for normative economics can arise when the possibilities are more open-ended. For example, we might ask how much should we control emissions of greenhouse gases (which contribute to climate change) and how should we achieve that degree of control? Or we might ask how much forest of various types should be preserved? Answering these questions requires us to consider the entire range of possible outcomes and to select the best or optimal one. Although that is a much more difficult question to answer than one that asks us only to compare two pre-defined alternatives, the basic normative analysis framework is the same in both cases.

Normative Criteria for Decision-Making

Evaluating Predefined Options

If you were asked to evaluate the desirability of some proposed action, you would probably begin by attempting to identify both the gains from that action and the losses. If the gains exceed the losses, then it seems natural to support the action.

That simple framework provides the starting point for the economic approach. Economists suggest that actions have both benefits and costs. If the benefits exceed the costs, then the action is desirable. On the other hand, if the costs exceed the benefits, then the action is not desirable.

We can formalize this in the following way. Let B be the benefits from a proposed action and C be the costs. Our decision rule would then be:

If $B > C$, then support the action.

Otherwise, oppose the action.[2]
As long as B and C are positive, an equivalent formulation would be:

If $B/C > 1$, support the action.

Otherwise, oppose the action.

So far so good, but how do we measure benefits and costs? In economics the system of measurement is anthropocentric, which simply means human-centered. All benefits and costs are valued in terms of their effects (broadly defined) on humanity. As shall be pointed out later, that does *not* imply (as it might first appear) that ecosystem effects are ignored unless they *directly* affect humans. The fact that large numbers of humans contribute voluntarily to organizations that are dedicated to

---

[2]Actually if $B = C$, it wouldn't make any difference if the action occurs or not; the benefits and costs are a wash.

DEBATE 2.1

Should Humans Place an Economic Value on the Environment?

Arne Naess, the late Norwegian philosopher, used the term "deep ecology" to refer to the view that the nonhuman environment has "intrinsic" value, a value that is independent of human interests. Intrinsic value is contrasted with "instrumental" value in which the value of the environment is derived from its usefulness in satisfying human wants.

Two issues are raised by the Naess critique: (1) what is the basis for the valuing the environment? and (2) how is the valuation accomplished? The belief that the environment may have a value that goes beyond its direct usefulness to humans is in fact quite consistent with modern economic valuation techniques. As we show in Chapter 3, economic valuation techniques now include the ability to quantify a wide range of "nonuse" values as well as the more traditional "use" values.

Controversies over how the values are derived are less easily resolved. As described in this chapter, economic valuation is based firmly upon human preferences. Proponents of deep ecology, on the other hand, would argue that allowing humans to determine the value of other species would have no more moral basis than allowing other species to determine the value of humans. Rather, deep ecologists argue, humans should only use environmental resources when necessary for survival; otherwise, nature should be left alone. And, because economic valuation is not helpful in determining survival necessity, deep ecologists argue that it contributes little to environmental management.

Those who oppose all economic valuation face a dilemma: when humans fail to value the environment, it may be assigned a default value of zero in calculations designed to guide policy. A value of zero, however derived, will tend to justify a great deal of environmental degradation that could not be justified with proper economic valuation. As a 1998 issue of *Ecological Economics* demonstrated, a number of environmental professionals now support economic valuation as a way to demonstrate just how valuable the environment is to modern society. At the very least, support seems to be growing for the proposition that economic valuation can be a very useful means of demonstrating when environmental degradation is senseless, even when judged from a limited anthropomorphic perspective.

Sources: R. Costanza, et al. "The Value of Ecosystem Services: Putting the Issues in Perspective," *Ecological Economics* Vol. 25, No. 1 (1998): 67–72 and the other articles on valuation in that issue; Gretchen Daily and Katherine Ellison. *The New Economy of Nature: The Quest to Make Conservation Profitable* (Washington, D.C.: Island Press, 2003).

environmental protection provides ample evidence that humans place a value on environmental preservation that goes well beyond any direct use they might make of it. Nonetheless, the notion that humans are doing the valuing is a controversial point (see Debate 2.1).

Benefits can be derived from the demand curve for the good or service provided by the action. Demand curves measure the amount of a particular good people would

FIGURE 2.2

The Individual Demand Curve

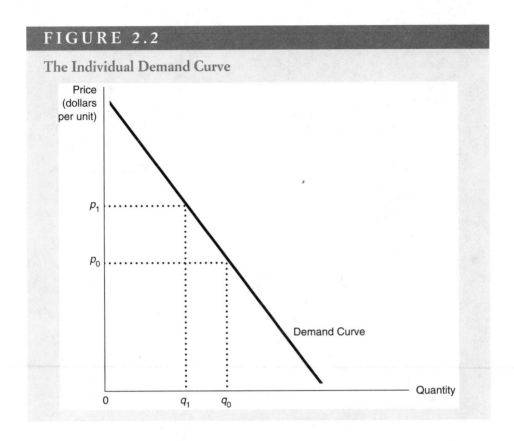

be willing to purchase at various prices. In a typical situation, a person will purchase less of a commodity (or environmental service) the higher is its cost. In Figure 2.2, when the price is p_0, q_0 will be purchased, but if the price rises to p_1, purchases will fall to q_1.

The meaning of these demand curves can be illustrated with this hypothetical experiment: suppose you were asked: At a price of X dollars, how much commodity Y would you buy? Your answer could be recorded as a point on a diagram such as Figure 2.2. By repeating the question many times for different prices, we could trace out a locus of points. Connecting these points would yield an individual *demand curve*. Adding up all of the individual amounts demanded by all individuals at some stipulated price yields one point on the market demand curve. Connecting the points for various prices reveals the market demand curve.

For each quantity purchased, the corresponding point on the market demand curve represents the amount of money some person is willing to pay for the last unit of the good. The *total willingness to pay* for some quantity of this good—say, three units—is the sum of the willingness to pay for each of the three units. Thus the total willingness to pay for three units would be measured by the sum of the willingness to pay for the first, second, and third units, respectively. It is now a simple extension to determine that the total willingness to pay is the area under the continuous market

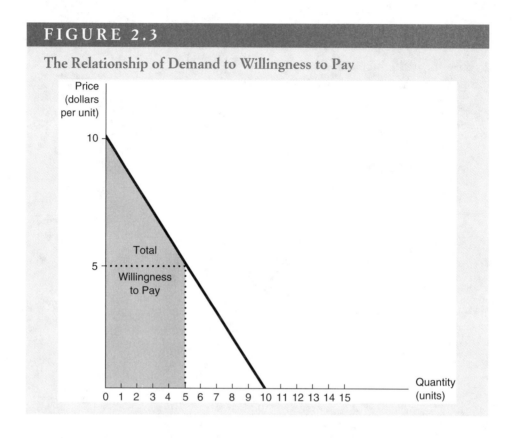

FIGURE 2.3

The Relationship of Demand to Willingness to Pay

demand curve to the left of the allocation in question. For example, in Figure 2.3 the total willingness to pay for five units of the commodity is the shaded area.[3] Total willingness to pay is the concept we shall use to define *total benefits*. Thus total benefits are equal to the area under the market demand curve from the origin to the allocation of interest.

Measuring total costs on the same set of axes involves logic similar to measuring total benefits. It is important to stress that environmental services have costs even though they are produced without any human input. All costs should be measured as opportunity costs.

As illustrated by Example 2.1, the *opportunity cost* for using resources in a new or an alternative way is the net benefit lost when specific environmental services are foregone in the conversion to the new use. The notion that it is costless to convert a forest to a new use is obviously wrong if valuable ecological services are lost in the process.

To firm up this notion of opportunity cost, consider another example. Suppose a particular stretch of river can be used either for white-water canoeing or to

---

[3]From simple geometry it can be noticed that for linear demand curves this area is the sum of the areas of the triangle on top plus the rectangle on the bottom. The area of a right triangle is $1/2 \times$ base $\times$ height. Therefore, in our example this area is $1/2 \times \$5 \times 5 + \$5 \times 5 = \$37.50$.

Example 2.1

VALUING ECOLOGICAL SERVICES FROM PRESERVED TROPICAL FORESTS

As Chapter 12 in this text will make clear, one of the main threats to tropical forests is the conversion of forested land to some other use (agriculture, residences, and so on). Whether economic incentives favor conversion of the land depends upon the magnitude of the value that would be lost through conversion. How large is that value? Is it large enough to support preservation?

A group of ecologists investigated this question for a specific set of tropical forest fragments in Costa Rica. They chose to value one specific ecological service provided by the local forest: wild bees using the nearby tropical forest as a habitat provided pollination services to aid coffee production. While this coffee (*C. Arabica*) can self-pollinate, pollination from wild bees has been shown to increase coffee productivity from 15 to 50%.

When the authors placed an economic value on this particular ecological service, they found that the pollination services from two specific preserved forest fragments (46 and 111 hectares, respectively) were worth approximately $60,000 per year for one large, nearby Costa Rican coffee farm. As the authors conclude:

> The value of forest in providing crop pollination service alone is . . . of at least the same order [of magnitude] as major competing land uses, and infinitely greater than that recognized by most governments (i.e. zero).

These estimates only partially capture the value of this forest because they consider only a single farm and a single type of ecological service. (This forest also provides carbon storage and water purification services, for example, and these were not included in the calculation.) Despite their partial nature, however, these calculations already begin to demonstrate the economic value of preserving the forest, even when considering only specific instrumental values.

Source: Taylor H. Ricketts, et al. "Economic Value of Tropical Forest to Coffee Production," *PNAS (Proceedings of the National Academy of Science)* Vol. 101, No. 34 (August 24, 2002): 12579–12582.

generate electric power. Since the dam that generates the power would flood the rapids, the two uses are incompatible. The opportunity cost of producing power is the foregone net benefit that would have resulted from the white-water canoeing.

In graphing costs, we shall use the marginal opportunity cost curve to correspond to the marginal willingness-to-pay function used previously to graph benefits. The *marginal opportunity cost curve* defines the additional cost of producing the last unit. In purely competitive markets, the marginal opportunity cost curve is identical to the supply curve.

FIGURE 2.4

The Relationship of Marginal Cost and Total Cost

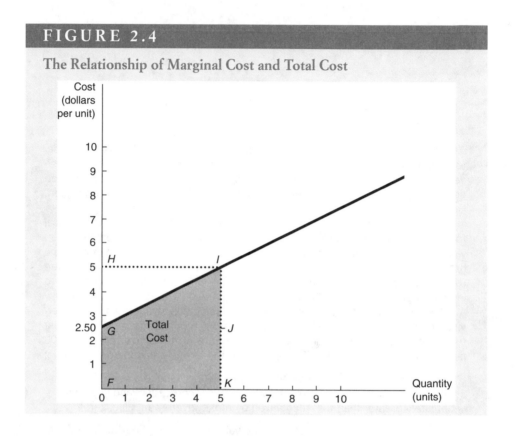

Total cost is simply the sum of the marginal costs.[4] The total cost of producing three units is equal to the cost of producing the first unit plus the cost of producing the second unit plus the cost of producing the third unit. As with total willingness to pay, the geometric representation of the sum of the individual elements of a continuous marginal cost curve is the area under the marginal cost curve, as illustrated in Figure 2.4 by the shaded area *FGIJK*.[5]

Since net benefit is defined as the excess of benefits over costs, it follows that net benefit is equal to that portion of the area under the demand curve that lies above the supply curve. Consider Figure 2.5, which combines the information in Figures 2.3 and 2.4.

Let's now use this apparatus to illustrate the use of the decision rules introduced earlier. Let's suppose for example that we are considering preserving a four-mile stretch of river and that the benefits and costs of that action are reflected in Figure 2.5. Should that stretch be preserved?

---

[4]Strictly speaking, the sum of the marginal costs is equal to total variable cost. In the short run, this is smaller than total cost by the amount of the fixed cost. For our purposes this distinction is not important.

[5]Notice again that this area is the sum of a right triangle and a rectangle. In Figure 2.4 the total variable cost of producing 5 units is $18.75. Why?

FIGURE 2.5

The Derivation of Net Benefits

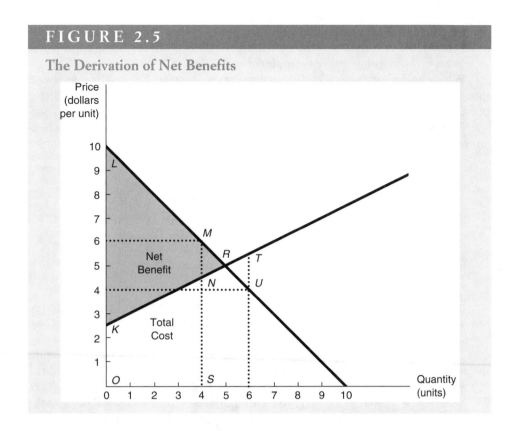

Comparing Benefits and Costs Across Time

The analysis we have covered so far is very useful for thinking about actions where time is not an important factor. Yet many of the decisions made now have consequences that persist well into the future. Time is a factor. Exhaustible energy resources, once used, are gone. Biological renewable resources (such as fisheries or forests) can be overharvested, leaving smaller and possibly weaker populations for future generations. Persistent pollutants can accumulate over time. How can we make choices when the benefits and costs may occur at different points in time?

Incorporating time into the analysis requires an extension of the concepts we have already developed. This extension provides a way for thinking not only about the magnitude of benefits and costs, but also about timing. In order to incorporate timing, the decision rule must provide a way to compare the net benefit received in one period with the net benefit received in another. The concept that allows this comparison is called *present value*. Therefore, before introducing this expanded decision rule, we must define present value.

Present value explicitly incorporates the time value of money. A dollar today invested at 10% interest yields $1.10 a year from now (the return of the $1 principal plus $0.10 interest). The present value of $1.10 received one year from now is, therefore, $1 because, given $1 now, you can turn it into $1.10 a year from now by investing it at 10% interest. We can find the present value of any amount of money (X) received one year from now by computing $X/(1 + r)$, where r is the appropriate interest rate (10% in our above example).

What could your dollar earn in two years at r% interest? Because of compound interest, the amount would be $\$1(1 + r)(1 + r) = \$1(1 + r)^2$. It follows then that the present value of X received two years from now is $X/(1 + r)^2$.

By now the pattern should be clear. The net present value of a *one-time* net benefit received n years from now is

$$NPV[B_n] = \frac{B_n}{(1+r)^n}$$

The net present value of a stream of net benefits $\{B_0, \ldots, B_n\}$ received over a period of n years is computed as

$$NPV[B_0,\ldots,B_n] = \sum_{i=0}^{n} \frac{B_i}{(1+r)^i}$$

where r is the appropriate interest rate and B_0 is the amount of net benefits received immediately. The process of calculating the present value is called *discounting*, and the rate r is referred to as the discount rate.[6]

The number resulting from a present-value calculation has a straightforward interpretation. Suppose you were investigating an allocation that would yield the following pattern of net benefits on the last day of each of the next five years: $3000, $5000, $6000, $10,000, $12,000. If you use an interest rate of 6% ($r = 0.06$) and the above formula, you will discover that this stream has a present value of $29,210.

What does that number mean? If you put $29,210 in a savings account earning 6% interest and wrote yourself checks, respectively, for $3000, $5000, $6000, $10,000, and $12,000 on the last day of each of the next five years, your last check would just restore the account to a $0 balance. Thus, you should be indifferent about receiving $29,210 now or in the specific five-year stream of benefits totaling $36,000; given one, you can get the other. Hence, the method is called present value because it translates everything back to its current worth.

It is now possible to show how this analysis can be used to evaluate actions. First calculate the present value of net benefits from the action. If the present value is greater than zero, the action should be supported. Otherwise it should not.

Finding the Optimal Outcome

In the preceding section we have examined how benefit/cost analysis can be used to evaluate the desirability of specific actions. In this section we want to examine how this approach can be used to identify "optimal" or best approaches.

---

[6]The discount rate should equal the social opportunity cost of capital. See Scheraga and Sussman (1998) for details on techniques for environmental discounting. We examine in Chapter 4 the questions of whether private firms can be expected to use the socially correct discount rate. In Chapter 3, we discuss how the discount rate is chosen by the government.

In subsequent chapters, which address individual environmental problems, the normative analysis will proceed in three steps. First we will identify an optimal outcome. Second we will attempt to discern the extent to which our institutions produce optimal outcomes and, where divergences occur between actual and optimal outcomes, to attempt to uncover the behavioral sources of the problems. Finally we can use both our knowledge of the nature of the problems and their underlying behavioral causes as a basis for designing appropriate policy solutions. Although how these three steps are applied to each of the environmental problems will reflect the uniqueness of each situation, the overarching framework used to shape that analysis will be the same.

To provide some concreteness of this approach, consider two examples, one drawn from natural resource economics and another from environmental economics. These are meant to be illustrative and to convey a flavor of the argument; the details are left to upcoming chapters.

Consider the rising number of depleted ocean fisheries. Depleted fisheries, which involve fish populations that have fallen so low as to threaten their viability as commercial fisheries, not only jeopardize oceanic biodiversity, but also pose a threat to both the individuals who make their living from the sea and the communities that have depended on fishing to support their local economies.

How would an economist attempt to understand and to resolve this problem? The first step would involve defining the optimal stock or the optimal rate of harvest of the fishery. The second step would compare this level with the actual stock and harvest levels. Once this economic framework is applied, not only does it become clear that stocks are much lower than optimal for many fisheries, but the reason for excessive exploitation becomes clear as well. Understanding the nature of the problem has led quite naturally to some solutions. Once implemented, these policies have allowed some fisheries to begin the process of renewal. The details of this analysis and the policy implications that flow from it are covered in Chapter 13.

Another problem involves solid waste. As local communities run out of room for landfills in the face of an increasing generation of waste, what can be done?

Economists start by thinking about how one would define the optimal amount of waste. The definition necessarily incorporates waste reduction and recycling as aspects of the optimal outcome. The analysis not only reveals that current waste levels are excessive, but also suggests some specific behavioral sources of the problem. Based upon this understanding, specific economic solutions have been identified and implemented. Communities that have adopted these measures have generally experienced lower levels of waste and higher levels of recycling. The details are spelled out in Chapter 9.

In the rest of the book, similar analysis is applied to population, energy, minerals, agriculture, air and water pollution, and a host of other topics. In each case the economic analysis helps to point the way toward solutions. To initiate that process we must begin by defining what is meant by optimal.

Static Efficiency

The chief normative economic criterion for choosing among various allocations occurring at the same point in time is called *static efficiency*, or merely *efficiency*.

An allocation of resources is said to satisfy the static efficiency criterion if the net benefit from the use of those resources is maximized by that allocation.

Let's show how this concept can be applied by returning to Figure 2.5. Previously we asked whether an action that preserved four miles of river was worth doing? The answer was yes because the net benefits from that action were positive.

Static efficiency, however, requires us to ask a rather different question, namely, what is the efficient number of miles to be preserved? We know from the definition that the efficient amount of preservation would maximize net benefits. Do four miles maximize net benefits?

We can answer that question by establishing whether it is possible to increase the net benefit by preserving more or less of the river. If the net benefit can be increased by preserving more miles, clearly, preserving four miles could not have maximized the net benefit and, therefore, could not have been efficient.

Consider what would happen if society were to choose to preserve five miles instead of four. What happens to the net benefit? It increases by area *MNR*. Since we can find another allocation with greater net benefit, four miles of preservation could not have been efficient. Are five? Yes. Let's see why.

We know that five miles of preservation convey more net benefits than four. If this allocation is efficient, then it must also be true that the net benefit is smaller for levels of preservation higher than five. Notice that the additional cost of preserving the sixth unit (the area under the marginal cost curve) is larger than the additional benefit received from preserving it (the corresponding area under the demand curve). Therefore, the triangle *RTU* represents the reduction in net benefit that occurs if six miles are preserved rather than five.

Since the net benefit is reduced, both by preserving less than five and by preserving more than five, we conclude that five units is the preservation level that maximizes net benefit. Therefore, from our definition, preserving five miles constitutes an efficient allocation.[7]

One implication of this example, which shall be very useful in succeeding chapters, is what we shall call the first equimarginal principle:

> First Equimarginal Principle (the "Efficiency Equimarginal Principle"): Net benefits are maximized when the marginal benefits from an allocation equal the marginal costs.

This criterion helps to minimize wasted resources, but is it fair? The ethical basis for this criterion is derived from a concept called *Pareto optimality*, named after the Italian-born Swiss economist Vilfredo Pareto, who first proposed it around the turn of the 20th century.

> Allocations are said to be Pareto optimal if no other feasible allocation could benefit some people without any deleterious effects on at least one other person.

---

[7] The monetary worth of the net benefit is the sum of two right triangles, and it equals $(1/2)(\$5)(5) + (1/2)(\$2.50)(5)$ or \$18.75. Can you see why?

Allocations that do not satisfy this definition are suboptimal. Suboptimal allocations can always be rearranged so that some people are better off and no one is hurt by the rearrangement. Therefore, the gainers could use a portion of their gains to compensate the losers sufficiently to ensure they were at least as well off as they were prior to the reallocation. Efficient allocations are Pareto optimal. Since net benefits are maximized by an efficient allocation, it is not possible to increase the net benefit by rearranging the allocation. Without an increase in the net benefit, there is no way the gainers could sufficiently compensate the losers; the gains to the gainers would necessarily be smaller than the losses to the losers.

Inefficient allocations are judged inferior because they do not maximize the net benefit. By failing to maximize net benefit, they are forgoing an opportunity to make some people better off without harming others.

Dynamic Efficiency

The static efficiency criterion is very useful for comparing resource allocations when time is not an important factor. How can we make choices when the benefits and costs may occur at different points in time?

The traditional criterion used to find an optimal allocation when time is involved is called *dynamic efficiency*, a generalization of the static efficiency concept already developed. In this generalization, the present-value criterion provides a way for comparing the net benefits received in one period with the net benefits received in another.

An allocation of resources across n time periods satisfies the dynamic efficiency criterion if it maximizes the present value of net benefits that could be received from all the possible ways of allocating those resources over the n periods.

Applying the Concepts

Having now spent some time developing the concepts we need, let's take a moment to examine some actual studies in which they have been used.

Pollution Control

Benefit/cost analysis has been used to assess the desirability of efforts to control pollution. Pollution control certainly confers many benefits, but it also has costs. Do the benefits justify the costs? That was a question the U.S. Congress wanted answered, so in Section 812 of the Clean Air Act Amendments of 1990, it required the U.S. Environmental Protection Agency (EPA) to evaluate the benefits and costs of the U.S. air pollution control policy over the 1970–1990 period (see Example 2.2).

In responding to this congressional mandate, the EPA set out to quantify and to monetize both the benefits and the costs of achieving the emissions reductions required by U.S. policy. Benefits quantified by this study included reduced death rates and lower incidences of chronic bronchitis, lead poisoning, strokes, respiratory diseases, and heart disease as well as the benefits of better visibility, reduced damage

Example   2.2

DOES REDUCING POLLUTION MAKE ECONOMIC SENSE?

In its 1997 report to Congress, the EPA presented the results of its attempt to discover whether the Clear Air Act had produced positive net benefits over the period 1970 to 1990. The results suggested that the present value of benefits (using a discount rate of 5%) was $22.2 trillion, while the costs were $0.523 trillion. Performing the necessary subtraction reveals that the net benefits were therefore equal to $21.7 trillion. According to this study, U.S. air pollution control policy during this period made very good economic sense.

TABLE 2.1

Monetized Benefits and Costs of the U.S. Clean Air Act, 1970–1990 (billions of 1990 dollars)

	1975	1980	1985	1990	Present Value
Benefits[a]	355	930	1,155	1,248	22,200
Costs[b]	14	21	25	26	523
Net Benefits	341	909	1,130	1,220	21,700

[a] These are the mean (average) benefits. Due to the uncertainties involved, EPA also calculated low and high estimates.

[b] These are the annualized costs. (Many investments in pollution control involve the purchase of durable equipment that lasts many years.) Rather than put all of the expense in the year of purchase, EPA distributed the costs over the useful lives of this equipment.

Source: Created by the author from information presented in U.S. Environmental Protection Agency, *The Benefits and Costs of the Clean Air Act, 1970 to 1990* (Washington, DC: Environmental Protection Agency, 1997): Table 18 on p. 56.

to structures, and improved agricultural productivity. They were unable to quantify many suspected ecosystem effects.

Two categories of costs were also quantified. The first category included the higher costs of goods and services as the costs of installing, operating, and maintaining pollution control equipment were passed on to the consumers in the form of higher prices. The second category included the costs associated with designing and implementing the regulations as well as monitoring and enforcing compliance with them.

Though we shall return to this study later in the book for a deeper look at how these estimates were derived, a couple of comments are relevant now. First, despite the fact that this study did not attempt to value the pollution damage to ecosystems that was avoided by this policy, the net benefits are strongly positive. While presumably the case for controlling pollution would have been even stronger had they been included, the case is strong enough even when they are not included. An inability to monetize everything does not necessarily jeopardize the ability to reach sound policy conclusions.

Although these results justify the conclusion that pollution control made economic sense, they do not justify the stronger conclusion that the policy was efficient. Notice that to justify that conclusion, the study would have to have shown that the present value of net benefits was maximized, not merely positive. In fact this study did not attempt to calculate the maximum net benefits outcome and if it had, it would have discovered that the policy during this period was not completely efficient. As we shall show later in Chapters 15 and 16, the costs of the chosen policy approach were higher than necessary to achieve the desired emission reductions. With an optimal policy mix, the net benefits would have been even higher.

Preservation Versus Development

One of the most basic conflicts faced by environmental policy occurs when a currently underdeveloped but ecologically significant piece of land becomes a candidate for development. If developed, the land may provide jobs for workers, wealth for owners, and goods for consumers, but it may also degrade the ecosystem, possibly in irreversible ways. Wildlife habitat may be eliminated, wetlands may be paved over, and recreational opportunities may be gone forever. On the other hand, if the land is preserved, the ecosystem benefits will be retained, but the opportunity for increased income and employment will have been lost. These conflicts become intensified if unemployment rates in the area are high and the local ecology is rather unique.

One such conflict arose in Australia from a proposal to mine a piece of land that was in an area known as the Kakadu Conservation Zone (KCZ). Decision-makers at that time had to decide whether it should be mined or preserved. One way to examine that question is to use the techniques above to examine the net benefits of the two alternatives (see Example 2.3).

Summary

The relationship between humanity and the environment requires many choices. Some basis for making rational choices is absolutely necessary. If not made by design, decisions will be made by default.

Example   2.3

CHOOSING BETWEEN PRESERVATION AND DEVELOPMENT IN AUSTRALIA

The Kakadu Conservation Zone (KCZ), a 50-square-kilometer area lying entirely within the Kakadu National Park (KNP), was initially set aside as part of a government grazing lease. The current issue was whether it should be mined (it was believed to contain significant deposits of gold, platinum, and palladium) or added to the KNP, one of Australia's major parks. In recognition of its unique ecosystem and extensive wildlife as well as its aboriginal archeological sites, much of the park has been placed on the U.N. World Heritage List. Mining would produce income and employment, but it could also cause the ecosystems in both the KCZ and KNP to experience irreversible damage. What value was to be placed on those risks? Would those risks outweigh the employment and income effects from mining?

To provide answers to these crucial questions, economists conducted a benefit/cost analysis using a technique known as contingent valuation. (We shall go into some detail about how this technique works in the next chapter, but for now it can suffice to note that this is a technique for eliciting "willingness-to-pay" information.) The value of preserving the site was estimated to be A$435 million, while the present value of mining the site was estimated to be A$102.

According to this analysis, preservation was the preferred option and it was the option chosen by the government.

Source: Richard T. Carson, Leanne Wilks, and David Imber. "Valuing the Preservation of Australia's Kakadu Conservation Zone," *Oxford Economic Papers* Vol. 46 Supplement (1994): 727–749.

The economics approach views the environment as a composite asset, supplying a variety of services to humanity. The intensity and composition of those services depend on the actions of humans as constrained by physical laws, such as the first and second laws of thermodynamics.

Economics has two rather different means of enhancing understanding of environmental and natural resource economics. Positive economics is useful in describing the actions of people and the impact of those actions on the environmental asset. Normative economics can provide guidance on how optimal service flows can be defined and achieved.

Normative economics invokes benefit/cost analysis for judging the desirability of the level and composition of provided services. A static efficient allocation is one that maximizes the net benefit over all possible uses of those resources. The dynamic efficiency criterion, which is appropriate when time is an important consideration, is satisfied when the outcome maximizes the present value of net benefits from all possible uses of the resources. Future chapters examine the degree to which our social institutions yield allocations that conform to these criteria.

Discussion Question

1. It has been suggested that we should use the "net energy" criterion to make choices among various types of energy. Net energy is defined as the total energy content in the energy source minus the energy required to extract, process, and deliver it to consumers. According to this criterion, we should use those sources with the highest net energy content first. Would the dynamic efficiency criterion and the net energy criterion be expected to yield the same choice? Why or why not?

Problem

1. One convenient way to express the willingness-to-pay relationship between price and quantity is to use the inverse demand function. In an inverse demand function, the price consumers are willing to pay is expressed as a function of the quantity available for sale. Suppose the inverse demand function (expressed in dollars) of a product is $P = 80 - q$, and the marginal cost (in dollars) of producing it is $MC = 1q$, where P is the price of the product and q is the quantity demanded and/or supplied. (a) How much would be supplied in a static efficient allocation? (b) What would be the magnitude of the net benefits (in dollars)?

Further Reading

Freeman, A. Myrick, III. *The Measurement of Environmental and Resource Values* (Washington, DC: Resources for the Future, Inc., 1993). A comprehensive and analytically rigorous survey of the concepts and methods for environmental valuation.

Hanley, Nick, and Clive L. Spash. *Cost-Benefit Analysis and the Environment* (Brookfield, VT: Edward Elgar Publishing Company, 1994). An up-to-date account of the theory and practice of benefit/cost analysis applied to environmental problems. Contains a number of specific case studies.

Norton, Bryan, and Ben A. Minteer. "From Environmental Ethics to Environmental Public Philosophy: Ethicists and Economists: 1973–Future," in T. Tietenberg and H. Folmer, eds. *The International Yearbook of Environmental and Resource Economics: 2002/2003* (Cheltenham, UK: Edward Elgar, 2002): 373–407. A review of the interaction between environmental ethics and economic valuation.

Scheraga, Joel D., and Frances G. Sussman. "Discounting and Environmental Management," in T. Tietenberg and H. Folmer, eds. *The International Yearbook of Environmental and Resource Economics 1998–1999* (Cheltenham, UK: Edward Elgar, 1998): 1–32. This article summarizes the "state of the art" for the use of discounting in environmental management.

Historically Significant References are available on this book's companion web site www.aw-bc.com/tietenberg.

Appendix

The Simple Mathematics of Dynamic Efficiency*

Assume that the demand curve for a depletable resource is linear and stable over time. Thus the inverse demand curve in year t can be written as:

$$P_t = a - bq_t \tag{1}$$

The total benefits from extracting an amount q_t in year t are then the integral of this function (the area under the inverse demand curve):

$$(\text{Total benefits})_t = \int_0^{q_t} (a - bq)dq$$

$$= aq_t - \frac{b}{2}q_t^2 \tag{2}$$

Further assume that the marginal cost of extracting that resource is a constant c and therefore the total cost of extracting any amount q_t in year t can be given by

$$(\text{Total cost})_t = cq_t \tag{3}$$

If the total available amount of this resource is $\bar{Q}$, then the dynamic allocation of a resource over n years is the one that satisfies the maximization problem:

$$\underset{q}{\text{Max}} \sum_{i=1}^{n} \frac{aq_i - bq_i^2/2 - cq_i}{(1+r)^{i-1}} + \lambda \left[\bar{Q} - \sum_{i=1}^{n} q_i \right] \tag{4}$$

Assuming that $\bar{Q}$ is less than would normally be demanded, the dynamic efficient allocation must satisfy

$$\frac{a - bq_i - c}{(1+r)^{i-1}} - \lambda = 0, \quad i = 1, \dots, n \tag{5}$$

$$\bar{Q} - \sum_{i=1}^{n} q_i = 0 \tag{6}$$

An implication is that $(P - MC)$ increases over time at rate r.

---

*Greater detail on the mathematics of constrained optimization can be found in any standard mathematical economics text.

Valuing the Environment: Methods

For it so falls out; That what we have we prize not to the worth; Whiles we enjoy it, but being lack'd and lost; Why, then we rack the value; then we find; The virtue that possession would not show us; Whiles it was ours.

—William Shakespeare, *Much Ado about Nothing*

Introduction

Soon after the Exxon Valdez oil tanker ran aground on the Bligh Reef in Prince William Sound off the coast of Alaska on March 24, 1989, spilling approximately 11 million gallons of crude oil, the Exxon corporation accepted the liability for the damage caused by the leaking oil. This liability consisted of two parts: (1) the cost of clearing up the spilled oil and restoring the site insofar as possible, and (2) compensation for the damage caused to the local ecology. Approximately $2.1 billion was spent in cleanup efforts and Exxon also spent approximately $303 million to compensate fishermen whose livelihoods were dramatically damaged for the five years following the spill.[1] Litigation on environmental damages settled with Exxon agreeing to pay $900 million over ten years. The punitive damages phase of this case began in May 1994. In January 2004, after many rounds of appeals, the U.S. District Court for the State of Alaska awarded punitive damages to the plaintiffs in the amount of $4.5 billion.[2]

In the last chapter we examined the concepts used by economists to calculate this damage. Yet implementing these concepts is far from a trivial exercise. While the costs of cleanup were fairly transparent (specific bills for labor, materials, and equipment appeared at Exxon corporate headquarters with great regularity), estimating the damage was more complex. For example, how was the number $900 million calculated? How can we move from the general concepts to the actual estimates of compensation required by the courts?

---

[1] U.S. District Court for the State of Alaska, Case Number A89-0095CV, January 28, 2004.
[2] Ibid.

A series of special techniques has been developed to value the benefits from environmental improvement or, conversely, to value the damage done by environmental degradation. Special techniques were necessary because most of the normal valuation techniques that have been used over the years cannot be applied to environmental resources. Benefit/cost analysis requires the monetization of all relevant benefits and costs of a proposed policy or project. As such, it is important to make sure a thorough analysis is conducted. The difficulties, however, are the monetization of those environmental goods and services that are not traded in any market. Even more difficult to grapple with are those nonmarket benefits associates with passive use or nonuse value.

In this chapter we shall examine these valuation methods. We begin with an examination of how benefit/cost can be implemented in an environmental context. In this section we identify and discuss the various valuation techniques that are used to value environmental resources in both *ex ante* and *ex post* settings. This is followed by a discussion of the strategies that exist for using economics to protect the environment when valuation information cannot reliably be obtained. One of these strategies, cost-effectiveness analysis, has become extremely important in guiding pollution control policy. Its popularity is not only due to the very practical consideration that it can be a valuable component of the policy process even when reliable valuation estimates cannot be obtained, but also because it responds to the concerns of those who reject the anthropomorphic basis for economic valuation. It has become the technique of choice for those who recognize the importance of economics for protecting the environment, but are skeptical of any efforts to monetize the value of environmental resources.

Why Value the Environment?

Debate Box 2.1 highlighted the debate on the monetization of ecosystem services. While it may prove difficult, if not impossible, to place an accurate value on certain environmental amenities, not doing so leaves us with $0 in the equation. Will a value of $0 lead us to the best policy decisions? Probably not!

Many federal agencies require benefit/cost analysis for decision-making. Ideally, the goal is to choose the most economically feasible projects, given limited budgets. A 1982 amendment to the Endangered Species Act, for example, required benefit/cost analysis for the listing of a species. This requirement was subsequently relaxed, however, due to a lack of defensible benefits measurements. The Federal Energy and Regulatory Commission (FERC) requires benefit/cost analysis for dam relicensing applications. These analyses, however, frequently fail to incorporate important nonmarket values associated with rivers. If the analysis does not include all the appropriate values, the results will be flawed. Have we made progress?

Valuing Benefits

While the valuation techniques we shall cover can be applied to both the damage caused by pollution and the services provided by the environment, each context offers its own unique problems. We begin our investigation of valuation techniques by exposing some of the difficulties associated with one of those contexts, pollution control.

In the United States, damage estimates are not only used in the design of policies, they have also become important in the courts. Under the Comprehensive Environmental Response, Compensation, and Liability Act, local, state, or federal governments can seek monetary compensation from responsible parties for natural resources that are injured or destroyed by spills and releases of hazardous wastes. Some basis for deciding the magnitude of the award is necessary.[3]

The damage caused by pollution can take many different forms. The first, and probably most obvious, is the effect on human health. Polluted air and water can cause disease when ingested. Other forms of damage include loss of enjoyment from outdoor activities and damage to vegetation, animals, and materials.

Assessing the magnitude of this damage requires (1) identifying the affected categories; (2) estimating the physical relationship between the pollutant emissions (including natural sources) and the damage caused to the affected categories; (3) estimating responses by the affected parties toward averting or mitigating some portion of the damage; and (4) placing a monetary value on the physical damages. Each step is often difficult to accomplish.

Because the experiments used to track down causal relationships are uncontrolled, identifying the affected categories is a complicated matter. Obviously we cannot run large numbers of people through controlled experiments. If people were subjected to different levels of some pollutant, such as carbon monoxide, so that we could study the short-term and long-term effects, some might become ill and even die. Ethical concern precludes human experimentation of this type.

This leaves us essentially two choices. We can try to infer the impact on humans from controlled laboratory experiments on animals, or we can do statistical analysis of differences in mortality or disease rates for various human populations living in polluted environments to see the extent to which they are correlated with pollution concentrations. Neither approach is completely acceptable.

Animal experiments are expensive, and the extrapolation from effects on animals to effects on humans is tenuous at best. Many of the significant effects do not appear for a long time. To determine these effects in a reasonable period of time, test animals must be subjected to large doses for a relatively short period of time. The researcher then extrapolates from the results of these high-dosage, short-duration experiments to estimate the effects of lower doses over a longer period of time on a human population. Because these extrapolations move well beyond the range of experimental experience, many scientists disagree on how the extrapolations should be accomplished.

Statistical studies, on the other hand, deal with human populations subjected to low doses for long periods, but, unfortunately, they have another set of problems—correlation does not imply causation. To illustrate, the fact that death rates are higher in cities with higher pollution levels does not prove that the higher pollution caused the higher death rates. Perhaps those same cities averaged older populations, which would tend to lead to higher death rates. Or perhaps they had more smokers.

---

[3]The rules for determining these damages are defined in Department of Interior regulations. See 40 Code of Federal Regulations 300:72–74.

The existing studies have been sophisticated enough to account for many of these other possible influences but, because of the relative paucity of data, they have not been able to cover them all.

The problems discussed so far arise when identifying whether a particular effect results from pollution. The next step is to estimate how strong the relationship is between the effect and the pollution concentrations. In other words, it is necessary not only to discover *whether* pollution causes an increased incidence of respiratory disease, but also to estimate *how much* reduction in respiratory illness could be expected from a given reduction in pollution.

The nonexperimental nature of the data makes this a difficult task. It is not uncommon for researchers analyzing the same data to come to remarkably different conclusions. Diagnostic problems are compounded when the effects are synergistic—that is, when the effect depends in a nonadditive way on what other elements are in the surrounding air or water at the time of the analysis.

Once physical damages have been identified, the next step is to place a monetary value on them. It is not difficult to see how complex an undertaking this is. Consider, for example, the difficulties in assigning a value to extending a human life by several years or to the pain, suffering, and grief borne by a cancer victim and the victim's family.

How can these difficulties be overcome? What valuation techniques are available not only to value pollution damage, but also to value the large number of services that the environment provides?

Types of Values

Depending upon the circumstance, we may need to place a value on either a *stock* or a *flow*. For example, the standing forest is a stock of trees, while the harvest of timber from that forest represents one of the service flows. The two are connected in that the value of a stock should be equal to the present value of the stream of services flowing from the stock. If the present value of the stream of services is maximized, then we say the resource is being used efficiently. This is equivalent to maximizing the value of that resource.

Economists have decomposed the total economic value conferred by resources into three main components: (1) use value, (2) option value, and (3) nonuse value. Use value reflects the direct use of the environmental resource. Examples would include fish harvested from the sea, timber harvested from the forest, water extracted from a stream for irrigation, even the scenic beauty conferred by a natural vista. Pollution can cause a loss of use value such as when air pollution increases the vulnerability to illness, an oil spill adversely affects a fishery, or when smog enshrouds a scenic vista.

A second category of value, the option value, reflects the value people place on a future ability to use the environment. Option value reflects the willingness to preserve an option to use the environment in the future even if one is not currently using it. Whereas use value reflects the value derived from current use, option value reflects the desire to preserve a potential for possible future use.

The third and final category of value, nonuse value, reflects the common observation that people are more than willing to pay for improving or preserving resources that they will never use. A pure nonuse value is also called *existence value*. When the Bureau of Reclamation began looking at sites for dams near the Grand Canyon, groups such as the Sierra Club rose up in protest of the potential loss of this unique resource. With Glen Canyon already flooded by Lake Powell, even those who never intended to visit recognized this potential loss. Because this value does not derive either from direct use or potential use, it represents a very different category of value.

These categories of value can be combined to produce the total willingness to pay (TWP):

$$TWP = \text{Use Value} + \text{Option Value} + \text{Nonuse value.}$$

Since nonuse values are derived from motivations other than personal use, they are obviously less tangible than use values. Furthermore, as Example 3.1 makes clear,

---

Example 3.1

VALUING THE NORTHERN SPOTTED OWL

The Northern Spotted Owl lives in an area of the Pacific Northwest where its habitat is threatened by logging. Its significance derives not only from its designation under the Endangered Species Act as a threatened species, but also from its role as an indicator of the overall health of the Pacific Northwest's old-growth forest.

In 1990 an interagency scientific committee presented a plan to withdraw certain forested areas from harvesting and preserve them as "habitat conservation areas." Would preserving these areas represent an efficient choice?

To answer this question, a national contingent valuation survey (this technique is described below) was conducted to estimate the nonuse value of preservation in this case. Conducted by mail, the survey went to 1,000 households.

The results suggested that the benefits of preservation outweighed the costs by at least 3 to 1, regardless of the assumptions necessitated by the need to resolve such issues as how to treat the nonresponding households. (One calculation, for example, included them all as a zero nonuse value.) Under the assumptions most favorable to preservation, the ratio of benefits to costs was 43 to 1. In this example the nonuse values were large enough to indicate that preservation was the preferred choice.

The authors also point out, however, that the distributional implications of this choice should not be ignored. While the benefits of preservation are distributed widely throughout the entire population, the costs are concentrated on a relatively small group of people in one geographic region. Perhaps the public should be willing to share some of the preservation costs by allocating tax dollars to this area to facilitate the transition and to reduce the hardship. This is ultimately what happened.

Source: Daniel A. Hagen, James W. Vincent, and Patrick G. Welle. "Benefits of Preserving Old-Growth Forests and the Spotted Owl," *Contemporary Policy Issues* Vol. 10 (April 1992): 13–26.

estimated nonuse values can be quite large. It is therefore not surprising that they are controversial. Indeed when the U.S. Department of Interior drew up its regulations on the appropriate procedures for performing natural resource damage assessment, it prohibited the inclusion of nonuse values unless use values for the incident under consideration were zero. A subsequent 1989 decision by the District of Columbia Court of Appeals (880 F. 2nd 432) overruled this decision and allowed nonuse values to be included as long as they could be measured.

Classifying Valuation Methods

Several methods are available to estimate these values. This section will provide a brief overview to convey some sense of the range of possibilities and how they are related. Subsequent sections will provide more specific information about how they are actually used.

The possibilities are presented in Table 3.1. Direct observation methods are those that are based on actual observable choices and from which actual resource values can be directly inferred. For example, in calculating how much local fishermen lost from the oil spill, the direct observation method might calculate how much the catch declined and the resulting value of the catch. In this case, prices are directly observable, and their use allows the direct calculation of the loss in value.

Compare this with the direct hypothetical case that might be used when the value is not directly observable. In Example 3.1, for example, the nonuse value of the Northern Spotted Owl was not directly observable. Hence the authors attempted to derive this value by using a survey that attempted to elicit the respondents' willingness to pay for the preservation of the species.

This approach, called contingent valuation, provides a means of deriving values that cannot be obtained in more traditional ways. The simplest version of this approach merely asks respondents what value they would place on an environmental change (such as the loss of a wetlands or increased exposure to pollution) or on preserving the resource in its current state. More complicated versions ask whether

TABLE 3.1

Economic Methods for Measuring Environmental and Resource Values

Methods	Observed Behavior	Hypothetical
Direct	Market Price	Contingent Valuation
	Simulated Markets	
Indirect	Travel Cost	Attribute-Based Models
	Hedonic Property Values	Conjoint Analysis
	Hedonic Wage Values	Choice Experiments
	Avoidance Expenditures	Contingent Ranking

Source: Modified by the author from Mitchell and Carson (1989).

the respondent would pay $X to prevent the change or preserve the species. The answers reveal either an upper bound (in the case of a "no" answer) or a lower bound (in the case of a "yes" answer).

The major concern with the use of the contingent valuation method has been the potential for survey respondents to give biased answers. Four types of potential bias have been the focus of a large amount of research: (1) strategic bias, (2) information bias, (3) starting-point bias, and (4) hypothetical bias.

Strategic bias arises when the respondent provides a biased answer in order to influence a particular outcome. If a decision to preserve a stretch of river for fishing, for example, depends on whether or not the survey produces a sufficiently large value for fishing, the respondents who enjoy fishing may be tempted to provide an answer that ensures a high value rather than a lower value that reflects their true valuation.

Information bias may arise whenever respondents are forced to value attributes with which they have little or no experience. For example, the valuation by a recreationist of a loss in water quality in one body of water may be based on the ease of substituting recreation on another body of water. If the respondent has no experience using the second body of water, the valuation will be based on an entirely false perception.

Starting-point bias may arise in those survey instruments in which a respondent is asked to check off his or her answers from a predefined range of possibilities. How that range is defined by the designer of the survey may affect the resulting answers. A range of $0 to $100 may produce a valuation by respondents different from, for example, a range of $10 to $100, even if no bids are in the $0 to $10 range.

The final source of bias, hypothetical bias, can enter the picture because the respondent is being confronted by a contrived, rather than an actual, set of choices. Since he or she will not actually have to pay the estimated value, the respondent may treat the survey casually, providing ill-considered answers. One survey of the field (Hanemann, 1994) found that ten studies have directly compared willingness-to-pay estimates derived from surveys with actual expenditures. Though some of the studies found that the willingness-to-pay estimates derived from surveys exceeded actual expenditures, the majority of those found that the differences were not statistically significant.[4]

Much experimental work has been done on contingent valuation to determine how serious a problem these biases may present. One survey (Carson, et al., 1994) uncovered 1,672 continent valuation studies. Are the results from these surveys reliable enough for the policy process?

Faced with the need to answer this question in order to compute damages from oil spills, the National Oceanic and Atmospheric Administration (NOAA) convened a panel of independent economic experts (including two Nobel Prize laureates) to evaluate the use of continent valuation methods for determining lost passive use or nonuse values. Their report, issued on January 15, 1993 (58 FR 4602), was cautiously supportive.

The committee made clear that it had several concerns with the technique. Among those concerns, the panel listed: (1) the tendency for contingent valuation

---

[4]For a much more skeptical view of this evidence, see Diamond and Hausman (1994).

willingness-to-pay estimates to seem unreasonably large; (2) the difficulty in assuring the respondents have understood and absorbed the issues in the survey; and (3) the difficulty in assuring that respondents are responding to the specific issues in the survey rather than reflecting general warm feelings about public-spiritedness or the "warm glow" of giving.[5]

But the panel also made clear its conclusion that suitably designed surveys could eliminate or reduce these biases to acceptable levels and it provided in an appendix specific guidelines for determining whether a particular study was suitably designed. The panel suggested that when practitioners follow these guidelines they:

> can produce estimates reliable enough to be the starting point of a judicial process of damage assessment, including lost passive-use values. . . . [A well-constructed contingent valuation study] contains information that judges and juries will wish to use, in combination with other estimates, including the testimony of expert witnesses.

The NOAA panel report has created an interesting dilemma. Although it has legitimized the use of contingent valuation for estimating passive-use (nonconsumptive use) and nonuse values, the panel has also set some rather rigid guidelines that reliable studies should follow. The cost of completing an "acceptable" contingent valuation study will be sufficiently high that they will only be useful for incidents in which the damages are high enough to justify their use. Yet due to the paucity of other techniques, the failure to use contingent valuation may, by default, result in passive-use values of zero, which isn't right either.[6]

One key to resolving this dilemma may be provided by a technique called meta-analysis. In this context meta-analysis would use a cross section of contingent valuation studies as a basis for isolating the determinants of nonuse value. Once these determinants have been isolated and related to specific policy contexts, it may be possible to transfer estimates from one context to another without incurring the time and expense of conducting new surveys each time.

The third category is indirect observable methods, which are "observable" because they involve actual (as opposed to hypothetical) behavior, and "indirect" because they infer a value rather than estimate it directly. Suppose, for example, a particular sportfishery is being threatened by pollution, and one of the damages caused by that pollution is a reduction in sportfishing. How is this loss to be valued when access to the fishery is free?

One way is through travel-cost methods. Travel-cost methods may infer the value of a recreational resource (such as a sportfishery, a park, or a wildlife preserve where visitors hunt with a camera) by using information on how much the visitors

---

[5]Mitchell (2002) discusses many of the methodological issues and concerns with contingent valuation with respect to the actual Exxon Valdez contingent valuation survey.

[6]Whittington (2002) examines the reasons why so many contingent valuation studies in developing countries are unhelpful. Poorly designed or rapidly implemented surveys could result in costly policy mistakes on topics that are very important in the developing world. The current push for cheaper, quicker studies is risky and researchers need to be very cautious.

spent in getting to the site to construct a demand curve for willingness to pay for a "visitor day."

Freeman (2003) identifies two variants of this approach. In the first, analysts examine the number of trips visitors make to a site. In the second, the analysts examine whether people decide to visit a site and, if so, which site. This second variant includes random utility models (RUM) used to value quality changes.

The first variant allows the construction of a travel-cost demand function. The value of the flow of services from that site is the area under the estimated demand curve for those services or for access to the site, aggregated over all who visit the site.

The second variant allows the analysis of how specific site characteristics influence choice and therefore indirectly how valuable those characteristics are. Knowledge of how the value of each site varies with respect to its characteristics allows the analyst to value how degradation of those characteristics (from pollution, for example) would lower the value of the site.

Travel-cost models have been used to value beach closures during oil spills, fish consumption advisories, and the cost of development that has eliminated a recreation area. Parsons (2003) details this methodology for both variants. In the RUM model, a person choosing a particular site takes into consideration site characteristics and its price (trip cost). Characteristics affecting the site choice include ease of access and environmental quality. Each site results in a unique level of utility and a person is assumed to choose the site giving the highest level of utility. Welfare losses from an event such as an oil spill can then be measured by the resulting change in utility should the person have to choose an alternate site.

Two other indirect observable methods are known as the hedonic property value and hedonic wage approaches. They share the characteristic that they use a statistical technique known as multiple regression analysis to "tease out" the environmental component of value in a related market. For example, it is possible to discover that, all other things being equal, property values are lower in polluted neighborhoods than in clean neighborhoods. (Property values fall in polluted neighborhoods because they are less desirable places to live.) Freeman (2003) examines the hedonic approach in detail. Hedonic property value models use market data (house prices) and then break down this price into its components including the house characteristics (for example, number of bedrooms, lot size, features), the neighborhood characteristics (crime rates, school quality, and so on), and environmental characteristics (for example, air quality, percentage of open space nearby, distance to a local landfill, and so forth). Hedonic models allow for the measurement of the marginal willingness to pay for discrete changes in an attribute. Numerous studies have utilized this approach to examine the effect on property value of such things as distance to a hazardous waste site (Michaels and Smith, 1990); large farm operations (Palmquist, et al., 1997); and open space and land use patterns (Bockstael, 1996; Geoghegan, et al., 1997; and Acharya and Bennett, 2001). Quite a few studies incorporate air quality variables. (See Smith and Huang (1993) for a meta-analysis using these studies.)

Hedonic wage approaches are similar except that they attempt to isolate the component of wages, which serves to compensate workers in risky occupations for taking on the risk. It is well known that workers in high-risk occupations demand higher wages in order to be induced to undertake the risks. When the risk is

Example 3.2

VALUING DAMAGE FROM GROUNDWATER CONTAMINATION USING AVERTING EXPENDITURES

How many resources should be allocated to the prevention of groundwater contamination? In part that depends on how serious a risk is posed by the contamination. How much damage would be caused? One way to obtain a lower-bound estimate on the damage caused is to discover how much people are willing to spend to defend themselves against the threat.

In late 1987 trichloroethylene (TCE) was detected in one of the town wells in Perkasie, a town in southeastern Pennsylvania. Concentrations of the chemical were 7 times the EPA's safety standard. Since no temporary solution was available to reduce concentrations to safe levels, the county required the town to notify customers of the contamination.

Once notified, consumers took 1 or more of the following actions: (1) they purchased more bottled water; (2) they started using bottled water; (3) they installed home water treatment systems; (4) they hauled water from alternative sources; and (5) they boiled water. Through a survey, analysts were able to discover the extent of each of these actions and combine that information with their associated costs.

The results indicated that residents spent between $61,313.29 and $131,334.06 over the 88-week period of the contamination. They further indicated that families with young children were more likely to take averting actions and, among those families who took averting actions, to spend more on those actions than childless families.

Source: Charles W. Abdalla, et al. "Valuing Environmental Quality Changes Using Averting Expenditures: An Application to Groundwater Contamination," *Land Economics* Vol. 68, No. 2 (1992): 163–169.

environmental (such as exposure to a toxic substance), the results of the multiple regression analysis can be used to construct a willingness to pay to avoid this kind of environmental risk. Additionally, the compensating wage differential can be used to calculate the value of a statistical life (Taylor, 2003).

A final example of an indirect observable method involves examining "averting or defensive expenditures." Averting expenditures are those designed to reduce the damage caused by pollution by taking some kind of averting or defensive action. An example would be to install indoor air purifiers in response to an influx of polluted air or to rely on bottled water as a response to the pollution of local drinking water supplies (Example 3.2). Since people would not normally spend more to prevent a problem than would be caused by the problem itself, averting expenditures can provide a lower-bound estimate of the damage caused by pollution.

A final category, indirect hypothetical methods, includes attribute-based methods and contingent ranking. Attribute-based methods such as choice-based, conjoint

TABLE 3.2

Attributes in the Maine Forest Harvesting Conjoint Analysis

Attribute	Level
Live trees after harvesting	No trees (clear-cut)
	153 trees/acre
	459 trees/acre
Dead trees after harvesting	Remove all
	5 trees/acre
	10 trees/acre
Percent of forest set aside from harvest	20%
	50%
	80%

Source: Boyle, et al. (2001) and Holmes and Adamovicz (2003).

models are useful when project options have multiple levels of different attributes. Like contingent valuation, conjoint analysis is also a survey-based technique, but instead of stating a willingness to pay, respondents choose between alternate states of the world. Each state of the world has a set of attributes, and a price.

Consider an example, Boyle, et al. (2001) surveyed Maine residents on their preferences for alternative forest harvesting practices. The State of Maine was considering purchasing a 23,000-acre tract of forest land to manage. Attributes used in the survey included the number of live trees, management practice for dead trees, percent of land set aside, and a tax payment. Three levels of each management attribute and 13 different tax prices were considered. Table 3.2 reproduces the attributes and levels.

Respondents were given a choice set of four different alternative management plans and the status quo (no purchase). Table 3.3 demonstrates a sample survey question. This type of survey has evolved from both contingent valuation and marketing studies. This approach allows the respondent to make a familiar choice (choose a bundle) and allows the researcher to derive marginal willingness to pay for an attribute from that choice.

Contingent ranking, another survey method, also falls within this final category. Respondents are given a set of hypothetical situations that differ in terms of the environmental amenity available (instead of a bundle of attributes) and are asked to rank order them (Example 3.3). These rankings can then be compared to see the implicit trade-offs between more of the environmental amenity and less of the other characteristics. When one or more of these characteristics can be expressed in terms of a monetary value, it is possible to use this information and the rankings to impute a value to the environmental amenity.

Sometimes a valuation exercise may use more than one of these techniques simultaneously. In some cases, that is necessary to capture the total economic value; in other cases it is done to provide independent estimates of the value being sought (see Example 3.4).

TABLE 3.3

A Sample Conjoint Analysis Survey Questionnaire

Attribute	Alternatives				
	A	B	C	D	No change
Live trees Remaining	No trees	459/acre	No trees	153/acre	
Dead Trees Remaining	Remove all	Remove all	5/acre	10/acre	
Percent Set Aside	80%	20%	50%	20%	
Tax	$40	$200	$10	$80	
I would vote for (please check off)	—	—	—	—	—

Source: Taken from Thomas P. Holmes and Wiktor L. Adamowicz. "Attribute-Based Methods," Chapter 6 in Ian Bateman, ed. *A Primer on Nonmarket Valuation* (New York: Kluwer Academic Publishers, 2003).

Example 3.3

VALUING DIESEL ODOR REDUCTION BY CONTINGENT RANKING

Emissions from diesel engines can adversely affect human health; they also produce an unpleasant odor. Reducing those emissions produces both a health benefit and reduction in odor. How much emission reduction is efficient therefore depends on how beneficial odor reduction is; if odor reduction is highly valued, more emission reduction is justified.

To discover whether odor reduction is valued sufficiently highly to make it an important component in diesel emission reduction decisions, a contingent ranking study was conducted in Philadelphia. Each respondent was required to smell two odors: odor A was a mild diesel smell, while odor B was a more intense smell. Respondents were then asked to rank the desirability of various options. Each option contained a level of exposure to odor and a level of annual transportation cost that was associated with reducing the number of exposures to the specified level. Higher transportation costs (reflecting the higher degree of control) were associated with lower exposure levels.

The analysis of these data revealed a willingness to pay between $3.03 and $5.49 per year to avoid one weekly contact with odor A and between $14.57 and $18.50 to avoid one weekly contact with odor B. Combining this information with the average number of weekly exposures to each of these odor types produced an estimate of $75 per year to avoid completely all odor exposures. Since EPA programs to control diesel emissions are estimated to cost about $3.60 per household, the value of diesel odor reduction seems significant.

Source: Thomas J. Lareau and Douglas A. Rae. "Valuing WTP for Diesel Odor Reductions: An Application of Contingent Ranking Technique," *Southern Economic Journal* Vol. 55, No. 3 (1989): 728–742.

Example 3.4

THE VALUE OF WILDLIFE VIEWING

One strategy we shall examine later in this book for preserving wildlife involves the use of ecotourism. Ecotourism tries to capture some of the willingness to pay for preserving wildlife as expressed by those who embark on safaris to view wildlife in their native habitat and uses that revenue to support wildlife preservation activities. How successful that strategy will be depends in part on how large that willingness to pay is.

One study attempted to find out how large the willingness to pay was for the Lake Nakuru National Park in Kenya. Originally established as a bird sanctuary in 1961, this park was expanded in 1969 and 1972. It is the home of some 1.4 million flamingos as well as some 360 other species of birds. Lately, however, the number of flamingos has diminished due to water pollution from increased farming activities.

Using both a travel-cost method and a contingent valuation method, the authors calculated the use value of visits to the park to view wildlife. The travel-cost estimates indicated that the annual value of recreational viewing in this park in 1991 was ($US) 13.7 to 15.1 million. Of that, ($US) 3.6 to 4.5 million was from residents of Kenya; the rest (the majority) was from nonresidents. The total value estimated by contingent valuation was ($US) 7.5 million.

Several points are worth noting:

- According to the travel-cost results, the majority of the value comes from nonresidents, which is not surprising given that the average nonresident visitor had a much higher income than the average resident visitor.
- Despite the fact that this study examined only use values and ignored nonuse values, the resulting estimates are quite high. Apparently ecotourism (in this park at least) could bring in significant revenue.
- The calculated values of wildlife viewing were much higher than the prevailing fees charged at the time, implying that more revenue for protecting wildlife could be extracted. (Recognizing this fact, the government raised nonresident entrance fees by 310% in 1993.)
- While it is normally recognized that controlling pollution costs money, this study points out that *not* controlling pollution *also* costs money (by killing the valuable wildlife). Although this study did not actually examine the cost of controlling the pollution, that would be an obvious next step.

Source: Ståle Navrud and E. D. Mungatana. "Environmental Valuation in Developing Countries: The Recreational Viewing of Wildlife," *Ecological Economics* 11 (November 1994): 135–151.

Valuing Human Life. One fascinating public policy area where these various approaches have been applied is in the valuation of human life. Many government programs, from those controlling hazardous pollutants in the workplace or in drinking water to those improving nuclear power plant safety, are designed to save human life as well as to reduce illness. How resources should be allocated among these programs depends crucially on the value of human life. How is life to be valued?

The simple answer, of course, is that life is priceless, but that turns out to be not very helpful. Because the resources used to prevent loss of life are scarce, choices must be made. The economic approach to valuing lifesaving reductions in environmental risk is to calculate the change in the probability of death resulting from the reduction in environmental risk and to place a value on the change. Thus, it is not life itself that is being valued but rather a reduction in the probability that some segment of the population could be expected to die earlier than otherwise. Debate 3.1 examines some of this controversy.

It is possible to translate the value derived from this procedure into an "implied value of human life." This is accomplished by dividing the amount each individual is willing to pay for a specific reduction in the probability of death by the probability reduction. Suppose, for example, that a particular environmental policy could be expected to reduce the average concentration of a toxic substance to which one million people are exposed. Suppose further that this reduction in exposure could be expected to reduce the risk of death from 1 out of 100,000 to 1 out of 150,000. This implies that the number of expected deaths would fall from 10 to 6.67 in the exposed population as a result of this policy. If each of the one million persons exposed is willing to pay $5 for this risk reduction (for a total of $5 million), then the implied value of a life is approximately $1.5 million ($5 million divided by 3.33).

What actual values have been derived from these methods? A survey (Viscusi, 1996) of a large number of studies examining reductions in a number of life-threatening risks found that most implied values for human life (in 1986 dollars) were between $3 million and $7 million. This same survey went on to suggest that the most appropriate estimates were probably closer to the $5 million estimate. In other words, all government programs resulting in risk reductions costing less than $5 million would be justified in benefit/cost terms. Those costing more might or might not be justified, depending on the appropriate value of a life saved in the particular risk context being examined.

How have health, safety, and environmental regulations lived up to this recommendation? As Table 3.4 suggests, not very well. A very large number of regulations listed in that table could be justified only if the value of a life saved were much higher than the upper value of $7 million.

Issues in Benefit Estimation[7]

The analyst charged with the responsibility for performing a benefit/cost analysis encounters many decision points requiring judgment. If we are to understand benefit/cost analysis, the nature of these judgments must be clear in our minds.

---

[7]This section relies heavily on Peskin and Seskin (1975).

DEBATE
3.1

Is Valuing Human Life Immoral?

In 2004 economist Frank Ackerman and lawyer Lisa Heinzerling teamed up to write a book that questions the morality of using benefit/cost analysis to evaluate regulations designed to protect human life. In *Priceless: On Knowing the Price of Everything and the Value of Nothing* (2004), they argue that benefit/cost analysis is immoral because it represents a retreat from the traditional standard that all citizens have an absolute right to be free from harm caused by pollution. When it justifies a regulation that will allow some pollution-induced deaths, benefits/cost analysis violates this absolute right.

Economist Maureen Cropper responds that it would be immoral not to consider the benefits of lifesaving measures. Resources are scarce and they must be allocated so as to produce the greatest good. If all pollution were reduced to zero, even if that were possible, the cost would be extremely high and the resources to cover that cost would have to be diverted from other beneficial uses. Professor Cropper also suggests that it would be immoral to impose costs on people about which they have no say—for example, the costs of additional pollution controls—without at least trying to consider what choices people would make themselves. Like it or not, hard choices must be made.

Cropper also points out that people are always making decisions that recognize a trade-off between the cost of more protection and the health consequences of not taking the protection. Thinking in terms of trade-offs is a familiar concept. She points out that people drive faster to save time, thereby increasing their risk of dying. They also decide how much money to spend on medicines to lower their risk of disease or they may take jobs that pose morbidity or even mortality risks.

In her response to Ackerman and Heinzerling. Cropper acknowledges that benefit/cost analysis has its flaws and that it should never be the only decision-making guide. Nonetheless she argues that it does add useful information to the process and throwing that information away could prove to be detrimental to the very people that Ackerman and Heinzerling seek to protect.

Sources: Frank Ackerman and Lisa Heinzerling. *Priceless: On Knowing the Price of Everything and the Value of Nothing* (New York: The New Press, 2004); *Frank Ackerman.* "Morality, Cost-Benefit and the Price of Life," *Environmental Forum* Vol. 21, No. 5 (2004): 46–47; and Maureen Cropper. "Immoral Not to Weigh Benefits Against Costs," *Environmental Forum* Vol. 21, No. 5 (2004): 47–48.

Primary Versus Secondary Effects. Environmental projects usually trigger both primary and secondary consequences. For example, the primary effect of cleaning a lake will be an increase in recreational uses of the lake. This primary effect will cause a further ripple effect on services provided to the increased number of users of the lake. Are these secondary benefits to be counted?

The answer depends upon the employment conditions in the surrounding area. If this increase in demand results in employment of previously unused resources, such as labor, the value of the increased employment should be counted. If, on the other hand, the increase in demand is met by a shift in previously employed

TABLE 3.4

The Cost of Risk-Reducing Regulations

	Agency Year and Status	Initial Annual Risk	Annual Lives Saved	Cost Per Life Saved (Millions of 1984 $)
Unvented Space Heaters	CPSC 1980 F	2.7 in 10^5	63.000	$.10
Cabin Fire Protection	FAA 1985 F	6.5 in 10^8	15.000	.20
Passive Restraints/Belts	NHTSA 1984 F	9.1 in 10^5	1,850.000	.30
Seat Cushion Flammability	FAA 1984 F	1.6 in 10^7	37.000	.60
Floor Emergency Lighting	FAA 1984 F	2.2 in 10^8	5.000	.70
Concrete & Masonry Constr.	OSHA 1988 F	1.4 in 10^5	6.500	1.40
Hazard Communication	OSHA 1983 F	4.0 in 10^5	200.000	1.80
Benzene/Fugitive Emissions	EPA 1984 F	2.1 in 10^4	0.310	2.80
Radionuclides/Uranium Mines	EPA 1984 F	1.4 in 10^4	1.100	6.90
Benzene	OSHA 1987 F	8.8 in 10^4	3.800	17.10
Asbestos	EPA 1989 F	2.9 in 10^5	10.000	104.20
Benzene/Storage	EPA 1984 R	6.0 in 10^7	0.043	202.00
Radionuclides/DOE Facilities	EPA 1984 R	4.3 in 10^6	0.001	210.00
Radionuclides/Elem. Phos.	EPA 1984 R	1.4 in 10^5	0.046	270.00
Benzene/Ethylbenzenol Styrene	EPA 1984 R	2.0 in 10^6	0.006	483.00
Arsenic/Low-Arsenic Copper	EPA 1986 R	2.6 in 10^4	0.090	764.00
Benzene/Maleic Anhydride	EPA 1984 R	1.1 in 10^6	0.029	820.00
Land Disposal	EPA 1988 F	2.3 in 10^8	2.520	3,500.00
Formaldehyde	OSHA 1987 F	6.8 in 10^4	0.010	72,000.00

In the "Agency Year and Status" column, R and F represent Rejected and Final rule, respectively. "Initial Annual Risk" indicates annual deaths per exposed population; an exposed population of 10^3 is 1000, 10^4 is 10,000, etc.

Source: Adapted from W. Kip Viscusi. "Economic Foundations of the Current Regulatory Reform Efforts," *The Journal of Economic Perspectives* 10 (1996): Tables 1 and 2: 124–125.

resources from one use to another, this is a different story. In general, secondary employment benefits should be counted in high unemployment areas or when the particular skills demanded are underemployed at the time the project is commenced. This should not be counted when the project simply results in a rearrangement of productively employed resources.

Tangible Versus Intangible Benefits. *Tangible* benefits are those that can reasonably be assigned a monetary value. *Intangible* benefits are those that cannot be assigned a monetary value, either because data are not available or reliable enough or because it is not clear how to measure the value even with data.[8]

How are intangible benefits to be handled? One answer is perfectly clear: They should not be ignored. To ignore intangible benefits is to bias the results. That benefits are intangible does not mean they are unimportant.

Intangible benefits should be quantified to the fullest extent possible. One frequently used technique is to conduct a sensitivity analysis of the estimated benefit values derived from less than perfectly reliable data. We can determine, for example, whether or not the outcome is sensitive, within wide ranges, to the value of this benefit. If not, then very little time has to be spent on the problem. If the outcome is sensitive, the person or persons making the decision bear the ultimate responsibility for weighing the importance of that benefit.

Approaches to Cost Estimation

Estimating costs is generally easier than estimating benefits, but it is not easy. One major problem for both derives from the fact that benefit/cost analysis is forward-looking and thus requires an estimate of what a particular strategy *will* cost, which is much more difficult than tracking down what an existing strategy *does* cost.

Another frequent problem is posed by collecting cost information when availability of that information is controlled by a firm having an interest in the outcome. Pollution control is an obvious example. Two approaches have been used to deal with this problem.

The Survey Approach. One way to discover the costs associated with a policy is to ask those who bear the costs, and presumably know the most about them, to reveal the magnitude of the costs to policy-makers. Polluters, for example, could be asked to provide control-cost estimates to regulatory bodies. The problem with this approach is the strong incentive not to be truthful. An overestimate of the costs can trigger less stringent regulation; therefore, it is financially advantageous to provide overinflated estimates.

The Engineering Approach. The engineering approach bypasses the source being regulated by using general engineering information to catalog the possible technologies that could be used to meet the objective and to estimate the costs of purchasing and using those technologies. The final step in the engineering approach

---

[8]The division between tangible and intangible benefits changes as our techniques improve. Recreation benefits were, until the advent of the travel-cost model, treated as intangible.

is to assume that the sources would use technologies that minimize cost. This produces a cost estimate for a "typical," well-informed firm.

The engineering approach has its own problems. These estimates may not approximate the actual cost of any particular firm. Unique circumstances may cause the costs of that firm to be higher, or lower, than estimated; the firm, in short, may not be typical.

The Combined Approach. To circumvent these problems, analysts frequently use a combination of survey and engineering approaches. The survey approach collects information on possible technologies, as well as special circumstances facing the firm. Engineering approaches are used to derive the actual costs of those technologies, given the special circumstances. This combined approach attempts to balance information best supplied by the source with that best derived independently.

In the cases described so far, the costs are relatively easy to quantify and the problem is simply finding a way to acquire the best information. This is not always the case, however. Some costs are not easy to quantify, though economists have developed some ingenious ways to secure monetary estimates even for those costs.

Take, for example, a policy designed to conserve energy by forcing more people to carpool. If the effect of this is simply to increase the average time of travel, how is this cost to be measured?

For some time, transportation analysts have recognized that people do value their time, and quite a literature has now evolved to provide estimates of this valuation. The basis for this valuation is opportunity cost—how the time might be used if it weren't being consumed in travel. Although the results of these studies depend on the amount of time involved, individuals seem to value their time at a rate not more than half their wage rates.

The Treatment of Risk

For many environmental problems, it is not possible to state with certainty what consequences a particular policy will have, because scientific estimates themselves often are imprecise. Determining the efficient exposure to potentially toxic substances requires obtaining results at high doses and extrapolating to low doses, as well as extrapolating from animal studies to humans. It also requires relying upon epidemiological studies that infer a pollution-induced adverse human health impact from correlations between indicators of health in human populations and recorded pollution levels.

Another illustration of the significance of scientific uncertainty is afforded by the climate change problem. Certain gases, when emitted into the atmosphere, are suspected of causing the planetary temperature to rise. If this suspicion is correct, it could have very serious implications. Among others, it could trigger a rise in the sea level and could result in the deaths of large numbers of plants no longer suited for the temperatures to which they would be subjected. The conjecture that increased emissions of carbon dioxide and other greenhouse gases are causing a rise in temperature is based upon a computer model that has only partially been validated. This is a prototypical example of a problem that is poorly understood but that, if the conjectures are true, could pose significant problems in the future.

The treatment of risk in the policy process involves two major dimensions: (1) identifying and quantifying the risks; and (2) deciding how much risk is acceptable. The former is primarily scientific and descriptive, while the latter is more evaluative or normative.

Benefit/cost analysis grapples with the evaluation of risk in several ways. Suppose, for example, that we have a range of policy options A, B, C, D and a range of possible outcomes E, F, G for each of these policies depending on how the economy evolves over the future. These outcomes, for example, might depend on whether the demand growth for the resource is low, medium, or high. Thus, if we choose policy A, we might end up with outcomes AE, AF, or AG. Each of the other policies has three possible outcomes as well, yielding a total of 12 possible outcomes.

We could conduct a separate benefit/cost analysis for each of the 12 possible outcomes. Unfortunately, the policy that maximizes net benefits for E may be different from that which maximizes net benefits for F or G. Thus, if we only knew which outcome would prevail, we could select the policy that maximized net benefits; the problem is that we don't. Furthermore, choosing the policy that is best if outcome E prevails may be disastrous if G results instead.

When a dominant policy emerges, this problem is avoided. A *dominant policy* is one that confers higher net benefits for every outcome. In this case, the existence of risk concerning the future is not relevant for the policy choice. Though this fortuitous circumstance is exceptional rather than common, it can occur.

Other options exist even when dominant solutions do not emerge. Suppose, for example, that we were able to assess the likelihood that each of the three possible outcomes would occur. Thus we might expect outcome E to occur with probability 0.5, F with probability 0.3, and G with probability 0.2. Armed with this information, we can estimate the expected present value of net benefits. The *expected present value of net benefits* for a particular policy is defined as the sum over outcomes of the present value of net benefits for that policy where each outcome is weighted by its probability of occurrence. Symbolically this is expressed as:

$$NPVNB_j = \sum_{i=0}^{I} P_i PVNB_{ij}, \qquad j = 1, \ldots, \mathcal{J}, \qquad (3.1)$$

where

$EPVNB_j$ = expected present value of net benefits for policy j
P_i = probability of the ith outcome occurring
$PVNB_{ij}$ = present value of net benefits for policy j if outcome i prevails
$\mathcal{J}$ = number of policies being considered
I = number of outcomes being considered

The final step is to select the policy with the highest expected present value of net benefits.

This approach has the substantial virtue that it weighs higher probability outcomes more heavily. It also, however, makes a specific assumption about society's preference for risk. This approach is appropriate if society is risk-neutral. *Risk-neutrality* can be defined most easily by the use of an example. Suppose you were allowed to choose between being given a definite $50 or entering a lottery in which you had a

50% chance of winning $100 and a 50% chance of winning nothing. (Notice that the expected value of this lottery is $50 = 0.5($100) + 0.5($0).) You would be said to be risk-neutral if you would be indifferent between these two choices. If you view the lottery as more attractive, you would be exhibiting *risk-loving* behavior, while a preference for the definite $50 would suggest *risk-averse* behavior. Using the expected present value of net benefits approach implies that society is risk-neutral.

Is that a valid assumption? The evidence is mixed. The existence of gambling suggests that at least some members of society are risk lovers while the existence of insurance suggests that at least for some risks, others are risk-averse. Since the same people may gamble and own insurance policies, it's likely that the type of risk may be important.

Even if individuals were demonstrably risk-averse, this would not be a sufficient condition for the government to forsake risk-neutrality in evaluating public investments. One famous article by Arrow and Lind (1970) argues that risk-neutrality is appropriate since "when the risks of a public investment are publicly borne, the total cost of risk-bearing is insignificant and, therefore, the government should ignore uncertainty in evaluating public investments." The logic behind this result suggests that as the number of risk bearers (and the degree of diversification of risks) increases, the amount of risk borne by any individual diminishes to zero.

When the decision is irreversible, as demonstrated by Arrow and Fisher (1974), considerably more caution is appropriate. Irreversible decisions may subsequently be regretted, but the option to change course will be lost forever. Extra caution also affords an opportunity to learn more about alternatives to this decision and its consequences before acting. Isn't it comforting to know that procrastination can occasionally be optimal?

There is a movement in national policy in both the courts and the legislature to search for imaginative ways to define acceptable risk.[9] In general, the policy approaches reflect a case-by-case approach. We shall see that current policy reflects a high degree of risk aversion toward a number of environmental problems.

Choosing the Discount Rate

In the previous chapter we discussed how the discount rate could be defined conceptually as the social opportunity cost of capital. This cost of capital can be divided further into two components: (1) the riskless cost of capital and (2) the risk premium.

As Example 3.5 indicates, this has been, and continues to be, an important issue. When the public sector uses a discount rate lower than that in the private sector, the public sector will find more projects with longer payoff periods worthy of authorization. And, as we have already seen, the discount rate is a major determinant of the allocation of resources among generations as well.

Traditionally, economists have used long-term interest rates on government bonds as one measure of the cost of capital, adjusted by a risk premium that would depend on the riskiness of the project considered. Unfortunately, the choice of how large an adjustment to make has been left to the discretion of the analysts.

---

[9]An excellent collection of essays on this subject is contained in Glickman and Gough (1990).

Example 3.5

THE HISTORICAL IMPORTANCE OF THE DISCOUNT RATE

For years the United States and Canada had been discussing the possibility of constructing a tidal power project in the Passamaquoddy Bay between Maine and New Brunswick. This project would have heavy initial capital costs, but low operating costs that presumably would hold for a long time into the future. As part of their analysis of the situation, a complete inventory of costs and benefits was completed in 1959.

Using the same benefit and cost figures, Canada concluded that the project should not be built, while the United States concluded that it should. Because these conclusions were based on the same benefit/cost data, the differences can be attributed solely to the use of different discount rates. The United States used 2.5% while Canada used 4.125%. The higher discount rate makes the initial cost weigh much more heavily in the calculation, leading to the Canadian conclusion that the project would yield a negative net benefit. Since the lower discount rate weights the lower future operating costs relatively more heavily, Americans saw the net benefit as positive.

There are a number of other examples, as well. During 1962, Congress authorized a number of water projects that had been justified by benefit/cost analysis using a discount rate of 2.63%. Upon examining these projects, economists Fox and Herfindahl (1964, p. 202) found that, at an 8% rate of discount, only 20% of the projects would have had favorable benefit/cost ratios.

The choice of the discount rate even played a major role following a highly publicized dispute between President Jimmy Carter and Congress. President Carter wanted to rescind authorization from many previously approved water projects that he viewed as wasteful. The President based his conclusions on a discount rate of 6.38% while Congress was using a lower one.

Far from being an esoteric subject, the choice of the discount rate is fundamentally important in defining the role of the public sector, the types of projects undertaken, and the allocation of resources across generations.

Source: Edith Stokey and Richard Zeckhauser. *A Primer for Policy Analysis* (New York: W. W. Norton, 1978): 164–165; Raymond Mikesell. *The Rate of Discount for Evaluating Public Projects* (Washington, DC: The American Enterprise Institute for Public Policy Research, 1977): 3–5; Irving K. Fox and Orris C. Herfindahl. "Attainment of Efficiency in Satisfying Demands for Water Resources," *American Economic Review* 54 (May 1964): 202.

This ability to affect the desirability of a particular project or policy by the choice of discount rate led to a situation in which government agencies were using a variety of discount rates to justify programs or projects they supported. One set of hearings conducted by Congress during the 1960s discovered that, at one time, agencies were using discount rates ranging from 0% to 20%.

During the early 1970s the Office of Management and Budget published a circular that required, with some exceptions, all government agencies to use a discount rate of 10% in their benefit/cost analysis. A revision issued in 1992 reduced the required discount rate to 7%. This circular also includes guidelines for benefit/cost analysis and specifies that certain rates will change annually.[10] This standardization reduces biases by eliminating the agency's ability to choose a discount rate that justifies a predetermined conclusion. It also allows a project to be considered independently of fluctuations in the true social cost of capital due to cycles in the behavior of the economy. On the other hand, when the social opportunity cost of capital differs from this administratively determined level, the benefit/cost analysis will not, in general, define the efficient allocation.

A Critical Appraisal

We have seen that it is sometimes, though not always, difficult to estimate benefits and costs. When this estimation is difficult or unreliable, it limits the value of a benefit/cost analysis. This problem would be particularly disturbing if biases tended to systematically increase or decrease net benefits. Do such biases exist?

In the early 1970s, economist Robert Haveman (1972) did a major study that sheds some light on this question. Focusing on Army Corps of Engineers water projects, such as flood control, navigation, and hydroelectric power generation, Haveman compared the *ex ante* (before the fact) estimate of benefits and costs with their *ex post* (after the fact) counterparts. Thus he was able to address the issues of accuracy and bias. He concluded that:

> In the empirical case studies presented, *ex post* estimates often showed little relationship to their *ex ante* counterparts. On the basis of the few cases and the *a priori* analysis presented here, one could conclude that there is a serious bias incorporated into agency *ex ante* evaluation procedures, resulting in persistent overstatement of expected benefits. Similarly in the analysis of project construction costs, enormous variance was found among projects in the relationship between estimated and realized costs. Although no persistent bias in estimation was apparent, nearly 50 percent of the projects displayed realized costs that deviated by more than plus or minus 20 percent from *ex ante* projected costs.[11]

In the cases examined by Haveman, at least, the notion that benefit/cost analysis is purely a scientific exercise was clearly not consistent with the evidence; the biases of the analysts were merely translated into numbers.

In a more recent review of benefit/cost analysis, Ackerman, et al. (2004) examine three policies that were imposed without *ex ante* benefit/cost analysis. For each of the three regulatory decisions, they look backward and ask, "What would have

---

[10]Annual rates can be found at http://www.whitehouse.gov/omb/.

[11]A more recent assessment of costs (Harrington, et al., 1999) found evidence of both overestimation and underestimation, although overestimation was more common. The authors attributed the overestimation mainly to a failure to anticipate technical innovation.

happened if benefit/cost analysis, based on the information available, had been the determining factor in the decision?" (Ackerman, et al., p. 2). They examine the removal of lead from gasoline, protecting the Grand Canyon from hydroelectric dams, and the regulation of allowable workplace exposure to vinyl chloride. These three regulatory decisions are all deemed successes today, yet according to their analysis none of them would have passed a benefit/cost analysis. Examining the reasons why they would not have passed a benefit/cost test is instructive. Benefit/cost analysis of the removal of lead from gasoline would have required a long waiting period to experience the health benefits. Benefit/cost analysis of hydroelectric dams near the Grand Canyon would have shown positive net benefits since the same amount of electricity from thermal powered plants would have been much more expensive. If a benefit/cost analysis had been done for exposure to vinyl chloride, the costs to industry would have been compared to the value of avoided deaths. Low values of life were typically used in the 1970s and 1 in 7 workers would have had to have died for this regulation to pass benefit/cost analysis! (Ackerman, et al., 2004).

Does their analysis mean that benefit/cost analysis is fatally flawed? Absolutely not! It does, however, highlight the importance of calculating an accurate value of life (vinyl chloride), of including all of the potential benefits and costs (for example, nonmarket values associated with the Grand Canyon) and of appropriately valuing health effects that may take time to appear (lead). It also serves to remind us, however, that benefit/cost analysis is not a stand-alone technique. It should be used in conjunction with other available information. Economic analysis including benefit/cost analysis can provide useful information, but it should not be the only determinant for all decisions.

Another shortcoming of benefit/cost analysis is that it does not really address the question of who reaps the benefits and who pays the cost. It is quite possible for a particular course of action to yield high net benefits, but to have the benefits borne by one group of society and the costs borne by another. This admittedly extreme case does serve to illustrate a basic principle—ensuring that a particular policy is efficient provides an important, but not always the sole, basis for public policy. Other aspects, such as who reaps the benefit or bears the burden, are also important.

In summary, on the positive side, benefit/cost analysis is frequently a very useful part of the policy process. Even when the underlying data are not strictly reliable, the outcomes may not be sensitive to that unreliability. In other circumstances, the data may be reliable enough to give indications of the consequences of broad policy directions, even when they are not reliable enough to fine-tune those policies. Benefit/cost analysis, when done correctly, can provide a useful complement to the other influences on the political process by clarifying what choices yield the highest net benefits to society.

On the negative side, benefit/cost analysis has been attacked as seeming to promise more than can actually be delivered, particularly in the absence of solid benefit information. There have been two responses to this kind of concern. First, regulatory processes have been developed that can be implemented with very little information and yet have desirable economic properties. The recent reforms in air pollution control, which we cover in Chapter 16, provide one powerful example.

The second approach involves techniques that supply useful information to the policy process without relying on controversial techniques to monetize environmental services that are difficult to value. The rest of this chapter deals with the two most prominent of these—cost-effectiveness analysis and impact analysis.

Even when benefits are difficult or impossible to quantify, economic analysis has much to offer. Policy-makers should know, for example, how much various policy actions will cost and what their impacts on society will be, even if the efficient policy choice cannot be identified with any certainty. Cost-effectiveness analysis and impact analysis both respond to this need, albeit in different ways.

Cost-Effectiveness Analysis

What can be done to guide policy when the requisite valuation for benefit/cost analysis is either unavailable or not sufficiently reliable? Without a good measure of benefits, making an efficient choice is no longer possible.

In such cases it frequently is possible, however, to set a policy target on some basis other than a strict comparison of benefits and costs. One example is pollution control. What level of pollution should be established as the maximum acceptable level? In many countries, studies of the effects of a particular pollutant on human health have been used as the basis for establishing that pollutant's maximum acceptable concentration. Researchers attempt to find a threshold level below which no damage seems to occur. That threshold is then further lowered to provide a margin of safety and that becomes the pollution target.

Approaches could also be based upon expert opinion. Ecologists, for example, could be enlisted to define the critical numbers of certain species or the specific critical wetlands resources that should be preserved.

Once the policy target is specified, however, economic analysis can have a great deal to say about the cost consequences of choosing a means of achieving that objective. The cost consequences are important not only because eliminating wasteful expenditures is an appropriate goal in its own right, but also to assure that they do not trigger a political backlash.

Typically, several means of achieving the specified objective are available; some will be relatively inexpensive, while others turn out to be very expensive. The problems are frequently complicated enough that identifying the cheapest manner of achieving an objective cannot be accomplished without a rather detailed analysis of the choices.

Cost-effectiveness analysis frequently involves an *optimization procedure*. An optimization procedure, in this context, is merely a systematic method for finding the lowest-cost means of accomplishing the objective. This procedure does not, in general, produce an efficient allocation because the predetermined objective may not be efficient. All efficient policies are cost-effective, but not all cost-effective policies are efficient.

In the preceding chapter we introduced the efficiency equimarginal principle. According to that principle, net benefits are maximized when the marginal benefit is equal to the marginal cost.

A similar, and equally important, equimarginal principle exists for cost-effectiveness:

> Second Equimarginal Principle (the Cost-Effectiveness Equimarginal Principle): The least-cost means of achieving an environmental target will have been achieved when the marginal costs of all possible means of achievement are equal.

Suppose, for example, we want to achieve a specific emission reduction across a region, and several possible techniques exist for reducing emissions. How much of the control responsibility should each technique bear? The cost-effectiveness equimarginal principle suggests that the techniques should be used such that the desired reduction is achieved and the cost of achieving the last unit of emission reduction (in other words, the marginal control cost) should be the same for all sources.

To demonstrate why this principle is valid, suppose that we have an allocation of control responsibility where marginal control costs are much higher for one set of techniques than for another. This cannot be the least-cost allocation since we could lower cost while retaining the same amount of emission reduction. Costs could be lowered by allocating more control to the lower marginal cost sources and less to the high marginal cost sources. Since it is possible to find a way to lower cost, then clearly the initial allocation could not have minimized cost. Once marginal costs are equalized, it becomes impossible to find any lower-cost way of achieving the same degree of emissions reduction; therefore that allocation must be the allocation that minimizes costs.

In our pollution control example, cost-effectiveness can be used to find the least-cost means of meeting a particular standard and its associated cost. Using this cost as a benchmark case, we can estimate how much costs could be expected to increase from this minimum level if policies that are not cost-effective are implemented. Cost-effectiveness analysis can also be used to determine how much compliance costs can be expected to change if the EPA chooses a more stringent or less stringent standard. The case study presented in Example 3.6 not only illustrates the use of cost-effectiveness analysis, it also shows that costs can be very sensitive to the regulatory approach chosen by the EPA.

Impact Analysis

What can be done when the information needed to perform a benefit/cost analysis or a cost-effectiveness analysis is not available? The analytical technique designed to deal with this problem is called *impact analysis*. An impact analysis, regardless of whether it focuses on economic impact or environmental impact or both, attempts to quantify the consequences of various actions.

In contrast to benefit/cost analysis, a pure impact analysis makes no attempt to convert all these consequences into a one-dimensional measure, such as dollars, to ensure comparability. In contrast to cost-effectiveness analysis, impact analysis does not necessarily attempt to optimize. Impact analysis places a large amount of relatively undigested information at the disposal of the policy-maker. It is up to the policy-maker to assess the importance of the various consequences and act accordingly.

Example 3.6

NO₂ CONTROL IN CHICAGO: AN EXAMPLE OF COST-EFFECTIVENESS ANALYSIS

In order to compare compliance costs of meeting a predetermined ambient air quality standard in Chicago, Seskin, Anderson, and Reid (1983) gathered information on the cost of control for each of 797 stationary sources of nitrogen oxide emissions in the city of Chicago, along with measured air quality at 100 different locations within the city. The relationship between ambient air quality at those receptors and emissions from the 797 sources was then modeled using mathematical equations. Once these equations were estimated, the model was calibrated to ensure that it was capable of re-creating the actual situation in Chicago. Following successful calibration, this model was used to simulate what would happen if EPA were to take various regulatory actions.

The results indicated that a cost-effective strategy would cost less than one-tenth as much as the traditional approach to control and less than one-seventh as much as a more sophisticated version of the traditional approach. In absolute terms, moving to a more cost-effective policy was estimated to save more than $100 million annually in the Chicago area alone. In Chapters 15 and 16 we shall examine in detail the current movement toward cost-effective polices, a movement triggered in part by studies such as this one.

On January 1, 1970, President Nixon signed the National Environmental Policy Act of 1969. This act, among other things, directed all agencies of the federal government to:

> include in every recommendation or report on proposals for legislation and other major Federal actions significantly affecting the quality of the human environment, a detailed statement by the responsible official on—
>
> (i)   the environmental impact of the proposed action.
> (ii) any adverse environmental effects which cannot be avoided should the proposal be implemented,
> (iii) alternatives to the proposed action,
> (iv) the relationships between local short-term uses of man's environment and the maintenance and enhancement of long-term productivity; and
> (v)   any irreversible and irretrievable commitments of resources which would be involved in the proposed action should it be implemented.[12]

This was the beginning of the environmental impact statement, which is now a familiar, if controversial, part of environmental policy-making.

---

[12]83 Stat. 853.

Current environmental impact statements are more sophisticated than their early predecessors and may contain a benefit/cost analysis or a cost-effectiveness analysis in addition to other more traditional impact measurements. Historically, however, the tendency had been to issue huge environmental impact statements that are virtually impossible to comprehend in their entirety.

In response, the Council on Environmental Quality, which, by law, administers the environmental impact statement process, has set content standards that are now resulting in shorter, more concise statements. To the extent that they merely quantify consequences, statements can avoid the problem of "hidden value judgments" that sometimes plague benefit/cost analysis, but they do so only by bombarding the policy-makers with masses of noncomparable information. All three of the techniques discussed in this chapter are useful, but none of them can stake a claim as being universally the "best" approach. The nature of the information that is available and its reliability make a difference.

Summary

In this chapter we have examined the most prominent but certainly not the only techniques available to supply policy-makers with the information needed to implement efficient policy. Finding the total economic value of the service flows requires estimating three components of value: (1) use value, (2) option value, and (3) nonuse or passive-use value.

Our review of these various techniques included direct observation, contingent valuation, contingent ranking, travel cost, hedonic property and wage studies and averting or defensive expenditures. Examples of actual studies using these techniques were presented.

Because benefit/cost analysis is both very powerful and very controversial, in 1996 a group of economists of quite different political persuasions got together to attempt to reach some consensus on its proper role in environmental decision-making. Their conclusion is worth reproducing in its entirety:

> Benefit-cost analysis can play an important role in legislative and regulatory policy debates on protecting and improving health, safety and the natural environment. Although formal benefit-cost analysis should not be viewed as either necessary or sufficient for designing sensible policy, it can provide an exceptionally useful framework for consistently organizing disparate information, and in this way, it can greatly improve the process and, hence, the outcome of policy analysis. If properly done, benefit-cost analysis can be of great help to agencies participating in the development of environmental, health and safety regulations, and it can likewise be useful in evaluating agency decision-making and in shaping statutes.[13]

---

[13]Kenneth Arrow, et al. "Is There a Role for Benefit-Cost Analysis in Environmental, Health and Safety Regulation?" *Science* 272 (April 12, 1996): 221–222.

Even when benefits are difficult to calculate, however, economic analysis in the form of cost effectiveness can be valuable. This technique can establish the least expensive ways to accomplish predetermined policy goals and to assess the extra costs involved when policies other than the least-cost policy are chosen. What it cannot do is answer the question of whether those predetermined policy goals are efficient.

At the end of the spectrum is impact analysis, which merely identifies and quantifies the impacts of particular policies without any pretense of optimality or even comparability of the information generated. Impact analysis does not guarantee an efficient outcome.

Discussion Questions

1. Is risk-neutrality an appropriate assumption for benefit/cost analysis? Why or why not? Does it seem more appropriate for some environmental problems than others? If so, which ones? If you were evaluating the desirability of locating a hazardous waste incinerator in a particular town, would the Arrow-Lind rationale for risk-neutrality be appropriate? Why or why not?
2. Was the executive order issued by President Bush mandating a heavier use of benefit/cost analysis in regulatory rule making a step toward establishing a more rational regulatory structure, or was it a subversion of the environmental policy process? Why?
3. Certain environmental laws prohibit EPA from considering the costs of meeting various standards when the levels of the standards are set. Is this a good example of "putting first things first" or simply an unjustifiable waste of resources? Why?

Problems

1. In Mark A. Cohen, "The Costs and Benefits of Oil Spill Prevention and Enforcement," *Journal of Environmental Economics and Management* 13 (June 1986), an attempt was made to quantify the marginal benefits and marginal costs of U.S. Coast Guard enforcement activity in the area of oil spill prevention. His analysis suggests (p. 185) that the marginal per-gallon benefit from the current level of enforcement activity is $7.50 while the marginal per-gallon cost is $5.50. Assuming these numbers are correct, would you recommend that the Coast Guard increase, decrease, or hold at the current level their enforcement activity? Why?
2. In Table 3.4, Professor Kip Viscusi estimates that the cost per life saved by current government risk-reducing programs ranges from $100,000 for unvented space heaters to $72 billion for a proposed standard to reduce occupational exposure to formaldehyde.
    (a) Assuming these values to be correct, how might efficiency be enhanced in these two programs?
    (b) Should the government strive to equalize the marginal costs per life saved across all lifesaving programs?

Further Reading

Barde, Jean-Philippe, and David W. Pearce. *Valuing the Environment: Six Case Studies* (London: Earthscan Publications, 1991). A series of essays describing the use of economic valuation of environmental resources to inform public policy. Includes case studies from Germany, Italy, the Netherlands, Norway, the United Kingdom, and the United States.

Boardman, Anthony E., David H. Greemberg, Aiden R. Vining, and David L. Weimer. *Cost-Benefit Analysis: Concepts and Practice* (Upper Saddle River, NJ: Prentice-Hall, 1996). An excellent basic text on the use of benefit/cost analysis.

Costanza, R., et al. "The Value of the World's Ecosystem Services and Natural Capital (Reprinted from *Nature* Vol. 387, p. 253, 1997)," *Ecological Economics* Vol. 25, No. 1 (1998): 3–15. An ambitious but ultimately flawed attempt to place an economic value on ecosystem services. This issue of *Ecological Economics* also contains a number of articles that demonstrate some of the flaws.

Cummings, Ronald G., David S. Brookshire, and William D. Schulze. *Valuing Environmental Goods: An Assessment of the Contingent Valuation Method* (Totowa, NJ: Rowman and Littlefield, 1986). A critical evaluation of the contingent valuation method by both practitioners and impartial reviewers.

Diamond, Peter A., and Jerry A. Hausman. "Contingent Valuation. Is Some Number Better than No Number?" *Journal of Economic Perspectives* Vol. 8, No. 4 (Fall 1994): 45–64.

Dixon, John A., and Maynard M. Hufschmidt. *Economic Valuation Techniques for the Environment* (Baltimore: The Johns Hopkins University Press, 1986). Several case studies on the application of valuation techniques to environmental problems in less developed countries.

Glickman, Theodore S., and Michael Gough, eds. *Readings in Risk* (Washington, DC: Resources for the Future, Inc., 1990).

Griffin, Ronald C. "The Fundamental Principles of Cost-Benefit Analysis," *Water Resources Research* Vol. 34, No. 8 (1998): 2063–2071.

Hausman, Jerry A., ed. *Contingent Valuation: A Critical Assessment* (Amsterdam: North-Holland, 1993). The critics of contingent valuation weigh in.

Kneese, Allen V. *Measuring the Benefits of Clean Air and Water* (Washington, DC: Resources for the Future, 1984). An accessible introduction to a large number of studies attempting to quantify the benefits of cleaner air and water.

Kopp, Raymond J., and V. Kerry Smith, eds. *Valuing Natural Assets: The Economics of Natural Resource Damage Assessment* (Washington, D.C.: Resources for the Future, Inc., 1993). A comprehensive set of essays by some of the chief practitioners in the field evaluating both the legal framework for damage assessment and the validity and reliability of the methods currently being used.

Mitchell, Robert Cameron, and Richard T. Carson. *Using Surveys to Value Public Goods: The Contingent Valuation Method* (Washington: Resources for the Future, 1989). A comprehensive examination of contingent valuation research with brief summaries of representative studies.

Viscusi, W. Kip. "Economic Foundations of the Current Regulatory Reform Efforts," *Journal of Economic Perspectives* Vol. 10, No. 3 (Summer 1996): 119–134.

Additional References and Historically Significant References are available on this book's companion Web site www.aw-bc.com/tietenberg.

Property Rights, Externalities, and Environmental Problems

The charming landscape which I saw this morning, is indubitably made up of some twenty or thirty farms. Miller owns this field, Locke that, and Manning the woodland beyond. But none of them owns the landscape. There is a property in the horizon which no man has but he whose eye can integrate all the parts, that is, the poet. This is the best part of these men's farms, yet to this their land deeds give them no title.

—Ralph Waldo Emerson, *Nature* (1836)

Introduction

In Chapter 2 we developed specific normative criteria for making rational choices about the relationship between the economic system and the environment. According to those criteria, an environmental problem exists when resource allocations are inefficient.

When would breaches of efficiency occur? Why would individual or group interests diverge from those of society at large? What circumstances give rise to this division of interests, and what can be done about it? One useful way to examine this question is based on the concept known as a *property right*. In this chapter we explore this concept and how it can be used to understand why the environmental asset can be undervalued by both the market and governmental policy. We also discuss how the government and the market can, on occasion, use knowledge of property rights and their effects on incentives to orchestrate a coordinated approach to resolving these difficulties.

Property Rights

Property Rights and Efficient Market Allocations

The manner in which producers and consumers use environmental resources depends on the property rights governing those resources. In economics, *property right* refers to a bundle of entitlements defining the owner's rights, privileges, and limitations for use of the resource. By examining such entitlements and how they affect human behavior, we will better understand how environmental problems arise from government and market allocations.

These property rights can be vested either with individuals, as in a capitalist economy, or with the state, as in a centrally planned socialist economy. It is not uncommon to hear that the source of environmental problems in a capitalist economy is the market system itself or, more specifically, the pursuit of profits. You may have heard this point of view expressed as, "Corporations are more interested in profits than in the needs of people." Those who espouse this view look longingly at centrally planned economies as a means of avoiding environmental excess.

Simple answers rarely suffice for complex problems; environmental and natural resource problems are not an exception. Centrally planned economies, such as the former Soviet Union, have not historically avoided pollution excesses (see Example 4.1). On the other hand, the pursuit of profits is not inevitably inconsistent with fulfilling the needs of the people. Though the pursuit of profits may sometimes be inconsistent with fulfilling these needs, it is not always inconsistent. In fact, this pursuit is often the essential ingredient in meeting people's needs. How can we tell when the pursuit of profits is consistent with societal objectives, such as efficiency, and when it is not?

Efficient Property Right Structures

Let's begin by describing the structure of property rights that could produce efficient allocations in a well-functioning market economy. An efficient structure has 3 main characteristics:

1. *Exclusivity*—All benefits and costs accrued as a result of owning and using the resources should accrue to the owner, and only to the owner, either directly or indirectly by sale to others.
2. *Transferability*—All property rights should be transferable from one owner to another in a voluntary exchange.
3. *Enforceability*—Property rights should be secure from involuntary seizure or encroachment by others.

An owner of a resource with a well-defined property right (one exhibiting these three characteristics) has a powerful incentive to use that resource efficiently because a decline in the value of that resource represents a personal loss. Farmers who own the land have an incentive to fertilize and irrigate it because the resulting increased

Example 4.1

POLLUTION IN CENTRALLY PLANNED ECONOMIES

Since environmental problems are thought to be caused by a divergence between individual incentives and collective incentives, the belief that centrally planned economies avoid environmental problems seems plausible. Centralizing power in the state, as occurs in a centrally planned economy, could potentially allow collective decisions to be made at the outset.

Studies of air and water pollution in the former Soviet Union and other Eastern European countries, however, suggest that the problems found in market economies occur with equal intensity in the Eastern bloc. Copsa Mica, Romania, for example, is called Europe's most polluted urban area. Weakened by acid rain, monuments in Krakow, Poland, are crumbling. Women with newborn babies in Czechoslovakia have priority access to bottled water because tap water is considered injurious to infant health.

How can this be? Goldman suggests that the centralized planning system creates different, but no less potent, divergences between individual and collective incentives. According to the State of the Environment in Russia report, two-thirds of Russia's population lives in territories where the air pollution level is unhealthy. By the year 2000 more than two billion tons of toxic waste had accumulated in Russia. Preventing this pollution was a low priority because the managers of the polluting factories were rewarded for output, not pollution control. The central plans, which established national priorities, emphasized growth over environmental protection.

In his summary Goldman states:

> . . . not private enterprise but industrialization is the primary cause of environmental disruption. This suggests that state ownership of all the productive resources is no cure-all.

Sources: Marshall I. Goldman. "Economics of Environmental and Renewable Resources in Socialist Systems," in Allen V. Kneese and James L. Sweeney, eds. *Handbook of Natural Resource and Energy Economics,* Vol. II (Amsterdam: North-Holland, 1985): 725–745; State of the Environment in Russia (http://eco.priroda.ru/); Louis Berney. "Black Town of Transylvania Is Called Europe's Most Polluted," *The Boston Globe* (March 28, 1990): 2; Hilary F. French. "Industrial Wasteland," *Worldwatch* (November/December 1988): 21–30; Vladimir Kotov and Elena Nikitina. "Russia in Transition: Obstacles to Environmental Protection," *Environment* 35 (December 1993): 10–19.

production raises income. Similarly, they have an incentive to rotate crops when that raises the productivity of their land.

When well-defined property rights are exchanged, as in a market economy, this exchange facilitates efficiency. We can illustrate this point by examining the incentives consumers and producers face when a well-defined system of property rights

FIGURE 4.1

The Consumer's Choice

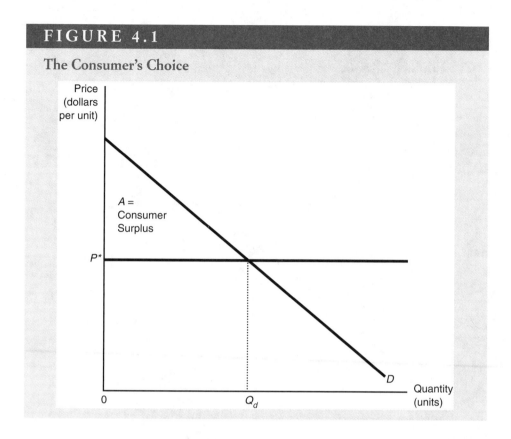

is in place. Because the seller has the right to prevent the consumer from consuming the product in the absence of payment, the consumer must pay to receive the product. Given a market price, the consumer decides how much to purchase by choosing the amount that maximizes his or her individual net benefit (see Figure 4.1).

The consumer's net benefit is the area under the demand curve minus the area representing cost. The cost to the consumer is the area under the price line, since that area represents the expenditure on the commodity. Obviously, for a given price P^*, consumer net benefit is maximized by choosing to purchase Q_d units. Area A is then the geometric representation of the net benefit received, known as *consumer surplus*. It is the area under the demand curve that lies above the price, bounded from the left by the vertical axis and from the right by the quantity of the good being considered.

Meanwhile, sellers face a similar choice (see Figure 4.2). Given price P^*, the seller maximizes his or her own net benefits by choosing to sell Q_s units. The net benefit received (Area B) by the seller is called *producer surplus*. It is the area under the price line that lies over the marginal cost curve, bounded from the left by the vertical axis and the right by the quantity of the good being considered.

FIGURE 4.2

The Producer's Choice

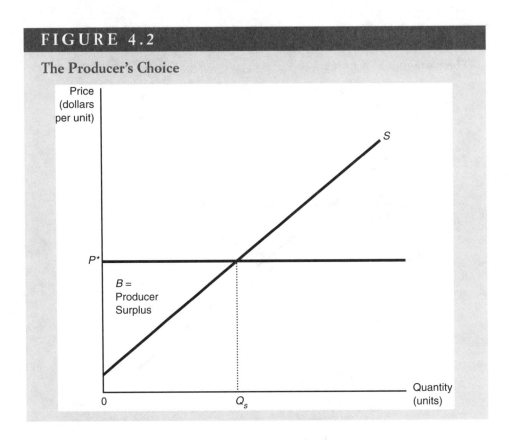

The price level that producers and consumers face will adjust until supply equals demand, as depicted in Figure 4.3. Given that price, consumers maximize their surplus, producers maximize their surplus, and the market clears.

Is this allocation efficient? According to our definition of static efficiency from the previous chapter, it is clear the answer is yes. The net benefit is maximized by the market allocation and, as seen in Figure 4.3, it is equal to the sum of consumer and producer surpluses. Thus, we have established a procedure for measuring net benefits, and a means of describing how the net benefits are distributed between consumers and producers.

This distinction is crucially significant. Efficiency is *not* achieved because consumers and producers are seeking efficiency. They aren't! In a system with well-defined property rights and competitive markets in which to sell those rights, producers try to maximize their surplus and consumers try to maximize their surplus. The price system, then, induces those self-interested parties to make choices that are efficient from the point of view of society as a whole. It channels the energy motivated by self-interest into socially productive paths.

Though familiarity may have dulled our appreciation, it is noteworthy that a system designed to produce a harmonious and congenial outcome could function

FIGURE 4.3

Market Equilibrium

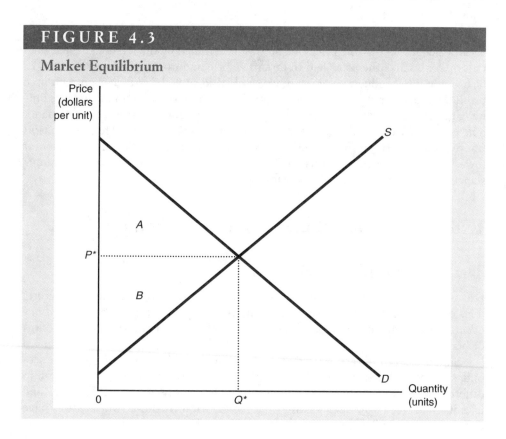

effectively while allowing consumers and producers so much individual freedom in making choices. This is truly a remarkable accomplishment.

Producer's Surplus, Scarcity Rent, and Long-Run Competitive Equilibrium

Since the area under the price line is total revenue, and the area under the marginal-cost curve is total variable cost, producer's surplus is related to profits. In the short run when some costs are fixed, producer's surplus is equal to profits plus fixed cost. In the long run when all costs are variable, producer's surplus is equal to profits plus rent, the return to scarce inputs owned by the producer. As long as new firms can enter into profitable industries without raising the profits of purchased inputs, long-run profits and rent will equal zero.

Scarcity Rent. Most natural resource industries, however, do give rise to rent and, therefore, producer's surplus is not eliminated by competition, even with free entry. This producer's surplus, which persists in long-run competitive equilibrium, is called *scarcity rent*.

David Ricardo was the first economist to recognize the existence of scarcity rent. Ricardo suggested that the price of land was determined by the least fertile marginal unit of land. Since the price had to be sufficiently high to allow the poorer land to be brought into production, other, more fertile land could be farmed at an economic profit. Competition could not erode that profit because the amount of land was limited and lower prices would serve only to reduce the supply of land below demand. The only way to expand production would be to bring additional, less fertile land (more costly to farm) into production; consequently, additional production does not lower price, as it does in a constant-cost industry. As we shall see, other circumstances also give rise to scarcity rent for natural resources.

Externalities as a Source of Market Failure

The Concept Introduced

Exclusivity is one of the chief characteristics of an efficient property rights structure. This characteristic is frequently violated in practice. One broad class of violations occurs when an agent making a decision does not bear all of the consequences of his or her action.

Suppose two firms are located by a river. The first produces steel, while the second, somewhat downstream, operates a resort hotel. Both use the river, though in different ways. The steel firm uses it as a receptacle for its waste, while the second uses it to attract customers seeking water recreation. If these two facilities have different owners, an efficient use of the water is not likely to result. Because the steel plant does not bear the cost of reduced business at the resort resulting from waste being dumped into the river, it is not likely to be very sensitive to that cost in its decision-making. As a result, it could be expected to dump too much waste into the river, and an efficient allocation of the river would not be attained.

This situation is called an externality. An *externality* exists whenever the welfare of some agent, either a firm or household, depends not only on his or her activities, but also on activities under the control of some other agent. In the example, the increased waste in the river imposed an external cost on the resort, a cost the steel firm could not be counted upon to consider appropriately in deciding the amount of waste to dump.

The effects of this external cost on the steel industry can be seen in Figure 4.4, which depicts the market for steel. Steel production inevitably involves producing pollution as well as steel. The demand for steel is shown by the demand curve D, and the private marginal cost of producing the steel (exclusive of pollution control and damage) is depicted as MC_p. Because society considers both the cost of pollution and the cost of producing the steel, the social marginal-cost function (MC_s) includes both of these costs as well.

If the steel industry faced no outside control on its emission levels, it would seek to produce Q_m. That choice, in a competitive setting, would maximize its private producer surplus. But that is clearly not efficient, since the net benefit is maximized at Q^* not Q_m.

FIGURE 4.4

The Market for Steel

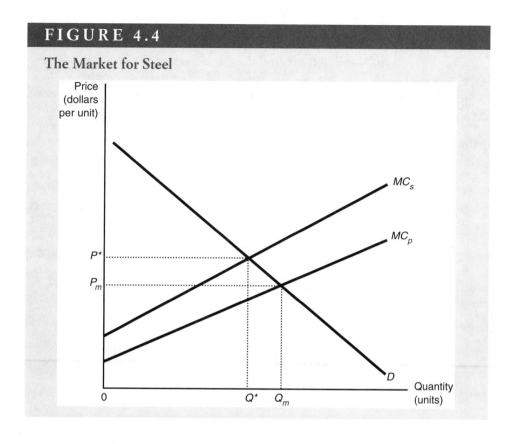

With the assistance of Figure 4.4, we can draw a number of conclusions about market allocations of commodities causing pollution externalities:

1. The output of the commodity is too large.
2. Too much pollution is produced.
3. The prices of products responsible for pollution are too low.
4. As long as the costs are external, no incentives to search for ways to yield less pollution per unit of output are introduced by the market.
5. Recycling and reuse of the polluting substances are discouraged since release into the environment is so inefficiently cheap.

The effects of a market imperfection for one commodity end up affecting the demands for raw materials, labor, and so on. The ultimate effects are felt through the entire economy.

Types of Externalities

External effects can be either positive or negative. Historically, the terms *external diseconomy* and *external economy* have been used to refer, respectively, to circumstances in which the affected party is damaged or benefited by the externality. Clearly, the water pollution example represents an external diseconomy. External economies are not hard to find, however. Private individuals who purchase a particularly scenic area provide an external economy to all who pass. Generally, when external economies are present, the market will undersupply the resources.

One other distinction is important. One class of externalities, known as *pecuniary externalities*, does not present the same kinds of problems as pollution does. Pecuniary externalities arise when the external effect is transmitted through altered prices. Suppose that a new firm moves into an area and drives up the rental price of land. That increase creates a negative effect on all those paying rent and, therefore, is an external diseconomy.

This pecuniary diseconomy, however, does not cause a market failure because the resulting higher rents are reflecting the scarcity of land. The land market provides a mechanism by which the parties can bid for land; the prices that result reflect the value of the land in its various uses. Without pecuniary externalities, the price signals would fail to sustain an efficient allocation.

The pollution example is *not* a pecuniary externality because the effect is not transmitted through prices. In this example, prices do not adjust to reflect the increasing waste load. The scarcity of the water resource is not signaled to the steel firm. An essential feedback mechanism that is present for pecuniary externalities is not present for the pollution case.

The externalities concept is a broad one covering a multitude of sources of market failure (see Example 4.2). The next step is to investigate some specific circumstances that can give rise to externalities.

Improperly Designed Property Rights Systems

Other Property Rights Regimes[1]

Private property is, of course, not the only possible way of defining entitlements to resource use. Other possibilities include state-property regimes (where the government owns and controls the property), common-property regimes (where the property is jointly owned and managed by a specified group of co-owners), and *res nullius* or open-access regimes (in which no one owns or exercises control over the resources). All of these create rather different incentives for resource use.

State-property regimes exist not only in former communist countries (as in Example 4.1), but also to varying degrees in virtually all countries of the world. Parks and forests, for example, are frequently owned and managed by the government in capitalist as well as in socialist nations. As Example 4.1 indicates, problems with both efficiency and sustainability can arise in state-property regimes when the incentives of bureaucrats who implement and/or make the rules for resource use diverge from collective interests.

Common-property resources are those that are managed in common rather than privately. Entitlements to use common-property resources may be formal, protected by specific legal rules, or they may be informal, protected by tradition or custom. Common-property regimes exhibit varying degrees of efficiency and

---

[1]This section relies on the classification system presented in Bromley (1991).

Example 4.2

SHRIMP FARMING EXTERNALITIES IN THAILAND

In the Tha Po village on the coast of Surat Thani Province in Thailand, more than half of the 1,100 hectares of mangrove swamps have been cleared for commercial shrimp farms. Although harvesting shrimp is a lucrative undertaking, mangroves serve as nurseries for fish and as barriers for storms and soil erosion. Following the destruction of the local mangroves, Tha Po villagers experienced a decline in fish catch and suffered storm damage and water pollution. Can market forces be trusted to strike the efficient balance between preservation and development for the remaining mangroves?

Calculations by two economists, Dr. Sathirathai and Dr. Barbier, demonstrated that the value of the ecological services that would be lost from further destruction of the mangrove swamps exceeded the value of the shrimp farms that would take their place. Preservation of the remaining mangrove swamps would be the efficient choice.

Would a potential shrimp-farming entrepreneur make the efficient choice? Unfortunately the answer is no. This study estimated the economic value of mangroves in terms of local use of forest resources, off-shore fishery linkages, and coastal protection to be in the range of $27,264 to $35,921 per hectare. In contrast, the economic returns to shrimp farming, once they are corrected for input subsidies and for the costs of water pollution, are only $194 to $209 per hectare. However, as shrimp farmers are heavily subsidized and do not have to take into account the external costs of pollution, their financial returns are typically $7,706.95 to $8,336.47 per hectare. In the absence of some sort of external control imposed by collective action, development would be the normal, if inefficient, result. The externalities associated with the ecological services provided by the mangroves support a biased decision that results in fewer social net benefits, but greater private net benefits.

Source: Suthawan Sathirathai and Edward B. Barbier. "Valuing Mangrove Conservation in Southern Thailand," Contemporary Economic Policy Vol. 19, No. 2 (April 2001): 109–122.

---

sustainability, depending on the rules that emerge from collective decision-making. While some very successful examples of common-property regimes exist, unsuccessful examples are even more common.[2]

One successful example of a common-property regime involves the system of allocating grazing rights in Switzerland. Though agricultural land is normally treated as private property in Switzerland, grazing rights on the Alpine meadows have been

---

[2]The two cases that follow, and many others, are discussed in Ostrom (1990).

treated as common property for centuries. Overgrazing is protected by specific rules, enacted by an association of users, which limit the amount of livestock permitted on the meadow. The families included on the membership list of the association have been stable over time as rights and responsibilities have passed from generation to generation. This stability has apparently facilitated reciprocity and trust, thereby providing a foundation for continued compliance with the rules.

Unfortunately, that kind of stability may be the exception rather than the rule, particularly in the face of heavy population pressure. The more common situation can be illustrated by the experience of Mawelle, a small fishing village in Sri Lanka. Initially, a complicated but effective rotating system of fishing rights was devised by villagers to assure equitable access to the best spots and best times while protecting the fish stocks. Over time, population pressure and the infusion of outsiders both raised demand and undermined the collective cohesion sufficiently that the traditional rules became unenforceable, producing overexploitation of the resource and lower incomes for all the participants.

Res nullius property resources, the main focus of this section, can be exploited on a first-come, first-served basis, because no individual or group has the legal power to restrict access. *Open-access resources*, as we shall henceforth call them, have given rise to what has become known popularly as the "tragedy of the commons."

The problems created by open-access resources can be illustrated by recalling the fate of the American bison. Bison are an example of "common-pool" resources. Common-pool resources are characterized by nonexclusivity and divisibility. Nonexclusivity implies that they can be exploited by anyone while divisibility means that the capture of part of the resource by one group subtracts it from the amount available to the other groups. (Note the contrast between common-pool resources and public goods in the next section.) In the early history of the United States, bison were plentiful; unrestricted hunting access was not a problem. Frontier people who needed hides or meat could easily get whatever they needed; the aggressiveness of any one hunter did not affect the time and effort expended by other hunters. In the absence of scarcity, efficiency was not threatened by open access.

As the years slipped by, however, the demand for bison increased and scarcity became a factor. As the number of hunters increased, eventually every additional unit of hunting activity increased the amount of time and effort required to produce a given yield of bison. In Figure 4.5, we depict the social benefits and costs of bison hunting. Total benefits are calculated by multiplying, for each level of hunting activity, the (assumed constant) price of bison by the amount harvested. The marginal benefit curve is downward sloping because as the amount of hunting effort expended increases, the resulting population size decreases. Smaller populations support smaller harvests per unit of effort expended.

The efficient level of hunting activity in this model (Q_1) is the level where the marginal benefit curve crosses the marginal-cost curve. At this level of harvest the marginal benefits would equal marginal cost implying that net benefits would be maximized.

With all hunters having completely unrestricted access to the bison, the resulting allocation would not be efficient. No individual hunter would have an incentive to protect scarcity rent by restricting hunting effort. Individual hunters, without

FIGURE 4.5

Bison Harvesting

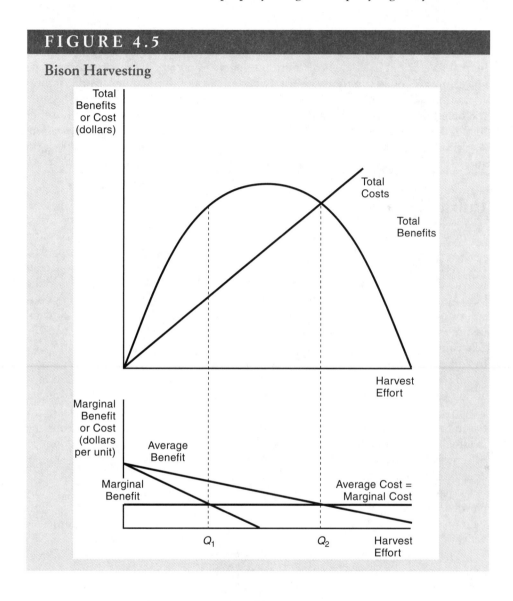

exclusive rights, would exploit the resource until their total benefit equaled total cost, implying a level of effort equal to (Q_2). Excessive exploitation of the herd occurs because individual hunters cannot appropriate the scarcity rent; therefore, they ignore it. One of the losses from further exploitation that could be avoided by exclusive owners—the opportunity cost of overexploitation—is not part of the decision-making process of open-access hunters.

Two characteristics of this formulation of the open-access allocation are worth noting: (1) In the presence of sufficient demand, unrestricted access will cause resources to be overexploited; (2) the scarcity rent is dissipated; no one appropriates the rent, so it is lost.

Why does this happen? Unlimited access destroys the incentive to conserve. A hunter who can preclude others from hunting this stock has an incentive to keep the herd at an efficient level. This restraint results in lower costs in the form of less time and effort expended to produce a given yield of bison. On the other hand, a hunter exploiting an open-access resource would not have an incentive to conserve because the benefits derived from restraint would, to some extent, be captured by other hunters. Thus unrestricted access to resources promotes an inefficient allocation. As a result of excessive harvest and the loss of habitat as land was converted to farm and pasture, the Great Plains bison herds nearly became extinct (Lueck, 2002).

Public Goods

Public goods, defined as those that exhibit both consumption indivisibilities and nonexcludability, present a particularly complex category of environmental resources. *Nonexcludability* refers to a circumstance where, once the resource is provided, even those who fail to pay for it cannot be excluded from enjoying the benefits it confers. Consumption is said to be *indivisible* when one person's consumption of a good does not diminish the amount available for others. Several common environmental resources are public goods, including not only the "charming landscape" referred to by Emerson, but also clean air, clean water, and biological diversity.[3]

Biological diversity includes two related concepts: (1) the amount of genetic variability among individuals within a single species, and (2) the number of species within a community of organisms. *Genetic diversity*, critical to species survival in the natural world, has also proved to be important in the development of new crops and livestock. It enhances the opportunities for crossbreeding and, thus, the development of superior strains. The availability of different strains was the key, for example, in developing a new, disease-resistant barley.

Because of the interdependence of species within ecological communities, any particular species may have a value to the community far beyond its intrinsic value. Certain species contribute balance and stability to their ecological communities by providing food sources or holding the population of the species in check.

The richness of diversity within and among species has provided new sources of food, energy, industrial chemicals, raw materials, and medicines. Yet there is considerable evidence that biological diversity is decreasing.

Can we rely on the private sector to produce the efficient amount of public goods such as biological diversity? Unfortunately, the answer is no! Suppose that in response to diminishing ecological diversity we decide to take up a collection to provide some means of preserving endangered species. Would the collection yield sufficient revenue to pay for an efficient level of ecological diversity? The general answer is no. Let's see why.

In Figure 4.6 individual-demand curves for preserving biodiversity have been presented for two consumers *A* and *B*. The market demand curve is represented by the

---

[3]Notice that public "bads," such as dirty air and dirty water, are also possible.

FIGURE 4.6

Efficient Provision of Public Goods

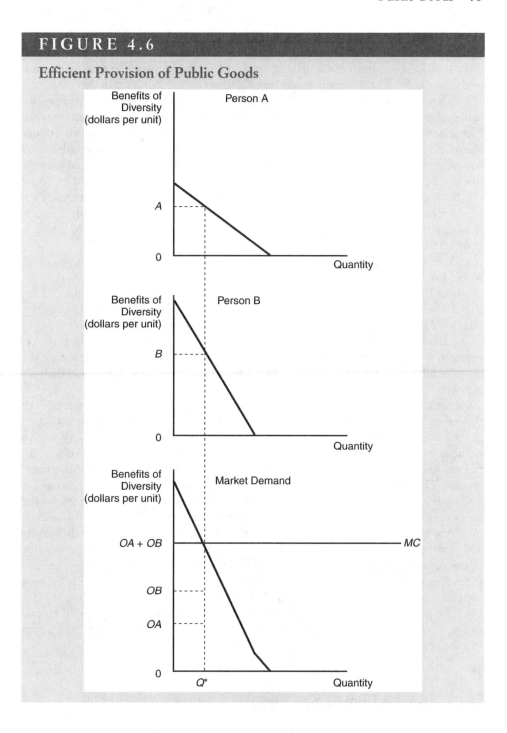

vertical summation of the two individual-demand curves. A vertical summation is necessary because everyone can simultaneously consume the same amount of biological diversity. We are therefore able to determine the market demand by finding the sum of the amounts of money they would be willing to pay for that level of diversity.

What is the efficient level of diversity? It can be determined by a direct application of our definition of efficiency. The efficient allocation maximizes net benefits. Net benefits, in turn, are represented geometrically by the portion of the area under the market demand curve that lies above the marginal-cost curve. The allocation that maximizes net benefits is Q^*, the allocation where the demand curve crosses the marginal-cost curve.

Both consumers consume this amount. At this level of availability, the marginal net benefit to person B is OB whereas the marginal net benefit to person A is OA. Adding these together produces $OA + OB$, society's marginal net benefit, which is equated to marginal cost.

Would a private market supply this amount? In general, the answer is that it would not. The typical market will undersupply diversity.

One further insight can be gained from Figure 4.6, and it is this insight that led to characterizing public-good problems as "complex" in the opening sentence of this section. The efficient market equilibrium for a public good requires different prices for each consumer. In Figure 4.6, if consumer A is charged price P_a ($=OA$), and consumer B is charged price P_b ($=OB$), then both consumers will be satisfied with the efficient allocation (the efficient allocation would have maximized their net benefits given the prices).

Furthermore, the revenue collected will be sufficient to finance the supply of the public good (because $P_b \times Q^* + P_a \times Q^* = MC \times Q^*$). Thus, although an efficient pricing system exists, it is very difficult to implement. The efficient pricing system requires charging a different price to each consumer; in the absence of excludability, consumers may not choose to reveal the strength of their preference for this commodity. Therefore, the producer could not possibly know what prices to charge.

Inefficiency results because each person is able to become a free rider on the other's contribution. A *free rider* is someone who derives the benefits from a commodity without contributing to its supply. Because of the consumption indivisibility and nonexcludability properties of the public good, consumers receive the benefits of any diversity purchased by other people. When this happens it tends to diminish incentives to contribute, and the contributions are not sufficiently large to finance the efficient amount of the public good; it would be undersupplied.

The privately supplied amount may not be zero. Some diversity would be privately supplied. Indeed, as suggested by Example 4.3, the privately supplied amount may be considerable.

Imperfect Market Structures

Environmental problems also occur when one of the participants in an exchange of property rights is able to exercise an inordinate amount of power over the outcome. This can occur, for example, when a product is sold by a single seller, or *monopoly*.

Example **4.3**

PUBLIC GOODS PRIVATELY PROVIDED: THE NATURE CONSERVANCY

Can a demand for a public good such as biological diversity be observed in practice? Would the market respond to that demand? Apparently so, according to the existence of an organization called The Nature Conservancy.

The Nature Conservancy was born of an older organization called the Ecologist Union on September 11, 1950, for the purpose of establishing natural area reserves to aid in the preservation of areas, objects, and fauna and flora that have scientific, educational, or aesthetic significance. This organization purchases, or accepts as donations, land that has some unique ecological or aesthetic significance, to keep it from being used for other purposes. In so doing they preserve many species by preserving the habitat.

From humble beginnings, The Nature Conservancy has, as of 2004, been responsible for the preservation of 117 million acres of forests, marshes, prairies, mounds, and islands around the world. These areas serve as home to rare and endangered species of wildlife and plants. The Conservancy owns and manages the largest privately owned nature preserve system in the world.

This approach has considerable merit. A private organization can move more rapidly than the public sector. Because it has a limited budget, The Nature Conservancy sets priorities and concentrates on acquiring the most ecologically unique areas. Yet the theory of public goods reminds us that if this were to be the sole approach to the preservation of biological diversity, it would preserve a smaller-than-efficient amount.

Source: The Nature Conservancy, http://nature.org/aboutus/.

It is easy to show that monopolies violate our definition of *efficiency* in the goods market (see Figure 4.7). According to our definition of *static efficiency* (Chapter 2), the efficient allocation would result when *OB* is supplied. This would yield net benefits represented by triangle *HIC*. The monopoly, however, would produce and sell *OA*, where marginal revenue equals marginal cost, and would charge price *OF*. At this point, the producer's surplus, albeit maximized, is clearly inefficient, because this choice causes society to lose net benefits equal to triangle *EDC*.[4] Monopolies supply an inefficiently small amount of the good.

---

[4]Producers would lose area *JDC* compared to the efficient allocation, but they would gain area *FEJG*, which is much larger. Meanwhile, consumers would be worse off, because they lose the area *FECJG*. Of these, *FEJG* is merely a transfer to the monopoly, whereas *EJC* is a pure loss to society. The total pure loss (*EDC*) is called a *deadweight loss*.

FIGURE 4.7

Monopoly and Inefficiency

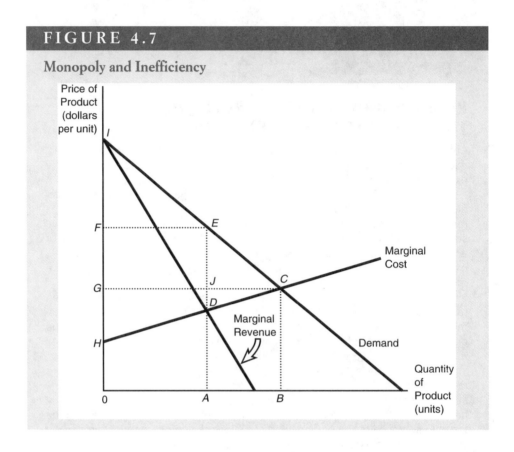

Imperfect markets clearly play some role in environmental problems. For example, the major oil-exporting countries have formed a cartel, resulting in higher-than-normal prices and lower-than-normal production. A *cartel* is a collusive agreement among producers to restrict production and raise prices. This collusive agreement allows the group to act as a monopolist. Note that the inefficiency in the goods market would be offset to some degree by the reduction in social costs caused by the lower levels of pollution resulting from the reduction in the combustion of oil. Example 4.4 examines the pricing activities of OPEC.

Divergence of Social and Private Discount Rates

We concluded earlier that producers, in their attempt to maximize producer surplus, also maximize the present value of net benefits under the "right" conditions, such as the absence of externalities, the presence of properly defined property rights, and the presence of competitive markets within which the property rights can be exchanged.

Now let's consider one more condition. If resources are to be allocated efficiently, firms must use the same rate to discount future net benefits as is appropriate for society at large. If firms were to use a higher rate, they would extract and sell

Example 4.4

HOW SHOULD OPEC PRICE ITS OIL?

As a cartel, OPEC (Organization of Petroleum Exporting Countries) has some control over its prices. And as Figure 4.7 suggests, it could increase its profits by restricting supply, a tactic that would cause prices to rise above their competitive levels. By how much should prices be raised?

The profit-maximizing price will depend upon several factors, including the price elasticity of demand (to determine how much the quantity demanded will fall in response to the higher price), the price elasticity of supply for non-OPEC members (to determine how much added production should be expected from outside producers), and the propensity for cheating (members producing more than their assigned quotas). Gately (1995) has modeled these and other factors and concluded that OPEC's interests would be best served by a policy of moderate output growth, defined as growth at a rate no faster than world income growth.

As Gately points out, however, OPEC historically has not always exercised this degree of caution. In 1979–80, succumbing to the lure of even higher prices, OPEC chose a price strategy that required substantial restrictions of cartel output. Not only did the price elasticities of demand and non-OPEC supply turn out to be much higher than anticipated by the cartel, but the higher oil prices also triggered a worldwide recession (which further lowered demand). OPEC lost not only revenue but also market share. Even for monopolies, the market imposes some discipline; the highest price is not always the best price.

Source: Dermot Gately. "Strategies for OPEC's Pricing and Output Decisions," *Energy Journal* Vol. 16, No. 3 (1995): 1–38.

resources faster than would be efficient. Conversely, if firms were to use a lower-than-appropriate discount rate, they would be excessively conservative.

Why might private and social rates differ? As stated in the previous chapter, the social discount rate is equal to the social opportunity cost of capital. This cost of capital can be separated into two components: risk-free cost of capital and the risk premium.[5] The *risk-free cost of capital* is the rate of return earned when there is absolutely no risk of earning more or less than the expected return. The *risk premium* is an additional cost of capital required to compensate the owners of this capital when the expected and actual returns may differ. Therefore, because of the risk premium, the cost of capital is higher in risky industries than in no-risk industries.

One difference between private and social discount rates may stem from a difference in social and private risk premiums. If the risk of certain private decisions is

---

[5]This point is discussed in more detail in Scheraga and Sussman (1998).

different from the risks faced by society as a whole, then the social and private risk premiums may differ. One obvious example is the risk *caused* by the government. If the firm is afraid its assets will be taken over by the government, it may choose a higher discount rate to make its profits before nationalization occurs. From the point of view of society—as represented by government—this is not a risk and, therefore, a lower discount rate is appropriate. When private rates exceed social rates, current production is higher than is desirable to maximize the net benefits to society. Energy production and forestry both have been subject to this source of inefficiency.

Though private and social discount rates do not always diverge, they may. When those circumstances arise, market decisions are not efficient.

Government Failure

Market processes are not the only sources of inefficiency. Political processes are fully as culpable. As will become clear in the chapters that follow, some environmental problems have arisen from a failure of political rather than economic institutions. To complete our study of the ability of institutions to allocate environmental resources, we must understand this source of inefficiency as well.

Government failure shares with market failure the characteristic that improper incentives are the root of the problem. Special interest groups use the political process to engage in what has become known as *rent seeking*. Rent seeking is the use of resources in lobbying and other activities directed at securing protective legislation. Successful rent-seeking activity will increase the net benefits going to the special interest group, but it will also frequently lower net benefits to society as a whole. In these instances it is a classic case of the aggressive pursuit of a larger slice of the pie leading to a smaller pie.

Why don't the losers rise up to protect their interests? One main reason is voter ignorance. It is economically rational for voters to remain ignorant on many issues simply because of the high cost of keeping informed and the low probability that any single vote will be decisive. In addition, it is difficult for diffuse groups of individuals, each of whom is affected only to a small degree, to organize a coherent, unified opposition. Successful opposition is, in a sense, a public good, with its attendant tendency for free riding on the opposition of others. Opposition to special interests would normally be underfunded.

Rent seeking can take many forms. Producers can seek protection from competitive pressures brought by imports or can seek price floors to hold prices above their efficient levels. Consumer groups can seek price ceilings or special subsidies to transfer part of their costs to the general body of taxpayers. Rent seeking is not the only source of inefficient government policy. Sometimes governments act without full information and establish policies that ultimately are very inefficient. For example, as you will see in Chapter 18, one technological strategy chosen by the government to control motor vehicle pollution involved adding the chemical substance MTBE to gasoline. Designed to promote cleaner combustion, this additive turned out to create a substantial water pollution problem.

Governments may also pursue social policy objectives that have the side effect of causing an environmental inefficiency. For example, in Chapter 8 we shall see how the desire to hold natural gas prices down for consumers led to massive shortages.

Whatever form government failure takes, it provides a direct challenge to the presumption that more direct intervention by the government automatically leads to either greater efficiency or greater sustainability.

These cases illustrate the general economic premise that environmental problems arise because of a divergence between individual and collective objectives. This is a powerful explanatory device because not only does it suggest why these problems arise, but it also suggests how they might be resolved—by realigning individual incentives to make them compatible with collective objectives. As self-evident as this approach may be, it is controversial. The controversy involves whether the problem is our improper values or the improper translation of our quite proper values into action.

Economists have always been reluctant to argue that values of consumers are warped, because that would necessitate dictating the "correct" set of values. Both capitalism and democracy are based on the presumption that the majority knows what it is doing, whether it is casting ballots for representatives or dollar votes for goods and services.

The Pursuit of Efficiency

We have seen that environmental problems arise when property rights are ill defined, when these rights are exchanged under something other than competitive conditions, and when social and private discount rates diverge. We can now use our definition of efficiency to explore possible remedies, such as private negotiation, judicial remedies, and regulation by the legislative and executive branches of government.

Private Resolution Through Negotiation

The simplest means to restore efficiency occurs when the number of affected parties is small, making negotiation feasible. Suppose, for example, we return to the case used earlier in this chapter to illustrate an externality—the conflict between the polluting steel company and the downstream resort.

Figure 4.8 reveals the answer. If the resort offers a bribe of $C + D$, they would experience damage reduction from the decrease in production from Q_m to Q^*. Let's assume that the bribe is equal to this amount. Would the steel company be willing to reduce production to the desired level? If they refused the bribe, their producer surplus would be $A + B + D$. If they accepted the bribe, their producer surplus would be $A + B$ plus the bribe, so their total return would be $A + B + C + D$. Clearly they are better off by C if they accept the bribe. Society as a whole is better off by amount C as well since net benefits from Q_m are $A - C$ and net benefits for Q^* are A.

Our discussion of individual negotiations raises two questions: (1) Should the property right always belong to the party who gained or seized it first (in this case the steel company)? (2) How can environmental risks be handled when prior negotiation is clearly impractical? These questions are routinely answered by the court system.

The Courts: Property Rules and Liability Rules

The court system can respond to environmental conflicts by imposing either property rules or liability rules. Property rules specify the initial allocation of the entitlement. The entitlements at conflict in our example are, on the one hand, the right

FIGURE 4.8

Efficient Output with Pollution Damage

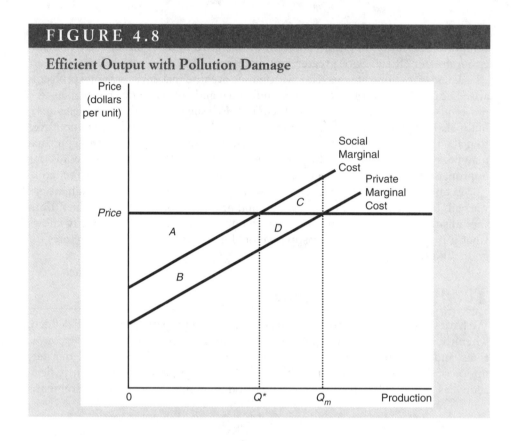

to add waste products to the river and, on the other, the right to an attractive river. In applying property rules, the court merely decides which right is preeminent and places an injunction against violating that right. The injunction is removed only upon obtaining the consent of the party whose right was violated. Consent is usually obtained in return for an out-of-court monetary settlement.

Notice that in the absence of a court decision, the entitlement is naturally allocated to the party that can most easily seize it. In our example the natural allocation would give the entitlement to the steel company. The courts must decide whether to overturn this natural allocation.

How would they decide? And what difference would their decision make? The answer may surprise you.

In a classic article, economist Ronald Coase (1960) held that as long as negotiation costs are negligible and affected consumers can negotiate freely with each other (when the number of affected parties is small), the court could allocate the entitlement to *either* party, and an efficient allocation would result. The only effect of the court's decision would be to change the distribution of costs and benefits among the affected parties. This remarkable conclusion has come to be known as the Coase theorem.

Why is this so? We have already shown (in Figure 4.8) that if the steel company has the property right, it is in the resort's interest to offer a bribe that results in the desired level of output. Suppose, now, the resort had the property right instead. To pollute in this case, the steel company must bribe the resort. Suppose it could pollute only if it compensated the resort for all damages. (In other words, it would agree to pay the difference between the two marginal-cost curves up to the level of output actually chosen.) As long as this compensation were required, the steel company would choose to produce Q^* since that is the level at which its private net benefits are maximized. (Notice that, due to the compensation, the curve the steel company uses to calculate its private net benefits is the social marginal cost curve.)

The difference between these two different ways of allocating property rights lies in how the cost of obtaining the efficient level of output is shared between the parties. When the property right is assigned to the steel company, the cost is borne by the resort (part of the cost is the damage and part is the bribe to reduce the level of damage). When the property right is assigned to the resort, the cost is borne by the steel company (it now must compensate for all damage). In either case the efficient level of production results. The Coase theorem shows that the very existence of an inefficiency triggers pressures for improvements. Furthermore, the existence of this pressure does not depend on the assignment of property rights.

This is an important point. As we shall see in succeeding chapters, private efforts triggered by inefficiency can frequently prevent the worst excesses of environmental degradation. Yet the importance of this theorem should not be overstated. Both theoretical and practical objections can be raised. The chief theoretical qualification concerns the assumption that wealth effects do not matter. The decision to confer the property right on a particular party results in a transfer of wealth to that party. This transfer might shift the demand curve for either steel or resorts out, as long as higher incomes result in greater demand. Whenever wealth effects are significant, the type of property rule issued by the court affects the outcome by shifting the level of the marginal benefit curve.

Wealth effects normally are small, so the zero-wealth-effect assumption is probably not a fatal flaw. Some serious practical flaws, however, do mar the usefulness of the Coase theorem. The first involves the incentives for polluting that result when the property right is assigned to the polluter. Since pollution would become a profitable activity with this assignment, other polluters might be encouraged to increase production and pollution in order to earn the bribes. That certainly would not be efficient.

Negotiation is also difficult to apply when the number of people affected by the pollution is large. You may have already noticed that in the presence of several affected parties, pollution reduction is a public good. The free-rider problem would make it difficult for the group to act cohesively and effectively for the restoration of efficiency.

When individual negotiation is not practical for one reason or another, the courts can turn to liability rules. These are rules that award monetary damages, after the fact, to the injured party. The amount of the award is designed to correspond to the amount of damage inflicted. Thus, returning to Figure 4.8, a liability rule would force the steel company to compensate the resort for all damages incurred. In this case it could choose any production level it wanted, but it would have to pay the resort an amount of money equal to the area between the two marginal-cost curves from the origin to the chosen level of output. In this case the steel plant would maximize its net benefits by choosing Q^*. (Why wouldn't the steel plant choose to produce more than that? Why wouldn't the steel plant choose to produce less than that?)

The moral of this story is that appropriately designed liability rules can also correct inefficiencies by forcing those who cause damage to bear the cost of that damage. Internalizing previously external costs causes profit-maximizing decisions to be compatible with efficiency.

Liability rules are interesting from an economics point of view because early decisions create precedents for later ones. Imagine, for example, how the incentives to prevent oil spills facing an oil company are transformed once it has a legal obligation to clean up after an oil spill and to compensate fishermen for reduced catches. It quickly becomes evident that accident prevention is cheaper than retrospectively dealing with the damage once it has occurred.

This approach, however, also has its limitations. It relies on a case-by-case determination based on the unique circumstances for each case. Administratively, such a determination is very expensive. Expenses, such as court time, lawyers' fees, and so on, fall into a category called *transaction costs* by economists. In the present context, these are the administrative costs incurred in attempting to correct the inefficiency. When the number of parties involved in a dispute is large and the circumstances are common, we are tempted to correct the inefficiency by statutes or regulations rather than court decisions.

Legislative and Executive Regulation

These remedies can take several forms. The legislature could dictate that no one produce more steel or pollution than Q^*. This dictum might then be backed up with sufficiently large jail sentences or fines to deter potential violators. Alternatively, the legislature could impose a tax on steel or on pollution. A per-unit tax equal to the vertical distance between the two marginal cost curves would work (see Figure 4.8).

Legislatures could also establish rules to permit greater flexibility and yet reduce damage. For example, zoning laws might establish separate areas for steel plants and resorts. This approach assumes that the damage is substantially smaller if nonconforming uses are kept apart.

They could also require the installation of particular pollution control equipment (as when catalytic converters were required on automobiles), or deny the use of a particular production ingredient (as when lead was removed from gasoline). In other words they can regulate outputs, inputs, production processes, emissions, and even the location of production in their attempt to produce an efficient outcome. In subsequent chapters we shall examine the various options policy-makers have to show how they can modify environmentally destructive behavior, but also to establish the degree to which they can promote efficiency.

Bribes are, of course, not the only means victims have at their disposal for lowering pollution. When the victims also consume the products produced by the polluters, consumer boycotts are possible. When the victims are employed by the producer, strikes or other forms of labor resistance are possible. In Chapter 19 we shall examine how likely these approaches are to restore efficiency.

An Efficient Role for Government

While the economic approach suggests that government action could well be used to restore efficiency, it also suggests that inefficiency is not a sufficient condition to justify government intervention. Any corrective mechanism involves transaction costs. If these transaction costs are high enough, and the benefit to be derived from correcting the inefficiency small enough, then it is best simply to live with the inefficiency.

Consider, for example, the pollution problem. Wood-burning stoves, which were widely used for cooking and heat in the late 1800s in the United States, were sources of pollution, but because of the enormous capacity of the air to absorb the emissions, no regulation resulted. In the 1980s, however, the resurgence of demand for wood-burning stoves precipitated in part by high oil prices resulted in strict regulations for wood-burning stove emissions.

As society has evolved, the scale of economic activity (and emissions) has expanded. Cities are experiencing severe problems from air and water pollutants because of the clustering of activities. Both the expansion and the clustering have increased the amount of emissions per unit volume of air or water. As a result, pollutant concentrations have caused perceptible problems with human health, vegetation growth, and aesthetics.

Historically, as incomes have risen, the demand for leisure activities has also risen. Many of these leisure activities, such as canoeing and backpacking, take place in unique, pristine environmental areas. With the number of these areas declining as a result of conversion to other uses, the value of remaining areas has increased. Thus, the benefits from protecting some areas have risen over time until they have exceeded the transaction costs of protecting them from pollution and/or development.

The level and concentration of economic activity, having increased pollution problems and driven up the demand for clean air and pristine areas, have created the preconditions for government action. Can government respond or will rent seeking prevent efficient political solutions? We devote much of this book to searching for the answer.

Summary

How producers and consumers use the resources making up the environmental asset depends on the nature of the property rights governing resource use. When property right systems are exclusive, transferable, and enforceable, the owner of a resource has a powerful incentive to use that resource efficiently, since the failure to do so results in a personal loss.

The economic system will not always sustain efficient allocations, however. Specific circumstances that could lead to inefficient allocations include externalities, improperly defined property-rights systems (such as open-access resources and public goods), imperfect markets for trading the property rights to the resources (monopoly), and the divergence of social and private discount rates (under the threat of nationalization). When these circumstances arise, market allocations do not maximize the present value of the net benefit.

Due to rent-seeking behavior by special interest groups or the less-than-perfect implementation of efficient plans, the political system can produce inefficiencies as well. Voter ignorance on many issues coupled with the public-good nature of any results of political activity tend to create a situation in which private, but not social, net benefits are maximized.

The efficiency criterion can be used to assist in the identification of circumstances in which our political and economic institutions lead us astray. It can also assist in the search for remedies by facilitating the design of regulatory, judicial, or legislative solutions.

Discussion Questions

1. In a well-known legal case, *Miller v. Schoene* (287 U.S. 272), a classic conflict of property rights was featured. Red cedar trees, used only for ornamental purposes, carried a disease that could destroy apple orchards within a radius of two miles. There was no known way of curing the disease except by destroying the cedar trees or by ensuring that apple orchards were at least two miles away from the cedar trees. Apply the Coase theorem to this situation. Does it make any difference to the outcome whether the cedar tree owners are entitled to retain their trees or the apple growers are entitled to be free of them? Why or why not?

2. In primitive societies the entitlements to use land were frequently possessory rights rather than ownership rights. Those on the land could use it as they wished, but they could not transfer it to anyone else. One could acquire a new plot by simply occupying and using it, leaving the old plot available for someone else. Would this type of entitlement system cause more or less incentive to conserve the land than an ownership entitlement? Why? Would a possessory entitlement system be more efficient in a modern society or a primitive society? Why?

Problems

1. Suppose the state is trying to decide how many miles of a very scenic river it should preserve. There are 100 people in the community, each of whom has an identical inverse demand function given by $P = 10 - 1.0q$, where q is the number of miles preserved and P is the per-mile price he or she is willing to pay for q miles of preserved river. (a) If the marginal cost of preservation is $500 per mile, how many miles would be preserved in an efficient allocation? (b) How large are the net benefits?

2. (a) Compute the consumer surplus and producer surplus if the product described by the first problem in Chapter 2 were supplied by a competitive industry. Show that their sum is equal to the efficient net benefits.

   (b) Compute the consumer surplus and the producer surplus assuming this same product was supplied by a monopoly. (*Hint:* The marginal revenue curve has twice the slope of the demand curve.)

   (c) Show that when this market is controlled by a monopoly, producer surplus is larger, consumer surplus is smaller, and net benefits are smaller than when it is controlled by competitive industry.

3. Suppose you were asked to comment on a proposed policy to control oil spills. Since the average cost of an oil spill has been computed as X, the proposed policy would require any firm responsible for a spill immediately to pay the government X. Is this likely to result in the efficient amount of precaution against oil spills? Why or why not?

4. "In environmental liability cases, courts have some discretion regarding the magnitude of compensation polluters should be forced to pay for the environmental incidents they cause. In general, however, the larger the required payments the better." Discuss.

Further Reading

Bromley, Daniel W. *Environment and Economy: Property Rights and Public Policy* (Oxford: Basil Blackwell, Inc., 1991). A detailed exploration of the property rights approach to environmental problems.

Bromley, Daniel W., ed. *Making the Commons Work: Theory, Practice and Policy* (San Francisco: ICS Press, 1992). An excellent collection of 13 essays exploring various formal and informal approaches to controlling the use of common-property resources.

Lueck, Dean. "The Extermination and Conservation of the American Bison," *Journal of Legal Studies* (2002). A fascinating look at the role property rights played in the fate of the American bison.

Ostrom, Elinor. *Crafting Institutions for Self-Governing Irrigation Systems* (San Francisco: ICS Press, 1992). Argues that common-pool problems are sometimes solved by voluntary organizations rather than by a coercive state. Among the cases considered are communal tenure in meadows and forests, irrigation communities, and fisheries.

Sandler, Todd. *Collective Action: Theory and Applications* (Ann Arbor: University of Michigan, 1992). A formal examination of the forces behind collective action's failures and successes.

Stavins, Robert N. "Harnessing Market Forces to Protect the Environment," *Environment* 31 (1989): 4–7, 28–35. An excellent, nontechnical review of the many ways in which the creative use of economic policies can produce superior environmental outcomes.

Several books of readings provide a wealth of additional material to interested readers. These include the following:

Bromley, Daniel W. *The Handbook of Environmental Economics* (Cambridge, MA: Blackwell, 1995).

Krishnan, Rajaram, Jonathan M. Harris, and Neva Goodwin, eds. *A Survey of Ecological Economics* (Washington, DC: Island Press, 1995).

Markandya, Anil, and Julie Richardson, eds. *Environmental Economics: A Reader* (New York: St. Martin's Press, 1992).

Oates, Wallace E., ed. *The Economics of the Environment* (Brookfield, VT: Edward Elgar, 1992).

van den Berg, Jeroen C. J. M., ed. *Handbook of Environmental and Resource Economics* (Cheltenham, UK: Edward Elgar, 1999).

Additional References and Historically Significant References are available on this book's companion Web site www.aw-bc.com/tietenberg.

Chapter 5

Sustainable Development: Defining the Concept

*We usually see only the things we are looking for—
so much so that we sometimes see them where they
are not.*

—Eric Hoffer, *The Passionate State of Mind* (1993)

Introduction

In previous chapters we have developed two specific means for identifying environmental problems. The first, static efficiency, allows us to evaluate those circumstances where time is not a crucial aspect of the allocation problem. Typical examples might include allocating resources such as water or solar energy where next year's flow is independent of this year's choices. The second, more complicated criterion, dynamic efficiency, is suitable for those circumstances where time is a crucial aspect. One typical example might include the combustion of depletable resources such as oil, since supplies used now are unavailable for use by future generations.

After defining these criteria and showing how they could be operationally invoked, we demonstrated how helpful they can be. They are useful not only in identifying environmental problems and ferreting out their behavioral sources, but also in providing a basis for identifying types of remedies. These criteria even help design the various policy instruments that might restore some sense of balance.

But the fact that these are powerful and useful tools in the quest for a sense of harmony between the economy and the environment does not imply that they are the only criteria in which we should be interested. In a general sense the efficiency criteria are designed to prevent wasteful use of environmental and natural resources. That is a desirable attribute, but it is not the only possible desirable attribute. We might care, for example, not only about the value of the environment (the size of the pie), but how this value is shared as well (the size of each piece to all recipients). In other words, fairness or justice concerns should accompany efficiency considerations.

In this chapter we investigate one particular fairness concern—the treatment of future generations. We begin by considering a specific, ethically challenging situation—the allocation of a depletable resource over time. Using a numerical example, we shall trace out the temporal allocation of a depletable resource and show how this allocation is affected by changes in the discount rate. To lay the groundwork for our evaluation of fairness, we then turn to the task of defining what we mean by a fair intertemporal allocation. Finally, we take this theoretical definition and consider how it can be made operationally measurable.

A Two-Period Model

Dynamic efficiency balances present and future uses of a depletable resource by maximizing the present value of the net benefits derived from its use. This implies a particular allocation of the resource across time. We can investigate the properties of this allocation and the influence of such key parameters as the discount rate with the aid of a simple numerical example. We begin with the simplest of models— deriving the dynamic efficient allocation across two time periods. In subsequent chapters we show how these conclusions generalize to longer time periods and to more complicated situations.

Assume that we have a fixed supply of a depletable resource to allocate between two periods. Assume further that demand is constant in the two periods, the marginal willingness to pay is given by the formula $P = 8 - 0.4q$, and marginal cost is constant at \$2 per unit (see Figure 5.1). Notice that if the total supply were 30 or greater, and we were concerned only with these two periods, an efficient allocation

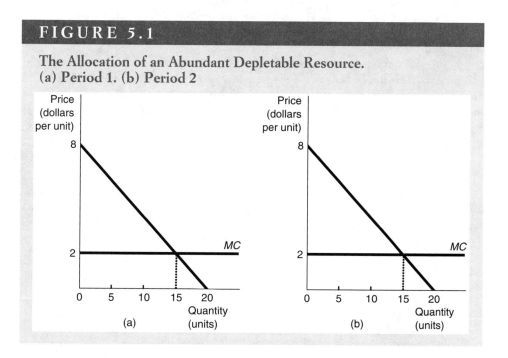

FIGURE 5.1

The Allocation of an Abundant Depletable Resource.
(a) Period 1. (b) Period 2

would produce 15 units in each period, *regardless of the discount rate*. The supply is sufficient to cover the demand in both periods; the consumption in Period 1 does not reduce the consumption in Period 2. In this case the static efficiency criterion is sufficient, since the allocations are not interdependent.

Examine, however, what happens when the available supply is less than 30. Suppose it is equal to 20. How do we determine the efficient allocation? According to the dynamic efficiency criterion, the efficient allocation is the one that maximizes the present value of the net benefit. The present value of the net benefit for both periods is simply the sum of the present values in each of the two periods. To take a concrete example, consider the present value of a particular allocation: 15 units in the first period and 5 in the second. How would we compute the present value of that allocation?

The present value in the first period would be that portion of the geometric area under the demand curve that is over the supply curve—$45.00.[1] The present value in the second period is that portion of the area under the demand curve that is over the supply curve from the origin to the five units produced multiplied by $1/(1 + r)$. If we use $r = 0.10$, then the present value of the net benefit received in the second period is $22.73,[2] and the present value of the net benefits for the two years is $67.73.

We now know how to find the present value of net benefits for any allocation. How does one find the allocation that maximizes present value? One way, with the aid of a computer, is to try all possible combinations of q_1 and q_2, that sum to 20. The one yielding the maximum present value of net benefits can then be selected. That is tedious and, for those who have the requisite mathematics, unnecessary.

The dynamically efficient allocation of this resource has to satisfy the condition that the present value of the marginal net benefit from the last unit in Period 1 equals the present value of the marginal net benefit in Period 2 (see appendix at the end of this chapter). Even without mathematics, this principle is easy to understand, as can be demonstrated with the use of a simple graphical representation of the two-period allocation problem.

Figure 5.2 depicts the present value of the marginal net benefit for each of the two periods. The net benefit curve for Period 1 is to be read from left to right. The net benefit curve intersects the vertical axis at $6; demand would be zero at $8 and the marginal cost is $2, so the difference (marginal net benefit) is $6. The marginal net benefit for the first period goes to zero at 15 units because, at that quantity, the willingness to pay for that unit exactly equals its cost.

The only tricky aspect of drawing the graph involves constructing the curve for the present value of net benefits in Period 2. Two aspects are worth noting. First, the zero axis for the Period 2 net benefits is on the right, rather than the left, side. Therefore, increases in Period 2 are recorded from right to left. This way, all points along the horizontal axis yields a total of 20 units allocated between the two periods. Any point on that axis picks a unique allocation between the two periods.[3]

---

[1] The height of the triangle is $6 [$8–$2] and the base is 15 units. The area is therefore $(1/2)($6)(15) = $45.

[2] The undiscounted net benefit is $25.00. The calculation is $(6 - 2) \times 5 + 1/2(8 - 6) \times 5 = $25. The discounted net benefit is therefore $25/1.10 = 22.73$.

[3] Note that the sum of the two allocations in Figure 5.2 is always 20. The left-hand axis represents an allocation of all 20 units to Period 2, and the right-hand axis represents an allocation entirely to Period 1.

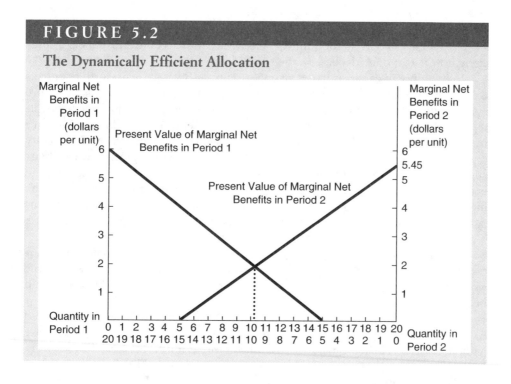

FIGURE 5.2

The Dynamically Efficient Allocation

Second, the present value of the marginal benefit curve for Period 2 intersects the vertical axis at a different point than does the comparable curve in Period 1. (Why?) This intersection is lower because the marginal benefits in the second period need to be discounted (multiplied by $1/(1 + r)$) to convert them into present value form since they occur one year later. Thus with the 10% discount rate we are using, the marginal net benefit is $6 and the present value is $6/1.10 = $5.45. Notice that larger discount rates rotate the Period 2 marginal benefit curve around the point of zero net benefit ($q_1 = 5$, $q_2 = 15$) toward the right-hand axis. We shall use this fact in a moment.

The efficient allocation is now readily identifiable as the point where the two curves representing present value of marginal net benefits cross. The total present value of net benefits is then the area under the marginal net benefit curve for Period 1 up to the efficient allocation, plus the area under the present value of the marginal net benefit curve for Period 2 from the right-hand axis up to its efficient allocation. Because we have an efficient allocation, the sum of these two areas is maximized.[4]

Since we have developed our efficiency criteria independent of an institutional context, these criteria are equally appropriate for evaluating resource allocations

---

[4]Demonstrate by first allocating slightly more to Period 2 (and therefore less to Period 1) and showing that the total area decreases. Conclude by allocating slightly less to Period 2 and showing that, in this case as well, total area declines.

generated by markets, government rationing, or even the whims of a dictator. While *any* efficient allocation method must take scarcity into account, the details of precisely how that is done depend on the context.

Intertemporal scarcity imposes an opportunity cost that we henceforth refer to as the *marginal user cost*. When resources are scarce, greater current use diminishes future opportunities. The marginal user cost is the present value of these forgone opportunities at the margin. To be more specific, uses of those resources, which would have been appropriate in the absence of scarcity, may no longer be appropriate once scarcity is present. Using large quantities of water to keep lawns lush and green may be wholly appropriate for an area with sufficiently large replenishable water supplies, but quite inappropriate when it denies drinking water to future generations. Failure to take the higher scarcity value of water into account in the present would lead to an inefficiency or an additional cost to society due to the additional scarcity imposed on the future. This additional marginal value that scarcity creates is the marginal user cost.

We can illustrate how this concept is used by returning to our numerical example. With 30 or more units, each period would be allocated 15 and the resource would not be scarce. With 30 or more units, therefore, the marginal user cost would be zero.

With 20 units, however, scarcity does exist. No longer can 15 units be allocated to each period; each period will have to be allocated less than would be the case without scarcity. The marginal user cost for this case is not zero. As can be seen from Figure 5.2, the present value of the marginal user cost, the additional value created by scarcity, is graphically represented by the vertical distance between the quantity axis and the intersection of the two present-value curves. It is identical to the present value of the marginal net benefit in each of the periods. This value can either be read off the graph or determined more precisely from the chapter appendix to be $1.905.

We can make this concept even more concrete by considering its use in a market context. An efficient market would have to consider not only the marginal cost of extraction for this resource, but the marginal user cost as well. Whereas in the absence of scarcity, the price would equal the marginal cost of extraction, with scarcity, the price would equal the sum of marginal extraction cost and marginal user cost.

To see this, solve for the prices that would prevail in an efficient market facing scarcity over time. Inserting the efficient quantities (10.238 and 9.762, respectively) into the willingness-to-pay function ($P = 8 - 0.4q$) yields $P_1 = 3.905$ and $P_2 = 4.095$. The corresponding supply-and-demand diagrams are given in Figure 5.3. Compare Figure 5.3 with Figure 5.1 to see the impact of scarcity on price. Note that in the absence of scarcity, marginal user cost is zero.

In an efficient market the marginal user cost for each period is the difference between the price and the marginal cost of extraction. Notice that it takes the value $1.905 in the first period and $2.095 in the second. In both years the present value of the marginal user cost is $1.905. In the second year the actual marginal user cost is $1.905(1 + r)$. Since $r = 0.10$ in this example, the marginal user cost for the second period is $2.095.[5] Thus, while the present value of marginal user cost is equal in both periods, the actual marginal user cost rises over time.

---

[5]You can verify this by taking the present value of $2.095 and showing it to be equal to $1.905.

FIGURE 5.3

The Efficient Market Allocation of a Depletable Resource: The Constant-Marginal-Cost Case. (a) Period 1. (b) Period 2

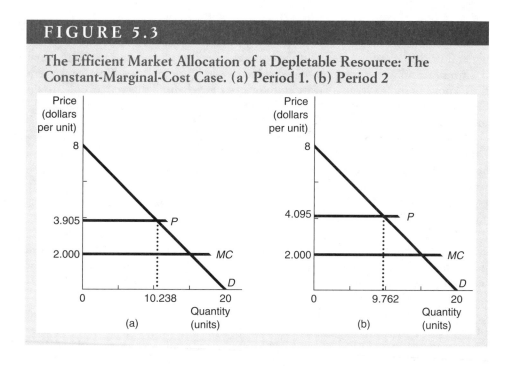

Both the size of the marginal user cost and the allocation of the resource between the two periods is affected by the discount rate. In Figure 5.2, because of discounting, the efficient allocation allocates somewhat more to Period 1 than to Period 2. A discount rate larger than 0.10 would be incorporated in this diagram by rotating the Period 2 curve an appropriate amount toward the right-hand axis, holding fixed the point at which it intersects the horizontal axis. (Can you see why?) The larger the discount rate, the greater the amount of rotation required. The amount allocated to the second period would be necessarily smaller with larger discount rates. The general conclusion, which holds for all models we consider, is that higher discount rates tend to skew resource extraction toward the present because they give the future less weight in balancing the relative value of present and future resource use.

Defining Intertemporal Fairness

While no generally accepted standards of fairness or justice exist, some have more prominent support than others. One such standard concerns the treatment of future generations. What legacy should earlier generations leave to later ones? This is a particularly difficult issue because, in contrast to other groups for which we may want to ensure fair treatment, future generations cannot articulate their wishes, much less negotiate with current generations ("We'll take your radioactive wastes, if you leave us plentiful supplies of titanium").

One starting point for intergenerational equity is provided by philosopher John Rawls in his monumental work *A Theory of Justice*. Rawls suggests one way to derive general principles of justice is to place, hypothetically, all people into an original position behind a "veil of ignorance." This veil of ignorance would prevent them from knowing their eventual position in society. Once behind this veil, people would decide on rules to govern the society that they would, after the decision, be forced to inhabit.

In our context this approach would suggest a hypothetical meeting of all members of present and future generations to decide on rules for allocating resources among generations. Because these members are prevented by the veil of ignorance from knowing the generation to which they will belong, they will not be excessively conservationist (lest they turn out to be a member of an earlier generation) or excessively exploitative (lest they become a member of a later generation).

What kind of rule would emerge from such a meeting? One possibility is the sustainability criterion. The *sustainability criterion* suggests that, at a minimum, future generations should be left no worse off than current generations. Allocations that impoverish future generations, in order to enrich current generations, are, according to this criterion, patently unfair.

In essence, the sustainability criterion suggests that earlier generations are at liberty to use resources that would thereby be denied to future generations as long as the well-being of future generations remains just as high as that of all previous generations. On the other hand, diverting resources from future use would violate the sustainability criterion if it reduced the well-being of future generations below the level enjoyed by preceding generations.

One of the implications of this definition of sustainability is that it is possible to use resources (even depletable resources) as long as the interests of future generations could be protected. Do our institutions provide adequate protection for future generations? We begin with examining the conditions under which efficient allocations satisfy the sustainability criterion. Are all efficient allocations sustainable?

Are Efficient Allocations Fair?

In the numerical example we have constructed, it certainly does not appear that the efficient allocation satisfies the sustainable criterion. In the two-period example, more resources are allocated to the first period than to the second. Therefore, net benefits in the second period are lower than in the first. Sustainability does not allow earlier generations to profit at the expense of later generations, and this example certainly appears to be a case where that is happening.

Yet choosing this particular extraction path does not prevent those in the first period from saving some of the net benefits for those in the second period. If the allocation is dynamically efficient, it will always be possible to set aside sufficient net benefits accrued in the first period for those in the second period, so that those in the second period will be at least as well off as they would have been with any other extraction profile.

We can illustrate this point with a numerical example that compares a dynamic efficient allocation with sharing to an allocation where resources are committed equally to each generation. Suppose, for example, you believe that setting aside half (10 units) of the available resources for each period would be a better allocation than the dynamic efficient allocation. The net benefits to each period from this alternative scheme would be $40.00. Can you see why?

Now let's compare this to an allocation of net benefits that could be achieved with the dynamic efficient allocation. If the dynamic efficient allocation is to satisfy the sustainability criterion, we must be able to show that it can produce an outcome such that each generation would be at least as well off as it would be with the equal allocation. Can that be demonstrated?

In the dynamic efficient allocation, the net benefits to the first period were 40.466, while those for the second period were 39.512.[6] Clearly, if no sharing between the periods took place, this example would violate the sustainability criterion; the second generation is worse off.

But suppose sharing took place. If the first generation keeps net benefits of $40.00 (thereby making it just as well off as if equal amounts were extracted in each period) and saves the extra $0.466 (the $40.466 net benefits earned during the first period in the dynamic efficient allocation minus the $40 reserved for itself) at 10% interest for those in the next period, this savings would grow to $0.513 by the second period [0.466(1.10)]. Add this to the net benefits received directly from the dynamic efficient allocation ($39.512), and the second generation would receive $40.025. Those in the second period would be better off by accepting the dynamic efficient allocation with sharing than they would if they demanded that resources be allocated equally between the two periods.

This example demonstrates that although dynamic efficient allocations do not automatically satisfy sustainability criteria, they are not automatically inconsistent with sustainability, even in an economy relying heavily on depletable resources. The possibility that the second period can be better off is not a guarantee; the required degree of sharing must take place. Example 5.1 points out that this sharing does sometimes take place. In subsequent chapters we shall examine both the conditions under which we could expect the appropriate degree of sharing to take place and the conditions under which it would not.

Applying the Sustainability Criterion

One of the difficulties in assessing the fairness of intertemporal allocations using this version of the sustainability criterion is that it is so difficult to apply. Discovering whether the well-being of future generations is lower than that of current generations requires us to know not only something about the allocation of resources over time, but also something about the preferences of future generations (in order to establish how valuable various resource streams are to them). That is a tall (impossible?) order!

---

[6]The supporting calculations are $(1.905)(10.238) + 0.5(4.095)(10.238)$ for the first period and $(2.095)(9.762) + 0.5(3.905)(9.762)$ for the second period.

Example 5.1

THE ALASKA PERMANENT FUND

One example of an intergenerational sharing mechanism that fits this sustainability notion currently exists in the state of Alaska. Extraction from Alaska's oil fields generates significant income, but it also depreciates one of the state's main environmental assets. To protect the interests of future generations as the Alaskan pipeline construction neared completion in 1976, Alaska voters approved a constitutional amendment that authorized the establishment of a dedicated fund: the Alaska Permanent Fund. This fund was designed to capture a portion of the rents received from the sale of the state's oil to share with future generations. The amendment requires:

> At least 25 percent of all mineral lease rentals, royalties, royalty sales proceeds, federal mineral revenue-sharing payments and bonuses received by the state be placed in a permanent fund, the principal of which may only be used for income-producing investments.

The principal of this fund cannot be used to cover current expenses without a majority vote of Alaskans.

The fund is fully invested in capital markets and diversified among various asset classes. It generates income from interest on bonds, stock dividends, real estate rents, and capital gains from the sale of assets. To date the legislature has used some of these annual earnings to provide dividends to every eligible Alaska resident, while using the rest to increase the size of the principal, thereby assuring that it is not eroded by inflation.

Though this fund does preserve some of the revenue for future generations, two characteristics are worth noting. First, the principal could be used for current expenditures if a majority of current voters agreed. To date that has not happened, but it has been discussed. Second, only 25% of the oil revenue is placed in the fund; full sustainability would require dedicating all 100%. The current generation gets 75% of the proceeds from oil as well as some portion of the income from the permanent fund.

Source: The Alaska Permanent Fund Web site: http://www.apfc.org/homeobjects/tabpermfund.cfm/.

Is it possible to develop a version of the sustainability criterion that is more operational? Fortunately it is, thanks to what has become known as the "Hartwick Rule." In an early article, John Hartwick (1977) demonstrated that a constant level of consumption could be maintained perpetually if all the scarcity rent were invested in capital. Furthermore, that level of investment would be sufficient to assure that the value of the total capital stock (defined below) would not decline.

Two important insights flow from this reinterpretation of the sustainability criterion. First, with this version it is possible to judge the sustainability of an allocation by examining whether or not the value of the total capital stock is nondeclining. That test can be performed each year without knowing anything about future allocations or preferences. Second, this analysis suggests the specific degree of sharing that would be necessary to produce a sustainable outcome, namely, all scarcity rent must be invested.

Let's pause a moment to make sure we understand what is being said here and why it is being said. Although we shall return to this subject later in the book, it is important now to have at least an intuitive understanding of the implications of this analysis. Consider an analogy. Suppose a grandparent left you an inheritance of $10,000, and you put it in a bank where it earns 10% interest.

What are the choices for allocating that money over time and what are the implications of those choices? If you spent exactly $1,000 per year, the amount in the bank would remain $10,000 and the income would last forever; you are spending only the interest, leaving the principal intact. If you spend more than $1,000 per year, the principal would necessarily decline over time and eventually the balance in the account would go to zero. In the language of this chapter, spending $1,000 per year or less would satisfy the sustainability criterion, while spending more would violate the sustainability criterion.

What does the Hartwick Rule mean in this context? It suggests that one way to tell whether an allocation (spending pattern) is sustainable or not is to examine what is happening to the principal over time. If the principal is declining, the allocation (spending pattern) is not sustainable. If the principal is increasing or remaining constant, the allocation (spending pattern) is sustainable.

How do we apply this to the environment? In general, the Hartwick Rule suggests that the current generation has been given an endowment. Part of the endowment consists of environmental and natural resources (known as "natural capital") and physical capital (such as buildings, equipment, schools, roads, and so on). Sustainable use of this endowment implies that we should keep the principal (the value of the endowment) intact and live off only the flow of services provided. We should not, in other words, chop down all the trees and use up all the oil, leaving future generations to fend for themselves. Rather we need to assure that the value of the total capital stock is maintained, not depleted.

The desirability of this version of the sustainability criterion depends crucially on how substitutable the two forms of capital are. If physical capital can readily substitute for natural capital, then maintaining the value of the sum of the two is sufficient. If, however, physical capital cannot completely substitute for natural capital, investments in physical capital may not be enough to assure sustainability.

How strong is the assumption of complete substitutability between physical and natural capital? Clearly it is untenable for certain categories of environmental resources. Though we can contemplate the replacement of natural breathable air with universal air-conditioning in domed cites, both the expense and the artificiality of this approach make it an absurd compensation device. Obviously intergenerational compensation must be approached carefully (see Example 5.2).

Example 5.2

NAURU: WEAK SUSTAINABILITY IN THE EXTREME

The weak sustainability criterion is used to judge whether the depletion of natural capital is offset by sufficiently large increases in physical or financial capital so as to prevent total capital from declining. It seems quite natural to suppose that a violation of that criterion does demonstrate *unsustainable* behavior. But does fulfillment of the weak sustainability criterion provide an adequate test of *sustainable* behavior? Consider the case of Nauru.

Nauru is a small Pacific island that lies some 3,000 kilometers northeast of Australia. It contains one of the highest grades of phosphate rock ever discovered. Phosphate is a prime ingredient in fertilizers.

Over the course of a century, first colonizers and then, after independence, the Nauruans decided to extract massive amounts of this rock. This decision has simultaneously enriched the remaining inhabitants (including the creation of a trust fund believed to contain over $1 billion) and destroyed most of the local ecosystems. Local needs are now mainly met by imports financed from the financial capital created by the sales of the phosphate.

However wise or unwise the choices made by the people of Nauru were, they could not be replicated globally. Everyone cannot subsist solely on imports financed with trust funds; every import must be exported by someone! The story of Nauru demonstrates the value of complementing the weak sustainability criterion with other, more demanding criteria. Satisfying the weak sustainability criterion may be a necessary condition for sustainability, but it is not always sufficient.

Source: J. W. Gowdy and C. N. McDaniel. "The Physical Destruction of Nauru: An Example of Weak Sustainability," *Land Economics* Vol. 75, No. 2 (1999): 333–338.

Recognizing the weakness of the constant total capital definition in the face of limited substitution possibilities has led some economists to propose a new definition—a sustainable allocation is one that maintains the value of the stock of *natural* capital. This definition assumes that it is natural capital that drives future well-being, and further assumes that little or no substitution between physical and natural capital is possible. To differentiate these two definitions, the maintenance of the value of total capital is now known as the "weak sustainability" definition, while maintaining the value of natural capital is known as the "strong sustainability" definition.

A final definition, known as "environmental sustainability," requires that certain *physical flows* of certain *individual* resources be maintained. This definition suggests that it is not sufficient to maintain the *value* of an *aggregate*. For a fishery, for example, this definition would emphasize assuring that catch levels did not exceed the growth of the biomass for the fishery. For a wetland, it would involve the preservation of the specific ecological functions.

Implications for Environmental Policy

In order to be useful guides to policy, our sustainability and efficiency criteria must be neither synonymous nor incompatible. Do these criteria meet that test?

They do. As we shall see later in the book, not all efficient allocations are sustainable and not all sustainable allocations are efficient. Yet some sustainable allocations are efficient and some efficient allocations are sustainable. Furthermore, market allocations may be either efficient or inefficient and either sustainable or unsustainable.

Do these differences have any policy implications? Indeed they do. In particular they suggest a specific strategy for policy. Among the possible uses for resources that fulfill the sustainability criterion, choose the one that maximizes either dynamic or static efficiency as appropriate. In this formulation the sustainability criterion acts as an overriding constraint on social decisions. Yet by itself, it is insufficient because it fails to provide any guidance on which of the infinite number of sustainable allocations should be chosen. That is where efficiency comes in. It provides a means for maximizing the wealth derived from all the possible sustainable allocations.

This combination of efficiency with sustainability turns out to be very helpful in guiding policy. Many unsustainable allocations are the result of inefficient behavior. Correcting the inefficiency can either restore sustainability or move the economy a long way in that direction. Furthermore, and this is important, correcting inefficiencies can frequently produce win-win situations. In win-win changes, the various parties affected by the change are all better off after the change than before. This contrasts sharply with changes in which the gains to the gainers are offset by losses to the losers.

Win-win situations are possible because removing an inefficiency increases net benefits. The increase in net benefits provides a means for compensating those who might otherwise lose from the change. Compensating losers reduces the opposition to change, thereby making change more likely. Do our economic and political institutions normally produce outcomes that are both efficient and sustainable? In future chapters we will provide explicit answers to this important question.

Summary

Both efficiency and ethical considerations can guide the desirability of private and social choices involving the environment. Whereas the former is concerned mainly with eliminating waste in the use of resources, the latter is concerned with assuring the fair treatment of all parties.

Previous chapters have focused on the static and dynamic efficiency criteria. A subsequent chapter will focus on the environmental justice implications of environmental degradation and remediation for members of the current generation. This chapter examines one possible characterization of the obligation previous generations owe to those generations that follow and the policy implications that flow from acceptance of that obligation.

The specific obligation examined in this chapter—sustainable development—is based upon the notion that earlier generations should be free to pursue their own well-being as long as in so doing they do not diminish the welfare of future generations. This notion gives rise to three alternative definitions of sustainable allocations:

Weak Sustainability. Resource use by previous generations should not exceed a level that would prevent subsequent generations from achieving a level of well-being at least as great. One of the implications of this definition is that the value of the capital stock (natural plus physical capital) should not decline. Individual components of the aggregate could decline in value as long as other components were increased in value (normally through investment) sufficiently to leave the aggregate value unchanged.

Strong Sustainability. According to this interpretation, the value of the remaining stock of natural capital should not decrease. This definition places special emphasis on preserving natural (as opposed to total) capital under the assumption that natural and physical capital offer limited substitution possibilities. This definition retains the focus of the previous definition on preserving value (rather than a specific level of physical flow) and on preserving an aggregate of natural capital (rather than any specific component).

Environmental Sustainability. Under this definition, the *physical* flows of *individual* resources should be maintained, not merely the *value* of the *aggregate*. For a fishery, for example, this definition would emphasize maintaining a constant fish catch (referred to as a sustainable yield), rather than a constant value of the fishery. For a wetland, it would involve preserving specific ecological functions, not merely its value.

It is possible to examine and compare the theoretical conditions that characterize various allocations (including market allocations and efficient allocations) to the necessary conditions for an allocation to be sustainable under these definitions. According to the theorem that is now known as the "Hartwick Rule," if all of the scarcity rent from the use of scarce resources is invested in capital, the resulting allocation will satisfy the first definition of sustainability.

In general, not all efficient allocations are sustainable and not all sustainable allocations are efficient. Furthermore market allocations can be: (1) efficient, but not sustainable; (2) sustainable, but not efficient; (3) inefficient and unsustainable; and (4) efficient and sustainable. One class of situations, known as "win-win" situations, provides an opportunity to increase simultaneously the welfare of both current and future generations.

We shall explore these themes much more intensively as we proceed through the book. In particular we shall inquire into when market allocations can be expected to produce allocations that satisfy the sustainability definitions and when they cannot. We shall also see how the skillful use of economic incentives can allow policymakers to exploit "win-win" situations to promote a transition onto a sustainable path for the future.

Discussion Questions

1. The notion of sustainability is not the same in the natural sciences as it is in economics. In the natural sciences, sustainability frequently means maintaining a constant physical flow of each and every resource (for example, fish from the

sea or wood from the forest), while in economics it means maintaining the *value* of those service flows. When might the two criteria lead to different choices? Why?

Problems

1. In the numerical example given in the text, the inverse demand function for the depletable resource is $P = 8 - 0.4q$ and the marginal cost of supplying it is $2.00. (a) If 20 units are to be allocated between two periods, in a dynamic efficient allocation how much would be allocated to the first period and how much to the second period when the discount rate is zero? (b) What would the efficient price be in the two periods? (c) What would the marginal user cost be in each period?

2. Assume the same demand conditions as stated in Question 1, but for this question let the discount rate be 0.10 and the marginal cost of extraction be $4.00. How much would be produced in each period in an efficient allocation? What would the marginal user cost be in each period? Would the static and dynamic efficiency criteria yield the same answers for this problem? Why?

3. Compare two versions of the two-period depletable resource model that differ only in the treatment of marginal extraction cost. Assume that in the second version the constant marginal extraction cost is lower in the second period than the first (perhaps due to the anticipated arrival of a new, superior extraction technology). The constant marginal extraction cost is the same in both periods in the first version and is equal to the marginal extraction cost in the first period of the second version. In a dynamic efficient allocation, how would the extraction profile in the second version differ from the first? Would relatively more or less be allocated to the second period in the second version than in the first version? Would the marginal user cost be higher or lower in the second version?

Further Reading

Atkinson, G., et al. *Measuring Sustainable Development: Macroeconomics and the Environment* (Cheltenham, UK: Edward Elgar, 1997). This book tackles the tricky question of how one can tell whether development is sustainable or not.

Desimone, L. D. *Eco-Efficiency: The Business Link to Sustainable Development* (Cambridge, MA: MIT Press, 1997). What is the role for the private sector in sustainable development? Is concern over the "bottom line" consistent with the desire to promote sustainable development?

May, P., and R. S. D. Motta, eds. *Pricing the Planet: Economic Analysis for Sustainable Development* (New York: Columbia University Press, 1996). Ten essays dealing with how sustainable development might be implemented.

Perrings, C. *Sustainable Development and Poverty Alleviation in Sub-Saharan Africa: The Case of Botswana* (New York: Macmillan, 1996). One of the leading practitioners in the field examines the problems and prospects for sustainable development in the African nation of Botswana.

Pezzey, J. V. C., and Michael A. Toman. "Progress and Problems in the Economics of Sustainability," in T. Tietenberg and H. Folmer, eds. *The International Yearbook of*

Environmental and Resource Economics: A Survey of Current Issues (Cheltenham, UK: Edward Elgar, 2002): 165–232. An excellent survey of the economics literature on sustainable development.

Additional References and Historically Significant References are available on this book's companion web site www.aw-bc.com/tietenberg.

Appendix

The Mathematics of the Two-Period Model

An exact solution to the two-period model can be derived using the solution equations derived in the appendix to Chapter 2.

The following parameter values are assumed by the two-period example:

$$a = 8, c = \$2, b = 0.4, Q = 20, \text{ and } r = 0.10.$$

Using these, we obtain:

$$8 - 0.4q_1 - 2 - \lambda = 0, \tag{1}$$

$$\frac{8 - 0.4q_2 - 2}{1.10} - \lambda = 0 \tag{2}$$

$$q_1 + q_2 = 20.$$

It is now readily verified that the solution (accurate to the third decimal place) is:

$$q_1 = 10.238, q_2 = 9.762, \lambda = \$1.905.$$

We can now demonstrate the propositions discussed in this text.

1. Verbally, equation (1) states that in a dynamic efficient allocation, the present value of the marginal net benefit in Period 1 ($8 - 0.4q_1 - 2$) has to equal λ. Equation (2) states that the present value of the marginal net benefit in Period 2 should also equal λ. Therefore, they must equal each other. This demonstrates the proposition shown graphically in Figure 5.2.
2. The present value of marginal user cost is represented by λ. Thus equation (1) states that price in the first period ($8 - 0.4q_1$) should be equal to the sum of marginal extraction cost ($\$2$) and marginal user cost ($\$1.905$). Multiplying (2) by $1 + r$, it becomes clears that price in the second period ($8 - 0.4q_2$) is equal to the marginal extraction cost ($\$2$) plus the higher marginal user cost [$\lambda (1 + r) = (1.905) (1.10) = \$2.905$] in Period 2. These results show why the graphs in Figure 5.3 have the properties they do. They also illustrate the point that, in this case, marginal user cost rises over time.

The Population Problem

The choices of the next ten years will decide the speed of population growth for much of the next century; . . . they will decide whether the pace of damage to the environment speeds up or slows down; . . . they may decide the future of the earth as habitation for humans.

—Dr. Nafis Sadik, Executive Director of the U.N. Population Fund, *The State of the World Population*, 1990

Introduction

In Chapter 1 we examined two strikingly different views of what the future holds for the world economic system. At the heart of those differences lie divergent views of the world population problem. One view sees population growth as continuing relentlessly, putting enormous pressure on food and environmental resources. The other view foresees human ingenuity erasing those limits as it has in the past.

These views are symptomatic of a debate that has deep historical roots. Thomas Malthus, a late-18th-century and early-19th-century classical economist, concluded that population growth posed a trap for nations seeking to develop. Temporary increases in income were seen as triggering increases in population until the land could no longer supply adequate food. Cornell University Professor David Pimentel (1994) has brought this argument into the 20th century by suggesting that the optimum global population, defined as the largest population that could be supported sustainably in relative prosperity, is about 2 billion people. Since this is approximately one-third of the current population, his analysis suggests the need for considerable reductions in current population *levels*, not merely growth.

Contrasting views are held by representatives of Third World countries and some prominent population economists. The late Julian Simon maintained that not only have the pessimists overstated the seriousness of the problem, but also that they fail to recognize that population growth in many of the developing countries is desirable. Clearly no consensus exists.

In this chapter we examine the manner in which population affects and is affected by the development process, as well as the microeconomic issues dealing with economic determinants of fertility. This economic perspective provides one basis for understanding the causes and consequences of population growth and provides an approach for controlling population.

Historical Perspective

World Population Growth

It has been estimated that at the beginning of the Common Era, world population stood at about 250,000,000 people and was growing at 0.04% per year (not 4%!). When the world's population passed 6 billion, it was growing at an annual rate around 1.5% per year. Since the beginning of time, the population has grown to over 6 billion people; at a 1.5% growth rate, the next 6 billion could take only 50 years.

In recent years, the average rate of population growth has declined (Table 6.1). This slowdown has been experienced in both developed and less developed countries, although rates remain higher in the less developed countries. The World Fertility Survey, a multinational survey of some 400,000 women in 61 countries, found several apparent causes, including increased use of contraception, a growing preference for fewer children, and couples marrying later.

Although the trend toward falling birthrates is pervasive, the fact remains that most developing countries still have, and can be expected to have in the future, substantial increases in their populations. Some 98% of the population growth between 1998 and 2025 is expected to occur in the poorer countries.

For example, in 1995–2000 Rwanda and Liberia had growth rates of 7.9% and 8.6%, respectively. During the same period, Italy and Portugal experienced growth rates of less than one-tenth of 1%. Hungary, Bulgaria, and Latvia all currently have declining populations.[1]

Population Growth in the United States

Population growth in the United States has followed the general declining pattern of most of the developed world, although in most periods American growth rates have exceeded the average for Europe by a substantial margin. These large reductions in American population growth rates have been due primarily to declines in the birthrate, which fell from a high of 55.2 live births per thousand population in 1820 to only 14.1 live births per thousand in 2001 (see Figure 6.1).

---

[1]The comparative population growth rate figures can be found in World Resources Institute. *World Resources: 1998–99* (New York: Oxford University Press, 1999): 244–245.

TABLE 6.1

Average Annual Rate of Growth by Region and Development Category: 1950–2050 [In percent]

Region	1950–60	1960–70	1970–80	1980–90	1990–2000	2000–10	2010–25	2025–50
WORLD	1.7	2.0	1.8	1.7	1.4	1.1	0.9	0.6
Less Developed Countries	2.0	2.4	2.2	2.0	1.7	1.3	1.1	0.7
More Developed Countries	1.2	1.0	0.7	0.6	0.4	0.3	0.1	(Z)
AFRICA	2.2	2.4	2.7	2.8	2.5	2.0	1.6	1.4
Sub-Saharan Africa	2.1	2.5	2.7	2.8	2.6	2.0	1.7	1.6
North Africa	2.4	2.4	2.5	2.7	2.1	1.7	1.3	0.8
NEAR EAST	2.7	2.6	3.0	2.9	2.3	2.2	1.9	1.4
ASIA	1.7	2.2	2.0	1.8	1.4	1.1	0.9	0.4
LATIN AMERICA AND THE CARIBBEAN	2.7	2.7	2.4	2.0	1.7	1.3	1.0	0.5
EUROPE AND THE NEW INDEPENDENT STATES	1.1	0.9	0.7	0.5	0.2	0.1	(Z)	−0.2
Western Europe	0.7	0.8	0.4	0.3	0.3	0.2	(Z)	−0.3
Eastern Europe	1.2	0.8	0.8	0.4	−0.1	−0.1	−0.2	−0.5
New Independent States	1.7	1.3	0.9	0.8	0.1	0.1	0.2	(Z)
NORTH AMERICA	1.8	1.3	1.1	1.0	1.2	0.9	0.8	0.7
OCEANIA	2.3	2.1	1.6	1.6	1.5	1.2	0.9	0.5
EXCLUDING CHINA:								
World	1.8	1.9	1.8	1.8	1.5	1.3	1.0	0.7
Less Developed Countries	2.2	2.4	2.4	2.3	1.9	1.6	1.3	0.9
Asia	1.9	2.2	2.2	2.0	1.7	1.4	1.1	0.6
Less Developed Countries	2.0	2.3	2.2	2.1	1.8	1.5	1.1	0.7

(Z) Between −0.05% and +0.05%.

Note: Reference to China encompasses China, Hong Kong S.A.R., Macau S.A.R., and Taiwan. Direct access to this table and the International Data Base is available through the Internet at www.census.gov/ipc/www.

Source: U.S. Census Bureau, International Programs Center, International Data Base.
Internet Release Date: March 22, 2004

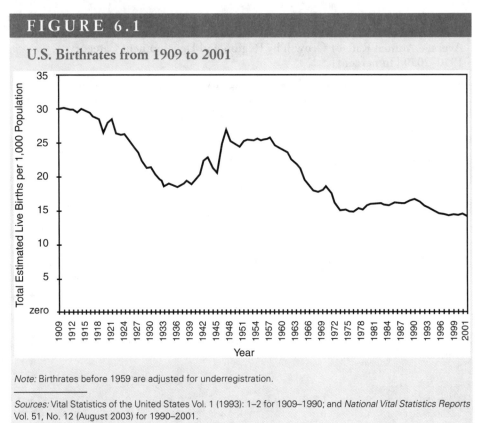

FIGURE 6.1

U.S. Birthrates from 1909 to 2001

Note: Birthrates before 1959 are adjusted for underregistration.

Sources: Vital Statistics of the United States Vol. 1 (1993): 1–2 for 1909–1990; and *National Vital Statistics Reports* Vol. 51, No. 12 (August 2003) for 1990–2001.

Birthrates, however, provide a rather crude measure of the underlying population trends, primarily because they do not account for age structure. To understand the effect of age structure, let's separate the birthrate experience into two components: (1) the number of persons in the childbearing years and (2) the number of children those persons are bearing.

To quantify the second of these components, the Census Bureau uses a concept known as the *total fertility rate*, which is the number of live births an average woman has in her lifetime if, at each year of age, she experiences the average birthrates occurring in the general population of similarly aged women. This concept can be used to determine what level of fertility would, if continued, lead to a stationary population. A *stationary population* is one in which age- and sex-specific fertility rates yield a birthrate that is constant and equal to the death rate, so the growth rate is zero. The level of the total fertility rate that is compatible with a stationary population is called the *replacement rate*. Rates higher than the replacement rate would lead to population growth, while rates lower would lead to population declines. Once the replacement fertility rate is reached, the World Bank

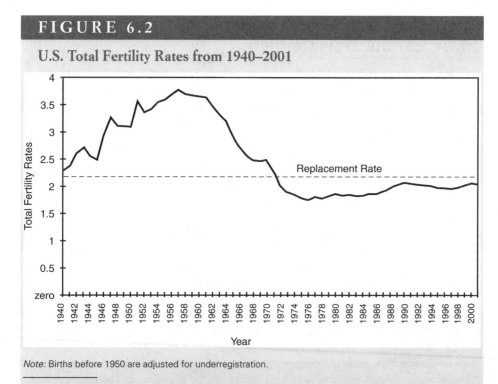

FIGURE 6.2

U.S. Total Fertility Rates from 1940–2001

Note: Births before 1950 are adjusted for underregistration.

Sources: The Statistical History of the United States, Colonial Times to the Present, p. 50; *Vital Statistics of the United States* Vol. 1 (1993): 10; and *National Vital Statistics Reports* Vol. 51, No. 12 (August 2003) for 1990–2001.

estimates that it takes approximately 25 years before the population stabilizes, due to the large numbers of families in the childbearing years. As the age structure reaches its older equilibrium, the growth rate declines until a stationary population is attained.

In the United States, the replacement rate is 2.11. The two children replace the mother and her mate, while the extra 0.11 is to compensate for those women who do not survive the childbearing years and because slightly more than 50% of births are males. The U.S. total fertility rate dropped below the replacement rate in 1972 and has remained below it ever since (see Figure 6.2). In 2001 (the latest year for which data were available) the rate stood at 2.034.

Two questions arise when we think about how population growth affects sustainability: (1) What is the relationship between population growth and economic development? and (2) How can the rate of population growth be altered when alteration is appropriate? The first question lays the groundwork for considering the effect of population growth on quality of life, including the effects of a stationary population. The second allows us to consider public policies geared toward manipulating the rate of population growth when desirable.

Effects of Population Growth on Economic Development

A number of questions guide our inquiry. Does population growth enhance or inhibit the opportunities of a country's citizens? Does the answer depend on the stage of development? Given that several countries are now entering a period of declining population growth, what are the possible effects of this decline on economic growth?

Population growth affects economic growth and, as long as each person contributes something, those effects generally are positively correlated. As long as their marginal product is positive, additional people mean additional output. Since this is not a very restrictive condition, it should usually hold true.

However, the existence of a positive marginal product is not a very appropriate test of the desirability of population growth! Perhaps a better one is to ask whether population growth positively affects the average citizen. Whenever the marginal product of an additional person is lower than the average product, adding more persons simply reduces the welfare of the average citizen. Why?

In the range of marginal productivities between zero and the average product, economic growth measured in aggregate terms would increase, but measured in per capita terms, would decrease. Similarly, there is a range of marginal productivities—those greater than the average product—where economic growth increases regardless of whether it is measured in aggregate or per capita terms. Whether or not the material status of the average citizen is improved by population growth becomes a question of whether the marginal product of additional people is higher or lower than the average product.

To facilitate our examination of the population-related determinants of economic development, let's examine a rather simple definition of output:

$$O = L \cdot X$$

where O is the output level, X is the output per worker, and L is the number of workers. This equation can be expressed in per capita terms by dividing both sides by population, denoted as P:

$$\frac{O}{P} = \frac{L}{P} \cdot X$$

This equation now states that output per capita is determined by the product of two factors: the share of the population that is in the labor force and the output per worker. Each of these two factors provides a channel through which population growth affects economic growth.

The most direct effect of population growth on the percentage of the population employed, the *age structure effect*, results from induced changes in the age distribution. Suppose that we were to compare two populations, one rapidly growing and one slowly growing. The one with the rapid growth would contain a much larger percentage of younger persons (see Figure 6.3).

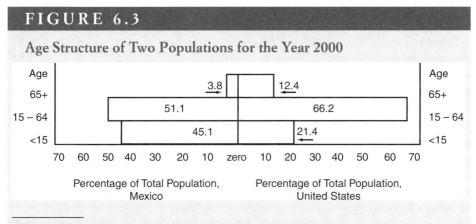

FIGURE 6.3

Age Structure of Two Populations for the Year 2000

Percentage of Total Population, Mexico

Percentage of Total Population, United States

Source: World Resources Institute, *World Resources: 1998–99* (New York: Oxford University Press, 1999): 246–247.

Due to its slow growth, the U.S. population is in general older than the population in Mexico. While approximately 45.1% of Mexico's population is 14 years of age or younger, the comparable figure for the United States is 21.4%. This is reinforced at the other end of the age structure, where some 12.4% of the U.S. population is 65 or older, compared with only 3.8% in Mexico.

These differences in the age structure have mixed effects on the percentage of the labor force available to be employed. The abundance of youth in a rapidly growing population creates a large supply of people too young to work, a situation referred to as the *youth effect*. On the other hand, a country characterized by slow population growth has a rather larger percentage of persons who have reached, or are past, the traditional retirement age of 65, a situation referred to as the *retirement effect*. Some developing countries are experiencing both effects simultaneously as better public health policies reduce death rates while birthrates remain high. How do the youth and retirement effects interact to determine the percentage of the population in the labor force? Does the youth effect dominate the retirement effect?

Examine the percentage of population in the prime working ages, 15–64. As Figure 6.3 shows, this percentage is much higher for the United States. A larger percentage of the population is in the working force in the United States than in Mexico. For Mexico, the youth effect dominates.

This dominance of the youth effect generalizes to other countries. For example, in 2000 the African countries had an average of 53.8% of the population in the prime working age while European countries averaged 65.5%.[2] High population growth retards per capita economic growth by decreasing the percentage of the population in the labor force.

Rapid growth also affects the percentage available to be employed through the *female availability effect*. With a slower growth rate and fewer children to care for,

[2]World Resources Institute. *World Resources: 1998–99* (New York: Oxford University Press, 1999): 246–247.

more women are available to join the labor force. Both the dominance of the youth effect (over the retirement effect) and the female availability effect suggest that rapid population growth reduces the percentage of the population in the labor force, which, in turn, has a depressing effect on economic growth per capita.

How about possible relationships between population growth and the second factor, the amount of output produced by the average worker? The most common way to enhance productivity is through the accumulation of capital. As the capital stock is augmented (for example, through the introduction of assembly lines or production machinery), workers become more productive. Is there any connection between population growth and capital accumulation?

One main connection involves the link between savings and capital accumulation. The availability of savings constrains the level of additions to the capital stock. Availability of savings, in turn, is affected in part by the age structure of the population. Older populations are presumed to save more because less is spent directly on the care and nurturing of children. Therefore, all other things being equal, societies with rapidly growing populations could be expected to save proportionately less. This lowered availability of savings would lead to lower amounts of capital stock augmentation and lower productivity per worker.

Apparently the magnitude of the effect of demographic change on savings in the 1960s and 1970s was small, but that has changed. A large study by Kelley and Schmidt (1994) has found that population growth and demographic dependency exerted a sizable negative impact on savings in the 1980s.

A final model suggesting a negative effect of population growth on economic growth involves the presence of some fixed essential factor for which limited substitution possibilities exist (land or raw materials, for example). In this case, the *law of diminishing marginal productivity* applies. This law states that in the presence of a fixed factor (land), successively larger additions of a variable factor (labor) will eventually lead to a decline in the marginal productivity of the variable factor. It suggests that in the presence of fixed factors, successive increases in labor will drive the marginal product down. When it falls below the average product, per capita income will decline with further increases in the population.

Not all arguments suggest that growth in output per capita will be restrained by population growth. Perhaps the most compelling arguments for the view that population growth enhances per capita growth are those involving technological progress and economies of scale (see Figure 6.4).

The vertical axis shows marginal productivity measured in units of output. The horizontal axis describes various levels of labor employed on a fixed amount of land. Population growth implies an increase in the labor force, which is recorded on the graph as a movement to the right on the horizontal axis.

The curve labeled $P(t_1)$ shows the functional relationship between the marginal product of labor and the amount of labor employed on a fixed plot of land at a particular point in time (t_1). Different curves represent different points in time because in each period of time there exists a unique state of the art in the knowledge of how to use the labor most effectively. Thus, as time passes, technological progress occurs, advancing the state of the art and shifting the productivity curves outward, as demonstrated by $P(t_2)$ and $P(t_3)$.

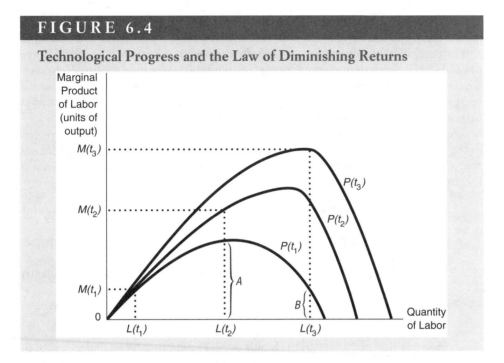

FIGURE 6.4

Technological Progress and the Law of Diminishing Returns

Three situations are demonstrated by Figure 6.4. At time t_1, an application of $L(t_1)$ yields a marginal product of $M(t_1)$. At times t_2 and t_3, the application of $L(t_2)$ and $L(t_3)$ units of labor respectively yield $M(t_2)$ and $M(t_3)$ marginal units of output. Marginal products have increased as larger amounts of labor were added.

Consider what would have happened, however, if the state of technical knowledge had not increased. The increase in labor from $L(t_2)$ to $L(t_3)$ would have been governed by the $P(t_1)$ curve, and the marginal product would have declined from A to B. This is precisely the result anticipated by the law of diminishing marginal productivity. Technological progress provides one means of escaping the law of diminishing marginal productivity.

The second source of increase in output per worker is economies of scale. Economies of scale occur when increases in inputs lead to a more-than-proportionate increase in output. Population growth, by increasing demand for output, allows these economies of scale to be exploited. In the United States, at least, this has historically been a potent source of growth. While it seems clear that the population level in the United States is already sufficient to exploit economies of scale, the same is not necessarily true for all developing countries.

In the absence of trade restrictions, however, the relevant market now is the global market, not the domestic market. The level of domestic population has little to do with the ability to exploit economies of scale in the modern global economy unless tariffs, quotas, or other trade barriers prevent the exploitation of foreign markets. If trade restrictions are a significant barrier, the appropriate remedy would be reducing trade restrictions, not boosting the local population.

Because these a priori arguments suggest that population growth could either enhance or retard economic growth, it is necessary to rely on empirical studies to sort out the relative importance of these effects. Several researchers have attempted to validate the premise that population growth inhibits per capita economic growth. Their attempts were based on the notion that if the premise were true, one should be able to observe lower growth in per capita income in countries with higher population growth rates, all other things being equal.

A study for the National Research Council (1986) conducted an intensive review of the evidence. Does the evidence support the expectations? In general they did not find a strong correlation between population growth and the growth in per capita income. They did find, however, that:

1. Slower population growth would raise the amount of capital per worker and, hence, the productivity per worker.
2. Slower population growth is unlikely to result in a net reduction in agricultural productivity and might well raise it.
3. National population density and economies of scale are not significantly related.
4. Rapid population growth puts more pressure on both depletable and renewable resources.

A subsequent study by Kelley and Schmidt (1994) found that "A statistically significant and quantitatively important negative impact of population growth on the rate of per capita output growth appears to have emerged in the 1980s." This result is consistent with the belief that population growth may initially be advantageous but ultimately, as capacity constraints become binding, becomes an inhibiting factor. Kelley and Schmidt also found that the net negative impact of demographic change diminishes with the level of economic development; the impact is larger in the relatively impoverished less developed countries. According to this analysis, those most in need of increased living standards are the most adversely affected by population growth.

Rapid population growth may also increase the inequality of income. High population growth can increase the degree of inequality for a variety of reasons, but the most important reason has a depressing effect on the earning capacity of children and on wages.

The ability to provide for the education and training of children, given fixed budgets of time and money, is a function of the number of children in the family—the fewer the children, the higher the proportion of income (and wealth, such as land) available to develop each child's earning capacity. Since low-income families tend to have larger families than high-income families do, the offspring from low-income families are usually more disadvantaged. The result is a growing gap between the rich and the poor.

What happens to the marginal cost of an additional child as the number of children increases? According to Table 6.2, the existing estimates suggest that child-rearing expenses rise from approximately a quarter of household expenditures for one-child families to approximately one-half for three-child families. These estimates also find that the total dollar amount spent on children increases with net income, but as a percentage of net income, it declines.

TABLE 6.2

Estimates of Child-Rearing Expenditures

Economist and Year of Study	Data Years[a]	Average Child-Rearing Expenditures as a Percent of Total Family Expenditure.		
		One Child	Two Children	Three Children
Espenshade (1984)	1972–73	24%	41%	51%
Betson (1990)	1980–86	25%	37%	44%
Lino (2000)	1990–92	26%	42%	48%
Betson[b] (2001)	1996–98	25%	35%	41%
Betson[b] (2001)	1996–98	30%	44%	52%

Notes: a. All estimates were developed using data from the Federal Bureau of Labor Statistics Consumer Expenditure Survey.

b. Betson (2001) developed two separate sets of estimates based on two somewhat different methodologies.

Source: Policy Studies, Inc. "Report on Improving Michigan's Child Support Formula" submitted to the Michigan State Court Administrative Office on April 12, 2002. Available on the Web at http://www.courts.mi.gov/scao/services/focb/formula/psireport.htm/.

Another link between population growth and income inequality results from the effect of population growth on the labor supply. High population growth could increase the supply of labor faster than otherwise, depressing wage rates vis à vis profit rates. Since low-income groups have a higher relative reliance on wages for their income than do the rich, this effect would also increase the degree of inequality.

After an extensive review of the historical record for the United States, historian Peter Lindert concludes that:

> There seems to be good reason for believing that extra fertility affects the size and "quality" of the labor force in ways that raise income inequalities. Fertility, like immigration, tends to reduce the average "quality" of the labor force, by reducing the amounts of family and public school resources devoted to each child. The retardation in the historic improvement in labor force quality has in turn held back the rise in the incomes of the unskilled relative to those enjoyed by skilled labor and wealth-holders. [p. 258]

Lindert's interpretation of the American historical record seems to be valid for developing countries as well. The National Research Council study found that slower population growth would decrease income inequality, and it would raise the education and health levels of the children. This link between rapid population growth and income inequality provides an additional powerful motivation for controlling population. Slower population growth reduces income inequality.

The Population/Environment Connection

Historically population growth has also been held up as a major source of environmental degradation. If supported by the evidence, this could provide another powerful reason to control population. What is the evidence?

On an individual country level, some powerful evidence has emerged on the negative effects of population density, especially when it is coupled with poverty. In some parts of the world, forestlands are declining as trees are cut down to provide fuel for an expanding population or to make way for the greater need for agricultural land to supply food. Lands that historically were allowed to recover their nutrients by letting them lay fallow for periods of 7 years or longer are now, of necessity, brought into cultivation before recovery is complete.

As the population expands and the land does not, new generations must either intensify production on existing lands or bring marginal lands into production. Inheritance systems frequently subdivide the existing family land among the children, commonly only male children. After a few generations the resulting parcels are so small and so intensively farmed as to be incapable of supplying adequate food for a family.

Migration to marginal lands can be problematic as well. Generally those lands are available for a reason. Many of them are highly erodible, which means that they degrade over time as the topsoil and the nutrients it contains are swept away. Migration to coastal river deltas may initially be rewarded by high productivity of this fertile soil, but due to their location, those areas may be vulnerable to storm surges resulting from cyclones.

In thinking about the long run, it is necessary to incorporate some knowledge of feedback effects. Would initial pollution pressure on the land result in positive (self-reinforcing) or negative (self-limiting) feedback effects? (Debate 6.1)

The traditional means of poverty reduction is economic development. What feedback effects on population growth would development be expected to have? Are development and the reduction of population pressure on the environment compatible or conflicting objectives? The next section takes up these issues.

Effects of Economic Development on Population Growth

Up to this point, we have considered the effect of population growth on economic development. We now have to examine the converse relationship. Does economic development affect population growth? Table 6.1 suggests that it may, since the higher-income countries are characterized by lower population growth rates.

This suspicion is reinforced by some further evidence. Most of the industrialized countries have passed through three stages of population growth. The conceptual framework that organizes this evidence is called the *theory of demographic transition*. This theory suggests that as nations develop, they eventually reach a point where birthrates fall (see Figure 6.5).

During Stage 1, the period immediately prior to industrialization, birthrates are stable and slightly higher than death rates, ensuring population growth.

Does Population Growth Inevitably Degrade the Environment?

Research in this area has traditionally been focused on two competing hypotheses.

Ester Boserup, a Danish economist, posited a negative feedback mechanism that has become known as the "induced innovation hypothesis." In her view, increasing populations trigger an increasing demand for agricultural products. As land becomes scarce relative to labor, incentives emerge for agricultural innovation. And this innovation results in the development of more intensive, yet sustainable land-management practices in order to meet the food needs. In this case the environmental degradation is self-limiting because human ingenuity is able to find ways to farm the land more intensively without triggering degradation.

The opposite view, called the "downward spiral hypothesis," envisions a positive feedback mechanism in which the degradation triggers a reinforcing response that only makes the problem worse. For example, suppose that poor families find that they are using up local wood fuel sources and therefore must travel farther to obtain the wood they need. The amount of time needed to gather a given amount of wood has risen. One way families react to this rising time cost of wood gathering is to increase the total labor time available to the family by having more children. While this strategy may make sense in the short run from the point of the view of each individual family, of course it only intensifies the communities' wood scarcity problem.

Clearly these very different visions have very different implications for the role of population in environmental degradation. Does the evidence suggest which is right?

Although quite a few studies have been conducted, neither hypothesis always dominates the other. Apparently the nature of the feedback mechanism is very context specific. Using a rather theoretical general model, Pender (1998) finds that either type of behavior could result depending upon the situation. Tiffen and Mortimore (2002) find that as family farms become smaller under conditions of population growth, some people migrate to new areas or take up new occupations, while others attempt to raise the value of output (crops or livestock) per hectare. According to their review, long-term data for selected countries and areas provide some evidence of negative feedback effects (as predicted by the Boserup hypothesis). Adaptive strategies of small farmers revealed by the case studies include "techniques to improve fertility, conserve water, manage trees, increase livestock, and take advantage of changing markets." However, they also found that investments in improving land and productivity are constrained by poverty.

Intensification of land use, even if it were sustainable, would not inevitably imply that poverty would be reduced. All of the effects cited in the previous section— including diminished wages from an increased labor supply, smaller investments in each child, a rise in the dependency ratio, and diminished savings—could all act to retard poverty reduction despite successful agricultural intensification. And diminished poverty reduction could put a brake on induced innovation. Hence induced innovation can occur (and has occurred), but it is certainly not automatic.

FIGURE 6.5

The Demographic Transition

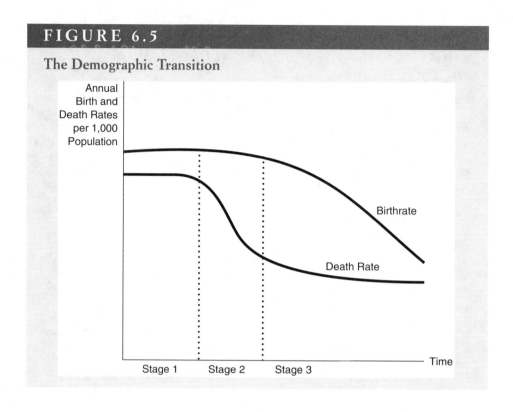

During Stage 2, the period immediately following the initiation of industrialization, death rates fall dramatically with no accompanying change in birthrates. This decline in mortality results in a marked increase in life expectancy and a rise in the population growth rate. In Western Europe, Stage 2 is estimated to have lasted somewhere around 50 years.

Stage 3, the period of demographic transition, involves large declines in the birthrate that exceed the continued declines in the death rate. Thus, the period of demographic transition involves further increases in life expectancy, but rather smaller population growth rates than characterized during the second stage. The Chilean experience with demographic transition is illustrated in Figure 6.6. Can you identify the stages?

One substantial weakness of the theory of the demographic transition as a guide to the future lies in the effect of HIV/AIDS on death rates. Demographic transition theory presumes that with development comes falling death rates and increasing life expectancy, producing an increase in population growth until the subsequent fall in birthrates. The AIDS pandemic is so pervasive in some Sub-Saharan African nations that the resulting large increase in death rates and decrease in life expectancy is causing population to decline, not increase. According to the U.S. Census Bureau, Botswana, South Africa, and Zimbabwe are in that position.

The theory of demographic transition is useful in countries where death rates have fallen because it suggests that reductions in population growth might accompany rising standards of living, at least in the long run. However, it also

FIGURE 6.6

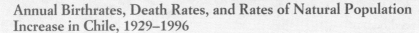

Annual Birthrates, Death Rates, and Rates of Natural Population Increase in Chile, 1929–1996

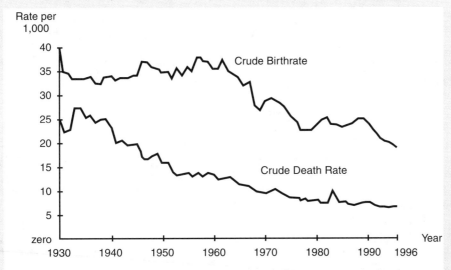

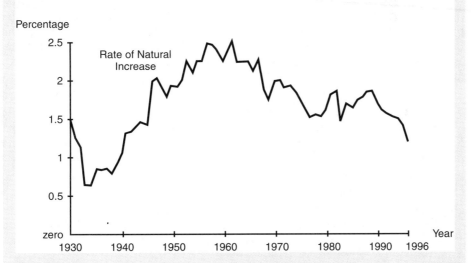

Sources: International Historical Statistics: The Americas (1750–1988) (New York: Stockton, 1993): 76 and 78, 1993 *Demographic Yearbook* (United Nations 1995): 294 and 321; 1997 *Demographic Yearbook* (United Nations 1999): 373 and 403. .

leaves many questions unanswered: Why does the fall in birthrates occur? Can the process be hastened? Will lower-income countries automatically experience demographic transition as living standards improve? Are industrialization or better-designed agricultural production systems possible solutions to "the population problem"?

To answer these questions it is necessary to begin to look more deeply into the sources of change behind the demographic transition. Once these sources are identified and understood, they can be manipulated in such a way as to produce the maximum social benefit.

The Economic Approach to Population Control

Is the current rate of population growth efficient? Is it sustainable? The issue of sustainability is most easily dealt with in specific natural resource settings (such as the ability to produce sufficient food), so intensive consideration of that question will be deferred until succeeding chapters.

The demonstration that population growth reduces per capita income, however, is not sufficient to prove that an inefficiency exists. If the reduced output is borne entirely by the families of the children, this reduction may represent a conscious choice by parents to sacrifice production in order to have more children. The net benefit gained from having more children would exceed the net benefit lost as output per person declined.

To establish whether or not population control is efficient, we must discover any potential behavioral biases toward overpopulation. Will parents always make efficient childbearing decisions?

A negative response seems appropriate for three specific reasons. In the first place, childbearing decisions impose external costs outside the family. Second, the prices of key commodities or services related to childbearing and/or rearing may be inefficient, thereby sending the wrong signals. And finally, parents may not be fully informed about, or may not have reasonable access to, adequate means for controlling births.

Two sources of market failure can be identified immediately. Adding more people to a limited space gives rise to "congestion externalities," higher costs resulting from the attempt to use resources at a higher-than-optimal capacity. Examples include too many people attempting to farm too little land and too many travelers attempting to use a specific roadway. These costs are intensified when the resource base is treated as free-access common property. And, as noted above, high population growth may exacerbate income inequality. Income equality is a public good. The population as a whole cannot be excluded from the degree of income equality that exists. Furthermore, it is indivisible because, in a given society, the prevailing income distribution is the same for all the citizens of that country.

Why should individuals care about inequality per se as opposed to simply caring about their own income? Aside from a purely humane concern for others, particularly the poor, people care about inequality because it can create social tensions. When these social tensions exist, society is a less pleasant place to live.

The demand to reduce income inequality clearly exists in modern society, as evidenced by the large number of private charitable organizations created to fulfill this demand. Yet because the reduction of income inequality is a public good, we also know that these organizations cannot be relied on to reduce inequality as much as would be socially justified.

Parents are not likely to take either the effect of more children on income inequality or congestion externalities into account when they make their childbearing decisions. Decisions that may well be optimal for individual families will result in inefficiently large populations.

Excessively low prices on key commodities can create a bias toward inefficiently high populations as well. Two particularly important ones are: (1) the cost of food, and (2) the cost of education. It is common for developing countries to subsidize food by holding prices below market levels. Lower-than-normal food prices artificially lower the cost of children as long as the quantities of food available are maintained by government subsidy (we discuss this further in Chapter 11).[3]

The second area in which the costs of children are not fully borne by the parents is education. Primary education is usually state-financed, with the funds collected by taxes. The point is *not* that parents do not pay these costs; in part they do. The point is rather that their level of contribution is not usually sensitive to the number of children they have. The school taxes parents pay are generally the same whether parents have two children, 10 children, or even no children. Thus the marginal educational expenditure for a parent—the additional cost of education due to the birth of a child—is certainly lower than the true social cost of educating that child.

Unfortunately, very little has been accomplished on assessing the empirical significance of these externalities. Despite this lack of evidence, the interest in controlling population is clear in many, if not most, countries.

The task is a difficult one. In many cultures the right to bear children is considered an inalienable right immune to influences outside the family. Indira Gandhi, the Prime Minister of India, lost an election in the late 1970s due principally to her aggressive and direct approach to population control. Though she subsequently regained her position, political figures in other democratic countries are not likely to miss the message. Dictating that no family can have more than two children is not politically palatable at this time. Such a dictum is seen as an unethical infringement on the rights of those who are mentally, physically, and monetarily equipped to care for larger families.

Yet the failure to control population growth can prove devastating to the quality of life, particularly in high-population-growth, low-income countries. Partha Dasgupta (1993) describes the pernicious, self-perpetuating process that can result:

> Children are borne in poverty, and they are raised in poverty. A large proportion suffer from undernourishment. They remain illiterate, and are often both stunted and wasted. Undernourishment retards their cognitive (and often motor) development. . . .

What, then, is a democratic country to do? How can it gain control over population growth while allowing individual families considerable flexibility in choosing their family size?

---

[3]Notice, however, that if the food is domestically produced and the effect of price controls is to lower the prices farmers receive for their crops, the effect is to lower the demand for children in the agricultural sector. (Why?)

Successful population control involves two components: (1) lowering the desired family size, and (2) providing sufficient access to contraceptive methods and family planning information to allow that size family to be realized.

The economic approach to population control *indirectly* controls population by lowering the desired family size. This is accomplished by identifying those factors that affect desired family size and changing those factors. To use the economic approach, we need to know how fertility decision-making is affected by the economic environment experienced by the family.

The major model attempting to assess the determinants of childbirth decision-making from an economic viewpoint is called the *microeconomic theory of fertility*. The point of departure for this theory is viewing children as consumer durables. The key insight is that the demand for children will, as with more conventional commodities, be downward sloping. All other things being equal, the more expensive children become, the fewer will be demanded.

With this point of departure, childbearing decisions can be modeled within a traditional demand-and-supply framework (see Figure 6.7). We shall designate the initial situation, before the imposition of any controls, as the point where marginal benefit, designated by MB_1, and marginal cost, designated by MC_1, are equal.

FIGURE 6.7

The Marginal Benefits and Marginal Costs of Children

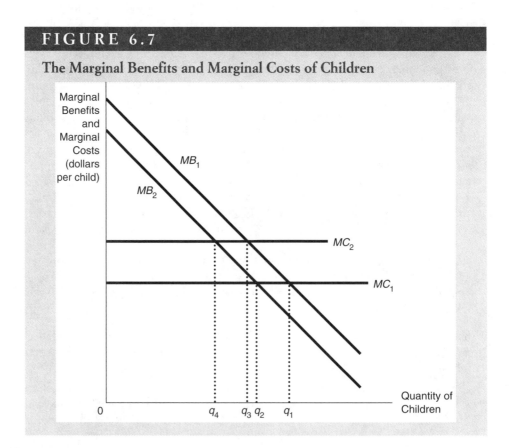

The desired number of children at this point is q_1. Notice that, according to the analysis, the desired number of children can be reduced either by an inward shift of the marginal benefit curve to MB_2, or an upward shift in the marginal cost of children to MC_2, or both. What would cause these to shift?

Let's consider the demand curve. Why might it have shifted inward during the demographic transition? Several sources of this change have emerged:

1. The shift from an agricultural to an industrial economy reduces the productivity of children. In an agricultural economy, extra hands are useful, but in an industrial economy, child labor laws result in children contributing substantially less to the family. Therefore the investment demand for children is reduced.

2. In countries with primitive savings systems, one of the very few ways a person can provide for old-age security is to have plenty of children to provide for him or her in the twilight years. One would not, at first glance, think of children as social security systems, but, in many societies, they are precisely that. When alternative means of providing for old-age security are developed, the marginal benefit from additional children decreases.

3. In some countries a woman's status is almost exclusively defined in terms of the number of children she bears. If personal status is positively correlated with desired family size, this will increase the marginal benefit from an additional child.

4. A decrease in infant mortality can also cause the marginal benefit curve to shift inward. When infant mortality is high, it takes more births to produce the desired number of children.

5. Some evidence also suggests that the amount the marginal benefit curve shifts inward as a result of economic growth depends on the manner in which the increased employment associated with development is shared among the members of society. Those countries that have typically entered into a phase of sustained fertility decline in spite of low levels of average per capita income levels are usually characterized by a relatively equal distribution of income and a relatively widespread participation in the benefits of growth. The rather dramatic fertility decline in Korea during the 1960–1974 period provides an historical illustration of this point.

Desired family size is also affected by changes in the cost of children. The costs of raising children can be changed as a means of controlling population.

1. One of the main components of the cost of children is the opportunity cost of the mother's time. By increasing the educational and labor market opportunities for women, the opportunity cost of raising children is increased. This can affect the observed fertility rate both by deferring the time of marriage and by causing a reduction in the desired number of children, once married.

2. As societies urbanize and industrialize, housing space becomes more expensive due to the concentrated demands in specific locations. Thus while the cost of extra space for children may be low in rural settings, it is much higher in urban settings.

3. The cost of children to parents may also be affected to a large extent by the cost of education. As nations struggle to improve their literacy rates by

universal compulsory education, they may simultaneously raise the cost of children. These costs rise not only because of direct additional parental expenditures on education but also because of the earnings that are forgone when the children are in school rather than working.

4. As development occurs, generally parents demand more education and a higher-quality education for their children. Depending on the system for financing education, providing this higher-quality education may raise the cost of every child even if the cost of a given quality of education is not rising.

All of this provides a menu of opportunities for population control. The reasons listed above represent potent forces for change. Yet these methods should be used with care. Inducing a family to have fewer children without assisting the family in satisfying the basic needs the children were fulfilling (such as old-age security) would be inequitable.

Policies in China illustrate just how far economic incentives can be carried. In announced regulations, one-child parents receive subsidized health expenditures; priority in education, health care, and housing; and additional subsidized food. Meanwhile, parents who have more than two children receive a reduction of 5% in the total income for the third child (6% for the fourth, and so on). Also, families were denied access to further subsidized grain beyond that which they would already receive for their two previous children. The total fertility rate, which had been 5.97 in 1968, had fallen to 1.8 by 2000.

Countries seeking to reduce fertility do not have to resort to such extreme measures. Policies such as enhancing the status of women, providing alternative sources of old-age security, and supplying employment opportunities that equalize the income distributions are both humane and effective. And, it is important to note that these policies can make headway even in very-low-income areas (see Example 6.1).

Studies that have evaluated the effects of this type of approach find that: (a) greater family wealth sustains higher education levels and better health; (b) a rise in the value of the mother's time has a positive effect on the demand for contraceptive services and a negative effect on fertility; (c) a rise in the value of the father's earnings has a positive effect on completed family size, child health, and child education; and (d) an increase in the mother's schooling has a negative effect on fertility and infant mortality and a positive effect on nutrition and children's schooling.

One way to empower women is to increase their income-earning potential. The typical way to increase income-earning potential is through investment in either human capital (education and training) or physical capital (looms, agricultural equipment, and so on). Funds for investment are normally obtained from banks. In order to minimize their risk, banks usually require collateral—property that can be sold to cover the proceeds of the loan in a case of failure to repay. In many developing countries women are not allowed to own property so they have no collateral. As a result, traditional credit facilities are closed to them and good investment opportunities are forgone.

Example 6.1

ACHIEVING FERTILITY DECLINES IN LOW-INCOME COUNTRIES: THE CASE OF KERALA

Conventional wisdom suggests that achieving fertility declines in low-income countries is very difficult. Stories about countries that overcome the income barrier can therefore be very revealing.

One such case is Kerala, one of the poorer states in India. Despite ranking near the bottom of India in terms of per capita income, the state has achieved the below replacement level of fertility two decades ahead of the all-India target year of 2011. The total fertility rate (TFR) declined from a high of 5.6 children per woman in the period 1951–1961 to about 1.7 in 1993.

Kerala apparently achieved this reduction in fertility because state and local governments focused on delivering reproductive and community health care, education (especially for females), and sanitation services to their citizens. The other key factor in this transition is the much higher social status accorded women in Kerala.

The advances in the field of social development have failed, however, to spur economic development. Kerala's per capita income and average annual growth rate during the decade of the 1980s were not only low; they were below the Indian average. The great potential for investments in human and social capital to spur sustainable development was not realized. Persistent problems included agricultural stagnation; massive "educated" unemployment; persistent poverty, especially among tribal populations, elderly women, and widows; high and still-rising suicide rate among young people; and continued environmental degradation.

Recognizing these deficiencies, the Indian government is now pursuing a more ambitious approach to improve both the economic condition of its inhabitants and the environment on which they depend. The new Kerala model relies on a community-based approach to sustainable development that draws upon the knowledge and aspirations of the various local populations.

Although it is too early to form a judgment on the success of this new approach, the early signs are encouraging. One project, for example, has been able to break the deadlock between decreasing land-use intensity and declining labor productivity. Two years after its implementation in 1998, the project has led to agricultural intensification and employment creation, and to a reversal of the environmentally unsound conversion of wetland. This institutional innovation has apparently been economically beneficial for both participating laborers and farmers.

This is one experiment worth keeping an eye on.

Source: S. Irudaya Rajan and K.C. Zachariah. "Long-Term Implications of Low Fertility in Kerala, India," *Asia-Pacific Population Journal* Vol. 13, No. 3 (1998): 41–66; and René Véron. "The 'New' Kerala Model: Lessons for Sustainable Development," *World Development.* Vol. 29, Issue 4 (April 2001): 601–617.

One innovative solution to this problem was developed by the Grameen Bank in Bangladesh. This bank uses peer pressure rather than collateral to lower the risk of nonpayment. Small loans are made to individual women who belong to a group of five or so members. Upon complete repayment of all individual loans within the group, the members of the group become eligible for additional loans. If any member of the group fails to repay, all members remain ineligible until the full loan is repaid. Not only have repayment rates reportedly been very high, but the increasing income-earning capacity generated by these loans has enhanced the effect of family planning programs (see Example 6.2).

In terms of population growth, child nutrition, and health, these studies indicate a large payoff to making women fuller partners in the quest for improved living standards in the Third World. According to Lawrence Summers (1992), who at the time held the post of Chief Economist at the World Bank, the rate of return on investments in power plants in developing countries (a common investment) averaged less than 4%, while investments in education for girls produced returns of 20% or more.

In the words of Dr. Nafis Sadik (1989), Executive Director of the U.N. Population Fund:

> The extent to which women are free to make decisions affecting their lives may be the key to the future, not only of the poor countries, but the rich ones too. As mothers; producers or suppliers of food, fuel and water; traders and manufacturers; political and community leaders, women are at the center of the process of change. (p. 3)

The desire to reduce family size, however, is not sufficient if access to birth control information and contraceptives is inadequate. The adequacy of family planning programs varies markedly among countries even within the same continent. Yet where access is very good, fertility has declined, particularly when access is coupled with better education and opportunities for women.

Summary

World population growth has slowed considerably in recent years. Population declines are already occurring in Germany and are expected in the near future in a number of northern European countries. The U.S. total fertility rate is now below the replacement level. If maintained for a number of years, this fertility behavior would usher in an era of zero or negative population growth for the United States as well.

Those countries experiencing declines in their population growth will also experience a rise in the average age of their population. This transition to an older population should boost income per capita growth by increasing the share of the population in the labor force and by allowing more family wealth to be concentrated on the nutrition, health, and education of the children.

Example 6.2

INCOME-GENERATING ACTIVITIES AS FERTILITY CONTROL: BANGLADESH

In Bangladesh the Grameen Bank and other organizations have begun to combine family planning programs with projects designed to generate income for women. Relying on peer pressure to encourage repayment of small loans, such programs have been successful, as loan recovery rates range between 96% and 100%. Results show that credit provision has been associated with productive self-employment, increase in income, accumulation of capital, and meeting basic needs of the poor borrowers.

A variety of income-generating activities is undertaken by participating women in order to pay back the loans. Such activities include: paddy husking, poultry raising, weaving, goat raising, and horticulture. In addition, other complementary government-financed social development activities such as sanitation, health care, nutrition, functional education, and population education are emphasized by all three programs. Family planning is actively and routinely promoted in group meetings, loan workshops, and training sessions that are financed by the agencies.

Results from this case study show that knowledge of contraceptive methods (through the population education component and group meetings with staff members) and the desire for no more children were higher among the beneficiaries of income-generating projects compared to the control group. About 60% of the beneficiaries were current users of contraceptives, compared to about 38% use by the control group. Also, about 80% of the beneficiaries desired no more children, while only 63% of the control group shared the same desire.

The income-generating projects led to an increase in contraceptive use regardless of their population education components. Over 50% who did not participate in their population education components were current users of contraceptives, compared to 38.4% of the control group. This suggests that the income-generating projects have an independent effect on the demand for fertility regulation and contraception.

Source: J. Chowdhury, Ruhul Amin, and A.U. Amhed. "Poor Women's Participation in Income Generating Projects and Their Fertility Regulation in Rural Bangladesh: Evidence from a Recent Survey," *World Development* (April 1994): 555–564; and the Web site: http://www.colby.edu/personal/thtieten/pop-ban.html.

All other things being equal, lower population growth should also help to reduce income inequality. On average this effect will be felt most strongly in lower-income families, since they typically are larger. This tendency for incomes of lower-income families to increase faster than those of higher-income families should be reinforced by the effects on labor supply. By preventing an excess supply of labor, which holds wages down, slower population growth benefits wage earners. Wages are a particularly important source of income for lower-income families.

Finally, while population growth is not the sole or perhaps even the most important source of nonsustainability, it definitely plays a significant role. If, as seems reasonable, there exists a maximum level of economic activity that can be sustained without undermining the resource base upon which it depends, population growth determines how the fruits of that activity are shared. While a smaller global population could experience relatively high individual standards of living, a larger population would have to settle for less.

Discussion Questions

1. Fertility rates vary widely among various ethnic groups in the United States. Black and Spanish-speaking Americans have above-average rates, for example, while Jews have below-average fertility rates. This may be due to different ethnic beliefs, but it may also be due to economic factors. How could you use economics to explain these fertility rate differences? What tests could you devise to see whether this explanation has validity?
2. The microeconomic theory of fertility provides an opportunity to determine how public policies that were designed for quite different purposes could affect fertility rates. Identify some public policies (for example, subsidies to people who own their own home, or subsidized day care) that could have an effect on fertility rates, and describe the relationship.

Problems

1. Some education is funded by property taxes, whereas other forms of education are funded by charging each student tuition. Suppose that within a community, more money is needed for education. Assuming that they raise the same amount of revenue, would the rising cost of education have the same effect on the desired number of children regardless of whether the system was funded by property taxes or tuition? Using the microeconomic theory of fertility, trace the expected impacts.
2. "According to the theory of the demographic transition, industrialization lowers population growth." Discuss.

Further Reading

Dasgupta, Partha. *An Inquiry into Well-Being and Destitution* (Oxford: Oxford University Press, 1993). A seminal work that deals comprehensively with the forces that create and accentuate poverty, including population growth.

Kelley, Allen C. "Economic Consequences of Population Change in the Third World," *Journal of Economic Literature* Vol. 26 (December 1988): 1685–1728. Excellent review of a complex literature with a detailed bibliography.

Kelley, Allen C., and Robert M. Schmidt. *Population and Income Change: Recent Evidence* (Washington, DC: The World Bank, 1994). An excellent review of the theory and evidence underlying the relationship between population growth and economic development. The review is complemented by some original empirical studies that reveal distinct new patterns.

Simon, Julian L. *Population and Development in Poor Countries: Selected Essays* (Princeton, NJ: Princeton University Press, 1992). A collection of essays from the primary proponent of the idea that moderate population growth (as opposed to zero or high) may be helpful to developing countries.

Additional References and Historically Significant References are available on this book's companion Web site www.aw-bc.com/tietenberg.

The Allocation of Depletable and Renewable Resources: An Overview

The whole machinery of our intelligence, our general ideas and laws, fixed and external objects, principles, persons, and gods, are so many symbolic, algebraic expressions. They stand for experience; experience which we are incapable of retaining and surveying in its multitudinous immediacy. We should flounder hopelessly, like the animals, did we not keep ourselves afloat and direct our course by these intellectual devices. Theory helps us to bear our ignorance of fact.

—George Santayana, *The Sense of Beauty* (1896)

Introduction

How do societies react when finite stocks of depletable resources become scarce? Is it reasonable to expect that self-limiting feedbacks would facilitate the transition to a sustainable, steady state? Or is it more reasonable to expect that self-reinforcing feedback mechanisms would cause the system to overshoot the resource base, ultimately precipitating a societal collapse?

We begin to seek answers to these questions by studying the implications of both efficient and profit-maximizing decision-making. What kinds of feedback mechanisms are implied by decisions motivated by efficiency and by profit maximization? Are they compatible with a smooth transition or are they more likely to produce overshoot and collapse?

We approach these questions in several steps, first by defining and discussing a simple but useful *resource taxonomy* (classification system), as well as explaining the dangers of ignoring the distinctions made by this taxonomy. We begin by defining an efficient allocation of an exhaustible resource over time when no renewable substitute is available. This is accomplished by exploring the conditions any efficient allocation must satisfy and using numerical examples to illustrate the meaning of these conditions.

We begin our treatment of renewable resources with the simplest possible case—the resource is supplied at a fixed, abundant rate and can be accessed at a constant marginal cost. Solar energy and replenishable surface water are two examples that seem roughly to fit this characterization. Combining this model of renewable resource supply with our basic depletable resource model allows us to characterize efficient extraction paths for both types of resources, assuming that they are perfect substitutes. We explore how these efficient paths are affected by changes in the nature of the cost functions as well as the nature of market extraction paths. Whether or not the market is capable of yielding a dynamically efficient allocation in the presence or absence of a renewable substitute provides a focal point for the analysis. Succeeding chapters will use these principles both to examine the allocation of energy, food, and water resources, and as a basis for developing more elaborate models of renewable biological populations such as fisheries and forests.

A Resource Taxonomy

Three separate concepts are used to classify the stock of depletable resources: (1) *current reserves*, (2) *potential reserves*, and (3) *resource endowment*. In the United States the Geological Survey (USGS) has the official responsibility for keeping records of the U.S. resource base, and has developed the classification system described in Figure 7.1.

Notice the two dimensions—one economic and one geological. A movement from top to bottom represents movement from cheaply extractable resources to those extracted at substantially higher prices. By contrast, a movement from left to right represents increasing geological uncertainty about the size of the resource base.

Current reserves (shaded area in Figure 7.1) are defined as known resources that can profitably be extracted at current prices. The magnitude of these current reserves can be expressed as a number.

Potential reserves, on the other hand, are most accurately defined as a function rather than a number. The amount of reserves potentially available depends upon the price people are willing to pay for those resources—the higher the price, the larger the potential reserves. For example, studies examining the amount of additional oil that could be recovered from existing oil fields by enhanced recovery techniques, such as injecting solvents or steam into the well to lower the density of the oil, find that as price is increased, the amount of oil that can be economically recovered also increases.

The *resource endowment* represents the natural occurrence of resources in the earth's crust. Since prices have nothing to do with the size of the resource endowment, it is a geological rather than an economic concept. This concept is important because it represents an upper limit on the availability of terrestrial resources.

The distinctions among these three concepts are significant. One common mistake in failing to respect these distinctions is using data on current reserves as if they represented the maximum potential reserves. This fundamental error can cause a huge understatement of the time until exhaustion.

A second common mistake is to assume that the entire resource endowment can be made available as potential reserves at some price people would be willing to pay.

FIGURE 7.1

A Categorization of Resources

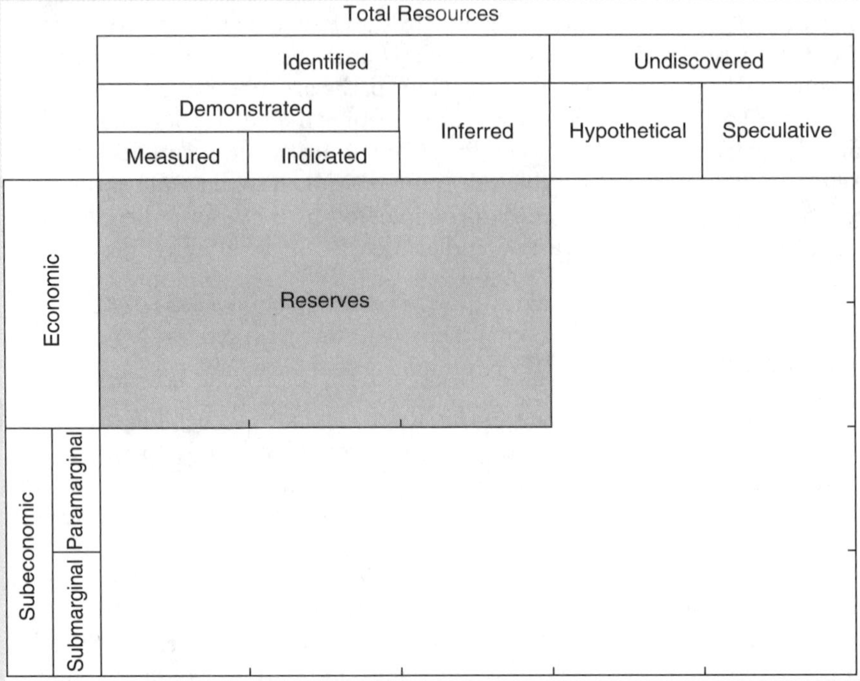

Total Resources					
Identified				Undiscovered	
Demonstrated		Inferred	Hypothetical	Speculative
Measured	Indicated				

(Left axis: Economic / Subeconomic; Subeconomic split into Paramarginal and Submarginal)

Reserves (shaded area covering Economic × Measured/Indicated/Inferred)

Terms

Identified resources: specific bodies of mineral-bearing material whose location, quality, and quantity are known from geological evidence, supported by engineering measurements.

Measured resources: material for which quantity and quality estimates are within a margin of error of less than 20 percent, from geologically well-known sample sites.

Indicated resources: material for which quantity and quality have been estimated partly from sample analyses and partly from reasonable geological projections.

Inferred resources: material in unexplored extensions of demonstrated resources based on geological projections.

Undiscovered resources: unspecified bodies of mineral-bearing material surmised to exist on the basis of broad geological knowledge and theory.

Hypothetical resources: undiscovered materials reasonably expected to exist in a known mining district under known geological conditions.

Speculative resources: undiscovered materials that may occur in either known types of deposits in favorable geological settings where no discoveries have been made, or in yet unknown types of deposits that remain to be recognized.

Source: U.S. Bureau of Mines and the U.S. Geological Survey. "Principle of the Mineral Resource Classification System of the U.S. Bureau of Mines and the U.S. Geological Survey," *Geological Survey Bulletin* (1976): 1450-A.

Clearly, if an infinite price were possible, then the entire resource endowment could be exploited. However, an infinite price is not likely.

For reasons that will be explained in Chapter 14, certain mineral sources are so costly to extract that it is inconceivable any current or future society would be willing to pay the price necessary to extract them. Thus it seems likely that the maximum feasible size of the potential reserves is smaller than the resource endowment. Exactly how much smaller cannot yet be determined with any degree of certainty, though Chapter 14 surveys the available evidence.

Other distinctions among resource categories are also useful. The first category includes all depletable, recyclable resources, such as copper. A *depletable resource* is one for which the natural replenishment feedback loop can safely be ignored. The rate of replenishment for these resources is so low that it does not offer a potential for augmenting the stock in any reasonable time frame.

A *recyclable resource* is one that, although currently being used for some particular purpose, exists in a form allowing its mass to be recovered once that purpose is no longer necessary or desirable. For example, copper wiring from an automobile can be recovered after the car has been shipped to the junkyard. The degree to which a resource is recycled is determined by economic conditions, a subject covered in Chapter 9.

The current reserves of a depletable, recyclable resource can be augmented by economic replenishment, as well as by recycling. Economic replenishment takes many forms, all sharing the characteristic that they turn previously unrecoverable resources into recoverable ones. One obvious stimulant for this replenishment is price. As price rises, producers find it profitable to explore more widely, dig more deeply, use lower-concentration ores, and so on.

Higher prices also stimulate technological progress. Technological progress simply means an advancement in the state of knowledge that allows us to do things we were not able to do before. One profound, if controversial, example can be found in the successful harnessing of nuclear power.

The other side of the coin for depletable, recyclable resources is that their potential reserves can be exhausted. The depletion rate is affected by the demand for and the durability of the products built with the resource, and the ability to reuse the products. Except where demand is totally price-inelastic (that is, insensitive to price), higher prices tend to reduce the quantity demanded. Durable products last longer, reducing the need for newer ones. Reusable products provide a substitute for new products. In the commercial sector, reusable soft-drink bottles provide one example, while flea markets (where secondhand items are sold) provide another for the household sector.

For some resources, the size of the potential reserves depends explicitly on our ability to store the resource. For example, helium is generally found commingled with natural gas in common fields. As the natural gas is extracted and stored, unless the helium is simultaneously captured and stored, it diffuses into the atmosphere. This results in such low concentrations that extraction of helium from the air is not economical at current or even likely future prices. Thus, the useful stock of helium depends crucially on how much we decide to store.

Not all depletable resources permit recycling or reuse. Depletable energy resources such as coal, oil, and gas are consumed as they are used. Once combusted and turned into heat energy, the heat dissipates into the atmosphere and becomes nonrecoverable.

The endowment of depletable resources is of finite size. Current use of depletable, nonrecyclable resources precludes future use; hence, the issue of how they should be shared among generations is raised in the starkest, least forgiving form.

Depletable, recyclable resources raise this same issue, though somewhat less starkly. Recycling and reuse make the useful stock last longer, all other things being equal. It is tempting to suggest that depletable, recyclable resources could last forever with 100% recycling, but unfortunately the physical theoretical upper limit on recycling is less than 100%—an implication of a version of the entropy law defined in Chapter 2. Some of the mass is always lost during recycling.

For example, copper pennies can be melted down to recover the copper, but the amount rubbed off during circulation would never be recovered. As long as less than 100% of the mass is recycled, the useful stock must eventually decline to zero. Even for recyclable, depletable resources, the cumulative useful stock is finite, and current consumption patterns still have an effect on future generations.

Renewable resources are differentiated from depletable resources primarily by the fact that natural replenishment augments the flow of renewable resources at a non-negligible rate. Solar energy, water, cereal grains, fish, forests, and animals are all examples of renewable resources. Thus it is possible, though not inexorable, that a flow of these resources could be maintained perpetually.[1]

For some renewable resources, the continuation and volume of their flow depend crucially on humans. Soil erosion and nutrient depletion reduce the flow of food. Excessive fishing reduces the stock of fish, which in turn reduces the rate of natural increase of the fish population. Newsprint can be recycled. Other examples abound. For other renewable resources, such as solar energy, the flow is independent of humans. The amount consumed by one generation does not reduce the amount that can be consumed by subsequent generations.

Some renewable resources can be stored; others cannot. For those that can, storage provides a valuable way to manage the allocation of the resource over time. We are not left simply at the mercy of natural ebbs and flows of the source. Food without proper care perishes rapidly, but with storage can be used to feed the hungry in times of famine. Unstored solar energy radiates off the earth's surface and dissipates into the atmosphere. While solar energy can be stored in many forms, the most common natural form of storage occurs when it is converted to biomass by photosynthesis.

Storage of renewable resources usually performs a different service from storage of depletable resources. Storing depletable resources extends their economic life; storing renewable resources, on the other hand, can serve as a means of smoothing out the cyclical imbalances of supply and demand. Surpluses are stored for periods when deficits may occur. Food stockpiles and the use of dams to store hydropower are two familiar examples.

---

[1]Even renewable resources are ultimately finite because their renewability depends on energy from the sun and the sun is expected to serve as an energy source for only the next 5 or 6 billion years. That fact does not eliminate the need to manage resources effectively until that time. Furthermore, the finiteness of renewable resources is sufficiently far into the future to make the distinction useful.

Managing renewable resources presents a different challenge from managing depletable resources, though an equally significant one. The challenge for depletable resources involves allocating dwindling stocks among generations while meeting the ultimate transition to renewable resources. In contrast, the challenge for managing renewable resources involves the maintenance of an efficient, sustainable flow. The next six chapters deal with how the economic and political sectors have responded to these challenges for particularly significant types of resources.

Efficient Intertemporal Allocations

If we are to judge the adequacy of market allocations, we must define what is meant by efficiency in relation to the management of depletable and renewable resource allocations. Because allocation over time is the crucial issue, dynamic efficiency becomes the core concept. The dynamic efficiency criterion assumes that society's objective is to maximize the present value of net benefits coming from the resource. For a depletable, nonrecyclable resource, this requires a balancing of the current and subsequent uses of the resource. In order to recall how the dynamic efficiency criterion defines this balance, we shall begin with an elaboration of the very simple two-period model developed in Chapter 5. We shall show how these conclusions generalize to longer planning horizons and more complicated situations.

The Two-Period Model Revisited

In Chapter 5 we defined a situation involving the allocation over two periods of a finite resource that could be extracted at constant marginal cost. With a stable demand curve for the resource, an efficient allocation meant that more than half of the resource was allocated to the first period and less than half to the second period. This allocation was affected both by the marginal cost of extraction and by the marginal user cost.

Due to the fixed and finite supplies of depletable resources, production of a unit today precludes production of that unit tomorrow. Therefore, production decisions today must take forgone future net benefits into account. Marginal user cost is the opportunity cost measure that allows intertemporal balancing to take place.

The marginal cost of extraction is assumed to be constant, but the current value of the marginal user cost rises over time. In fact, as was demonstrated mathematically in the appendix to Chapter 5, when the demand curve is stable over time and the marginal cost of extraction is constant, the rate of increase in the current value of the marginal user cost is equal to r, the discount rate. Thus, in Period 2, the marginal user cost would be $1 + r$ times as large as it was in Period 1.[2] Marginal user cost rises at rate r in an efficient allocation in order to preserve the balance between present versus future production.

In summary, our two-period example suggests that an efficient allocation of a finite resource with a constant marginal cost of extraction involves rising marginal

---

[2]The condition that marginal user cost rises at rate r is true only when the marginal cost of extraction is constant. Later in this chapter, we show how the marginal user cost is affected when marginal extraction cost is not constant.

FIGURE 7.2

(a) Constant Marginal Extraction Cost with No Substitute Resource: Quantity Profile. (b) Constant Marginal Extraction Cost with No Substitute Resource: Marginal Cost Profile

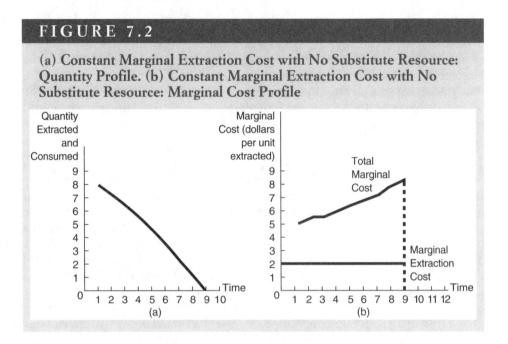

user cost and falling quantities consumed. We can now generalize to longer time periods and different extraction circumstances.

The *N*-Period Constant-Cost Case

We begin this generalization by retaining the constant-marginal-extraction-cost assumption while extending the time horizon within which the resource is allocated. In the numerical example shown in Figures 7.2a and 7.2b, the demand curves and the marginal-cost curve from the two-period case are retained. The only changes in this numerical example from the two-period case involve spreading the allocation over a large number of years and increasing the total recoverable supply from 20 to 40. (The mathematics behind this and subsequent examples is presented in the chapter appendix.)

Figure 7.2a demonstrates how the efficient quantity extracted varies over time, while Figure 7.2b shows the behavior of the marginal user cost and the marginal cost of extraction. Total marginal cost refers to the sum of the two. The marginal cost of extraction is represented by the lower line, and the marginal user cost is depicted as the vertical distance between the marginal cost of extraction and the total marginal cost. To avoid confusion, note that the horizontal axis is defined in terms of time, not the more conventional designation, quantity.

Several trends are worth noting. First of all, in this case as in the two-period case, the efficient marginal user cost rises steadily in spite of the fact that the marginal cost of extraction remains constant. This rise in the efficient marginal user cost reflects increasing scarcity and the accompanying rise in the opportunity cost of current consumption.

In response to these rising costs over time, the quantity extracted falls over time until it finally goes to zero, which occurs precisely at the moment when the total marginal cost becomes $8. At this point total marginal cost is equal to the highest price anyone is willing to pay, so demand and supply simultaneously equal zero. Thus, even in this difficult case involving no increase in the cost of extraction, an efficient allocation envisions a smooth transition to the exhaustion of a resource. The resource does not "suddenly" run out, although in this case it does run out.

Transition to a Renewable Substitute

So far we have discussed the allocation of a depletable resource when no substitute is available to take its place. Suppose, however, we consider the nature of an efficient allocation when a substitute renewable resource is available at constant marginal cost. This case, for example, could describe the efficient allocation of oil or natural gas with a solar substitute or the efficient allocation of exhaustible groundwater with a surface-water substitute. How could we define an efficient allocation in this circumstance?

Since this problem is very similar to the one already discussed, we can use what we have already learned as a foundation for mastering this new situation. The depletable resource would be exhausted in this case, just as it was in the previous case, but that will be less of a problem, since we'll merely switch to the renewable one at the appropriate time. For the purpose of our numerical example, assume the existence of a perfect substitute for the depletable resource that is infinitely available at a cost of $6 per unit. The transition from the depletable resource to this renewable resource would ultimately transpire because its marginal cost ($6) is less than the maximum willingness to pay ($8). (Can you figure out what the efficient allocation would be if the marginal cost of this substitute resource was $9 instead of $6?)

The total marginal cost for the depletable resource in the presence of a $6 perfect substitute would never exceed $6, because society could always use the renewable resource instead, whenever it was cheaper. Thus, while the maximum willingness to pay (the *choke price*) sets the upper limit on total marginal cost when no substitute is available, the marginal cost of extraction of the substitute sets the upper limit when one is available at a marginal cost lower than the choke price. The efficient path for this situation is given in Figures 7.3a and 7.3b.

In this efficient allocation, the transition is once again smooth. Quantity extracted is gradually reduced as the marginal user cost rises until the switch is made to the substitute. No abrupt change is evident in either marginal cost or quantity profiles.

Because the renewable resource is available, more of the depletable resource would be extracted in the earlier periods than was the case in our previous numerical example without a renewable resource. As a result, the depletable resource would be exhausted sooner than it would have been without the renewable resource substitute. In this example the switch is made during the sixth period, whereas in the last example the last units were exhausted at the end of the eighth period.

At the transition point, called the switch point, consumption of the renewable resource begins. Prior to the switch point, only the depletable resource is consumed, while after the switch point only the renewable resource is consumed. This sequencing

FIGURE 7.3

(a) Constant Marginal Extraction Cost with Substitute Resource: Quantity Profile. (b) Constant Marginal Extraction Cost with Substitute Resource: Marginal Cost Profile

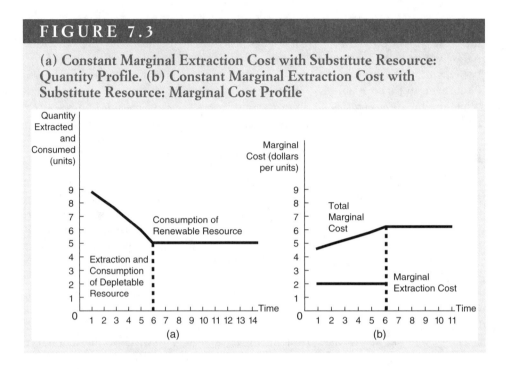

of consumption pattern results from the cost patterns. Prior to the switch point, the depletable resource is cheaper. At the switch point, the marginal cost of the depletable resource (including marginal user cost) rises to meet the marginal cost of the substitute, and the transition occurs. Due to the availability of the substitute resource, consumption never drops below five units in any time period. This level is maintained because five is the amount that maximizes the net benefit when the marginal cost equals $6 (the price of the substitute). (Convince yourself of the validity of this statement by substituting $6 into the willingness-to-pay function and solving for the quantity demanded.)

Though we shall not show the numerical example here, it is not difficult to see how an efficient allocation would be defined when the transition is from one constant marginal-cost depletable resource to another depletable resource with a constant, but higher, marginal cost (see Figure 7.4). The total marginal cost of the first resource would rise over time until it equaled that of the second resource at the time of transition. In the period of time prior to transition (T^*), only the cheapest resource would be consumed; all of it would have been consumed by T^*.

A close examination of the total-marginal-cost path reveals two interesting characteristics worthy of our attention. First, even in this case, the transition is a smooth one; total marginal cost never jumps to the higher level. Second, the rate of increase in total marginal cost slows down after the time of transition.

The first characteristic is easy to explain. The total marginal costs of the two resources have to be equal at the time of transition. If they weren't equal, the net benefit could be increased by switching to the lower-cost resource from the more

FIGURE 7.4

The Transition from One Constant-Cost Depletable Resource to Another

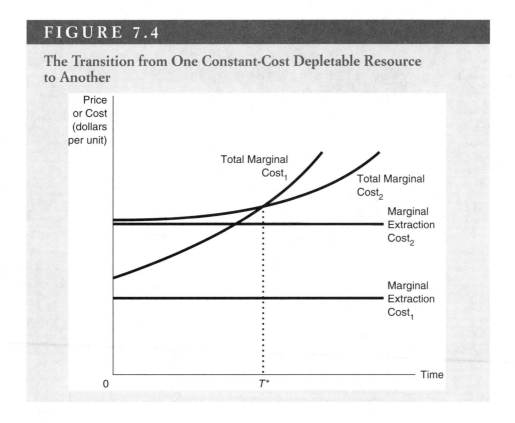

expensive resource. Total marginal costs are not equal in the other periods. In the period before transition, the first resource is cheaper and therefore used exclusively, whereas after transition the first resource is exhausted, leaving only the second resource.

The rate of increase in marginal cost is slower after transition simply because the component of total marginal cost that is growing (the marginal user cost) represents a smaller portion of the total marginal cost of the second resource than of the first. The total marginal cost of each resource is determined by the marginal extraction cost plus the marginal user cost. In both cases the marginal user cost is increasing at rate r, and the marginal cost of extraction is constant. As seen in Figure 7.4, at the time of transition the marginal cost of extraction, which is constant, constitutes a much larger proportion of total marginal cost for the second resource than for the first. Hence, total marginal cost rises more slowly for the second resource, at least initially.

Increasing Marginal Extraction Cost

We have now expanded our examination of the efficient allocation of depletable resources to include longer time horizons and the availability of other depletable or renewable resources that could serve as perfect substitutes. As part of our trek toward

FIGURE 7.5

(a) Increasing Marginal Extraction Cost with Substitute Resource: Quantity Profile. (b) Increasing Marginal Extraction Cost with Substitute Resource: Marginal Cost Profile

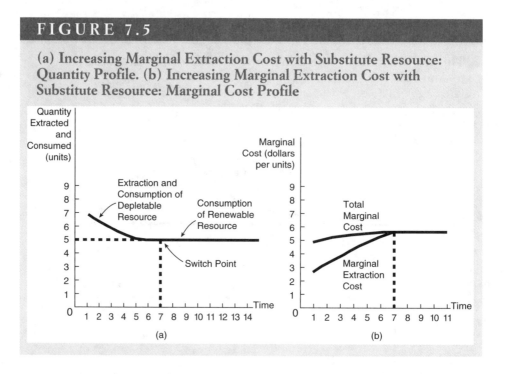

increasing realism, we will next consider a situation in which the marginal cost of extracting the depletable resource rises with the cumulative amount extracted. This is commonly the case, for example, with minerals, where the higher-grade ores are extracted first, followed by an increasing reliance on lower-grade ones.

Analytically, this case is handled in the same manner as the previous case except that the function describing the marginal cost of extraction is slightly more complicated.[3] It increases with the cumulative amount extracted. The dynamic efficient allocation of this resource is found by maximizing the present value of the net benefits using this modified cost of extraction function. The results of that maximization are portrayed in Figures 7.5a and 7.5b.

The most significant difference between this case and the others lies in the behavior of marginal user cost. In the previous case we said that marginal user cost rose over time at rate r. When the marginal cost of extraction increases with the cumulative amount extracted, marginal user cost *declines* over time until, at the time of transition to the renewable resource, it goes to zero. Why is that?

Remember that marginal user cost is an opportunity cost reflecting forgone future marginal net benefits. In contrast to the constant marginal-cost case, in the increasing-cost case every unit extracted raises the cost of extraction. Therefore, as the current marginal cost rises over time, the sacrifice made by future generations (as an additional unit is consumed earlier) diminishes; the net benefit that would be

---

[3]The marginal cost of extraction is $MC_t = \$2 + 0.1Q_t$ where Q_t is cumulative extraction to date.

received by a future generation if a unit of the resource were saved for them gets smaller and smaller as the marginal extraction cost of that resource gets larger and larger. By the last period the marginal extraction cost is so high that earlier consumption of one more unit imposes virtually no sacrifice at all. The opportunity cost of current extraction drops to zero, and total marginal cost equals the marginal extraction cost at the switch point.[4]

The increasing-cost case differs from the constant-cost case in another important way as well. In the constant-cost case, the depletable resource reserve is completely exhausted. In the increasing-cost case, however, the reserve is not exhausted; some is left in the ground because it is too expensive to take out.

Up to this point in our analysis, we have examined how an efficient allocation would be defined in a number of circumstances. First we examined a situation in which a finite amount of a resource was to be extracted at constant marginal cost. Despite the absence of increasing extraction cost, an efficient allocation involves a smooth transition to a substitute, when one is available, or to abstinence, when one is not. The complication of increasing marginal cost changes the time profile of the marginal user cost, but it does not alter the basic finding of declining consumption of depletable resources coupled with rising total marginal cost.

As a look at the historical record reveals, the consumption patterns of most depletable resources have involved increases, not decreases, in consumption over time. Is this prima facia evidence that the resources are not being allocated efficiently?

Exploration and Technological Progress

Using the historical patterns of increasing consumption to conclude that depletable resources are not being allocated efficiently would not represent a valid use of the theory of depletable resources. The models considered to this point have not yet included a consideration of the role of exploration for new resources or the role of technological progress, historically two significant factors in the determination of actual consumption paths.

The search for new resources is expensive. As easily discovered resources are exhausted, we must search in less rewarding environments, such as the bottom of the ocean or locations deep within the earth. This suggests the *marginal cost of exploration*, which is the marginal cost of finding additional units of the resource, should be expected to rise over time, just as the marginal cost of extraction does.

As the total marginal cost for a resource rises over time, society should actively explore possible new sources of that resource. The higher the marginal cost of

---

[4]Total marginal cost cannot be greater than the marginal cost of the substitute. Yet, in the increasing marginal extraction cost case, at the time of transition the marginal extraction cost also must equal the marginal cost of the substitute. If that weren't true, it would imply that some of the resource that was available at a marginal cost lower than the substitute would not be used. This would clearly be inefficient, since net benefits could be increased by simply using less of the more expensive substitute. Hence, at the switch point, in the rising marginal-cost case, the marginal extraction cost has to equal total marginal cost, implying a zero marginal user cost.

extraction for known sources is expected to rise, the larger is the potential increase in net benefits from exploration.

Some of this exploration would be successful; new sources of the resource would be discovered. If the marginal extraction cost of the newly discovered resources is low enough, these discoveries could lower, or at least retard, the increase in the total marginal cost of production. As a result, the new finds would tend to encourage more consumption. Compared to a situation with no exploration possible, the model with exploration would show a smaller and slower decline in consumption, while the rise in total marginal cost would be dampened.

It is also not difficult to expand our concept of efficient resource allocations to include *technological progress*, the general term economists give to advances in the state of knowledge. In the present context, technological progress would be manifested as reductions in the cost of extraction. For a resource that can be extracted at constant marginal cost, a one-time breakthrough lowering the marginal cost of extraction would hasten the time of transition. Furthermore, for an increasing-cost resource, more of the total available resource would be recovered in the presence of technological progress than would be recovered without it. (Why?)

The most pervasive effects of technological progress involve continuous downward shifts in the cost of extraction over some time period. The total marginal cost of the resource could actually fall over time if the cost-reducing nature of technological progress became so potent that, in spite of increasing reliance on inferior ore, the marginal cost of extraction decreased (see Example 7.1). With a finite amount of this resource, the fall in total marginal cost would be transitory, since ultimately it would have to rise, but, as we shall see in the next few chapters, this period of transition can last quite a long time.

Market Allocations

In the preceding sections we have examined in detail how the efficient allocation of substitutable, depletable, and renewable resources over time would be defined in a variety of circumstances. We must now address the question of whether actual markets can be expected to produce an efficient allocation. Can the private market involving millions of consumers and producers each reacting to his or her own unique preferences ever result in a dynamically efficient allocation? Is profit maximization compatible with dynamic efficiency?

Appropriate Property Right Structures

The most common misconception of those who believe that even a perfect market could never achieve an efficient allocation is a belief that producers want to extract and sell the resources as fast as possible, since that is how they derive the value from the resource. This misconception makes people see markets as myopic and unconcerned about the future.

As long as the property rights governing natural resources have the characteristics of exclusivity, transferability, and enforceability (Chapter 4), the markets in

Example 7.1

TECHNOLOGICAL PROGRESS IN THE IRON ORE INDUSTRY

The term *technological progress* plays an important role in the economic analysis of mineral resources. Yet, at times, it can appear abstract, even mystical. It shouldn't! Far from being a blind faith detached from reality, technological progress refers to a host of ingenious ways in which people have reacted to impending shortages with sufficient imagination that the available supply of resources has been expanded by an order of magnitude and at reasonable cost. To illustrate how concrete a notion technological progress is, consider one example of how it has worked in the past.

In 1947 the president of Republic Steel, C. M. White, calculated the expected life of the Mesabi range of northern Minnesota (the source of some 60% of iron ore consumed during World War II) as being in the range from five to seven years. By 1955, only eight years later, *U.S. News and World Report* was able to conclude that worry over the scarcity of iron ore could be forgotten. The source of this remarkable transformation of a problem of scarcity into one of abundance was the discovery of a new technique, called *pelletization,* of preparing iron ore.

Prior to pelletization, the standard ores from which iron was derived contained from 50% to more than 65% iron in crude form. There was a significant percentage of taconite ore available containing less than 30% iron in crude form, but no one knew how to produce it at reasonable cost. Pelletization is a process by which these ores are processed and concentrated at the mine site prior to shipment to the blast furnaces. The advent of pelletization allowed the profitable use of the taconite ores.

While expanding the supply of iron ore, pelletization reduced its cost in spite of the inferior grade being used. There were several sources of the cost reduction. First, substantially less energy was used; the shift in ore technology toward pelletization produced net energy savings of 17% in spite of the fact that the pelletization process itself required more energy. The reduction came from the discovery that the blast furnaces could be operated much more efficiently using pelletization inputs. The process also reduced labor requirements per ton by some 8.2% while increasing the output of the blast furnaces. A blast furnace owned by Armco Steel in Middletown, Ohio, which had a rated capacity of approximately 1,500 tons of molten iron per day, was able by 1960 to achieve production levels of 2,700 and 2,800 tons per day when fired with 90% pellets. Pellets nearly doubled the blast furnace productivity!

Source: Peter J. Kakela. "Iron Ore: Energy Labor and Capital Changes with Technology," *Science* Vol. 202 (December 15, 1978): 1151–1157; Peter J. Kakela. "Iron Ore: From Depletion to Abundance," *Science* Vol. 212 (April 10, 1981): 132–136.

which those resources are bought and sold will not necessarily lead to myopic choices. When bearing the marginal user cost, the producer acts in an efficient manner. A resource in the ground has two potential sources of value to its owner: (1) a use value when it is sold (the only source considered by those diagnosing inevitable myopia) and (2) an asset value when it remains in the ground. As long as the price of a resource continues to rise, the resource in the ground is becoming more valuable. The owner of this resource accrues this capital gain, however, only if the resource is conserved. A producer who sells all resources in the earlier periods loses the chance to take advantage of higher prices in the future.

A prescient, profit-maximizing producer attempts to balance present and future production in order to maximize the value of the resource. Since higher prices in the future provide an incentive to conserve, a producer who ignores this incentive would not be maximizing the value of the resource. We would expect the resource then to be bought by someone willing to conserve and prepared to maximize its value. As long as social and private discount rates coincide, property right structures are well defined, and reliable information about future prices is available, a producer who selfishly pursues maximum profits simultaneously provides the maximum present value of net benefits for society.

The implication of this analysis is that, in prescient competitive resource markets, the price of the resource equals the total marginal cost of extracting and using the resource. Thus, Figures 7.2a through 7.5b can illustrate not only an efficient allocation but also the allocation produced by an efficient market. When used to describe an efficient market, the total marginal-cost curve describes the time path that prices could be expected to follow.

Environmental Costs

One of the most important situations in which property right structures may not be well defined is that in which the extraction of a natural resource imposes an environmental cost on society not internalized by the producers. The aesthetic costs of strip mining, the health risks associated with uranium tailings, and the acids leached into streams from mine operations are all examples of associated environmental costs. Not only is the presence of environmental costs empirically important, it is also conceptually important, since it forms one of the bridges between the traditionally separate fields of environmental economics and natural resource economics.

Suppose, for example, that the extraction of the depletable resource caused some damage to the environment not adequately reflected in the costs faced by the extracting firms. This would be, in the language of Chapter 4, an external cost. The cost of getting the resource out of the ground, as well as processing and shipping it, is borne by the resource owner and considered in the calculation of how much of the resource to extract. The environmental damage, however, is not borne by the owner and, in the absence of any outside attempt to internalize that cost, will not be part of the extraction decision. How would the market allocation, based on only the former cost, differ from the efficient allocation, which is based on both?

We can examine this issue by modifying the numerical example used earlier in this chapter. Suppose the environmental damage can be included by increasing the

FIGURE 7.6

(a) Increasing Marginal Extraction Cost with Substitute Resource in the Presence of Environmental Costs: Quantity Profile. (b) Increasing Marginal Extraction Cost with Substitute Resource in the Presence of Environmental Costs: Price Profile (Solid Line—without Environmental Costs; Dashed Line—with Environmental Costs)

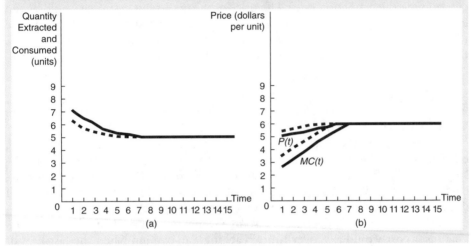

(a)   (b)

marginal cost by $1.00.[5] The additional dollar reflects the cost of the environmental damage caused by producing another unit of the resource. What effect do you think this would have on the efficient time profile for quantities extracted?

The answers are given in Figures 7.6a and 7.6b. The result of including environmental cost on the timing of the switch point is interesting because it involves two different effects that work in opposite directions. On the demand side, the inclusion of environmental costs results in higher prices, which tend to dampen demand. This lowers the rate of consumption of the resource, which, all other things being equal, would make it last longer.

All other things are not equal, however. The higher marginal cost also means that a smaller cumulative amount of the depletable resource would be extracted in an efficient allocation. (Why?) In our example depicted in Figures 7.6a and 7.6b, the efficient cumulative amount extracted would be 30 units instead of the 40 units extracted in the case where environmental costs were not included. This supply-side effect tends to hasten the time when a switch to the renewable resource is made, all other things being equal. Which effect dominates—the demand effect or the supply effect? In our numerical example the supply-side effect dominates and, as a result, the time of transition for an efficient allocation is sooner than for the market allocation.

---

[5]Including environmental damage, the marginal cost function would be raised to $3 + 0.1Q$ instead of $2 + 0.1Q$.

In general, the answer depends on the shape of the marginal-extraction-cost function. With constant marginal cost, for example, there would be no supply-side effect and the market would transition later. If the environmental costs were associated with the cost of the renewable resource rather than the depletable resource, the time of transition for the efficient allocation would have been later than the market allocation.

What can we learn from these graphs about the allocation of depletable resources over time when environmental side effects are not borne by the agent determining the extraction rate? The price of the depletable resource would be too low and too much of the resource would be extracted. This once again shows the interdependencies among the various decisions we have to make about the future. Environmental and natural resource decisions are intimately and inextricably linked.

Summary

The efficient allocation of depletable and renewable resources depends on the circumstances. When the resource can be extracted at a constant marginal cost, the efficient quantity of the depletable resource extracted declines over time. If no substitute is available, the quantity declines smoothly to zero. If a renewable constant-cost substitute is available, the quantity of the depletable resource extracted will decline smoothly to the quantity available from the renewable resource. In both cases, all of the available depletable resource would be eventually used up and marginal user cost would rise over time, reaching a maximum when the last unit of depletable resource was extracted.

The efficient allocation of an increasing marginal-cost resource is similar in that the quantity extracted declines over time, but differs with respect to the behavior of marginal user cost and the cumulative amount extracted. Whereas marginal user cost typically rises over time when the marginal cost of extraction is constant, it declines over time when the marginal cost of extraction rises. Furthermore, in the constant-cost case the cumulative amount extracted is equal to the available supply; in the increasing-cost case it is less.

Introducing technological progress and exploration activity into the model tends to delay the transition to renewable resources. Exploration expands the size of current reserves, while technological progress keeps marginal extraction cost from rising as much as it otherwise would. If these effects are sufficiently potent, marginal cost could actually decline for some period of time, causing the quantity extracted to rise.

Market allocations of depletable resources can, when property right structures are properly defined, be efficient. Self-interest and efficiency are not necessarily incompatible.

When the extraction of resources imposes an external environmental cost, however, market allocations will not generally be efficient. The market price of the depletable resource would be too low, and too much of the resource would be extracted.

In an efficient market allocation, the transition from depletable to renewable resources is smooth and exhibits no overshoot-and-collapse characteristics. Whether the actual market allocations of these various types of resources are efficient remains to be seen. To the extent they are, a laissez-faire policy would represent an appropriate response by the government. On the other hand, if the market is not capable of yielding an efficient allocation, then some form of government intervention may be necessary.

In the next few chapters we shall examine these questions for a number of different types of depletable and renewable resources. We shall then return to the issue of aggregate scarcity and a survey of the empirical evidence on whether resource scarcity in a general sense is increasing.

Problems

1. To anticipate subsequent chapters where more complicated renewable resource models are introduced, consider a slight modification of the two-period depletable resource model. Suppose a biological resource is renewable in the sense that any of it left unextracted after period 1 will grow at rate k. Compared to the case where the total amount of a constant-MEC resource is fixed, how would the efficient allocation of this resource over the two periods differ? (*Hint:* It can be shown that $MNB_1/MNB_2 = (1 + k)/(1 + r)$, where MNB stands for marginal net benefit.)

2. Consider an increasing marginal-cost depletable resource with no effective substitute. (a) Describe in general terms how the user cost for this resource in the earlier time periods would depend on whether the demand curve for that resource was stable or shifting outward over time. (b) How would the allocation of that resource over time be affected?

3. Many states are now imposing severance taxes on resources being extracted in their states. In order to understand the effect of these on the allocation of the mineral over time, assume a stable demand curve. (a) How would the competitive allocation of an increasing marginal-cost depletable resource be affected by the imposition of a per-unit tax (for example, $4.00 per ton) if there exists a constant-marginal-cost substitute? (b) Comparing the allocation without a tax to one with a tax, in general terms what are the differences in cumulative amounts extracted and the price paths?

4. For the increasing marginal-extraction-cost model of the allocation of a depletable resource, how would the ultimate cumulative amount taken out of the ground be affected by: (a) an increase in the discount rate, (b) extraction by a monopoly rather than a competitive industry, and (c) a per-unit subsidy paid by the government for each unit of the abundant substitute used.

Further Reading

Bohi, Douglas R., and Michael A. Toman. *Analyzing Nonrenewable Resource Supply* (Washington, DC: Resources for the Future, 1984). A reinterpretation and evaluation of research that attempts to weave together theoretical, empirical, and practical insights concerning the management of depletable resources.

Chapman, Duane. "Computation Techniques for Intertemporal Allocation of Natural Resources," *American Journal of Agricultural Economics* Vol. 69 (February 1987): 134–142. Shows how to find numerical solutions for the types of depletable resource problems considered in this chapter.

Conrad, Jon M., and Colin W. Clark. *Natural Resource Economics: Notes and Problems* (Cambridge: Cambridge University Press, 1987). This book reviews techniques of dynamic optimization and shows how they can be applied to the management of various resource systems.

Toman, Michael A. "'Depletion Effects' and Nonrenewable Resource Supply," *Land Economics* Vol. 62 (November 1986): 341–353. An excellent, nontechnical discussion of the increasing-cost case with and without exploration and additions to reserves.

Additional References and Historically Significant References are available on this book's companion Web site www.aw-bc.com/tietenberg.

Appendix

Extensions of the Basic Depletable Resource Model

In the appendix to Chapter 5 we derived a simple model to describe the efficient allocation of a constant-marginal-cost depletable resource over time and presented the numerical solution for a two-period version of that model. In this appendix, the mathematical derivations for the Chapter 7 extension to that basic model will be documented, and the resulting numerical solutions for these more complicated cases will be explained.

The N-Period, Constant-Cost, No-Substitute Case

The first extension involves calculating the efficient allocation of the depletable resource over time when the number of time periods for extraction is unlimited. This is a more difficult calculation because how long the resource will last is no longer predetermined; the time of exhaustion must be derived as well as the extraction path prior to exhaustion of the resource.

The equations describing the allocation that maximizes the present value of benefits derived in the appendix to Chapter 2 are

$$\frac{a - bq_t - c}{(1+r)^{t-1}} - \lambda = 0, \quad t = 1, \ldots, T \tag{1}$$

$$\sum_{t=1}^{T} q_t - \bar{Q} = 0 \tag{2}$$

The parameter values assumed for the numerical example presented in the text are

$$a = \$8, \, b = 0.4, \, c = \$2, \, \bar{Q} = 40, \text{ and } r = 0.10$$

The allocation that satisfies these conditions is

$q_1 = 8.004$	$q_4 = 5.689$	$q_7 = 2.607$	$T = 9$
$q_2 = 7.305$	$q_5 = 4.758$	$q_8 = 1.368$	$\lambda = 2.7983$
$q_3 = 6.535$	$q_6 = 3.733$	$q_9 = 0.000$	

The optimality of this allocation can be verified by substituting these values into the above equations. (Due to rounding, these add to 39.999, rather than 40.000.)

Practically speaking, solving these equations to find the optimal solution is not a trivial matter, but neither is it very difficult. One method of finding the solution involves developing a computer algorithm (computation procedure) that converges on the correct answer. One such algorithm for this example can be constructed as follows: (1) assume a value for λ; (2) using equation set (1) solve for all q's based upon this λ; (3) if the sum of the calculated q's exceeds $\bar{Q}$, adjust λ upward or if the sum of the calculated q's is less than $\bar{Q}$, adjust λ downward (the adjustment should use information gained in previous steps to ensure that the new trial will be closer to the solution value); (4) repeat steps (2) and (3) using the new λ; (5) when the sum of the q's is sufficiently close to $\bar{Q}$, stop the calculations. As an exercise, those interested in computer programming might construct a program to reproduce these results.

Constant Marginal Cost with an Abundant Renewable Substitute

The next extension assumes the existence of an abundant, renewable, perfect substitute, available in unlimited quantities at a cost of $6 per unit. To derive the dynamically efficient allocation of both the depletable resource and its substitute, let q_t be the amount of a constant-marginal-cost depletable resource extracted in year t and q_{st} the amount used of another constant-marginal-cost resource that is perfectly substitutable for the depletable resource. The marginal cost of the substitute is assumed to be d.

With this change the total benefit and cost formulas become

$$\text{Total benefit} = \sum_{t=1}^{T} a(q_t q_{st}) - \frac{b}{2}(q_t + q_{st})^2 \tag{3}$$

$$\text{Total cost} = \sum_{t=1}^{T} cq_t + dq_{st} \tag{4}$$

The objective function is thus:

$$PVNB = \sum_{t=1}^{T} \frac{a(q_t + q_{st}) - \frac{b}{2}(q_t^2 + q_{st}^2 + 2q_t q_{st}) - cq_t - dq_{st}}{(1+r)^{t-1}}$$

subject to the constraint on the total availability of the depletable resource:

$$\bar{Q} - \sum_{t=1}^{T} q_t \geq 0 \tag{6}$$

Necessary and sufficient conditions for an allocation maximizing this function are expressed in equations (7), (8), and (9):

$$\frac{a - b(q_t + q_{st}) - c}{(1+r)^{t-1}} - \lambda \leq 0, \quad t = 1, \ldots, T \tag{7}$$

(Any member of equation set (7) will hold as an equality when $q_t > 0$ and will be negative when

$$a - b(q_t + q_{st}) - d \leq 0, \quad t = 1, \ldots, T \tag{8}$$

Any member of equation set (8) will hold as an equality when $q_{st} > 0$ and will be negative when $q_{st} = 0$.)

$$\bar{Q} - \sum_{t=1}^{T} q_t \geq 0 \tag{9}$$

For the numerical example used in the test, the following parameter values were assumed: $a = \$8$, $b = 0.4$, $c = \$2$, $d = \$6$, $Q = 40$, and $r = 0.10$. It can be readily verified that the optimal conditions are satisfied by

$$q_1 = 8.798 \qquad q_3 = 7.495 \qquad q_5 = 5.919$$

$$q_2 = 8.177 \qquad q_4 = 6.744$$

$$q_{s6} = 2.137 \qquad q_{st} = \begin{cases} 5.000 \text{ for } t > 6 \\ 0 \text{ for } t < 6 \end{cases}$$

$$q_6 = 2.863 \qquad \lambda = 2.481$$

The depletable resource is used up before the end of the sixth period and the switch is made to the substitute resource at that time. From equation set (8), in competitive markets the switch occurs precisely at the moment when the resource price rises to meet the marginal cost of the substitute.

The switch point in this example is earlier than in the previous example (the sixth period rather than the ninth period). Since all characteristics of the problem except for the availability of the substitute are the same in the two numerical examples, the difference can be attributed to the availability of the renewable substitute.

Increasing Marginal Cost Case

In this case the cost function for the depletable resource differs from the previous case. Specifically, instead of $TC_t = cq_t$ the function is

$$TC_t = cq_t \cdot \sum_{i=1}^{t-1} q_i + \frac{f}{2} q_t^2$$

prior to the switch point and $TC_1 = dq_{st}$ after. In addition, there is no availability constraint; availability in this case is determined by cost, not by a finite limit on the amount available. With this change the objective function is

$$PVNB = \sum_{t=1}^{T} \frac{a(q_t + q_{st}) - \dfrac{b}{2}(q_t^2 + q_{st}^2 + 2q_t q_{st}) - cq_t - dq_{st}}{(1+r)^{t-1}}$$

$$- c \sum_{t=2}^{T} \frac{q_i \cdot \sum_{i=1}^{t-1} q_i}{(1+r)^{t-1}} - \frac{f}{2} \sum_{t=1}^{T} \frac{q_t^2}{(1+r)^{t-1}} \tag{10}$$

Necessary and sufficient conditions for any allocation satisfying this function are

$$\frac{a - b(q_t + q_{st}) - c - f\left(\sum_{i=1}^{t} q_i\right)}{(1+r)^{t-1}} - \sum_{i=t+1}^{T} \frac{fq_i}{(1+r)^{i-1}} \leq 0, \quad t = 1,\ldots,T \quad (11)$$

(Any member of equation set (11) will hold as an equality when $q_t > 0$ and will be negative when $q_t = 0$.)

$$a - b(q_t + q_{st}) - d \leq 0$$

(Any member of equation set (12) will hold as an equality when $q_{st} > 0$ and will be negative when $q_{st} = 0$.)

In equation set (11) the term immediately before the $\leq$ sign is the marginal user cost. Note that it diminishes over time as t approaches the switch point.

For the increasing-cost numerical example that ignores environmental costs, the assumed parameter values were $a = \$8$, $b = 0.4$, $c = \$2$, $d = \$6$, $r = 0.10$, and $f = 0.10$. It is easily verified that the following solution satisfies the optimal conditions:

$$q_1 = 7.132 \qquad q_3 = 6.017 \qquad q_5 = 5.304 \qquad q_7 = 4.316$$
$$q_2 = 6.523 \qquad q_4 = 5.610 \qquad q_6 = 5.099 \qquad n = 7$$

$$q_{st} = \begin{cases} 0 & \text{for } t < 7 \\ 0.684 & \text{for } t = 7 \\ 5.000 & \text{for } t > 7 \end{cases}$$

All of the depletable resource that is available at a cost lower than the substitute is used up prior to the switch point, which occurs during the seventh period.

Including Environmental Cost

For the case with environmental costs all formulas are the same, and only one parameter value is changed. Specifically, the environmental cost simulation assumes $c = \$3$ rather than $c = \$2$, as had been true in the previous simulation. The difference is presumed to reflect the environmental costs associated with extracting this resource.

With this parameter change, the new solutions become:

$$q_1 = 6.297 \qquad q_3 = 5.470 \qquad q_5 = 5.048$$
$$q_2 = 5.834 \qquad q_4 = 5.207 \qquad q_6 = 2.144 \quad \text{for } t > 6, q_{st} = 5.0$$
$$n = 6 \qquad Q = 30 \qquad q_{s6} = 2.856 \quad \text{for } t < 6, q_{st} = 0.00$$

Chapter 8

Depletable, Nonrecyclable Energy Resources: Oil, Gas, Coal, and Uranium

If it ain't broke, don't fix it!

—Old Maine Proverb

Introduction

Energy is one of our most critical resources; without it, life would cease. We derive energy from the food we eat. Through photosynthesis, the plant life we consume—both directly and indirectly when we eat meat—depends on energy from the sun. The materials we use to build our houses and produce the goods we consume are extracted from the earth's crust, then transformed into finished products with expenditures of energy.

Currently, most industrialized countries depend on oil and natural gas for most of their energy needs. Worldwide, these two resources together supply 62% of all energy consumed. Both are depletable, nonrecyclable sources of energy. Crude oil proven reserves peaked during the 1970s and natural gas peaked in the 1980s in the United States and Europe, and since that time, the amount extracted has exceeded additions to reserves.[1]

Kenneth Deffeyes (2001) and Campbell and Laherrere (1998) estimate that *global* oil production will peak in the first decade of the 21st century. As Example 8.1 points out, however, due to the methodology used, these predictions are controversial.

If we cannot estimate with precision when the fuels on which we currently depend so heavily will run out, at least we can begin to think about the process of transition to new energy sources. According to depletable resource models, oil and natural gas would be used until the marginal cost of further use exceeded the marginal cost of substitute resources—either more abundant depletable resources such as coal, or renewable sources such as solar energy.[2] In an efficient market path, the transition to these

---

[1] In contrast, world reserves of oil and gas have continued to increase during the 1980s. See U.S. Energy Information Administration. *International Energy Annual* (Washington, DC: Government Printing Office): various issues.

[2] When used for other purposes, oil can be recyclable. Waste lubricating oil is now routinely recycled.

150

Example *8.1*

HUBBERT'S PEAK

When can we expect to run out of oil? It's a simple question with a complex answer. In 1956, geophysicist M. King Hubbert, then working at the Shell research lab in Houston, predicted that U.S. oil production would reach its peak in the early 1970s. Though Hubbert's analysis failed to win much acceptance from experts either in the oil industry or among academics, his prediction came true in the early 1970s. With some modifications this methodology has since been used to predict the timing of a downturn in global annual oil production as well as when we might run out of oil.

These forecasts and the methods that underlie them are controversial, in part because they ignore such obvious economic factors as prices. The Hubbert model assumes that the annual rate of production follows a bell-shaped curve, regardless of what is happening in oil markets; oil prices don't matter. It seems reasonable to believe, however, that by affecting the incentive to explore new sources and to bring them into production, prices should affect the shape of the production curve.

How much difference would incorporating prices make? Pesaran and Samiei (1995) find, as expected, that modifying the model to include price effects causes the estimated ultimate resource recovery to be larger than implied by the basic Hubbert model. Moreover, a study by Kaufman and Cleveland (2001) finds that forecasting with a Hubbert-type model is fraught with peril:

> . . . production in the lower 48 states stabilizes in the late 1970's and early 1980's, which contradicts the steady decline forecast by the Hubbert model. Our results indicate that Hubbert was able to predict the peak in US production accurately because real oil prices, average real cost of production, and [government decisions] co-evolved in a way that traced what appears to be a symmetric bell-shaped curve for production over time. A different evolutionary path for any of these variables could have produced a pattern of production that is significantly different from a bell-shaped curve and production may not have peaked in 1970. In effect, Hubbert got lucky. (p. 46)

Does this mean we are not running out of oil? No. It simply means we have to be cautious when interpreting forecasts of the timing of the transition to other sources of energy.

Sources: M. Pesaran and H. Samiei. "Forecasting Ultimate Resource Recovery," *International Journal of Forecasting* Vol. 11, No. 4 (1995): 543–555; and R. Kaufman and C. Cleveland. "Oil Production in the Lower 48 States: Economic, Geological, and Institutional Determinants," *Energy Journal* Vol. 22, No. 1 (2001): 27–49.

alternative sources would be smooth and harmonious. Have the allocations of the last several decades been efficient or not? Is the market mechanism flawed in its allocation of depletable, nonrecyclable resources? If so, is the flaw fatal? If not, what caused the inefficient allocations? Is the problem correctable?

In this chapter we shall examine some of the major issues associated with the allocation of energy resources over time and explore how economic analysis can clarify our understanding of both the sources of the problems and their solutions. Because energy is too complex a subject to treat comprehensively in one chapter, however, additional references are provided.

Natural Gas: Price Controls

In the United States during the winter of late 1974 and early 1975, serious shortages of natural gas developed. Customers who had contracted for and were willing to pay for natural gas were unable to get as much as they wanted. The shortage (or curtailments, as the Federal Energy Regulatory Commission calls them) amounted to 2.0 trillion cubic feet of natural gas in 1974–1975, which represented roughly 10% of the marketed production in 1975. In an efficient allocation, shortages of that magnitude would never have happened. Why did they?

The source of the problem can be traced directly to government controls over natural gas prices. This story begins, oddly enough, with the rise of the automobile, which traditionally has not used natural gas as a fuel. The increasing importance of the automobile for transportation created a rising demand for gasoline, which in turn stimulated a search for new sources of crude oil. This exploration activity uncovered large quantities of natural gas (known as associated gas), in addition to large quantities of crude oil, which was the object of the search.

As natural gas was discovered, it replaced manufactured gas—and some coal—in the geographic areas where it was found. Then, as a geographically dispersed demand developed for this increasingly available gas, a long-distance system of gas pipelines was designed and constructed. In the period following World War II, natural gas became an important source of energy for the United States.

The regulation of natural gas began in 1938 with the passage of the Natural Gas Act. This act transformed the Federal Power Commission (FPC) into a federal regulatory agency charged with maintaining "just" prices. In 1954, a Supreme Court decision in *Phillips Petroleum Co. v. Wisconsin* forced the FPC to extend their price control regulations to the producer. Prior to that time, they had merely limited their regulation to pipeline companies.

Because the process of setting price ceilings proved cumbersome, the hastily conceived initial "interim" ceilings remained in effect for almost a decade before the Commission was able to impose more carefully considered ceilings. What was the effect of this regulation?

By returning to our models in the previous section, we can see the havoc this would raise. The ceiling would prevent prices from reaching their normal levels. Since price increases are the source of the incentive to conserve, the lower prices would cause more of the resource to be used in earlier years. Consumption levels in those years would be higher under price controls than without them.

FIGURE 8.1

(a) Increasing Marginal Extraction Cost with Substitute Resource in the Presence of Price Controls: Quantity Profile. (b) Increasing Marginal Extraction Cost with Substitute Resource in the Presence of Price Controls: Price Profile

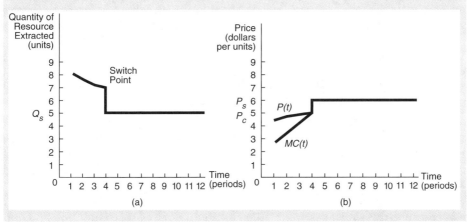

(a)

(b)

Effects on the supply side are also significant. Producers would produce the resource only when they could do so profitably. Once the marginal cost rose to meet the price ceiling, no more would be produced, in spite of the large demand for the resource at that price. Thus, as long as price controls were permanent, less of the resource would be produced with controls than without. Furthermore, more of what would be produced would be used in the earlier years.

The combined impact of these demand-and-supply effects would be to distort the allocation significantly (see Figures 8.1a and 8.1b). While a number of aspects differentiate this allocation from an efficient one, two are of particular importance: (1) the time of transition is earlier under price controls; and (2) the transition is abrupt, with prices suddenly jumping to new, higher levels. Both are detrimental. The first effect means we would not be using all of the natural gas available at prices consumers were willing to pay. Among other things, this could cause a transition to the substitute before the technologies to use it were adequately developed.

The discontinuous jump to a new technology, which results from price controls, can place quite a burden on consumers. Attracted by artificially low prices, consumers would invest in equipment to use natural gas, only to discover—after the transition—that natural gas was no longer available.

One interesting characteristic of price ceilings is that they affect behavior even when they are not binding (when the market price is lower than the price ceiling, for example).[3] This effect is clearly illustrated in Figures 8.1a and 8.1b in the earlier years. Even though the price in the first year is lower than the price ceiling, it is not

_____
[3]For a complete analysis of this point, see Lee (1978).

equal to the efficient price. The price ceiling causes a reallocation of resources toward the present, which, in turn, affects prices in the earlier years.

Price controls may cause other problems as well. Up to this point, we have discussed permanent controls. Not all price controls are permanent; they can change at the whim of the political process in unpredictable ways. The fact that prices could suddenly rise when the ceiling is lifted also creates unfortunate incentives. If producers expect a large price increase in the near future, they have an incentive to stop production and wait for the higher prices. This circumstance could cause severe problems for consumers.

For legal reasons the price controls on natural gas were placed solely on gas shipped across state lines. Gas consumed within the states where it was produced could be priced at what the market would bear. As a result, gas produced and sold within the state received a higher price than that sold in other states. Consequently, the share of gas in the interstate market fell over time as producers found it more profitable to commit reserve additions to the *intrastate*, rather than the *interstate*, market. In the 1964–1969 period, about 33% of the average annual reserve additions were committed to the interstate market. By 1970–1974, this commitment had fallen to a little less than 5%.

The practical effect of charging less for gas destined for the interstate market was to cause the shortages to be concentrated in states served by pipeline and dependent on the interstate shipment of gas. As a result, the damage caused was greater than it would have been if all consuming areas had shared somewhat more equitably in the shortfall. The price control system not only caused the damage, it intensified it!

It seems fair to conclude that, by sapping the economic system of its ability to respond to changing conditions, price controls on natural gas created a significant amount of turmoil. If this kind of political control is likely to recur with some regularity, perhaps the overshoot and collapse scenario might have some validity. In this case it would be caused by government interference rather than any pure market behavior. If so, the proverb that opens this chapter becomes particularly relevant!

Why did Congress embark on such a counterproductive policy? The answer is found in rent-seeking behavior that can be explained through the use of our consumer and producer surplus model. Let's examine the political incentives in a simple model.

Consider Figure 8.2. An efficient market allocation would result in Q^* supplied at price P^*. The net benefits received by the country would be represented by the total geometric area encompassed by the areas denoted as A and B. Of these net benefits, area A would be received by consumers as consumer surplus and B would be received by producers as a producer surplus.

Suppose now that a price ceiling were established. From the above discussion we know that this ceiling would reduce the marginal user cost because higher future prices would no longer be possible. In Figure 8.2, this has the effect for current producers of lowering the perceived supply curve, due to the lower marginal user cost. As a result of this shift in the perceived supply curve, current production would expand to Q_c and price would fall to P_c. Current consumers would unambiguously be better off, since consumer surplus would be area $A + B + C$ instead of area A. They would have gained a net benefit equal to $B + C$.

FIGURE 8.2

The Effect of Price Controls

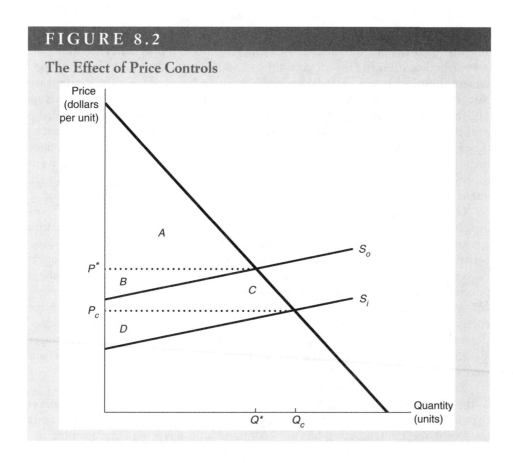

It may appear that producers could also gain if $D > B$, but that is not correct. Because producers would be overproducing, they would be giving up the scarcity rent they could have gotten without price controls. Area D measures only current profits without considering scarcity rent. When the loss in scarcity rent is considered, producers unambiguously lose net benefits.

Future consumers are also unambiguously worse off. In the terms of Figure 8.2, which represents the allocation in a given year, as the resource was depleted, the supply curve for each subsequent year would shift up, thereby reflecting the higher marginal extraction costs for the remaining endowment of the resource. When the marginal extraction cost ultimately reached the level of the price control, the amount supplied would drop to zero. Extracting more would make no sense to suppliers because their cost would exceed the controlled price. Since the demand would not be zero at that price, a shortage would develop. Although consumers would be willing to pay higher prices and suppliers would be happy to supply more of the resource at those higher prices (if they were not prevented from doing so by the price control), the price ceiling would keep those resources in the ground.

Congress may view scarcity rent as a possible source of revenue to transfer from producers to consumers. As we have seen, however, scarcity rent is an opportunity cost that serves a distinct purpose—the protection of future consumers. When a government attempts to reduce this scarcity rent through price controls, the result is an overallocation to current consumers and an underallocation to future consumers. Thus, what appears to be a transfer from producers to consumers is, in large part, also a transfer from future consumers to present consumers. Since current consumers mean current votes and future consumers may not know whom to blame by the time shortages appear, price controls are politically attractive. Unfortunately, they are also inefficient; the losses to future consumers and producers are greater than the gains to current consumers. Because controls distort the allocation toward the present, they are also unfair. Thus, markets in the presence of price controls are indeed myopic, but the problem lies with the controls, not the market.

Over the long run, price controls end up harming consumers rather than helping them. Scarcity rent plays an important role in the allocation process, and attempts to eliminate it can create more problems than are solved. After long debating the price control issue, Congress passed the Natural Gas Policy Act on November 9, 1978. This act initiated the eventual phased decontrol of natural gas prices. Included among its other provisions was a movement away from the average-cost pricing of substitute gas for industrial customers and the imposition of price controls for the first time on intrastate gas, until such time as all prices are decontrolled. On July 27, 1989, President George H. Bush signed a bill removing in stages all remaining controls on natural gas. By January 1993, no sources of natural gas were subject to price controls.

Since that time, the demand for natural gas has been increasing (due in part to the fact that its combustion products cause fewer adverse air-quality impacts than either oil or coal) and domestic production in many industrialized nations (including the United States) has not kept pace. This has put an upward pressure on prices. For example, in the United States the residential price of natural gas rose from $5.89 per thousand cubic feet in 1992 to $9.51 per thousand cubic feet in 2003.

Necessarily, imports have risen. While some imports come from contiguous countries through pipelines, the bulk of increasing imports has come in the form of liquefied natural gas (LNG). Liquefied natural gas is created when natural gas is cooled to −259 degrees Fahrenheit (−161 degrees Celsius). In this state it becomes a clear, colorless, odorless liquid. The superchilled LNG is transported over water in specially built carriers that are up to 1,000 feet long, and require a minimum water depth of 40 feet when fully loaded.

Although LNG is relatively attractive from an air-quality point of view, the transport and storage of LNG poses some significant potential hazards. According to the U.S. Congressional Research Service, if LNG spills near an ignition source, the evaporating gas in a combustible gas-air concentration will burn much hotter and much more rapidly than oil or gasoline fires. These fires cannot be extinguished—all the LNG must be consumed before they go out. Because LNG fires are so hot, the heat from the fireball may injure people and damage property a considerable distance from the fire itself.

Though historically the safety record of LNG has been quite good, the enhanced potential for terrorism has raised security concerns. Since experts believe that LNG facilities would pose tempting targets for terrorists, those facilities have been identified as high-security risks. In light of these dangers, attempts to locate new LNG terminals in coastal communities have normally aroused considerable local opposition. These political considerations are having, and presumably will continue to have, as much impact on the supply of LNG available to importing nations in the future as the size of the worldwide reserves.

Oil: The Cartel Problem

Since we have considered similar effects on natural gas, we merely note that price controls have been responsible for much mischief in the oil market as well.[4] A second source of misallocation in the oil market, however, deserves further consideration. Most of the world's oil is produced by a cartel called the Organization of Petroleum Exporting Countries (OPEC). The members of this organization collude to exercise power over oil production and prices. As established in Chapter 4, seller power over resources due to a lack of effective competition leads to an inefficient allocation. When sellers have market power, they can restrict supply and thus force prices higher than otherwise.

Though these conclusions were derived in Chapter 4 for nondepletable resources, they are valid for depletable resources as well. A monopolist can extract more scarcity rent from a depletable resource base than competitive suppliers can, simply by restricting supply. The monopolistic transition results in slower production and higher prices.[5] The monopolistic transition to a substitute, therefore, occurs later than a competitive transition. It also reduces the net present value society receives from these resources.

The cartelization of the oil suppliers has been very effective. Why? Are the conditions that make it profitable unique to oil, or could oil cartelization be the harbinger of a wave of natural resource cartels? To answer these questions, we must isolate those factors that make cartelization possible. Though many factors are involved, four stand out: (1) the price elasticity of demand for OPEC oil in both the long run and the short run; (2) the income elasticity of demand for oil; (3) the supply responsiveness of the oil producers who are not OPEC members; and (4) the compatibility of interests among members of OPEC.

Price Elasticity of Demand

The elasticity of demand is an important ingredient because it determines how responsive demand is to price. When demand elasticities are between 0 and –1.0, price increases lead to increased revenue. Exactly how much revenue would increase

---

[4]The price controls on oil were similar to, but not the same as, price controls on natural gas.

[5]The conclusion that a monopoly would extract a resource more slowly than a competitive mining industry is not perfectly general. It is possible to construct demand curves such that the extraction of the monopolist is greater than or equal to that of a competitive industry. As a practical matter, these conditions seem unlikely. That a monopoly would restrict output, while not inevitable, is the most likely conclusion to draw.

when prices increase depends on the price elasticity of demand. In general, the smaller the absolute value of the price elasticity of demand, the larger the gains to be derived from forming a cartel.

The price elasticity of demand for oil depends on the opportunities for conservation, as well as on the availability of substitutes. As storm windows cut heat losses, the same temperature can be maintained with less heating oil. Smaller automobiles reduce the amount of gasoline needed to travel a given distance. The larger the set of these opportunities and the smaller the cash outlays required to exploit them, the more price-elastic the demand. This suggests that demand will be more price-elastic in the long run (when sufficient time has passed to allow adjustments) than in the short run.

The availability of substitutes is important because it limits the degree to which prices can be raised by a producer cartel. Abundant quantities of substitutes available at prices not far above competitive oil prices can set an upper limit on the cartel price. Unless OPEC controls those sources as well—and it doesn't—any attempts to raise prices above those limits would cause the consuming nations to simply switch to these alternative sources; OPEC would have priced itself out of the market.

Alternative sources clearly exist, although they are expensive and the time of transition is long. Although petroleum can be extracted from unconventional sources—such as deep offshore wells, wells in the polar seas, heavy oils, enhanced recovery techniques, oil shales, tar sands, and synthetic oils—these sources are very expensive. While coal is clearly a substitute for some uses and is available in large supplies, as we shall see in the next section, coal use triggers a number of environmental problems.

Clearly, the ultimate substitute is solar energy, and it is the cost of solar energy that will set the long-run upper limit on the ability of OPEC to raise its prices. Since in many parts of the United States solar energy is currently cost-competitive for space and hot-water heating, that limit is probably not substantially higher than recent OPEC prices. Although it will take a significant amount of time for these new technologies to get all the bugs worked out and begin to penetrate the market on a massive scale, the transition seems under way.

Income Elasticity of Demand

The income elasticity of oil demand is important because it indicates how sensitive oil demand is to growth in the world economy. At constant prices, as income grows, oil demand should grow. This continual increase in demand fortifies the ability of OPEC to raise its prices. High income elasticities of demand support the cartelization of oil. All other things being equal, the higher the demand, the higher the price would have to rise to bring demand to zero (in the absence of substitutes) or the more rapidly it would rise to the level of the substitute resource when one is available.

The income elasticity of demand is also important because it registers how sensitive demand is to the business cycle. The higher the income elasticity of demand, the more sensitive demand is. This was major source of the weakening of the cartel, which occurred during 1983, and its subsequent strengthening. A recession caused a large reduction in the demand for oil, putting new pressure on the cartel to absorb these demand reductions. When worldwide demand for oil recovered and expanded, the cartel benefitted disproportionately.

Non-OPEC Suppliers

Another key factor in the ability of producer nations to exercise power over a natural resource market is their ability to prevent new suppliers, not part of the cartel, from entering the market and undercutting the price. Currently OPEC produces about two-thirds of the world's oil. If the remaining producers were able, in the face of higher prices, to expand their supply dramatically, they would increase the amount of oil supplied and cause the prices to fall, decreasing OPEC's market share. If this response were large enough, the allocation of oil would approach the competitive allocation.

Currently only Mexico appears to have large enough reserves to make an individual difference in the world oil market. Since both the size of its reserve and its production profile are uncertain, it is difficult to assess Mexico's ultimate impact on the future world market.

This does not mean, however, that non-OPEC members collectively do not have an impact on price. They do. The cartel must take the nonmembers into account when setting prices. Salant (1976) proposed an interesting model of monopoly pricing in the presence of a fringe of small nonmember producers that serves as a basis for exploring this issue. His model includes a number of suppliers. Some form a cartel. Others, a smaller number, form a "competitive fringe." The cartel is assumed to set the price of oil to maximize its collective profits by restricting production, taking the competitive fringe production into account. The competitive fringe cannot directly set the price, but since it is free to choose the level of production, which maximizes its own profits, its output does affect the cartel's pricing strategy.

What conclusions does this model yield? The model concludes that a resource cartel would set different prices when faced with a competitive fringe than when it is not. With a competitive fringe, it would set the initial price somewhat lower and allow price to rise more rapidly than would otherwise be the case. This strategy maximizes cartel profits by forcing the competitive fringe to produce more in the earlier periods (in response to higher demand) and eventually to exhaust their supplies. After the competitive fringe has depleted its reserves, the cartel would raise the price and thereafter prices would increase much more slowly.

Thus, the optimal strategy, from the point of view of the cartel, is to hold back on its own sales during the initial period, letting the other suppliers exhaust their supplies. Sales and profits of the competitive fringe, in this optimal cartel strategy, decline over time, while sales and profits of the cartel increase over time as prices rise and the cartel captures a larger share of the market.

One fascinating implication of this model is that the formation of the cartel raises the present value of competitive fringe profits by an even greater percentage than the present value of cartel profits. Those without the power gain more in percentage terms than those with the power!

Though this may seem counterintuitive, it is actually easily explained. The cartel, in order to keep the price up, must cut back on its own production level.

The competitive fringe, however, is under no such constraint and is free to take advantage of the high prices without cutting back its own production. Thus, the profits of the competitive fringe are higher in the earlier period. All the cartel can do is wait until the competitive suppliers become less of a force in the market. The implication of this model is that the competitive fringe is a collective force in the oil market, even if it controls as little as one-third of the production.

The impact of this competitive fringe on OPEC behavior was dramatically illustrated by events in the 1985–1986 period. In 1979, OPEC accounted for approximately 50% of world oil production, while in 1986 this had fallen to approximately 30%. Taking account of the fact that total world oil production was down during this period over 10% for all producers, the pressures on the cartel mounted and prices ultimately fell. The real cost of crude oil imports in the United States fell from $34.95 per barrel in 1981 to $11.41 in 1986 (see Figure 8.3). OPEC simply was not able to hold the line on prices because the necessary reductions in production were too large for the cartel members to sustain.

In 2004 the price of crude oil soared to over $50.00 a barrel (over $27.00 a barrel in real prices). The price increase was due to strong worldwide demand coupled with restricted supply from Iraq because of the war. However, these high prices also underscored the major oil companies' difficulty finding new sources outside of OPEC countries. High oil prices in the 1970s drove Western multinational oil companies away from low-cost Middle-Eastern oil to high-cost new oil in places such as the North Sea and Alaska. Most of these oil companies are now running out of big non-OPEC opportunities, which diminishes their ability to moderate price.

FIGURE 8.3

Real Crude Oil Price (1973–2003)

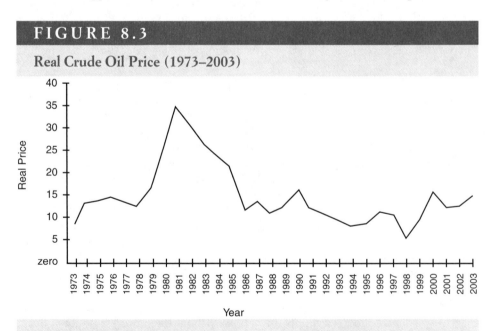

Sources: Price of Crude Oil: monthly Energy Review Online (http://www.eia.doe.gov/); CPI: Bureau of Labor Statistics (http://www.bls.gov/cpi/home.htm data).

Compatibility of Member Interests

The final factor we shall consider in determining the potential for cartelization of natural resource markets is the internal cohesion of the cartel. When there is only one seller, the objective of that seller can be pursued without worrying about alienating others who could undermine the profitability of the enterprise. In a cartel composed of many sellers, that freedom is no longer as wide-ranging. The incentives of each member and the incentives of the group as a whole may diverge.

Cartel members have a strong incentive to cheat. A cheater, if undetected by the other members, could surreptitiously lower its price and steal part of the market away from the others. Formally, the price elasticity of demand facing an individual member is substantially higher than that for the group as a whole, because some of the increase in individual sales at a lower price represents sales reductions for other members. With a higher price elasticity, lower prices maximize profits. Thus, successful cartelization presupposes a means for detecting cheating and enforcing the collusive agreement.

In addition to cheating, however, there is another threat to the stability of cartels—the degree to which members fail to agree on pricing and output decisions. Oil provides an excellent example of how these dissensions can arise. Since the 1974 rise of OPEC as a world power, Saudi Arabia has exercised a moderating influence on the pricing decisions of OPEC. Why?

One highly significant reason is the size of Saudi Arabia's oil reserves (see Table 8.1). Saudi Arabia holds approximately 33% of the OPEC proved reserves; its reserves are larger than those of any other member. Hence Saudi Arabia has an incentive to preserve the value of those resources. It is worried about setting prices so high as to

TABLE 8.1

The World's Largest Oil Reserves

Country	Reserves (in billions of barrels)
Saudi Arabia	261.5
Iraq	112.5
United Arab Emirates	97.8
Kuwait	96.5
Iran	93.0
Venezuela	71.7
Russia	48.6
Mexico	40.0
Libya	29.5
China	24.0
United States	22.5
Nigeria	16.8

Source: Oil and Gas Journal (http://www.eia.doe.gov/emeu/iea/table81.htm).

undercut the future demand for its oil. As already stated, the demand for oil in the long run is more price-elastic than in the short run. Countries with smaller reserves, meanwhile, know that in the long run their reserves will be gone and are more concerned about the near future. Since alternative sources of supply are not much of a threat in the near future because of long development times, other countries want to extract as much rent as possible now.

The size of Saudi Arabia's production also gives it the potential to make its influence felt. Its capacity to produce is so large that it can unilaterally affect world prices.

Cartelization is not an easy path to pursue for producers, but when possible it can be very profitable. When the resource is a strategic and pervasive raw material, cartelization can be very costly for consuming nations.

Strategic-material cartelization also confers on the members political, as well as economic, power. Economic power can become political power when the revenue is used to purchase weapons or the capacity to produce weapons. The producer nations can also use an embargo of the material as a lever to cajole reluctant adversaries into foreign policy concessions. When the material is of strategic importance, the potential for embargoes casts a pall over the normally clear and convincing case for free trade of raw materials among nations. What is an efficient resolution of this problem?

Oil: National Security Problem

From an economic point of view, vulnerable strategic imports have an added cost that is not reflected in the marketplace. National security is a classic public good. No individual importer correctly represents our collective national security interests in making a decision on how much to import. Thus, leaving the determination of the appropriate balance between imports and domestic production to the market generally results in an excessive dependence on imports (see Figure 8.4).

Three supply curves are relevant. The first, S_d, is the long-run domestic supply curve. Its upward slope reflects increasing availability of domestic oil at higher prices, given sufficient time to develop those resources. There are two supply curves for imported foreign oil: S_{f0} reflects the world price, and S_{f1} includes a "vulnerability premium" in addition to the world price. This premium reflects the additional national security costs caused by imports. Both curves are drawn horizontally to the axis to reflect the assumption that any importing country's action on imports is unlikely to affect the world price for oil.

In Figure 8.4 the market would generally demand and receive Q_5 units of oil. Of this total amount, Q_1 would be domestically produced and $Q_5 - Q_1$ would be imported. (Why?) However, in an efficient allocation incorporating the national security costs, only Q_4 units would be consumed. Of these, Q_2 would be domestically produced and $Q_4 - Q_2$ would be imported. Notice that when national security is an issue, the market in general tends to consume too much oil and domestic production is too small. Both of these factors raise vulnerable imports above their efficient level.

What would happen during an embargo? Be careful! At first glance you would guess that we would consume Q_3 relying solely on domestic production. We may

FIGURE 8.4

The National Security Problem

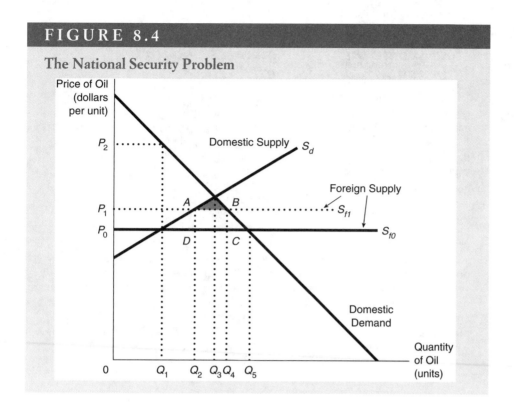

well rely solely on domestic production; yet, the amount consumed would be Q_1 and the price, P_2. Why?

Remember that S_d is the domestic supply curve, *given enough time to develop the resources*. If an embargo hits, there is not enough time to develop additional resources (six-year time lags are common). Therefore, in the short run, the supply curve becomes perfectly inelastic (vertical) at Q_1. The price will rise to P_2 to equate supply and demand. As the graph indicates, the loss in consumer surplus during an embargo can be very large indeed.

How can importing nations react to this inefficiency? As Debate 8.1 shows, several strategies are available.

Should the importing country become self-sufficient? If the situation is adequately represented by Figure 8.4, then the answer is clearly no. The net benefit from self-sufficiency (the allocation in which consumption is Q_3 and imports are zero) is clearly lower than the net benefits from the efficient allocation (Q_4). The size of the efficiency loss is indicated by the shaded area in Figure 8.4.

Why, you might ask, is self-sufficiency so inefficient when embargoes obviously impose so much damage and self-sufficiency could grant immunity from this damage? Why would we want any imports at all when national security is at stake?

The simple answer is that the vulnerability premium is lower than the cost of becoming self-sufficient, but that response merely begs the question. Why is the vulnerability premium lower? It is lower for three primary reasons: (1) embargoes

**DEBATE
8.1**

How Should the United States Deal with the Vulnerability of Its Imported Oil?

The United States currently imports most of its oil and its dependence on OPEC is growing. Since oil is such a strategic material, how can that vulnerability be addressed? The 2004 presidential campaign outlined two very different approaches.

President George W. Bush articulated a strategy of increasing domestic production, not only of oil, but also of natural gas and coal. His vision included opening up a portion of the Arctic National Wildlife Refuge for oil drilling. Tax incentives and subsidies were to be used to promote production.

Senator John Kerry's vision, on the other hand, promoted a much larger role for energy efficiency and energy conservation. Pointing out that expanded domestic production could exacerbate environmental problems (including climate change), he supported such strategies as mandating standards for fuel economy in automobiles and energy efficiency standards in appliances. He was strongly opposed to drilling in the Arctic National Wildlife Refuge.

Over the long run both candidates favored a transition to a greater reliance on hydrogen as an alternative fuel. Although hydrogen is a clean-burning fuel, its creation can have important environmental impacts; some hydrogen-producing processes (such as those based on coal) pollute much more than others (such as when the hydrogen is created using solar power).

are not certain events—they may never occur; (2) domestic steps can be taken to reduce vulnerability of the remaining imports; and (3) accelerating domestic production would incur a user cost by lowering the amounts available to future users.

The expected damage caused by one or more embargoes depends on the likelihood of occurrence, as well as the intensity and duration. This means that the S_{f1} curve will be lower for imports having a lower likelihood of being embargoed. Imports from countries less hostile to our interests are more secure and the vulnerability premium on those imports is smaller.[6]

For vulnerable imports, we can adopt certain contingency programs to reduce the damage an embargo would cause. The most obvious measure is to develop a domestic stockpile of oil to be used during an embargo. The United States has taken this route. The stockpile, called the *strategic petroleum reserve*, was designed to contain 1 billion barrels of oil. It would replace 3 million barrels a day for slightly less than one year or a larger number of barrels per day for a shorter period of time. This reserve would serve as an alternative source of supply, which, unlike our other oil resources, could be rapidly deployed on short notice. It is, in short, a form of insurance protection. The less expensive this protection is, the lower S_{f1} is and the more attractive imports are.

---

[6]It is this fact that explains the tremendous U.S. interest in Mexican oil, in spite of the fact that, historically, it has not been cheaper.

To understand the third and final reason that paying the vulnerability premium would be less costly than self-sufficiency, we must consider vulnerability in a dynamic, rather than static, framework. Because oil is a depletable resource, there is a user cost associated with its efficient use. To reorient the extraction of that resource toward the present, as a self-sufficiency strategy would do, reduces future net benefits. Thus the self-sufficiency strategy tends to be myopic, in that it solves the short-term vulnerability problem by creating a more serious one in the future. Paying the vulnerability premium creates a more efficient balance between the present and future, as well as between current imports and domestic production.

We have established the fact that government can reduce our vulnerability to imports, which tends to keep the risk premium as low as possible. Certainly for oil, however, even after the stockpile has been established, the risk premium is not zero; S_{f0} and S_{f1} will not coincide. Consequently, the government must also concern itself with achieving both the efficient level of consumption and the efficient share of that consumption borne by imports. Let's examine some of the policy choices.

Energy conservation is one popular approach to the problem. One way to accomplish additional conservation is by means of a tax on energy consumption, such as the widely used gasoline tax. Graphically, this approach would be reflected as a shift inward of the after-tax demand curve. Such a tax would reduce consumption (an efficient result) but would not achieve the efficient share of imports (an inefficient result). An energy tax falls on *all* energy consumption, whereas the security problem involves only imports. While energy conservation may increase the net benefit, it cannot ever be the sole policy instrument used or an efficient allocation will not be attained.

Another possible strategy employs the subsidization of domestic supply. Diagrammatically, this would be portrayed in Figure 8.4 as a shift of the domestic supply curve to the right. Notice that the effect would be to reduce the share of imports in total consumption (a desired effect) but not reduce consumption (an inefficient result). While subsidies may be better than nothing, they cannot be the sole solution to the problem, either.

A final approach would tailor the response more closely to the problem. One could use either a tariff on imports equal to the vertical distance between S_{f0} and S_{f1} or a quota on imports equal to $Q_4 - Q_2$. With either of these approaches, the price to consumers would rise to P_1, total consumption would fall to Q_4, and imports would be $Q_4 - Q_2$. In short, when either tariffs or quotas are used correctly with the contingency programs discussed earlier, an efficient allocation may be attained.

The use of tariffs or quotas has some redistributive consequences. Suppose a tariff were imposed on imports equal to $P_1 - P_0$. The area $ABCD$ would then represent tariff revenue collected by the government.

If a quota system were used instead of a tariff and the quotas were simply given to importers, area $ABCD$ in Figure 8.4 would represent the value of those quotas to the importers, the difference between the cost of the oil and the price at which it can be sold. This explains why importers prefer quotas to a tariff system.

The effect of either system on domestic producer surplus should also be noticed. Producers of domestic oil would be better off with a tariff or quota on imported oil than without it. Each raises the cost or reduces the availability of the foreign substitute, which results in higher domestic prices for the product. This result induces producers to produce more, but it also means that they earn higher profits on the oil that would have been produced anyway, echoing the premise that public policies may restore efficiency, but also tend to redistribute wealth.

Transition Fuels: Environmental Problems

Currently the industrialized world depends on oil and gas for most of our energy. In the distant future we shall make a transition to renewable sources of energy. How about the intermediate time period?

Though some observers believe the transition to renewable sources will proceed so rapidly that no transition fuels will be necessary, most believe that transition fuels will probably play a significant role. Though there are other contenders, such as natural gas from deep wells, the fuels receiving the most attention as transition fuels are coal and uranium. Coal, in particular, is abundantly available and frees us from dependencies on foreign countries.

The role of technology is an important part of the picture. Resource availability is a problem with uranium as long as we depend on conventional reactors. However, if countries move to a new generation of breeder reactors, which can use a wider range of fuel, availability would cease to be an important issue. In the United States, for example, on a heat-equivalent basis, domestic uranium resources are 4.2 times as great as domestic oil and gas resources if they are used in conventional reactors. With breeder reactors, the U.S. uranium base is 252 times the size of its oil and gas base.

The main issue defining the role for these two fuels involves their environmental impact. Coal's main drawback is its contribution to air pollution. Its high sulfur content makes it a potentially large source of sulfur dioxide emissions, one of the chief culprits in the acid-rain problem. It is also a major source of particulate emissions and carbon dioxide, one of the greenhouse gases implicated in climate change. Since a detailed analysis of these environmental problems follows in Chapters 15 and 16, we shall not consider them any further here except to note that if those who burn coal fail to consider these environmental costs, the market will foster an excessive reliance on it.

The other main transition fuel, uranium, used in nuclear electrical generation stations, has its own limitations, principally safety. Two sources of concern stand out: (1) nuclear accidents, and (2) the storage of radioactive waste. Is the market likely to make the correct decisions on these questions? In both cases the answer is no, given the current decision-making environment. Let's consider these issues one by one.

The production of electricity by nuclear reactors requires radioactive elements. If these elements escape into the atmosphere and come in contact with humans in sufficient concentrations, they produce birth defects, cancer, or death. Some radioactive elements may also escape during the normal operation of a plant, but the greatest risk of nuclear power is still the threat of nuclear accidents.

Nuclear accidents may inject large doses of radioactivity into the environment. The most dangerous of these possibilities is the core meltdown. Unlike other types of electrical generation, nuclear processes continue to generate heat even after the reactor is turned off. This means that the nuclear fuel must be continuously cooled, or the heat levels will escalate beyond the design capacity of the reactor shield. If, in this case, the reactor vessel fractures, clouds of radioactive gases and particulates would be released into the atmosphere.

For some time conventional wisdom had held that nuclear accidents involving a core meltdown were a remote possibility. On April 25, 1986, however, a serious core meltdown occurred at the Chernobyl nuclear plant in the Soviet Union. Though safety standards are generally conceded to be much higher in the Western industrialized world than in the Soviet Union, this incident has added yet another burden for an already-troubled industry to bear.

Nuclear power has been beset by economic as well as political forces. New nuclear power plant construction has become much more expensive, in part due to the increasing regulatory requirements designed to provide a safer system. Its economic advantage over coal has dissipated and the demand for new nuclear plants has been eliminated. In the United States, for example, in 1973, 219 nuclear power plants were either planned or in operation. By the end of 1998 that number had fallen to 104, the difference being explained by cancellations. No new applications for nuclear plants are pending, though high oil prices and concern over greenhouse gases have caused a resurgence of interest.

Not all nations are making the same choice with respect to the nuclear option. Sweden not only has pledged not to build any new nuclear plants, but also plans to shut down those currently in operation early in the 21st century. In France and Japan, however, standardized plant design and regulatory stability have resulted in electricity generating costs for nuclear power that are lower than for coal. Both countries are expanding the role of nuclear power.

An additional concern relates to storing nuclear wastes. The waste-storage issue relates to both ends of the nuclear fuel cycle—the disposal of uranium tailings from the mining process and spent fuel from the reactors, though the latter receives most of the publicity. Uranium tailings contain several elements, the most prominent being thorium-230, which decays with a half-life of 78,000 years to a radioactive, chemically inert gas, radon-222. Once formed, this gas has a very short half-life (38 days).

The spent fuel from nuclear reactors contains a variety of radioactive elements with quite different half-lives. In the first few centuries, the dominant contributors to radioactivity are fission products, principally strontium-90 and cesium-137. After approximately 1,000 years, most of these elements will have decayed, leaving the transuranic elements, which have substantially longer half-lives. These remaining elements would remain a risk for up to 240,000 years. Thus, decisions made today affect not only the level of risk borne by the current generation—in the form of nuclear accidents—but also that borne by a host of succeeding generations (due to the longevity of radioactive risk from the disposal of spent fuel).

Can we expect the market to make the correct choice with respect to nuclear power? We might expect the answer for the problem of nuclear accidents to be no, because this seems to be a clear case of externalities. Third parties, those living near the reactor, would receive the brunt of the damage from a nuclear accident. Would the utility have an incentive to choose the efficient level of precaution?

FIGURE 8.5

The Efficient Level of Precaution

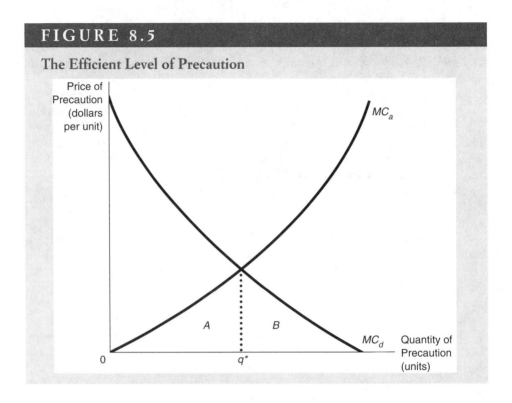

If the utility had to compensate fully for all the damages caused, then the answer would be yes. To see why, consider Figure 8.5. Curve MC_a is the marginal cost of damage avoidance. The more precautions that are taken, the higher is the cost of additional measures. Curve MC_d is the marginal cost of damage, suggesting that as more precautionary measures are taken, the additional reduction in damages obtained from those measures declines.

The efficient level of precaution is the one minimizing the sum of the costs of precaution and the costs of the unabated damage. In Figure 8.5 that point is q^*, and the total cost to society from that choice is the sum of area A and area B.

Will a private utility choose q^*? Presumably it would, if the curves it actually faces are MC_a and MC_d. The utility would be responsible for the costs of precautionary behavior, so it would face MC_a. How about MC_d? We might guess that the utility would face MC_d because people incurring damages could, through the judicial system, sue for damages. In the United States that guess is not correct for two reasons: (1) the role of the government in sharing the risk, and (2) the role of insurance.

When the government first allowed private industry to use atomic power to generate electricity, there were no takers. No utility could afford the damages if an accident occurred. No insurance company would underwrite the risk. Then in 1957, with the passage of the Price-Anderson Act, the government underwrote the liability. That act provided for a liability ceiling of $560 million (once that amount had been paid out, no more claims would be honored), of which the government would bear $500 million. The industry would pick up the remaining $60 million. The act was originally designed to expire in 10 years, at which time the industry would assume full responsibility for the liability.

The act didn't expire, though over time a steady diminution of the government's share of the liability has occurred. Currently the liability ceiling still exists, albeit at a higher level; the amount of private insurance has increased; and a system has been set up to assess all utilities by retrospective premium in the event an accident occurs.

The effect of the Price-Anderson Act is to shift inward the marginal damage curve that any utility faces. Both the liability ceiling and the portion of the liability borne by government reduce the potential compensation the utility would have to pay. As the industry assumes an increasing portion of the liability burden, the risk-sharing embodied in the retrospective premium system (the means by which it assumes that burden) breaks the link between precautionary behavior by the individual utility and the compensation it might have to pay. Under this system, increased safety by the utility does not reduce its premiums.

The individual utilities pay into a fund that compensates victims. The important point is that the actual cost of an accident to the utility is not sensitive to the level of precautions it takes. The cost to all utilities, whether they have accidents or not, is the premium paid both before and after any accident. These premiums do not reflect the amount of precautionary measures taken by an individual plant; therefore, individual utilities have little incentive to provide an efficient amount of safety.

In recognition of the utilities' lower-than-efficient concern for safety, the U.S. government has established the Nuclear Regulatory Commission to oversee the safety of nuclear reactors, among its other responsibilities. In the aftermath of the nuclear accident at Three Mile Island on March 28, 1979, a presidential commission was established to provide an independent evaluation of this system of safety regulation. Their final report, issued on October 30, 1979, was highly critical of the existing system and made a series of recommendations to improve it. While the problem of nuclear accidents is manageable in principle, it may or may not be manageable in practice.

To further complicate the problem, the private sector is not the only source of excessive nuclear waste. The U.S. Department of Energy, for example, presides over a nuclear weapons complex containing 15 major facilities and a dozen or so smaller ones.

Both the operating safety and the nuclear waste storage issue can be viewed as a problem of determining appropriate compensation. Those who gain from nuclear power should be forced to compensate those who lose. If they can't, in the absence of externalities, the net benefits from adopting nuclear power are not positive. If nuclear power is efficient, by definition the gains to the gainers will exceed the losses to the losers. Nonetheless, it is important that this compensation actually be paid because without compensation, the losers can block the efficient allocation.

A compensation approach is already being taken in those countries still expanding the role of nuclear power. The French government, for example, has announced a policy of reducing electricity rates by roughly 15% for those living near nuclear stations. And in Japan during 1980, the Tohoku Electric Power Company paid the equivalent of $4.3 million to residents of Ojika, in northern Japan, to get them to withdraw their opposition to a nuclear power plant being built there.

This approach could also help resolve the current political controversy over the location of nuclear waste disposal sites. Most plans currently focus on burying the waste in some geologically stable formation. Current and future generations of people living near the chosen sight would have a tendency to oppose nuclear power, since the costs to them appear to outweigh the benefits. To others, however, who may enjoy nuclear-produced electricity and may live far from the sites, the benefits might exceed the costs. This rationale prompted a number of states to pass laws permitting nuclear power but prohibiting the permanent storage of waste in their state.

Under a compensation scheme, those consuming nuclear power would be taxed to compensate those who live in the areas of the disposal site. If the compensation is adequate to induce them to accept the site, then nuclear power is a viable option and the costs of disposal are ultimately borne by the consumers. Some towns, such as Naurita, Colorado, have actively sought to become disposal sites. If taxes to obtain a sufficient number of disposal sites are so high that nuclear energy becomes non-competitive, then nuclear energy is not an efficient source.

Are future generations adequately represented in this transaction? The quick answer is no, but that answer is not correct. Those living around the sites will experience declines in the market value of land, reflecting the increased risk of living or working there. The payment system is designed to compensate those who experience the reduction, the current generation. Future generations, should they decide to live near a disposal site, would be compensated by lower land values. If the land values were not cheap enough to compensate them, they would not have to live there. As long as full information on the risks posed is available, those who do bear the cost of locating near the sites do so only if they are willing to accept the risk in return for lower land values.

Electricity

As the previous discussion indicated, environmental problems associated with the transition fuels present particular difficulties for generating electric power. While alternative fuels and solar power will eventually play an increasing role, most experts seem to feel that they will penetrate the market slowly as they become more familiar and accessible. How then is the transition to these long-term solutions to be managed by the electrical utilities sector in light of the problems associated with the transition fuels?

For a number of utilities, conservation has assumed an increasing role. To a major extent, conservation has already been stimulated by market forces. High oil and natural gas prices, coupled with the rapidly increasing cost of both nuclear and coal-fired generating stations, have reduced electrical demand significantly. Yet many regulatory authorities are coming to the conclusion that more conservation is needed.

Perhaps the most significant role for conservation is its ability to defer capacity expansion. Each new electrical generating plant tends to cost more than the last, and frequently the cost increase is substantial. When the new plants come on line, rate increases to finance the new plant are necessary. By reducing the demand for electricity, conservation delays the date when the new capacity is needed to satisfy the higher demand. Delays in the need to construct new plants translate into delays in rate increases as well.

The dominant regulated electricity pricing system is ill-designed to stimulate the efficient amount of conservation. Average-cost pricing is common. This pricing system implies that the new higher-cost sources are averaged in with the lower-cost sources, yielding a rate that is substantially lower than the true marginal cost of the power being generated. Thus, the consumer considering investing in conservation would save less money by conserving with average-cost pricing than would be the case if the energy saved were priced at its true marginal cost. Less than an efficient amount of conservation would be the expected outcome.

Utilities are reacting to this situation in a number of ways. One is to consider investing in conservation, rather than in new plants, when conservation is the cheaper alternative. Typical programs have established systems of rebates for residential customers to install conservation measures in their homes, have provided free home weatherization to qualified low-income home owners, have offered owners of multifamily residential buildings incentives for installing solar water heating systems, and have provided subsidized energy audits to inform customers about money-saving conservation opportunities. Similar incentives have been provided to the commercial, agricultural, and industrial sectors. Though the costs of these investments must also be recovered from customers, utilities report that the savings have been dramatic and customer satisfaction has been high. Less power consumed means available energy supplies last longer.

The total amount of electric energy demanded in a given year is not the only concern utilities have. They are also concerned with how that energy demand is spread out over the year. The capacity of the system must be high enough to satisfy the demand even during the periods when the energy demand is highest (called *peak periods*). During other periods, much of the capacity remains underutilized.

Demand during the peak period imposes two rather special costs on utilities. First, the peaking units, those generating facilities fired up only during the peak periods, produce electricity at a much higher marginal cost than do base-load plants, those fired up virtually all the time. Typically, peaking units are cheaper to build than base-load plants, but they have higher operating costs. Second, it is the growth in peak demand that frequently triggers the need for capacity expansion. Slowing the growth in peak demand can delay the need for new, expensive capacity expansion, and a higher proportion of the power needs can be met by the most efficient generating plants.

Utilities respond to this problem by adopting load-management techniques to produce a more balanced use of this capacity over the year. One economic load-management technique is called *peak-load pricing*. Peak-load pricing attempts to impose the full (higher) marginal cost of supplying peak power on those consuming peak power by charging higher prices during the peak period.

While many utilities have now begun to use simple versions of this approach, some are experimenting with innovative ways of implementing rather refined versions of this system. One system, for example, transmits electricity prices every five minutes over regular power lines. In a customer's household, the lines attached to one or more appliances can be controlled by switches that turn the power off any time the prevailing price exceeds a limit established by the customer. Other less sophisticated pricing systems simply inform consumers in advance of the prices that will prevail in predetermined peak periods.

Studies by economists indicate that even the rudimentary versions of peak-load pricing work. The greatest shifts were registered by the largest residential customers and those with several electrical appliances. Interestingly, the gains from peak-load pricing in the United States are somewhat lower than those reported for European customers, who have been exposed to peak-load pricing for a longer period of time.

A third innovation in the utility sector involves procedures for internalizing the environmental costs. Those who have typically been assigned the responsibility for regulating utility prices have focused almost exclusively on holding down prices by choosing the cheapest sources of power. Unfortunately, only generating and distribution costs were considered; the damage caused by emissions was ignored. The resulting choices turned out not to be the cheapest when all costs were considered.

To rectify this imbalance in the procedures for choosing generating sources, some states began explicitly incorporating environmental costs in their decision-making process. New York State, for example, added 1.4 cents per kilowatt hour to the estimated cost of electricity produced from fossil fuel sources to account for the various negative environmental effects. By creating a more level playing field for competing sources, this technique has increased competitiveness of renewable sources such as hydro, solar, and wind.

One of the newest developments in the energy field is the movement to deregulate electricity production. Historically, electricity was generated by regulated monopolies. In return for accepting both government control of prices and an obligation to service all customers, utilities were given the exclusive rights to service specific geographic areas.

Recently it has been recognized that while electricity distribution has elements of a natural monopoly, generation does not. Therefore several states and a number of national governments have deregulated the generation of electricity, while keeping the distribution under the exclusive control of a monopoly. In the United States electricity deregulation officially began in 1992 when Congress allowed independent energy companies to sell power on the wholesale electricity market. Forcing generators to compete for customers, it was believed, would produce lower electricity bills for customers. That has not always been the case (see Example 8.2).

Electricity deregulation has also raised some environmental concerns, however (Palmer and Burtraw 1997). Since electricity costs typically do not include all the costs of environmental damage, the sources that could offer the lowest prices could well be highly polluting sources. In this case environmentally benign generation sources could not compete on a level playing field.

One policy approach for dealing with these concerns involves tradable energy certificates. Renewable energy sources, such as wind or solar, are frequently characterized by relatively large capital costs, relatively low variable costs (since the fuel is costless); and low pollution emissions. Energy markets may ignore the advantages of low pollution emissions (since pollution imposes an external cost) and are likely to be characterized by short-term energy sales and price volatility (to the detriment of investors, who usually prefer investments with low capital costs and short payback periods). Under these circumstances, sufficient investments in capital-intensive, renewable energy technologies are unlikely to take place.

Tradable energy certificates (TECs) are designed to facilitate the transition to renewable power by overcoming these obstacles. Under this system, certified production of qualified renewable power is recorded via certificates that are granted to producers in proportion to the amounts of qualified power produced. The certificates are transferable and can be sold separately from the power. Since renewable

Example   8.2

ELECTRICITY DEREGULATION IN CALIFORNIA: WHAT HAPPENED?

In 1995 the state legislature in California reacted to electricity rates that were 50% higher than the U.S. average by unanimously passing a bill to deregulate electricity generation within the state. The bill had three important features: (1) all utilities would have to divest themselves of their generation assets; (2) retail prices of electricity would be capped until the assets were divested; and (3) the utilities were forced to buy power in a huge open-auction market for electricity, known as a spot market, where supply and demand were matched every day and hour.

The system was seriously strained by a series of events that restricted supplies and raised prices.

Despite the fact that demand had been growing rapidly, no new generating facility had been built over a decade and much of the existing capacity was shut down for maintenance. An unusually dry summer reduced generating capacity at hydroelectric dams and electricity generators in Oregon and Washington, traditional sources of imported electricity. In addition, prices rose for the existing supplies of natural gas, a fuel that supplied almost one-third of the state's electricity.

This combination of events gave rise to higher wholesale prices, as would be expected, but the price cap prevented them from being passed on to consumers. Since prices could not equilibrate the retail market, blackouts (involving a complete loss of electricity to certain areas at certain times) resulted. To make matters worse, the evidence suggests that wholesale suppliers were able to take advantage of the short-term inflexibility of supply and demand to withhold some power from the market, thereby raising prices more and creating some monopoly profits. And on April 6, 2001, Pacific Gas and Electric, a utility that served a bit more than one-third of all Californians, declared bankruptcy.

Why had a rather simple quest for lower prices resulted in such a tragic outcome? Are the deregulation plans in other states headed for a similarly dismal future? Time will tell, of course, but that outcome seems unlikely. A reduction of supplies could affect other areas, though the magnitude of the confluence of events in California seems unusually harsh. Furthermore, the design of the California deregulation plan was clearly flawed. The price cap, coupled with the total dependence on the spot market, created a circumstance in which the market could not respond to the shortage and in some ways made it worse. Since neither of those features is an essential ingredient of a deregulation plan, other areas can chose more prudent designs.

Sources: Severin Borenstein, Jim Bushnell, and Frank Wolak. "Measuring Market Inefficiencies in California's Restructured Wholesale Electricity Market," a paper presented at the American Association meetings in Atlanta, January 2001; and P. L. Joskow. "California's Electricity Market Meltdown," *Economies et Sociétés* Vol. 35, No. 1–2 (Jan.–Feb. 2001): 281–296.

energy and conventional energy are physically indistinguishable, both are sold in the energy market at the same price. Producers can seek to recover the additional cost of producing renewable power through the sale of certificates (since the renewable energy producer will receive the revenue from the sale of both the physical energy and the certificates). Whether the revenue is sufficient to cover the extra cost obviously depends on the certificate price, and the certificate price, in turn, depends on the strength of demand.

Demand for these certificates is usually driven by government directives. For example, in September 2001 the European Union Council of Ministers and the European Parliament adopted a directive designed to promote electricity from renewable energy sources in their internal electricity market. The EU target specifies that 22% of electricity should be produced from qualified renewable sources by 2010. These EU-wide requirements result in quotas being assigned to individual countries and, ultimately, even to individual companies.

Compliance with the quota requirements can be demonstrated by surrendering an appropriate number of certificates at the end of each compliance period. The certificates can be acquired directly via production of qualified energy or indirectly through purchase of certificates from the producer. The price of certificates will be determined in part by demand, which in this case is driven by the stringency of the government directive, and part by supply, which depends on the availability and cost of renewable energy options. The transferability of these certificates reduces the cost of the mandate by increasing the flexibility of how the directive can be met; requiring every company to meet the 22% target on its own would typically be much more expensive. Some companies, due to their location, have many more available options (such as more sunny days or access to stronger, more frequent winds) and can more easily (and more cheaply) fulfill their quota.

TECs are no panacea. Experience in several U.S. states shows that a poorly designed system does little to increase renewable generation (Rader, 2000). On the other hand, appropriately designed systems can provide a significant boost to renewable energy (Example 8.3).

A final approach, adopted by some jurisdictions, involves consumer right-to-know laws. These laws require generators to disclose not only the types of fuels they use, but the emissions that result from their energy production as well. Usually these are compared to regional benchmarks to provide some reasonable basis for comparison. The hope is that this information will allow environmentally conscious consumers to base their electricity purchase choice on environmental considerations as well as on costs.

The Long Run

Ultimately our energy needs will have to be fulfilled from renewable energy sources, either because the depletable energy sources have been exhausted or, as is more likely, the environmental costs of using the depletable sources have become so high that renewable sources will be cheaper.

Example **8.3**

TRADABLE ENERGY CERTIFICATES: THE TEXAS EXPERIENCE

Texas has rapidly emerged as one of the leading wind power markets in the United States, in no small part due to a well-designed and carefully implemented government directive (known as a renewable portfolio standard, or RPS) coupled with transferable energy certificates. The renewable portfolio standard specifies targets and deadlines for producing specific proportions of electricity from renewable resources (wind, in this case) while the certificates lower compliance cost by increasing the options available to any party required to comply.

The early results have been impressive. Initial RPS targets in Texas were easily exceeded by the end of 2001, with 915MW of wind capacity installed in that year alone. The response has been sufficiently strong that it has become evident that the RPS capacity targets for the next few years would be met early. RPS compliance costs are reportedly very low, in part due to a complementary production tax credit (a subsidy to the producer), the especially favorable wind conditions in Texas, and an RPS target that was ambitious enough to allow economies of scale to be exploited. The fact that the cost of administering the program is also low, due to an efficient Web-based reporting and accounting system, also helps.

Finally, and significantly, retail suppliers have been willing to enter into long-term contracts with renewable generators, reducing exposure of both producers and consumers to potential volatility of prices and sales. Long-term contracts ensure developers a stable revenue stream and, as a result, access to low-cost financing, while offering customers a reliable, steady supply of electricity.

Sources: O. Langniss and R. Wiser. "The Renewables Portfolio Standard in Texas: An Early Assessment," *Energy Policy* Vol. 31 (2003): 527–535; N. Rader. "The Hazards of Implementing Renewable Portfolio Standards," *Energy and Environment* Vol. 11, No. 4 (2000): 391–405; and L. Nielsen and T. Jeppesen. "Tradable Green Certificates in Selected European Countries—Overview and Assessment," *Energy Policy* Vol. 31 (2003): 3–14.

Depending on how the scientific uncertainty is resolved, the most compelling case for the transition may well be made by the mounting evidence that the global climate is being jeopardized by current and prospective energy consumption patterns. (A detailed analysis of this problem is presented in Chapter 17.) If the Third World were to follow the energy-intensive, fossil-fuel-based path to development pioneered by the industrialized nations, the amount of carbon dioxide emissions injected into the air would be unprecedented. According to the U.S. Agency for International Development (1986), half of all developing nations rely on imported oil for more than 75% of their commercial energy needs. A transition away from fossil fuels to other energy forms in both the industrialized and Third World nations would be an important component in any strategy to reduce carbon dioxide emissions. Can our institutions manage that transition in a timely and effective manner?

Renewable energy comes in many different forms. Hydropower can be derived from flowing water; biomass can be burned; solar energy can be used to produce heat used to drive steam turbines or converted directly into electricity by means of photovoltaics; wind energy can drive turbines; hydrogen extracted from the air by solar energy could fuel cars or furnaces; and geothermal energy can be captured from the bowels of the earth and put to useful work.

The extent to which these sources will penetrate the market will depend upon their relative cost and consumer acceptance. Relative cost will no doubt change over time as research uncovers better ways to harness the power of renewable sources. Perhaps the best example of how research can lower costs is provided by the experience with photovoltaics.

Photovoltaics involve the direct conversion of solar energy to electricity (as opposed to indirect conversions, such as when steam energy is used to drive a turbine). Anticipating a huge potential market, private industry has been very interested in photovoltaics and has poured a lot of research dollars into improving its commercial viability. The research has paid off. In 1976, the average market price for photovoltaic modules was $30.00. By 2002 this price had fallen to $3.75.[7] Rural electrification projects using photovoltaics are slowly spreading into developing countries. Their attractiveness is especially high in regions that have not already established a traditional grid system of large generators and distribution lines. Photovoltaic systems allow these countries to provide electricity to remote regions while avoiding the very high capital cost associated with expanding traditional grid systems into those areas.

Wind power is also beginning to penetrate the market on a rather large scale. New turbine technology has reduced the cost and increased the reliability of wind-generated electricity to the point that it now can compete with conventional sources in favorable sites even when environmental costs have not been internalized. (Favorable sites are those with sufficiently steady, strong winds.) Although many unexploited favorable sites still exist around the world, the share of wind power in the total energy mix will ultimately be limited by the diminishing availability of those sites.

One fuel that is currently receiving intense interest for the long run is hydrogen. (Iceland, for example, has announced its intention to become a hydrogen-fueled economy.) Although hydrogen is the most plentiful element in the universe, it is normally combined with other elements. Water, for example, combines two atoms of hydrogen with one of oxygen (H_2O). Hydrogen is also found in "hydrocarbons" that make up many of the fossil fuels, such as gasoline, natural gas, methanol, and propane.

"Reformed" hydrogen can be made by separating it from hydrocarbons using heat. Currently, most hydrogen is made this way from natural gas. Alternatively, it can be produced from water. If an electric current (produced by photovoltaics,

---

[7]U.S. Department of Energy Renewable Energy Annual (REA): http://www.eia.doe.gov/cneaf/solar.renewables/page/pubs.html/.

for example) is conducted through a reservoir of water, the liquid splits into its constituent elements, hydrogen and oxygen. NASA has used liquid hydrogen since the 1970s to propel the space shuttle and other rockets into orbit.

In addition to being directly combusted, hydrogen can be used in fuel cells. Fuel cells offer a promising technology for use as a source of heat and electricity for buildings, and as an electrical power source for electric vehicles. Hydrogen fuel cells power the NASA space shuttle's electrical systems, producing a clean by-product—pure water, which the crew drinks.

Although fuel cells would ideally run off pure hydrogen, in the near term they may be fueled by hydrogen that comes in natural gas, methanol, or even gasoline. Although using these fossil fuels as feedstock results in more pollution than pure hydrogen fuel cells, reforming these fuels to create hydrogen would allow the use of much of our current energy infrastructure—gas stations, natural gas pipelines, and so on—while fuel cells are phased in.

Several barriers must be dealt with if the hydrogen-based economy is to become a reality. The technologies that use hydrogen as a fuel are currently very expensive, and the infrastructure needed to get the hydrogen to users is undeveloped.

It is unlikely that hydrogen will be fully competitive with more conventional fuels in the absence of a specific role for government. One potentially substantial cost savings from using hydrogen, the reduction in air pollution damage, is an externality. Since consumers are likely to ignore, or at least weigh less, external costs in their choice of fuels, in the absence of corrective government policy (such as a tax on more polluting fuels), demand will be biased away from hydrogen, and potential suppliers will be discouraged from entering the market.

Consumer acceptance is an important ingredient in the transition to any alternative source of energy. New systems are usually less reliable and more expensive than old systems. Once they become heavily used, reliability normally increases and cost declines; experience is a good teacher. Since the early consumers, the pioneers, experience both lower reliability and higher costs, procrastination can be an optimal individual strategy. Waiting until all the bugs have been worked out and costs come down reduces uncertainty. If every consumer procrastinates about switching, however, the industry will not be able to operate at a sufficient scale and will not be able to gain enough experience to produce the reliability and lower cost that will ensure a large, stable market. How can this initial consumer reluctance be overcome?

One strategy involves using tax dollars to subsidize purchases by the pioneers. Once the market is sufficiently large that it can begin to take advantage of economies of scale and can eliminate the initial sources of unreliability, the subsidies could be eliminated. The available empirical evidence (Durham, et al., 1988; Fry, 1986) suggests that the tax credit approach significantly increased the degree of market penetration of solar equipment in the United States.

In the United States, substantial tax credits authorized at both the federal and state levels were influential in inducing independent producers to accept the financial and engineering risks associated with developing wind power. Although the federal tax credits expired in 1985, a 1.5¢/kwh production incentive for producers of electricity generated from wind power was reinstated in 1992. Since that time it has elapsed and been reinstated irregularly.

In contrast with the "on-again, off-again" nature of the U.S. subsidies, European nations have been steadily increasing the economic incentives for encouraging wind power, with the result that Europe is beginning to dominate the production of wind power. England, Denmark, Germany, and the Netherlands are expected to lead the way.

An alternative approach would involve removing inefficient subsidies in order to create a level playing field for sustainable energy sources. Typical subsidies take many forms. Governments currently subsidize the production of some fuels through tax breaks or, in the case of nuclear energy, they absorb a significant portion of the cost of liability for accidents (thereby significantly lowering insurance premiums). Governments also subsidize the research and development costs associated with the future use of these fuels.

In the sense that subsidies create an uneven playing field, uninternalized externalities act like a subsidy as well. Since these costs are not born by the producer, they create a bias toward polluting sources and away from less polluting sources. Since energy is a major source of pollution, to the extent that these externalities are not internalized (carbon dioxide, an unregulated gas that contributes to climate change, provides an obvious example), decisions that depend on private, not social, costs will inefficiently favor polluting sources.

How significant are these subsidies? Would their removal make a difference? One study (Myers and Kent, 2001) concludes that the worldwide subsidies to fossil fuels and nuclear energy are on the order of $131 billion per year and that uninternalized externalities for the same energy sources run about $200 billion per year. An over $300 billion annual subsidy is a substantial barrier that less-favored energy sources, such as renewable resources, have to overcome.

Removing subsides has a certain political appeal. Removal can lower government expenditures (or raise tax revenue in the case of eliminating tax breaks), welcome news during periods of tight budgets. The fact that removal could improve efficiency does not, however, mean that this step is easily taken. The producers of favored energy sources clearly benefit from those subsidies and would fight their removal.

The penetration by renewable energy resources would have been even greater if the cartel had been able to sustain the very high oil prices that were in effect at the beginning of the 1980s. As oil prices fell in real terms, both residential and commercial enthusiasm for making the transition to solar energy was undermined. Since saving money is a primary motivation for making the switch and low oil prices translate into relatively low or even negative savings, uncertainty associated with the path of future oil and natural gas prices could continue to be a barrier to the transition, even as oil and gas prices rise.

Summary

We have seen that the relationship between government and the market is not always harmonious and efficient. In the past, price controls have tended to reduce energy conservation, to discourage exploration and supply, to cause biases in the substitution among fuel types that penalize future consumers, and to create the potential for abrupt, discontinuous transitions to renewable sources. This important area makes a clear case for less, not more, regulation.

This is not universally true, however. Other dimensions of the energy problem suggest the need for some government role. In particular, insecure foreign sources require tariffs and stockpiles to reduce vulnerability and to balance the true costs of imported and domestic sources. In addition, government should ensure that the costs of energy fully reflect the potentially large environmental costs and that fluctuating resource prices and inefficient subsidies do not undermine the transition to energy resources that make sense in the long run. Government should also oversee nuclear reactor safety and should ensure that communities accepting nuclear waste disposal sites are fully compensated. Given the environmental difficulties with both of the traditional transition fuels (coal and uranium), conservation and load-management techniques are now playing and will continue to play a larger role in the electric utilities sector. Subsidizing conservation, where it is cheaper for the utility than capacity expansion, and peak-load pricing are two economic measures that have been instrumental in ushering in this greater role. The potential for an efficient allocation of energy resources by the economic and political institutions clearly exists, even if historically it has not always occurred.

Discussion Questions

1. Should benefit/cost analysis play the dominant role in deciding the proportion of electric energy to be supplied by nuclear power? Why or why not?
2. Economist Abba Lerner once proposed a tariff on oil imports equal to 100% of the import price. This tariff is designed to reduce dependence on foreign sources as well as to discourage OPEC from raising prices (since, due to the tariff, the delivered price would rise twice as much as the OPEC increase, causing a large subsequent reduction in consumption). Should this proposal become public policy? Why or why not?

Problems

1. During a worldwide recession in 1983, the oil cartel began to lower prices. Why would a recession make the cartel more vulnerable to price cutting? How would the reduced demand be shared between the competitive fringe and the cartel members in the absence of this price cutting?
2. Assume the demand and marginal cost conditions given in the first problem in Chapter 2 as well as a competitive market to allocate the product. In addition, assume that the government imposes a price control at $P = \$80/3$. (a) Find the consumer and producer surplus associated with the resulting allocation. (b) Compare this allocation to the monopoly allocation in the second problem in Chapter 4.
3. Not long ago, a conflict between a paper company and a coalition of environmental groups arose over the potential use of a Maine river for hydroelectric

power generation. As one aspect of its case for developing the dam, the paper company argued that without hydroelectric power the energy cost of operating five particular paper machines would be so high that they would have to be shut down. Environmental groups countered that the energy cost was estimated to be too high by the paper company only because it was assigning all of the high-cost (oil-fired) power to these particular machines. That was seen as inappropriate because all machines were connected to the same electrical grid and therefore drew power from all sources, not merely the high-cost sources. They suggested, therefore, that the appropriate cost to assign to the machines was the much lower average cost. Revenue from these machines was expected to be sufficient to cover this average cost. Who was right?

4. In the section of this chapter dealing with load management by the utilities, it was mentioned that peaking plants are typically cheap to build (compared to base-load plants), but that they have relatively high operating costs. Explain why it makes sense for utilities to use this lower-capital, high-operating-cost type of plant for peaking and the high-capital, lower-operating-cost type of plant for base load.

Further Reading

Goldemberg, J. "Solving the Energy Problems in Developing Countries," *Energy Journal* Vol. 11, No. 1 (1990): 19–24. The energy-development connection from a developing-country perspective.

Griffin, James M., and Steven L. Puller. *Electricity Deregulation: Choices and Challenges* (Chicago: University of Chicago Press, 2005). Bringing together leading experts from academia, government, and big business, this comprehensive volume provides a timely and thoughtful discussion of the many risks and rewards of electricity deregulation in practice.

International Energy Agency. *Renewable Energy: Market and Policy Trends in IEA Counties* (Paris: International Energy Agency, 2004). This book examines policies and measures that have been introduced in IEA countries to increase the cost-effective deployment of renewables and evaluates the results.

International Energy Agency. *Taxing Energy: Why and How?* (Paris: OECD, 1993). Examines energy taxation in five OECD countries.

Additional References and Historically Significant References are available on this book's companion Web site www.aw-bc.com/tietenberg.

Recyclable Resources: Minerals, Paper, Glass, and More

*Man is endowed with reason and creative powers
to increase and multiply his inheritance; yet up
to now he has created nothing, only destroyed.
The forests grow ever fewer; the rivers parch; the
wild life is gone; the climate is ruined; and with
every passing day the earth becomes uglier
and poorer.*

—Anton Chekhov (1896) *Uncle Vanya, Act I*

Introduction

Once used, energy resources dissipate into heat energy. They cannot be recycled. Other resources, in contrast, retain their basic physical and chemical properties during use and under the proper conditions can be recycled or reused. They therefore represent a separate category for us to examine.

What is an efficient amount of recycling? Will the market automatically generate this amount in the absence of government intervention? How does the efficient allocation over time differ between recyclable and non-recyclable resources? The phrase *planned obsolescence* is sometimes used to suggest that industries have an incentive to produce products with a short life span. Does the market produce an efficient level of product durability? What impact does product durability have on the allocation of virgin and recycled materials?

We begin our investigation by describing how an efficient market in recyclable, depletable resources would work. We then use this as a benchmark to examine recycling in some detail. We close by relating our findings back to the central questions of development in a finite environment.

An Efficient Allocation of Recyclable Resources

Extraction and Disposal Cost

How would an efficient market, one devoid of any imperfections, allocate a recyclable depletable resource? The models developed in Chapter 7 provide a point of departure for answering this question. In the earliest periods, reliance would generally be exclusively on the virgin ore, because it is cheapest. As more concentrated ores are extracted, the mining industry would turn to the lower-grade ore and to foreign sources for higher-grade ores.

In the presence of technological progress, the increasing reliance on the lower-grade ores would not necessarily precipitate an increase in cost (as shown in Example 7.1), at least initially. Eventually, however, as the sources became increasingly difficult to extract, a point would be reached at which the costs of extraction and prices of the virgin material would begin to rise.

At the same time, the costs of disposing of the products would probably rise as population density became more pronounced and wealth levels supported higher levels of waste. Over the last two centuries the world has experienced a large increase in the geographic concentration of people. The attraction of cities and exodus from rural areas led an increasingly large number of people to live in urban or near-urban environments.

This concentration creates waste disposal problems. Historically, when land was plentiful and the waste stream was less hazardous, the remnants could be buried in landfills. But as land became scarce, burial became increasingly expensive. In addition, concerns over environmental effects on water supplies and economic effects on the value of surrounding land have made buried waste less acceptable.

The rising costs of virgin materials and of waste disposal increase the attractiveness of recycling. By recovering and reintroducing materials into the system, recycling provides an alternative to virgin ores and reduces the waste disposal load (see Example 9.1).

Consumers, as well as manufacturers, play a role on both the demand and supply sides of the market. On the demand side, consumers would find that products depending exclusively on virgin raw materials are subject to higher prices than those relying on recycled materials. Consequently, consumers would have a tendency to switch to products made with the cheaper, recycled raw materials, as long as quality is not adversely affected. This powerful incentive is called the *composition of demand effect*.

As long as consumers bear the cost of disposal, they have the additional incentive to return their used recyclable products to collection centers. By doing so they avoid disposal costs, while at the same time reaping financial rewards for supplying a product someone wants.

This highly stylized version of how the market should work has to be complemented by some hard realities that must be faced in setting up actual markets. For the cycle to be complete, it is essential that a demand exist for the recycled products. New markets may ultimately emerge, but the transition may prove somewhat turbulent. Simply returning recycled products to the collection centers accomplishes little if they are simply dumped into a nearby landfill or if the supply is increased so

Example 9.1

POPULATION DENSITY AND RECYCLING: THE JAPANESE EXPERIENCE

Since Japan has a much greater population density than any of the industrialized nations, it has been forced by necessity to come to grips with its solid waste problems somewhat earlier than counties with more land area available for disposal. It has done this with a combination of technological solutions, reduction strategies, and recycling.

Currently Japan recycles about 50% of its paper, 80% of its steel cans, and 75% of its glass bottles. For the sake of comparison, similar numbers for the United States are 45%, 59%, and 21%.

Since the early 1970s, Japanese citizens have been forced to separate combustible from noncombustible trash. Burnable waste, which is some 72% of the total, is burned in some 1,850 incinerators. (This compares to about 140 large incinerators in the United States.) About 80% of the volume of incinerated waste in Japan is used to generate power. What's left, about 9% of the total waste generated, ends up in landfills. (In the United States about 56% of the waste generated ends up in landfills.)

In addition Japan has been a leader in mandating the return of appliances (washing machines, refrigerators, televisions, and air conditioners) for recycling. In April 2001 the Home Appliances Recycling Law was enacted. While it places most of the responsibility on manufacturers, it requires consumers to deliver the appliances to the appropriate collection sites and to provide the financing. When consumers trade in an old appliance for a new one or they deliver their used appliances to a collection site, they must pay a fee to cover the cost of recycling. Manufacturers have the responsibility for recycling the appliances and for ensuring that future products are both easier to recycle and incorporate materials supplied by the recycling program.

Sources: Japanese recycling statistics http://web-japan.org/stat/stats/19ENV51.html; U.S. statistics http://www.epa.gov/epaoswer/non-hw/muncpl/facts.htm/.

much by mandatory recycling laws that prices for recycled materials fall through the floor. The purity of the recycled products also plays a key role in explaining the strength of demand for them. One of the reasons for the high rate of aluminum recycling and much lower rate of plastics recycling is the differential difficulty with which a high-quality product can be produced from scrap. Whereas bundles of aluminum cans have a relatively uniform quality, waste plastics tend to be highly contaminated with nonplastic substances, and the plastics manufacturing process has little tolerance for impurities. Remaining contaminants in metals can frequently be eliminated by high-temperature combustion, but plastics are destroyed by high temperatures.

Recycling: A Closer Look

The model in the preceding section would lead us to expect that recycling would increase over time as virgin ore and disposal costs rose. This seems to be the case. Take copper, for example. During 1910, recycled copper accounted for about 18% of the total production of refined copper in the United States. By 2001, this percentage had risen to 70%.

In most cases recycling is not cheap. Several types of costs are involved. Transport and processing costs are usually significant. The sources of scrap may be concentrated around cities where most of the products are used, while for historical reasons the processing facilities are near the sources of the virgin ores. The scrap must be transported to the processing facility and the processed scrap to the market.

Labor costs are also important. Collecting, sorting, and processing scrap is typically very labor intensive. Higher labor costs can make the recycled scrap less competitive in the input market. Recognizing the importance of labor costs raises the possibility that recycling rates would be higher in regions where labor costs are lower, which does seem to be the case. Porter (1997), for example, shows how vibrant markets for scrap have emerged in Africa.

And, finally, since the processing of scrap as input into the production process can produce its own environmental consequences, compliance with environmental regulations can add to the cost of recycled input. In the United States, for example, relatively low world copper prices, coupled with high environmental compliance costs, created a cost squeeze that contributed to the closure of all U.S. secondary smelters and associated electrolytic refineries by 2001.

When recycling markets operate smoothly, however, and scrap becomes a cost-competitive input, rather dramatic changes occur in the manufacturing process. Not only do manufacturers rely more heavily on recycled inputs, they also begin to design their products to facilitate recycling. Facilitating recycling through product design is already important in industries where the connection between the manufacturer and disposal agent is particularly close. Aircraft manufacturers, which are often asked to scrap old aircraft, may stamp the alloy composition on parts during manufacturing to facilitate recycling. The idea is beginning to spread to other industries. Ski boot manufacturers in Switzerland are also beginning to stamp all individual boot parts with a code to identify their composition.

Recycling and Virgin Ore Depletion

How does the efficient allocation of a recyclable resource compare with that of a nonrecyclable resource over time? Thinking back to the models in Chapter 7, perhaps the most important difference occurs in the timing of the switch point. As long as the resource can be recycled at a marginal cost lower than that of the substitute, the market tends to rely on the recyclable resource longer than it does on a nonrecyclable resource with an identical extraction cost curve. This should not be surprising, since one effect of recycling is simply to add more of the resource.

This point can be illustrated using a simple numerical example. Suppose 100 units of a resource are contained in a product with a useful life of one year. Suppose further that 90% of the resource could be recovered and reused after one year. During the first year, the full 100 units could be used. At the end of the second year, 90% of the remaining 90 units could once again be recovered, leaving 81 units for the third year, and so on.

How much more of this resource was made available by recycling? Algebraically, if we let the original stock be A, and the recovery rate be a, then the total amount used would be an infinite sum of the form $A + Aa + Aa^2 + Aa^3$. It turns out that the sum of this series as time becomes infinitely long is $A/(1 - a)$.[1] Notice that non-recyclable resources are represented by the special case where $a = 0$. In this case the sum of resource use equals the available stock. Whenever $a > 0$, however, as it would be when any of the resource was recycled, the sum of the resource flows exceeds the size of the stock. The closer to 1.0 a is, the larger the sum of the resource flows. For example, if $a = 0.9$, as it was in our example, the sum of the flows is 10 times the size of the stock. The effect of recycling is to increase the size of the available resources by a factor of 10.

This formulation also points out another feature of recycling. Unless the recycling rate is 100% ($a = 1.0$), the sum of the resource flows is finite. This means that while some recycled materials can be recycled forever, the amount will become infinitesimally small as time goes on.

An efficient economic system will orchestrate a balance between the consumption of depletable and recycled materials, between disposing of used products and recycling, and between imports and domestic production. Example 9.2 provides an example of how changing economic circumstances can lead to an increase in recycling.

How close are we to efficiency? Have we achieved an efficient balance between imports and domestic production? Is the common pejorative notion that we are a "throwaway society" an accurate one? If so, is the market behaving efficiently—in the sense that the time for recycling has not yet come—or are there clearly identified sources of market failure, implying that the wrong price signals are being sent? The next few sections investigate these issues. Let's begin by examining the balance between domestic and foreign sources.

The Strategic-Material Problem Revisited

General Principles

Oil is not the only substance for which U.S. demand has outpaced domestic supply, necessitating an increased importation. Certain strategic minerals also meet this criteria. When imports are of strategic importance in wartime situations and/or are supplied by a relatively few foreign producers, they require special treatment. As we saw in the last chapter, this situation implies that the true social cost of these resources is higher than their market price. If this divergence is large enough, some government corrective action may be appropriate.

---

[1]Note the similarity of $1/(1 - a)$ to the familiar multiplier used in introductory macroeconomics, $1/(1 - MPC)$.

Example 9.2

LEAD RECYCLING

The domestic demand for lead has changed significantly over the last 30 years. In 1972, dissipative, nonrecyclable uses of lead (primarily gasoline additives, pigments in paint, and ammunition) accounted for about 30% of reported consumption. And only about 30% of all produced lead came from recycled material.

Over the last three decades, however, congressional recognition of lead's negative health effects on children has led to a series of laws limiting the amount of allowable lead in gasoline and paints. Not only has this resulted in a decline in the total amount of lead used, but the decline has been most dramatic for the dissipative uses (which, by 1997, had fallen to only 13% of total demand). A declining role for dissipative uses implies that an increasing proportion of the production is available to be recycled. And, in fact, more is now recycled. By 2002, 77% of the domestic lead consumption came from recycled scrap.

Old scrap accounts for some 96% of the total lead scrap recovered. Used batteries supply about 90% of that old scrap. Battery manufacturers have begun entering buyback arrangements with retail outlets, both as a marketing tool for new batteries and as a means of ensuring a supply of inputs to their downstream manufacturing operations.

Source: U.S. Department of the Interior. *Minerals Yearbook* available on the Web at: http://minerals.usgs.gov/minerals/pubs/commodity/lead/.

The appropriate policy response would be to establish a tariff on imports of the strategic material and use the proceeds to finance a stockpile. This stockpile would provide a form of insurance against supply disruptions by providing a rapid-response alternative source of supply. The tariff would signal the social cost of the resources and thereby encourage domestic production and a search for substitutes. By using the tariff revenues to finance the stockpile, those who are creating the vulnerability, by demanding the resource, would pay the cost of protecting against it.

The first step in defining a list of vulnerable strategic minerals is to identify those for which foreign sources of supply are particularly important. While the specifics of this list will differ for each importing nation, some rather intense dependencies will normally emerge from any list.

For the 42 most critical minerals, as defined by the government, the United States depends on foreign sources for more than 50% of 24 of them. Four of these—cobalt, chromium, manganese, platinum—receive the lion's share of attention. South Africa, a country with which the United States has had turbulent relations over its former policy of apartheid, is a major supplier of three of the four minerals. The fourth, cobalt, comes primarily from the African nations of Zambia and Zaire. Clearly the strategic-minerals problem is not a trivial one for the United States.

Government Response

How has the U.S. government reacted to this dependency? The Strategic and Critical Materials Stockpiling Act of 1946 initiated the first major government program to protect defense needs during a wartime. Since that time, the program has had a checkered history. In 1954, for example, the Agricultural Trade Development and Assistance Act authorized the acquisition of strategic materials with the foreign currencies obtained from the sale of surplus agricultural commodities. This authority was subsequently revoked in 1966 by the Food for Peace Act.

The two main laws currently guiding materials policy are the Strategic and Critical Materials Stockpiling Revision Act of 1979 and the National Materials and Minerals Policy, Research and Development Act of 1980. These laws consolidated a number of separately mandated stockpiles into a single program and provided specific guidance to the president on determining the materials to be included in the stockpile and the quantities of each to be stockpiled.

The 1979 Act also created a National Defense Stockpile Transaction Fund to receive funds from sales of resources in the stockpile and to support purchases of resources for the stockpiles when actual levels fell below desired levels. Currently the national defense stockpile goals require a reserve adequate to supply the material requirements of the first three years of a conventional war, after subtracting the amounts available from domestic sources and secure foreign sources.

Cobalt: A Case Study

Cobalt is a particularly interesting mineral because it is generally considered to be one of the most strategic and vulnerable of our imported minerals. To what extent is government policy efficient?

Cobalt alloys are important to a number of American industries, especially aerospace and defense. Its properties make it particularly useful in high-temperature environments such as jet engines. Short-term substitution possibilities are limited.

At present the United States produces none of its own cobalt. Therefore, all supplies come from reduction in stockpiles, recycling, or foreign producers. Currently about 28% of American consumption comes from recycling.

The supply situation has been volatile. During the 1970s, for example, cobalt prices rose from $5.50 per pound to $25 per pound; spot prices went as high as $50 at one point. The price in 2003 was $9.40 a pound.

The American government has responded erratically; although a cobalt stockpile has existed for some time, the appropriateness of its size has been the subject of much debate. Major purchases occurred throughout the 1950s, but in 1973, during the Nixon administration, millions of pounds of cobalt were sold from the stockpile. In late 1976 the Ford administration effectively reversed that decision, and a new goal of 85.4 million pounds was established.

That the stockpile has not reached the target level is not the only problem with current policy. As of January 1, 2004, all cobalt ores and concentrates could enter the country free of tariffs. Since a tariff is an important part of an efficient policy package for strategic minerals, we have not yet achieved an efficient allocation of this resource.

Substitution and Vulnerability

The vulnerability of a nation importing a strategic mineral depends not only on the severity of the shortfall the nation could experience, but also on its ability to cope with the shortfall. Coping in this context may be accomplished either by substituting other materials for the one in short supply or suffering the resulting reduction in output. In assessing vulnerability, therefore, it is important to take the costs of both substitution and abstinence into account.

Hazilla and Kopp (1984) attempt to accomplish this difficult task within the context of a detailed econometric model of the production process. The various production processes involving five specific strategic minerals—titanium, vanadium, cobalt, columbium, and cadmium—were modeled. These models included not only substitution possibility and the associated costs but the costs to society from any resulting reduced output as well. To quantify the degree of vulnerability, the authors estimated the total cost to the U.S. economy that would be expected to result from various levels of shortfalls of these strategic materials (see Table 9.1).

Two interesting insights emerge from this information. First, small disruptions, loosely defined as those involving 35% or less of the available supply, could be handled without serious impact on the economy, but larger disruptions could be quite serious. Second, the vulnerability ranking depends on the size of the shortfall. For small shortfalls, the scarcity of titanium imposes the largest cost on society. Notice, however, that when the shortage is in the range of 50%, cobalt presents a more serious problem. For shortfalls of 85%, the largest costs are imposed by shortages of vanadium. No one mineral imposes the highest cost in all shortfall scenarios.

This econometric approach has the substantial virtue that it allows the analyst to ask the kind of "what if" questions that give rise to the estimates in Table 9.1. It also has the disadvantage, however, that it is so general that the particular details of substitution are buried in the mathematics. Other authors therefore have attempted to learn more of the details by doing case studies of particular minerals.

TABLE 9.1

Mineral Supply Disruption Scenarios (cost in millions of 1974 dollars)

Shortfall %	Titanium	Vanadium	Cobalt	Columbium	Cadmium
5	23	19	6	6	—
15	69	38	12	11	—
25	140	98	30	35	—
35	198	159	49	46	1
50	340	21,532	25,667	17,136	2
85	33,475	80,752	74,976	78,800	4

Source: Data extracted from Michael Hazilla and Raymond J. Kopp. "Assessing U.S. Vulnerability to Raw Material Supply Disruptions: An Application to Non-fuel Minerals," *Southern Economic Journal* Vol. 52 (Southern Economic Association: October 1984): Table IV, p. 351.

One such study by Tilton (1985) examined the substitution effects resulting from the rapid rise of tin prices during the 1970s. Three uses of tin were selected for study—beverage containers, solder, and tin-based chemicals used in manufacturing plastic pipe. Substantial substitution was uncovered. The tinplate beverage can, for example, after years of increasing its share of the market, began in the 1960s to lose market share, first to aluminum cans and ultimately to plastic bottles. As this was going on, new technologies reduced the amount of tin in the average tinplate beverage can by over 93% between 1950 and 1977. Even the use of solder, thought by many to be impervious to substitution, was reduced as the introduction of low-tin alloys reduced the need for high-tin-content solder in automobile bodies. Similarly, in the plastic pipe industry, the introduction of new second- and third-generation stabilizers reduced the tin content by over 50%.

Based on this analysis, the Tilton study concluded that changes in material prices seem to have had little effect on materials usage in the short run, because producers are constrained by existing technologies and equipment. Over the long run, however, they seemed to have a significant effect.

Waste Disposal and Pollution Damage

The strategic-mineral problem suggests that an imperfection may arise in the way the market reacts to imports vis à vis domestically produced minerals. When the imports are critically important and come from risky sources, the market perceives a price ratio that fails to incorporate some of these social costs of imports. The result would be an inefficient and excessive reliance on imports.

Other market imperfections are apparent as well. The treatment of waste by producers and consumers can lead to biases in the market balance between recycling and the use of virgin ores. Since disposal cost is a key ingredient in determining the efficient amount of recycling, the failure of an economic agent to bear the full cost of disposal implies a bias toward virgin materials and away from recycling. We begin by considering how the method of financing the disposal of potentially recyclable waste affects the level of recycling.

Disposal Cost and Efficiency

We must be clear about the relationship of the marginal disposal cost to the efficient level of recycling. Suppose, for example, it costs a community $20 per ton to recycle a particular waste product that can ultimately be sold to a local manufacturer for $10 per ton. Can we conclude that this is an inefficient recycling venture because it is losing money? No, we can't! In addition to earning the $10 per ton from selling the recycled product, the town is avoiding the cost of disposing of the product. This avoided marginal cost is appropriately considered a marginal benefit from recycling. Suppose the marginal avoided disposal cost was $20 per ton. In this case the benefits to the town from recycling would be $30 per ton ($20 per ton avoided cost plus $10 per ton resale value) and the cost would be $20 per ton; this would be an efficient recycling venture. Both marginal disposal costs and the prices of recycled materials directly affect the efficient level of recycling.

The Disposal Decision

Potentially recyclable waste can be divided into two types of scrap: old scrap and new scrap. *New scrap* is composed of the residual materials generated during production. For example, as steel beams are formed, the small remnants of steel left over are new scrap. *Old scrap* is recovered from products used by consumers.

To illustrate the relative importance of new scrap and old scrap, consider that in the U.S. aluminum industry, about 40% of the recovered aluminum scrap comes from old scrap. The difficulties in recycling new scrap are significantly less than those in recycling old scrap. New scrap is already at the place of production, and with most processes it can simply be reentered into the input stream without transportation costs. Transport costs tend to be an important part of the cost of using old scrap.

Equally important are the incentives involved. Since new scrap never leaves the factory, it remains under the complete control of the manufacturer. Having the joint responsibility of creating a product and dealing with the scrap, the manufacturer now has an incentive to design the product with the use of the scrap in mind. It would be advantageous to establish procedures guaranteeing the homogeneity of the scrap and minimizing the amount of processing necessary to recycle it. For all these reasons, it is likely the market for new scrap will work efficiently and effectively.

Unfortunately, the same is not true for old scrap. The market works inefficiently because the product users do not bear the full marginal social costs of disposing of their product. As a result, the market is biased away from recycling old scrap and toward the use of virgin materials.

The key to understanding why these costs are not internalized lies in the incentives facing individual product users. Suppose you had some small aluminum products that were no longer useful to you. You could either recycle them, which usually means driving to a recycling center, or you could toss them into your trash. In comparing these two alternatives, notice that recycling imposes one cost on you (transport cost), while the second imposes another (disposal cost).

It is difficult for consumers to act efficiently because of the way trash collection has traditionally been financed (see Figure 9.1). Urban areas have generally financed trash collection with taxes, if publicly provided, or a flat-rate fee, if privately provided. Neither of these approaches directly relates the size of an individual's payment to the amount of waste. The *marginal* cost to the homeowner of throwing out one more unit of trash is negligible, even when the cost to society is not. The marginal private disposal cost and the cost to society as a whole diverge (see Figure 9.2).

When the private marginal cost of disposal (MC_p) is lower than the marginal social cost of disposal (MC_s), the market level of recycling (where the marginal cost of recycling (MC_R) is equal to the marginal private disposal cost) is inefficient. Only if all social costs are included in the marginal cost of disposal will the efficient amount of recycling (Q_s) be attained.[2]

---

[2]According to Figure 9.2, would 100% recycling normally be efficient? Does that conclusion make sense to you? Why or why not?

FIGURE 9.1

Description of User Charges on Municipal Waste, Selected Countries

Country	Charge calculation	Target groups
Australia	Flat rate	Households; firms
Belgium	Flat rate or volume	Households
Canada	Flat rate	Households
	Flat rate + volume over threshold	Firms
Denmark	Flat rate	Households
	Waste volume	Firms
Finland	Waste volume	Households
	id + type + transport distance	Firms
France	Dwelling size (80% of population)	Households; firms
(or)	Waste volume (4% of population)	Households; firms
(or)	(None: Waste collection paid for from public budget)	
Italy	Dwelling size	Households; firms
Netherlands	Flat rate	Households; firms
Norway	Flat rate	Households; firms
Sweden	Flat rate (53% of municipalities)	Households; firms
(or)	Collection structure (45% of m.)	Households; firms
United Kingdom	Flat rate	Households
	Waste volume	Firms

Sources: Adapted from Table 3.9 in J. B. Opschoor and Dr. Hans B. Vos. *Economic Instruments for Environmental Protection* (Paris: Organization for Economic Cooperation and Development): 53.

This point can be reinforced by a numerical example. Suppose your city provides trash pickup for which you pay $150 a year in taxes. Your cost will be $150 regardless (within reasonable limits) of how much you throw out. In that year your additional (marginal) cost from throwing out these items is *zero*. Certainly the marginal cost to society is not zero, and, therefore, the balance between these alternatives as seen by the individual homeowner is biased in favor of throwing things out.[3]

Littering is an extreme example of what we have been talking about. In the absence of some kind of government intervention, the cost to society of littering is the aesthetic loss plus the risk of damage to automobile tires and pedestrians caused by sharp edges of discarded cans or glass. Tossing used containers outside the car is relatively costless for the individual, but costly for society.[4]

---

[3]The problem is not that $150 is too low; indeed it may be too high! The point is that the cost of waste disposal does not increase with the amount of waste to be disposed.

[4]Using economic analysis, would you expect transients or residents to have a higher propensity to litter? (Why?)

FIGURE 9.2

The Efficient Level of Recycling

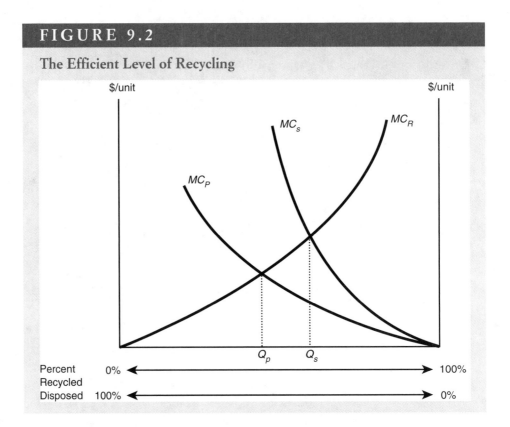

Disposal Costs and the Scrap Market

How would the market respond to a policy forcing product users to bear the true marginal disposal cost? The major effect would be on the supply of materials to be recycled. Consumers would now be able to avoid disposal costs and might even be paid for discarded products. This would cause the diversion of some materials to recycling centers, where they could be reintegrated into the materials process. If this expanded supply allows dealers to take advantage of previously unexploited economies of scale, this expansion could well result in a lower average cost of processing, as well as more recycled materials.

The total consumption of inputs would increase because the price falls. The use of recycled materials increases as well. The amount of virgin ore falls. Thus the correct inclusion of disposal cost would tend to increase the amount of recycling and extend the useful economic life for depletable, recyclable resources.

Subsidies on Raw Materials

Disposal costs are only part of the story. Inputs derived from recycling can only compete with raw materials if the playing field is level. Subsidies on raw materials are another troubling source of inefficiencies that create a bias away from recycled inputs.

Subsides can take many forms. One form is illustrated by the U.S. Mining Law of 1872. This law, which was originally passed over 150 years ago to promote mining on public lands, is still on the books. Under this law, miners can stake lode claims (for subsurface minerals) and placer claims (for surface minerals) for mineral prospecting on public lands. A claim can be maintained for a payment of only $100 a year. If minerals are discovered in a claim area and at least $500 has been invested in development or extraction, the land could actually be bought for $5 an acre on lode claims or $2.50 an acre on placer claims. In 1999 the U.S. Congress enacted a moratorium on land purchases, but not on staking claims.

These prices for access to public lands are so low relative to market prices that they constitute a considerable subsidy. As a result of this subsidy, taxpayers not only don't receive the true value of the mining services provided by public lands, but the subsidy is lowering the cost of extracting these raw minerals. As a result, raw materials are artificially cheap and can inefficiently undermine the market for recycled inputs.

Corrective Public Policies

Why are recycling rates so low? No doubt some of the responsibility lies in improper incentives created by inappropriate pricing. Can the misallocation resulting from inefficiently low disposal cost be corrected?

One approach, volume pricing, would impose disposal charges reflecting the true social cost of disposal (see Example 9.3). A preimplementation concern about volume pricing was that it might impose a hardship on the poor residents of the area. Strategies based on higher prices always raise the specter that they will end up placing an intolerable burden on the poor.

That concern was apparently misplaced. Under the old system of financing trash collection, every household pays the same fee regardless of how much trash is produced. Since lower-income households produce less trash, they are in effect subsidizing wealthier households. Under the new system, lower-income households pay only a flat fee since they don't need to purchase stickers for additional disposal. The expense of these stickers is less than the average cost of disposal, which was the basis for the previous fee. Poor households have turned out to be better off, not worse off, under the new pricing system.

Another suggestion for promoting recycling now being applied in many areas is the refundable deposit. Already widely accepted for beverage containers, such deposits could become a remedy for many other products.

A refund system is designed to accomplish two purposes: (1) the initial charge reflects the cost of disposal and produces the desired composition of demand effect; and (2) the refund, attainable upon turning the product in for recycling, helps conserve virgin materials. Such a system is already employed in Sweden and Norway to counter the problem of abandoned automobiles.

The recycling of aluminum beverage cans has been one clear beneficiary of deposit refund schemes.[5] Although not all states have passed bottle bills, over 50% of aluminum beverage cans are now recycled in the United States. As a result,

---

[5] A very strong demand for aluminum scrap was also influential. In fact, the price for aluminum scrap went so high in 1988 that pilferers were stealing highway sings and guardrails for their aluminum content.

Example 9.3

PRICING TRASH IN MARIETTA, GEORGIA

In 1994 the people of Marietta, Georgia, participated in a demonstration project that changed the way in which waste was priced. The traditional $15 monthly fee for trash pickup was cut to $8 per month. In addition, half of the residents faced a per-bag price on waste ($.75 per bag), while the rest faced a monthly fee for pickup that depended on the maximum number of cans per month that the customer wished to have picked up per month. This number was contracted in advance by the customer and did not vary from month to month. The fee was $3 or $4 per can (depending upon the number).

Economic theory suggests that while both plans should reduce waste and increase recycling, the per-bag fee should promote more. (Can you see why?)

And indeed that is what happened. The can program reduced nonrecycled waste by about 20%, whereas the bag program reduced it by as much as 51%. Both programs had an equally strong effect on encouraging households to recycle. Both programs not only diverted waste into recycling, they also reduced the amount of waste generated.

Could the costs associated with the program be justified in benefit/cost terms? According to the economists who conducted the study, they were. The net benefits for the city were estimated to be $586 per day for the bag program and $234 per day for the can program.

Source: G. L. Van Houtven and G. E. Morris. "Household Behavior Under Alternative Pay-as-You-Throw Systems for Solid Waste Disposal," *Land Economics*, Vol. 75, No. 4 (November 1999): 515–537.

aluminum old scrap has become an increasingly significant component of total aluminum supplies. Recycling aluminum saves about 95% of the energy that is needed to make new aluminum from ore. The magnitude of these energy savings has had a significant influence on the demand for recycled aluminum as cost-conscious producers search for new ways to reduce energy costs.

Beverage can recycling also reduces littering because an incentive is created to bring the bottle to a recycling center. In some cities, scavenging and returning these bottles has provided a significant source of income to the homeless. One Canadian study found that recycling creates six times as many jobs as landfilling.

Deposit-refund systems are also being used for batteries and tires. New Hampshire and Maine, for example, place a surcharge on new car batteries. Consumers in these states receive a rebate if they trade in their used battery for a new one. Oklahoma places a $1.00 fee on each new tire sold and then returns 50 cents to certified processing facilities for each tire handled.

Some states in the United States, as well as some developing countries, also use deposit-refund systems to assure that pesticide containers are returned after use. Since these containers usually contain toxic residues after use, which can contaminate water and soil, collecting the containers and either reusing them or properly decontaminating them can eliminate this contamination threat.

Some areas attempt to enlist economic incentives by imposing a disposal or recycling surcharge on the product. Paid at the time of purchase of a new product, this surcharge would normally be designed to recover the costs of recycling the product at the end of its useful life; more-difficult-to-recycle products would have larger fees. These fees would normally be coupled with a requirement that the revenue be used by sellers to set up recycling systems. Assuming these fees correctly internalize the costs of recycling, they will provide consumers with incentives to take the recycling and disposal costs into account, since easier-to-recycle products would have a lower price (including the fee). Notice, however, that these purchase surcharges do not provide any incentive against illegal disposal (littering) since the consumer gets no rebate for dropping the product off at a collection center. On the other hand, unlike a trash collection charge it provides no specific disincentive for illegal disposal either. Since the fee is paid up front, it cannot be avoided by illegal disposal. In this sense the deposit-refund system is clearly superior to either purchase surcharges or volume pricing of trash.

The tax system can also be used to promote recycling by taxing virgin materials and by subsidizing recycling activities. The European approach to waste oil recycling, reinforced by the high cost of imported crude oil, was to require both residential and commercial users to recycle all waste oil they generate. Virgin lubricating oils are taxed, and the resulting income is used to subsidize the recycling industry. As a result, many countries collect up to 65% of the available waste oil.

In the United States, which does not subsidize waste oil recycling, the waste oil market has been rather less successful. Currently only about 15% of waste oil is recovered. The waste oil industry has been in a relative decline since World War II with the exception of the period immediately following the oil crisis during the 1970s, when oil prices rose dramatically.

Many areas are now using tax policy to subsidize the acquisition of recycling equipment in both the public and private sectors. Frequently taking the form of sales-tax exemptions or investment tax credits to private industries or loans or grants to local communities, these approaches are designed to get recycling programs off the ground with the expectation that they will ultimately be self-sustaining. The pioneers are being subsidized.

Examining Oregon's program can serve to illustrate how a tax approach works. From 1981 to 1987, to reduce energy consumption as well as to promote recycling, the Oregon Department of Energy granted tax credits to 163 projects. Being granted this credit allows companies a five-year period in which to deduct from their taxes an amount equal to 35% of the cost of any equipment used solely for recycling. Oregon also offers a broader tax credit that covers equipment, land, and building purchases. Paper companies, the major recipients of both types of credits, have used them to increase the capacity to use recycled newsprint and cardboard in the paper-making process. According to Shea (1988), these incentives helped to raise Oregon's newspaper recycling rate (65%) to twice the national average.

Any long-run solution to the solid waste problem must not only influence consumer choices about purchasing, packaging, and disposal, it must also influence producer choices about product design (to increase recyclability), product packaging, and the use of recycled (as opposed to virgin materials) in the production process. One general approach is called expanded producer responsibility, and it involves requiring producers to take back packaging, and even their products, at the end of their useful life (see Example 9.4).

This approach is now spreading rapidly to the United States as well. Recognizing the dangers from improperly disposed electronic equipment, some states have enlisted economic incentives to promote recycling. For example, California passed a bill in 2003 that charges consumers a fee for buying computer monitors or televisions and pays recyclers to dispose of the displays safely when users no longer want them. In 2004 California passed a bill that makes it unlawful for retailers to sell mobile phones without the establishment of a collection, reuse, and recycling system for proper disposal of used cell phones by July 2006. This bill places the responsibility for recycling squarely upon the industry, but leaves the implementation details up to them. While this approach allows the industry to minimize recycling costs, it remains to be seen whether the resulting policy promotes reuse of the materials in a manner that is safe for human health and the environment.

Pollution Damage

One other situation influences the use of recycled and virgin ores. When environmental damage results from extracting and using virgin materials and not from the use of recycled materials, the market allocation will be biased away from recycling. The damage might be experienced at the mine, such as the erosion and aesthetic costs of strip mining, or at the point of processing, where the ore is processed into a usable resource.

Suppose that the mining industry was forced to bear the cost of this environmental damage. What difference would the inclusion of this cost have on the scrap market? The internalizing of this cost results in a leftward shift in the supply curve for the virgin ore. This would, in turn, cause a leftward shift in the total supply curve. The market would be using less of the resource—due to higher price—while recycling more. Thus the correct treatment of these environmental costs would share with disposal costs a tendency to increase the role for recycling.

Disposal also imposes external environmental costs in the form of odors, pests, and contaminants leaching into water supplies; obstruction of visual landscapes; and so on. Kinnaman and Fullerton (2000) note that while the number of landfills in the United States has been decreasing, the aggregate capacity of these landfills has been increasing as small-town facilities are replaced by large regional sanitary landfills. Since local opposition from potential host communities is likely to rise with landfill size, locating these facilities can be extremely contentious.

While governments now regulate landfills to protect public safety, these regulations rarely eliminate all unpleasant aspects of these landfills for the host communities. As a result many communities are all for the existence of these facilities as

Example 9.4

IMPLEMENTING THE "TAKE-BACK" PRINCIPLE

According to the "take-back" principle, all producers should be required to accept responsibility for their products—including packaging—from cradle to grave by taking them back once they have outlived their useful lives. In principle this requirement was designed to encourage the elimination of inessential packaging, to stimulate the search for products and packaging that are easier to recycle, and to support the substitution of recycled inputs for virgin inputs in the production process.

Germany has required producers (and retailers as intermediaries) to accept all packaging associated with products, including such different types of packaging as the cardboard boxes used for shipping hundreds of toothbrushes to retailers, to the tube that toothpaste is sold in. Consumers are encouraged to return the packaging by means of a combination of convenient drop-off centers, refundable deposits on some packages, and high disposal costs for packaging that is thrown away.

Producers responded by setting up a new, private, nonprofit corporation, the Duales System Deutschland (DSD), to collect the packaging and to recycle the collected materials. This corporation is funded by fees levied on producers. The fees are based on the number of kilograms of packaging the producers use. The DSD accepts only packaging that it has certified as recyclable. Once certification is received, producers are allowed to display a green dot on their product, signaling consumers that this product is accepted by the DSD system. Other packaging must be returned directly to the producer or to the retailer, who returns it to the producer.

The law has apparently reduced the amount of packaging produced and has diverted a significant amount of packaging away from incineration and landfills. A most noteworthy failure, however, was the inability of the DSD system to find markets for the recycled materials it collected. Some German packaging even ended up in neighboring countries, causing some international backlash. The circumstance where the supply of recycled materials far exceeds the demand is so common—not only in Germany but in the rest of the world as well—that further efforts to increase the degree of recycling will likely flounder unless new markets for recycled materials are forthcoming.

Despite the initial difficulties with implementing the "take-back" principle, the idea that manufacturers should have ultimate responsibility for their products has a sufficiently powerful appeal that it has moved beyond an exclusive focus on packaging and is now expanding to include the products themselves. In 2002, the European Union passed a law that makes manufacturers financially responsible for recycling the appliances they produce.

Sources: A.S. Rousso and S.P. Shah. "Packaging Taxes and Recycling Incentives: The German Green Dot Program," *National Tax Journal* Vol. 47, No. 3 (September 1994): 689–701; Meagan Ryan. "Packaging a Revolution," *World Watch* (September–October 1993): 28–34; and Christopher Boerner and Kenneth Chilton, "False Economy: The Folly of Demand-Side Recycling," *Environment* Vol. 36 (January/February 1994): 6–15, 32–33.

long as they are not located in their community. If every community feels this way, locating new facilities can be difficult, if not impossible.

One technique for resolving this problem relies on the imposition of host fees. Host fees compensate the local community (and sometimes surrounding communities) for accepting the location of a waste facility within their community. This approach gives local communities veto power over the location, but it also attempts to share the benefits of the regional facility in such a way that makes the net benefits sufficiently positive for them that the communities will accept the facility.

In one example, Porter (2002) reports that a host fee agreement between Browning Ferris Industries and the township of Salem, Michigan, involves sharing with the town 2.5% of all landfill revenues and 4% of all compost revenues. The town also shares in the revenues derived from the sale of landfill gases (used for energy) and it can use the site free of charge for all town refuse, without limit on volume. These benefits are estimated to be worth about $400 per person per year, apparently enough to overcome local opposition.

Host fees are not a perfect resolution of the siting problem. Notice, for example, that the fact that Salem can dispose of its waste free of charge provides no incentive for source reduction. In addition, it is important to ensure that locating these facilities does not raise environmental justice concerns. Though we consider this issue in much greater depth in Chapter 21, let it suffice here to point out that at a minimum, the local community has to be fully informed of the risks they will face from a regional sanitary landfill and must be fully empowered to accept or reject the proposed compensation package. As we shall see, those preconditions frequently didn't exist in the past.

Tax Treatment of Minerals

Built into the U.S. tax code is a series of special provisions for selected extractive industries. These provisions were designed to avoid taxing as profits returns that really represented a liquidation of assets. The assets in this case are the reserves of natural resources being depleted. Thus these provisions, chiefly known as the depletion allowance, expand the conventional treatment of capital assets to include depletable resources. They stimulate the extraction of targeted minerals and fuels by providing implicit tax reduction subsidies to extractive industries.

While the subsidy has taken several forms, the overall effect is to lower the after-tax cost of extraction for virgin ores. According to our models, this should have the effect of increasing the amount of virgin ore mined.

Other effects of the tax treatment of minerals can be identified as well. Because these tax breaks are accrued by some minerals, they create a bias in favor of those minerals whose lobbying groups were sufficiently strong that they were able to get favorable tax treatment. One provision, the foreign tax credit, which stipulates favorable tax treatment of foreign sources of minerals produced by U.S. corporations, may exacerbate the strategic-mineral problem. Favorable tax treatment for these minerals also creates a bias against recycling, since recycled materials are not eligible for the special tax treatment.

Not all tax treatment, however, is favorable to the virgin ores. One in particular, the *severance tax*, tends to counteract these biases induced by other portions of the tax code. The severance tax is levied on minerals as they are extracted. Areas imposing severance taxes argue that the revenues compensate current citizens for localized environmental damage caused by extraction and compensate future generations for the loss of the resource by financing public investments. Others suspect that severance taxes are also used to export their tax liability to consumers in other states. Regardless of the reason for implementation, the rates were not designed to eliminate a bias against recycling.

While severance taxes may be useful in raising revenue for whatever purpose, they do little to correct the lack of balance between environmental and virgin resources. Furthermore, they may well make the strategic-mineral problem worse. Only domestic ore suppliers are taxed; foreign ore suppliers can avoid the tax.

Product Durability

In a memorable passage from *Death of a Salesman*, Willy Loman laments:

> Once in my life I would like to own something outright before it's broken! I'm always in a race with the junkyard! I just finish paying for the car and it's on its last legs. The refrigerator consumes belts like a goddamn maniac. They time those things. They time them so when you've finally paid for them, they're used up.

Willy is not alone in his anguish. In the early 1960s popular author Vance Packard came out with a book called *The Waste Makers*, which suggested that Willy's plight was the product of a conscious marketing strategy by corporations. If products wear out faster, the argument goes, consumers have to buy them more often and sales are increased. Is this a valid argument? If it is, the drain on the resource base is artificially high, and we have another reason for corrective measures.

Packard identifies three possible types of product obsolescence. *Functional obsolescence* occurs when a new product can perform the function in a superior manner to an older product. The vacuum tube became functionally obsolescent when it was replaced by the transistor. *Fashion obsolescence* occurs when consumers prefer a new product for reasons of taste. Wide ties and short skirts become obsolete when tastes shift to narrow ties and long skirts. *Durability obsolescence* occurs when the product can no longer perform its function because of wear and tear. A refrigerator becomes obsolete when it can no longer keep its inside temperature stable and cool. The economic implications of these three types of obsolescence are quite different.

Functional Obsolescence

Because functional obsolescence is not really a problem, we will spend little time on it. A vigorous amount of inventive activity is a natural and desirable consequence of a market economy. Those who find better ways of doing things can become wealthy from the sales of their product, whether it be a tastier way to fry chicken or a cheaper, higher-quality method of copying documents. Far from representing a problem, functional obsolescence is the natural consequence of the successful search for better products.

Fashion Obsolescence

Fashion obsolescence is trickier. On the one hand, if fashion is a valued characteristic for consumers, then it is possible to conceive fashion obsolescence as merely a special case of functional obsolescence. New fashions replace old because they are more satisfying to the consumer. In this view there is no problem with fashion obsolescence because it is merely the result of the market continually doing a superior job of satisfying consumer preference.

The opposite point of view starts from the premise that those consumer preferences being satisfied by the market are *created* by the market. If consumer preferences are created by producers, then it is appropriate to question whether consumers are legitimately being made better off or are merely being manipulated into believing they are better off.

The apparel industry is certainly one where fashion obsolescence plays a strong role. However, it is not clear that fashion obsolescence is as important for other products. The automobile has certainly had its share of fashion obsolescence, perhaps best epitomized by the era in the 1950s when pronounced tail fins were in vogue. Yet, clearly the auto industry can go only so far. It would be very difficult, for example, to explain the shift in consumer buying toward small imported automobiles in the late 1970s and early 1980s as reflecting a shift in what was fashionable.

Indeed, some observers believe that a significant portion of the malaise of the domestic auto industry in the 1980s was caused by its inability to anticipate and respond to consumer preferences. That is important because the automobile market is one in which consumer preferences were thought to be dominated by the big-three American automakers. Clearly that is not the case.

Even when fashion influences consumer preferences, it is not clear that taste is dictated by the manufacturer or that it relates solely to new products. Antique furniture and antique cars are fashionable, but these fashions certainly are not created by manufacturers and do not help sell new cars or new furniture.

In looking at the totality of consumer decisions, we cannot conclude that consumer tastes are systematically manipulated by industry. Markets do exist for which a strong case can be made, but they seem to be isolated examples.

Durability Obsolescence

We come then to the final category, the one that triggered Willy Loman's lament. We must answer two questions: (1) What is an efficient level of durability? (2) Will the market supply that level? The *efficient level of durability* is the one that maximizes the net benefit from the product. Products that last longer confer more benefits on society, but they also cost more. Therefore, it is not obvious that the most durable product is also the most efficient. Can we trust the market to find the efficient level of durability? To examine that issue, let's look at both the demand and supply sides of the market.

On the demand side, the consumer makes his or her choices by discounting benefits and costs. The capital costs of consumer durables are borne immediately (although payments can be spread out by borrowing money), while the benefits (flow of services), as well as operating and maintenance costs, are accrued as a flow over time. He or she will purchase the commodity only if the net benefit is maximized by that level of durability (the additional cost of making a more durable commodity is justified by the additional benefit received). In performing this balancing between cost and durability, will the consumer make efficient choices or, because of lack of information or some other market imperfection, will durability be undervalued or overvalued?

One way to test this is to examine a case in which the benefits and costs are relatively easy to quantify, thereby allowing a comparison of the discount rate implied by consumer purchases of durable goods with market rates. If their individual discount rates are higher than the social opportunity cost of capital (as measured by interest rates), consumers are undervaluing durability. If they use lower discount rates, they are overvaluing it.

Kooreman (1996) conducted a fascinating study that relates to this issue. He was able to acquire data on individual purchases of electric lightbulbs. For each of these purchases he could calculate the benefits (longer life plus energy savings resulting from higher energy efficiency) and cost (purchase price as well as expected operating and maintenance costs). From this information he could calculate the discount rates implied by the purchase made by the average consumer. High discount rates indicate a special sensitivity to the initial cost.

Interestingly, in his sample, the implied discount rates were higher than the market rates. Furthermore, he found that discount rates were highest for the lowest-income people. This suggests that consumers—particularly low-income consumers—purchase less durability and less energy efficiency than is dictated by the dynamic efficiency criterion.

To be able to structure the appropriate policy response the government would have to know more about the reasons for the higher implied discount rates. If the reason is inadequate consumer information, then the appropriate policy might well be increasing the flow of reliable information through testing, labeling requirements, and so on. If it is purely that the market rate of interest is higher for low-income consumers because they have a higher probability of defaulting on loan repayments, then some means of providing easier access to capital markets might be called for. In other cases, measures such as tax subsidies or enforced standards might be appropriate.

We must also consider the supply side of the market. If they can get away with it, producers as a group have an incentive to reduce product durability below the efficient level. By doing so, they would reduce their cost per unit and they would sell many more units over time. For example, a household could satisfy its demand over a 10-year period with one appliance lasting 10 years, but would have to purchase two if the appliance lasted only five years. As long as the profit were higher on the sale of two rather than one (the presumption), firms would be better off with planned obsolescence.

But the key question is whether they can get away with it. As long as competitive suppliers, or even potential competitive suppliers, could enter the market to supply more durable goods, the consumer could turn to these alternative suppliers instead. In a normal market process, competition prevents individual firms from producing insufficiently durable products. Those who sell products that don't last find their markets drying up.

This market process may not work efficiently in two cases. The first case occurs when consumers are not well informed about the differences in durability, so they do not have enough information to make efficient decisions. To the extent they face ignorant consumers, producers would have an incentive to position themselves in the lower-initial-price portion of the market by lowering the durability of their products.

In recognition of the importance of this information, organizations have been set up to supply it. Consumers' Union, the publisher of *Consumer Reports*, is one such organization. It performs its own independent testing and evaluating, a service that can rectify this lack of information at reasonable cost. Its chief limitation probably relates to products undergoing rapid technological change. For rapidly changing products, by the time the testing lab acquires the product, tests it, and reports the results, other untested but potentially superior products are already on the market. This flaw, however, is not fatal; it merely means the rate of adoption would be more sluggish than would be dictated by efficiency.

The second case where a firm could profit by producing a good with an inefficiently low durability is when it does not face competition. This would require either a monopoly—which is very rare—or explicit collusion to cut corners by all the members of the industry. Since competition comes from foreign, as well as domestic, firms and from potential entrants as well as existing firms, this must be a relatively rare circumstance.

The American automobile industry provides an interesting subject for examining the hypothesis that increased competition can increase durability because that industry has faced increasingly intense foreign competition. The share of the U.S. market captured by imports rose from 14.8% in 1976 to 29.2% in 1988.[6] Did this lead to increased durability?

According to two possible measures, durability did increase. Durable cars should last longer and be safer. The average age of passenger cars increased from 6.2 years in 1976 to 7.6 years in 1988. And the deaths per 100,000,000 vehicle miles traveled decreased from 3.33 in 1976 to 2.46 in 1988. Though other factors were certainly also at work, competition probably did play a major role in increasing durability.

Summary

Market mechanisms automatically create pressures for recycling and reuse that are generally in the right direction, though not always of the correct intensity. Higher disposal costs and increasing scarcity of virgin materials do create a larger demand for recycling. This is already evident for a number of products, such as those containing copper or aluminum.

---

[6]The data in this and the following paragraph came from Motor Vehicles Manufacturing Association, *Motor Vehicle Facts and Figures, 1989* (Detroit: Motor Vehicles Manufacturing Association, 1989): 16, 26, and 90.

Yet there are also a number of imperfections in the market that tend to suggest that the degree of recycling we are currently experiencing is less than the efficient amount. The absence of sufficient stockpiles and the absence of tariffs mean that our national security interests are not being adequately considered in market decisions involving strategic minerals. From the perspective of efficiency, the reliance on vulnerable imports is excessive.

Artificially low disposal costs, and tax breaks for ores combine to depress the role that old scrap can, and should, play. Severance taxes provide a limited if poorly targeted redress for some minerals.

One imperfection, the supposed tendency of American manufacturers to produce products less durable than efficient, seems overstated. Yet the Kooreman study indicates that some people purchase products less durable than would be efficient, implying that the market penetration of more energy-efficient devices may be lower than efficient. This is a more limited view of product durability problems than is usually espoused by writers such as Vance Packard, but a troubling one nonetheless.

One cannot help but notice that many of these problems—such as pricing municipal disposal services and tax breaks for virgin ores result from government actions. It therefore appears in this area that the appropriate role for government is selective disengagement complemented by some fine-tuning adjustments.

This is not true, however, for environmental damage due to littering, air and water pollution, and strip mining. When a product is produced from virgin materials rather than recycled or reusable materials, and the cost of any associated environmental damage is not internalized, some government action may be called for.

The selective disengagement of government in some areas must be complemented by the enforcement of programs to internalize the costs of environmental damage. The commonly heard ideological prescriptions suggesting that environmental problems can be solved either by ending government interference or by increasing the amount of government control are both inaccurate. The efficient role for government in achieving a balance between the economic and environmental systems requires less control in some areas and more in others.

Discussion Questions

1. Glass bottles can either be recycled (crushed and remelted) or reused. The market will tend to choose the cheapest path. What factors will tend to affect the relative cost of these options? Is the market likely to make the efficient choice? Are the "bottle bills" passed by many of the states requiring deposits on bottles a move toward efficiency? Why?

2. Many areas have attempted to increase the amount of recycled waste lubricating oil by requiring service stations to serve as collection centers or by instituting deposit-refund systems. On what grounds, if any, is government intervention called for? In terms of the effects on the waste lubrication oil market, what differences should be noticed among those states that do nothing, those that require all service stations to serve as collection centers, and those that implement deposit-refund systems? Why?

3. What are the income-distribution consequences of "fashion"? Can the need to be seen driving a new car by the rich be a boon to those with lower incomes who will ultimately purchase a better, lower-priced used car as a result?

Problems

1. Suppose a product can be produced using virgin ore at a marginal cost given by $MC_1 = 0.5q_1$ and with recycled materials at a marginal cost given by $MC_2 = 5 + 0.1q_2$. (a) If the inverse demand curve were given by $P = 10 - 0.5(q_1 + q_2)$, how many units of the product would be produced with virgin ore and how many units with recycled materials? (b) If the inverse demand curve were $P = 20 - 0.5(q_1 + q_2)$, what would your answer be?
2. When the government allows private firms to extract minerals offshore or on public lands, two common means of sharing in the profits are bonus bidding and production royalties. The former awards the right to extract to the highest bidder, while the second charges a per-ton royalty on each ton extracted. Bonus bids involve a single, up-front payment, while royalties are paid as long as minerals are being extracted.
   (a) If the two approaches are designed to yield the same amount of revenue, will they have the same effect on the allocation of the mine over time? Why or why not?
   (b) Would either or both be consistent with an efficient allocation? Why or why not?
   (c) Suppose the size of the mineral deposit and the future path of prices are unknown. How do these two approaches allocate the risk between the mining company and the government?
3. "As society's cost of disposing of trash increases over time, recycling rates should automatically increase as well." Discuss.

Further Reading

Dinan, Terry. "Economic Efficiency Aspects of Alternative Policies for Reducing Waste Disposal," *Journal of Environmental Economics and Management* Vol. 25 (1993): 242–256. Argues that a tax on virgin materials is not enough to produce efficiency. A subsidy on reuse is also required.

Jenkins, Robin R. *The Economics of Solid Waste Reduction: The Impact of User Fees* (Cheltenham, UK: Edward Elgar, 1993). An analysis that examines whether user fees do, in fact, encourage people to recycle waste. Using evidence derived from nine U.S. communities, the author concludes that they do.

Kinnaman, T. C., and D. Fullerton. "The Economics of Residential Solid Waste Management," in T. Tietenberg and H. Folmer, eds. *The International Yearbook of Environmental and Resource Economics 2000/2001* (Cheltenham, UK: Edward Elgar, 2000): 100–147. A comprehensive survey of the economic literature devoted to household solid waste collection and disposal.

Porter, Richard C. *The Economics of Waste* (Washington, DC: Resources for the Future, Inc., 2002). A highly readable, thorough treatment of how economic principles and policy instruments can be used to improve the management of a diverse range of both business and household waste.

Reschovsky, J. D., and S. E. Stone. "Market Incentives to Encourage Household Waste Recycling: Paying for What You Throw Away," *Journal of Policy Analysis and Management* Vol. 13 (1994): 120–139. An examination of ways to change the zero marginal cost of disposal characteristics of many current disposal programs.

Tilton, John E., ed. *Mineral Wealth and Economic Development* (Washington, DC: Resources for the Future, Inc., 1992). Explores why a number of mineral-exporting countries have seen their per capita incomes decline or their standards of living stagnate over the last several decades.

Additional References is available on this book's companion Web site www.aw-bc.com/tietenberg.

Chapter 10

Replenishable but Depletable Resources: Water

You'll never miss the water; Till your well runs dry.
—William Christopher Handy, *Joe Turner's Blues* (1915)

Introduction

To the red country and part of the gray country of Oklahoma, the last rains came gently, and they did not cut the scarred earth. . . . The sun flared down on the growing corn day after day until a line of brown spread along the edge of each green bayonet. The clouds appeared and went away, and in awhile they did not try anymore.

With these words John Steinbeck (1939) sets the scene for his powerful novel *The Grapes of Wrath*. Drought and poor soil conservation practices combined to destroy the agricultural institutions that had provided nourishment and livelihood to Oklahoma residents since settlement in that area had begun. In desperation, those who had worked that land were forced to abandon not only their possessions, but their past. Moving to California to seek employment, they were uprooted only to be caught up in a web of exploitation and hopelessness.

Based on an actual situation, the novel demonstrates how the social fabric can tear when subject to tremendous stress, such as an inadequate availability of water, and how painful those tears can be.[1] Clearly problems such as these should be anticipated and prevented as much as possible.

Water is one of the essential elements of life. We humans depend not only on an intake of water to replace the continual loss of body fluids, but also on food sources that themselves need water to survive. This resource deserves special attention.

In this chapter we examine how our economic and political institutions have allocated this important resource in the past and how they might improve on its allocation in the future. We initiate our inquiry by examining the likelihood and severity of water scarcity. Turning to the management of our water resources, we define the efficient allocation of ground- and

---

[1]Popular films such as *The Milagro Beanfield War* and *Chinatown* have addressed similar themes.

surface water over time and compare these allocations to current practice, particularly in the United States. Finally, we examine the menu of opportunities for meaningful institutional reform.

The Potential for Water Scarcity

The earth's renewable supply of water is governed by the hydrologic cycle, a system of continuous water circulation (see Figure 10.1). Enormous quantities of water are cycled each year through this system, though only a fraction of circulated water is available each year for human use.

Of the estimated total volume of water on Earth, only 2.5% (1.4 billion km³) of the total volume is freshwater. Of this amount, only 200,000 km³, or less than 1% of all freshwater resources (and only 0.01% of all the water on Earth), is available for human consumption and for ecosystems (Gleick, 1993).

FIGURE 10.1

The Hydrologic Cycle

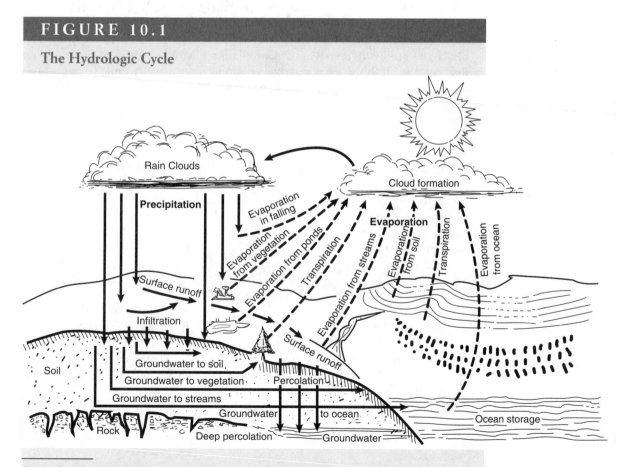

Source: Council on Environmental Quality, *Environmental Trends* (Washington, DC: Government Printing Office, 1981): 210.

If we were simply to add up the available supply of freshwater (total runoff) on a global scale and compare it with current consumption, we would discover that the supply is currently about 10 times larger than consumption. Though comforting, that statistic is also misleading because it masks the impact of growing demand and the rather severe scarcity situation that already exists in certain parts of the world. Taken together, these insights suggest that in many parts of the world, water scarcity is already upon us, and other areas, including several parts of the United States, can be expected to experience water scarcity in the next few decades.

Available supplies are derived from two rather different sources—surface water and groundwater. As the name implies, *surface water* consists of the freshwater in rivers, lakes, and reservoirs that collects and flows on the earth's surface. *Groundwater* by contrast collects in porous layers of underground rock known as aquifers. Though some groundwater is renewed by percolation of rain or melted snow, most was accumulated over geologic time and, because of its location, cannot be recharged once it is depleted.

According to the UN Environment Program (2002), 90% of the world's readily available freshwater resources is groundwater. And only 2.5% of this is available on a renewable basis. The rest is a finite, depletable resource.

Surface water withdrawals in the United States in 2000 amounted to 262 billion gallons per day. Of this, approximately 83 billion gallons per day came from groundwater. Water withdrawals, both surface and groundwater, vary considerably geographically. Figure 10.2 shows how surface and groundwater withdrawals for the United States vary by state. California, Texas, Nebraska, Arkansas, and Florida are the states with the largest groundwater withdrawals.

While surface water withdrawals in the United States have been relatively constant since 1985, groundwater withdrawals are up 14% (Hutson et al., 2004). Globally, annual water withdrawal is expected to grow by 10 to 12% every 10 years. Most of this growth is expected to occur in South America and Africa (UNESCO, 1999).

Approximately 1.5 billion people in the world depend on groundwater for their drinking supplies (UNEP, 2002). Agriculture is still the largest consumer of water. In the United States, irrigation accounts for approximately 65% of total water withdrawals and over 80% of water consumed (Hudson et al., 2004). This number is much higher in the Southwest. Worldwide in 2000, agriculture accounted for 67% of world freshwater withdrawal and 86% of its use (UNESCO, 2000).[2]

Tucson, Arizona, demonstrates how western communities cope. Tucson, which averages about 11 inches of rain a year, was (until the completion of the Central Arizona Project, which diverts water from the Colorado River) the largest city in the United States to rely entirely on groundwater. The water levels in some wells in the Tucson area have dropped 100 feet in 10 years. Tucson annually pumped five times as much water out of the ground as nature put back in. At current consumption rates the aquifers supplying Tucson would have been exhausted in less than 100 years. Despite the rate at which its water supplies were being depleted, Tucson continued to grow at a rapid rate. To head off this looming gap between increasing water

---

[2]"Use" is measured as the amount of water withdrawn that does not return to the system in the form of return or unused flow.

FIGURE 10.2

Estimated Use of Water in the United States in 2000 Including Surface Water and Groundwater Withdrawals

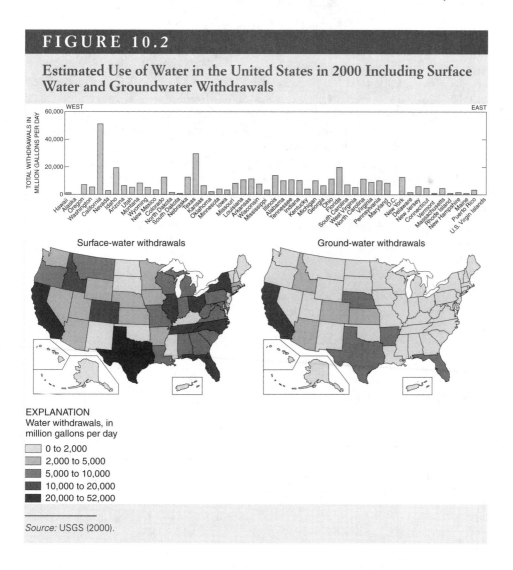

EXPLANATION
Water withdrawals, in
million gallons per day

0 to 2,000
2,000 to 5,000
5,000 to 10,000
10,000 to 20,000
20,000 to 52,000

Source: USGS (2000).

consumption and declining supply, a giant network of dams, pipelines, tunnels, and canals known as the Central Arizona Project was constructed to transfer water from the Colorado River to Tucson. Water diversion has been a common, but increasingly unavailable, policy response.

Though the discussion thus far has focused on the quantity of water, quality is also a problem. Much of the available water is polluted with chemicals, radioactive materials, salt, or bacteria. Though we shall reserve a detailed look at the water pollution problem for Chapter 19, it is important to keep in mind that water scarcity has an important qualitative dimension that further limits the supply of potable water.

The depletion and contamination of water supplies are not the only problems. Excessive withdrawal from aquifers is a major cause of land subsidence. (Land subsidence is a gradual settling or sudden sinking of the earth's surface owing to subsurface movement of Earth materials, in this case water.) In 1997, the USGS estimated subsidence amounts of 6 feet in Las Vegas, 9 feet in Houston, and approximately 18 feet near Phoenix, Arizona.

In Mexico City, land has been subsiding at a rate of 1–3 inches per year. The city has sunk 30 feet over the last century! The Monumento a la Independencia, a monument built to celebrate the 100th anniversary of Mexico's War of Independence, now needs 23 additional steps to reach its base. The monument was built in 1910. Mexico City, with its population of approximately 20 million, is facing large water problems. Not only is the city sinking, but with an average population growth of 350,000 per year, the city is running out of water (Rudolph, 2001).

What this brief survey of the evidence suggests is that in certain parts of the world, groundwater supplies are being depleted to the potential detriment of future users. Supplies that for all practical purposes will never be replenished are being "mined" to satisfy current needs. Once used, they are gone. Is this allocation efficient, or are there demonstrable sources of inefficiency? Answering this question requires us to be quite clear about what is meant by an efficient allocation of surface water and groundwater.

The Efficient Allocation of Scarce Water

What efficiency means for the allocation of water depends crucially on whether surface water or groundwater is being tapped. In the absence of storage, the problem with surface water is the allocation of a renewable supply among competing users. Intergenerational effects are less important because future supplies depend on natural phenomena (such as precipitation) rather than on current withdrawal practices. For groundwater, on the other hand, withdrawing water now does affect the resources available to future generations. In this case, the allocation over time is a crucial aspect of the analysis. Because it represents a somewhat simpler analytical case, we shall start by considering the efficient allocation of surface water.

Surface Water

An efficient allocation of surface water: (1) must strike a balance among a host of competing users and (2) must supply an acceptable means of handling the year-to-year variability in surface water flow. The former issue is acute because so many different potential users have legitimate competing claims. Some withdraw the water for consumptive use (such as municipal drinking water suppliers or farmers), while others use but do not consume the water (such as swimmers or boaters). The latter challenge arises because surface water supplies are not constant from year to year or month to month. Since precipitation, runoff, and evaporation all change from year to year, in some years less water will be available for allocation than in others. Not only must a system be in place for allocating the average amount of water, but also above-average and below-average flows must be anticipated and allocated.

With respect to the first problem, the dictates of efficiency are quite clear—the water should be allocated so that the marginal net benefit is equalized for all uses. (Remember that the marginal net benefit is the vertical distance between the demand

FIGURE 10.3

The Efficient Allocation of Surface Water

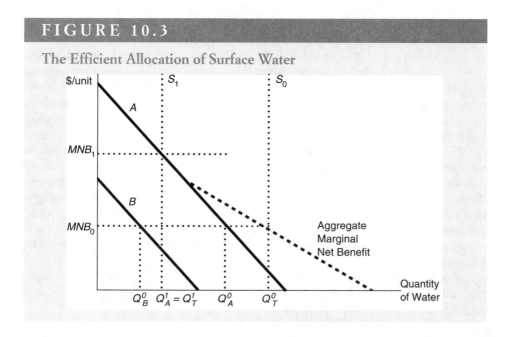

curve for water and the marginal cost of extracting and distributing that water for the last unit of water consumed.) To demonstrate why efficiency requires equal marginal net benefits, consider a situation in which the marginal net benefits are not equal. We shall show that in this situation it is always possible to find some reallocation of the water that increases net benefits. Since net benefits could be increased by this reallocation, the initial allocation could not have maximized net benefits. Since an efficient allocation maximizes net benefits, any allocation that fails to equalize net benefits could not have been efficient.

If marginal net benefits have not been equalized, it is always possible to increase net benefits by transferring water from those users with low net marginal benefits to those with higher net marginal benefits. By transferring the water to the users who value the marginal water more, the net benefits of the water use are increased; those losing water are giving up less than those receiving the additional water are gaining. When the marginal net benefits are equalized, no such transfer is possible without lowering net benefits. This can be seen in Figure 10.3.

Two individual net benefit curves (A and B) are depicted along with the aggregate net benefit curve for both individuals.[3] For supply situation S_T^0, the amount of water available is Q^0. An efficient allocation would give Q_B^0 to use B and Q_A^0 to use A. By construction, $Q_A^0 + Q_B^0 = Q_T^0$. For this allocation, notice that the marginal net benefit (MNB_0) is equal for the 2 users.

Notice also that the marginal net benefit for both users is positive in Figure 10.3. This implies that water sales should involve a positive marginal scarcity rent. Could

---

[3]Remember that the net benefit curve for an individual would be derived by plotting the vertical distance between the demand curve and the marginal cost of getting the water to that individual.

we draw the diagram so that the marginal net benefit (and, hence, marginal scarcity rent) would be zero? How?

Marginal scarcity rent would be zero if water were not scarce. If the availability of water as presented by the supply curve were greater than the amount represented by the point where the aggregate marginal net benefit curve intersects the axis, water would not be scarce. Both users would get all they wanted; their demands would not be competing with one another. Their marginal net benefits would still be equal, but in this case they would both be zero.

Now let's consider the second problem—dealing with fluctuations in supply. As long as the supply level can be anticipated, the equal marginal net benefit rule still applies, but different supply levels may imply very different allocations among users. This is an important attribute of the problem because it implies that simple allocation rules, such as each user receiving a proportion of the available flow or high-priority users receiving a guaranteed amount, are not likely to be efficient.

Consider Figure 10.3 again, but this time focus on the water supply labeled S_1, a condition of restricted supply. With S_1, a very different efficient allocation prevails; specifically, use B receives no water, while use A receives it all. Why does the efficient allocation change so radically between S_0 and S_1? The answer lies in the shape of the two demand curves for water.

The marginal net benefit curve for water in use A lies above that for B, implying that as supplies diminish, the cost (the forgone net benefits) of doing without water is much higher for A than for B. To minimize this cost, more of the burden of the shortfall is allocated to B than A. In an efficient allocation, users who can most easily find substitutes or conserve water receive proportionately smaller allocations when supplies are diminished than those who have few alternatives. In practice this can be handled using a spot market (Zarnikau, 1994).

Groundwater

Extending this analysis to encompass groundwater requires that the depletable nature of groundwater supplies be explicitly taken into account. When withdrawals exceed recharge from a particular aquifer, the resource will be mined over time until either supplies are exhausted or the marginal cost of pumping additional water becomes prohibitive. The similarity of this case to the increasing-cost, depletable-resource model discussed in Chapter 7 allows us to exploit that similarity to learn something about the efficient allocation of groundwater over time.

The first transferable implication is that a marginal user cost is associated with mining groundwater, reflecting the opportunity cost associated with the unavailability in the future of any unit of water used in the present. An efficient allocation considers this user cost.

The efficient extraction path for constant demand involves declining use of groundwater over time. The marginal extraction cost (the cost of pumping the last unit to the surface) would rise over time as the water table fell. Pumping would stop either when (1) the water table ran dry or (2) when the marginal cost of pumping was either greater than the marginal benefit of the water or greater than the marginal cost of acquiring water from some other source.

Abundant surface water in proximity to the location of the groundwater could serve as a substitute for groundwater, effectively setting an upper bound on the marginal cost of extraction. The user would not pay more to extract a unit of groundwater than it would cost to acquire surface water. Unfortunately in many parts of the country where groundwater overdrafts are particularly severe, the competition for surface water is already keen; a cheap source of surface water doesn't exist.

In efficient groundwater markets, the water price would rise over time. The rise would continue until the point of exhaustion, the point at which the marginal pumping cost becomes prohibitive or when the marginal cost of pumping becomes equal to the next-least-expensive source of water. At that point the marginal pumping cost and the price would be equal. In all three cases the net price, the difference between the price of the water and the marginal extraction cost, would decline over time, reaching zero at the switch point (if a substitute were available) or the point of exhaustion (if it were not). This expectation of a declining net price seems consistent with the evidence. (See Table 3 in Torrell, Libbin, and Miller, 1990).

In some regions, groundwater and surface water supplies are not physically separate. For example, due to the porous soils in the Arkansas River Valley, groundwater withdrawals in the region affect surface water flows near the Colorado-Kansas border (Bennett, 2000). Lack of conjunctive use management led the State of Kansas to sue the State of Colorado for depleted surface water flows at the border. (*Conjunctive use* refers to the combined management of surface and groundwater resources to optimize their joint use and to minimize adverse effects of excessive reliance on a single source.) The hydrologic nature of the water source must be taken into consideration when designing a water allocation scheme if problems like this are to be avoided.

The Current Allocation System

Riparian and Prior Appropriation Doctrines

Within the United States, the means of allocating water differ from one geographic area to the next, particularly with respect to the legal doctrines that govern conflicts. In this section we shall focus on the allocation systems that prevail in the arid Southwest, which must cope with the most potentially serious and imminent scarcity of water.

In the earliest days of settlement in the American Southwest and West, the government had a minimal presence. Residents were pretty much on their own in creating a sense of order. Property rights played a very important role in reducing conflicts in this potentially volatile situation.

As water was always a significant factor in the development of an area, the first settlements were usually oriented near bodies of water. The property rights that evolved, called *riparian rights*, allocated the right to use the water to the owner of the land adjacent to the water. This was a practical solution because by virtue of their location, these owners had easy access to the water. Furthermore, there were enough sites with access to water that virtually all who sought water could be accommodated.

With population growth and the consequent rise in the demand for land, this allocation system became less appropriate. As demand increased, the amount of land adjacent to water became scarce, forcing some spillover onto land that was not adjacent to water. The owners of this land began to seek means of acquiring water to make their land more productive.

About this time, with the discovery of gold in California, mining became an important source of employment. With the advent of mining came a need to divert water away from streams to other sites. Unfortunately, riparian property rights made no provision for water to be diverted to other locations. The rights to the water were tied to the land and could not be separately transferred.

As economic theory would predict, this situation created a demand for a change in the property right structure from riparian rights to one that was more congenial to the need for transferability. The waste resulting from the lack of transferability became so great that it outweighed any transition costs of changing the system of property rights. The evolution that took place in the mining camps became the fore-runner of what has become known as the *prior appropriation doctrine.*

The miners established the custom that the first person to arrive had the supe-rior claim on the water. In practice, this severed the relationship that had existed under the riparian doctrine between the rights to land and the rights to water. As this new doctrine became adopted in legislation, court rulings, and seven state constitutions, widespread diversion of water based on prior appropriation became possible. Stimulated by the profits that could be made in shifting water to more valu-able uses, private companies were formed to construct irrigation systems, and to transport water from surplus to deficit areas. Agriculture flourished.

Although prior to 1860 the role of the government was rather minimal, it began to change—slowly at first, but picking up momentum as the 20th century began. The earliest incursions involved establishing the principle that the ownership of water properly belonged to the state. Claimants were accorded a right to use, known as a *usufructory right*, rather than an ownership right. The establishment of this prin-ciple of public ownership was followed in short order by the establishment of state control over the rates charged by the private irrigation companies, by imposing restrictions on the ability to transfer water out of the district, and by creating a cen-tralized bureaucracy to administer the process.

This was only the beginning. The demand for land in the arid West and South-west was still growing, creating a complementary demand for water to make the desert bloom. The tremendous profits to be made from large-scale water diversion created the political climate necessary for federal involvement.

The federal role in water resources originated in the early 1800s, largely out of concern for the nation's regional development and economic growth. Toward these ends, the federal government built a network of inland waterways to provide trans-portation. Since The Reclamation Act of 1902, the federal government has built almost 700 dams to provide water and power to help settle the West.

To promote growth and regional development, the federal government has paid an average of 70% of the combined construction and operating costs of such proj-ects, leaving states, localities, and private users to carry the remaining 30%. Such subsidies have even been extended to cover some of the costs of providing marketable water services. For example, according to Rubin (1983), the federal government pays 81% of the cost of supplying irrigation water and 64% of municipal water costs.

This, in a nutshell, is the current situation for water in the southwestern United States. Both the state and federal governments play a large role. State laws may vary considerably, especially with respect to groundwater withdrawal. Though the prior appropriation doctrine stands as the foundation of this allocation system, it is heavily circumscribed by government regulations and direct government appropriation of a substantial amount of water.

Sources of Inefficiency

The current system is not efficient. The prime source of inefficiency involves restrictions that have been placed on water transfers, preventing their gravitation to the highest valued use, though other sources, such as charging inefficiently low prices, must bear some of the responsibility.

Restrictions on Transfers.

To achieve an efficient allocation of water, the marginal net benefits would have to be equalized across all uses (including nonconsumptive instream uses) of the water. With a well-structured system of water property rights, efficiency can be a direct result of the transferability of the rights (Griffin and Hsu, 1993). Users receiving low marginal net benefits from their current allocation would trade their rights to those who would receive higher net benefits. Both parties would be better off. The payment received by the seller would exceed the net benefits forgone, while the payment made by the buyer would be less than the value of the water acquired.

Unfortunately, the existing mixed system of prior appropriation rights coupled with quite restrictive federal and state laws have diminished the degree of transferability that can take place. Diminished transferability in turn reduces the market pressures toward equalization of the marginal net benefits. By itself this indictment is not sufficient to demonstrate the inefficiency of the existing system. If it could be shown that this regulatory system were able to substitute some bureaucratic process for finding and maintaining this equalization, efficiency would still be possible. Unfortunately, that has not been the case, as can be seen by examining in more detail the specific nature of these restrictions. The allocation is inefficient.

One of the earliest restrictions required users to fully exercise their water rights or else they would lose them. The principle of "beneficial use" was typically applied to offstream consumptive uses. It is not difficult to see what this "use it or lose it" principle does to the incentive to conserve. Particularly careful users who, at their own expense, find ways to use less water would find their allocations reduced accordingly. The regulations strongly discourage conservation.

A second restriction, known as "preferential use," attempts to establish bureaucratically a value hierarchy of uses. With this doctrine, the government attempts to establish allocation priorities across categories of water. Within categories (irrigation for agriculture, for example), the priority is determined by prior appropriation ("first in time—first in right"), but among categories the preferential-use doctrine governs.

The preferential-use doctrine supports three rather different kinds of inefficiencies. First, it substitutes a bureaucratically determined set of priorities for market priorities, resulting in a lower likelihood that marginal net benefits would be equalized. Second, it reduces the incentive to make investments that complement water use in lower preference categories for the simple reason that their water could be involuntarily withdrawn as the needs in higher-level categories grow. Finally, it allocates the risk of shortfalls in an inefficient way.

Although the first two inefficiencies are rather self-evident, the third merits further explanation. Because water supplies fluctuate over time, unusual scarcities can occur in any particular year. With a well-specified system of property rights, damage caused by this risk would be minimized by allowing those most damaged by a shortfall to purchase a larger share of the diminished amount of water available during a drought from those suffering the increased shortfall with smaller consequences.

By diminishing, and in some cases eliminating, the ability to transfer rights from so-called "high preferential use" categories to "lower preferential use" categories during times of acute need, the damage caused by shortfalls is higher than necessary. In essence, the preferential-use doctrine fails to adequately consider the marginal damage caused by temporary shortfalls, something a well-structured system of property rights would do automatically.

Inhibiting transfers has very practical implications. Due to low energy costs and federal subsidies, agricultural irrigation became the dominant use of water in the West. Yet, the marginal net benefits from agricultural uses are lower, sometimes substantially lower, than the marginal net benefits of water use by municipalities and industry. A transfer of water from irrigated agriculture to these other uses would raise net benefits. It is therefore not surprising that transfers from agriculture to municipalities are becoming more common.

Federal Reclamation Projects and Agricultural Water Pricing. By providing subsidies to approved projects, federal reclamation projects have diverted water to these projects even when the net benefits were negative. Why was this done? What motivated the construction of inefficient projects?

Some work by Howe (1986) provides a possible explanation. He examined the benefits and costs of constructing the Big Thompson Project in Northeastern Colorado. With this project the water is pumped to an elevation that allows it to flow through a tunnel to the eastern side of the mountains. On that side, electric power is produced at several points. At lower elevations, the water is channeled into natural streams and feeder canals for distribution to irrigation districts and front-range cities.

Howe calculated that the national net benefits for this project, which includes all benefits and costs, were either –$341.4 million or –$237.0 million, depending on the number of years included in the calculations. The project cost substantially more to construct than it returned in benefits. However, regional net benefits for the geographic region served by the facility were strongly positive ($766.9 million or $1,187 million, respectively). This facility was an extraordinary boon for the local area because a very large proportion of the total cost had been passed on to national taxpayers. The local political pressure was able to secure project approval despite its inherent inefficiency.

While the very existence of these facilities underwritten by the federal government is a source of inefficiency, the manner in which the water is priced is another. The subsidies have been substantial. Frederick (1989) reported on some work done by the Natural Resources Defense Council to calculate the subsidies to irrigated agriculture in the Westlands Water District, one of the world's richest agricultural areas located on the west side of California's San Joaquin Valley. The Westlands Water District paid about $10 to $12 per acre-foot, less than 10% of the unsubsidized cost of delivering water to the district. (An acre-foot is the amount of water it would take to flood an acre of level land to a depth of one foot.) The resulting subsidy was estimated to be $217 per irrigated acre or $500,000 per year for the average-sized farm.

Municipal and Industrial Water Pricing.

Restrictions on transfer are not the only source of inefficiency in the current allocation system. The prices charged by water distribution utilities do not promote efficiency of use either.

Both the level of prices and the rate structure are at fault. In general, the price level is too low and the rate structure does not adequately reflect the costs of providing service to different types of customers. Water utilities apply a variety of fees and charges to water. Some are better at reflecting cost than others. Water fees and charges reflect the costs of storage, treatment, and distribution of the water to customers. Rarely, however, does the rate reflect the actual value of water.

In part, perhaps because water is considered an essential commodity, the prices charged by public water companies are too low. For surface water the rates are too low for two rather distinct reasons: (1) historic average costs are used to determine rates and (2) marginal scarcity rent is rarely included.

Efficient pricing requires the use of marginal, not average, cost. In order to adequately balance conservation with use, the customer should be paying the marginal cost of supplying the last unit of water. Yet regulated utilities are typically allowed to charge prices just high enough to cover the costs of running the operation as revealed by figures from the recent past. Water utilities are capital intensive with very large fixed costs in the short run. This means that short-run average costs will be falling, implying a marginal cost that falls below average cost. In this circumstance, marginal-cost pricing would cause the utility to fail to generate enough revenue to cover costs. (Can you see why?)

Circumstances may be changing, however. Now long-run costs may be rising since new supplies are typically much more expensive to develop and the old supplies are limited by their fixed capacity. (Hanneman, 1998).

The second source of the problem is the failure of regulators overseeing the operations of water distribution companies to allow a scarcity rent to be incorporated in the calculation of the appropriate price, a problem that is even more severe when groundwater is involved. One study by Martin, et al. (1984) found that due to a failure to include a user cost, rates in Tucson, Arizona, were about 58% too low, despite increases. Debate 10.1 illustrates the inconsistencies in both agricultural and municipal pricing.

Both low pricing and ignoring the marginal scarcity rent promote an excessive demand for water. Simple actions, such as fixing leaky faucets or planting native lawn

DEBATE 10.1

What Is the Value of Water?

As mentioned earlier in this chapter, the Colorado Big-Thompson (C-BT) project moves water from the Colorado River to the eastern slope of Colorado. The Northern Colorado Conservancy District distributes the approximately 250,000 acre-feet of water per year to irrigators, towns, cities, and industries in northeastern Colorado. Irrigators with original rights pay approximately $3.50 per share. (A share is, on average, 0.7 acre-foot per year.) Cities pay approximately $7.00 per share if they hold original rights.

Shares of C-BT water are transferable and are actively traded in the district. Market prices have been at a minimum of $1,800 per share, which translates to approximately $2,600 per acre-foot for perpetual supply or about $208 per year using an 8% discount rate. Additionally, prices in the rental market (for users who want to sell or buy water on a one-year basis) range from $7.50 to $25.00 per acre-foot.

The cities that use the water charge a variety of prices to their customers. Boulder utilizes an increasing block rate structure with an initial block at $1.65 per thousand gallons for the first 5,000 gallons, $3.30 per thousand gallons for the next 16,000 gallons, and $5.50 per thousand gallons over 21,000 gallons per month. Ft. Collins has some unmetered customers, who pay a fixed monthly fee, but no marginal cost for additional use. Its metered customers pay a fixed charge of $12.72 plus water charges determined by an increasing block rate. In the first block the charge is $1.72 per thousand gallons for the first 7,000 gallons. The highest block rate in Ft. Collins is $3.07 for users consuming more than 20,000 gallons per month. Longmont has both metered and unmetered customers and utilizes an *increasing* block rate for its residential customers and a *decreasing* block rate for its small commercial customers.

Economic theory not only makes clear that the marginal net benefits for all uses and users of a given water project should be equal, but also that the common marginal net benefit metric provides a useful indication of the value of the marginal water unit to all users of this resource.

What do we make of the huge variation in these prices? The only difference in observed prices should be a difference in the marginal cost of delivering water to those customers (since marginal net benefit should be the same for all users). The prices from the C-BT project exhibit much more variation than could be explained by marginal conveyance cost, so they clearly are not only inefficient, but they are sending very mixed signals about the value of this water.

Source: Charles Howe. "Forms and Functions of Water Pricing: An Overview," in Baumann, Boland, and Hanneman, eds. *Urban Water Demand Management and Planning* (McGraw-Hill, Inc.: New York, 1998). With rate updates from the cities of Boulder, Longmont, and Ft. Collins, Colorado, and the Northern Colorado Conservancy District (2004).

grasses, are easy to overlook when water is excessively cheap. Yet in a city such as New York, leaky faucets can account for a significant amount of wasted water.

Instream Flows.   Conflicts between offstream and instream uses of water are not uncommon. In 2001, the federal government cut off water to farmers in the Klamath River Basin to protect threatened coho salmon, which are protected under the

Federal Endangered Species Act. Farmers responded by forcing open irrigation gates and forming a bucket brigade to dump water on their fields. Secretary of the Interior Gale Norton subsequently decided to resume the traditional diversion of water to the more than 1,400 farmers using Klamath River water. Six months later, a huge fish kill (estimated to be at least 35,000 salmon) was blamed on the low flows in the river. This ongoing dispute provides an illustration of the problem with the legal and institutional structures governing water resources. Without formal recognition of instream flow rights, the value of species, including salmon, cannot be properly incorporated into the allocation decision.

Common Property Problems.   The allocation of groundwater must confront one additional problem. When many users tap the same aquifer, that aquifer can become an open-access resource. Tapping an open-access resource will tend to deplete it too rapidly; users lose the incentive to conserve. The marginal scarcity rent will be ignored.

The incentive to conserve a groundwater resource in an efficient market is created by the desire to prevent pumping costs from rising too rapidly and the desire to capitalize on the higher prices that could reasonably be expected in the future. With open-access resources, neither of these desires translates into conservation for the simple reason that water conserved by one party may simply be used by someone else because the conserver has no exclusive right to the water that is saved. Water saved by one party to take advantage of higher prices can easily be pumped out by another user before the higher prices ever materialize.

For open-access resources, economic theory suggests several direct consequences. Pumping costs would rise too rapidly, initial prices would be too low, and too much water would be consumed by the earliest users. The burden of this waste would not be shared uniformly. Because the typical aquifer is bowl-shaped, users on the periphery of the aquifer would be particularly hard hit. When the water level declines, the edges go dry first, while the center can continue to supply water for substantially longer periods. Future users would also be hard hit relative to current users.[4] For coastal aquifers, salt water intrusion is an additional potential cost.

Potential Remedies

Economic analysis points the way to a number of possible means of remedying the current water situation in the southwestern United States. These reforms would promote efficiency of water use while affording more protection to the interests of future generations of water users.

The first reform would reduce the number of restrictions on water transfers. The "use it or lose it" component that often accompanies the prior appropriation doctrine can promote the extravagant use of water and discourage conservation. Typically, water saved by conservation is forfeited. Allowing users to capture the value of water saved by permitting them to sell it would stimulate water conservation and allow the water to flow to higher valued uses (see Example 10.1).

---

[4]In *Salt River User's Association v. Kavocovich* [411 P. 2d 201(1966)], the Arizona Court of Appeals ruled that irrigators who lined their ditches could not apply "saved" water to adjacent land.

Example   10.1

USING ECONOMIC PRINCIPLES TO CONSERVE WATER IN CALIFORNIA

In 1977, when then-California governor Jerry Brown negotiated a deal to settle one of the state's perennial water fights by building a new water diversion project, environmental groups were opposed. The opposition was expected. What was not expected was the form it took. Rather than simply block every imaginable aspect of the plan, the Environmental Defense Fund (EDF) set out to show project supporters how the water needs could be better supplied by ways that put no additional pressure on the environment.

According to this strategy, if the owners of the agricultural lands to the west of the water district seeking the water could be convinced to reduce their water use by adopting new, water-saving irrigation techniques, the conserved water could be transferred to the district in lieu of the project. But the growers had no incentive to conserve because conserving the water required the installation of costly new equipment and as soon as the water was saved it would be forfeited under the "use it or lose it" regulations. What could be done?

On January 17, 1989, largely through the efforts of EDF, an historic agreement was negotiated between the growers association, a major user of irrigation water, and the Metropolitan Water District (MWD) of California, a public agency that supplies water to the Los Angeles area. Under that agreement the MWD bears the capital and operating costs, as well as the indirect costs (such as reduced hydropower), of a huge program to reduce seepage losses as the water is transported to the growers and to install new water-conserving irrigation techniques in the fields. In return the MWD will get all of the conserved water. Everyone gains. The district gets the water it needs at a reasonable price; the growers retain virtually the same amount of irrigation benefits without being forced to bear large additional expenditures.

Because the existing regulatory system created a very large inefficiency, moving to a more efficient allocation of water necessarily increased the net benefits. By using those additional net benefits in creative ways, it was possible to eliminate a serious environmental threat.

The success of this agreement has spawned others. For example, two water transfer agreements, finalized in October 2003, provide an additional 200,000 acre-feet of water annually to the San Diego region as a result of conservation measures taken in the Imperial Valley and financed by the municipal payments for the water.

Sources: Robert E. Taylor. *Ahead of the Curve: Shaping New Solutions to Environmental Problems* (New York: Environmental Defense Fund, 1990); San Diego County Water Authority http://www.sdcwo.org/manage/pdf/QSA_2004.pdf

Water markets and water banks are being increasingly utilized to transfer water seasonally via short-term leases or on a long-term basis, either by multiple-year leases or permanent transfers. While most markets and banks are restricted to certain geographic areas, water is allowed to move to its higher valued uses to some extent. Drought-year banks have been successful in California (Howitt, 1994; Israel and Lund, 1995). The transfer of water, however, can incur high transaction costs, both in the time necessary for approval (up to two years in some cases) and in potential downstream impacts (Saliba, 1987).

Achieving a balance between instream and consumptive uses is not easy. As the competition for water increases, the pressure to allocate larger amounts of the stream for consumptive uses increases as well. Eventually the water level becomes too low to support aquatic life and recreation activities.

Though they do exist (see Example 10.2), water rights for instream flow maintenance are few in number relative to rights for consumptive purposes. Those few instream rights that typically exist have a low priority relative to the more senior consumptive rights. As a practical matter this means that in periods of low water flow, the instream rights lose out and the water is withdrawn for consumptive uses. As long as the definition of "beneficial use" requires diversion, as it does in many states, water left for fish habitat or recreation is undervalued.

This undervaluation of instream uses is not inevitable, however, as some enterprising fishermen have discovered.[5] In the Yellowstone River Valley in Montana, several spring creeks are wholly contained within the boundaries of property owned by a single landowner. Since these creeks are not subject to the same legal restrictions as waterways crossing property boundaries, landowners can sell the daily fishing rights. The revenues from these sales provide owners with an incentive to develop spawning beds, protect the fish habitat, and in general, make the fishing experience as desirable as possible. By limiting the number of fishermen, the owners prevent overexploitation of the resource.

In England and Scotland, markets are relied upon to protect instream uses more than they are in the United States. Private angling associations have been formed to purchase fishing rights from landowners. Once these rights have been acquired, the associations charge for fishing, using some of the revenues to preserve and to improve the fish habitat. Since fishing rights in England sell for as much as $220,000, the holders of these rights have a substantial incentive to protect their investments. One of the forms this protection takes is illustrated by the Anglers Cooperative Association, which has taken on the responsibility of monitoring the streams for pollution and alerting the authorities to any potential problems.

Getting the prices right is another avenue for reform. Recognizing the inefficiencies associated with subsidizing the consumption of a scarce resource, the U.S. Congress passed the Central Valley Project Improvement Act in 1992. The act raises prices that the federal government charges for irrigation water, though the full-cost rate is imposed only on the final 20% of water received. Collected revenues will be placed in a fund to mitigate environmental damage in the Central Valley. The act also allows water transfers to new uses.

---

[5]These examples were drawn from Anderson (1983).

Example 10.2

PROTECTING INSTREAM USES THROUGH ACQUIRING WATER RIGHTS

Attempts by environmental groups to protect instream water uses must confront two problems. First, any acquired rights are usually public goods, implying that others can free ride on their provision without contributing to the cause. Consequently the demand for instream rights will be inefficiently low. The private acquisition of instream rights is not a sufficient remedy. Second, once the rights have been acquired, their use to protect instream flows may not be considered "beneficial use" (and therefore could be confiscated and granted to others for consumptive use) or they could be so junior as to be completely ineffective in times of low flow, the times when they would most be needed.

Some movement toward protecting instream rights has occurred, however. In 1979, in what was then a precedent-setting action, The Nature Conservancy, an environmental, public-interest organization, applied to Arizona's Department of Water Resources for a permit for "instream flow" at the Ramsey Canyon Preserve, asking essentially for both the right to a certain amount of water and for the right simply to leave it in the stream. When the permit was approved in 1983, this was the first legal recognition in Arizona of the right to appropriate water for wildlife and recreational uses without diverting water from a streambed. Protected by these water rights and other conservation measures, the preserve has become a haven for one of the largest arrays of plant and animal species of any preserve in the United States. Some 210 species of birds (including 14 species of hummingbirds), 420 species of plants, 45 species of mammals, and 20 species of reptiles and amphibians can be found in the canyon. Modest supplemental financial support is now derived from the access fees paid by the many visitors.

What worked at Ramsey Canyon was simple and straightforward, but it is not an adequate protection device in many places. Under the prior appropriation doctrine, any rights that predate the 1983-granted instream flow right would have entitled the holder to priority for the water.

Another approach has been followed in Colorado. Several years ago a subsidiary of the Chevron corporation gave The Nature Conservancy a gift entitling it to a 300 cubic-feet-per-second flow rate of water in the Black Canyon of Colorado's Gunnison River. Although Chevron held consumptive rights to the water, The Nature Conservancy was interested in instream rights. Because Colorado law stipulates that instream flow rights can be held only by the state, The Conservancy was faced with the "use it or lose it" rule under the prior appropriation doctrine. Taking the only step available, a transfer of the instream flow rights to the state was negotiated.

Sources: Ken Wiley. "Untying the Western Water Knot," *The Nature Conservancy* Vol. 40 (March/April 1990): 5–13; and Bonnie Colby Saliba and David B. Bush. *Water Markets in Theory and Practice: Market Transfers and Public Policy* (Boulder, CO: Westview Press, 1987): 74–77.

TABLE 10.1

Pricing Methods and Their Properties

Pricing Scheme	Implementation	Efficiency Achieved	Time Horizon of Efficiency	Ability to Control Demand
Volumetric	Complicated	First-best	Short-run	Easy
Output	Relatively easy	Second-best	Short-run	Relatively easy
Input	Easy	Second-best	Short-run	Relatively easy
Per-area	Easiest	None	n.a.	Hard
Block-rate (tiered)	Relatively Complicated	First-best	Short-run	Relatively easy
Two-part	Relatively Complicated	First-best	Long-run	Relatively easy
Water market	Difficult without preestablished institutions	First-best	Short-run	n.a.

n.a. not applicable.

Source: Tsur Yacov, Terry Roe, Rachid Doukkali, and Ariel Dinar. *Pricing Irrigation Water Principles and Cases from Developing Countries* (Washington, DC: Resources for the Future, 2004).

Tsur, et al. (2004) review and evaluate actual pricing practices for irrigation water in developing countries. Table 10.1 summarizes their findings with respect to both the types and properties of pricing systems they discovered. As the table reveals, they found some clear trade-offs between what efficiency would dictate and what was possible given the limited information available to water administrators.

Two-part charges and volumetric pricing, while quite efficient, require information on the amount of water used by each farmer and are rarely used in developing countries. (The two-part charge combines volume pricing with a monthly fee that doesn't vary with the amount of water consumed. The monthly fee is designed to help recover fixed costs.) Individual-user water meters can provide information on the volume of water used, but they are relatively expensive. Output pricing (where the charge for water is linked to agricultural output, not water use), on the other hand, is less efficient, but only requires data on each water user's production. Input-based pricing is even easier because it doesn't require monitoring either water use or output. Block-rate or tiered pricing is most common when demand has seasonal peaks. Tiered pricing examples can be found in Israel and California. Under input pricing, irrigators are assessed taxes on water-related inputs, such as a per-unit charge on fertilizer. Area pricing is probably the easiest to implement since the only information necessary is the amount of irrigated land and the type of crop produced on that land. Although this method is the most common, it is not efficient since the marginal cost of extra water use is zero.

Tsur, et al. propose a set of water reforms for developing countries, including pricing at marginal cost where possible and using block-rate prices to transfer wealth between water suppliers and farmers. This particular rate structure puts the burden of fixed costs on the relatively wealthier urban populations, who would, in turn, benefit from less expensive food.

For water distribution utilities, the traditional practice of recovering only the costs of distributing water and treating the water itself as a free good should be abandoned. Instead, utilities should adopt a pricing system that reflects increasing marginal cost and that includes a scarcity value for groundwater. Since scarce water is not in any meaningful sense a free good, the user cost of that water must be imposed on current users. Only in this way will the proper incentive for conservation be created and the interests of future generations of water users be preserved.

Including this user cost in water prices is rather more difficult than it may first appear. Water utilities are typically regulated because they have a monopoly in the local area. One typical requirement for the rate structure of a regulated monopoly is that it earn only a "fair" rate of return. Excess profits are not permitted. Charging a uniform price for water to all users where the price includes a user cost would generate profits for the seller. (Remember the discussion of scarcity rent in Chapter 4?) The scarcity rent accruing to the seller as a result of incorporating the user cost would represent revenue in excess of operating and capital costs.

Water utilities have a variety of options to choose from when charging their customers for water. Figure 10.4 illustrates the most common volume-based price structures. A surprisingly large number of U.S. utilities are using a flat fee, which from a scarcity point of view is the worst possible form of pricing. Since a flat fee is not based on volume, the marginal cost of additional water consumption is zero. ZERO! Water use by individual customers is not even metered.

While more complicated versions of a flat-fee system are certainly possible, they do not solve the incentive-to-conserve problem. At least up until the late 1970s Denver, Colorado, used eight different factors (including number of rooms, number of persons, number of bathrooms, and so on) to calculate the monthly bill. Despite the complexity of this billing system, because the amount of the bill was unrelated to actual volume used (water use was not metered), the marginal cost of additional water consumed was still zero.

Declining block pricing, another inefficient pricing system, is much more prevalent than increasing block pricing. By charging customers a higher marginal cost for low levels of water consumption and a lower marginal cost for higher levels, regulators are placing an undue financial burden on low-income people who consume little water, and confronting high-income people with a marginal cost that is too low to provide adequate incentives to conserve. Declining block rates were popular in cities with excess capacities, especially in the eastern United States, because they encouraged higher consumption as a means of spreading the fixed costs more widely. Additionally, municipalities attempting to attract business may find this rate appealing.

One way that water utilities are attempting to respect the rate of return requirement while promoting water conservation is through the use of an inverted (increasing) block rate. Under this system, the price per unit of water consumed rises as the amount consumed rises.

This type of structure encourages conservation by ensuring that the marginal cost of consuming additional water is high. At the margin, where the consumer makes the decision of how much extra water to be used, quite a bit of money can be

FIGURE 10.4

Overview of the Various Variable Charge Rate Structures

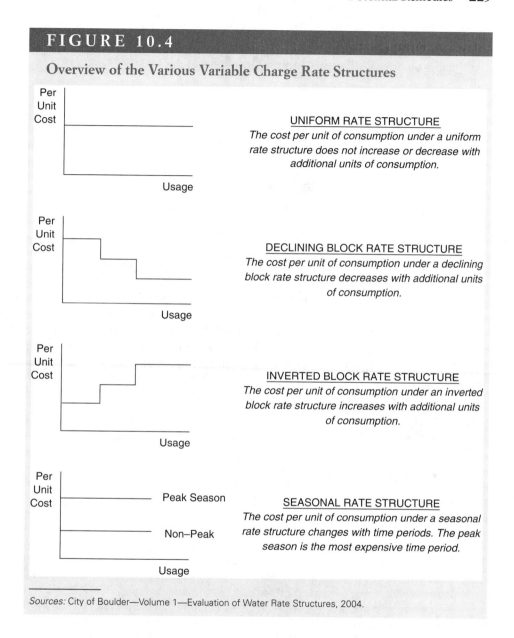

UNIFORM RATE STRUCTURE

The cost per unit of consumption under a uniform rate structure does not increase or decrease with additional units of consumption.

DECLINING BLOCK RATE STRUCTURE

The cost per unit of consumption under a declining block rate structure decreases with additional units of consumption.

INVERTED BLOCK RATE STRUCTURE

The cost per unit of consumption under an inverted block rate structure increases with additional units of consumption.

SEASONAL RATE STRUCTURE

The cost per unit of consumption under a seasonal rate structure changes with time periods. The peak season is the most expensive time period.

Sources: City of Boulder—Volume 1—Evaluation of Water Rate Structures, 2004.

saved by being frugal with water use. It also, however, holds revenue down by charging a lower price for the first units consumed. This has the added virtue that those who need some water, but cannot afford the marginal price paid by more extravagant users, can have access to water without placing their budget in as much jeopardy as would be the case with a uniform price. Many utilities base the first block on average winter (indoor) use.

How many U.S. utilities are using increasing block pricing? As Table 10.2 indicates, not many. Some evidence from Europe suggests that increasing block pricing

TABLE 10.2

Pricing Structures for Public Water Systems in the United States (1982–1997)

	1982 %	1987 %	1991 %	1997 %	2002 %
Flat Fee	1	—	3	2	2
Uniform Volume Charge	35	32	35	33	36
Decreasing Block	60	51	45	34	30
Increasing Block	4	17	17	31	32
Total	100	100	100	100	100

Sources: Household Water Pricing in OECD Countries. Copyright OECD 1999 and 2002 water and Wastewater Rate Survey, Raftelis Financial Consulting, 2002.

is not common there either (Harrington, 1987), although in individual cities like Zurich, Switzerland, it has made a considerable difference (see Example 10.3).

Other aspects of the rate structure are important as well. Efficiency dictates that prices equal the marginal cost of provision (including marginal user cost when appropriate). Several practical corollaries follow from this theorem. First, prices

Example 10.3

WATER PRICING IN ZURICH, SWITZERLAND

In 1975, largely in response to local groundwater pollution, Zurich instituted an excess charge that would be applied only if a customer exceeded a predefined consumption threshold. Households, for example, could consume up to 1,000 liters/day at the basic price. Every unit over that threshold, however, would be charged the much higher (initially double) per-unit rate. Other categories of consumers (such as commercial or industrial) faced a similar pricing system with unique thresholds and rates defined for each category.

Together with important changes in the wastewater pricing system, this rate structure seems to have made quite an impact. From 1970 to 1997, despite population increases, total water consumption in Zurich fell by 23%. (During this same period, Switzerland only achieved a 1% reduction.) In Zurich the amount of "excess" water consumed (the amount over the thresholds) fell from 7.3% to 3.7% of total consumption.

Source: Paul Harrington. *Household Water Pricing in OECD Countries* (Paris: Organization for Economic Co-operation and Development, 1999): 28–29.

during peak demand periods should exceed prices during off-peak periods. For water, peak demand is usually during the summer. It is peak use that strains the capacity of the system and therefore triggers the needs for expansion. Therefore, seasonal users should pay the extra costs associated with system expansion by being charged higher rates. Few current water pricing systems satisfy this condition in practice though some cities in the Southwest are beginning to use seasonal rates. Also, for municipalities using increasing block rates with the first block equal to average winter consumption, one could argue that this is essentially a seasonal rate for the average user. The average user is unlikely to be in the second or third blocks, except during summer months. The last graph in Figure 10.4 illustrates a seasonal uniform rate.

Another corollary of the marginal cost pricing theorem is that when it costs a water utility more to serve one class of customers than another, each class of customers should bear the costs associated with its respective service. Typically this implies, for example, that those farther away from the source or at higher elevations (requiring more pumping) should pay higher rates. In practice, utility water rates make fewer distinctions among customer classes than would be efficient. As a result, higher-cost water users are in effect subsidized; they receive too little incentive to conserve and too little incentive to locate in parts of the city that can be served at lower cost.

Until very recently, desalinized seawater has been prohibitively expensive and thus not a viable option outside of the Middle East. Recently, however, technological advances in reverse osmosis and distillation methods have reduced the price of desalinized water, making it a potential new source for water-scarce regions. Reverse osmosis works by pumping seawater at high pressure through permeable membranes. According to the World Bank, the cost of desalinized water has dropped from $1.00 per cubic meter to $0.50 per cubic meter in a period of five years (World Bank, 2004). Costs are expected to continue to fall, though not as rapidly. San Diego, California, and Tampa Bay, Florida, are examples of U.S. cities that have recently turned to this new technology for providing drinking water to their residents. While desalination holds some appeal as an option, it is only currently economically feasible for coastal cities, and concerns about the environmental impacts such as energy usage and brine disposal remain to be addressed (World Bank, 2004; California Coastal Commission, 1993).

In general, any solution should involve more widespread adoption of the principles of marginal cost pricing. More-expensive-to-serve users should pay higher prices for their water than their cheaper-to-serve counterparts. Similarly, when new, much-higher-cost sources of water are introduced into a water system to serve the needs of a particular category of user, those users should pay the marginal cost of that water, rather than the lower average cost of all water supplied. Finally, when a rise in the peak demand triggers a need for expanding either the water supplies or the distribution system, the peak demanders should pay the higher costs associated with the expansion.

These principles suggest a much more complicated rate structure for water than merely charging everyone the same price. As Example 10.4 demonstrates, the political consequences of introducing these changes may be rather drastic.

Example 10.4

POLITICS AND THE PRICING OF SCARCE WATER

As economics can make specific recommendations about the level and structure of water prices, politics can provide insights on the implementation of those recommendations. The implementation process is not always smooth or predictable, as the people of Tucson, Arizona, found out.

In 1976, the city of Tucson faced what it perceived as a water crisis. The development of its service capacity had not kept pace with rapid population growth, and artificially low prices reduced the incentive to conserve. The groundwater supplies on which the city depended were being depleted.

The utility, assisted by a newly elected city council, instituted a new rate structure involving higher water prices overall and more attention to the cost of service in determining the rate structure. An unexpectedly dry year (creating an abnormally high demand), coupled with a newly implemented increasing block rate structure, conspired to ensure that water bills increased tremendously soon after the change. The resulting anger of the residents spawned a recall campaign in which the councillors responsible for the rate increase were retired from office.

Are major changes in prices politically infeasible? The authors of the Tucson study believe not, though they do believe that feasible increases also have to be implemented with greater care. In particular, they believe that local politicians must be willing to take risks, that local residents must be convinced that a real problem exists, and that the burden of the increases must be distributed so no one group is asked to bear too large a share.

Under extreme circumstances, such as extreme drought, cities are more likely to be successful in passing large rate changes that are specifically designed to facilitate coping with that drought. During the period from 1987 to 1992, Santa Barbara, California, experienced one of the most severe droughts of the century. To deal with the crisis of excess demand the city of Santa Barbara changed both its rates and rate structures 10 times between 1987 and 1995 (Loaiciga and Renehan, 1997). Between March and October of 1990, an increasing block rate rose to $29.43 per ccf (748 gallons) in the highest block! Rates were subsequently lowered, but the higher rates were successful in causing water use to drop almost 50%. It seems that when a community is faced with extreme drought and community support for using pricing to cope is apparent, major changes in price are indeed possible.

Sources: William E. Manin, Helen M. Ingram, Nancy K. Laney, and Adrian H. Griffin. *Saving Water in a Desert City* (Washington, DC: Resources for the Future, 1984) and Hugo A. Loaiciga and Stephen Renehan. "Municipal Water Use and Water Rates Driven by Severe Drought: A Case Study," *Journal of the American Water Resources Association* Vol. 33, No. 6 (1997): 1313–1326.

Should Water Systems Be Privatized?

Faced with crumbling water supply systems and the financial burden from water subsidies, many urban areas in both industrialized and developing countries have privatized their water systems. Generally this is accomplished by selling the publicly owned water supply and distribution assets to a private company. The impetus behind this movement is the belief that private companies can operate more efficiently (thereby lowering costs and, hence, prices) and do a better job of improving both water quality and access by infusing these systems with new investment.

The problem with this approach is that water suppliers in many areas can act as a monopoly, using their power to raise rates beyond competitive levels, even if those rates are, in principle, subject to regulation. What happened in Cochabamba, Bolivia, illustrates just how serious a problem this can be.

After privatization in Cochabamba, water rates increased immediately, in some cases by 100 to 200%. The poor were especially hard hit. In January 2000, a four-day general strike in response to the water privatization brought the city to a total standstill. In February, the Bolivian government declared the protests illegal and imposed a military takeover on the city. Despite over 100 injuries and one death, the protests continued until in April the government agreed to terminate the contract.

Is Cochabamba typical? It certainly isn't the only example of privatization failure. Failure (in terms of a prematurely terminated privatization contract) also occurred in Atlanta, Georgia. The evidence is still out on its overall impact in other settings and whether we can begin to extract preconditions for its successful introduction, but it is very clear that privatization of water systems is no panacea and can be a disaster.

One strategy that has received more attention in the last couple of decades is the privatization of water supplies. The controversies that have arisen around this strategy are intense (see Debate 10.2).

However, it is important to distinguish between the different types of privatization since they can have quite different consequences. Privatization of water supplies creates the possibility of monopoly power and excessive rates, but privatization of access rights (such as discussed in Examples 10.1, 10.2, and 10.4 and Debate 10.1) does not.

Whereas privatization of water supplies turns the entire system over to the private sector, privatization of access rights only establishes specific quantified rights to use the publicly supplied water. As discussed earlier in this chapter, privatization of access rights is one way to solve the excesses that follow from the free-access problem, since the amount of water allocated by these rights would be designed to correspond to the amount available for sustainable use. And if these access rights are allocated fairly (a big if!) and if they are enforced consistently (another big if!), the security that enforceability provides can protect users, including poor or indigenous users, from encroachment. The question then becomes, "Are these rights allocated fairly and enforced consistently?" When they are, privatization of access rights can become beneficial for all users, not merely the rich.

Summary

Though on a global scale the amount of available water exceeds the demand, at particular times and in particular locations, water scarcity is already a serious problem. In a number of locations, the current use of water exceeds replenishable supplies, implying that aquifers are being irreversibly drained.

Efficiency dictates that replenishable water be allocated so as to equalize the marginal net benefits of water use even when supplies are higher or lower than normal. The efficient allocation of groundwater requires that the user cost of that depletable resource be considered. When marginal cost pricing (including marginal user cost) is used, water consumption patterns strike an efficient balance between present and future uses. Typically, the marginal pumping cost would rise over time until either it exceeded the marginal benefit received from that water or the reservoir runs dry.

In earlier times in the United States, markets played the major role in allocating water. But more recently governments have begun to play a much larger role in allocating this crucial resource.

Several sources of inefficiency are evident in the current system of water allocation in the southwestern United States. Transfers of water among various users are restricted so that the water remains in low-valued uses while high-valued uses are denied. Instream uses of water are actively discouraged in many western states. Prices charged for water by public suppliers typically do not cover costs, and the rate structures are not designed to promote efficient use of the resource. For groundwater, user cost is rarely included, and for all sources of water, the rate structure does not usually reflect the cost of service. These deficiencies combine to produce a situation in which we are not getting the most out of the water we are using and we are not conserving sufficient amounts for the future.

Reforms are possible. Allowing conservers to capture the value of water saved by selling it would stimulate conservation. Creating separate fishing rights that can be sold or allowing environmental groups to acquire and retain instream water rights would provide some incentive to protect streams as fish habitats. More utilities could adopt increasing block pricing as a means of forcing users to realize and to consider all of the costs of supplying the water.

Water scarcity is not merely a problem to be faced at some time in the distant future. In many parts of the world it is already a serious problem and unless preventive measures are taken, it will get worse. The problem is not insoluble, though to date the steps necessary to solve it have not yet been taken.

Discussion Questions

1. What pricing system best describes the pricing system used to price the water you use at your college or university? Does this pricing system affect your behavior about water use (length of showers, etc.)? How? Could you recommend a better pricing system in this circumstance? What would it be?
2. In your hometown what system is used to price the publicly supplied water? Why was that pricing system chosen? Would you recommend an alternative?
3. Suppose you come from a part of the world that is blessed with abundant water. Demand never comes close to the available amount. Should you be careful about the amount you use or should you simply use whatever you want whenever you want it? Why?

Problems

1. Suppose that in a particular area the consumption of water varies tremendously throughout the year, with average household summer use exceeding winter use by a great deal. What effect would this have on an efficient rate structure for water?
2. Is a flat-rate or flat-fee system more efficient for pricing scarce water? Why?

Further Reading

Anderson, Terry L. *Water Crisis: Ending the Policy Drought* (Washington, DC: Cato Institute, 1983): 81–85. A provocative survey of the political economy of water, concluding that we have to rely more on the market to solve the crisis.

Dinar, Ariel, and David Zilberman, eds. *The Economics and Management of Water and Drainage in Agriculture* (Norwell, MA: Kluwer Academic Publishers, 1991). Examines the special issues associated with water use in agriculture.

Easter, K. William, M. W. Rosegrant, and Ariel Dinar, eds. *Markets for Water: Potential and Performance* (Dordrecht: Kluwer Academic Publishers, 1998). This book not only develops the necessary conditions for water markets and illustrates how they can improve both water management and economic efficiency, but it also provides an up-to-date picture of what we have learned about water markets in a wide range of countries, from the United States to Chile and India.

Gibbons, Diana. *The Economic Value of Water* (Washington, DC: Resources for the Future, 1986). A detailed survey and synthesis of existing studies on the economic value of water in various uses.

Harrington, Paul. *Pricing of Water Services* (Organization for Economic Cooperation and Development, 1987). An excellent survey of the water pricing practices in the OECD countries.

MacDonnell, L. J., and D. J. Guy. "Approaches to Groundwater Protection in the Western United States," *Water Resources Research* Vol. 27 (1991): 259–265. Discusses groundwater protection in practice.

Martin, William E., Helen M. Ingram, Nancy K. Laney, and Adrian H. Griffin. *Saving Water in a Desert City* (Washington, DC: Resources for the Future, 1984). A detailed look at the political and economic ramifications of an attempt by Tucson, Arizona, to improve the pricing of its diminishing supply of water.

Saliba, Bonnie Colby, and David B. Bush. *Water Markets in Theory and Practice: Market Transfers and Public Policy* (Boulder, CO: Westview Press, 1987): 74–77. A highly recommended, accessible study of the way western water markets work in practice in the United States.

Spulber, Nicholas, and Asghar Sabbaghi. *Economics of Water Resources: From Regulation to Privatization* (Hingham, MA: Kluwer Academic Publishers, 1993). Detailed analysis of the incentive structures created by alternative water management regimes.

Additional References is available on this book's companion Web site www.aw-bc.com/tietenberg.

Reproducible Private-Property Resources: Agriculture

The Rome Declaration calls upon us to reduce by half the number of chronically undernourished people on the Earth by the year 2015. . . . If each of us gives his or her best I believe that we can meet and even exceed the target we have set for ourselves.

—H. E. Romano Prodi, President of the Council of Ministers of the Italian Republic and Chairman of the World Food Summit, 1996

We have the possibility to do it. We have the knowledge. We have the resources. And with the Rome Declaration and the Plan of Action, we've shown that we have the will.

—Dr. Jacques Diouf, Director-General of FAO, World Food Summit, 1996

Introduction

In 1974, the World Food Conference set a goal of eradication of hunger, food insecurity, and malnutrition within a decade. This goal was never met. The Food and Agriculture Organization of the United Nations (FAO) estimated that without faster progress, 680 million people would still face hunger by the year 2010 and that more than 250 million of these people would be in Sub-Saharan Africa. Amidst growing concern about widespread undernutrition and about the capacity of agriculture to meet future food needs, a World Food Summit was called. The World Food Summit was held at FAO headquarters in Rome in November 1996. Ten thousand participants representing 185 countries and the European community attended.

The Rome Declaration on World Food Security, which came out of the Food Summit, set a target of reducing by half the number of undernourished people by 2015. In June 2002, at a subsequent World Food Summit, some delegates from 179 countries plus the European Commission reiterated their pledge to meet this goal. How close are we to meeting this goal? The evidence is not encouraging.

According to the U.N. Hunger Project, the International Fund for Agricultural Development (2002), and FAO (2003),

- More than 800 million people in the world still suffer from chronic hunger and malnutrition.
- More than one-quarter of these, or 215 million, are children.
- From 1995–1997 to 1999–2001, the number of undernourished actually increased by 18 million.
- About 24,000 people die each day from hunger or hunger-related causes. Malnutrition is a factor in more than half of the 10.8 million child deaths per year.
- One-third of all the children in the developing countries are malnourished. The problem is most severe in South Asia and Sub-Saharan Africa.

In the United States, approximately one in ten households (or 33.6 million people) experience hunger or the risk of hunger (Nord et al., 2002).

According to the Food and Agriculture Organization, the total amount of available food is not the problem; the world produces plenty of food to feed everyone. World agriculture produces 17% more calories *per person* today than 30 years ago, despite the fact that population has increased by 70% over the same time period (FAO, 2002; FAO, 1998). If this is the case, why are so many people hungry?

Cereal grain, the world's chief supply of food, is a renewable private-property resource that, if managed effectively, could be sustained as long as we receive energy from the sun. Are current agricultural practices sustainable? Are they efficient? Because land is typically not a free-access resource, farmers have an incentive to invest in irrigation and other means of increasing yield because they can appropriate the additional revenues generated. On the surface, a flaw in the market process is not apparent. We must dig deeper to uncover the sources of the problem.

In this chapter we shall explore the validity of three common hypotheses used to explain widespread malnourishment: (1) a persistent global scarcity of food; (2) a maldistribution of that food both among nations and within nations; and (3) temporary shortages caused by weather or other natural causes. These hypotheses are not mutually exclusive; they could all be valid sources of a portion of the problem. As we shall see, it is important to distinguish among these sources and assess their relative importance because each implies a different policy approach.

Global Scarcity

To some, this onset of a food crisis suggests a need for dramatic changes in the relationship between the agricultural surplus nations and other nations. Garrett Hardin (1974), a human ecologist, has suggested the situation is so desperate that our conventional ethics, which involve sharing the available resources, are not only insufficient, but are also counterproductive. He argues we must replace these dated notions of sharing with more stern "lifeboat ethics."

The allegory he invokes envisions a lifeboat adrift in the sea that can safely hold 50 or, at most, 60 persons. Hundreds of other persons are swimming about, clamoring to get into the lifeboat, their only chance for survival. Hardin suggests that if passengers in the boat were to follow conventional ethics and allow swimmers into the boat, it would eventually sink, taking everyone to the bottom of the sea. In contrast, he argues, lifeboat ethics would suggest a better resolution of the dilemma; the 50 or 60 should row away, leaving the others to certain death, but saving those fortunate enough to gain entry into the lifeboat. The implication is that food sharing is counterproductive. It would encourage more population growth and ultimately would cause inevitable, even more serious shortages in the future.

The existence of a global scarcity of food is the premise that underlies this view; when famine is inevitable, sharing can become counterproductive. In the absence of global scarcity (the lifeboat has a large enough capacity for all), then a worldwide famine can be avoided by a sharing of resources. How accurate is the global scarcity premise?

Formulating the Global Scarcity Hypothesis

Most authorities seem to agree that an adequate amount of food is currently being produced. Because the evidence is limited to a single point in time, however, it provides little sense of whether scarcity is decreasing or increasing. If we are to identify and evaluate trends, we must develop more precise, measurable notions of how the market allocates food.

As a renewable resource, cereal grains could be produced indefinitely, if managed correctly. Yet two facets of the world hunger problem have to be taken into account. First, while population growth has slowed down, it has not stopped. Therefore, it is reasonable to expect the rising demand for food to continue. Second, the primary input for growing food is land, and land is ultimately fixed in supply. Thus, our analysis must explain how a market reacts in the presence of rising demand for a renewable resource that is produced using a fixed factor of production.

A substantial and dominant proportion of the Western world's arable land is privately owned. Access to this land is restricted; the owners have the right to exclude others and can reap what they sow. The typical owner of farmland has sufficient control over the resource to prevent undue depreciation, but not enough control over the market as a whole to raise the specter of monopoly profits.

What kind of outcome could we expect from this market in the face of rising demand and a fixed supply of land? What do we mean by scarcity and how could we perceive its existence? The answer depends crucially on the nature of the supply curve (see Figure 11.1).

Suppose the market is initially in equilibrium with quantity Q_0 supplied at price P_0. Let the passage of time be recorded as outward shifts in the demand curve. Consider what would happen in the fifth time period. If the supply curve were S_a, the quantity would rise to Q_{5a}. However, if the supply curve were S_b, the quantity supplied would rise to Q_{5b}, but price would rise to P_{5b}.

This analysis sheds light on what is meant by scarcity in the world food market. It does not mean a shortage. Even under relatively adverse supply circumstances pictured by the supply curve S_b, the amount of food supplied would equal the amount demanded. As prices rose, potential demand would be choked off and additional supplies would be called forth.

FIGURE 11.1

The Market for Food

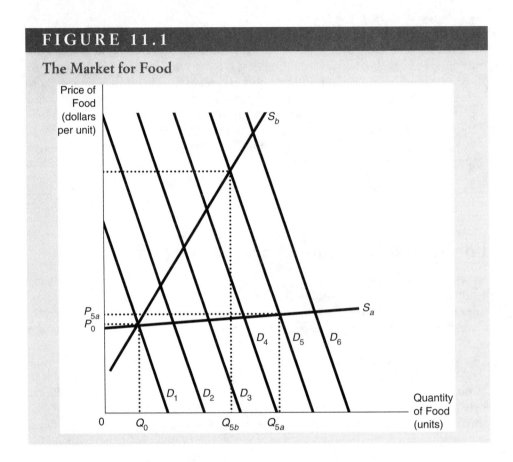

Some critics argue that the demand for food is not price sensitive. Since food is a necessary commodity for survival, they say, its demand is inflexible and doesn't respond to prices. While some food is necessary, not all food fits that category. We don't have to gaze very long at an average vending machine in a developed country to conclude that some food is far from a necessity.

Examples of food purchases being price-responsive abound. One occurred during the 1960s when the price of meat skyrocketed for what turned out to be a relatively short period. It wasn't long before hamburger substitutes made entirely out of soybean meal, appeared in supermarkets. The result was a striking reduction in meat consumption. This is a particularly important example because the raising of livestock for meat in Western countries consumes an enormous amount of grain. This evidence suggests that the balance between the direct consumption of cereal grains and the indirect consumption through meat is affected by prices.

But enough about the demand side; what do we know of the supply side? What factors would determine whether S_a or S_b is a more adequate representation of the past and the future?

While rising prices certainly stimulate a supply response, the question is: how much? As the demand for food rises, the supply can be increased either by expanding the amount of land under cultivation, or by increasing the yields on the land already under cultivation, or some combination of the two. Historically, both sources have been important.

Typically, the most fertile land is cultivated first. That land is then farmed more and more intensively until it is cheaper, at the margin, to bring additional, less fertile land into production. Because it is less fertile, the additional land is brought into production only if the prices rise enough to make farming it profitable. Thus the supply curve for arable land (and hence for food, as long as land remains an important factor of production) can be expected to slope upward.

Two forms of the global scarcity hypothesis can be tested against the available evidence. The *strong form* suggests that per capita food production is declining. In terms of Figure 11.1, the strong form of the hypothesis would imply that the slope of the supply curve is sufficiently steep that production does not keep pace with increases in demand brought about by population growth. If the strong form is valid, we should witness declining per capita food production. If valid, this form could provide some support for lifeboat ethics.

The *weak form* of the global scarcity hypothesis can hold even if per capita production is increasing over time. It suggests that the supply curve is sufficiently steeply sloped that food prices are increasing more rapidly than other prices in general; the relative price of food is rising over time. If the weak form is valid, per capita welfare is declining, even if production is rising. The problem is related more to the cost of food than the availability of food; as supplies of food increase, the cost of food rises relative to the cost of other goods.

Testing the Hypothesis

Now that we have a testable hypothesis, we can assess the degree to which the historical record supports the existence of increasing global scarcity. The evidence for per capita production is clear. Food production has increased faster than population in both the developed and developing countries. Per capita production has increased, although the increase has been small. Thus, at least for the recent past, we can rule out the strong form of the global scarcity hypothesis.

How about the weak form? According to the evidence, the supply curve for agricultural products is more steeply sloped than the supply curve for products in general in about half the countries. The experience of those countries, at least, provides some support for the weak form of the global scarcity hypothesis. Since not all market prices are efficient, as we shall see later in this chapter, we must not place too much faith in studies based purely on prices. Even so, the evidence suggests that agricultural supplies have increased faster than population but at an increasing relative cost.

Outlook for the Future

What factors will influence the future relative costs of food? A continuation of past trends would suggest a major role for the developing nations to supply an increasing share of world food production to meet their increasing shares of population and also on the ability of the developed nations to continue their role as a major food exporter. The ability of developing nations to expand their role is considered in the next section as a part of the food-distribution problem. In this section, therefore, we deal with forces affecting productivity in the industrialized nations.

Rather dramatic historic increases in crop productivity were stimulated by improvements in machinery; increasing utilization of commercial fertilizers, pesticides and herbicides; developments in plant and animal breeding; expanding use of irrigation water; and adjustments in location of crop production. For example, in the United States, corn is produced on more acreage than any other crop. Yields per acre quadrupled between 1930 and 2000 from approximately 30 bushels per acre to about 130 bushels per acre. Milk and dairy production is another industry showing marked productivity improvements. In 1944, average production per cow was 4,572 pounds. By 1971, the average had risen to 10,000 pounds. By the end of the 20th century, the average had risen to 17,000 pounds per cow! Other areas of the livestock industry show similar trends.

Table 11.1 shows some of the trends in agriculture that have occurred during the 20th century. Among other aspects, it points out that a huge shift to mechanization has occurred as farm equipment dependent upon depletable fossil fuels is substituted for animal power, which was fueled by renewable biological resources. This trend has provided the foundation for an increase in scale of the average farm and a reduction in the number of farms, but it also raises questions about the sustainability of that path.

Technological Progress.   Technological progress provides the main source of support for optimism about continued productivity increases. Three techniques appear particularly promising: (1) recombinant DNA, which permits recombining genes from one species with those of another; (2) tissue culture, which allows whole plants to be grown from single cells; and (3) cell fusion, which involves uniting the cells of species that would not normally mate to create new types of plants different from "parent" cells. Applications for these generic engineering techniques include:

1. Making food crops more resistant to diseases and insect pests.
2. Creating hardy, new crop plants capable of surviving in marginal soils.
3. Giving staple food crops such as corn, wheat, and rice the ability to make their own nitrogen-rich fertilizers by using solar energy to make ammonia from nitrogen in the air.
4. Increasing crop yields by improving the way plants use the sun's energy during photosynthesis.

Five concerns have arisen regarding the ability of the industrial nations to achieve further productivity gains: the declining share of land allocated to agricultural use, the rising cost of energy, the rising environmental cost of traditional forms of agriculture, the role of price distortions in agricultural policy, and potential side effects from the new genetically modified crops. A close examination of these concerns reveals that current agricultural practices in the industrial nations may be neither efficient nor sustainable and a transition to agriculture that is both efficient and sustainable could involve lower productivity levels.

TABLE 11.1

Trends in U.S. Agriculture A 20th-Century Time Capsule

	Beginning of the Century (1900)	End of the Century (1997)
Number of Farms	5,739,657	1,911,859
Average Farm Acreage	147 acres	487 acres
Crops		
Percent of Farms Growing:		
Corn	82%	23%
Hay	62%	46%
Vegetables	61%	3%
Irish potatoes	49%	1%
Orchards[1]	48%	6%
Oats	37%	5%
Soybeans	- 0 -	19%
Livestock		
Percent of Farms Raising:		
Cattle	85%	55%
Milk cows	79%	6%
Hogs & pigs	76%	6%
Chickens[2]	97%	5%
Farm Mechanization		
Percent of Farms with:		
Wheel Tractors[3]	4%	89%
Horses	79%	20%
Mules	26%	2%
Government Payments	- 0 -	$5 billion
Percent Population Living on Farms[4]	39.2%	1.8% (1990)
Percent Labor Force on Farms[5]	38.8%	1.7% (1990)

Source: USDA, National Agricultural Statistics Service on Web at http://www.usda.gov/nass/pubs/trends/timecapsule.htm/.

[1]1929 Census of Agriculture.

[2]1910 Censuscensus of Agriculture.

[3]1920 Census of Agriculture.

[4]Bureau of the Census.

[5]Bureau of Labor Statistics.

Allocation of Agricultural Land.   According to the 2002 Census of U.S. Agriculture, land in farms was estimated at 938 million acres, down from approximately 955 million acres in 1997. The corresponding acreage in 1974 was 1.1 million acres. Total cropland in 2002 was approximately 434 million acres, 55 million of which was irrigated. The corresponding irrigated acreage in 1974 was approximately 41 million acres. While total land in farms has dropped considerably, irrigated acreage has been rising.

More than 50% of the agricultural cropland has been converted to nonagricultural purposes since 1920. A simple extrapolation of this trend would certainly raise questions about our ability to increase productivity at historical rates. Is a simple extrapolation reasonable? What determines the allocation of land between agricultural and nonagricultural uses?

Agricultural land will be converted to nonagricultural land when its profitability in nonagricultural uses is higher. If we are to explain the historical experience, we must be able to explain why the relative value of land in agriculture has declined.

Two factors stand out. First, an increasing urbanization and industrialization of society rapidly raised the value of nonagricultural land. Second, rising productivity of the remaining land allowed the smaller amount of land to produce a lot more food. Less agricultural land was needed to meet the demand for food.

It seems unlikely that simple extrapolation of the decline in agricultural land of the magnitude since 1920 would be accurate. Since the middle of the 1970s, the urbanization process has diminished to the point that many urban areas are experiencing declining population. This shift is not merely explained by suburbia spilling beyond the boundaries of what was formerly considered urban. For the first time in our history, a significant amount of population has moved from urban to rural areas.

Furthermore, as increases in food demand are accompanied by increased prices of food, the value of agricultural land should increase. Higher food prices would tend to slow conversion and possibly even reverse the trend. To make this impact even greater, several states have now allowed agricultural land to either escape the property tax (until it is sold for some nonagricultural purpose) or to pay lower rates. Confirming evidence for this generally optimistic assessment can be found in the fact that most of the conversion to nonagricultural uses actually occurred prior to World War II.

Energy Costs.   Agricultural production in the industrial nations is very energy intensive. Some major portion of the productivity gains resulted from energy—using mechanization and the increased use of pesticides and fertilizers, which are derived from petroleum feedstocks and natural gas. As we saw in Chapter 8, the costs of petroleum and natural gas have risen substantially and probably can be expected to continue to rise in real terms as the available supplies of fossil fuels are exhausted or global warming concerns diminish their use. To the extent that energy-intensive producers cannot develop cheaper substitutes, the supply curve must shift to the left to reflect the increasing costs of doing business.

As suggested by Table 11.1, energy and capital have become complements in industrialized country agriculture. Due to this complementary relationship, energy price increases could be expected to trigger some reduction in capital, as well as some reduction in energy on the typical energy-intensive farm, reducing the yield per acre.

Environmental Costs.   Part of the past improvements in agricultural productivity has come at the cost of intensifying the environmental problems caused by agriculture. Not only has the use of land intensified (with a resulting increase in the use of chemicals and fertilizers), but grasslands and forests have been converted to farming.

Another source of environmental problems, soil erosion, has a different origin. Some soil erosion is natural, of course, and within certain tolerance limits does not harm productivity. The concern arises because some farm practices partially responsible for increasing productivity (continuous cropping rather than rotations with pasture or other soil-retaining crops) have tended to exacerbate soil erosion. The fears are further intensified by the belief that these losses are irreversible within one generation.

If increased soil erosion is taking place, why would a private-property owner allow this depletion? In the past, soil conservation simply did not pay. The techniques to avoid it were expensive and the ready availability of cheap fertilizer to replace lost nutrients meant that the cost of soil depletion was low. Further, the damage caused to rivers and streams by this eroding soil was not borne by the farmers who could best control it.

The factors that prevented erosion from being checked are now disappearing. As the level of topsoil reaches lower tolerance limits, the fertility of the land is affected. Rising cost and pollution concerns are making fertilizers a less desirable substitute for soil conservation, and public policy has begun to subsidize soil erosion control techniques. In 1985, the U.S. Congress authorized the Conservation Reserve Program, which was designed to reduce soil erosion and to stimulate tree planting. Average enrollment in the program peaked at 36.4 million acres in 1996. It is expected to reduce soil erosion by hundreds of millions of tons per year, to decrease sediment in reservoirs and streams, to increase the protection of recreational resources, and to preserve the long-term productivity of the land. In the near future we may see more soil conservation techniques practiced because they are becoming profitable.

Some past agricultural practices have caused environmental damage, and the continuation of these would cause rising environmental costs. In recent years the frequency and quantity of agricultural chemicals have increased dramatically. One effect of this has been using levels of nitrates in drinking water. In addition, some of the nutrients from fertilizers leak into lakes and stimulate the excessive growth of algae. Aside from the aesthetic cost to a body of water choked with plant life, this nutrient excess can deprive other aquatic life-forms of the oxygen they need to survive.

Pesticide use has also increased. A great deal of pest control in the recent past has relied upon pesticides. Many of these persist in the environment, and some toxicity extends to species other than the target population. The herbicides and pesticides can contaminate water supplies, rendering them unfit for drinking and for supporting normal populations of fish.

Throughout all Organisation for Economic Co-operation and Development (OECD) countries, "sustainable agriculture" is being increasingly associated with the reduced use of pesticides and mineral fertilizers. And policies have been established to facilitate the transition. Denmark and Sweden are pursuing ambitious agricultural chemical reduction targets. In Austria, Finland, the Netherlands, and Sweden a variety of input taxes and input levies have recently been introduced. The charges provide an incentive to use smaller amounts of agricultural chemicals while the revenue is used to ease the transition by funding research on alternative approaches and the dissemination of information. According to the OECD (1988), many OECD countries expect little or no effect on crop yields.

While most European countries are focusing on eliminating input subsidies (on pesticides or fertilizers, for example), taxing inputs or directly limiting their use, New Zealand has taken a more radical step by scrapping most of its agricultural supports. According to a study conducted for the New Zealand Ministry of Agriculture (Reynolds, et al., 1993), the environmental consequences were rather profound. Fertilizer use declined, farms have become more diversified, most marginal land is now grazed less intensively, and the excessive conversion of land has stopped.

Irrigation can increase yields of most crops by 100 to 400%. The FAO estimates that over the next 30 years, 70% of the gains in cereal production will come from irrigated land, and irrigated land in the developing countries will increase by 27% by 2030.

However, irrigation, a traditional source of productivity growth, is also running into limits, particularly in the western United States. Some traditionally important underground sources used to supply water are not being replenished at a rate sufficient to offset the withdrawals. Encouraged by enormous subsidies that transfer the cost to the taxpayers, these water supplies are being exhausted. Those that remain are subject to rising levels of salt. Irrigation of soils with naturally occurring salts causes a concentration of the salts near the surface. This salty soil is less productive and, in extreme cases, kills the crops.

The organic foods industry is the fastest-growing U.S. food segment. Growth has been at about 20% annually since 1990 when the USDA National Organic Program was established. Acreage of certified organic cropland in the United States more than doubled between 1992 and 1997 alone. Projections of organic product sales anticipate that they will triple over a four-year period.

Organic food sales represent approximately 2% of total U.S. food sales. Of this 2%, fresh fruits and vegetables make up 43%; breads and grains, 13%; and dairy products, 11%. The remainder is made up of packaged and prepared foods, beverages, soy products, and meat and poultry. Although meat and poultry represents less than 3% of organic sales, it is the fastest-growing portion of this market at a rate of 78%.[1]

A recent source of encouragement for organic farms has been the demonstrated willingness of consumers to pay a premium for organically grown fruits and vegetables.[2] Since it would be relatively easy for producers to claim their produce was organically grown, even if it were not, organic growers need a reliable certification process to assure the consumers that they are indeed getting what they pay for. Additionally, fear of lost access to important foreign markets such as the European Union led to an industry-wide push for mandatory labeling standards. Since the value of labeling depends in large degree on the credibility of the labeling service, a nationally uniform seal was sought. Voluntary U.S. certification programs had not ensured access to foreign markets such as the European Union since they were highly variable by state.

In response to these pressures, the Organic Foods Production Act (OFPA) was enacted in the 1990 Farm Bill. Title 21 of that law states the following

---

[1]USDA and Organic Trade Associations's 2004 Manufacturer Survey.

[2]Thompson and Kidwell (1998) found premiums ranged from 40 to 175% for fresh organic fruits and vegetables.

objectives: "1) to establish national standards governing the marketing of certain agricultural products as organically produced; 2) to assure consumers that organically produced products meet a consistent standard; and 3) to facilitate interstate commerce in fresh and processed food that is organically produced."[3]

The USDA National Organic Program, established as part of this Act, is responsible for a mandatory certification program for organic production. The Act also established the National Organic Standards Board (NOSB) and charged it with defining the "organic" standards. The new rules, which took effect in October 2002, require certification by the USDA for labeling. Foods labeled as "100 percent organic" must contain only organic ingredients. Foods labeled as "organic" must contain at least 95% organic agricultural ingredients, excluding water and salt. Products labeled as "Made with Organic Ingredients" must contain at least 70% organic agricultural ingredients.

The European Union has followed a similar, but by no means identical, policy. Table 11.2 compares the U.S. and EU programs. With the U.S. standards now in place, U.S. and EU officials are working on developing an equivalency agreement to expedite and facilitate trade between the two regions.

Is labeling the best policy approach? Does it create efficient incentives? As Example 11.1 points out, labeling certainly represents a movement toward efficiency, but because it does not internalize all important externalities, it is unlikely to get us all the way.

The Role of Agricultural Policies

Past gains in agricultural productivity have come at a large environmental cost. Why? Part of the answer, of course, can be found in an examination of the externalities associated with agriculture. Many of the costs of farming are not borne by the farmers, but by others subjected to contaminated groundwater and polluted streams. But that is not the whole story. Government policies must bear some of the responsibility as well.

Government policies have completely subverted the normal functioning of the price system. Three types of agricultural policies are involved: (1) subsidies for specific farming inputs such as equipment, fertilizers, or pesticides; (2) guaranteed prices for outputs; and (3) trade barriers to protect against competition from imports.

Subsidies have helped to create a dependence on purchased inputs.[4] One study (Anderson and Blackhurst, 1992) examined whether the size of the farm subsidy (as measured by its proportion to total income) across countries was correlated with fertilizer use in those countries. It was. Countries with the largest subsidies used considerably more fertilizer than those with little or no subsidies. The subsidies made it possible to use inefficient and unsustainable levels of fertilizer.

---

[3]Golan, et al. (2001).

[4]It has also been argued that these subsidies have been designed to help poor farmers, but this argument is not persuasive. Because they produce only one-tenth of the output, poor farmers receive only $1 from every $10 of subsidies paid. See "The Economist Survey of Agriculture" (1993): 7.

TABLE 11.2

Comparison of EU and U.S. Standards

I. Both systems share the following:
   1. Third-Party Certification
   2. Audit Trails
   3. Annual Inspections
   4. Accreditation
   5. Materials Lists
   6. Defined Conversion Periods
   7. Sustainable Farm Plan

II. Agriculture Conversion Period
   1. U.S.—requires a three-year conversion period with no exceptions
   2. EU—generally requires two years for annuals and three years for perennials, with some exceptions.

III. Manure Restrictions—The EU has load limits on manure applications for livestock and other organic cropping operations, while the U.S. requires minimum periods prior to harvest.

IV. Buffer Zones—The U.S. requires buffer zones; the EU does not require buffer zones.

V. Milk Production—May be certified as organic in the U.S. after 12 months on 100% organic program, whereas EU rules allow for organic production at 6 months.

VI. Organic Feedstuffs—In-conversion allowances (30–60%) of transitional and conventional feedstuffs for organic livestock production in the EU are not found in the U.S. (requiring 100%).

VII. Healthcare—No antibiotics or hormones are allowed in the U.S., however, the EU does include exemptions for synthetic veterinary medicines and allows for treatments up to three times per year.

VIII. Labeling requirements are similar.
   1. "Organic"—Both agree that at least 95% of the ingredients must be organic.
   2. "Made With"—Both agree that 70% of the ingredients must be organic. In the EU the remaining 30% must be on published lists of "not commercially available ingredients." This list is subject to interpretation by the certifier or Member State.
   3. "Below 70%—EU does not allow "organic" to appear anywhere on the label. U.S. allows identification of organic ingredients on the information panel in products containing 50% or more organic ingredients.
   4. Percent organic declarations in the U.S. are not mandatory, but in some EU situations declaration may be required.
   5. Under EU regulations, "transition to organic" labeling is allowed. In the U.S. such labeling is not allowed.

Source: Organic Trade Association, 2003.

Example **11.1**

DO MANDATORY LABELS CORRECT EXTERNALITIES?

Governments have a variety of policy tools available to address issues of asymmetric information and to control externalities, such as those associated with conventional farming. Policy options include Pigouvian taxes, bans, quotas, educational programs, disclosure strategies (such as labeling), and direct regulation of production or marketing. Theory suggests that labeling will be a sufficient policy tool only if all costs and benefits of consumption choices are borne by the consumer. However, if the consumption of a food creates an externality, then information-based policy will not result in efficient choices.

Are externalities involved? They clearly are. Consider, for example, the potential effects of choosing to purchase organic foods on the quality of drinking water. If conventional agriculture affects local drinking water by its application of fertilizers and pesticides, switching production to organically grown food will diminish the environmental damage. Do consumers of organic products reap all the benefits? In general, they do not. All users of that drinking water benefit, whether or not they purchase organic foods. Consumers of organic food confer an external benefit on the others.

Mandatory food labeling does alleviate problems of asymmetric information (where the producer knows the production techniques, but in the absence of labeling, the consumer does not). In this case consumer can use this information to make superior choices in terms of their own preferences. However, labeling is rarely effective in addressing problems related to environmental externalities or other spillover effects associated with food production or consumption.

Source: Elise Golan, et al. "Economics of Food Labeling," *Journal of Consumer Policy* Vol. 24, No. 2 (2001): 117–184.

Subsidies have become an important component of farm income, making them difficult to eliminate. Agricultural subsidies in the United States and the European Union are responsible for about one-third and one-half of all farm income, respectively. In Japan farmers earn twice as much income from subsidies as from the practice of agriculture. In Switzerland the comparable figure is four times agricultural income.

Recently, however, governments have begun to encourage sustainable agriculture, not only by discouraging the harmful side effects of traditional agriculture, but also by learning more about sustainable practices and disseminating the information derived from this research. In addition, both the United States and the European Union offer financial assistance for the transition to sustainable agriculture.

A Summing Up

Agricultural productivity in the industrialized countries can be expected to rise in the future, but at lower rates. Part of the large historic increases in agricultural productivity was based upon unsustainable, inefficient, and environmentally destructive agricultural practices, which were supported and encouraged by agricultural subsidies. In the future we can expect that as farmers become less insulated from the energy and environmental costs as subsidies are removed, some of the expected gains from technological progress will be offset.

In addition to changes in the productivity of agriculture in the future, we can also expect changes in agricultural practices. A transition to alternative agriculture appears to be under way. While the growth of the organic foods industry provides one example, new technology in the form of genetically modified organisms is another. Genetically modified foods have sparked a great debate (Debate 11.1). Since the economic, social, and economic costs and benefits of GMOs are multifaceted and uncertain, it remains to be seen whether consumers will support or reject this new technology (Example 11.2).

Distribution of Food Resources

The second hypothesis used to explain widespread malnourishment holds that the problem may stem more from food distribution than from global availability. According to this outlook, the basic problem is poverty. We would expect, therefore, that the poorest segments of society would be the most malnourished and that the poorest countries would contain the largest proportion of malnourished people.

If accurate, this representation suggests a very different policy orientation from that suggested by global scarcity. If the problem is maldistribution rather than shortage, the issue is how to get the food to the poorest people. The alleviation of poverty, increasing the ability to pay for food, is a strategy that could alleviate the problem. If the problem were a lack of food, this strategy would be totally ineffectual.

Defining the Problem

Considerable and persuasive evidence suggests that the problem is one of distribution (see Table 11.3). Though the data are far from perfect, a number of interesting conclusions can be drawn. Looking at the top line first, we find that the average member of the developing world has a sufficient caloric intake. This reinforces our conclusion that the problem is not one of global scarcity. It is also clear, however, that the food is not uniformly distributed among the world's peoples. For the least developed countries, the average diet contained fewer calories than necessary to prevent nutritional deficiency.

Equally revealing, however, is the trend. Though clear progress has been made in the developing countries as a whole in increasing per capita food production, production in the least developed countries failed to keep pace with population. For the poorest countries, not only was the average diet woefully inadequate at the beginning of the period, but the situation has deteriorated during the intervening 20 years. Furthermore, their dependency on food imports has grown.

Should Genetically Modified Organisms Be Banned?

One controversy surrounding genetically modified organisms (GMOs) is whether the commercialization of these plants or animals should be banned or delayed because of their potentially damaging environmental impacts. Because they contain genetic combinations that do not occur in nature through normal evolution, GMOs are exotic species. When introduced into open, complex ecosystems, they raise the possibility of imposing significant social externalities. Since these modified plants or animals are new to the ecosystem, their effects on all the other elements of the ecosystem are simply unknown. Some of these effects could prove to be very detrimental and irreversible (NRC, 2002). Even if these effects could in principle be managed (a controversial point), successful management would crucially depend upon what many see as an unrealistic degree of oversight and control by farmers.

Economic concerns have been raised as well. Some observers believe the new technologies could favor large farmers or multinational corporations to the detriment of smaller farmers (Nelson, et al., 1999).

In contrast, supporters suggest that genetically modified plants and animals have the potential to considerably boost world food production at a reasonable cost. Reducing the cost of food and fiber production would reduce the threat posed by the weak scarcity hypothesis. Using GMOs to reduce the rate of application of chemical pesticides could lessen the chemical contamination of water supplies and reduce the exposure of farm workers to pest-control chemicals. Genetically modified food organisms offer the possibility of introducing more nutrients and reducing health-threatening substances (such as saturated fats) into traditional food sources as well as the possibility of creating plants that grow more productively in less hospitable climates or soil types.

Banning the use of GMOs could prevent the externalities and the possible associated irreversible damage, but it could also reduce food availability and increase cost.

Sources: Sandra S. Batie. "The Environmental Impacts of Genetically Modified Plants: Challenges to Decision-Making," *American Journal of Agricultural Economics* Vol. 85, No. 5 (2003): 1107–1111; Wallace E. Huffman. "Consumers' Countries: Effects of Labels and Information in an Uncertain Environment," *American Journal of Agricultural Economics* Vol. 85, No. 5 (2003): 1112–1118; National Research Council (NRC). *Environmental Effects of Transgenic Plants: The Scope and Adequacy of Regulation* (Washington, DC: National Academy Press, 2002); and Gerald Nelson, et al. *The Economics and Politics of Genetically Modified Organisms: Implications for WTO 2000* (University of Illinois, Bulletin 809, 1999).

As we stated in the chapter on population growth, poverty, population growth, and the sufficiency of food production may well be related. High poverty levels are generally conducive to high population growth, and high population growth rates may increase the degree of income inequality. Furthermore, excessive population levels and poverty both increase the difficulty of achieving food sufficiency. Since we have examined population-control strategies in Chapter 6, we shall now focus on strategies to increase the amount of food available to the poorest people. What can be done?

Example 11.2

ARE CONSUMERS WILLING TO PAY A PREMIUM FOR GMO-FREE FOODS?

In the European Union, any food product containing an ingredient that consists of more than 1% genetically modified organisms (GMOs) must be labeled as "contains GMOs." Though biotechnology may help to increase crop yields, improve pest resistance, and enhance nutrition, the introduction of GMOs into food products has faced considerable hostility, particularly among consumers in Europe. How widespread is this hostility? And might it suggest that consumers might be willing to pay a price premium for GMO-free food?

Economists Charles Noussair, Stéphane Robin, and Bernard Ruffieux reported that 79% of French survey respondents agreed with the statement "GMOs should be banned" and 89% were opposed to the presence of GMOs in food products. Wondering whether this apparent anti-GMO sentiment would be reflected in purchase behavior led them to design an experiment to find out.

Due to the lack of field data, they utilized an experimental method designed to elicit and compare the willingness to pay for GMO-free products with those containing GMOs. In particular, the laboratory experiment was designed to measure how the willingness to pay would change in response to new information about GMO content. Approximately 100 French consumers participated in the experiments.

Interestingly, in contrast to early studies, only 35% of the subjects completely refused to purchase a product containing GMOs. Some 42% turned out to be willing to purchase a product containing GMOs if it was sufficiently inexpensive. The remaining 23% were indifferent.

This study suggests the advantages of using labels to segment the market. The authors found that survey respondents were willing to pay 8% more for a product labeled GMO-free compared to a product with an unknown GMO status. However, respondents were willing to pay 46.7% more for a GMO-free product compared to a product that they knew to contain GMOs.

Sources: Charles Noussair, Stéphane Robin, and Bernard Ruffieux. "Do Consumers Really Refuse to Buy Genetically Modified Food?" *The Economic Journal* Vol. 114 (January 2004): 102–120; and W. E. Huffman, M. Rousu, J. F. Shogren, and A. Tegene. "The Public Good Value of Information from Agribusinesses on Genetically Modified Foods," *American Journal of Agricultural Economics* Vol. 85, No. 5 (2003): 1309–1315.

Domestic Production in Less Developed Countries

The first issue to be addressed concerns the relative merits of increasing domestic production in the less developed countries (LDCs) as opposed to importing more from abroad. There are several reasons for believing that many developing countries can profitably increase the percentage of their consumption domestically produced. One of the most important is that food imports use up precious foreign exchange.

TABLE 11.3

Food Situation in Developing Countries

	Food Production 1988–90 (per capita index) (1989–91 = 100)	Daily Calorie Supply 1996 (per capita)
All Developing Countries	132	2,628
Least Developed Countries	115	2,095
Sub-Saharan Africa	116	2,205

Source: United Nations Development Programme, *Human Development Report 1993* (New York: Oxford University Press, 1999) Table 20, p. 214.

Most developing countries cannot pay for imports with their own currencies. They must pay in an internationally accepted currency, such as the American dollar, earned through the sale of exports. As more foreign exchange is used for agricultural imports, less is available for imports such as capital goods, which could raise the productivity (and hence incomes) of local workers.

The lack of foreign exchange has been exacerbated during periods of high oil prices. Many developing nations must spend large portions of export earnings merely to import energy. In 1993, for example, fuel imports made up one-third of all imports for Kenya. Little remains for capital goods or agricultural imports.

While this pressure on foreign exchange suggests a need for greater reliance on domestic agricultural production, it would be incorrect to carry that argument to its logical extreme by suggesting that all nations should become self-sufficient in food. The reason why self-sufficiency is not always efficient is suggested by *the law of comparative advantage*.

Nations are better off specializing in those products for which they have a comparative advantage. If its comparative advantage is not in food but in textiles, for example, a country would be better off producing and exporting textiles and using the earnings to purchase food (see Table 11.4). The opportunity costs of producing textiles and wheat (measured in hours of labor per unit output) are given for a hypothetical less developed country and a developed country (DC). Suppose we are

TABLE 11.4

A Hypothetical Example of the Law of Comparative Advantage

	Hours to Produce One Unit of Textiles	Hours to Produce One Unit of Wheat
Less Developed Country	1	3
Developed Country	1	1

considering an eight-hour day in each country. If the average worker in each country were to spend four hours of each day on each activity, then 8 units of textile (four by the LDC and four by the DC) and $5\frac{1}{3}$ units of wheat ($1\frac{1}{3}$ by the LDC and four by the DC) would be produced by the two countries each day. (Be sure you can see how these numbers can be derived from the table.)

Suppose, however, that the LDC in this case were to specialize in textiles (by allocating all eight hours to textile production) while the DC specialized in wheat. It is easy to verify that the total world production would now be 8 units of textiles and 8 units of wheat. When countries specialize in those products in which they have a comparative advantage, total production can increase!

Why did this happen in our example? It happened because the opportunity cost of making textiles in LDC (in terms of forgone wheat) was lower than in DC, while the opportunity cost of growing wheat in DC (in terms of forgone textile production) was lower than that in LDC. By freeing labor in DC from making textiles, LDC would be able to reap some of the benefits of the increased wheat production.

Although this example is hypothetical, the principle it conveys is real. Total self-sufficiency in food for all nations is not an appropriate goal. Those nations with a comparative advantage in agriculture due to climate, soil type, available land, and so on, such as the United States, should be net exporters, while those nations such as Japan with comparative advantage in other commodities, should remain net food importers. This balance should not be allowed to get out of line, however, by creating an excessive reliance on either domestic production or imports.

Due to price distortions and externalities in the agricultural sector, most developing countries have developed an excessive dependency on imports. What kind of progress has been made in reducing this dependency? According to Table 11.3 dependency has increased, not fallen. And the lowest-income countries as a group are having trouble even keeping up with population growth, much less making headway in reducing imports. Progress on this front is elusive, it seems.

The Undervaluation Bias

Why has food production barely kept pace with population growth for so many years? Accumulating evidence suggests that the limits to further production are primarily economic and political, not physical or biological. Agriculture in the low-income countries has been undervalued, implying that the rate of return on investment in agriculture is well below what it would be if agricultural output were allowed to receive its full social value. As a result, investments in agriculture were lower than they would otherwise have been and productivity has suffered.

Governments have used many mechanisms having the undesirable side effect of undervaluing agriculture and destroying incentives in the process. Two stand out—marketing boards and export taxes.

National marketing boards have been established in many developing countries to stabilize agricultural prices and hold food prices down in order to protect the poor from malnutrition. Typically, a marketing board sells food at subsidized prices. As the subsidy grows, the board looks around for ways to reduce the amount of subsidy.

Two strategies regularly employed by marketing boards are the wholesale importation of artificially cheap food from the United States (available under the food aid program originally designed to eliminate wheat surpluses) and holding down prices paid to domestic farmers. Both, of course, have the long-term effect of disrupting local production.

Many developing countries depend on export taxes, levied on all goods shipped abroad, as a principal source of revenue. Some of these taxes fall on cash-crop food exports (bananas, coca beans, coffee, and so on). The impact of export taxes is to raise the cost to foreign purchasers, reducing the amount of demand. A reduction in demand generally means lower prices and lower incomes for the farmers. Thus, this strategy also impairs food production incentives.

Government policies in developing countries not only affect the level of agricultural production, they affect the techniques employed as well. A study by the World Bank (1987) reported that in nine developing countries, pesticide subsidies ranged from 15% to 90% of full retail cost, with a median of 44%. Agricultural mechanization has also been stimulated by subsidies. As a result of this distortion of prices, farmers have been encouraged to rely heavily on pesticides and to embrace mechanization, strategies that make little sense in the long run. Having proceeded down this path and become dependent on the subsidies, it becomes difficult for these farmers to transition to sustainable agricultural practices.

Nonetheless, some basis for optimism exists. Agricultural techniques that are both sustainable and profitable in a developing country setting can be identified. The World Resources Institute conducted a series of studies in India, the Philippines, and Chile (Faeth, 1993) to study the effects on farmer income of transitioning to a more sustainable form of agriculture. The conclusion was that sustainable agriculture could be profitable, but usually not without changing the current pricing structure to reflect the full environmental costs of production. Better means of diffusing information about sustainable agricultural techniques among farmers would also be needed.

Feeding the Poor

The undervaluation bias was caused by a misguided attempt to use price controls as the way to provide the poor with access to an adequate diet. It backfired because the price controls served to reduce the availability of food. Is there a way to reduce the nutritional gap among the poor while maintaining adequate supplies of food?

Some countries such as Sri Lanka, Colombia, and the United States are using food stamp programs to subsidize food purchases by the poor. Currently, in Colombia, this is being accomplished by issuing food coupons to low-income women and children, who are particularly vulnerable to nutritional deficiency. The coupons can be used by recipients to purchase a number of high-nutrition, low-cost foods. By boosting the purchasing power of those with the greatest need, these programs provide access to food while protecting the incentives of farmers. Those countries lowering food prices for everyone necessitate substantially higher payments by the government to finance them. When governments search for ways to finance these subsidies, they are tempted to reduce the subsidy by paying below-market prices to farmers or to rely more heavily on artificially low-cost imported food aid. In the long run, either of these strategies can be self-defeating.

Targeting the assistance to those who need it is one strategy that works. Another approach to feeding the poor is an attempt to ensure that the income distribution effects of agricultural policies benefit the poor. One great hope associated with the "green revolution" was that new varieties of seeds produced by scientific research would expand the supply of food, holding down prices and making a better diet accessible to the poor, while at the same time providing expanding employment opportunities for the poor to supply more grain. How did it work out?

The green revolution started with maize hybrids adapted in the 1950s from the United States and Rhodesia and later spread across large parts of Central America and East Africa. Since the mid-1960s short-stalk, fertilizer-responsive varieties of rice have spread throughout East Asia and varieties of wheat have spread through Mexico, and the Indian and Pakistan Punjabs.

In many areas with access to these hybrids, productivity doubled or tripled over a 30-year period. Short-duration varieties have permitted many farmers to harvest two crops a year where only one was formerly possible. The transformation was historically unprecedented.

The effects were impressive. According to Lipton and Longhurst (1989), in most areas with access to these modern varieties, small farmers adopted them no less widely, intensively, or productively than others. Labor use per acre was increased with a consequent increase in the wage bill received by the poor. Poor people's consumption and nutrition were better with the new varieties than without them.

Yet the adoption of these varieties has had a darker side as well. As the Irish potato famine of the mid-1800s made clear, reliance on a few species of hybrid cereal grains increases the risk of disease and pests. Risk can be lowered by holding a diverse collection of stocks. The security offered by diversity of agricultural species has diminished as larger and larger areas are planted in these new varieties. In other areas, those without access to the new varieties have probably lost out as large quantities of new grain enter the market, eliminating by competition some of the more traditional sources. Small farmers were not always the beneficiaries of these new agricultural hybrids.

We are now in a position to define the role for aid from the developed nations. Temporary food aid is helpful when traditional sources are completely inadequate due to natural disasters or when the food aid does not interfere with the earnings of domestic producers. In the long run, developed nations could provide both appropriate technologies (such as solar-powered irrigation systems) and the financial capital to get farmer-owned local cooperatives off the ground. These cooperatives would then provide some of the advantages of scale (such as risk sharing and distribution), while maintaining the existing structure of small-scale farms. Coupled with a balanced development program designed to raise the general standard of living and effective population-control efforts, this approach could provide a solution to the distributional portion of the world food problem.

Feast and Famine Cycles

The remaining dimension of the world food problem concerns the year-to-year fluctuations in food availability caused by vagaries of weather and planting decisions. Even if the average level of food availability were appropriate, the fact that the average consists of a sequence of overproduction and underproduction years means that society as a whole can benefit from smoothing out the fluctuations.

The point is vividly depicted by an analogy. If a person were standing in two buckets of water—the first containing boiling-hot water, the second, ice-cold water—his misery would not be assuaged in the least by a friend telling him that on average the temperature was perfect. The average does not tell the whole story.

The fluctuations of supplies of food seem to be rather large and the swings in prices even larger. Why? One characteristic of the farming sector suggests that farmers' production decisions may actually make the fluctuations worse or at least prolong them. This tendency is explored via the *cobweb model* (see Figure 11.2). The source of the name is obvious, though no spider would own up to having created such a pathetic specimen.

Suppose, due to a weather-induced shortage, Q_0 is supplied, driving the price up to P_0. For the next growing season, farmers have to plant well in advance of harvest time. Their decisions about how much to plant will depend on the price they expect to receive. Let us suppose they use this year's price as their guess of what next year's price will be.

They will plan to supply (and in the absence of further weather aberrations *will* supply) Q_1. At price P_0, the market cannot absorb that much of the commodity, so the price falls to P_1. If farmers use that price to plan the following year's crop, they will produce Q_3. This will cause the price to rise to P_3 and so on.

FIGURE 11.2

The Cobweb Model

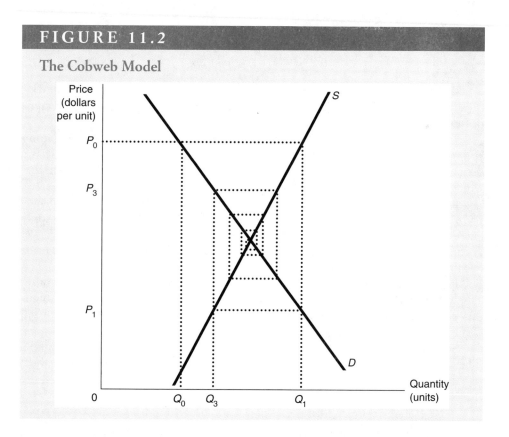

FIGURE 11.3

Price Elasticity of Demand and the Size of Price Fluctuations

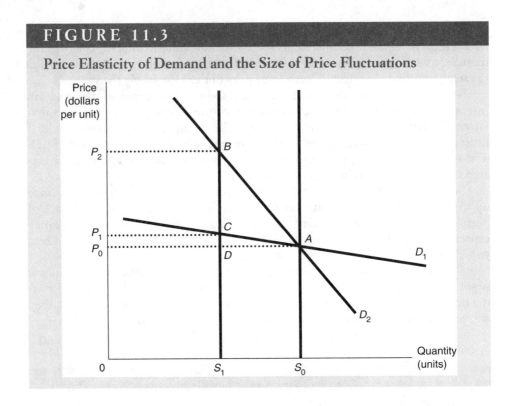

What is occurring is a *damped oscillation*. In the absence of further supply shocks, the amplitude of price and quantity fluctuations decreases over time until the equilibrium price and quantity are obtained.[5]

The demand for food tends to be price-inelastic, particularly in developing countries. This has some important implications. The more price-inelastic the demand curve, the higher the price has to go in order to bring the demand into line with supply when a weather-induced shortage occurs (see Figure 11.3).

Figure 11.3 records an initial equilibrium situation where demand D_1 and supply S_0 are equal to point A. A supply shortfall is registered as a shift in the supply curve from S_0 to S_1. In the two demand curves shown, D_1 is the most price-elastic. Notice that the more inelastic the demand curve, such as D_2, the higher the price has to go to clear the market.

Figure 11.3 also shows the effects of price shifts on producer revenues. How do supply shocks affect the incomes of farmers? At first glance the result seems ambiguous, since during shortages they get higher prices (a plus!) but also have less to sell (a minus!). Which effect dominates?

Since producer revenue is price times quantity, it is represented as a rectangle. The size of the rectangle depends on the circumstances. Before the supply shift, revenues received are depicted by the rectangle OP_0AS_0. After the supply shift, the

---

[5]Theoretically speaking, undamped oscillations that increase in amplitude over time are possible under certain conditions, but this pattern does not seem to characterize existing food markets.

revenues for the elastic demand curve (D_1) are OP_1CS_1 and for the inelastic demand curve are OP_2BS_1.

Have revenues increased with the supply shift? To answer the question, we have to compare areas P_0P_1CD (the net amount gained with the elastic demand curve) or P_0P_2BD (the net amount gained with the inelastic demand curve) to DAS_0S_1 (the revenue lost due to the lower production levels).

One conclusion is immediately obvious—the more inelastic the demand curve, the more likely farmers as a group are to gain from the shortfall. As long as the demand curve is price-inelastic in the relevant range (a condition commonly satisfied in the short run by food products), farmers as a group will be better off by supply shortfalls.[6]

For consumers, a quite different picture emerges. Consumers are unambiguously hurt by shortfalls and helped by situations with excess supply. The more price-inelastic the demand curve, the greater the loss is in consumer surplus from shortfalls and the greater the gain in consumer surplus from excess supply.

This creates some interesting (and from the policy point of view, difficult) incentives. Producers as a group do not have any particular interest in protecting against supply shortfalls, but they have a substantial interest in protecting against excess supply. Consumers, on the other hand, have no quarrel with excess supply, but want to guard against supply shortfalls.

While society as a whole would gain from the stabilization of prices and quantities, the different segments of society have rather different views of how that stabilization should come about. Farmers would be delighted with price stabilization as long as the average price were high, while consumers would be delighted if the average price were kept low.

The main means of attempting to stabilize prices and quantities is by creating stockpiles. These can be drawn down during periods of scarcity and built up during periods of excess supply. Currently, two different types of food stockpiles exist. The first is a special internationally held emergency stockpile that would be used to alleviate the hunger caused by natural disasters (such as drought). Established in 1975 by the Seventh Special Session of the U.N. General Assembly, with an annual target of 500,000 tons, the World Emergency Stockpile has the potential to greatly reduce suffering without having any noticeable disruptive effect on the world grain market (involving some 70 million tons traded). Unfortunately, its full potential has not yet been reached. The bulk of reserves is distributed annually to needy nations in that same year, leaving little in reserve.

The second kind of stockpile represents the stocks held individually by the various countries. While it was hoped that these stockpiles would be internationally coordinated, that has proved difficult to achieve. Food stockpiles can potentially increase food security on a worldwide basis, but implementation of an effective system has proved difficult. Significant difficult political decisions on stockpile management, such as timing purchases and sales, have yet to be agreed upon. Until that time, because the interests of producers and consumer nations are so different, it is unlikely that any uncoordinated system will be fully effective.

---

[6]This is not necessarily true for every farmer, of course. If the supply reduction is concentrated on a few, they will unambiguously be worse off while the remaining farmers will be better off. The point is that the revenue gains received by the latter group will exceed the losses suffered by the former group.

Summary

The world hunger problem is upon us and it is real. Serious malnutrition is currently being experienced in many parts of the world. The root of the chronic problem is poverty—an inability to afford the rising costs of food. The harm caused by poverty is intensified by fluctuations in the availability of food.

These problems are not unsolvable and do not call for a massive retrenchment by the developed world. The main barriers to a solution are political and economic, rather than physical.

The FAO has concluded that developing countries *could* increase their food production by around 4% per year in the near future, well in excess of population growth. They conclude, however, that this will occur only if the developed nations share technology and provide the developing countries access to their markets and if the developing countries show a willingness to adopt pricing policies that do not restrict output. This can be accomplished without jeopardizing the poor by using direct food purchase subsidies (such as a food stamp program) rather than price controls.

Because a major part of the world hunger problem is poverty, it is not enough to simply produce more food. The ability of the poor to afford food has also to be improved. This is particularly important in light of the rapidly rising cost of agricultural inputs such as fertilizer. Reducing poverty can be accomplished by bolstering nonfarm employment opportunities, as well as by enhancing the returns of smaller-scale farmers.

The available evidence suggests that, with respect to scale economies, there does not seem to be a trade-off between efficiency and equity; small-scale farming can compete effectively, given access to credit markets and new, improved technologies.

Food stockpiles—key elements in a program to provide food security—exist but are not yet fully effective. The emergency stockpile has not achieved its designed capacity and the system of national stockpiles is large but not effectively managed. The light is visible at the end of the tunnel and the train is moving, but the journey is distressingly slow.

Discussion Questions

1. "By applying modern technology to agriculture, the United States has become the most productive food-producing nation in the world. The secret to solving the world food problem lies in transferring this technology to developing countries." Discuss.

2. Under Public Law 480, the United States sells surplus grains to developing countries, which pay in local currencies. Since the United States rarely spends all of these currencies, much of this grain transfer is *de facto* an outright gift. Is this an equitable and efficient way for the United States to dispose of surplus grain? Why or why not?

Problems

1. The two countries Norland and Souland can produce commodities A and B per hour of labor expended according to the following table:

	Amount of A Produced in One Hour	Amount of B Produced in One Hour
Norland	4	8
Souland	2	6

   Which country, if either, has the comparative advantage in producing A? Why?

2. "Food stamp programs serve only to drive food prices higher, not increase the quantity of food available to the poor." What would the elasticity of supply have to be for this statement to be true? What would the elasticity of supply have to be for a food stamp program to increase the availability of food to the poor with no price increase?

3. A 1985 *Wall Street Journal* article suggested that absentee landlords may be one source of soil erosion problems. (Assume for the purposes of this problem that absentee landlords rent the land to the farmer for a fixed annual price.) Use your knowledge of property rights to discuss whether or not soil erosion could be expected to be a more serious problem with absentee landlords.

Further Reading

Carlson, Gerald R., David Zilberman, and John A. Miranowski, eds. *Agricultural and Environmental Resource Economics* (New York: Oxford University Press, 1993). A textbook that provides considerably more detail about issues raised in this chapter.

Crosson, Pierre R., and Sterling Brubaker. *Resource and Environmental Effects of U.S. Agriculture* (Baltimore: Johns Hopkins University Press for Resources for the Future, 1982). This book identifies the environmental costs associated with future increases in production and suggests measures to deal with them.

Meier, Gerald M. *Leading Issues in Economic Development*, 5th ed. (New York: Oxford University Press, 1989). A highly regarded, extensive collection of integrated short articles on various aspects of the development process. Contains an excellent section of agricultural development with an extensive bibliography.

Streeten, Paul. *What Price Food? Agricultural Policies in Developing Countries* (New York: St. Martin's Press, 1987). An excellent study of agricultural policies in developing countries.

Williams, Jeffrey C., and Brian D. Wright. *Storage and Commodity Markets* (Cambridge: Cambridge University Press, 1991). A primarily theoretical treatment of such issues as how large stockpiles should be, whether stockpiles are more useful in raw or processed form, and how the existence of stockpiles affect commodity prices and production.

Additional References and Historically Significant References are available on this book's companion Web site www.aw-bc.com/tietenberg.

Chapter 12

Storable, Renewable Resources: Forests

There is nothing more difficult to carry out, nor more doubtful of success, nor more dangerous to handle, than to initiate a new order of things. For the reformer has enemies in all who profit by the old order, and only lukewarm defenders in all those who would profit from the new order. The lukewarmness arises partly from fear of their adversaries who have law in their favor; and partly from the incredulity of mankind, who do not truly believe in anything new until they have had actual experience of it.

—Niccolò Machiavelli, *The Prince* (1513)

Introduction

Forests provide a variety of products and services. The raw materials for housing and wood products are extracted from the forest. In many parts of the world, wood is an important fuel. Paper products are derived from wood fiber. Trees cleanse the air by absorbing carbon dioxide and adding oxygen. Forests provide shelter and sanctuary for wildlife and they play an important role in maintaining the watersheds that supply much of our drinking water.

Although the contributions that trees make to our everyday life are easy to overlook, even the most rudimentary calculations indicate their significance. Almost one-third of the land in the United States is covered by forests, the largest category of land use with the exception of pasture and grazing land. In Maine, an example of a heavily forested state, 95% of the land area is covered by forest. In 1995, the comparable figure for the world was 31.7% (OECD, 1997: 111).

Managing these forests is no easy task. In contrast to cereal grains, which are planted and harvested on an annual cycle, trees mature very slowly. The manager must decide not only how to maximize yields on a given amount of land, but also when to harvest and replant. A delicate balance must be established among the various possible uses of forests. Since harvesting the resource diminishes other values (such as protecting the aesthetic value of forested vistas), establishing the proper balance requires some means of comparing the value of potentially conflicting uses. The efficiency criterion is one obvious method.

A glance at some of the vital signs of the forest resource does not inspire confidence that it is being managed either efficiently or sustainably. Deforestation is currently proceeding at an unprecedented rate. In 1992 the World Resources Institute reported that 42 million acres of tropical forests, an area about the size of the state of Washington, are being destroyed each year as trees are cut for timber and for clearing land for agriculture and development. This estimate, which was based upon remote-sensing data from satellites, was 50% higher than the previous global estimate prepared by the United Nations Food and Agricultural Organization in 1980.

Deforestation is a serious problem because it has intensified climate change, has decreased biodiversity, has caused agricultural productivity to decline, has increased soil erosion and desertification, and has precipitated the decline of traditional cultures of people indigenous to the forests. Instead of forests being used on a sustainable basis to provide for the needs of subsequent generations as well as current generations, the forests are being "cashed in." In its Global Forest Resources Assessment 2000, the Food and Agricultural Organization of the United Nations reports that during the 1990s, the world lost 4.2% of its natural forests through deforestation. During the same time period, the world gained 1.8% of natural forests through reforestation (with plantations), afforestation the conversion of unforested land to forest), and the natural expansion of forests. The result has been a net reduction in natural forests of 2.4% over the 10-year period.[1] Current forestry practices seem to violate both the sustainability and efficiency criteria. Why is this occurring and what can be done about it?

In the remainder of this chapter we shall explore how economics can be combined with forest ecology to assist in efficiently managing this important resource. We begin by characterizing what is meant by an efficient allocation of the forest resource when the value of the harvested timber is the only concern. Starting simply, we first model the efficient decision to cut a single stand or cluster of trees with a common age by superimposing economic considerations on a biological model of tree growth. This model is then refined to demonstrate how the multiple values of the forest resource should influence the harvesting decision and how the problem is altered if planning takes place over an infinite horizon, with forests being harvested and replanted in a continual sequence. Turning to matters of institutional adequacy, we shall then examine the inefficiencies that have resulted or can be expected to result from both public and private management decisions and strategies for restoring efficiency.

---

[1]In this context, sustainability refers to harvesting no more than would be replaced by growth; sustainable harvest would preserve the interests of future generations by assuring that the volume of remaining timber was not declining over time. This is consistent with the environmental sustainability criterion in Chapter 5, but is stronger than needed to satisfy the weak sustainability criterion. It would conceivably be possible to make future generations better off even if the volume of wood were declining over time by providing a compensating amount of some commodity or service they value even more.

Characterizing Forest Harvesting Decisions

Special Attributes of the Timber Resource

While timber shares many characteristics with other living resources, it also has some unique aspects. Timber shares with many other animate resources the characteristic that it is both an output and a capital good. Trees, when harvested, provide a salable commodity, but left standing they are a capital good, providing for increased growth the following year. Each year, the forest manager must decide whether to harvest a particular stand of trees or to wait for the additional growth. In contrast to many other living resources, however, the time period between initial investment (planting) and recovery of that investment (harvesting) is especially long. Intervals of 25 years or more are common in forestry, but not in many other industries. Finally, forestry is subject to an unusually large variety of externalities, which are associated with either the standing timber or the act of harvesting timber. These externalities not only make it difficult to define the efficient allocation, they also play havoc with incentives, reducing the ability of institutions to manage efficiently.

The Biological Dimension

Tree growth is measured on a volume basis, typically cubic feet, on a particular site. This measurement is taken of the stems, exclusive of bark and limbs, between the stump and a 4-inch top. For larger trees, the stump is 24 inches from the ground. Only standing trees are measured; those toppled by wind or age are not included. In this sense the volume is measured in net rather than gross terms.

Based on this measurement of volume, the data reveal that tree stands go through distinct growth phases. Initially, when the trees are very young, growth is rather slow in volume terms, though the tree may experience a considerable increase in height. A period of sustained, rapid growth follows, with volume increasing considerably. Finally, slower growth sets in as the stand fully matures, until growth stops or even reverses.

The actual growth of a stand of trees depends on many factors, including the weather, the fertility of the soil, susceptibility to insects or disease, the type of tree, the amount of care devoted to the trees, and vulnerability to forest fire or air pollution. Thus, tree growth can vary considerably from stand to stand. Some of these growth-enhancing or growth-retarding factors are under the influence of foresters; others are not.

Abstracting from these differences, it is possible to develop a hypothetical but realistic biological model of the growth of a stand of trees. Our model (see Figure 12.1) is based on the growth of a stand of Douglas fir trees in the Pacific Northwest.[2]

---

[2]The numerical model in the text is based loosely on the data presented in Marion Clawson. "Decision Making in Timber Production, Harvest, and Marketing," Research Paper R-4 (Washington, DC: Resources for the Future, 1977): 13, Table 1. The mathematical function relating volume to age stand in Figure 12.1 is a third-degree polynomial of the form $v = a + bt + ct^2 + dt^3$, where v = volume in cubic feet, t = the age of the stand in years, and a, b, c, and d are parameters that take on the values 0, 40, 3.1, and −0.016, respectively.

FIGURE 12.1

Model of Tree Growth in a Stand of Douglas Fir

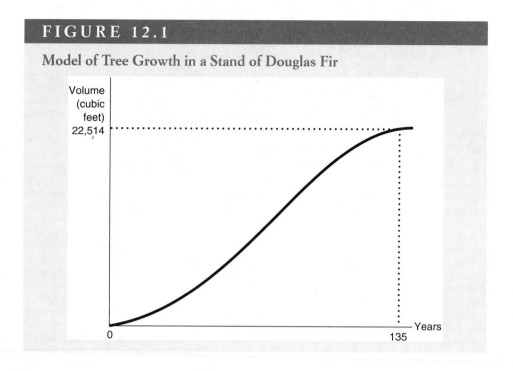

Notice that the figure is consistent with the growth phases listed above, following an early period of limited growth in the middle ages, with growth ceasing after 135 years.

When should this stand be harvested? Foresters have come up with a calculation called the *mean annual increment* (MAI) that provides the basis for a biological approach to answering this question. Developing this concept provides a useful contrast to the economic approach that is presented in subsequent sections.

The MAI is calculated by dividing the cumulative volume of the stand at the end of each decade by the cumulative number of years the stand has been growing up to that decade. For tree growth patterns like the ones represented by Figure 12.1, the MAI rises during the early ages and then falls during the later ages (see Table 12.1).

According to the biological decision rule, the forest should be harvested at the age when the MAI is maximized. For our Douglas fir example, this occurs when the stand is 100 years old. Column 4 in Table 12.1 helps us to understand what is special about this age. Annual incremental growth rises until the trees are about 70 years old, declining thereafter. The MAI rises for the first 100 years because the annual incremental growth is above the MAI during that period; it falls in the following years because the annual incremental growth is below the MAI.

The Economics of Forest Harvesting

To an economist, this biological criterion seems rather arbitrary; it fails to consider any of the factors such as the value of the timber, the time value of money, or costs associated with planting and harvesting, which would play a central role in an

TABLE 12.1

The Biological Harvesting Decision: Douglas Fir

Age (years) (1)	Volume[a] (cubic feet) (2)	MAI[b] (cubic feet) (3)	Annual Incremental Growth[c] (cubic feet) (4)
10	694	69.4	69.4
20	1,912	95.6	121.8
30	3,558	118.6	164.6
40	5,536	138.4	197.8
50	7,750	155.0	221.4
60	10,104	168.0	235.4
70	12,502	178.6	239.8
80	14,848	185.6	234.6
90	17,046	189.4	219.8
100	19,000	190.0	195.4
110	20,614	187.4	161.4
120	21,792	181.6	117.8
130	22,438	172.6	64.6
135	22,514	166.8	11.6

[a]Calculated from the equation used to produce Figure 12.1. See Footnote 2.

[b]Column 2 divided by Column 1.

[c]Change over intervening period in Column 2 divided by change in number of years in Column 1.

efficient harvesting decision. It is possible, however, to use the basic biological model of growth portrayed in Figure 12.1 as the basis for an economic model of the harvesting decision.

From the definition of efficiency, the optimal time to harvest this stand would be the time that maximizes the present value of the net benefits from the wood. The size of the net benefits from the wood depends on whether the land will be perpetually committed to forestry or left to natural processes after harvest. For our first model, we will assume that the stand will be harvested once and the land will be left as is following the harvest. This model will serve to illustrate how the economic principles of forestry can be applied to the simplest case, while providing the background necessary to move to more complicated and more realistic examples.

Two costs are presumed to be important in this decision—planting costs and harvesting costs. Apart from their magnitudes, these costs differ in one significant characteristic—the time at which they are borne. Planting costs are borne immediately, while harvesting costs are borne at the time of harvest. In a present-value calculation, harvesting costs are discounted (as is the value of the wood) because they are paid (received) in the future, whereas planting costs are not discounted because they are paid immediately. For the sake of our example, assume that planting this stand costs $1,000 and harvesting costs $0.30 per cubic foot of wood harvested.

With these additions to the model, it is now possible to calculate the present value of net benefits that would be derived from harvesting this stand at various ages (see Table 12.2). The net benefits are calculated by subtracting the present value of costs from the value of the timber at that age. Three different discount rates are used to illustrate the influence of discounting on the harvesting decision. The undiscounted calculations ($r = 0.0$) simply indicate the actual values that would prevail at each age, while the positive discount rate takes the time value of money into account.

Some interesting conclusions can be gleaned from Table 12.2. First, discounting shortens the time until the stand is harvested. Whereas the maximum undiscounted net benefits occur at 135 years, when a discount rate of only 0.02 is used, the maximum occurs at 68 years, roughly half the time of the undiscounted case.

Second, changing the magnitude of the planting and harvesting costs does not change the optimal harvesting point. Notice that the maximum of the value of timber row and the net benefit row occur in precisely the same year for each of the discount rates. In other words, even if costs were zero, the harvesting decision would occur at the same point. Third, with high enough discount rates, replanting may not be efficient. Note that with $r = 0.04$, the present value of net benefits is uniformly negative due to the assumed $1,000 planting cost. Harvesting a naturally reseeded forest in this case would occur when the trees were about 40 years old, but the costs of replanting would exceed the benefits.

Higher discount rates imply shorter harvesting periods because they are less tolerant of the slow timber growth that occurs as the stand reaches maturity. The use of a positive discount rate implies a direct comparison between the increase in the value of the timber that occurs prior to harvesting and the increase in value that would occur if the forest were harvested and the money from the sale invested at rate r. In the undiscounted case, the opportunity cost of capital is zero, so it pays to leave the money invested in trees as long as some growth is occurring. As long as r is positive, however, the trees will be harvested as soon as the growth rate declines sufficiently that more will be earned from financial investments.

The fact that neither harvesting nor planting costs affect the harvesting period results from the form of costs that we have used in the model. Because they are paid immediately, the present value of planting costs is equal to the actual expenditure; it does not vary with the age at which the stand is harvested. Essentially, a constant is being subtracted from the value of timber at any age. The age of the stand that maximizes the value of the timber necessarily maximizes the difference between the present value of the timber and the (constant) present value of the planting cost.

This does not imply, however, that planting costs are irrelevant to the harvesting decision. If planting costs are sufficiently high, they can exceed the maximum value of the timber. In this case, the net benefits would be negative for all possible ages and it would not be efficient to plant this type of tree for commercial harvest.

Harvesting costs are a different matter. They differ from planting costs in two respects. Not only are they borne at the time of harvest, but total harvesting costs are also proportional to the amount of timber harvested ($0.30 for each cubic foot). The present value of total harvesting costs changes with the harvesting period both because costs are discounted an amount determined by the harvesting date and because costs rise as the volume of wood to be harvested rises.

TABLE 12.2

Economic Harvesting Decision: Douglas Fir

Age (years)	10	20	30	40	50	60	68	70	80	90	100	110	120	130	135
Volume (cubic feet)	694	1,912	3,558	5,536	7,750	10,104	12,023	12,502	14,848	17,046	19,000	20,614	21,792	22,438	22,514
Undiscounted ($r = 0.0$)															
Value of Timber ($)	694	1,912	3,558	5,536	7,750	10,104	12,023	12,502	14,848	17,046	19,000	20,614	21,792	22,438	22,514
Cost ($)	1,208	1,574	2,067	2,661	3,325	4,031	4,607	4,751	5,454	6,114	6,700	7,184	7,538	7,731	7,754
Net Benefits ($)	-514	338	1,491	2,875	4,425	6,073	7,416	7,751	9,394	10,932	12,300	13,430	14,254	14,707	14,760
Discounted ($r = 0.01$)															
Value of Timber ($)	628	1,567	2,640	3,718	4,712	5,562	6,112	6,230	6,698	6,961	7,025	6,899	6,603	6,155	5,876
Cost ($)	1,188	1,470	1,792	2,115	2,414	2,669	2,833	2,869	3,009	3,088	3,107	3,070	2,981	2,846	2,763
Net Benefits ($)	-560	97	848	1,603	2,299	2,893	3,278	3,361	3,689	3,873	3,917	3,830	3,622	3,308	3,113
Discounted ($r = 0.02$)															
Value of Timber ($)	567	1,288	1,964	2,507	2,879	3,080	3,128	3,126	3,046	2,868	2,623	2,334	2,024	1,710	1,449
Cost ($)	1,170	1,386	1,589	1,752	1,864	1,924	1,938	1,938	1,914	1,860	1,787	1,700	1,607	1,513	1,435
Net Benefits ($)	-603	-98	375	755	1,015	1,156	1,190	1,188	1,132	1,008	836	634	417	197	14
Discounted ($r = 0.04$)															
Value of Timber ($)	469	873	1,097	1,153	1,091	960	835	803	644	500	376	276	197	137	113
Cost ($)	1,141	1,262	1,329	1,346	1,327	1,288	1,251	1,241	1,193	1,150	1,113	1,083	1,059	1,041	1,034
Net Benefits ($)	-672	-389	-232	-193	-237	-328	-415	-438	-549	-650	-737	-807	-862	-904	-921

Volume of timber from Table 12.1.

Value of timber = price × volume/(1 + r)^t

Cost = $1,000 + $0.30 × volume/(1 + r)^t

Net benefits = value of timber – cost

Price = $1.00

The impact of this type of cost on the harvesting decision can most easily be seen by realizing that the net benefits of a cubic foot of wood harvested at any given age is the price of that wood minus the marginal cost of harvesting that cubic foot, appropriately discounted. By assumption, the price and the marginal cost of a cubic foot of wood do not vary with age; they are constants. In the case of our numerical example, this constant net value before discounting is $0.70 (the $1.00 price minus the $0.30 marginal harvest cost). If the marginal cost of harvesting were zero, this value would be $1.00. Regardless what the marginal cost of harvesting is, this net value before discounting is a constant that is multiplied by the volume of timber at each age divided by $(1 + r)^t$. Its role is merely to raise or lower the net benefits curve; it does not change its shape. Therefore net benefits will be maximized at the same age of the stand regardless of the value of the marginal harvesting cost, as long as marginal harvesting cost is less than the price received; a rise in the marginal cost of harvesting will not affect the optimal age of harvest.

What would be the effect of a $0.20 tax levied on each cubic foot of wood harvested in this simple model? Since this tax would raise the marginal cost of harvesting from $0.30 per cubic foot to $0.50 per cubic foot, it would have the same effect as a rise in harvesting cost; it would also leave the optimal harvesting age unchanged.

The final conclusion that can be drawn from our numerical example relates to the decision to plant trees for subsequent harvest. When high discount rates combine with high replanting costs, planting trees for commercial harvest may not yield positive net benefits. For this specific set of circumstances, tree growth is simply too slow to justify the planting expense; profit-maximizing foresters would favor cutting down the forest without replanting it.

Extending the Basic Model

Our basic model is somewhat unrealistic in several respects. Perhaps most importantly, it considers the harvest as a single event rather than a part of an infinite sequence of harvesting and replanting. Typically in the forest industry, harvested lands are restocked and the sequence starts over again in a never-ending cycle.

At first glance it may appear that this is really no different from the case just considered. After all, can't one merely use this model to characterize the efficient interval between planting and harvest for each of the periods? The mathematics tells us (Bowles and Krutilla, 1985) that this is not the correct way to think about the problem, and with a bit of reflection it is not difficult to see why.

The single-harvest model we developed would be appropriate for an infinite planning period if and only if all periods were independent. If interdependencies exist among time periods, the harvesting decision must reflect those interdependencies.

Interdependencies do exist. The decision to delay a harvest imposes an additional cost on an infinite planning model that has no counterpart in our single-harvest model—the cost of delaying the onset of the next planting and harvesting cycle. In our single-harvest model, the optimum time to harvest occurs when the marginal benefit of an additional year's growth equals the marginal opportunity cost of capital. When the capital gains from letting the trees grow another year become equal to the return that could be obtained from harvesting the trees and investing the gains, the stand is harvested. In the infinite-planning horizon case, the opportunity cost of delaying the next cycle must also be covered by the gain in tree growth.

The effect of including this new cost can be rather profound. Assuming that all other aspects of the problem (such as planting and harvesting costs, discount rate, growth function, and price) are the same, the optimal time to harvest (called the *optimal rotation* in the infinite-planning case) is shorter in the infinite-planning case than in the single-harvest case. This follows directly from the fact that the marginal cost of a delay is higher due to the existence of the opportunity cost of starting the cycle later. The efficient forester will harvest a stand sooner when he or she is planning to replant the same area than when the plot will be left inactive after the harvest.

This more complicated model also yields some rather different conclusions from our original model, a valuable reminder of a point made in the first chapter—conclusions flow from a specific view of the world and are valid only to the extent that view captures the essence of a problem. Consider, for example, the effect of a rise in planting costs. In our single-harvest model, they had no effect on the optimal time to harvest. In the infinite-planning case, the optimal rotation is affected. Specifically, higher planting costs reduce the marginal opportunity cost of delaying the cycle. By doing so, they allow positive net benefits to accrue from delaying the cycle, compared to the case with lower planting costs. As a result, the optimal rotation (the time between planting and harvest) would increase as planting costs increase. A similar result would be obtained when harvesting costs are increased. The optimal rotation period would be lengthened.

Since increased harvesting costs in the infinite-horizon model lengthen the optimal rotation period, a per-unit tax on harvested timber would lengthen the optimal rotation period in this model as well. Furthermore, lengthening the rotation period implies that the harvested trees would be somewhat older and therefore each harvest would involve a somewhat larger volume of wood.

The vision of a fully regulated forest that emerges from these models involves a series of forest plots, each with trees of a different age. A sufficient number of plots would be available to provide trees at every age up to the age at which they are harvested. When the trees on a particular plot reach the age stipulated by the optimal rotation, they are harvested and the plot is restocked. The following year a different plot is harvested as its trees reach economic maturity. In this way harvesting activity can take place every year without endangering the sustainability of the forest.

Another limitation of our basic model lies in its assumption of a constant relative price for the wood over time. In fact, the relative prices of timber have been rising over time. Introducing relative prices for timber that rise at a constant rate in the infinite-horizon model causes the optimal rotation period to increase. In essence, prices that are rising at a fixed rate act to offset the effect of discounting. Since we have already established that lower discount rates imply longer rotation periods, it immediately follows that rising prices also lead to longer efficient rotation periods.

A final issue with the models as elaborated so far is that they all are concerned solely with the sale of timber as a product. In fact, forests serve several other purposes as well, such as providing habitat for wildlife, supplying recreational opportunities, and stabilizing watersheds. For these uses, additional benefits accrue to the standing timber that are lost or diminished when the stand is harvested.

It is possible to incorporate these benefits into our model to demonstrate the effect they would have on the efficient rotation. Suppose that the amenity benefits conveyed by a standing forest are positively related to the age of the forest. In this case the optimal rotation would once again occur when the marginal benefit of delay equaled the marginal cost of delay. In the case being considered, the marginal benefit of delay would be higher than in the models considered above because of the additional amenity benefit. For this reason, considering amenity benefits would lengthen the optimal rotation. If the amenity benefits are sufficiently large, it may be efficient to delay harvest forever, leaving the forest as a wilderness area.

Land Conversion

The previous section showed how high discount rates can increase harvests (by shortening the age at harvest) and discourage replanting. In this section we deal with the deforestation that occurs when forested land is converted to other uses. In particular we examine the economics of land conversion in order to understand not only why it is occurring, but also why the rate of conversion may be inefficiently high.

In general, as with other resources, land should be allocated to its highest valued use. Conversion from one use to another takes place when the relative values of the competing uses change.

Consider Figure 12.1, which graphs two hypothetical land uses—agriculture and forest. The left-hand side of the horizontal axis represents the location of the market. Moving to the right on that axis reflects an increasing distance away from the market.

The vertical axis represents value per acre. Each of the two functions records the relationship between distance to the market and the net benefits received from each type of land use. Both functions are downward sloping because transport costs to the market lower profits per acre more for distant locations. For the specific situation reflected in this graph, agricultural land has a higher value per acre close to the market, but forests have a higher value per acre farther away.

A market process that allocates land to its highest valued use would allocate the land closest to the market to agriculture (a distance of A) and the land farthest away from the market would remain as forest (from A to $A + B$). This allocation maximizes the net benefits received from the land.

Shifts in the benefit functions could trigger a land-use conversion. Conversion of forests to agricultural land could be stimulated either when the net benefit function for agricultural use shifted up or the net benefit function for forest use shifted down, or any combination of those two changes.

Increases in the net benefits for agriculture could result from:

- Domestic population growth that increase the domestic demand for food.
- Opening of export markets for agriculture that increase the foreign demand for local crops.
- Shifting from subsistence crops to cash crops (such as coffee or cocoa) for exports.
- The introduction of new crops that increase the yield per acre.

FIGURE 12.2

Allocating Land to Competing Uses

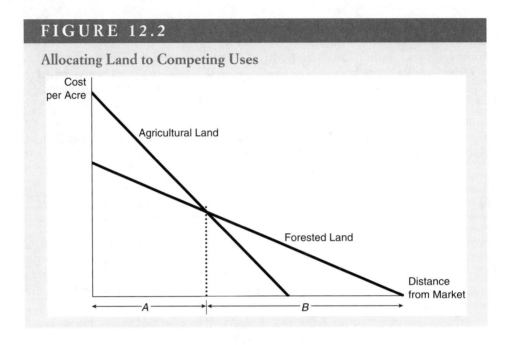

- New technologies that lower the costs and increase the profitability of producing crops.
- Lower agricultural transport costs due, for example, to the building of new
  roads into forested land.

Decreases in the net benefits for forests could result from:

- A decline in the demand for forest products from either domestic or foreign
  markets.
- Policies that increase the cost of harvesting or replanting.
- Diseases that reduce the yield of timber from forests
- Increases in the discount rate that reduce the present value of net benefits.

And, of course, factors not considered in Figure 12.2 might trigger land-use conversions as well. The most obvious of these is the value of land in other land uses
such as residential or industrial development. When the net benefits from these land
uses exceed those from forested land, conversion can be expected.

Sources of Inefficiency

The two previous sections considered the nature of both harvesting and land-use
conversion decisions. In this section we shall discover sources of inefficiency in those
decisions. These inefficiencies have the effect of biasing profit-maximizing decisions
toward excess rates of deforestation.

Perverse Incentives for the Landowner

Profit maximization does not produce efficient outcomes when the pattern of incentives facing decision makers is perverse. Forestry provides an unfortunately large number of situations where perverse incentives have produced very inefficient and unsustainable outcomes.

Privately owned forests are a significant force all over the world, but in some countries, such as the United States, they are the dominant force. Private forest decisions are plagued by external costs of various types. Yields can be adversely affected by such external factors as air pollution. When heavy investments in forested lands can be wiped out by factors totally out of the control of the owners, the incentive to invest is undermined.

Providing a sustainable flow of timber is not the sole *social* purpose of the forest, however. When the act of harvesting timber imposes costs on other valued aspects of the forest (for example, watershed maintenance, prevention of soil erosion, and protection of biodiversity), these costs may not (and normally will not) be adequately considered in the decision.

The fact that the value of the standing forest as wildlife habitat or as a key element in the local ecosystem is an *external* cost can lead to inefficient decisions that threaten biodiversity. Failure to recognize all of the social values of the standing forest not only provides an incentive to harvest an inefficiently large amount of timber in working forests, but it also provides an incentive to harvest timber even when preservation is the preferred alternative. For example, the controversy that erupted in the Pacific Northwest of the United States between environmentalists concerned with protecting the habitat of the Northern Spotted Owl and loggers can, in part, be explained by the different values these two groups put on habitat destruction. Loggers treat the loss of the Northern Spotted Owl as an external cost, while environmentalists treat the loss of timber harvest that results from habitat protection as an external cost.

Government policies can also create perverse incentives for landowners. Historically the rapid rate of deforestation in the Amazon, for example, was in part promoted by the Brazilian government (Binswager, 1991; Mahar, 1989). When the Brazilian government reduced taxes on income derived from agriculture (primarily cattle ranching), this discriminatory treatment of agricultural income overvalued agriculture and made it profitable to cut down forests and convert the land to agriculture even when, in the absence of discriminatory tax relief, agriculture in these regions would not have been profitable. This system of taxation encouraged higher-than-efficient rates of conversion of land from forests to pasture and subsidized an activity that, in the absence of tax discrimination, would not normally have been economically viable. In essence, Brazilian taxpayers were subsidizing deforestation.

The Brazilian system of property rights over land also played a role in the early history of deforestation. Acquiring land by squatting had been formally recognized since 1850. A squatter acquired a usufruct right (the right to continue using the land) by (1) living on a plot of unclaimed public land and (2) using it "effectively" for the required period of time. If these two conditions were met for 5 years, the squatter acquired ownership of the land, including the right to transfer it to others. A claimant received a title for an amount of land up to three times the amount cleared of forest;

hence, the more deforestation the squatter engaged in, the larger the amount of land he or she acquired. In effect, landless peasants could only acquire land by engaging in deforestation.

Government polices no longer encourage deforestation by requiring that land be cleared for ownership, and it has also abandoned its practice of subsiding cattle. Property rights are now generally well established in the original government settlements; however, in many other regions of the Amazon that can and may be settled, this is not the case. In addition, laws have been passed that make it illegal to burn more than 50% of the lot, but still deforestation continues, suggesting that other reasons may exist for the high rate of clearing.

Government settlement plans have certainly played a role. In addition to providing a free distribution of land, these resettlement programs have promoted the expansion of paved roads into Central Amazonia, and the construction of ports, waterways, railways, and hydroelectric power plants. All of these government policies radically changed the value of land uses that were competing with preserved forest, and the result was deforestation.

As a result of the resettlement program, many migrants engage in agriculture. Studying the decisions made by these farmers, Caviglia-Harris (2004) found that, as the land conversion model would suggest, the degree to which these farmers contribute to deforestation is impacted by market conditions as well as government polices. Market forces not only affect incentives to expand the scale of operations, but they also affect incentives to choose particular forms of agriculture. For example, her empirical results show that cattle ownership significantly increases the percentage of deforestation. Therefore as the market for cattle and its related products—milk and meat—advanced, deforestation levels also increased.

Even natural conditions affect land conversion since they affect the profitability of agriculture. Chomitz and Thomas (2003), for example, found that the probability that land in Amazonia is used for agriculture or intensively stocked with cattle declines markedly with increasing rainfall, other things equal. This point is significant since it suggests that due to its high humidity, Western Amazonia may be less suitable for agricultural development and therefore less vulnerable to deforestation from the conversion of forested land into agriculture.

In the Far East and in the United States, perverse incentives take another form. Logging is the major source of deforestation in both regions. Why don't loggers act efficiently? One reason, as noted above, is the fact that many values of the standing forest are external to loggers and hence do not play much if any role in their decision-making.

Another source of inefficiency can be found in the concession agreements, which define the terms under which public forests can be harvested. To loggers, existing forests have a substantial advantage over planting new forests: Old growth can be harvested immediately for profit. By virtue of the commercial value of larger, older trees, considerable economic rent (called *stumpage value* in the industry) is associated with a standing forest.

In principle, governments have a variety of policy instruments at their disposal to capture this rent from the concessionaires, but they have typically given out the concessions to harvest this timber without capturing anywhere near all of the rent.[3] As a result, the cost of harvesting is artificially reduced and loggers can afford to harvest much more forest than is efficient. The failure of government to capture this rent also means that the wealth tied up in these forests has typically gone to a few now-wealthy individuals and corporations rather than to the government to be used for the alleviation of poverty or other worthy social objectives.

The failure to capture the rent from concession agreements is not the only problem. Other contractual terms in these concession agreements have a role to play as well. Because forest concessions are typically awarded for limited terms, concession holders have little incentive to replant, to exercise care in their logging procedures, or even to conserve younger trees until they reach the efficient harvest age. The future value of the forest will not be theirs to capture. The resulting logging practices can destroy much more than simply the high-value species due to the destruction of surrounding species by: (1) the construction of access roads, (2) the felling and dragging of the trees, and (3) the elimination of the protective canopy. Although sustainable forestry would be possible for many of these nations, limited term concession agreements make it unlikely.[4]

The list of losers from inefficient forestry practices frequently includes indigenous peoples who have lived in and derived their livelihood from these forests for a very long time. As the loggers and squatters push deeper and deeper into forests, the indigenous people, who lack the power to stem the tide, are forced to relocate farther and farther away from their traditional lands.

Perverse Incentives for Nations

Another source of deforestation involves external costs that transcend national borders, making it unrealistic to expect national policy to solve the problem. Some international action would normally be necessary.

Biodiversity. Due to species extinction, the diversity of the forms of life that inhabit the planet is diminishing at an unprecedented rate. And the extinction of species is an irreversible process. Deforestation, particularly the destruction of the tropical rain forests, is a major source of species extinction because it destroys the most biologically active habitats. In particular, Amazonia has been characterized by Norman Myers (1984) as the "single richest region of the tropical biome."

---

[3]One way for the government to capture this rent would be to put timber concessions up for bid. Bidders would have an incentive to pay up to the stumpage value for these concessions. The more competitive the bidding was, the higher the likelihood that the government would capture all of the rent. In practice, many of the concessions have been given to those with influence in the government at far below market rates. See Jeffrey R. Vincent. "Rent Capture and the Feasibility of Tropical Forest Management," *Land Economics* Vol. 66, No. 2 (May 1990): 212–223.

[4]Currently, foresters believe that the sustainable yield for closed tropical rain forests is zero, because they have not yet learned how to regenerate the species in a harvested area once the canopy has been destroyed. Destroying the thick canopy allows the light to penetrate and changes the growing conditions and the nutrient levels of the soil sufficiently that even replanting is unlikely to regenerate the types of trees included in the harvest.

The quantity of bird, fish, plant, and insect life that are unique to that region is unmatched anywhere else on the planet.

One of the tragic ironies of the situation is that these extinctions are occurring at precisely the moment in history when we would be most able to take advantage of the gene pool this biodiversity represents. Modern techniques now make it possible to transplant desirable genes from one species into another, creating species with new characteristics such as enhanced disease- or pest-resistance. But the gene pool must be diverse to serve as a source of donor genes. Tropical forests have already contributed genetic material to increase disease resistance of cash crops such as coffee and cocoa, and have been the source of some entirely new foods. Approximately one-quarter of all prescription drugs have been derived from substances found in tropical plants. Future discoveries, however, are threatened by deforestation's deleterious effect on habitat.

Climate Change.   Deforestation also contributes to climate change. Since trees absorb carbon dioxide, a major greenhouse gas, deforestation eliminates a potentially significant means of ameliorating the rise in carbon dioxide emissions. Furthermore, burning trees, an activity commonly associated with agricultural land clearing, adds carbon dioxide to the air, by liberating the carbon sequestered within the trees.

Why is deforestation occurring so rapidly when the benefits conferred by a standing forest are so significant by virtually anyone's reckoning? The concept of externalities provides the key to resolving this paradox. Both the climate change and biodiversity benefits are largely external to the nation containing the forest, while the costs of preventing deforestation are largely internal. The loss of biodiversity precipitated by deforestation is perhaps most deeply felt by the industrialized world, not the countries that control the forests. Currently, the technologies to exploit the gene pool this diversity represents are in widest use in the industrialized countries. Similarly, most of the damage from climate change would be felt outside the borders of the country being deforested. Yet stopping deforestation means giving up the jobs and income derived from harvesting the wood or harvesting the land made available by clearing the forests. It is therefore not surprising that the most vociferous opposition to the loss of biodiversity is mounted in the industrialized nations, not the tropical forest nations. With global externalities, we have not only a clear rationale for market failure, but also a clear rationale for why the governments involved cannot be expected to solve the problem by themselves.

Poverty and Debt

Poverty and debt are also major sources of pressure on the forests. Peasants see unclaimed forest land as an opportunity to become landowners. Nations confronted with masses of peasants see unowned or publicly owned forests as a politically more viable source of land for the landless than taking it forcibly from the rich. Without land, peasants descend upon the urban areas in search of jobs in larger numbers than can be accommodated by urban labor markets. Politically explosive tensions, created and nourished by the resulting atmosphere of frustration and hopelessness, force governments to open up forested lands to the peasants or at least to look the other way as peasants stake their claim.

In eastern and southern Africa, positive feedback loops have created a downward cycle in which poverty and deforestation reinforce each other. Most natural forests have long since been cut down for timber, fuelwood, and cleared land for agricultural purposes. As forests disappear, the rural poor divert more time toward locating fuelwood. When fuelwood is no longer available, animal waste is burned, thereby eliminating it as a source of fertilizer to nourish depleted soils. Fewer trees hasten soil erosion. Depleted soils lead to diminished nutrition, as does an inability to find or afford fuelwood or animal waste for cooking and for boiling unclean water. Lower nutrition saps energy, increases susceptibility to disease, and reduces productivity. Survival strategies may necessarily sacrifice long-term goals simply to ward off starvation or death; the forests are typically an early casualty.

Poverty at the national level takes the form of staggering levels of debt to service in comparison to the capacity to generate foreign exchange earnings. In periods of high real interest rates, servicing these debts commands most if not all foreign exchange earnings. Using these foreign exchange earnings to service the debt eliminates the possibility of using them to finance imports for sustainable activities to alleviate poverty.

The large debts owed by many developing countries also encourage these countries to overexploit their resource endowments to raise the necessary foreign exchange. Timber exports represent a case in point. As Gus Speth (1989), the former president of the World Resources Institute, points out, "By an accident of history and geography, half of the Third World external debt and over two-thirds of global deforestation occur in the same 14 developing countries."

Sustainable Forestry

We have examined two types of decisions by landowners—the harvesting decision and the conversion decision—that affect the rate of deforestation. The first type of decision involves how much timber to harvest, how often to harvest it, and whether to replant after a harvest. The second type of decision concerns whether and when to convert a forest to a different land use.

In both cases profit-maximizing decisions may not be efficient and these inefficiencies tend to create a bias toward higher rates of deforestation. These cases present both a challenge and an opportunity. The current level of deforestation is the challenge. The opportunity arises from the realization that correcting these inefficiencies can promote both efficiency and sustainability.

Does the restoration of efficiency guarantee sustainable outcomes? The answer depends on what is meant by sustainable forestry. If the possibility of compensation is entertained along with the "nondeclining welfare among generations" definition, then efficiency is fully compatible with sustainability as long as the economic gains from harvest are invested and shared with future generations. In this case, even when efficiency results in some deforestation, future generations will not suffer.

Let's suppose, however, that we consider sustainable forestry to be realized only when the forests are sufficiently protected that harvests can be realized perpetually. Under this definition, sustainable forestry would occur as long as harvests were limited to the growth of the forest, leaving the volume of wood unaffected over some specified period of time.

Efficiency is not necessarily compatible with this definition of sustainable forestry. Maximizing the present value involves an implicit comparison between the increase in value from delaying harvest (largely because of the growth in volume) and the increase in value from harvesting the timber and investing the earnings (largely a function of r, the interest rate earned on invested savings). With slow-growing species, the growth rate in volume is small; maximizing the present value may well involve harvest volumes higher than the net growth of the forest.

The search for sustainable forestry practices that are also economically sustainable has led to a focus on rapidly growing tree species and plantation forestry. Rapidly growing species raise the attractiveness of replanting, because the invested funds are tied up for a shorter period of time. Species raised in plantations can be harvested and replanted at a low cost. Forest plantations have been established for such varied purposes as supplying fuelwood in developing countries and supplying pulp for paper mills in both the industrialized and developing countries.

Plantation forestry is controversial, however. Not only do plantation forests typically involve a single species of tree, which results in a poor wildlife habitat, they also require typically large inputs of fertilizer and pesticides.

In some parts of the world the natural resilience of the forest ecosystem is sufficiently high that sustainability is ultimately achieved, despite decades of earlier unsustainable levels of harvest. In the United States, for example, sometime during the 1940s, the net growth of the nation's timberlands exceeded timber removals. Subsequent surveys have confirmed that net growth has exceeded harvests, in spite of a rather large and growing demand for timber. The total volume of forest biomass in the United States has been growing since at least World War II; for the country as a whole, harvests during that period have been sustainable, although the harvests of some specific species in some specific areas have not.

Public Policy

Does public ownership of forest provide an answer? With the large amount of resources at its disposal, plus the ability to acquire land through eminent domain proceedings, the government can achieve the efficient scale rather easily. Furthermore, since it is not obligated to maximize profits, it can more easily account for external effects on wildlife or recreation. Unfortunately, if the U.S. experience is typical, the potential to solve these problems by public ownership is more illusory than real.

Public ownership of lands in the United States started even before the fledgling nation had a constitution. The first public land, much of it forest land, was accepted as a donation by the Confederation of Congress on October 29, 1782. Though these lands were owned by the government, they were not managed by the government until more than a century later. The forest was treated as common property.

By the second half of the 19th century, a number of voices began to decry the apparent wanton destruction of the forests and to call for more enlightened use of the resource. The first piece of legislation designed to respond to this outcry was the Forest Reserve Act of 1891, which authorized the first permanent system of forest reserves. No provision for private harvesting of trees on the forest reserves was included. It was not until 1897, with the passage of a general administration bill, that Congress provided the funds and a process to manage this system. This act authorized private harvesting on forest reserves under other restrictive conditions.

The management for these reserves was transferred in 1905 to the U.S. Department of Agriculture's Forest Service. The ambitious chief of the USDA Forest Service at that time, Gifford Pinchot, was to have an enormous influence over Forest Service management for several decades. Unlike other contemporaries such as John Muir, who wanted to withdraw these lands from use, Pinchot vigorously pursued a philosophy that they should be used. Focusing first on timber production, his goal was the promotion of a sustainable level of harvest from the national forests. Concern over wildlife and recreation would come much later.

The desire for the maintenance of a sustained level of harvest gave rise to the acceptance of a number of operation procedures by the Forest Service that were explicitly biologically based. Chief among these were the maximum average annual increment described earlier and the requirement to keep the allowable cut on the national forests steady through time. This would reduce the potential instability faced by private forest owners caused by flooding the market with timber from the public lands.

Although the Forest Service had, to some extent, followed a multiple-use philosophy since its inception, in the period following World War II, public interest in nontimber uses grew sufficiently that the rather ad hoc methods of the Forest Service for achieving a balance were no longer deemed sufficient.

The Multiple-Use Sustained Yield Act mandated a multiple-use philosophy, without giving much guidance on how to implement that philosophy. In part, this act had been sought by the Forest Service to protect its multiple-use philosophy from attack by those seeking congressional or judicial support for single interests. Subsequent legislation, however, would force the Forest Service to be much more systematic in how it sought to define and implement a multiple-use philosophy.

The Wilderness Act set aside specific forest areas to be preserved in their pristine state. No roads were permitted and timber harvests were prohibited in wilderness areas. Although initially limited to designating specific areas that had by tradition not been harvested, the act has in fact ushered in much more wilderness land than was envisioned by those discussing it in Congress at the time the bill was passed.

Though the management of public forests in the United States has been evolving since 1782, it has not yet reached the point where it yields efficient outcomes. Harvests from the public forests are subsidized by taxpayers.[5] The benefits of the

---

[5] A review of several studies estimating the size of these subsidies can be found in Repetto (1988).

forests to wildlife and recreation are inadequately protected.[6] Too many political pressures influence the process. Other policy approaches offer the prospect of a more rapid transition to efficiency.

Changing Incentives

One such approach involves restoring efficient incentives. Concessionaires should pay the full cost for their rights to harvest publicly controlled lands, including compensating for damage to the forests surrounding the trees of interest. The magnitude of land transferred to squatters should not be a multiple of the amount of cleared forest. The rights of indigenous peoples should be respected.

Another approach involves enlisting the power of consumers in the cause of sustainable forestry. The process typically involves the establishment of standards for sustainable forestry, employing independent certifiers to verify compliance with these standards, and allowing certified suppliers to display a label designating compliance (see Example 12.1).

For this system to work well, several preconditions need to be met. Consumers must trust the certification process and it must address issues consumers care about. In addition, consumers must be sufficiently concerned about sustainable forestry to pay a price premium (over prices for otherwise comparable, but uncertified products) that is large enough to make certification an attractive option for forestry companies. This means that the revenue should be sufficient to at least cover the higher costs associated with producing certified wood. Nothing guarantees that these conditions would be met in general.

Most of these changes could be implemented by individual nations to protect their own forests. And to do so would be in their interests. By definition, inefficient practices cost more than the benefits received. The move to a more efficient set of policies would necessarily generate more net benefits, which could be shared in ways that build political support for the change. But what about the global inefficiencies? How can those be resolved?

Several economic strategies exist. They share the characteristic that they all involve compensating the nations conferring external benefits so as to encourage conservation actions consistent with global efficiency.

Debt-Nature Swaps.   One strategy involves reducing the pressure on the forests caused by the international debt owed by many developing countries. Private banks hold most of the debt, and they are not typically motivated by a desire to protect biodiversity. Nonetheless it is possible to find some common ground for negotiating strategies to reduce the debt. Banks realize that complete repayment of the loans is probably not possible. Rather than completely write off the loans, an action that not only causes harm to the income statement but creates adverse incentives for repayment of future loans, they are willing to consider alternative strategies.

---

[6]The below-cost sales of timber to harvesters is usually justified by the Forest Service in terms of the associated public benefits of harvesting (enhanced recreation opportunities and wildlife protection). This argument is difficult to accept since, as Repetto puts it, "The supposed beneficiaries, including both environmental groups and fish and wildlife agencies in affected states, loudly oppose and are suing the Forest Service to stop it from providing the benefits they are allegedly receiving" (op. cit., p. 97).

Example **12.1**

PRODUCING SUSTAINABLE FORESTRY THROUGH CERTIFICATION

The Forest Stewardship Council (FSC) is an international, not-for-profit organization headquartered in Oaxaca, Mexico. The FSC was conceived in large part by environmental groups, most notably the World Wide Fund for Nature (WWF). The goal of the FSC is to foster "environmentally appropriate, socially beneficial, and economically viable management of the world's forests." It pursues this goal through independent third-party certification of well-managed forests.

The FSC has developed standards to assess the performance of forestry operations. These standards address environmental, social, and economic issues. Forest assessments require one or more field visits by a team of specialists representing a variety of disciplines typically including forestry, ecology/wildlife management/biology, and sociology/anthropology. In addition, the FSC requires that forest assessment reports be subject to independent peer review. Any FSC assessment may be challenged through a formal complaints procedure. FSC certified products are identified by an on-product label and/or off-product publicity materials.

Although the FSC is supported by a broad coalition of industry representatives, social justice organizations, and environmental organizations, it is opposed by some mainstream industry groups, particularly in North America, and by some landowners associations in Europe. One unresolved issue is how to certify small and medium-sized landholdings since conventional certification is expensive.

Source: The Forest Stewardship Web site: http://www.fsc.org/fsc (Accessed 11/18/04).

One of the more innovative policies that explores common ground in international arrangements has become known as the debt-nature swap. It is innovative in two senses: (1) the uniqueness of the policy instrument, and (2) the direct involvement of nongovernmental organizations (NGOs) in implementing the policy. A debt-nature swap involves the purchase (at a discounted value in the secondary debt market) of a developing country debt usually by a nongovernmental environmental organization. The new holder of the debt, the NGO, offers to cancel the debt in return for an environmentally related action on the part of the debtor nation.

The first debt-nature swap took place in Bolivia in 1987. Since then debt-for-nature swaps have been arranged or explored in many developing countries including Ecuador, the Philippines, Zambia, Jamaica, Madagascar, Guatemala, Venezuela, Argentina, Honduras, and Brazil.

A brief examination of the Madagascar case can illustrate how these swaps work. Recognized as a prime source of biodiversity, the overwhelming majority of

Madagascar's land mammals, reptiles, and plants are found nowhere else on Earth. Madagascar is also one of the poorest countries in the world, burdened with high levels of external debt. Because of its limited domestic financial resources, Madagascar could not counter the serious environmental degradation it was experiencing. Between 1989 and 1996, Conservation International, the Missouri Botanical Garden, and the World Wildlife Fund negotiated nine commercial debt-for-nature swaps in Madagascar. These arrangements generated $11.7 million in conservation funds. Agreements signed by Madagascar's government and the participating conservation organizations identified the programs to be funded. One such program trained over 320 nature protection agents, who focused on involving local communities in forest management.

Other arrangements involving different governments and different environmental organizations have since followed this lead. The main advantage of these arrangements to the debtor nation is that a significant foreign exchange obligation can be paid off with domestic currency. Debt-nature swaps offer the realistic possibility to turn what has been a major force for unsustainable economic activity (the debt crisis) into a force for resource conservation.

Extractive Reserves.   One strategy designed to protect the indigenous people of the forest as well as to prevent deforestation involves the establishment of extractive reserves. These areas would be reserved for the indigenous people to engage in the traditional hunting-gathering activities.

Extractive reserves have already been established in the Acre region of Brazil. Acre's main activity comes from the thousands of men who tap the rubber trees scattered throughout the forest, a practice dating back 100 years. Under the leadership of Chico Mendes, a leader of the tappers who was subsequently assassinated, four extractive reserves were established in June 1988 by the Brazilian government to protect the rubber tappers from encroaching development.

Conservation Easements and Land Trusts.   One approach to preserving land, which is increasingly being used around the world, is known as a conservation easement. A conservation easement is a legal agreement between a landowner and a land trust or government agency that permanently limits uses of the land in order to protect its conservation values. (A land trust is an organization specifically established to hold land and to ensure that use of the land is in conformance with the easement agreement.)

Conservation easements can be either sold or donated. If the donation benefits the public by permanently preserving important resources and meets other federal tax code requirements, it can qualify as a tax-deductible charitable donation. The tax-deductible amount is the different between the land's value with and without the easement.

From an economic point of view, a conservation easement allows the bundle of rights that is associated with land ownership to be separated into transferable units. Separating the rights and allowing them to flow to the highest valued user may allow the value to be derived from the land to be increased, while preserving it at the same time.

Suppose, for example, a landowner wants to continue to harvest timber from her land, but not to convert it to housing. In the absence of a conservation easement, the owner is likely to face property taxes on the land that are based on highest valued use rather than its current use. Depending on its location, the assessed value of the land (the property tax base) could well be based on its conversion to a housing development rather than on its current use. If, however, the owner executes an agreement with a land trust to administer a conservation easement on the land, property taxes will fall (since the assessed value is now lower), and she will either get a substantial income tax break (in the case of a charitable donation of the easement) or the revenue (in the case of a sale of the easement). Meanwhile the land is protected in perpetuity from development, and the current owner can use her land for all purposes except those explicitly precluded by the easement agreement.

Conservation easements have much to recommend them. Since they are voluntary transactions, no one is forced to part with the development rights; consent is required for any transfer. This approach also allows land trusts to preserve land from development much more cheaply than would be possible if the only option were to purchase the land itself, rather than just the development rights.

Easements, however, can also introduce problems. The land trust has to monitor the land to ensure that the terms of the agreement are being upheld and, if they are not, to bear the costs of a legal action to enforce compliance with the agreement. These legal actions are not cheap. In addition, the perpetual nature of conservation easements could also be a problem if and when, in the far distant future, development became the preferred use.

The World Heritage Convention.   The *World Heritage Convention* came into being in 1972 with the primary mission of identifying and preserving the cultural and natural heritage of outstanding sites throughout the world, and ensuring their protection through international cooperation. Currently some 178 countries have ratified the convention.

Ratifying nations have the opportunity to have their natural properties of outstanding universal value added to the World Heritage List. The motivation for taking this step is to gain international recognition for this site, using the prestige that comes from this designation to raise awareness for heritage preservation and the likelihood that the site can be preserved. A ratifying nation may receive both financial assistance and expert advice from the World Heritage Committee as support for promotional activities for the preservation of its properties as well as for developing educational materials.

Responsibility for providing adequate protection and management of these sites falls on the host nations, but a key benefit from ratification, particularly for developing countries, is access to the World Heritage Fund. This Fund is financed by mandatory contributions from ratifying nations, calculated at 1% of the country's contribution to UNESCO, the administering agency. Annually, about three million U.S. dollars are made available, mainly to low-income countries to finance technical assistance and training projects, as well as for assistance preparing their nomination proposals or to develop conservation projects. Emergency assistance may also be made available for urgent action to repair damage caused by human-made or natural disasters.

Royalty Payments

One potential source of revenue for biodiversity preservation involves taking advantage of the extremely high degree of interest by the pharmaceutical industry in searching for new drugs derived from these biologically diverse pools of flora and fauna. Establishing the principle that nations containing these biologically rich resources within their borders would be entitled to a stipulated royalty on any and all products developed from genes obtained from these preserves provides both an incentive to preserve the resources and some revenue to accomplish the preservation.

Nations harboring rich, biological preserves have begun to realize their value and to extract some of that value from the pharmaceutical industry. The revenue is in part used for inventorying and learning more about the resource as well as preserving it. For example, in 1996, Medichem Research, an Illinois-based pharmaceutical company, entered into a joint venture with the Sarawak government. The organization created by this joint venture has the right to file exclusive patents on two compounds that offer some promise as cancer treatments. Currently the agreement specifies a 50-50 split from royalties once the drug is marketed. The Sarawak government has been given the exclusive right to supply the latex raw material from which the compounds are derived. Sarawak scientists are involved in screening and isolating the compounds, and Sarawak physicians are involved in the clinical trials. This agreement not only provides a strong rationale for protecting the biological source, but also enables the host country to build its capacity for capturing the value of its biodiversity in the future (Laird and ten Kate, 2002). These arrangements are particularly significant because they facilitate transboundary sharing of the costs of preservation. It is unrealistic to expect that countries harboring these preserves should be required to shoulder the entire cost of preservation when the richer countries of the world are the major beneficiaries. It may also be unrealistic to assume that pharmaceutical demand is sufficient for preservation (see Example 12.2).

Debt-nature swaps, extractive reserves, royalty payments, and conservation easements all involve a recognition of the fact that resolving the global externalities component of deforestation requires a rather different approach from resolving the other aspects of the deforestation problem. In general this approach involves financial transfers from the industrialized nations to the tropical nations, transfers that are constructed so as to incorporate global interests into decisions about the future of tropical forests.

Recognizing the limited availability of international aid for the preservation of biodiversity habitat, nations have begun to tap other revenue sources. Tourist revenues have become an increasingly popular source, particularly where the tourism is specifically linked to the resources that are targeted for preservation. Rather than mixing these revenues with other public funds, nations are earmarking them for preservation (see Example 12.3).

Summary

Forests represent an example of a storable, renewable source. Typically, tree stands have three distinct growth phases—slow growth in volume in the early stage, followed by rapid growth in the middle years and slower growth as the stand reaches

Example 12.2

DOES PHARMACEUTICAL DEMAND OFFER SUFFICIENT PROTECTION TO BIODIVERSITY?

The theory is clear—incentives to protect plants are stronger when the plants are valuable to humans. Is the practice equally clear?

The case of Taxol is instructive. Derived from the slow-growing Pacific yew, Taxol is a substance that has been proved effective in treating advanced forms of breast and ovarian cancers. As of 1998, it was the best-selling anti-cancer drug ever.

Since the major site for this tree was in the old-growth forests of the Pacific Northwest, the hope of environmental groups was that the rise in the importance of Taxol might provide both sustainable employment and some protection for old-growth forests.

In fact, that is not how it worked out. The Taxol for the chemical trials was derived from the bark of the tree. Stripping the tree of its bark killed it. And supplying enough bark for the chemical trials put a tremendous strain on the resource.

Ultimately, the private company that marketed Taxol, Bristol-Squibb, developed a semi-synthetic substitute that could be made from imported renewable tree parts.

The Pacific yew, the original source of one of the most important medical discoveries in the 20th century, was left completely unprotected. And the industry that had grown up to supply the bark collapsed. In the end, its value proved transitory and its ability to support a sustainable livelihood in the Pacific Northwest was illusory.

Source: Jordan Goodman and Vivian Walsh. *The Story of Taxol: Nature and Politics in the Pursuit of an Anti-Cancer Drug* (New York: Cambridge University Press, 2001).

full maturity. The owner who harvests the timber receives the income from its sale, but the owner who delays harvest will receive additional growth. The amount of growth depends on the part of the growth cycle the stand is in.

From an economic point of view, the efficient time to harvest a stand of timber is when the present value of net benefits is maximized—that is, when the marginal gain from delaying the harvest one more year is equal to the marginal cost of the delay. For longer-than-efficient delays, the additional costs outweigh the increased benefits, while for earlier-than-efficient harvests, more benefits (in terms of the increased value of the timber) are given up than costs saved. For many species the efficient age at harvest is 25 years or older.

The efficient harvest age depends on the circumstances the owner faces. When the plot is to be left fallow after the harvest, the efficient harvest occurs later than when the land is immediately replanted to initiate another cycle. With immediate replanting,

Example 12.3

TRUST FUNDS FOR HABITAT PRESERVATION

How can local governments finance biodiversity preservation when faced with limited availability of both international and domestic funds? One option being aggressively pursued by the World Wildlife Fund involves trust funds. Trust funds are moneys that are legally restricted to be used for a specific purpose (as opposed to being placed in the general government treasury). They are administered by trustees to assure compliance with the terms of the trust. Most, but not all, trust funds are endowments, meaning that the trustees can spend the interest and dividends from the funds, but not the principal. This assures the continuity of funds for an indefinite period.

Where does the money come from? Many nations that harbor biodiversity preserves can ill afford to spend the resources necessary to protect them. One possibility is to tap into foreign demands for preservation. In Belize, the revenue comes from a "conservation fee" charged to all arriving foreign visitors. The initial fee, U.S.$ 3.75, was passed by Belize's parliament in January 1996, raising $500,000 in revenues each year for the trust fund. Similar fees are being designed in Namibia and Papua, New Guinea.

Income from the trust funds can be used for many purposes, including training park rangers, developing biological information, paying the salaries of key personnel, and conducting environmental education programs, depending on the terms of the trust agreement.

Biodiversity preservation that depends on funds from the general treasury becomes subject to the vagaries of budgetary pressures. When the competition for funds intensifies, the funds may disappear or be severely diminished. The virtue of a trust fund is that it provides long-term, sustained funding for the protection of biodiversity.

Source: Barry Spergel. "Trust Funds for Conservation," *FEEM Newsletter* Vol. 1 (April 1996): 13–16.

---

delaying the harvest imposes an additional cost—the cost of delaying the next harvest—which, when factored into the analysis, makes it more desirable to harvest earlier.

A number of other factors affect the size of the efficient rotation as well. In general the larger the discount rate, the earlier the harvest. With an infinite-planning horizon model, increases in planting and harvesting costs tend to lengthen the optimal rotation, while in a single-harvest model, they have no effect on the length of the efficient rotation. If the price of timber grows at a constant rate over time, the efficient rotation is longer than if prices remain constant over time. Finally, if standing timber provides amenity services (such as for recreation or wildlife management) in proportion to the volume of the standing timber, the efficient rotation will be longer than it would be in the absence of any amenity services.

Profit maximization can be compatible with efficient forest management under the right circumstances. In particular, profit-maximizing private owners have an incentive to adopt the efficient rotation when amenity services are small and to undertake investments that increase the yield of the forest.

In reality, not all private firms will follow efficient forest management practices because they may choose not to maximize profits, they may be operating at too small a scale of operation, or externalities may create inefficient incentives. Many forest owners are simply not acting like profit maximizers. Even if they were, small-scale plots cannot normally be operated efficiently because of the importance of economies of scale both in learning about scientific forestry and in implementing it. The costs of acquiring this knowledge and putting it into practice may be so large as to eliminate any potential benefits. Finally, when amenity values are large and not captured by the forest owner, the private rotation period may fail to consider these values, leading to an inefficiently short rotation period.

Inefficient deforestation has been encouraged by a failure to incorporate global benefits from standing forests; by concession agreements that provide incentives to harvest too much, too soon and that fail to provide adequate incentives to protect the interests of future generations; by land property right systems that make the amount of land acquired by squatters a multiple of cleared forestland; and by tax systems that discriminate against standing forests.

Substantial strides toward restoring efficiency as well as sustainability can be achieved simply by recognizing and correcting the perverse incentives, actions that can be and should be taken by the tropical forest nations. But these actions will not, by themselves, provide adequate protection for the global interests in the tropical forests. Five schemes designed to internalize some of these benefits—debt-nature swaps, extractive reserves, royalty payments, forest certification, and conservation easements—have already begun to be implemented.

Discussion Questions

1. Should U.S. national forests become "privatized" (sold to private owners)? Why or why not?
2. In his book *The Federal Land Revisited*, Marion Clawson proposed what he called the "pullback concept":

Under the pullback concept any person or group could apply, under applicable law, for a tract of federal land, for any use they chose; but any other person or group would have a limited time between the filing of the initial application and granting other lease or the making of the sale in which to "pull back" a part of the area applied for. . . . The user of the pullback provision would become the applicant for the area pulled back, required to meet the same terms applicable to the original application, . . . but the use could be what the applicant chose, not necessarily the use proposed by the original applicant (p. 216).

Evaluate the pullback concept as a means for conservationists to prevent some mineral extraction or timber harvesting on federal lands.

Problems

1. Suppose there are two forest plots that are identical except that one will be harvested and left while the second will be cleared after the harvest and turned into a housing development. In terms of efficiency, which should have the oldest harvest age? Why?
2. In Table 12.2, when $r = 0.02$, the present value of the cost rises for 68 years and then subsequently declines. Why?

Further Reading

Bowles, Michael D., and John V. Krutilla. "Multiple Use Management of Public Forestlands," in Allen V. Kneese and James L. Sweeney, eds. *Handbook of Natural Resource and Energy Economics* Vol. 11 (Amsterdam: North-Holland, 1985). Excellent analytical treatment of the multiple-use strategy as it applies to U.S. forest policy. Somewhat mathematical.

Deacon, R. T. "The Simple Analytics of Forest Economics," in R. T. Deacon and M. B. Johnson, eds. *Forestlands: Public and Private* (San Francisco: Pacific Institute for Public Policy Research, 1985). An especially accessible treatment of forestry economics.

Gregory, G. Robinson. *Resource Economics for Foresters* (New York: Wiley, 1987). Undergraduate text in forest economics that could be used to go beyond the material in this chapter.

Pagiola, Stefano, Joshua Bishop, and Natasha Landell-Mills. *Selling Forest Environmental Services: Market-Based Mechanisms for Conservation and Development* (London, UK: Earthscan, 2002) Market-based approaches are thought to offer considerable promise as a means to promote forest conservation and as a new source of income for rural communities. Based on extensive research and case studies, this book demonstrates the feasibility and effectiveness of payment systems and their implications for the poor.

Price, Colin. *The Theory and Application of Forest Economics* (Oxford: Basil Blackwell, 1989). A text aimed at "students of forestry and of natural resource management at both undergraduate and graduate levels."

Repetto, Robert. *The Forest for the Trees? Government Policies and the Misuse of Forest Resources* (Washington, DC: World Resources Institute, 1988). A highly recommended study of forestry practices in several different countries.

VanKooten, G. C., R. A. Sedjo, et al. "Tropical Deforestation: Issues and Policies," in T. Tietenberg and H. Folmer, eds. *The International Yearbook of Environmental and Resource Economics 1999/2000* (Cheltenham UK: Edward Elgar, 1999) 198–249. A survey of what we have learned about tropical deforestation.

Wibe, Sören, and Tom Jones, eds. *Forests: Market and Intervention Failures* (London: Earthscan Publications Ltd., 1992). Case studies of forest policy in the United Kingdom, Sweden, Italy, Germany, and Spain.

Additional References are available on this book's companion Web site www.aw-bc.com/tietenberg.

Appendix

The Harvesting Decision: Forests

Suppose that an even-aged stand of trees is to be harvested at an age that maximizes the present value of the harvested timber. That age can be found by: (1) defining the present value of the harvested timber as a function of the age of the stand, and (2) maximizing the function with respect to age.

$$\text{Present Value} = [P \cdot V(t) - C_b \cdot V(t)] \cdot e^{rt} - C_p \tag{1}$$

Where:

P = the price received per unit of harvested volume
$V(t)$ = the volume of timber harvested at age t
C_b = the per-unit cost of harvesting the timber
T = the age of the timber, and
C_p = the fixed cost of planting

Taking the derivative of the function with respect to age and setting it equal to zero yields:*

$$(P - C_b)\frac{dV(t)}{dt} = (P - C_b) \cdot V(t) \cdot r \tag{2}$$

or rewriting yields:

$$\frac{\frac{dV(t)}{dt}}{V(t)} = r \tag{3}$$

Translated into English, this condition implies that the rate of return from letting the stand grow over the last increment of age should be equal to the market rate of return.

Notice that the fixed planting cost has no effect on the choice of harvesting age. While it raises or lowers the present value by the exact amount of the cost of planting, it does not change where the function reaches its maximum. If it is high enough, however, it can make the function reach its maximum at a negative number. In this case, not planting trees would maximize the present value even if that meant no future harvest. (A present value of zero would be larger than the present value that would necessarily be negative with planting.)

Note also that neither the price nor the harvesting cost affects the optimal choice. Mathematically this is due to the fact that they cancel out in equation (2). Economically it is because the value of a harvested unit does not vary with age; therefore the *change* in present value as the stand ages is due to the change in *volume*, not the change in the *value* of each unit of volume (since the change in value is zero).

---

*If we had used a discrete time framework (i.e., $(1 + r)^t$ were used for discounting instead of e^{rt}), then the optimal condition would be the same except r would be replaced by $\ln(1 + r)$. You can verify that for the values of r we are using, these two expressions are approximately equal.

Chapter 13

Renewable Common-Pool Resources: Fisheries and Other Species

In an overpopulated (or overexploited) world, a system of the commons leads to ruin.... Even if an individual fully perceives the ultimate consequences of his actions he is most unlikely to act in any other way, for he cannot count on the restraint his conscience might dictate being matched by a similar restraint on the part of all others.

—Garrett Hardin, *Carrying Capacity as an Ethical Concept* (1967)

Introduction

Humans share the planet with many other living species. How those biological populations are treated depends on whether they are commercially valuable and on whether those who are best positioned to protect them have sufficient incentives.

As we have seen in the previous chapter, one major threat to wildlife is the destruction of its habitat. Undervaluing an existing habitat or overvaluing a competing use of the land can cause excessive destruction of habitat as the land is converted to other uses. Changing those perverse incentives can serve as a means of indirectly protecting wildlife by protecting its habitat.

Protecting habitat is not enough, however, when the species becomes commercially valuable. Commercially valuable species are like a double-edged sword. On the one side, the value of the species to humans provides a strong, current reason for human concern about its future. On the other hand, the level of exploitation may be excessive; commercially exploited biological resources can also be depleted if not managed effectively. If, through human activities, the population is drawn down beyond a critical threshold, even commercially valuable species can become extinct.

Extinction, though important, is not the only critical renewable resource-management issue. Since any sustainable level of harvest will avoid extinction, how do we choose among them? What sustainable level of harvest is appropriate?

Biological populations belong to a class of renewable resources we will call *interactive resources*, wherein the size of the resource stock (population) is determined jointly by biological considerations and by actions taken by society. The post-harvest size of the population, in turn, determines the availability of resources for the future. Thus, humanity's actions determine the flow of these resources over time. Because this flow is not purely a natural phenomenon, the rate of harvest has intertemporal effects. Tomorrow's harvesting choices are affected by today's harvesting behavior.

Using the fishery as a case study, we begin by examining what is meant by an efficient sustainable level of harvest. We then investigate whether efficiency is a sufficiently strong criterion to avoid extinction. Will efficient harvests always result in sustainable outcomes?

Having developed the social choice criteria in some detail, we then turn to an examination of how well our institutions fulfill those criteria. Are normal incentives compatible with efficient sustainable harvest levels?

Unfortunately we shall discover that in many cases normal incentives are compatible with neither efficiency nor sustainability. Focusing on those cases where prevailing incentives are incompatible, the chapter then demonstrates how policy reform incorporating different economic incentives could restore both efficiency and sustainability. Finally, we show how other types of commercial opportunity that do not involve harvesting can be used to protect certain types of wildlife.

Efficient Allocations

The Biological Dimension

Like many other studies, our characterization of the fishery rests on a biological model originally proposed by Schaefer (1957). The Schaefer model posits a particular average relationship between the growth of the fish population and the size of the fish population. This is an average relationship in the sense that it abstracts from such influences as water temperature and the age structure of the population. The model therefore does not attempt to characterize the fishery on a day-to-day basis, but rather in terms of some long-term average in which these various random influences tend to counterbalance each other (see Figure 13.1).

The size of the population is represented on the horizontal axis and the growth of the population on the vertical axis. The graph suggests that there is a range of population sizes ($\underline{S}$ to S^*) where population growth increases as the population increases and a range (S^* to $\bar{S}$) where initial increases in population lead to eventual declines in growth.

We can shed further light on this relationship by examining more closely the two points ($\underline{S}$ and $\bar{S}$) where the function intersects the horizontal axis and therefore growth in the stock is zero. $\bar{S}$ is known as the *natural equilibrium*, since this is population size that would persist in the absence of outside influences. Reductions in

FIGURE 13.1

Relationship between the Fish Population and Growth

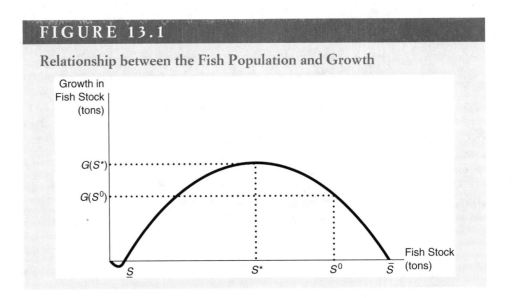

the stock due to mortality or out-migration would be exactly offset by increases in the stock due to births, growth of the fish in the remaining stock, and in-migration.

This natural equilibrium would persist because it is stable. A *stable equilibrium* is one in which movements away from this population level set forces in motion to restore it. If, for example, the stock temporarily exceeded $\bar{S}$, it would be exceeding the capacity of its habitat (called carrying capacity). As a result, mortality rates or out-migration would increase until the stock was once again within the confines of the carrying capacity of its habitat at $\bar{S}$.

This tendency for the population size to return to $\bar{S}$ works in the other direction as well. Suppose the population is temporarily reduced below $\bar{S}$. Because the stock is now smaller, growth would be positive and the size of the stock would increase. Over time, the fishery would move along the curve to the right until $\bar{S}$ is reached again.

What about the other points on the curve? $\underline{S}$, known as the *minimum viable population*, represents the level of population below which growth in population is negative (deaths and out-migration exceed births and in-migration). In contrast to $\bar{S}$, this equilibrium is unstable. Population sizes to the right of $\underline{S}$ lead to positive growth and a movement along the curve to $\bar{S}$ and away from $\underline{S}$. When the population moves to the left of $\underline{S}$, the population declines until it eventually becomes extinct. In this region no forces act to return the population to a viable level.

A catch level is said to represent a *sustainable yield* whenever it equals the growth rate of the population, since it can be maintained forever. As long as the population size remains constant, the growth rate (and hence the catch) will remain constant as well.

S^* is known in biology as the *maximum sustainable yield population*, defined as the population size that yields the maximum growth; hence the maximum sustainable yield is equal to this maximum growth and it represents the largest catch that can be perpetually sustained. Since the catch is equal to the growth, the sustainable yield for any population size (between $\underline{S}$ and $\overline{S}$ can be determined by drawing a vertical line from the stock size of interest on the horizontal axis to the point at which it intersects the function, and drawing a horizontal line over to the vertical axis. The sustainable yield is the growth in the biomass defined by the intersection of this line with the vertical axis. Thus, in terms of Figure 13.1, $G(S^0)$ is the sustainable yield for population size S^0. Since the catch is equal to the growth, population size (and next year's growth) remains the same.

It should now be clear why $G(S^*)$ is the maximum sustainable yield. Larger catches would be possible in the short run, but these could not be sustained; they would lead to reduced population sizes and eventually, if the population were drawn down to a level smaller than $\underline{S}$, to the extinction of the species.

Static Efficient Sustainable Yield

Is the maximum sustainable yield synonymous with efficiency? The answer is no. Recall that efficiency is associated with maximizing the net benefit from the use of the resource. If we are to define the efficient allocation, we must include the costs of harvesting as well as the benefits.

Let's begin by defining the efficient sustainable yield without worrying about discounting. The static efficient sustainable yield is the catch level that if maintained perpetually, would produce the largest annual net benefit. We shall refer to this as the *static efficient sustainable yield* to distinguish it from the *dynamic efficient sustainable yield*, which incorporates discounting. The initial use of this static concept enables us to fix the necessary relationships firmly in mind before dealing with the more difficult role discounting plays. Subsequently, we raise the question of whether or not efficiency always dictates the choice of a sustainable yield as opposed to a catch that changes over time.

We condition our analysis on three assumptions that simplify the analysis without sacrificing too much realism: (1) the price of fish is constant and does not depend on the amount sold; (2) the marginal cost of a unit of fishing effort is constant; and (3) the amount of fish caught per unit of effort expended is proportional to the size of fish population (the smaller the population, the fewer fish caught per unit of effort).

In any sustainable yield, catches, population, effort levels, and net benefits remain constant over time. The static efficient sustainable yield allocation maximizes the constant net benefit.

In Figure 13.2, the benefits (revenues) and costs are portrayed as a function of fishing effort and can be measured in vessel years, hours of fishing, or some other convenient metric. The shape of the revenue function is dictated by the shape of the function in Figure 13.1, since the price of fish is assumed constant. To avoid confusion, notice that increasing fishing effort in Figure 13.1 would result in smaller population sizes and would be recorded as a movement from right to left. As shown by equation (5) in the chapter appendix, the population size is a negatively sloped linear function of the level of effort. The maximum population size (with zero effort) is equal to the carrying capacity, while the minimum population size is zero. Because the variable on the horizontal axis in Figure 13.2 is effort, and not population, an increase in fishing effort is recorded as a movement from left to right.

FIGURE 13.2

Efficient Sustainable Yield for a Fishery

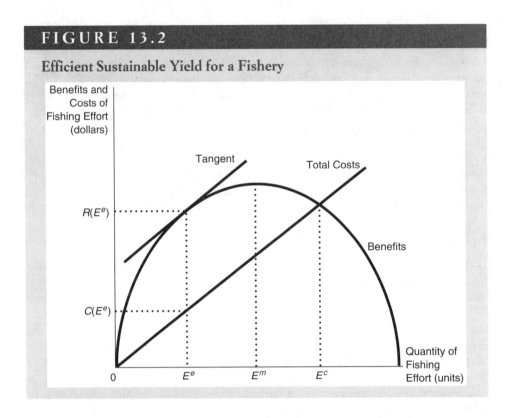

As sustained levels of effort are increased, eventually a point is reached (E^m) at which further effort reduces the sustainable catch and revenue for all years. That point, of course, corresponds to the maximum sustainable yield on Figure 13.1, which involves identical population and growth levels. Every effort level portrayed in Figure 13.2 corresponds to a population level in Figure 13.1.

The net benefit is presented in the diagram as the difference (vertical distance) between benefits (prices times the quantity caught) and costs (the constant marginal cost of effort times the units of effort expended). The efficient level of effort is E^e, that point in Figure 13.2 at which the vertical distance between benefits and costs is maximized.

E^e is the efficient level of effort because it is where marginal benefit (which graphically is the slope of the total benefit curve) is equal to marginal cost (the *constant* slope of the total cost curve). Levels of effort higher than E^e are inefficient because the additional cost associated with them exceeds the value of the fish obtained. Can you see why lower levels of effort are inefficient?

Now we are armed with sufficient information to determine whether or not the maximum sustainable yield is efficient. The answer is clearly no. The maximum sustainable yield would be efficient only if the marginal cost of additional effort were zero. Can you see why? (*Hint:* What is the marginal benefit at the maximum sustainable yield?) Since this is not the case, the efficient level of effort is *less* than that necessary to harvest the maximum sustainable yield. Thus the static efficient level of effort leads to a *larger* fish population than the maximum sustainable yield level of effort.

To fix these concepts firmly in mind, consider what would happen to the static efficient sustainable yield if a technological change were to occur (for example, sonar detection), lowering the marginal cost of fishing. The lower marginal cost would result in a rotation of the total cost curve to the right. With this new cost structure, the old level of effort is no longer efficient. The marginal cost of fishing (slope of the total cost curve) is now lower than the marginal benefit (slope of the total benefit curve). Since the marginal cost is constant, the equality of marginal cost and marginal benefit can result only from a decline in marginal benefits. This implies an increase in effort. The new static efficient sustainable yield equilibrium implies more effort, a lower population level, a larger catch, and a higher net benefit for the fishery.

Dynamic Efficient Sustainable Yield

The static efficient sustainable yield turns out to be the special case of the dynamic efficient sustained yield where the discount rate is zero. It is not difficult to understand why; the static efficient sustained yield is the allocation that maximizes the (identical) net benefit in every period. Any effort levels higher than this would yield temporarily larger catches (and net benefit), but this would be more than offset by a reduced net benefit in the future as the stock reached its new lower level. Thus the undiscounted net benefits would be reduced.

The effect of a positive discount rate for the management of a fishery is similar to its influence on the allocation of depletable resources—the higher the discount rate, the higher the cost (in terms of forgone current income) to the resource owner of maintaining any given resource stock. When positive discount rates are introduced, the efficient level of effort would be increased beyond that suggested by the static efficient sustained yield with a corresponding decrease in the equilibrium population level.

The increase in the yearly effort beyond the efficient sustained yield level would *initially* result in an increased net benefit from the increased catch. (Remember that the amount of fish caught per unit effort expended is proportional to the size of the population.) However, since this catch exceeds the sustained yield for that population size, the population of fish would be reduced and future population and catch levels would be lower. Eventually, as that level of effort is maintained, a new, lower equilibrium level would be attained when the size of the catch once again equals the growth of the population. Colin Clark (1976) has shown mathematically that in terms of Figure 13.2, as the discount rate is increased, the dynamic efficient level of effort is increased until, with an infinite discount rate, it becomes equal to E^c, the point at which net benefits go to zero.

It is easy to see why the use of an infinite discount rate to define the dynamic efficient sustained yield results in allocation E^c. We have seen that interdependent allocations over time give rise to a marginal user cost measuring the opportunity cost of increasing current effort. This opportunity cost reflects the forgone future net benefits when more resources are extracted in the present. For efficient interdependent allocations, the marginal willingness to pay is equal to the marginal user cost plus the marginal cost of extraction.

With an infinite discount rate, this marginal user cost is zero, because no value is received from future allocations. This implies: (1) the marginal cost of extraction equals the marginal willingness to pay, which equals the constant price, and (2) total benefits equal total costs.[1] Earlier we demonstrated that the static efficient sustained yield implies a larger fish population than the maximum sustained yield. Once discounting is introduced, it is inevitable that the dynamic efficient sustained yield would imply a smaller fish population than the static efficient sustained yield and it is possible, though not inevitable, that the sustained catch would be smaller. Can you see why? In Figure 13.2 the sustained catch clearly is lower for an infinite discount rate.

The likelihood of the population being reduced below the level supplying the maximum sustainable yield depends on the discount rate. In general, the lower the extraction costs and the higher the discount rate, the more likely it is that the dynamic efficient level of effort will exceed the level of effort associated with the maximum sustainable yield. This is not difficult to see if we remember the limiting case discussed earlier. When the marginal extraction cost is zero, the static efficient sustainable yield and the maximum sustainable yield are equal.

Thus, with zero marginal extraction costs and a positive discount rate, the dynamic efficient level of effort necessarily exceeds the static efficient level of effort and the level of effort associated with the maximum sustainable yield. Higher extraction costs reduce the static efficient sustainable yield but not the maximum sustainable yield. Higher extraction costs reduce the likelihood that discounting would cause the population to be drawn below the maximum sustainable yield level.

Would a dynamically efficient management scheme lead to extinction of the fishery? As Figure 13.2 shows, it would not be possible under the circumstances described here because E^c is the highest dynamically efficient level possible in this model, and that level falls well short of the level needed to drive the population to extinction. It is possible under other circumstances, however (Cheng, et al., 1981).

For extinction to occur under a dynamic efficient management scheme, the benefit from extracting the very last unit would have to exceed the cost of extracting that unit (including the costs on future generations). As long as the population growth rate exceeds the discount rate, this will not be the case. If, however, the growth rate is lower than the discount rate, extinction can occur in an efficient management scheme if the costs of extracting the last unit are sufficiently low.

Why does the biomass rate of growth have anything to do with whether or not an efficient catch profile leads to extinction? Rates of growth determine the productivity of conservation efforts.[2] With high rates of growth, future generations can be easily satisfied. On the other hand, when the rate of growth is very low, it takes

---

[1] This is not difficult to demonstrate mathematically. In our model, the yield (h) can be expressed as $h = qES$, where q is the proportion of the population harvested with one unit of effort, s is the size of the population, and E is the level of effort. One of the conditions a dynamic efficient allocation has to satisfy with an infinite discount rate is $P = \frac{a}{qE}$, where P is the constant price, a is the constant marginal cost per unit of effort, and qE is the number of fish harvested per unit of effort. By multiplying both sides of this equation by h and collecting terms, we obtain $Ph = aE$. The left-hand side is total benefits, while the right is total cost, implying net benefits are zero.

[2] Note the parallel with the role of the growth rate in efficient timber harvesting in the previous chapter.

a large sacrifice by current generations to produce more fish for future generations. In the limiting case, where the rate of growth is zero, we have a resource with fixed supply and therefore no different from an exhaustible resource. Total depletion would occur whenever the price commanded by the resource is high enough to cover the marginal cost of extracting the last unit.

We have shown that the dynamic efficiency criterion is not automatically consistent with sustaining constant yields perpetually for an interactive renewable resource, since it is mathematically possible for an efficient allocation of a fishery to lead to extinction of the resource. How likely are these criteria to conflict in practice?

Although the information is sketchy, most empirical studies suggest that because of the importance of extraction costs, the dynamic efficient catch rate is usually smaller than the maximum sustainable yield and extinction is rarely, if ever, efficient.[3] The cost of catching the last few fish is usually well in excess of the price received for them. The two criteria are usually completely compatible, although we must bear in mind that they are not inevitably compatible.

Appropriability and Market Solutions

We have now defined an efficient allocation of the fishery over time. The next step is to characterize the normal market allocation and to contrast these two allocations. Where they differ we can entertain the possibility of various public policy corrective means.

Let's first consider the allocation resulting from a fishery managed by a competitive sole owner. A sole owner would have a well-defined property right to the fish. We can establish the behavior of a sole owner by elaborating on Figure 13.2, as is done in Figure 13.3. Notice that the two panels share a common horizontal axis that allows us to examine the effect of various fishing effort levels on both graphs.

A sole owner would want to maximize his or her profits. Ignoring discounting for the moment, the owner can increase profits by increasing fishing effort until marginal revenue equals marginal cost. Clearly this is effort level E^e, the static efficient sustainable yield. This will yield positive profits equal to the difference between $R(E^e)$ and $C(E^e)$.

In ocean fisheries, however, sole owners are unlikely. Ocean fisheries are typically open-access resources—no one exercises complete control over them. Since the property rights to the fishery are not conveyed to any single owner, no fisherman can exclude others from exploiting the fishery.

What problems arise when access to the fishery is completely unrestricted? Open-access resources create two kinds of external costs: a contemporaneous external cost and an intergenerational external cost. The contemporaneous external cost, which is borne by the current generation, involves the overcommitment of resources to fishing—too many boats, too many fishermen, too much effort. As a result,

---

[3]See, for example, the discussion in Clark (1976).

FIGURE 13.3

Market Allocation in a Fishery

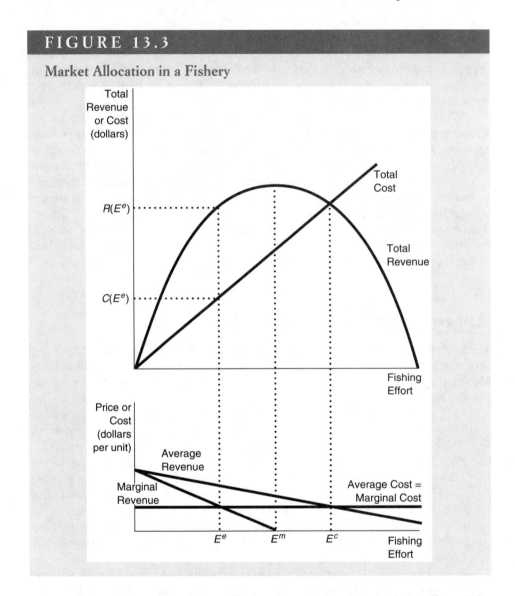

current fishermen earn a substantially lower rate of return on their efforts. The intergenerational external cost, borne by future generations, occurs because over-fishing reduces the stock, which, in turn, lowers future profits from fishing.[4]

We can use Figure 13.3 to see how these external costs arise.[5] Once too many fishermen have unlimited access to the same common-pool fishery, the property

---

[4]This will result in fewer fish for future generations as well as smaller profits if the resulting effort level exceeds that associated with the maximum sustainable yield. If the open-access effort level is lower than the maximum sustainable yield effort level (when extraction costs are very high), then reductions in stock would increase the growth in the stock, thus supplying more fish (albeit lower net benefits) to future generations.

[5]This type of analysis was first used in Gordon (1954).

rights to the fish are no longer efficiently defined. At the efficient level, each boat would receive a profit equal to its share of the scarcity rent. This rent, however, serves as a stimulus for new fishermen to enter, drawing up costs and eliminating the rent. Open access results in overexploitation.

The sole owner chooses not to expend more effort than E^e because to do so would reduce the profits of the fishery, resulting in a personal loss to her. When access to the fishery is unrestricted, a decision to expend effort beyond E^e reduces profits to the fishery as a whole but not to that individual fisherman. Most of the decline in profits falls on the other fishermen.

In an open-access resource, the individual fisherman has an incentive to expend further effort until profits are zero. In Figure 13.3, that point is at effort level E^c, at which average benefit and average cost are equal. It is now easy to see the contemporaneous external cost—too much effort is being expended to catch too few fish, and the cost is substantially higher than it would be in an efficient allocation.

If this point seems abstract, it shouldn't. Many fisheries are currently plagued by precisely these problems. In a productive fishery in the Bering Sea and Aleutian Islands, for example, one study (Huppert, 1990) found significant overcapitalization. While the efficient number of motherships (used to take on and process the catch at sea, so the catch boats do not have to return to port as often) was estimated to be 9, the actual level was 140. As a result, a significant amount of net benefits was lost ($124 million a year). Had the fishery been harvested more slowly, the same catch could have been achieved with fewer boats used closer to their capacity.

An intergenerational external cost occurs because the size of the population is reduced, causing future profits to be lower than would otherwise be the case. As the existing population is overexploited, the open-access catch would initially be higher, but as population growth rates are affected, the steady-state profit level, once attained, would be lower.

We stated in Chapter 7 that the resource owner with exclusive property rights balances the use value against the asset value. When access to the resource is unrestricted, exclusivity is lost. As a result, it is rational for a fisherman to ignore the asset value, since he or she can never appropriate it, and simply maximize the use value. In the process, all the scarcity rent is dissipated. The allocation that results from allowing unrestricted access to the fishery is identical to that resulting from a dynamic efficient sustainable yield when an infinite discount rate is used.

Open-access resources do not automatically lead to a stock lower than that maximizing the sustained yield. We can draw a cost function with a slope sufficiently steep that it intersects the benefit curve at a point to the left of E^m. Nonetheless, it is not unusual for mature, open-access fisheries to be exploited well beyond the point of maximum sustainable yield.

Open-access fishing may or may not pose the threat of species extinction. It depends on the nature of the species and the benefits and costs of harvesting below the minimum viable population. Since the threat of extinction can be determined only in the context of empirical studies, it must be determined on a case-by-case basis (Example 13.1).

Are open-access resources and common-property resources synonymous concepts? They are not. On the one hand, governments can restrict entry, a topic we

Example 13.1

OPEN-ACCESS HARVESTING OF THE MINKE WHALE

Amundsen, Bjørndal, and Conrad examined the effects of open-access fishing on the minke whale using an economic model that is very similar to the model developed in this chapter. Their model was designed to capture harvesting behavior, stock dynamics, and the response of the size of the fishing fleet to profitability. Their model was able to simulate both efficient and open-access equilibria.

While the minke whale is found in both the northern and southern hemispheres, this study examined the North Atlantic stock, which can be found in the areas around Spitzbergen, in the Barents Sea, along the Norwegian coast, and the areas around the British Isles.

Their results suggest that the efficient stock size is in the range of 52,000 to 82,000 adult males, whereas the open-access stock level is in the range 10,000 to 41,000. According to these results, open access does cause substantial depletion of the stock, but it does not cause extinction. The benefits of further harvesting are lower than the costs.

Because the minke whale hunt went unregulated until 1973 (and was only loosely regulated for a while after that), it is possible for results from this simulation to be compared to the preregulation (open-access) historical experience with the fishery. In fact the results of the model seem to conform rather well to that experience. While a substantial increase in harvest was experienced after World War II, the harvest declined to a relatively stable level of 1,700 to 1,800 whales by 1973 and continued at approximately that level for some time until effective regulation ultimately restricted fishing efforts.

The regulation apparently worked. The Scientific Committee of the North Atlantic Marine Mammal Commission (NAMMCO) estimates the current stock of minke whales at 72,130, which is at the high end of the efficient stock size.

Source: Eirik S. Amundsen, Trond Bjørndal, and Jon M. Conrad. "Open Access Harvesting of the Northeast Atlantic Minke Whale," *Environmental and Resource Economics* Vol. 6, No. 2 (September 1995), 167–185.

address in the next section. On the other hand, informal arrangements among those harvesting the common-property resource can also serve to limit access[6] (Example 13.2).

Open-access resources generally violate both the efficiency and sustainability criteria. If these criteria are to be fulfilled, some restructuring of the decision-making environment is necessary. The next section examines how that could be accomplished.

---

[6]For other examples of these arrangements, see Berkes, et al. (1989).

Example   *13.2*

HARBOR GANGS OF MAINE

Unlimited access to common-pool resources reduces net benefits so drastically that this loss encourages those harvesting the resource to restrict access if possible. The Maine lobster fishery is one setting where those informal arrangements have served to limit access with some considerable success.

Key among these arrangements is a system of territories that establishes boundaries between fishing areas. Particularly near the off-shore islands, these territories tend to be exclusively harvested by close-knit, disciplined groups of harvesters. These "gangs" restrict access to their territory by various means. (Some methods are covert and illegal, such as the practice of cutting the lines to lobster traps owned by new entrants, which renders the traps irretrievable.)

Acheson (2003) found that in every season of the year, the pounds of lobster caught per trap and the size of those lobsters were greater in defended areas. Not only did the larger number of pounds result in more revenue, but the bigger lobsters brought in a higher price per pound.

While it would be a mistake to assume that all common-pool resources are characterized by open access, it would also be a mistake to assume that all informal arrangements automatically provide sufficient social means for producing efficient harvests, thereby eliminating any need for public policy. The Maine lobster stock, for example, is also protected by regulations limiting the size of lobsters that can be taken (imposing both minimum and maximum sizes) and prohibiting the harvest of egg-bearing females. The main role for the informal arrangements has been to diminish the pressure on the resource and to prevent overcapitalization. When fewer fishermen harvest the available yield and conservation efforts can increase the size of the stock, income levels for harvesters are higher.

Source: J. M. Acheson. *Capturing the Commons: Devising Institutions to Manage the Maine Lobster Fishery* (Hanover, NH: University Press of New England, 2003).

Public Policy Toward Fisheries

What can be done? A variety of public policy responses is possible. Perhaps it is appropriate to start with allowing the market to work.

Aquaculture

Having demonstrated that inefficient management of the fishery results from treating it as common, rather than private, property, we have one obvious solution—allowing some fisheries to be privately rather than commonly held. This approach can work when the fish are not very mobile, when they can be confined by artificial barriers, or when they instinctively return to their place of birth to spawn.

The advantages of such a move go well beyond the ability to preclude overfishing. The owner is encouraged to invest in the resource and undertake measures that will increase the productivity (yield) of the fishery. (For example, adding certain nutrients to the water or controlling the temperature can markedly increase the yields of some species.) This movement toward controlled raising and harvesting of fish is called *aquaculture*, and there are some noteworthy examples of success. Probably the highest yields ever attained through aquaculture resulted from using rafts to raise mussels. Some 300,000 kilograms per hectare of mussels, for example, have been raised in this manner in the Galician bays of Spain.[7] This productivity level approximates those achieved in poultry farming, widely regarded as one of the most successful attempts to increase the productivity of farm-produced animal protein.

In the United States, aquaculture has been thwarted by treating bodies of water as open-access resources. This need not be the case, of course. Some oysters are raised in the United States in open-access beds and others are raised in private beds. As fish in the open-access resource become more scarce, triggering price increases, aquaculture probably would become more profitable and prevalent.

In some ways, Japan, as a densely populated country depending heavily on fish for protein, has reached the point where merely harvesting what the sea offers is no longer sufficient to satisfy the market at low cost. Consequently, Japan has become a leader in aquaculture, undertaking some of the most advanced aquaculture ventures in the world. The government has been supportive, mainly by creating private-property rights for waters formerly held commonly. The prefecture governments (comparable to states in the United States) initiate the process by designating the areas to be used for aquaculture. The local fishermen's cooperative associations then partition these areas and allocate the subareas to individual fishermen for exclusive use. This exclusive control allows the owner to invest in the resource and to manage it effectively and efficiently.

Another market approach to aquaculture involves fish ranching rather than fish farming. Whereas fish farming involves cultivating fish over their lifetime in a controlled environment, fish ranching involves holding them in captivity only for the first few years of their lives.

Fish ranching relies on the strong homing instincts in certain fish such as Pacific salmon or ocean trout to permit their ultimate capture. The young salmon or ocean trout are hatched and confined in a convenient catch area for approximately two years. When released, they migrate to the ocean. Upon reaching maturity, they return by instinct to the place of their births where they are harvested.

Fish farming has certainly made an impact on the total supply of harvested fish. In 1984 it was estimated that 8% of fish consumed around the world were raised on farms. By 1995 this proportion had already risen to 20%. About one-third of the seafood consumed in the United States comes from fish farms.

---

[7] A hectare is a measure of surface area equal to 10,000 square meters. It is equal to 2.471 acres.

Aquaculture is certainly not the answer for all fish. Although today it works well for certain species, other species will probably never be harvested domestically. Furthermore, fish farming can create environmental problems, ranging from the pollution caused by the fish wastes, to the destruction of ecologically valuable sites to develop fish farms. Nonetheless it is comforting to know that aquaculture can provide a safety valve in some regions and for some fish, and in the process take some of the pressure off the overstressed natural fisheries.[8]

Raising the Real Cost of Fishing

Perhaps one of the best ways to illustrate the virtues of using economic analysis to help design policies is to show the harsh effects of policy approaches that ignore it. Because the earliest approaches to fishery management had a single-minded focus on attaining the maximum sustainable yield with little or no thought given to maximizing the net benefit, they provide a useful contrast.

Perhaps the best concrete example is the set of policies originally designed to deal with overexploitation of the Pacific salmon fishery in the United States. The Pacific salmon is particularly vulnerable to overexploitation and even extinction because of its migration patterns. Pacific salmon are spawned in the gravel beds of rivers. As juvenile fish, they migrate to the ocean, only to return as adults to spawn in the rivers of their birth. After spawning, they die. When the adults swim upstream with an instinctual need to return to their native streams, they can easily be captured by traps, nets, or other catching devices.

Recognizing the urgency of the problem, the government took action. To reduce the catch, they raised the cost of fishing. Initially this was accomplished by preventing the use of any barricades on the rivers and by prohibiting the use of traps (the most efficient catching devices) in the most productive areas. These measures proved insufficient, since mobile techniques (trolling, nets, and so on) proved quite capable by themselves of overexploiting the resource. Officials then began to close designated fishing areas and suspend fishing in other areas for certain periods of time. In Figure 13.3 these measures would be reflected as a rotation of the cost curve to the left until it intersected the benefits curve at a level of effort equal to E^e. The aggregate of all these regulations had the desired effect of curtailing the yield of salmon.

Were these policies efficient? They were not and would not have been even had they resulted in the efficient catch! This statement may seem inconsistent, but it is not. Efficiency implies not only that the catch must be at the efficient level, but it must also be extracted at the lowest possible cost. This latter condition was violated by these policies (see Figure 13.4).

Figure 13.4 reflects the total cost in an efficient allocation (TC_1) and the total cost after these policies were imposed (TC_2). The net benefit received from an efficient policy is shown graphically as the vertical distance between total cost and

---

[8]In another example Frederick Bell (1986) shows that the social welfare losses from the overexploitation of open-access wild crawfish were reduced by an estimated $1,068,933 in 1978 by the existence of private-property crawfish farms. Without them, social welfare losses would have been 4.16 times greater.

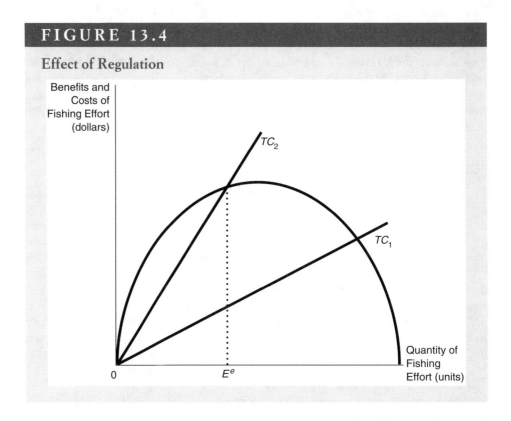

FIGURE 13.4

Effect of Regulation

total benefit. After the policy, however, the net benefit was reduced to zero; the net benefit (represented by vertical distance) was lost to society. Why?

The net benefit was squandered on the use of excessively expensive means to catch the desired yield of fish. Rather than use traps to reduce the cost of catching the desired number of fish, traps were prohibited. Larger expenditures on capital and labor were required to catch the same number of fish. This additional capital and labor represent one source of the waste.

The limitations on fishing times had a similar effect on cost. Rather than allowing fishermen to spread their effort out over time so the boats and equipment could be more productively utilized, fishermen were forced to buy larger boats to allow them to take as much as possible during the shorter seasons. (As one extreme example, Tillion (1985) reported that the 1982 herring season in Prince William Sound lasted only four hours and the catch still exceeded the area quota.) Significant over-capitalization resulted.

Regulation imposed other costs as well. It was soon discovered that while the above regulations were adequate to protect the depletion of the fish population, they had no effect on the incentive for individual fishermen to increase their share of the take. Even though the profits would be small because of high costs, new technological change would allow adopters to increase their shares of the market and put others out of business. To protect themselves, the fishermen were successful in introducing bans on new technology. These restrictions took various forms, but two seem particularly noteworthy. The first was the banning of the use of thin-stranded, monofilament net. The course-stranded net it would have replaced was visible to the salmon in the daytime and therefore could be avoided by them. As a result, it was useful only at night. By contrast, the thinner monofilament nets could be successfully used during the daylight hours as well as at night. Monofilament nets were banned in both Canada and the United States soon after they appeared.

The most flagrantly inefficient regulation was one in Alaska that barred gill netters in Bristol Bay from using engines to propel their boats. This regulation lasted until the 1950s and heightened the public's awareness of the anachronistic nature of this regulatory approach. The world's most technologically advanced nation was reaping its harvest from the Bering Sea in sailboats, while the rest of the world—particularly Japan and the Soviet Union—was modernizing its fishing fleets at a torrid pace!

Time-restriction regulations had a similar effect. Limiting fishing time provides an incentive to use that time as intensively as possible. Huge boats facilitate large harvests within the period and therefore are profitable but are very inefficient; the same harvest could have been achieved with fewer, smaller boats used to their optimum capacity.

Guided by a narrow focus on the maximum sustainable yield that ignored costs, these policies led to a substantial loss in the net benefit received from the fishery. Costs are an important dimension of the problem, and when they are ignored, the incomes of fishermen suffer. When incomes suffer, further conservation measures become more difficult to implement, and incentives to violate the regulations are intensified.

Technical change presents a further problem with attempts to use cost-increasing regulations to reduce fishing effort. Technical innovations can lower the cost of fishing, thereby offsetting the increases imposed by the regulations. In the New England fishery, for example, Jin, et al. (2002) report that the introduction of new technologies such as fishfinders and electronic navigation aids in the 1970s and 1980s led to higher catches and declines in the abundance of the stocks despite the extensive controls in place at the time.

Taxes

Is it possible to provide incentives for cost reduction while assuring that the yield is reduced to the efficient level? Can a more efficient policy be devised? Economists who have studied the question believe that more efficient policies are possible.

Consider a tax on effort. In Figure 13.4, taxes on effort would also be represented as a rotation of the TC line, and the after-tax cost to the fishermen would be adequately represented by line TC_2. Since the after-tax curve coincides with TC_2, the cost curve for all those inefficient regulations, doesn't this imply that the tax system is just as inefficient? No! The key to understanding the difference is the distinction between *transfer costs* and *real-resource costs*.

Under a regulation system of the type described earlier in this chapter, all of the costs included in TC_2 are real-resource costs, which involve utilization of resources.

Transfer costs, by contrast, involve transfers of resources from one part of society to another, rather than their use. Transfers do represent costs to that part of society bearing them, but are exactly offset by the gain received by the recipients. Resources are not used up; they are merely transferred. Thus the calculation of the size of the net benefit should subtract real-resource costs, but not transfer costs, from benefits. For society as a whole, transfer costs are retained as part of the net benefit.

In Figure 13.3, the net benefit under a tax system is identical to that under an efficient allocation. The net benefit represents a transfer cost to the fisherman that is exactly offset by the revenues received by the tax collector. This discussion should not obscure the fact that, as far as the individual fisherman is concerned, these are very real costs. Rent normally received by a sole owner is now received by the government. Since the tax revenues involved can be substantial, fishermen wishing to have the fishery efficiently managed may object to this particular way of doing it. They would prefer a policy that restricts catches while allowing them to keep the rents. Is that possible?

Individual Transferable Quotas (ITQs)

One policy making it possible is a properly designed quota on the number of fish that can be taken from the fishery. The "properly designed" caveat is important because there are many different types of quota schemes and not all are of equal merit. An efficient quota system has several identifiable characteristics:[9]

1. The quotas entitle the holder to catch a specified share of the total authorized catch of a specified type of fish;
2. The catch authorized by the quotas held by all fishermen should be equal to the efficient catch for the fishery; and
3. The quotas should be freely transferable among fishermen.

Each of these three characteristics plays an important role in obtaining an efficient allocation. Suppose, for example, the quota were defined in terms of the right to own and use a fishing boat rather than in terms of catch—not an uncommon type of quota. Such a quota is not efficient, because under this type of quota an inefficient incentive still remains for each boat owner to build larger boats, to place extra equipment on them, and to spend more time fishing. These actions would expand the capacity of each boat and cause the actual catch to exceed the target (efficient) catch. In a nutshell, the boat quota limits the number of boats fishing but does not limit the amount of fish caught by each boat. If we are to reach and sustain an efficient allocation, it is the catch that must ultimately be limited.

While the purpose of the second condition is obvious, the role of transferability deserves more consideration. With transferability, the entitlement to fish flows naturally to those gaining the most benefit from it because their costs are lower. Because it is valuable, the transferable quota commands a positive price. Those who

---

[9]The ITQ system is fully efficient only in the absence of stock externalities (Boyce, 1992). Stock externalities exist when the productivity of a unit of harvesting effort depends on the density of the stock. The presence of stock externalities creates incentives for excessive fishing early in the season (when catches are higher per unit effort) before the biomass gets depleted.

have quotas but also have high costs find they make more money selling the quotas than using them. Meanwhile, those who have lower costs find they can purchase more quotas and still make money.

Transferable quotas also encourage technological progress. Adopters of new cost-reducing technologies can make more money on their existing quotas and make it profitable to purchase new quotas from others who have not adopted the technology. Therefore, in marked contrast to the earlier regulatory methods used to raise costs, both the tax system and the transferable quota system encourage the development of new technologies.

How about the distribution of the rent? In a quota system the distribution of the rent depends crucially on how the quotas are initially allocated. There are many possibilities with different outcomes. The first possibility is for the government to auction off these quotas. But the government would then appropriate all the rent, and the outcome would be very similar to the outcome of the tax system. If the fishermen do not like the tax system, they would not like the auction system either.

In an alternative approach, the government could give the quotas to the fishermen, say, in proportion to their historical catch. The fishermen could then trade among themselves until a market equilibrium is reached. All the rent would be retained by the current generation of fishermen. Fishermen who might want to enter the market would have to purchase the quotas from existing fishermen. Competition among the potential purchasers would drive up the price of the transferable quotas until it reflected the market value of future rents, appropriately discounted.[10]

Thus this type of quota system allows the rent to remain with the fishermen, but only the current generation of fishermen. Future generations see little difference between this quota system and a tax system; in either case, they have to pay to enter the industry, whether it be through the tax system or by purchasing the quotas.

In 1983 a limited individual transferable quota system was established in New Zealand to protect its deepwater trawl fishery (Muse and Schelle, 1988). Though this was far from being the only, or even the earliest, application of ITQs (see Table 13.1), it provides an unusually rich opportunity to study how this approach works in practice.

Because this fishery was newly developed, allocating the quotas proved relatively easy. The total allowable catches for the seven basic species were divided into individual transferable quotas and were allocated to existing firms on the basis of investment in harvesting equipment, investment in on-shore production equipment, and recent on-shore production. The rights to harvest were denominated in terms of a specific amount of fish, but were granted only for a 10-year period.

At the same time as the deep-sea fishery policy was being considered, the inshore fishery began to fall on hard times. Too many participants were chasing too many fish. Some particularly desirable fish species were being seriously overfished. While the need to reduce the amount of pressure being put on the population was rather

---

[10]This occurs because the maximum bid any potential entrant would make is the value to be derived from owning that permit. This value is equal to the present value of future rents (the difference between price and marginal cost for each unit of fish sold). Competition will force the purchaser to bid near that maximum value, lest he or she lose the quota.

TABLE 13.1

Countries with Individual Transferable Quota Systems

Countries	Number of Species Covered
Australia	4
Canada	14
Chile	3
Iceland	16
Netherlands	4
New Zealand	33
United States	4

Sources: Information compiled from OECD. *Implementing Domestic Tradable Permits for Environmental Protection* (Paris: Organisation for Economic Co-operation and Development, 1999): 19 and P. Bernal and B. Aliaga. "ITQs in Chilean Fisheries," in A. Hatcher and K. Robinson, eds. *The Definition and Allocation of Use Rights in European Fisheries*. Proceedings of the Second Concerted Workshop on Economics and the Common Fisheries Policy. (Brest, France. May 5–7, 1999). (University of Portsmouth, UK: Center for the Economics and Management of Aquatic Resources): 117–130.

obvious, the means to accomplish that reduction was not at all obvious. Although it was relatively easy to prevent new fishermen from entering the fisheries, it was harder to figure out how to reduce the pressure from those who had been fishing in the area for years or even decades. Because fishing is characterized by economies of scale, simply reducing everyone's catch proportionately wouldn't make much sense. That would simply place higher costs on everyone and waste a great deal of fishing capacity as all boats sat around idle for a significant proportion of time. A better solution would clearly be to have fewer boats harvesting the stock. That way each boat could be used closer to its full capacity without depleting the population. Which fishermen should be asked to give up their livelihood and leave the industry?

The economic incentive approach addressed this problem by having the government buy back catch quotas from those willing to sell them. While initially this was financed out of general revenues, subsequently it was financed by a fee on catch quotas. Essentially each fisherman stated the lowest price that he or she would accept for leaving the industry; the regulators selected those who could be induced to leave at the lowest price, paid the stipulated amount from the fee revenues, and retired their licenses to fish for this species. It wasn't long before a sufficient number of licenses had been retired and the population was protected. Because the program was voluntary, those who left the industry did so only when they felt they had been adequately compensated. Meanwhile, those who paid the fee realized that this small investment would benefit them greatly in the future as the population recovered. A difficult and potentially dangerous pressure on a valuable natural resource had been alleviated by the creative use of an approach that changed the economic incentives.

Toward the end of 1987, however, a new problem emerged. The original stock of one species (orange roughy) turned out to have been seriously overestimated by biologists. Since the total allocation of quotas was derived from this estimate, the practical implication was that an unsustainably high level of quotas had been issued; the stock was in jeopardy. Faced with the unacceptably large budget implications of buying back a significant amount of quota, the government ultimately shifted to a percentage-share allocation of quota. Under this system, instead of owning quota defined in terms of a specific quantity of fish, fishermen own percentage shares of a total allowable catch. The total allowable catch is determined annually by the government. In this way the government can annually adjust the total allowable catch, based on the latest stock assessment estimates, without having to buy back (or sell) large amounts of quota. This approach affords greater protection to the stock but increases the financial risk to the fishermen.

Some other implementation problems have emerged as well. Fishing effort is frequently not very well targeted. Species other than those sought (known as "bycatch") may well end up as part of the catch. If those species are also regulated by quotas and the fishermen do not have sufficient ITQs to cover the bycatch, they are faced with the possibility of being fined when they land the unauthorized fish. Dumping the bycatch overboard avoids the fines, but since the jettisoned fish frequently do not survive, this represents a double waste—not only is the stock reduced, but the harvested fish are wasted.

"High-grading" is another problem managers have had to deal with. High-grading can occur when quotas specify the catch in terms of weight of a certain species, but the value of the catch is affected greatly by the size of the individual fish. To maximize the value of the quota, fishermen have an incentive to throw back the less valuable (typically smaller) fish, keeping only the most valuable individuals. As with bycatch, when release mortality is high, high-grading results in both smaller stocks and wasted harvests.

Some fisheries managers have successfully solved both problems by allowing fishermen to cover temporary overages with allowances subsequently purchased or leased from others. As long as the market value of the "extra" fish exceeds the cost of leasing quota, the fishermen will have an incentive to land and market the fish and the stock will not be placed in jeopardy.

Though ITQ systems are far from perfect, they frequently do offer the opportunity to improve on traditional fisheries management (see Example 13.3). The fact that they are spreading to new fisheries so rapidly suggests that their potential is being increasingly recognized.

Marine Reserves

Regulating the amount of catch does not control either the type of gear that is used or locations where the harvests take place. Failure to control those elements can lead to environmental degradation of the habitat on which the fishery depends. Some gear may be particularly damaging, not only on the targeted species (for example, by capturing juveniles that cannot be sold, but that don't survive capture) but also to nontargeted species (bycatch). Similarly, harvesting in some geographic areas (such as those used for spawning) might have a disproportionately large detrimental effect on the sustainability of the fishery.

Example 13.3

THE RELATIVE EFFECTIVENESS OF TRANSFERABLE QUOTAS AND TRADITIONAL SIZE AND EFFORT RESTRICTIONS IN THE ATLANTIC SEA SCALLOP FISHERY

Theory suggests that transferable quotas will produce more cost-effective outcomes in fisheries than traditional restrictions, such as minimum legal size and maximum effort controls. Is this theoretical expectation compatible with the actual experience in implemented systems?

In a fascinating study, economist Robert Repetto (2001) examines this question by comparing Canadian and American approaches to controlling the sea scallop fishery off the Atlantic coast. While Canada adopted a transferable quota system, the United States adopted a mix of size, effort, and area controls. The comparison provides a rare opportunity to exploit a natural experiment since scallops are not migratory and the two countries used similar fishing technologies. Hence it is reasonable to presume that the differences in experience are largely due to the difference in management approaches.

What were the biological consequences of these management strategies for the two fisheries?

- The Canadian fishery was not only able to maintain the stock at a higher level of abundance; it was also able to deter the harvesting of undersized scallops (p. 257).
- In the United States, stock abundance levels declined and undersized scallops were harvested at high levels (p. 257).

What were the economic consequences?

- Revenue per sea-day increased significantly in the Canadian fishery, due largely to the sevenfold increase in catch per sea-day made possible by the larger stock abundance (pp. 258–260).
- In the United States, fishery revenue per sea-day fell, due not only to the fall in the catch per day that resulted from the decline in stock abundance, but also to the harvesting of undersized scallops (pp. 258–260).
- Although the number of Canadian quota holders was reduced from nine to seven over a fourteen-year period, 65% of the quota remained in its original hands. The evidence suggests that smaller players were apparently not at a competitive disadvantage (p. 262).

What were the equity implications?

- Both U. S. and Canadian fisheries have traditionally operated on the "lay" system, which divides the revenue among crew, captain, and owner according to preset percentages, after subtracting certain operating expenditures. This means that all parties remaining in the fishery after regulation shared in the increasing rents (p. 261).

In this fishery at least, it seems that the theory was supported by experience.

Source: Robert Repetto. "A Natural Experiment in Fisheries Management," *Marine Policy* Vol. 25 (2001): 252–264.

Conservation biologists have suggested complementing current policies with the establishment of a system of marine reserves. A marine reserve is an area that prohibits harvesting and enjoys a very high level of protection from other threats such as pollution.

Biologists believe that marine reserves can perform several maintenance and restorative functions. First, they protect *individual species* by preventing harvest within the reserve boundaries. Second, they reduce *habitat damage* caused by fishing gear or practices that alter biological structures. Third, in contrast to quotas on single species, reserves can promote *ecosystem balance* by protecting against the removal of ecologically pivotal species (whether targeted species or bycatch) that could throw an ecosystem out of balance by altering its diversity and productivity (Palumbi, 2002).

Reducing harvesting in these areas protects the stock, the habitat, and the ecosystem on which it depends. This protection results in a larger population and, ultimately, if the species swim beyond the boundaries of the reserve, larger catches in the remaining harvest areas.

How reserves promote sustainability seems clear since it allows the population to recover. Their relationship to the welfare of current users, however, is less clear. Proponents of marine reserves suggest that they can promote sustainability in a win-win fashion (meaning current users benefit as well). This is an important point since users who did not benefit might mount opposition to marine reserve proposals, thereby making their establishment very difficult.

Would the establishment of a marine reserve maximize the present value of net benefits for fishermen? If marine reserves work as planned, they reduce harvest in the short run (by declaring areas previously available for harvest off-limits), but they increase it in the long run (as the population recovers). However, the delay would impose costs. (Remember the discount rate?) To take one concrete example of the costs of delay, harvesters may have to pay off a mortgage on their boat. Even if the bank grants them a delay in making payments, total payments will rise. So, by itself, a future rise in harvests does not guarantee that establishing the reserve maximizes present value unless the rise in catch is large enough and soon enough to compensate for the costs imposed by the delay.

Since the present value of this policy depends on the specifics of the individual cases, a case study can be revealing. In their interesting case study of the California sea urchin industry, Smith and Wilen (2003) find:

> Our overall assessment of reserves as a fisheries policy tool is more ambivalent than the received wisdom in the biological literature. . . . We find . . . that reserves can produce harvest gains in an age-structured model, but only when the biomass is severely overexploited. We also find . . . that even when steady state harvests are increased with a spatial closure, the discounted returns are often negative, reflecting slow biological recovery relative to the discount rate. (p. 204)

Does this mean marine reserves are a bad idea? Certainly not! In some areas they may be a necessary step for achieving sustainability; in others they may represent the most efficient means of achieving sustainability. It does mean, however, that we should be wary of the notion that they always create win-win situations; sacrifices by local harvesters might be required. Marine reserve policies must recognize the possibility of this burden and deal with it directly, not just assume it doesn't exist.

The 200-Mile Limit

The final policy dimension concerns the international aspects of the fishery problem. Obviously the various policy approaches to effective management of fisheries require some governing body to have jurisdiction over a fishery so that it can enforce its regulations.

This is not currently the case for many of the ocean fisheries. Much of the open water of the oceans is a common-pool resource to governments as well as to individual fishermen. No single body can exercise control over it. As long as that continues to be the case, the corrective action will be difficult to implement. In recognition of this fact, there is an evolving law of the sea defined by international treaties. One of the concrete results of this law, for example, has been some limited restrictions on whaling. Whether this process ultimately yields a consistent and comprehensive system of management remains to be seen.

Countries bordering the sea have declared that their ownership rights extend some 200 miles out to sea. Within these areas, the countries have exclusive jurisdiction and implement effective management policies. These declarations have been upheld and are now firmly entrenched in international law. Thus, very rich fisheries in coastal waters can be protected, while those in the open waters await the outcome of an international negotiations process.

The Economics of Enforcement

Enforcement is an area that traditionally has not received much analytical treatment but is gradually becoming recognized as a key aspect of fisheries management. Policies can be designed to be perfectly efficient as long as everyone follows them voluntarily, but these same policies may look rather tragic in the harsh realities of costly and imperfect enforcement.

Fisheries policies are especially difficult to enforce. Coastlines are typically long and rugged; it is not difficult for fishermen to avoid detection if they are exceeding their limits or catching species illegally.

Recognizing these realities immediately suggests two implications. First, policy design should take enforcement into consideration, and, second, what is efficient when enforcement is ignored may not be efficient once enforcement is considered.

Policies should be designed to make compliance as inexpensive as possible. Regulations that impose very high costs are more likely to be disobeyed than regulations that impose costs in proportion to the purpose. Regulations should also contain provisions for dealing with noncompliance. A common approach is to levy monetary sanctions against those failing to comply. The sanctions should be set at a high enough level to bring the costs of noncompliance (including the sanction) into balance with the costs of compliance.

The enforcement issue points out another advantage of private-property approaches to fisheries management—they are self-enforcing. Fish farmers or fish ranchers have no incentive to deviate from the efficient scheme because they would only be hurting themselves. No enforcement activity is necessary. Noncompliance with some kind of regulatory constraint, on the other hand, could, in the absence of effective enforcement, be beneficial to those fishing in common-pool resources. Mounting this enforcement effort is yet another cost associated with the public management of fisheries.

Since enforcement activity is costly, it follows that it should be figured into our definition of efficiency. How would our analysis be changed by incorporating enforcement costs? One study (Sutinen and Anderson, 1985) suggests that the incorporation of realistic enforcement cost considerations tends to reduce the efficient population below the level declared efficient in the presence of perfect, costless enforcement.

The rationale is not difficult to follow. Assume that some kind of quota system is in effect to ration access. Enforcement activity would involve monitoring compliance with these quotas and assigning penalties on those found in noncompliance.[11] If the quotas are so large as to be consistent with the free-access equilibrium, enforcement cost would be zero; no enforcement would be necessary to ensure compliance. Moving the fishery away from the free-access equilibrium increases both net benefits and enforcement costs. For this model, as the steady-state population size is increased, marginal enforcement costs increase and marginal net benefits decrease. At the efficient population size (considering enforcement cost), the marginal net benefit equals the marginal enforcement cost. This necessarily involves a smaller population size than the efficient population size ignoring enforcement costs, because the latter occurs when the marginal net benefit is zero.

Preventing Poaching

A second type of threat to commercially valuable species comes from poaching, the illegal harvest of a species. Poaching can introduce the possibility of unsustainability even when a legal structure to protect the population has been enacted.

From an economic point of view poaching can be discouraged if it is possible to raise the relative cost of illegal activity. While that can be accomplished in principle by increasing the sanctions levied against poachers, that is only effective if monitoring can detect the illegal activity and apply the sanctions to those who engage in it. In many places that is a tall order, given the large size of the habitat to be monitored and the limited budgets for funding enforcement. Example 13.4 shows, however, how economic incentives can be enlisted to promote more monitoring by local inhabitants as well as to provide more revenue for enforcement activity.

Example 13.4 also points out that many species are commercially valuable even in the absence of any harvest. The rise of the *ecotourism* industry suggests that large numbers of people will pay considerable sums of money simply to witness these magnificent creatures in their native habitat. This revenue, when shared with local people, can provide an incentive to protect the species and decrease the incentive to

---

[11]In theory it would be possible to set the penalty so high that only a limited amount of enforcement activity would be necessary. Since large penalties are rarely imposed in practice, the model rules these out and assumes that increasing enforcement expenditures are necessary to enforce increasingly stringent quotas.

Example 13.4

LOCAL APPROACHES TO WILDLIFE PROTECTION: ZIMBABWE

In 1989 an innovative program was initiated in Zimbabwe that stands out as a success among other African wildlife protection schemes. It transformed the role of wildlife from a state-owned treasure to be preserved, into an active resource controlled and used by both commercial farmers and smallholders in communal lands. The transformation has been good for the economy and the wildlife.

The initiative is called the Communal Areas Management Program for Indigenous Resources, or CAMPFIRE. It was originally sponsored by several different agencies in cooperation with the Zimbabwen government, including the University of Zimbabwe's Center for Applied Study, the Zimbabwe Trust, and The World-wide Fund for Nature (WWF).

Under the CAMPFIRE system, villagers collectively utilize local wildlife resources on a sustainable basis. Trophy hunting by foreigners is perhaps the most important source of revenue, because hunters require few facilities and are willing to pay substantial fees to kill a limited number of large animals. The government sets the prices of hunting permits as well as quotas for the number of animals that can be taken per year in each locality. Individual communities sell the permits and contract with safari operators who conduct photographic and hunting expeditions on community lands.

The associated economic gains accrue to the villages, which then decide how the revenues should be used. The money may either be paid to households in the form of cash dividends, which may amount to 20% or more of an average family's income, or they may be used for capital investments in the community, such as schools, clinics, or labor saving. In at least one area, revenues compensate citizens who have suffered property loss due to wild animals. Households may also receive nonmonetary benefits, such as meat from problem animals or culled herds. By consistently meeting their needs from their own resources on a sustainable basis, local communities have become self-reliant. This voluntary program has been steadily expanding since its inception, and now includes about half of Zimbabwe's 55 districts.

Sources: Edward Barbier. "Community Based Development in Africa," in Timothy Swanson and Edward Barbier, eds. *Economics for the Wilds: Wildlife, Diversity, and Development* (Washington, DC: Island Press, 1992): 107–118; Jan Bojö. "The Economics of Wildlife: Case Studies from Ghana, Kenya, Namibia and Zimbabwe," AFTES Working Paper No. 19 (the World Bank, February 1996); and the Web site http://www.colby.edu/personal/thtieten/end-zim.html.

participate in illegal poaching activity that would threaten the source of the eco-tourism revenue.

Not all countries are availing themselves of this opportunity. For example, Kenya, a country with large declines in its elephant population, has no such system. Whereas in Zimbabwe villagers have a very large stake in protecting the source of this income, the elephant herd, Kenyans have little stake in their protection. The potential revenue that could be used to institutionalize a protection system is enormous. Economists Gardner Brown and Wes Henry (1989) have estimated that some $25 million per year would be available in Kenya from tourists seeking to view and photograph elephants.

Rearranging the economic incentives so that local groups have an economic interest in their preservation can provide a powerful means of protecting some biological populations. Open access undermines those incentives.

Summary

Unrestricted access to commercially valuable species will generally result in overexploitation. This overexploitation, in turn, results in overcapitalization, depressed incomes for harvesters, and depleted stocks. Even extinction of the species is possible, particularly for populations characterized by particularly low extraction costs (such as the Pacific salmon fishery). Where extraction costs are higher, extinction is unlikely, even with unrestricted access.

Both the private and public sectors have moved to ameliorate the problems associated with past mismanagement of wildlife populations. By reasserting private-property rights, Japan and other countries have stimulated the development of aquaculture. Governments in Canada and the United States have moved to limit overexploitation of the Pacific salmon. International agreements have been instituted to place limits on whaling. It is doubtful that these programs fully satisfy the efficiency criterion, although it does seem clear that sustainable catches will result.

Creative strategies for sharing the gains from moving to an efficient level of use could prove to be a significant weapon in the arsenal of techniques designed to protect a broad class of biological resources from overexploitation. An increasing reliance on individual transferable quotas offers the possibility of preserving stocks without jeopardizing the incomes of those men and women currently harvesting those stocks. Furthermore, giving local communities a stake in preserving elephant herds has provided a vehicle for building political coalitions to prevent overexploitation of this resource.

It would be folly to ignore barriers to further action, such as the reluctance of individual harvesters to submit to many forms of regulation, the lack of a firm policy governing open-ocean waters, and the difficulties of enforcing various approaches. Whether these barriers will fall before the pressing need for effective management remains to be seen.

Discussion Questions

1. Is the establishment of the 200-mile limit a sufficient form of government intervention to ensure that the tragedy of the commons does not occur for fisheries within the 200-mile limit? Why or why not?
2. With discounting, it is possible for the efficient fish population to fall below the level required to produce the maximum sustained yield. Does this violate the sustainability criterion? Why or why not?

Problems

1. Assume that the relationship between the growth of a fish population and the population size can be expressed as $g = 4P - 0.1P^2$, where g is the growth in tons and P is the size of the population (in thousands of tons). Given a price of \$100 a ton, the marginal benefit of smaller population sizes (and hence larger catches) can be computed as $20P - 400$. (a) Compute the population size that is compatible with the maximum sustainable yield. What would be the size of the annual catch if the population were to be sustained at this level? (b) If the marginal cost of additional catches (expressed in terms of the population size) is $MC = 2(160 - P)$, what is the population size that is compatible with the efficient sustainable yield?

2. Assume that a local fisheries council imposes an enforceable quota of 100 tons of fish on a particular fishing ground for one year. Assume further that 100 tons per year is the efficient sustained yield. Once the 100th ton has been caught, the fishery would be closed for the remainder of the year. (a) Is this an efficient solution to the common-property problem? Why or why not? (b) Would your answer be different if the 100-ton quota were divided up into 100 transferable quotas, each entitling the holder to catch one ton of fish, and distributed among the fishermen in proportion to their historical catch? Why or why not?

3. In the economic model of the fishery developed above, compare the effect on fishing effort of an increase in cost of a fishing license with an increase in a per-unit tax on fishing effort that raises the same amount of revenue. Assume the fishery is private property. Repeat the analysis assuming that the fishery is a free-access common-property resource.

Further Reading

Acheson, James M. *Capturing the Commons: Devising Institutions to Manage the Maine Lobster Industry* (Hanover, NH: University Press of New England, 2003). An impressive synthesis of theory and empirical work, combined with an insider's knowledge of the institutions and the people who run them, makes this a compelling examination of the history of one of America's most important fisheries.

Clark, Colin W. *Mathematical Bioeconomics: The Optimal Management of Renewable Resources*, 2nd ed. (New York: Wiley-Interscience, 1990). Careful development of the mathematical models that underlie current understanding of the exploitation of renewable resources under a variety of property right regimes.

National Research Council Committee to Review Individual Fishing Quotas. *Sharing the Fish: Toward a National Policy on Fishing Quotas*. (Washington, D.C.: National Academy Press, 1999). A detailed look at the experience with ITQs around the world.

Schlager, Edella, and Elinor Ostrom. "Property Right Regimes and Natural Resources: A Conceptual Analysis," *Land Economics* Vol. 68 (1992): 249–262. The authors develop a conceptual framework for analyzing a number of property rights regimes and use this framework to interpret findings from a number of empirical studies.

Swanson, Timothy M., and Edward Barbier, eds. *Economics for the Wilds* (Washington, DC: Island Press, 1992). The authors of this book argue that an economic system that properly values wildlife offers the best security for its preservation. Shows how this can be accomplished.

Townsend, Ralph E. "Entry Restrictions in the Fishery: A Survey of the Evidence," *Land Economics* Vol. 66 (1990): 361–378. Reviews the relevant experience with about 30 limited-entry programs around the world. Identifies features of limited-entry programs that seem to contribute to success and failure.

Additional References and Historically Significant References are available on this book's companion Web site www.aw-bc.com/tietenberg.

Appendix

The Harvesting Decision: Fisheries

Defining the efficient sustainable yield for a fishery begins with a characterization of the biological relationship between the growth for the biomass and the size of the biomass. The standard representation of this relationship is:

$$g = rS\left(1 - \frac{S}{k}\right), \tag{1}$$

where

g = the growth rate of the biomass,
r = the intrinsic growth rate for this species,
S = the size of the biomass, and
k = the carrying capacity of the habitat.

Since we want to choose the most efficient *sustained* yield, we must limit the possible outcomes we shall consider to those that are sustainable. Here we define a sustainable harvest level, h_s, as one that equals the growth of the population. Hence:

$$h_s = rS\left(1 - \frac{S}{k}\right). \tag{2}$$

The next step is to define the size of the harvest as a function of the amount of effort expended. This is traditionally modeled as:

$$h = qES \tag{3}$$

where:

q = a constant (known as the "catchability coefficient"), and
E = the level of effort.

The next step is to solve for sustained yields as a function of effort. This can be derived using a two-step procedure. First we express S in terms of E. Then we use this newly derived expression for S along with the relationship in (3) to derive the sustained yield expressed in terms of effort.

To define S in terms of E, we can substitute (3) into (2):

$$qES = rS\left(1 - \frac{S}{k}\right). \tag{4}$$

Rearranging terms yields:

$$S = k\left(1 - \frac{qE}{r}\right). \tag{5}$$

Using $S = h/qE$ from (3) and rearranging terms to solve for h yields:

$$h_s = qEk - \frac{q^2 kE^2}{r}. \tag{6}$$

It is now possible to find the maximum sustainable effort level by taking the derivative of the right-hand side of (6) with respect to effort (E) and setting the result equal to zero.

The maximum condition is:

$$qk - 2\frac{q^2 kE}{r} = 0. \tag{7}$$

So:

$$E_{msy} = \frac{r}{2q}, \tag{8}$$

where:

E_{msy} = the level of effort that is consistent with the maximum sustained yield.

Can you see how to solve for the maximum sustainable yield, h_{msy}? (*Hint:* Remember how the maximum sustained yield was defined in terms of effort in (6)?)

To conduct the economic analysis, we need to convert this biological information to a net benefits formulation. The benefit function can be defined by multiplying (6) by P, the price received for a unit of harvest. Assuming a constant marginal cost of effort, a, allows us to define total cost as equal to aE. Subtracting the total cost of effort from the revenue function produces the net benefits function:

$$\text{Net benefits} = PqEk - \frac{Pq^2 kE^2}{r} - aE. \tag{9}$$

Since the efficient sustained effort level is the level that maximizes (9), we can derive it by taking the derivative of (9) with respect to effort (E) and setting the derivative equal to zero:

$$Pqk - \frac{2Pkq^2 E}{r} - a = 0. \tag{10}$$

Rearranging terms yields:

$$E = \frac{r}{2q}\left(1 - \frac{a}{Pqk}\right).$$

(11)

Note that this effort level is smaller than that needed to produce the maximum sustainable yield. Can you see how to find the efficient sustainable harvest level? Finally we can derive the free-access equilibrium by setting the net benefits function (9) equal to zero and solving for the effort level.

Rearranging terms yields:

$$E = \frac{r}{q}\left(1 - \frac{a}{Pqk}\right).$$

(12)

Notice that this is larger than the efficient sustained level of effort. It may or may not be larger than the level of effort needed to produce the maximum sustained yield. That comparison depends on the specific values of the parameters.

Chapter

14

Generalized Resource Scarcity

As a nation, we have always faced choices and always will. What matters is the range of choice we have and the urgency with which the need to choose is thrust upon us.

—Commission on Population Growth and the American Future

Introduction

Public concern over natural resource scarcity is not new. The National Conservation Commission, formed during the Theodore Roosevelt administration and headed by noted conservationist Gifford Pinchot, conducted the first national inventory of natural resources in 1908. This commission was established in response to a growing concern about natural resource scarcity. Its mandate was to provide data so that the situation could be assessed and appropriate public policies could be charted. This initial inquiry has been followed by a number of others with a similar focus.

A number of concerns suggest the need for continued vigilance. We have seen, for example, that even though world fertility rates are now falling, the current age structure of the population creates an inertia for population growth that will not, even in the most optimistic projections, allow for a stable world population in the immediate future. These increases in the population will cause the demand for resources to increase faster than it would if the population were stable. The implications of this increasing growth on the demand can be profound, particularly in industrial countries such as the United States, where per capita consumption levels are high.

Previous chapters have demonstrated that while markets automatically provide some corrective responses to scarcity, market and public policy imperfections have reduced the efficiency of these responses. These imperfections include price controls, open-access resources, externalities, and the tax treatment of resources. We were able to suggest a public policy response to the particular resource problem under investigation. In some cases, the appropriate response is to remove restrictions previously placed on the market.

316

Individual mines or wells will be exhausted in the face of this rising demand. But will these remain isolated incidents or will they add up to a pattern of generalized resource scarcity? Generalized scarcity would have a detrimental impact on the quality of life for this and succeeding generations.

Our search for evidence of generalized scarcity begins with a review and elaboration of the manner in which a market economy copes with increasing scarcity, particularly the roles of exploration and discovery, technological progress, and the substitution of abundant resources for scarce ones. We then examine how resource scarcity can be detected. What indicators can be used? What are their strengths and weaknesses? Once we have gained an appreciation for avenues of detection, we turn to the evidence revealed by these indicators and discuss how this evidence may be interpreted.

This chapter serves two purposes: an end in itself and a means to understanding more global concerns. It is an end in that the existence or nonexistence of a generalized resource scarcity is inherently important. It also represents a point of departure in the larger debate about the desirability and inevitability of future economic growth. We pursue this concern in Chapter 22, when we explore the process of economic growth in the context of limited environmental and natural resources.

Factors Mitigating Resource Scarcity

The ability of a market economy to cope with pressures on the environmental asset caused by population and income growth depends on alternatives for diffusing these pressures. Three alternatives have been particularly important: (1) exploration and discovery, (2) technological progress, and (3) substitution.

Exploration and Discovery

A profit-maximizing firm will undertake exploration activity until the marginal discovery cost equals the marginal scarcity rent received from a unit of the resource sold.[1] Since the marginal scarcity rent—the difference between the price received and the marginal cost of extraction—is the marginal benefit received by the firm engaging in exploration activity, the level of activity should be increased to maximize profits until this marginal benefit is equal to the marginal cost.

An understanding of this relationship between scarcity rent and marginal discovery cost allows us to think about how exploration activity would respond to population and income growth. Since both of these factors contribute to rising demand over time, they raise the marginal user cost and the scarcity rent, stimulating producers to undertake larger marginal discovery costs.

How much this demand pressure is relieved depends upon the amount of exploration activity and the amount of resources discovered per unit of exploration activity undertaken. If the marginal discovery cost curve is flat (implying a large amount of relatively available resources), increases in scarcity rent can stimulate large amounts of successful exploration activity. If the marginal discovery cost curve is

---

[1]This is strictly true only when no uncertainty is associated with exploration. Even with uncertainty, however, marginal discovery cost is highly related to scarcity rent. See Devarajan and Fisher (1982).

steeply sloped (as would be the case when exploration had to take place in increasingly hostile and unproductive environments), increases in scarcity rent stimulate less successful exploration activity.

Technological Progress

Technological progress reduces the cost of ore by discovering new ways to extract, process, and use the ore. In Chapter 7, for example, we showed the significant impact of pelletization on the cost of producing steel from iron ore. The effect was so dramatic that production costs actually fell over time in spite of the need to use a lower-grade ore.

It is important to realize that the rate and type of technological progress are influenced by the degree of resource scarcity. Rising extraction costs create new profit opportunities for the development of new technologies. These profit opportunities are largest for technologies that economize on scarce resources and utilize abundant ones. In periods when labor is scarce and capital abundant, new technologies tend to use capital and save labor. If population growth were to reverse the relative scarcity, subsequent technological progress would concentrate on using labor and saving capital. In the past, when fossil-fuel energy was abundant and cheap, newly discovered technologies relied heavily on this energy source. As fossil-fuel supplies decline, technological progress can be expected to economize by increasing the amount of useful energy received per unit of fossil-fuel input and by replacing fossil-fuel energy with forms of solar energy.

Substitution

The final way in which adverse consequences of resource scarcity can be mitigated is by substituting abundant resources for scarce ones. The easier the substitution of abundant depletable or renewable resources, the smaller will be the impact of declining availability and rising costs (see Figure 14.1).

In the graph three isoquants (S_1, F_1, F_2) are pictured. An *isoquant* portrays all the possible combinations of inputs that can produce a given level of output. The two right-angled isoquants $(F_1$ and $F_2)$ depict the fixed-proportions case, the case in which no input substitution is possible. The fixed-proportions isoquant nearer the original (F_2) refers to a lower output level than the other fixed-proportion isoquant (F_1). The third isoquant (S_1) does admit of some possibility for input substitution and is drawn in such a way as to produce the same output level (O_1) as F_1. Naturally it implies a different production technology or set of technologies from F_1.

We can illustrate the significance of input substitution on output using Figure 14.1. Assume that the amount of some input Y (a depletable resource) is reduced from Y_1 to Y_2. If the technology involved is characterized by S_1, the constant output level (O_1) can be maintained by increasing the amount of the other resource used from X_1 to X_3. This increase in X compensates for the reduction in Y, leaving output unaffected.

Notice what happens, however, when the production process is characterized by F_1 instead of S_1. A reduction in the availability of Y from Y_1 to Y_2 necessitates a reduction in output from O_1 to O_2. No substitution of X for Y is possible. In addition,

FIGURE 14.1

Output Levels and the Possibilities for Input Substitution

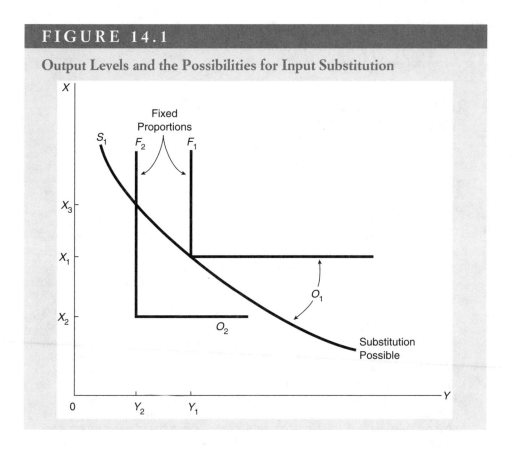

because inputs must be used in fixed proportions, the amount of X would be reduced from X_1 to X_2. Any more X would be redundant; it would not result in any additional output.

These examples serve to illustrate a basic premise—the wider the array of substitution possibilities, the smaller the impact of resource scarcity on output. Timber scarcity illustrates an important historical example (see Example 14.1) that serves to remind us that our review of the evidence must be sensitive to mitigating circumstances such as substitution possibilities and technological progress.

This short review suggests that some factors (rising population and incomes) increase the likelihood of resource scarcity, while others (exploration and discovery, technological progress, and input substitution) mitigate the seriousness of scarcity. To determine which set of factors dominates, we must examine the evidence.

Detecting Resource Scarcity

Selecting a means for detecting scarcity is the first step in assessing the seriousness of resource scarcity. While this may sound like a straightforward exercise, it is not. We begin by considering what properties the ideal indicators should have and the degree to which commonly used indicators live up to these standards.

Example *14.1*

RESOURCE SCARCITY IN HISTORICAL PERSPECTIVE: TIMBER

Early in our history timber was very abundant. For those who wanted to farm and had to clear the land, it was too abundant! As a result of low timber prices, Americans began to develop new technologies that relied more heavily on this vast resource. These included a whole range of wood-working machines for sawing, planing, shaping, and boring, as well as design improvements in the ax.

The use of these machines economized on labor—at that time a scarce commodity—at the cost of much wood. The saws of that period were easy to use, but they made such a wide swath that much of the log ended up as sawdust. It is interesting to note that in England, where labor was abundant and wood was scarce, the production process relied more heavily on labor and used a greater amount of the log.

When rising demand put pressure on the American forest resource base and prices began to rise, the incentive to economize on wood was increased. Wood-burning stoves became popular for increasing the thermal efficiency of wood burning. Substitutes (some of superior quality) came into use. Coal replaced wood for energy. Steel began to replace wood in bridges. Concrete began to replace wood in buildings. Plastics began to replace wood in packaging and toys. New products, such as particleboard, were created to use previously wasted wood by-products.

Meanwhile, other technological changes served to increase the size of the forest resource base. Forest scientists discovered a number of ways to increase tree growth, and the lumber industry found better ways to use what was available. Improvements in the process of making paper during the 1920s is one example of this latter change. This process modification made possible the use of a fast-growing southern pine that previously had been unusable.

The moral of the story seems to be that technological progress has opened new avenues that previously were only dimly perceived. Rising prices triggered the development of these avenues, as well as their exploitation. Increasing scarcity automatically creates incentives to increase inventive activity and innovation. Whether these incentives are sufficient to call forth such timely and beneficial responses in the future remains an open question.

Source: Nathan Rosenberg. "Innovative Responses to Materials Shortages," *American Economic Review* Vol. 63 (May 1983): 111–125.

Criteria for an Ideal Scarcity Indicator

An ideal indicator would have at least the three following properties:

1. *Foresight.* The ideal indicator should be forward-looking. It should anticipate scarcity and not merely record the scarcity once it has occurred. Thus, the ideal indicator should incorporate such things as future demand patterns, alternative sources of the resource, changes in extraction cost, and so on.

2. *Comparability*. The ideal indicator should allow direct comparisons to be made among resources for the purpose of identifying the most serious problems. This comparison should facilitate an assessment not only of the degree of scarcity, but also of its seriousness. Thus the indicator should be able to incorporate such differences as the importance of the resource and the availability of substitutes.

3. *Computability*. The ideal indicator should be readily calculated from reliable, published sources of information or should depend on information that could be readily collected.

Applying the Criteria

The Physical Indicators.   Before moving on to the four types of economic indicators, let's use these criteria to evaluate reserve-to-use ratios. Dividing known reserves by current consumption can be conveniently interpreted as the time until exhaustion. On the surface, this indicator appears to satisfy all three of our criteria. It is forward-looking, it allows comparisons to be made, and it is readily calculable.

This surface appearance, however, is deceiving. While reserve-to-use ratios are forward-looking, their view of the future is a narrow one on several counts. Their derivation makes no provision for stock augmentation. As a result, when past predictions using these indicators are compared with the actual experience, these predictions have been uniformly and excessively pessimistic. As the little boy tending the flocks discovered, if you cry "wolf!" often when the wolf is not there, people stop listening. When the wolf actually appears, no one reacts. Thus, reserve-to-use ratios satisfy the foresight criterion only in a very limited way.

In a similar vein, reserve-to-use ratios do allow comparisons to be made, but the resulting rankings provide no guide to the seriousness of the problems. These ratios not only yield an inaccurate estimated time to exhaustion, but they also provide no estimate of how serious a matter exhaustion would be. For example, running out of an ingredient that is used solely in cosmetics and has an available substitute is less serious than running out of a substance such as helium, which is used for important scientific research and has no known substitute for that use. Reserve-to-use ratios are powerless to make this kind of crucial distinction. Therefore, the comparability that is achieved is not a very useful one for setting resource management priorities.

Reserve-to-use ratios are also powerless to draw conclusions about the seriousness of *renewable* resource scarcity. They focus on a fixed resource reserve, a concept of limited validity when applied to depletable resources that is meaningless when applied to renewable resources. As we have seen in the preceding two chapters, the problem of scarcity with renewable resources can be even more serious than that with depletable resources. Thus the fact that this indicator allows us to draw no conclusions about scarcity in this important class of resource problems—much less integrate them into a comparable, comprehensive scheme to evaluate all resources—is a serious deficiency.

The outstanding virtue of the reserve-to-use ratio is that it is readily calculated from published data. That fact, along with its easy (but mistaken) interpretation by the general public as "time until exhaustion," probably accounts for its success.

The fact that standard physical indicators are not ideal is interesting and important, but it does not totally discredit their use unless we can show that something better exists. Does it?

Four candidate economic indicators have been suggested by the analysis in this and preceding chapters: trends in (1) resource price, (2) scarcity rent, (3) marginal discovery cost, and (4) marginal extraction cost. To determine whether these are superior indicators, we must consider their properties in a variety of circumstances.

Resource Prices.   In previous chapters we found it useful to distinguish between efficient resource prices, which maximize the net benefits to society, and market prices, which may or may not be efficient. We shall retain that distinction here.

Efficient resource prices satisfy both the foresight and comparability criteria. Current prices are forward-looking. They are affected by such factors as rising demand, the possibilities for stock augmentation and substitution, and changes in the cost of extraction. Relative prices are also affected by the price elasticity of demand—the greater the difficulty of doing without the resource, the higher the price. Therefore, price levels and relative price changes allow us to make direct comparisons of depletable and renewable resources that reflect the seriousness of the problem.

The problem with using trends in efficient resource prices as the sole indicator is that in certain markets they are not directly observable or calculable. This occurs whenever the readily available indicator, the market price, is not equal to the efficient price. In preceding chapters we discussed cases in which these two prices might not be equal—open-access resource markets, markets with government price controls or artificial subsidies, and markets with significant externalities (such as pollution) that have not been internalized.

In these cases, market price trends may not even be a valid approximation of efficient price trends. For example, take the situation with open-access resources. The problem with these resources is overexploitation in the earlier periods, followed (because the stock is so diminished) by underexploitation in the latter years. Thus, the problem is not that price would not rise to reflect scarcity. It will, eventually. The problem is that the lower earlier prices (due to the glut on the market) send a false signal of abundance. In markets where resources are treated as open-access resources, market prices fail to exhibit the foresight property.

A similar problem occurs with uninternalized externalities. We have already seen that when the market fails to recognize these externalities, market prices are too low. And in contrast to the open-access resource problem, no automatic adjustment mechanism ever causes market prices to reflect this increasing scarcity. Since scarcity in this case (indicated by the rising cost of extraction and reflected in the increasing damage caused by pollution) affects nonmarketed commodities (clean air and water), market prices do not signal the problem.

One further concern arises about the anticipatory role of market prices. The ability of resource markets to exhibit foresight depends, in turn, on the ability of suppliers to assess the future. If they cannot correctly anticipate future substitution possibilities, technological changes, demand patterns, and so on, market prices will fail to reflect these considerations. The information content of prices is only as rich as the information available to those who, by their collective actions, determine prices.

In conclusion, for those resources traded in efficient or nearly efficient markets, resource prices serve as a superior indicator. When markets are not efficient, the dominance of this indicator is no longer obvious. Other indicators become useful either to complement or replace resource prices in those markets.

Scarcity Rent. A second economic indicator involves trends in *scarcity rent,* the payment accruing to a resource owner when the user cost is positive. The efficient scarcity rent is forward-looking; indeed, if the future did not matter, there would be no scarcity rent! Use of scarcity rent should anticipate future increases in demand as well as changes in extraction cost as the resource is used up. Scarcity rent can be used as an indicator for both renewable and depletable resource scarcity.

As you can see, up to this point, scarcity rent trends sound roughly comparable to resource price trends as indicators. For certain types of resources, however, scarcity rent may be superior to the price of the extracted product, the most readily available price. A forestry economist, L. C. Irland (1974), provides a useful historical example:

> From the Civil War to about 1900, lumber prices were stable while timber prices rose. Prominent forces were the decline in transport costs and improvements in milling.

The use of *lumber* prices as a measure of timber scarcity would lead to an erroneous conclusion. The scarcity reflected in the rising price of timber was camouflaged by declining transportation and milling costs. Only the scarcity rent of the timber (called *stumpage* in the industry) correctly detected the scarcity.[2]

With respect to other resources, however, scarcity rent may well represent a less-than-adequate measure. As shown earlier, the scarcity rent for open-access resources is zero for all time periods. For that class of resources it is a deficient indicator of scarcity.

Even for efficient markets, the relationship between scarcity rent and the degree of resource depletion is not always well defined. For depletable resources having a constant marginal cost of extraction, we expect scarcity rent to *rise* with the depletion. On the other hand, when extraction costs rise with the amount extracted, scarcity rent should *decline* with increasing scarcity. To interpret the behavior of scarcity rent, we need to know the underlying structure of extraction costs.

As a result, interpretation becomes an important problem. Declining scarcity rent could represent either increasing availability of the resource, which is desirable, or rising extraction cost, which is undesirable. Since it makes a difference which interpretation is correct, it is risky to base conclusions on this one indicator.

---

[2]Stumpage is the price an extractor pays to the owner of forest land for the privilege of cutting and taking the timber.

Marginal Discovery Cost.   Scarcity rent is not always directly observable, even in those circumstances where it might prove to be a useful indicator. Earlier we derived a relationship capable of resolving this dilemma. We noted that marginal discovery cost, which can be observed, should be equal to marginal scarcity rent. Therefore, marginal discovery cost could be used as a proxy for marginal scarcity rent when information on discovery cost is available and information on scarcity rent is not. Unfortunately, very little public information on marginal discovery cost is available.

Marginal Extraction Cost.   The final indicators of resource scarcity suggested by conventional analysis are trends in the marginal cost of extraction. For a given technology of extraction, as lower-grade ores are extracted, we normally expect the marginal cost of extraction to rise. Rising marginal extraction cost should, therefore, serve as a signal of the amount of sacrifice needed to procure each unit of the resource. It is noteworthy that the usefulness of this indicator of scarcity is not undermined when the resources are treated as free-access, common property. Thus, it is perhaps the best indicator to be used for free-access, common-property resources, such as fish and whales.

Extraction cost, however, is far from a flawless indicator. Of the three economic indicators we have considered so far, extraction cost is the only one that does not fulfill the foresight criterion. Since it is based on the current cost of extraction, it provides no indication of future problems, such as rapidly rising demand or future increases in extraction cost, which may be just around the corner. Business or government leaders wishing to anticipate scarcity, rather than merely react to it once it occurs, do not get much help from this indicator.

Unit extraction cost is also a difficult concept to measure precisely with published information. As a result, analysts have developed means of approximating it with available information. Perhaps the most widely cited example is the unit-extraction-cost measure developed by Harold Barnett and Chandler Morse (1963):

$$C_i = (\alpha_i L_i + \beta_i K_i)/Q_i$$

where

C_i = the unit extraction cost for resources i
L_i = labor in industry i, as measured by employment
K_i = reproducible capital (equipment and structures)
Q_i = net amount of the ith resource extracted
α_i, β_i = weights used to aggregate the dissimilar capital and labor inputs

The logic behind this formulation suggests that capital and labor are primary inputs to the extraction of resources; as society begins the transition to increasingly inferior sources, larger inputs of capital and labor are required per unit of resource extracted. This is recorded as a rise in the index. Conversely, a fall over time in this index suggests either that new, low-cost sources have continually been discovered, or that technological progress has reduced the amount of capital and labor required to extract a unit of the resource to the extent of counteracting the increasing inferiority of the grades used.

Some problems with this particular specification would not arise if the true extraction-cost data were available. One of the most blatant problems is the omission of factors other than capital and labor that would be involved in the extraction of resources. Energy is one obvious example. If capital equipment consumed more energy over time—which is the expected response to the falling energy prices that occurred until 1974—then the Barnett-Morse measure would fail to pick one possible source of rising extraction cost: the cost of energy.

Combining this omission with the failure of this measure to include (presumably rising) environmental costs, it is, therefore, difficult to put our complete faith in this approximation.

In conclusion, no indicator of resource scarcity dominates the others in all cases. Trends in real resource prices probably dominate in efficient markets. Scarcity rent trends probably dominate in those markets, such as timber, where the open-access problem does not exist and where the values of the in situ resources are routinely collected. Marginal discovery cost trends may usefully approximate marginal scarcity rent when it is not directly observable. Trends in the cost of extraction are superior for those resources treated as free-access resources. The moral seems to be that we cannot trust any single indicator to provide the desired information. Judgments have to be made on a case-by-case basis using a variety of indicators.

Evidence on Resource Scarcity

A number of studies have attempted to assess the degree of scarcity now facing us. Since these have relied on quite different approaches, it is not surprising to discover that they come to rather different conclusions. Our review of these studies begins with those relying mainly on the physical indicators and closes with those using economic indicators.

Physical Indicators

To open our discussion of physical indicators, let's consider illustrative data on reserve-to-use ratios as of 1970. Resources that had a ratio of less than 30 years included gold, lead, mercury, silver, tin, and zinc. The 30 years have now passed, but we have not exhausted reserves of those minerals.

One key on the demand side lies in the ability to substitute renewable for depletable natural resources. One way we can assess the potential degree of substitutability between natural resources and other commodities is to estimate a construct known as the *elasticity of substitution*. The elasticity of substitution (σ) is a measure of the degree to which two factor inputs complement or substitute for each other in the production process.[3]

---

[3] The elasticity of substitution between two factors of production (say, X and Y) is defined as the ratio of the percentage change in the factor ratio to the percentage change in their relative prices (P_x and P_y). Thus

$$\sigma = \frac{(\Delta X/Y)(P_y/P_x)}{(\Delta P_y/P_x)(X/Y)}$$

When σ is positive, the factors are substitutes, and when σ is negative, they are complements.[4] The larger the positive number, the easier and more complete the substitution will be. Generally an elasticity of substitution greater than 1 indicates considerable ease in substitution. The elasticity of substitution is zero for the fixed-proportions isoquant in Figure 14.1. Though a thorough review of the voluminous literature on input substitution would carry us too far afield, it seems fair to summarize the evidence as suggesting that capital and resources are substitutes and sometimes strong substitutes (Berndt and Field, 1981). The relationship between capital and energy, however, is another matter indeed.

A number of studies examining the substitutability of energy with resources and with labor have been accomplished for the United States and other countries (Berndt and Wood, 1975; Halvorsen and Ford, 1978; Fuss, 1977; Atkinson and Halvorsen, 1976; Fisher, 1981). Generally the results are mixed. Energy and labor appear uniformly to be substitutes, with the size of elasticities ranging from 0.48 to 3.80, depending on the industry and country. The story about energy and capital is more complicated. Studies based on data for a single country usually find capital and energy to be complements, rather than substitutes. This is relatively easy to understand. Historically, when relative energy prices were falling, the natural response by the economic system was to construct and use energy-using capital. This does not necessarily mean that capital and energy remain complements in a period when relative energy prices are rising. We discuss this further in Chapter 22.

What can be said about substitution possibilities? In general, they seem quite good, though problems may erupt in particular industries. Both capital and labor are able to serve as substitutes for each other and for resources within reasonable limits. The complementarity of capital and energy would be troubling if it were inevitable, but this historic relationship could well be transformed to one of substitutability in the future as energy becomes much more expensive.[5]

How about the supply side and the longer term? Perhaps the most searching assessment of the future long-term availability of resources was conducted by two physical scientists, Goeller and Weinberg (1978). These authors went through the entire periodic table of elements and some of the more important compounds to derive estimates of current use and future availability. Their definition of future availability was expansive, including all potential sources of supply from the atmosphere, the ocean, and the crust of the earth down to a depth of one kilometer. Essentially their estimate of supply corresponds to what we called resource endowment in Chapter 7.

Using the resource endowment as their definition of reserves, Goeller and Weinberg computed static reserve indices for each substance. The resource we would run out of first, phosphorus, according to their calculation would last another 1,300 years. For most other resources, their indices suggest exhaustion horizons in

---

[4]Two factors are said to be complements if an increase in one leads to an increase in the other. If an increase in the first factor leads to a decrease in the second, then those factors are said to be substitutes.

[5]Consider, for example, the use of computers to control heating systems more efficiently, allowing substantial savings in energy.

the millions of years. On the basis of this and a complementary analysis, Goeller and Weinberg draw two main conclusions:

1. With three exceptions—phosphorus, a few trace elements for agriculture, and energy fossil fuels—there is virtually an unlimited supply of resources.
2. The transition away from these truly limited resources can be accomplished with relatively little, if any, loss in living standards. In most cases it can be accomplished with real-resource prices no more than double current levels.

If we were somehow able to peer into the future with a crystal ball, we would probably find that the actual situation would lie somewhere between the pessimism of the reserve-to-use ratio and the optimism of the Goeller and Weinberg forecast. The optimism of the Goeller and Weinberg analysis rests in part on an assumption that all of the resource endowment they identify could, in fact, be recovered and could be used without causing other environmental problems, such as changes in the climate. This expectation is fully compatible with a traditional geological view of the manner in which resources are distributed within the earth's crust. This view suggests that the lower the grade, the larger the supply of the resource available. It posits a rather smooth supply curve devoid of any sharp discontinuities.

The traditional view, however, is not unanimously held. One well-known geo-chemist, B. J. Skinner, has suggested that a rather different distribution may under-lie certain geochemically scarce elements in the earth's crust. This analysis suggests that minerals can be classified into three groups. For the first group—iron, alu-minum, titanium, magnesium, and silicon—the distribution of ores results in an inverse relationship between grade and tonnage of the ores. As grade is reduced by depleting the higher-grade ores, even larger tonnages of the lower-grade ores become available.

For the second group of resources—manganese, barium, vanadium, zirconium, sulfur, phosphorus, fluorine, and chlorine—limits to this inverse grade-tonnage rela-tionship are present, but the supplies of ores are so great to suggest that these limits do not constrain resource availability for the foreseeable future.

For all other metals—which Skinner calls the geochemically scarce metals, such as copper, lead, zinc, molybdenum, and gold—the distribution of ores is quite dif-ferent. A comparison of the traditional view with that of Skinner is presented as Figure 14.2. The left panel presents the traditional (single-peaked) function gener-ally found for the more abundant resources. The bimodal function is presented in the right panel.

The implication of the Skinner hypothesis is that as we mine lower grades of geochemically scarce resources, we shall find less, not more, lower-grade ore avail-able over some considerable range of grades. Skinner further suggests the existence of a *mineralogical threshold* between the two peaks. This mineralogical threshold delineates a sharp discontinuity in the manner by which minerals are extracted to the left and to the right of this threshold. His characterization of this threshold is presented as Figure 14.3.

With abundant elements, the energy used per unit output rises smoothly as the grade of the ore is decreased. For the geochemically scarce resources, Skinner posits a sharp discontinuity in energy use when the supply of separate minerals (as represented

FIGURE 14.2

Alternative Views of Ore Distribution

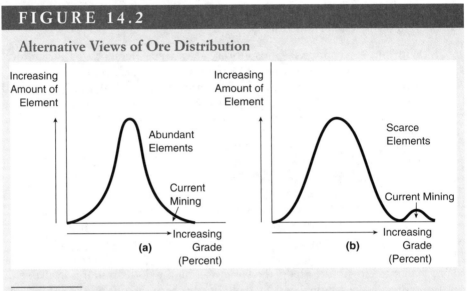

Source: B. J. Skinner. "A Second Iron Age Ahead?" American Scientist Vol. 64 (1976): 263.

FIGURE 14.3

Nature of the Mineralogical Threshold

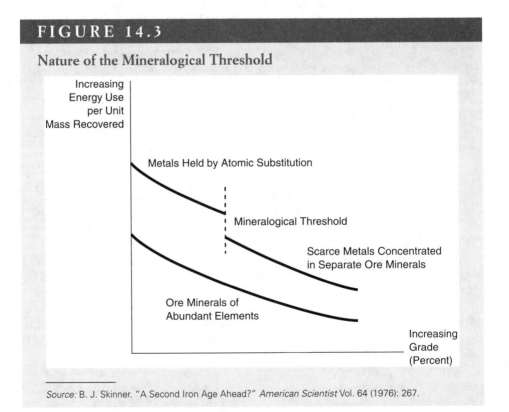

Source: B. J. Skinner. "A Second Iron Age Ahead?" American Scientist Vol. 64 (1976): 267.

TABLE 14.1

Energy Used To Mine and Process a Copper Ore in Which All Copper Is Present in Biotite

	Energy Used (BTU/lb. Cu)		
Grade, percent Cu	0.7	0.1	0.01
Mining plus			
Concentration	19,300	135,000	1,250,000
Preparation of a			
Copper Salt	326,858	2,288,010	22,880,100
Smelting	20,000	20,000	20,000
Total	366,158	2,443,010	24,250,100
Equivalent Thermal			
Energy in Bituminous			
Coal, in Pounds of Coal	28	188	1,866

Source: V. Kerry Smith and John V. Krutilla, Explorations in Natural Resource Economics, pp. 1 fig. ©1982. (Baltimore, MD: Johns Hopkins University Press).

by the smaller peak of Figure 14.2) is exhausted and the remaining sources are trapped as atomic substitutes for more abundant metals in the crystal structure of minerals.

Traditional mineral concentration processes could no longer be used to separate these minerals. The host ore would have to be broken down in order to release the tightly bound metals. Some estimates (Brobst, 1979) have suggested that the successful negotiation of this transition would require energy use per unit output some 100 or 1000 times higher than current use. Table 14.1 demonstrates this relationship for copper.

To the extent that the Skinner hypothesis is valid, barring the arrival of unlimited cheap energy, the Goeller and Weinberg analysis will be excessively optimistic, particularly for the geochemically scarce metals. How would the economy react to the very high prices necessary to extract these metals? Example 14.2 presents one study conducted specifically to answer this question. It seems to suggest that increasing scarcity will usher in some dramatic changes, but these changes will cushion the shock to the economy. Only the complete or near-complete disappearance of copper from the scene would cause large economic losses.

Economic Indicators

Extraction Cost.   The original work that spawned serious investigation of natural resource scarcity, by Barnett and Morse in 1963, *was Scarcity and Growth: The Economics of Natural Resource Availability*. This pioneering work is noteworthy both for the methodology it developed and for the conclusions it derived.

The Barnett-Morse empirical evaluations concentrated on two measures constructed using data from 1870 to 1957. The first, called the unit-cost measure, was

Example   *14.2*

GEOCHEMICALLY SCARCE METALS: HOW WOULD THE ECONOMY REACT?

Geochemically scarce metals such as copper present a special challenge to the economic system as the supplies of ore decline. To understand how the economy might respond to this challenge, a team that included three economists and a geochemist constructed a model of the future copper market in the United States. This model included a wide range of current and anticipated demands for copper, a host of substitution possibilities, and estimates of supplies available from production and recycling.

From their model they draw the following conclusions:

1. The rate of extraction of copper from the earth grows rapidly over the next 100 years. Extraction peaks in about 2100 and then declines slowly. The peak extraction rate is about eight times the current rate of production of new copper.
2. The ores containing copper minerals are largely exhausted by 2070. Thereafter, copper is obtained from copper rock, which has a maximum grade of 0.05%, compared with 0.5% today. Once copper is obtained from copper rock, the intrinsic scarcity of copper disappears; copper is then very expensive but no longer "scarce" in the sense of being exhaustible.
3. As time passes, the services currently or historically provided by copper are progressively provided by greater amounts of substitute materials such as aluminum, titanium, stainless steel, plastics, and glass. By the end of the 21st century, only a handful of today's uses survive.
4. Recycling becomes big business. By the middle of the next century, virtually all copper available from waste is recovered and reused.
5. Copper prices rise dramatically over the next century, growing exponentially from $2 per kilogram in the early periods to $120 per kilogram when the backstop resources (common rock) are brought into play; thereafter prices remain stable in real terms.
6. Even though the price of copper metal rises 50-fold over the next century, the cost of copper-equivalent services rises only 10-fold.
7. The overall cost of copper scarcity is estimated to be somewhat less than 0.5% of national income. However, the overall cost of completely doing without copper is estimated to be a whopping 22% of national income.

Source: Robert B. Gordon, Tjalling C. Koopmans, William D. Nordhaus, and Brian J. Skinner. *Toward a New Iron Age? Quantitative Modeling of Resource Exhaustion* (Cambridge, MA: Harvard University Press, 1987).

an attempt to capture any increase in effort required to extract an output of a given quality. This measure was described in the preceding section. The second measure recorded the trends in natural resource prices relative to an index of prices for nonextractive resources. The authors made it clear that they preferred the former measure.

After examining the trends of these two indicators, Barnett and Morse conclude that, with the exception of the forestry sector, no evidence of increasing scarcity was apparent. Furthermore, they found that this conclusion was insensitive to the various subjective judgments they had been forced to make during the analysis, such as defining the weights used to combine labor and capital and the choice of indices used to capture price trends in the nonextractive sector. Different calculations based on other reasonable judgments yielded the same conclusions.

What interpretation can be placed on these results? Barnett and Morse offer four explanations for the absence of any evidence of scarcity in the face of increasing demand and a finite resource base: (a) historically, when higher-grade resources were exhausted, lower-grade resources became available in even greater abundance; (b) as the possibility for scarcity emerged, resource users began to switch to other, less scarce resources; (c) as prices rose, exploration for new sources was encouraged and this exploration was remarkably successful; and (d) technological change reduced the costs of extraction and expanded the universe of recoverable resources. They suggest that, historically, the combined effect of these mitigating factors was so strong that they eliminated evidence of current or future scarcity, except for forest products.

This generally optimistic view of the past was complemented by an equally optimistic view of the future. They suggested:

> That man will face a series of particular scarcities as the result of growth is a foregone conclusion; that these will impose general scarcity—increasing cost—is not a legitimate corollary. The twentieth century's discovery of the uniformity of energy and matter has increased the possibilities of substitution to an unimaginable degree and placed at man's disposal an indefinitely large number of alternatives from which to choose. To suppose that these alternatives must eventually become so restricted, relative to man's wants, that increasing cost will be inescapable, is not justified by the evidence. An absolute limit to the possibilities of escape may exist, but it cannot be defined or specified. The finite limits of the globe, so real in their unqueried simplicity, lose definition under examination.

Skepticism may be appropriate for as sweeping a conclusion as this one. Barnett and Morse's failure to consider energy costs in measuring the cost of extraction, for example, has already been mentioned. How serious an omission is this? Cleveland (1991) has repeated the Barnett-Morse analysis using energy costs to measure changes in marginal extraction cost. Examining trends in physical output per unit energy input, Cleveland finds that for many resources, large increases in fossil-fuel use were the apparent source of the declines in capital and labor costs over time. By increasing labor and capital productivity, these infusions of energy lowered extraction costs measured purely in terms of capital and labor. Whether impending scarcity is occurring, therefore, would depend on the scarcity of energy, not merely on the availability and cost of labor and capital.

Other concerns about the interpretation of the Barnett-Morse results include the time frame of the analysis (the Barnett-Morse data end in 1957) and a singular focus on the United States. Would studies using later data, a wider geographic frame of reference, and a richer set of indicators tend to support the Barnett-Morse conclusions?

Such studies have provided some support for at least the historical interpretation of the Barnett-Morse data. Johnson, Bell, and Bennett (1980) extended the analysis on American unit extraction costs by incorporating data through 1970 (1966 in a few cases). By performing traditional hypothesis tests, they found:

1. The Barnett-Morse finding of increasing scarcity in forestry was reversed in the 1958–1970 period.
2. Of the 15 agricultural commodity groups studied, *all* had declining unit extraction cost during the 1958–1972 period. Of these, only three—food grains, oil crops, and vegetables—had smaller declines during this period than the earlier period studied by Barnett and Morse.
3. Of the eleven mineral and fuel commodity groups studied, *all* had declining unit extraction costs during the 1958–1972 period. Of these, only copper registered a smaller decline during the later period.
4. Since 1962, unit extraction costs have risen in commercial fishing. This was the only documented case of increasing scarcity that these three authors found and, after reading Chapter 13, this particular scarcity should surprise no one.

Harold Barnett (1979), one of the authors of *Scarcity and Growth*, has also expanded his earlier analysis by using more recent data covering the global resource situation, rather than merely that in the United States. After analyzing a wide variety of data, he found that:

1. Unit extraction cost, measured as labor per unit output, declined over all time periods, all countries, and all commodities.
2. Of 20 cases examined, the unit extraction cost, measured as labor per unit output, declined more slowly in mineral industries than it did in manufacturing for only three cases.

Subsequent studies have not generally contradicted these rather optimistic findings. Though Hall and Hall (1984) found a statistically significant increase in extraction cost for U.S. coal and petroleum in the 1970s, whether this is due to scarcity or to OPEC behavior is not clear. For other substances such as ferro alloys and non-ferrous metals, they found that extraction cost continued to decline in the 1970s. A subsequent study by Uri and Boyd (1995) failed to find any increase in unit extraction costs for several mineral resources.

Thus even when examination of extraction costs is expanded to include other countries and other time periods, the conclusion of declining extraction costs seems to be robust. Extraction costs are not forward-looking, however, so if we are to assess future resource scarcity, we must examine the behavior of resource prices as well. Extraction costs are not enough.

Example 14.3

THE BET

In 1980 each of two distinguished protagonists in the scarcity debate "put his money where his mouth is." Paul Ehrlich, an ecologist with a strong belief in impending scarcity, answered a challenge from Julian Simon, an economist known for his equally strong belief that concerns about impending scarcity were groundless. According to the terms of the bet, Ehrlich would hypothetically invest $200 in each of any five commodities he selected. (He picked copper, chrome, nickel, tin, and tungsten.) Ten years later the aggregate value of the same amounts of those five commodities would be calculated in real terms (after accounting for normal inflation). If the value increased, Simon would send Ehrlich a check for the difference. If the value decreased, Ehrlich would send Simon a check for the difference.

In 1990 Ehrlich performed the calculations and sent Simon a check for $576.07. Real prices for each of the five commodities were lower; some were less than half their former levels. New sources of the minerals had been discovered, substitutions away from these minerals had occurred in many of their uses (particularly computers), and the tin cartel, which had been holding up tin prices, collapsed.

Does this evidence provide a lesson for the future? You be the judge.

Source: John Tierney. "Betting the Planet," *New York Times Magazine* (December 2, 1990): 52–53, 74, 76, 78, 80–81.

Studies of Resource Price Trends.   If resource scarcity is increasing in some sense, we should be able to discover that natural resource prices are rising more rapidly than prices in general (see Example 14.3).

In the Harold Barnett study mentioned earlier, resource prices were examined, as well as unit extraction costs. His price findings were that:

1. Of 53 cases examined, agricultural prices rose faster than a general wholesale price index in 23 cases.
2. In West Germany over the period 1950 to 1971, prices of minerals and raw materials rose faster than prices in general in three out of the six cases studied.

This provides some evidence that prices are rising more rapidly in the natural resource sectors than in others, a finding that is compatible with projections of future increases in resource scarcity.

Work by V. Kerry Smith (1978, 1979, 1980) complements Barnett's study by examining somewhat more recent relative price data for the United States. Using more sophisticated statistical analyses than used in other previous studies, Smith found that conclusions concerning the rise or fall of natural resource prices were very sensitive to the choice of time periods used in the analysis. Different periods yielded different results. Even so, historical decline in relative resource prices appeared to be smaller in more recent periods with some reversals (and hence, increases in prices) evident for some resources. He concluded:

> The analysis in this paper has raised questions as to whether the conclusions drawn from the empirical data considered by Barnett and Morse were warranted, both in terms of the inherent limitation in the use of the outcome measure and the data themselves. Our analysis with updated data indicates that this evidence alone is not sufficient to arrive at what is [sic] commonly accepted interpretation of Barnett and Morse—namely, there is no evidence of natural-resource scarcity. [1978, p. 165]

The work described above relies upon linear functions that do not allow for relative prices to initially decline and then increase. Yet our description of the role of technological progress in Chapter 7 would lead us to expect precisely this kind of pattern. Can the presence of this nonlinear price pattern be refuted or confirmed?

Margaret Slade (1982) has specifically investigated this question for a variety of types of resources. Using statistical techniques, she fitted a quadratic equation of the form:

$$P_{it} = (b_{0i} + b_{1i}t + b_{2i}t^2 + V_{it})$$

where

P_{it} = deflated price of the ith commodity at time t
t = time measured in years (1800 = 0)
V_{it} = a random error term

The virtues of this simple approach are the use of a function that can first decline and then rise,[6] the existence of this pattern can be statistically verified,[7] and if the relationship is validated, the parameters can be used to determine the year in which the decline stopped and the increase began.[8]

In fact, Slade found that the quadratic function fitted the data better than the linear function for all but one of the resources examined (lead), implying that the minimum point on the U-shaped curve had already been passed.[9] For these resources, at least, the pattern of falling followed by rising relative prices seems

---

[6]This pattern results when $b_0 > 0$, $b_1 < 0$, and $b_2 > 0$.

[7]If $b_2 = 0$, then the equation is linear. Thus the test is to see whether $b_2 = 0$ or $b_2 > 0$.

[8]Using calculus, the bottom of the price decline can be found to be when $t = -b_1/2b_2$. Since $b_1 < 0$, this will be a positive number.

[9]Those interested in the process by which knowledge proceeds might wish to investigate the controversy about these results. See the criticism in Mueller and Gorin (1985) and the response in Slade (1985).

to be the rule rather than the exception, and the turning point seems to have passed.

Slade sums up this evidence by saying: "Therefore, if scarcity is measured by relative prices, the evidence indicates that nonrenewable natural-resource commodities are becoming scarce [p. 136]."

This early work has not generally been confirmed by subsequent studies using more recent data. Examining updated data–Krautkramer (1998) reports finding a negative (not quadratic) time trend for eight of the eleven resources examined, although the negative coefficient is statistically significant only for copper, lead, and tin. Coal, natural gas, and petroleum prices have a positive (not quadratic) time trend, although only the estimated coefficient for natural gas is statistically significant. He reports no resources that follow the quadratic trend found by Slade. A similar exercise performed by Howie (unpublished, but reported in Tilton (2003)) found that only nickel prices fit the quadratic trend. In terms of history, the argument that prices are signalling scarcity is not compelling.

Discovery Cost.   To shed more light on the final measure, discovery cost, Fisher (1981) compares price information with average discovery costs in the United States for oil and gas for the years 1950 to 1971 (expressed in constant 1947 to 1949 dollars). Because the preferred indicator, marginal discovery cost, was not available, average discovery cost was used instead.

Despite the fact that no real increase in crude oil prices occurred over the period, which suggests the absence of scarcity, Fisher found a different pattern for discovery costs. Though the pattern was somewhat erratic, the latter years seemed to show a distinct increase in discovery costs. The message seemed clear; the discovery costs were picking up an impending scarcity by the early 1970s that price information had missed.

Little later research has followed Fisher's work, but the reasons for that should counsel caution in interpreting any discovery cost results, including these. As M. A. Adelman (1997), one of the most prominent oil experts in our time, has noted, solid estimates of marginal discovery costs are impossible because the magnitude of any given year's discoveries remains unknown. While it is clear each year if exploration activity was successful in discovering oil, the amount of oil the discovery has uncovered is only known within a wide band of possibilities.

Juxtaposing Alternative Measures.   Since it seems clear that no single indicator universally dominates all others, it makes sense, where possible, to use several indicators, deriving as much useful information from them, both individually and in concert, as feasible. Cleveland (1993) has done precisely this for oil and gas in the United States. His analysis supports the proposition, advanced by Slade, that we have experienced a period of declining scarcity followed by a period of increasing scarcity. Given the pivotal importance of oil and gas in fueling modern society, these results may suggest a generalized scarcity that transcends the individual scarcities associated merely with oil and natural gas.

Summary

In view of the rapidly developing state of the art in the assessment of resource scarcity, can any concrete conclusions be drawn? Fortunately they can.

1. The problem is not whether we shall run out of resources. As the work of Goeller and Weinberg makes clear, the air, water, and crust of the earth provide a storehouse of the very resources we use. For most resources, this storehouse would not be exhausted for literally millions of years. The problem is not the existence of adequate physical amounts of resources, but whether we are willing to pay the price to extract and use them.
2. Although the evidence on resource scarcity is mixed, the historical evidence provides no compelling case that resource scarcities are upon us with the possible exception of oil and natural gas.
3. Our ability to detect resource scarcity is currently limited by the nonexistence of any single indicator that is forward-looking, comprehensive, and computable. While several indicators are currently being used, none is appropriate for all resources and all market situations.
4. One of the most serious deficiencies in both our detection system and our ability to respond to scarcity is the failure of the market system to incorporate the various environmental costs of increasing resource use, be they radiation hazards, the loss of genetic diversity or aesthetics, polluted air and drinking water, or climate modification. Without including these costs, our detection indicators give falsely optimistic signals, and the market makes choices that put society inefficiently at risk.
5. The fact that historical indicators do not indicate systematic resource scarcity does not rule out its appearance in the future.
   As Neumayer (2000) puts it:

   The world economy has so far exhibited a most remarkable capability to overcome resource constraints. Resources that were feared to become scarce at one time, often turned out to be abundantly available only a few years later. This gives reason to hope. And yet there are good reasons to be cautious as well: Never can there be any guarantee that the fortunate experiences of the past will replicate in the future. This holds especially true in times of rapid change as ours. Whether the limited availability of natural resources will ever constrain economic growth, we simply do not know. (p. 328)

Further Reading

Adelman, M. A. (1997). "My Education in Mineral (Especially Oil) Economics" *Annual Review of Energy and the Environment* (November): 13–46.

Howie, P. (Unpublished). "Long-Run Price Behavior of Nonrenewable Resources Using Time-Series Models" Golden, CO: Colorado School of Mines.

Krautkramer, J. A. (1998). "Nonrenewable Resource Scarcity" *Journal of Economic Literature* Vol. 36(4): 2065–2107. A thorough examination of the theory and empirical work evaluating natural resource scarcity.

Neumayer, E. (2000). "Scarce or Abundant? The Economics of Natural Resource Availability." *Journal of Economic Surveys* Vol. 14(3): 307–335. Another excellent survey of the literature in the field covered by this chapter.

Norgard, Richard B. "Economic Indicators of Resource Scarcity: A Critical Essay," *Journal of Environmental Economics and Management* Vol. 19 (July 1990): 19–25. Presents and defends the proposition that economic measures of resource scarcity are fundamentally flawed.

Tilton, J. E. (2003). *On Borrowed Time? Assessing the Threat of Mineral Depletion*. Washington, DC, Resources for the Future, Inc. A book-length assessment of the evidence on resource scarcity by a leading mineral economist.

Uri, N. D. and R. Boyd (1995). "Scarcity and Growth Revisited." *Environment and Planning* Vol. A 27(11): 1815–1832.

Additional References and Historically Significant References are available on this book's companion Web site www.aw-bc.com/tietenberg.

Chapter 15

Economics of Pollution Control: An Overview

Democracy is not a matter of sentiment, but of foresight. Any system that doesn't take the long run into account will burn itself out in the short run.

—Charles Yost, The Age Of Triumph And Frustration

Introduction

In Chapter 2 we introduced a schematic describing the relationship between the natural and the economic systems. One side depicted the flow of mass and energy to the economic system, while the other depicted the flow of waste products back to the environment. In the last few chapters we dealt extensively with achieving a balanced set of mass and energy flows; it now remains to discuss how a balance can be achieved in the reverse flow of waste products back to the environment. Because the waste flows are inexorably intertwined with the flow of mass and energy into the economy, establishing a balance for waste flows will have feedback effects on the input flows as well.

Two questions must be addressed: (1) what is the appropriate level of flow? (2) how should the responsibility for achieving this flow level be allocated among the various sources of the pollutant when reductions are needed?

In this chapter we lay the foundation for understanding the policy approach to controlling the flow of these waste products by developing a general framework for analyzing pollution control. This framework allows us to define efficient and cost-effective allocations for a variety of pollutant types, to compare these allocations to market allocations, and to demonstrate how efficiency and cost-effectiveness can be used to formulate desirable policy responses. This overview is then followed by a series of chapters that apply these principles by examining the policy approaches that have been taken in the United States and in the rest of the world to establish control over waste flows.

A Pollutant Taxonomy

The amount of waste products emitted determines the load upon the environment. The damage done by this load depends on the capacity of the environment to assimilate the waste products (see Figure 15.1). We call this ability of the environment to absorb pollutants its *absorptive capacity*. If the emissions load exceeds the absorptive capacity, then the pollutant accumulates in the environment.

Pollutants for which the environment has little or no absorptive capacity are called *stock pollutants*. Stock pollutants accumulate over time as emissions enter the environment. Examples of stock pollutants include nonbiodegradable bottles tossed by the roadside; heavy metals, such as lead, that accumulate in the soils near the emission source; and persistent synthetic chemicals such as dioxin and PCBs (polychlorinated biphenyls).

Pollutants for which the environment has some absorptive capacity are called *fund pollutants*. For these pollutants, as long as the emission rate does not exceed the absorptive capacity of the environment, the pollutants do not accumulate. Examples of fund pollutants are easy to find. Many organic pollutants injected into an oxygen-rich stream will be transformed by the resident bacteria into less harmful inorganic matter. Carbon dioxide is absorbed by plant life and the oceans.

The point is *not* that the mass is destroyed; the law of conservation of mass suggests this cannot be the case. Rather, when fund pollutants are injected into the air or water, they may be transformed into substances that are not considered harmful to people or to the ecological system, or they may be so diluted or dispersed that the resulting concentrations are not harmful.

Pollutants can also be classified by their zone of influence, defined both horizontally and vertically. The horizontal dimension deals with the domain over which damage from an emitted pollutant is experienced. The damage caused by *local* pollutants is experienced near the source of emission, while the damage from *regional* pollutants is experienced at greater distances from the source of emission. The local and regional categories are not mutually exclusive; it is possible for a pollutant to be

FIGURE 15.1

Relationship Between Emissions and Pollution Damage

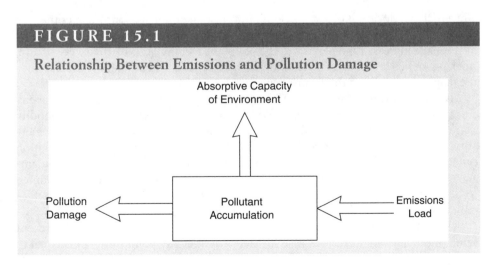

both. Sulfur oxides and nitrogen oxides, for example, are both local and regional pollutants.

The vertical zone of influence describes whether the damage is caused mainly by ground-level concentrations of an air pollutant or by concentrations in the upper atmosphere. When the damage caused by a pollutant is determined mainly by concentrations of the pollutant near the earth's surface, it is called a *surface pollutant*. When its damage is related more to its concentration in the upper atmosphere, the substance is called a *global pollutant*.

Water pollutants are obviously surface pollutants, but air pollutants can be surface pollutants, global pollutants, or both. One common global pollutant, carbon dioxide injected into the atmosphere as a product of fossil-fuel combustion, has been implicated in climate change via the "greenhouse effect." In addition, chlorofluoro-carbon emissions play a role in the destruction of the ozone layer, which protects the earth's surface from harmful solar radiation. As we shall see, the appropriate policy responses for global and surface pollutants are quite different.

This taxonomy will prove useful in designing policy responses to these various types of pollution problems. Each type of pollutant requires a unique policy response. The failure to recognize these distinctions leads to counterproductive policy.

Defining the Efficient Allocation of Pollution

Pollutants are the residuals of production and consumption. These residuals must eventually be returned to the environment in one form or another. Since their presence in the environment may depreciate the service flows received, an efficient allocation of resources must take this cost into account. What is meant by the efficient allocation of pollution depends on the nature of the pollutant.

Stock Pollutants

The efficient allocation of a stock pollutant must take into account the fact that the pollutant accumulates in the environment over time and that the damage caused by its presence increases and persists as the pollutant accumulates. By their very nature, stock pollutants create an interdependency between the present and the future, since the damage imposed in the future depends on current actions.

It is not hard to establish what is meant by an efficient allocation in these circumstances. Suppose, for example, that we consider the allocation of a commodity that we refer to as X. Suppose further that the production of X involves the generation of a proportional amount of a stock pollutant. The amount of this pollution can be reduced, but that takes resources away from the production of X. The damage caused by the presence of this pollutant in the environment is further assumed to be proportional to the size of the accumulated stock. As long as the stock of pollutants remains in the environment, the damage persists.

The efficient allocation, by definition, is the one that maximizes the present value of the net benefit. In this case the net benefit at any point in time t is equal to the benefit received from the consumption of X minus the cost of the damage caused by the presence of the stock pollutant in the environment.

This damage is a cost that society must bear, and in terms of its effect on the efficient allocation, this cost is not unlike that associated with extracting minerals or fuels. While for minerals the extraction cost rises with the cumulative amount of the depletable resource extracted, the damage cost associated with a stock pollutant rises with the cumulative amount deposited in the environment. The accretion of the stock pollutant is proportional to the production of X, which creates the same kind of linkage between the production of X and this pollution cost as exists between the extraction cost and the production of a mineral. They both rise over time with the cumulative amount produced. The one major difference is that the extraction cost is borne only at the time of extraction, while damage occurs as long as the stock pollutant exists in the environment.

We can exploit this similarity to infer the efficient allocation of a stock pollutant from our knowledge of the efficient allocation of a depletable resource with rising extraction cost. As discussed in Chapter 7, when extraction cost rises, the efficient quantity of a depletable resource extracted and consumed declines over time.

Exactly the same pattern would emerge for a commodity that is produced jointly with a stock pollutant. The efficient quantity of X (and therefore, the addition to the accumulation of this pollutant in the environment) would decline over time as the marginal cost of the damage rises. The price of X would rise over time, reflecting the rising social cost of production. To cope with the increasing marginal damage, the amount of resources committed to controlling the pollutant would increase over time. Ultimately, a steady state would be reached where additions to the amount of the pollutant in the environment would cease and the size of the stock would stabilize. At this point all further emission of the pollutant created by the production of X would be controlled (through recycling). The price of X and the quantity consumed would remain constant. The damage caused by the stock pollutant would persist.

As was the case with rising extraction cost, technological progress could modify this efficient allocation. Specifically, technological progress could reduce the amount of pollutant generated per unit of X produced; it could create ways to recycle the stock pollutant rather than injecting it into the environment; or it could develop ways of rendering the pollutant less harmful. All of these responses would lower the marginal damage cost associated with a given level of production of X. Therefore, more of X could be produced with technological progress than without it.

Stock pollutants are, in a sense, the other side of the intergenerational equity coin from depletable resources. With depletable resources it is possible for current generations to create a burden for future generations by using up resources, thereby diminishing the remaining endowment. Stock pollutants can create a burden for future generations by passing on damage that persists well after the benefits received from incurring that damage have been forgotten. Though neither of these situations automatically violates our sustainability criterion, they clearly require further scrutiny. We examine the relationship between stock pollutants and sustainability as well as depletable resources and sustainability in Chapter 23.

Fund Pollutants

To the extent that the emission of fund pollutants exceeds the assimilative capacity of the environment, they accumulate and share some of the characteristics of stock pollutants. When the emission rate is low enough, however, the discharges can be assimilated by the environment, with the result that the link between present emissions and future damage may be broken.

When this happens, current emissions cause current damage and future emissions cause future damage, but the level of future damage is independent of current emissions. This independence of allocations among time periods allows us to explore the efficient allocation of fund pollutants using the concept of static, rather than dynamic, efficiency. Because the static concept is simpler, this affords us the opportunity to incorporate more dimensions of the problem without unnecessarily complicating the analysis.

The normal starting point for the analysis would be to maximize the net benefit from the waste flows. However, pollution is more easily understood if we deal with an equivalent formulation involving the minimization of two rather different types of costs: damage costs and control or avoidance costs.

To examine the efficient allocation graphically, we need to know something about how control costs vary with the degree of control and how the damages vary with the amount of pollution emitted. Though our knowledge in these areas is far from complete, economists generally agree on the shapes of these relationships.

Generally the marginal damage caused by a unit of pollution increases with the amount emitted. When small amounts of the pollutant are emitted, the marginal damage is quite small. However, when large amounts are emitted, the marginal unit can cause significantly more damage. It is not hard to understand why. Small amounts of pollution are easily diluted in the environment, and the body can tolerate small quantities of substances. However, as the amount in the atmosphere increases, dilution is less effective and the body is less tolerant.

Marginal control costs commonly increase with the amount controlled. For example, suppose a source of pollution tries to cut down on its particulate emissions by purchasing an electrostatic precipitator that captures 80% of the particulates as they flow past in the stack. If the source wants further control, it can purchase another precipitator and place it in the stack above the first one. This second precipitator captures 80% of the remaining 20%, or 16% of the uncontrolled emissions. Thus the first precipitator would achieve an 80% reduction from uncontrolled emissions, while the second precipitator, which costs the same as the first, would achieve only a further 16% reduction. Obviously each unit of emission reduction costs more for the second precipitator than for the first.

In Figure 15.2 we use these two pieces of information on the shapes of the relevant curves to derive the efficient allocation. A movement from right to left refers to greater control and less pollution emitted. The efficient allocation is represented by Q^*, the point at which the damage caused by the marginal unit of pollution is exactly equal to the marginal cost of avoiding it.[1]

---

[1]At this point, we can see why this formulation is equivalent to the net benefit formulation. Since the benefit is damage reduction, another way of stating this proposition is that marginal benefit must equal marginal cost. That is, of course, the familiar proposition derived by maximizing net benefits.

FIGURE 15.2

Efficient Allocation of a Fund Pollutant

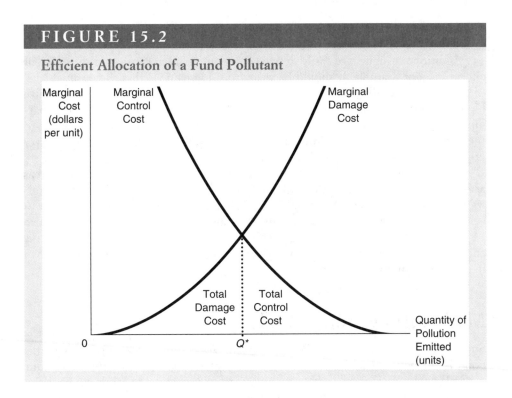

Greater degrees of control (points to the left of Q^*) are inefficient because the further increase in avoidance costs would exceed the reduction in damages. Hence total costs would rise. Similarly, levels of control lower than Q^* would result in a lower cost of control but the increase in damage costs would be even larger, yielding an increase in total cost. Either increasing or decreasing the amount controlled causes an increase in total costs. Hence Q^* must be efficient.

The diagram suggests that, under the conditions presented, the optimal level of pollution is not zero. If you find this disturbing, remember that we confront this principle every day. Take the damage caused by automobile accidents, for example. Obviously, a considerable amount of damage is caused by automobile accidents. Yet we do not reduce that damage to zero because the cost of doing so would be too high.

The point is *not* that we do not know how to stop automobile accidents. All we would have to do is eliminate automobiles! Rather, the point is that since we value the benefits of automobiles, we take steps to reduce accidents (using speed limits) only to the extent that the costs of accident reduction are commensurate with the damage reduction achieved. The efficient level of automobile accidents is not zero.

The second point to be made is that in some circumstances the optimal level of pollution *may* be zero, or close to it. This situation occurs when the damage caused by even the first unit of pollution is so severe that it is higher than the marginal cost of controlling the last unit of pollution. This would be reflected in Figure 15.2 as a leftward shift of the damage cost curve of sufficient magnitude that its intersection with the vertical axis would lie above the point where the marginal cost curve intersects the vertical axis. This circumstance seems to characterize the treatment of highly dangerous radioactive pollutants such as plutonium.

Additional insights are easily derived from our characterization of the efficient allocation. For example, it should be clear from Figure 15.2 that the optimal level of pollution generally is not the same for all parts of the country. Areas that have higher population levels or are particularly sensitive to pollution would have a marginal damage cost curve that intersected the marginal control cost curve close to the vertical axis. This would imply lower levels of pollution. Areas that have lower population levels or are less sensitive should have more.

Examples of ecological sensitivity are not hard to find. For instance, some areas are less sensitive to acid rain than others because the local geological strata neutralize moderate amounts of the acid. Thus, the marginal damage caused by a unit of acid rain is lower in those fortunate regions than in others less tolerant. It can also be argued that pollutants affecting visibility are more damaging in national parks and other areas where visibility is an important part of the aesthetic experience than in other more industrial areas.

Market Allocation of Pollution

Since air and water are treated in our legal system as common-pool resources, at this point in the book it should surprise no one that the market misallocates them. Our general conclusion that free-access resources are overexploited certainly applies here. Air and water resources have been overexploited as waste repositories. However, this conclusion only scratches the surface; much more can be learned about market allocations of pollution.

When firms create products, rarely does the process of converting raw material into outputs use 100% of the mass. Some of the mass, called a *residual,* is left over. If the residual is valuable, it is simply reused. However, if it is not valuable, the firm has an incentive to deal with it in the cheapest manner possible.

The typical firm has several alternatives. It can control the amount of the residual by using inputs more completely so that less is left over. It can also produce less output, so that smaller amounts of the residual are generated. Recycling the residual is sometimes a viable option, as is removing the most damaging components of the waste stream and disposing of the rest.

Because damage costs are externalities but control costs are not, what is cheapest for the firm is not always cheapest for society as a whole. When pollutants are injected into water courses or the atmosphere, they cause damages to those firms and consumers downstream or downwind of the source. These costs are *not* borne by the emitting source and hence not considered by it, although they certainly are borne by society at large.[2] As with other services that are systematically undervalued, the disposal of wastes into the air or water becomes inefficiently attractive.

---

[2]Actually the source certainly considers some of the costs, if only to avoid adverse public relations. The point, however, is that this consideration is likely to be incomplete; the source is unlikely to internalize all of the damage cost.

As we saw in Chapter 4, inefficient pollution control choices lead to further inefficiencies in product and input markets.

In the case of stock pollutants, the problem is particularly severe. Uncontrolled
markets would lead to an excessive production of X, too few resources committed
to pollution control, and an inefficiently large amount of the stock pollutant in the
environment. Thus the burden on future generations caused by the presence of this
pollutant would be inefficiently large.

There are important differences between the inefficiencies associated with pollution control and the previously discussed inefficiencies associated with the extraction or production of minerals, energy, and food. For private-property resources,
the market forces provide automatic signals of impending scarcity. These forces may
be understated (as when the vulnerability of imports is ignored), but they operate
in the correct direction. Even when some resources are treated as open-access
(fisheries), the possibility for a private-property alternative (fish farming) is
enhanced. When private-property and open-access resources sell in the same market,
the private-property owner tends to ameliorate the excesses of those who exploit
open-access properties. Efficient firms are rewarded with higher profits.

With pollution, no comparable automatic amelioration mechanism is evident.[3]
Because this cost is borne partially by innocent victims rather than producers, it does
not find its way into product prices. Firms that attempt unilaterally to control their
pollution are placed at a competitive disadvantage; due to the added expense, their
costs of production are higher than those of their less conscientious competitors.
Not only does the unimpeded market fail to generate the efficient level of pollution
control, it penalizes those firms that might attempt to control an efficient amount.
Hence the case for some sort of government intervention is particularly strong for
pollution control.

Efficient Policy Responses

Our use of the efficiency criterion has helped demonstrate why markets fail to
produce an efficient level of pollution control as well as trace out the effects of this
less-than-optimal degree of control on the markets for related commodities. It can
also be used to define efficient policy responses.

Efficiency is achieved when the marginal cost of control is equal to the marginal
damage caused by the pollution for each emitter. One way to achieve this equilibrium would be to impose a legal limit on the amount of pollution allowed by each
emitter. If the limit were chosen precisely at the level of pollution where marginal
control cost equals marginal damage (Q^* in Figure 15.2), efficiency would have been
achieved.

An alternative approach would be to internalize the marginal damage caused
by each unit of emissions by means of a tax or charge on each unit of emissions

---

[3]Affected parties do have an incentive to negotiate among themselves, a topic covered in Chapter 4. As
pointed out there, however, that approach works well only in cases where the number of affected parties
is small.

Example *15.1*

ENVIRONMENTAL TAXATION IN CHINA

China has extremely high pollution levels that are causing considerable damage to human health. Traditional means of control have not been particularly effective. To combat this pollution, China has instituted a wide-ranging system of environmental taxation with tax rates that are quite high by historical standards.

The program involves a two-rate tax system. Lower rates are imposed on emissions below an official standard and higher rates on all emissions over that standard. The tax is expected not only to reduce pollution and the damage it causes, but also to provide needed revenue to local Environmental Protection Bureaus.

According to the World Bank (1997) this strategy makes good economic sense. Conducting detailed analyses of air pollution in two Chinese cities (Beijing and Zhengzhou) and relying on "back of the envelope" measurements of benefits, they found that the marginal cost of further abatement was significantly less than the marginal benefit for any reasonable value of human life. Indeed in Zhengzhou they found that achieving an efficient outcome (based upon an assumed value of a "statistical life" of $8,000 per person) would require reducing current emissions by some 79%. According to their results, the current low abatement level makes sense only if China's policy-makers value the life of an average urban resident at approximately $270. It is hard to imagine that such a low value could be justified.

Source: Robert Bohm et al. "Environmental Taxes: China's Bold Initiative," *Environment* Vol. 40, No. 7 (September 1998):10–13, 33–38; Susmita Dasgupta, Hua Wang, and David Wheeler. "Surviving Success: Policy Reform and the Future of Industrial Pollution in China" (Washington, DC: The World Bank 1997) available online at http://www.worldbank.org/NIPR/work_paper/survive/china-htmp6.htm (August 1998).

(see Example 15.1). Either this per-unit charge could increase with the level of pollution (following the marginal damage curve for each succeeding unit of emission) or the tax rate could be constant as long as the rate were equal to the marginal social damage at the point where the marginal social damage and marginal control costs cross (see Figure 15.2). Since the emitter is paying the marginal social damage when confronted by these fees, pollution costs would be internalized. The efficient choice would also be the cost-minimizing choice for the emitter.[4]

However, while the efficient levels of these policy instruments can be easily defined in principle, they are very difficult to implement in practice. To implement either of these policy instruments, we must know the level of pollution at which the two marginal cost curves cross for every emitter. That is a tall order, one that imposes

---

[4]Another policy choice is to remove the people from the polluted area. The government has used this strategy for heavily contaminated toxic waste sites such as Times Beach, Missouri, and Love Canal, New York. See Chapter 20.

an unrealistically high information burden on control authorities. Control authorities typically have very poor information on control costs and little reliable information on marginal damage functions.

How can environmental authorities allocate pollution control responsibility in a reasonable manner when the information burdens are apparently so unrealistically large? One approach, the choice of several countries including the United States, is to select specific legal levels of pollution based on some other criterion such as providing adequate margins of safety for human or ecological health. Once these thresholds have been established by whatever means, only half of the problem has been resolved. The other half deals with deciding how to allocate the responsibility for meeting predetermined pollution levels among the large numbers of emitters.

This is precisely where the cost-effectiveness criterion comes in. Once the objective is stated in terms of meeting the predetermined pollution level at minimum cost, it is possible to derive the conditions that any cost-effective allocation of the responsibility must satisfy. These conditions can then be used as a basis for choosing among various kinds of policy instruments that impose more reasonable information burdens on control authorities.

Cost-Effective Policies for Uniformly Mixed Fund Pollutants

Defining a Cost-Effective Allocation

We begin our analysis with uniformly mixed fund pollutants, which analytically are the easiest to deal with. The damage caused by these pollutants depends on the amount entering the atmosphere. In contrast to nonuniformly mixed pollutants, the damage caused by uniformly mixed pollutants is relatively insensitive to where the emissions are injected into the atmosphere. Thus the policy can focus simply on controlling the total weight of emissions in a manner that minimizes the cost of control. What can we say about the cost-effective allocation of control responsibility for uniformly mixed fund pollutants?

Consider a simple example. Assume that there are two emission sources currently emitting a total 30 units of emissions. Assume further that the control authority determines that the environment can assimilate 15 units, so that a reduction of 15 units is necessary. How should this 15-unit reduction be allocated between the two sources in order to minimize the total cost of the reduction?

With the aid of Figure 15.3 we can demonstrate the answer. Figure 15.3 is drawn by measuring the marginal cost of control for the first source from the left-hand axis (MC_1) and the marginal cost of control for the second source from the right-hand axis (MC_2). Notice that a total 15-unit reduction is achieved for every point on this graph; each point represents some different combination of reduction by the two sources. Drawn in this manner, the diagram represents all possible allocations of the 15-unit reduction between the two sources. The left-hand axis, for example, represents an allocation of the entire reduction to the second source, while the right-hand

FIGURE 15.3

Cost-Effective Allocation of a Uniformly Mixed Pollutant

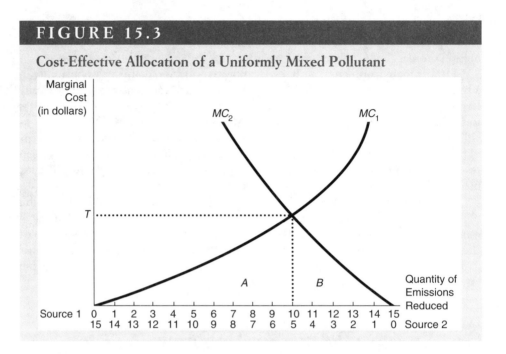

axis represents a situation in which the first source bears the entire responsibility. All points in between represent different degrees of shared responsibility. What allocation minimizes the cost of control?

In the cost-effective allocation, the first source cleans up 10 units, while the second source cleans up 5 units. The total variable cost of control for this particular assignment of the responsibility for the reduction is represented by area *A* plus area *B*. Area *A* is the cost of control for the first source; area *B* is the cost of control for the second. Any other allocation would result in a higher total control cost. (Convince yourself that this is true.)

Figure 15.3 also demonstrates the Cost-Effectiveness Equimarginal Principal introduced in Chapter 3. The cost of *achieving a given reduction in emissions will be minimized if and only if the marginal costs of control are equalized for all emitters.*[5] This is demonstrated by the fact that the marginal cost curves cross at the cost-effective allocation.

Cost-Effective Pollution Control Policies

This proposition can be used as a basis for choosing among the various policy instruments that the control authority might use to achieve this allocation. Sources have a large menu of options for controlling the amount of pollution they inject into the

---

[5]This statement is true when marginal cost increases with the amount of emissions reduced (see Figure 15.3). Suppose that for some pollutants the marginal cost were to decrease with the amount of emissions reduced. What would be the cost-effective allocation in that admittedly unusual situation?

environment. The cheapest method of control will differ widely not only among industries but also among plants in the same industry. The selection of the cheapest method requires detailed information on the possible control techniques and their associated costs.

Generally, plant managers are able to acquire this information for their plants when it is in their interest to do so. However, the government authorities responsible for meeting pollution targets are not likely to have this information. Since the degree to which these plants would be regulated depends on cost information, it is unrealistic to expect these plant managers to transfer unbiased information to the government. Plant managers would have a strong incentive to overstate control costs in hopes of reducing their ultimate burden.

This situation poses a difficult dilemma for control authorities. The cost of incorrectly assigning the control responsibility among various polluters is likely to be large. Yet the control authorities do not have the information at their disposal to make a correct allocation. Those who have the information—the plant managers—are not inclined to share it. Can the cost-effective allocation be found? The answer depends on the approach taken by the control authority.

Emission Standards.   We start our investigation of this question by supposing that the control authority pursues a traditional legal approach by imposing a separate emission standard on each source. In the economics literature this approach is referred to as the "command-and-control" approach. An *emission standard* is a legal limit on the amount of the pollutant an individual source is allowed to emit. In our example it is clear that the two standards should add up to the allowable 15 units, but it is not clear how, in the absence of information on control costs, these 15 units are to be allocated between the two sources. The easiest method of resolving this dilemma—and the one chosen in the earliest days of pollution control—would be simply to allocate each source an equal reduction. As is clear from Figure 15.3, this strategy would not be cost-effective. While the first source would have lower costs, this cost reduction would be substantially smaller than the increase faced by the second source. Compared to a cost-effective allocation, total costs would increase if both sources were forced to clean up the same amount.

When emission standards are used, there is no reason to believe that the authority will assign the responsibility for emission reduction in a cost-minimizing way. This is probably not surprising. Who would have believed otherwise?

Surprisingly enough, however, some policy instruments do allow the authority to allocate the emission reduction in a cost-effective manner even when it has no information on the magnitude of control costs. These policy approaches rely on economic incentives to produce the desired outcome. The two most common approaches are known as emission charges and transferable emission permits.

Emission Charges.   An *emission charge* is a fee, collected by the government, levied on each unit of pollutant emitted into the air or water. The total payment any source would make to the government could be found by multiplying the fee times

FIGURE 15.4

Cost-Minimizing Control of Pollution with an Emission Charge

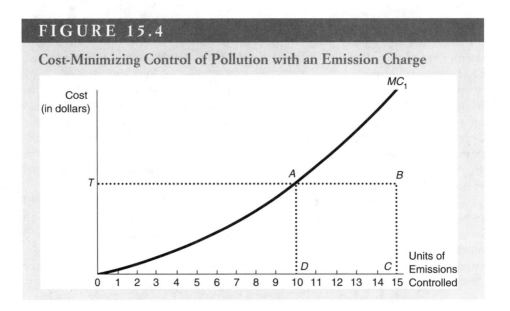

the amount of pollution emitted. Emission charges reduce pollution because pollution costs the firm money. To save money, the source seeks ways to reduce its pollution.

How much pollution control would the firm choose to purchase? A profit-maximizing firm would control, rather than emit, pollution whenever it proved cheaper to do so. We can illustrate the firm's decision with Figure 15.4. The level of uncontrolled emission is 15 units and the emission charge is T. Thus, if the firm were to decide against controlling any emissions, it would have to pay T times 15, represented by area 0TBC.

Is this the best the firm can do? Obviously not, since it can control some pollution at a lower cost than paying the emission charge. It would pay the firm to reduce emissions until the marginal cost of reduction is equal to the emission charge. The firm would minimize its cost by choosing to clean up 10 units of pollution and emitting 5 units. At this allocation the firm would pay control costs equal to area 0AD and total emission charge payments equal to area $ABCD$ for a total cost of 0ABC. This is clearly less than 0TBC, the amount the firm would pay if it chose not to clean up any pollution.

Let's carry this one step further. Suppose that we levied the same emission charge on both sources discussed in Figure 15.3. Each source would then control its emissions until its marginal control cost equaled the emission charge. (Faced with an emission charge T, the second source would clean up 5 units.) Since they both face the same emission charge, they will *independently choose* levels of control consistent with equal marginal control costs. This is precisely the condition that yields a cost-minimizing allocation.

This is a remarkable finding. We have shown that as long as the control authority imposes the same emission charge on all sources, the resulting reduction allocation *automatically* minimizes the costs of control. This is true in spite of the fact that the control authority may not have any knowledge of control costs.

However, we have not yet dealt with the issue of how the appropriate level of the emission charge is determined. Each level of a charge will result in *some* level of emission reduction. Furthermore, the responsibility for meeting that reduction will be allocated in a manner that minimizes control costs. How high should the charge be set to ensure that the resulting emission reduction is the *desired* level of emission reduction?

Without knowing the cost of control, the control authority cannot establish the correct tax rate on the first try. It is possible, however, to develop an iterative, trial-and-error process to find the appropriate charge rate. This process is initiated by choosing an arbitrary charge rate and observing the amount of reduction that occurs when that charge is imposed. If the observed reduction is larger than desired, it means the charge should be lowered; if the reduction is smaller, the charge should be raised. The new reduction that results from the adjusted charge can then be observed and compared with the desired reduction. Further adjustments in the charge can be made as needed. This process can be repeated until the actual and desired reductions are equal. At that point the correct emission charge would have been found.

The charge system not only causes sources to choose a cost-effective allocation of the control responsibility, it also stimulates the development of newer, cheaper means of controlling emissions, as well as promoting technological progress. This is illustrated in Figure 15.5.

The reason for this is rather straightforward. Control authorities base the emission standards on specific technologies. As new technologies are discovered by the

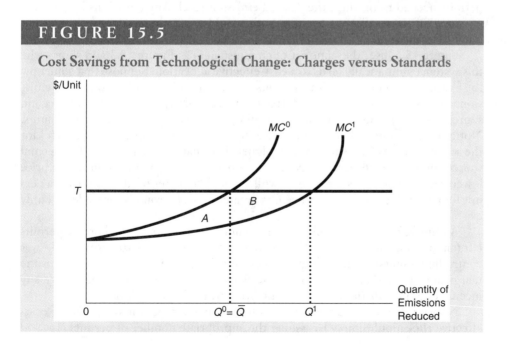

FIGURE 15.5

Cost Savings from Technological Change: Charges versus Standards

control authority, the standards are tightened. These stricter standards force firms to bear higher costs. Therefore, with emissions standards, firms have an incentive to hide technological changes from the control authority.

With an emissions charge system, the firm saves money by adopting cheaper new technologies. As long as the firm can reduce its pollution at a marginal cost lower than T, it pays to adopt the new technology. In Figure 15.5 the firm saves A and B by adopting the new technology and voluntarily increases its emissions reduction from Q^0 to Q^1.

With an emissions charge, the minimum cost allocation of meeting a predetermined emission reduction can be found by a control authority even when it has no information on control costs. An emission charge also stimulates technological advances in emission reduction. Unfortunately, the process for finding the appropriate rate takes some experimenting. During the trial-and-error period of finding the appropriate rate, sources would be faced with a volatile emission charge. Changing emission charges would make planning for the future difficult. Investments that would make sense under a high emission charge might not make sense when it falls. From either a policy-maker's or business manager's perspective, this process leaves much to be desired.

Transferable Emission Permits.
Is it possible for the control authority to find the cost-minimizing allocation without going through a trial-and-error process? It is possible if a *transferable emission permit system* is used to control pollution. Under this system, all sources are required to have permits to emit. Each permit specifies exactly how much the firm is allowed to emit. The permits are freely transferable; they can be bought and sold. The control authority issues exactly the number of permits needed to produce the desired emission level. Any emissions by a source in excess of those allowed by its permit would cause the source to face severe monetary sanctions.

Figure 15.6, uses the same set of circumstances as Figure 15.3 and shows why this system automatically leads to a cost-effective allocation. Suppose that somehow the first source found itself with 7 permits. Since it has 15 units of uncontrolled emissions, this would mean it must control 8 units. Similarly, suppose that the second source has the remaining 8 permits, meaning that it would have to clean up 7 units. Notice that both firms have an incentive to trade. The marginal cost of control for the second source (C) is substantially higher than that for the first (A). The second source could lower its cost if it could buy a permit from the first source at a price lower than C. The first source, meanwhile, would be better off if it could sell a permit for a price higher than A. Since C is greater than A, grounds for trade certainly exist.

A transfer of permits would take place until the first source had only 5 permits left (and is controlling 10 units), while the second source had 10 permits (and was controlling 5 units). At this point, the permit price would equal B, since that is the marginal value of that permit to both sources, and neither source would have any incentive to trade further. The permit market would be in equilibrium.

Notice that the market equilibrium for an emission permit system is the cost-effective allocation! Simply by issuing the appropriate number of permits (15) and

FIGURE 15.6

Cost-Effectiveness and the Emission Permit System

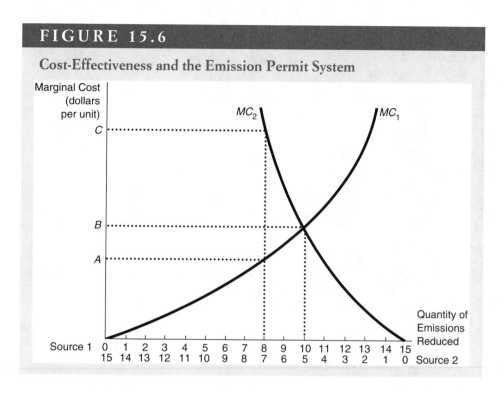

letting the market do the rest, the control authority can achieve a cost-effective allocation without having even the slightest knowledge about control costs. This system allows the government to meet its policy objective while allowing greater flexibility in how that objective is met.

The incentives created by this system ensure that sources use this flexibility to achieve the objective at the lowest possible cost. As we shall see in the next two chapters, this remarkable property has been responsible for the prominence of this type of approach in current attempts to reform the regulatory process. How far can the reforms go? Can developing countries use the experience of the industrialized countries to move directly into using these market-based instruments to control pollution? As Debate 15.1 points out, that may be easier said than done.

Cost-Effective Policies for Nonuniformly Mixed Surface Pollutants

The problem becomes more complicated when dealing with nonuniformly mixed surface pollutants rather than uniformly mixed pollutants. For these pollutants the policy must be concerned not only with the weight of emission entering the atmosphere, but also with the location of emissions. For nonuniformly mixed pollutants, it is the concentration in the air, soil, and water that counts. The concentration is

DEBATE 15.1

Should Developing Countries Rely on Market-Based Instruments to Control Pollution?

Since the case for using market-based instruments seems so strong in principle, some observers, most prominently the World Bank (2000, pp. 40 and 43), have suggested that developing countries should capitalize on the experience of the industrialized countries to move directly to market-based instruments to control pollution. The desirability of this strategy is seen as flowing from the level of poverty in developing countries; abating pollution in the least expensive manner would seem especially important to poorer nations. Furthermore, since developing countries are frequently also starved for revenue, revenue-generating instruments (such as emissions charges or auctioned permits) would seem to serve two significant social purposes at once. Proponents also point out that a number of developing countries already use market-based instruments.

Another school of thought (for example, Russell and Vaughan, 2003) suggests that the differences in infrastructure between the developing and industrialized countries make the transfer of lessons from one context to another fraught with peril. To illustrate their more general point, they note that the effectiveness of market-based instruments presumes an effective monitoring and enforcement system, something that is frequently not present in developing countries. In their absence, the superiority of market-based instruments is much less obvious.

Some middle ground is clearly emerging. Russell and Vaughan do not argue that market-based instruments should never be used in developing countries, but rather that they may not be as universally appropriate as the most enthusiastic proponents suggest. They see themselves as telling a cautionary tale. And proponents are certainly beginning to see the crucial importance of infrastructure. Recognizing that some developing countries may be much better suited (by virtue of their infrastructure) to implement market-based systems than others, proponents are beginning to see capacity building as a logical prior step for those countries that need it.

For market-based instruments, as well as for other aspects of life, if it looks too good to be true, it probably is.

Source: World Bank. *Greening Industry: New Roles for Communities, Markets and Governments* (Washington, DC: World Bank and Oxford University Press, 2000) and C. S. Russell and W. J. Vaughan. "The Choice of Pollution Control Policy Instruments in Developing Countries: Arguments, Evidence and Suggestions," in H. Folmer and T. Tietenberg, eds. *The International Yearbook of Environmental and Resource Economics 2003/2004* (Cheltenham, UK: Edward Elgar, 2003): 331–371.

measured as the amount of pollutant found in a given volume of air, soil, or water at a given location and at a given point in time.

It is easy to see why pollutant concentrations are sensitive to the location of emissions. Suppose that three emission sources are clustered and emit the same amount as three separate but otherwise identical sources. The emissions from the clustered sources generally cause higher pollution levels because they are all entering the same volume of air or water. Because the two sets of emission do not share a common receiving volume, those from the dispersed sources result in lower con-centrations. This is the main reason why cities generally face more severe pollution problems than do rural areas; urban sources tend to be more densely clustered.

Since the damage caused by nonuniformly mixed surface pollutants is related to their concentration levels in the air, soil, or water, it is natural that our search for cost-effective policies for controlling these pollutants focuses on the attainment of ambient standards. *Ambient standards* are legal ceilings placed on the concentration level of specified pollutants in the air, soil, or water. They represent the target con-centration levels that are not to be exceeded. A cost-effective policy results in the lowest cost allocation of control responsibility consistent with ensuring that the pre-determined ambient standards are met at specified locations called receptor sites.

The Single-Receptor Case

We can begin the analysis by considering a simple case in which we desire to con-trol pollution at one, and only one, receptor location. We know that all units of emissions from sources do not have the same impact on pollution measured at that receptor. Consider, for example, Figure 15.7.

Suppose that we hypothetically allow each of the four sources individually, at different points in time, to inject 10 units of emission into the stream. Suppose fur-ther that we measured the pollutant concentration resulting from each of these injec-tions at receptor R. In general, we would find that the emissions from A or B would cause a larger rise in the recorded concentration than would those from C and D, even though the same amount was emitted from each source. The reason for this is that the emissions from C and D would be substantially diluted by the time they arrived at R, while those from A and B would arrive in a more concentrated form.

Since emissions are what can be controlled, but the concentrations at R are the policy target, our first task must be to relate the two. This can be accomplished by using a transfer coefficient. A transfer coefficient (a_i) captures the constant amount the concentration at the receptor will rise if source i emits one more unit of

FIGURE 15.7

Effect of Location on Local Pollutant Concentration

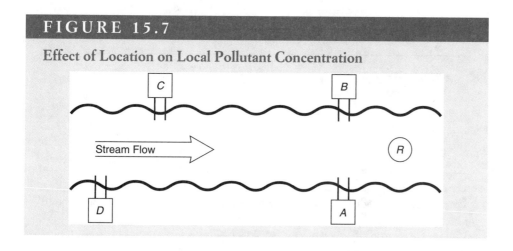

pollution. Using this definition and the knowledge that the a_is are constant, we can relate the concentration level at R to emissions from all sources:

$$K_R = \sum_{i=1}^{I} a_i E_i + B, \qquad (1)$$

where

K_R = concentration at the receptor
E_i = emission level of the ith source
I = total number of sources in the region
B = background concentration level (resulting from natural sources or sources outside the control region)

We are now in a position to define the cost-effective allocation of responsibility. A numerical example involving two sources is presented in Table 15.1. In that

TABLE 15.1

Cost-Effectiveness for Nonuniformly Mixed Pollutants:
A Hypothetical Example

Source 1($a_1 = 1.0$)			
Emissions Units Reduced	Marginal Cost of Emission Reduction (dollars per unit)	Concentration Units Reduced[a]	Marginal Cost of Concentration Reduction (dollars per unit)[b]
1	1	1.0	1
2	2	2.0	2
3	3	3.0	3
4	4	4.0	4
5	5	5.0	5
6	6	6.0	6
7	7	7.0	7
Source 2($a_1 = 0.5$)			
1	1	0.5	2
2	2	1.0	4
3	3	1.5	6
4	4	2.0	8
5	5	2.5	10
6	6	3.0	12
7	7	3.5	14

[a]Computed by multiplying the emission reduction (column 1) by the transfer coefficient (a_i).
[b]Computed by dividing the marginal cost of emission reduction (column 2) by the transfer coefficient (a_i).

example, the two sources are assumed to have the same marginal cost curves for cleaning up emissions. This assumption is reflected in the fact that the first two corresponding columns of the table for each of the two sources are identical.[6] The main difference between the two sources is their location vis à vis the receptor. The first source is closer to the receptor, so it has a larger transfer coefficient than the second (1.0 as opposed to 0.5).

The objective is to meet a given concentration target at minimum cost. Column 3 of the table translates emission reductions into concentration reductions for each source, while column 4 records the marginal cost of each unit of concentration reduced. The former is merely the emission reduction times the transfer coefficient, while the latter is the marginal cost of the emission reduction divided by the transfer coefficient (which translates the marginal cost of *emission* reduction into a marginal cost of *concentration* reduction).

Suppose the concentration at the receptor has to be reduced by 7.5 units in order to comply with the ambient standard. The cost-effective allocation would be achieved when the marginal costs of concentration reduction (*not* emission reduction) are equalized for all sources. In Table 15.1 this occurs when the first source reduces 6 units of emissions (and 6 units of concentration) and the second source reduces 3 units of emissions (and 1.5 units of concentration). At this allocation the marginal cost of concentration reduction is equal to $6 for both sources. By adding up all marginal costs for each unit reduced, we calculate the total variable cost of this allocation to be $27. From the definition of cost-effectiveness, no other allocation resulting in 7.5 units of concentration reduction would be cheaper.

Policy Approaches.   This framework can now be used to evaluate various policy approaches that the control authority might use. We begin with the *ambient charge*, the charge used to produce a cost-effective allocation of a nonuniformly mixed pollutant. This charge takes the form:

$$t_i = a_i F, \qquad (2)$$

where t_i is the per-unit charge paid by the ith source on each unit emitted, a_i is the ith source's transfer coefficient, and F is the marginal cost of a unit of concentration reduction, which is the same for all sources. In our example F is $6, so the first source would pay a per-unit emission charge of $6, while the second source would pay $3. *Note that sources will, in general, pay different charges when the objective is to meet an ambient standard at minimum cost because their transfer coefficients differ.* This contrasts with the uniformly mixed pollutant case in which a cost-effective allocation required that all sources pay the same charge.

How can the cost-effective t_i be found by a control authority with no information on control costs? The transfer coefficients can be calculated using knowledge of hydrology and meteorology, but what about F? Here a striking similarity to the uniformly mixed case becomes evident. Any level of F would yield a cost-effective allocation of control responsibility for achieving *some* level of concentration

---

[6]This assumption has no bearing on the results we shall achieve. It serves mainly to illustrate the role location plays on eliminating control-cost difference as a factor.

reduction at the receptor. That level might not, however, be compatible with the ambient standard.

We could ensure compatibility by changing F in an iterative process until the desired concentration is achieved. If the actual pollutant concentration is below the standard, the tax could be lowered; if it is above, the tax could be raised. The correct level of F would be reached when the resulting pollution concentration is equal to the desired level. That equilibrium allocation would be the one that meets the ambient standard at minimum cost.

Table 15.1 allows us to consider another issue of significance. The cost-effective allocation of control responsibility for achieving surface-concentration targets places a larger information burden on control authorities; they have to calculate the transfer coefficients. What is lost if the simpler emission charge system (where each source faces the same charge) is used to pursue a surface-concentration target? Can location be safely ignored?

In Table 15.1 a uniform emission charge equal to $5 would achieve the desired 7.5 units of reduction (5 from the first source and 2.5 from the second). Yet the total variable cost of this allocation (calculated as the sum of the marginal costs) would be $30 ($15 paid by each source). This is $3 higher than the allocation resulting from the use of ambient charge discussed earlier. In subsequent chapters we present empirical estimates of the size of this cost increase in actual air and water pollution situations. In general, they show the cost increases to be large; location matters.

Table 15.1 also helps us understand why location matters. Notice that with a uniform emissions charge, 10 units of emission are cleaned up, whereas with the ambient charge only 9 units are cleaned up. Both achieve the concentration target, but the uniform-emission charge results in fewer emissions. The ambient charge results in a lower cost allocation than the emission charge because it results in less emission control. Those sources having only a small effect on the recorded concentration at the receptor location are forced to control less than they would with a uniform charge.

With the ambient charge, we have the same problem that we encountered with emission charges in the uniformly mixed pollutant case—the cost-effective level can be determined only by an iterative process. Can a permit system get around this problem when dealing with nonuniformly mixed pollutants?

It can, by designing the permits in the correct way. An ambient permit entitles the owner to cause the concentration to rise at the receptor by a specified amount, rather than allowing the same amount of emissions to each owner. Using ΔK_R to represent this permitted rise and E to indicate the units of emissions allowed by each permit held by the ith source, we can see from equation (1) that:

$$\frac{\Delta K_R}{a_i} = \Delta E_i. \tag{3}$$

The larger the transfer coefficient (that is, the closer the source is to the receptor), the smaller the amount of emissions legitimized by a permit. Proximate sources must purchase more permits than distant sources to legitimize a given level of emissions. In this version of the permit system, the sources pay the same price for each permit, but the amount of emission allowed by each permit varies from location to location. The market automatically determines this common price, and the resulting allocation of permits is cost-effective. With respect to Table 15.1, the ambient permit price would be \$6. This cost-effective system is called an *ambient permit system* to differentiate it from the *emission permit system*, which is used to achieve a cost-effective allocation of control responsibility for uniformly mixed pollutants.

We can reinforce our understanding of what is going on with the ambient permit system by examining a specific trade. Suppose our two sources in Table 15.1 want to trade permits with the first source buying from the second. To maintain the same concentration level before and after the trade, we must ensure that:

$$a_1 \Delta E_1 = a_2 \Delta E_2$$

where the subscripts refer to the first source and second source and the ΔE_i refers to a change in emissions by the ith source. Solving this for the allowable increase in emission by the buyer yields:

$$\Delta E_1 = \frac{a_2}{a_t} \Delta E_2. \tag{4}$$

For $a_2 = 0.5$ and $a_1 = 1.0$, this equation suggests that for each permit traded, the buyer (the first source) is allowed to emit only one-half the amount of emissions allowed by that same permit when it was used by the seller. After this trade, the total amount of emissions by both sources goes down.[7] This could not happen in an emissions permit system, since the design of those permits causes all trades to leave emissions (but not concentrations!) unchanged.

The Many-Receptors Case

This analysis generalizes easily to the many-receptors case. The cost-effective ambient charge paid by any source would in this case be:

$$T_i = \sum_{j=1}^{J} a_{ij} F_j,$$

where

T_i = charge paid by the ith source for each unit of emissions
a_{ij} = transfer coefficient that translates emissions by source i into concentration increases at the jth receptor
J = number of receptors
F_j = monetary fee associated with the jth receptor

Thus the source has to pay a charge that incorporates its effect on all receptors. The control authority could manipulate F_j for each receptor location until the desired concentration level is achieved at that receptor.[8]

---

[7]Emissions could rise with ambient permit trades as well. This would occur whenever the transfer coefficient of the seller was larger than that of the buyer.

[8]Because any higher F_j reduces concentrations at several locations, not just at the jth receptor, not all selections of F_j that result in the ambient standards being met will result in cost-effective allocations. In the single-receptor case, the charge equilibrium is unique and equal to the cost-effective one. This is a further burden on the control authority of using an emission charge system as opposed to the permit system where the equilibrium is unique and cost-effective. The permit system equilibrium is unique because all equilibria other than the cost-effective one involve higher costs and, therefore, further opportunities for trade.

The extension of the ambient permit system to the many-receptor case requires that a separate permit market be created *for each receptor*. The price prevailing in each of these markets would reflect the difficulty of meeting the ambient standard at that receptor. All other things being equal, permit markets associated with receptors in heavily congested areas could be expected to sustain higher prices than those affected by relatively few emitters.

Since both the ambient permit system and the ambient charge system take location into account, when these policies are chosen, the marginal cost of emission control varies from location to location. Sources located in heavily populated portions of the region pay higher marginal costs, since their emissions have a greater impact on the receptors of interest. Having control costs depend on location provides incentives for new sources to choose their location carefully. Since heavily polluted areas have high control costs, there is some incentive to locate elsewhere, even though pollution control expenditures are only part of the costs a firm considers when deciding where to locate. For nonuniformly mixed pollution problems, where the emissions occur is important. Therefore, it is also important that the location component of the cost be internalized by relocating sources. With the ambient permit and charge systems, this is precisely what occurs.

As a practical matter, however, ambient charge and permit systems have proved to be excessively complex to implement. As a result, control authorities have developed a number of rule-of-thumb procedures designed to deal adequately with spatial issues while promoting cost-effectiveness. One approach allows unrestricted trading within predefined zones on a "one-for-one" basis, but allows trading between zones only after adjusting the trading ratios to take location into account. Another approach allows unrestricted *trading*, but restricts use, depending on the conditions around the acquiring source. A review of these approaches, where they have been applied, and the evidence on their success can be found in Tietenberg (1995).

Other Policy Dimensions

Two main pollution control policy instruments rely on economic incentives—charges and transferable permits. Both of these allow the control authority to distribute the responsibility for control in a cost-effective manner. The major difference between them we have discussed so far is that the appropriate charge can be determined only by an iterative trial-and-error process over time, while the permit price can be determined immediately by the market. Can other differences be identified?

The Revenue Effect

One of the differentiating characteristics of these instruments is their ability to raise revenue. Environmental taxes and auctioned permits raise revenue, but permit schemes that allocated the permits to users free of charge do not. Does this difference matter?

It does for at least two reasons.[9] First, a number of authors (Parry, 1995; Boven-berg and Goulder, 1996; and Goulder, 1997) have noted that the revenue from this source could be substituted for the revenue from distortionary taxes, thereby reducing those taxes and the distortions they cause. When this substitution is made, the calculations indicate that it allows an increase in the present value of net benefits from the application of this instrument, an effect that has been called the "double dividend." This effect creates a preference for instruments that can raise revenue as long as both the implementation of a revenue-raising instrument and this particular use of revenue from that instrument are politically feasible.

The second consequence involves precisely the political feasibility issue. It also seems quite clear that, to date at least, using a free-distribution approach to the initial allocation of permits has been a necessary ingredient in building the political support necessary to implement the approach (Raymond, 2003). Existing users frequently have the power to block implementation while potential future users do not. This has made it politically expedient to allocate a substantial part of the economic rent that these resources offer to existing users as the price of securing their support (Example 15.2). While this strategy reduces the adjustment costs to existing users, it generally raises them for new users. Interestingly in the climate-change case, the empirical evidence suggests that only a small fraction of the total revenue would be needed to hold the profits of carbon suppliers unchanged (Bovenberg and Goulder, 2001). Allocating all permits free of charge therefore may not be inevitable in principle, even if political feasibility considerations affect the design.

Responses to Changes in the Regulatory Environment

One major additional difference concerns the manner in which these two systems react to changes in external circumstances in the absence of further decisions by the control authority. This is an important consideration, because bureaucratic procedures are notoriously sluggish and changes in policies are usually rendered slowly.[10] We consider three such circumstances: growth in the number of sources, inflation, and technological progress.

If the number of sources were to increase in a permit market, the demand for permits would shift to the right. Given a fixed supply of permits, the price would rise, as would the control costs, but the amount of emissions or pollution concentrations (in the case of the ambient permit system) would remain the same. If charges were being used, in the absence of additional action by the control authority, the charge level would remain the same. This implies that the existing sources would control only what they would control in the absence of growth. Therefore, the arrival of new sources would cause a deterioration of air or water quality in the

---

[9]The literature contains a third reason. It suggests that unless emitters cover all external costs via a revenue-raising instrument, the cost of production will be artificially low, production will be artificially high, and the industry will contain too many firms. As Pezzey (2003) shows, however, this conclusion is sensitive to the manner in which subsidies and property rights are defined. Treating some level of allowed emission as a property right (as some current laws seem to, at least implicitly) means that free-distribution permits equal to that amount of emissions is not a subsidy and therefore does not trigger industry inefficiency.

[10]This is probably particularly true when the modification involves a change in the rate at which firms are charged for their emissions.

Example *15.2*

THE SWEDISH NITROGEN CHARGE

One of the dilemmas facing those who wish to use charges to control pollution is that the amounts of revenue extracted from those subject to the tax can be considerable and that additional expense can produce a lot of political resistance to the policy. This resistance can be lowered if the revenue is rebated to those who pay it, but if all firms know they are getting their money back, the economic incentive to limit emissions is lost. Is it possible to design a system of rebates that will promote political feasibility without undermining abatement incentives?

The Swedish Nitrogen Charge was designed specifically to resolve this dilemma. Sweden's nitrogen oxide emission charge was first imposed in 1992 on large energy sources. Some 120 heating plants and industrial facilities with about 180 boilers were subject to the tax.

It was intended from the beginning to have a significant incentive effect, not to raise revenue. Although the charge rate is high by international standards (thereby producing an effective economic incentive), the revenue from this tax is not retained by the government, but rather is rebated to the emitting sources (thereby promoting acceptance of the policy of the regulated sources). It is the form of this rebate that makes this an interesting scheme. While the tax is collected on the basis of *emissions,* it is rebated on the basis of *energy production.* In effect this system rewards plants that emit little per unit of energy and penalizes plants that emit more per unit of energy, thereby providing incentives to reduce emissions per unit of energy produced.

As expected, emissions per unit of energy produced fell rather dramatically. The Swedish Ministry of the Environment and Natural Resources has estimated that the benefits exceeded the costs by a factor of more than 3 to 1. Notice, however, that rebating the revenue means that this tax cannot produce a double dividend and it provides no incentives to reduce energy consumption.

Sources: R. Anderson and A. Lohof. "Foreign Experience with Incentive Systems," Section 11 in *The United States Experience with Economic Incentives in Environmental Pollution Control Policy* (Washington, DC: Environmental Law Institute, 1997) and T. Sterner. *Policy Instruments for Environmental and Natural Resource Management* (Washington, DC: Resources for the Future, 2003): 286–288.

region. The costs of abatement would rise, since the costs of control paid by the new sources must be considered, but by a lesser amount than in a permit market, because of the lower amount of pollution being controlled. If the choice is between a fixed fee and a fixed number of permits in a growing economy, the dominance of the permit system over the fixed-fee system increases over time (Butler and Maher, 1982).

With a permit system, inflation in the cost of control would automatically result in higher permit prices, but with a charge system it would result in lower control. Essentially the real charge (the nominal charge adjusted for inflation) declines with inflation if the nominal charge remains the same.

We should not, however, conclude that, over time, charges always result in less control than permits. Suppose, for example, technological progress in designing pollution control equipment were to cause the marginal cost of abatement to fall. In a permit system, this would result in lower prices and lower abatement costs but the same aggregate degree of control. With a charge system the amount controlled would actually increase (remember Figure 15.5?) and would, therefore, result in more control than a permit system that, prior to the fall in costs, controlled the same amount.

If the control authority were to adjust the charge in each of the above cases appropriately, the outcome would be identical to that achieved by a permit market. The permit market reacts automatically to these changes in circumstances, while the charge system requires a conscious administrative act to achieve the same result.

Instrument Choice Under Uncertainty

Another major difference between permits and charges involves the cost of being wrong. Suppose that we have very imprecise information on damages caused and avoidance costs incurred by various levels of pollution and yet we have to choose either a charge level or a permit level and live with it. What can be said about the relative merits of permits versus charges in the face of this uncertainty?

The answer depends on the circumstances. Permits offer a greater amount of certainty about the quantity of emissions, while charges confer more certainty about the marginal cost of control. Therefore, permits are the only system that allow an ambient standard or an aggregate emission standard to be met with certainty. In other cases, however, when the objective is to minimize total costs (the sum of damage cost and control costs), permits would be preferred when the costs of being wrong are more sensitive to changes in the quantity of emission than to change in the marginal cost of control. Charges would be preferred when control costs were more important. When would that be the case?

When the marginal damage curve is steeply sloped and the marginal cost curve is rather flat, certainty about emissions is more important than certainty over control costs. Smaller deviations of actual emissions from expected emission can cause a rather large deviation in damage costs, whereas control costs would be relatively insensitive to the degree of control. Permits would prevent large fluctuations in these damage costs and would, therefore, yield a lower cost of being wrong than charges.

Suppose, however, that the marginal control cost curve was steeply sloped, but the marginal damage curve was flat. Small changes in the degree of control would have a large effect on abatement costs but would not affect damages very much. In this case it makes sense to rely on charges to give more precise control over control costs, accepting the less dire consequences from possible fluctuations in damage costs.

These cases suggest that a preference either for permits or for charges in the face of uncertainty is not universal; it depends on the circumstances. Theory is not strong enough to dictate a choice. Empirical studies are necessary to establish a preference for particular situations.

One interesting case involves the control of the greenhouse gases (GHG) that intensify climate change. Though both the costs and benefits of control are subject to uncertainty, the long atmospheric lives of most greenhouse gases almost certainly make the marginal benefit cost curve (in present-value terms) much flatter than the marginal control cost curve (Pizer, 2002). Therefore, following Weitzman (1974), it would be better to use a tax-based instrument to control the price of GHG emissions, than to use permits to control the quantity of emissions. As we shall see, the Kyoto Protocol, the international agreement to control greenhouse gases, does not follow this prescription.

Product Charges: Another Form of Environmental Taxation

The use of emission charges presumes that it is possible to monitor and keep track of the level of emissions so the appropriate tax can be levied. Sometimes that is either impossible or impractical.

One strategy that has been employed in this circumstance is to tax the commodity that is most directly responsible for the emissions, rather than the emissions themselves. For example, one might tax gasoline rather than attempt to measure (and tax) the emissions from every gasoline-powered vehicle. And several counties tax fertilizer rather than attempt to measure the amount of contamination of groundwater sources from each bag sold. The Irish have even taxed plastic bags to prevent littering (Example 15.3).

While product charges frequently are simpler to administer, it is important to keep in mind that they are not equivalent to emissions charges. Not every unit of the taxed product may have the same impact on the environment. For example, some purchased fertilizer may be used in sensitive areas (and therefore should be heavily taxed for efficiency), while other may be used in areas with lots of natural buffering (and therefore should not be taxed as heavily). Since the product charge would be the same per bag, it would not be able to make these kinds of distinctions. Product charges are most efficient when all purchased units of that product cause exactly the same marginal damage. Although full efficiency is probably rarely achieved by product charges, they may be better (even much better) than doing nothing.

Summary

In this chapter we developed the conceptual framework needed to evaluate current approaches to pollution control policy. We have seen that there are many different types of pollutants, and different policy approaches are appropriate for each one.

Stock pollutants pose the most serious intertemporal problems. The efficient production of a commodity that generates a stock pollutant could be expected to decline over time. Eventually, a point would be reached when all of the pollutant would be recycled. After this point the amount of the pollutant in the environment would not increase. The amount already accumulated, however, would continue to cause damage perpetually unless some natural process could reduce the amount of the pollutant over time.

The efficient amount of a fund pollutant was defined as the amount that minimizes the sum of damage and control costs. Using this definition, we were able to derive two propositions of interest: (1) the efficient level of pollution would vary from region to region; and (2) the efficient level of pollution would not generally be zero, although in some particular circumstances it might.

Example 15.3

THE IRISH BAG LEVY

Rapid economic growth in Ireland in the 1990s was marked by a significant increase in the amount of solid waste per capita. The lack of adequate landfill sites resulted in escalating costs of waste disposal, which in turn led to more illegal dumping and littering. It was feared that tourism, one of Ireland's largest industries, would be negatively affected as a consequence of the degradation of the environment. The food industry, which based a significant amount of their marketing strategies on a healthy, wholesome reputation, also suffered as a result of the public perception of their role in the increased litter.

The most visible element of litter was plastic bags, so in 2002 the government introduced the Plastic Bag Environmental Levy on all plastic shopping bags, with a few exceptions that were sanctioned for health and safety reasons. Retailers were charged a fee of 15¢ per plastic bag, which they were obliged, by the government, to pass on to the consumer. This levy was designed to alter consumer behavior by creating financial incentives for consumers to choose more environmentally friendly alternatives to plastic, such as "bags-for-life." (Bags-for-life are heavy-duty, reusable cloth or woven bags, which are available in all supermarkets, at an average cost of €1.27.)

Expectations, that this levy would bring about a 50% reduction in the number of plastic bags used were exceeded when the estimated actual reduction turned out to be 95%! In a single year, Irish consumers reduced their consumption of plastic bags from 1.26 billion to 120,000, while concurrently raising approximately €10 million in revenue for the government. The revenue was placed in the Environmental Fund, which finances environmental initiatives such as recycling, waste management, and, most importantly, antilitter campaigns.

This levy has been viewed as a major success by the government and environmental groups alike. It has also been enthusiastically embraced by Irish consumers, thanks to an intensive environmental-awareness campaign that was launched in conjunction with the levy. Irish retailers, although skeptical in the beginning, have also recognized the huge benefits of this levy. Estimates suggest that their costs were offset by the savings from no longer providing disposable bags to customers free of charge, as well as the profit margin earned on the sale of "bags-for-life," whose sales have increased by 600%–700% since the introduction of the levy. The amount of plastic being sent to Irish landfills has been dramatically reduced, bringing about a clear visual improvement.

Source: Linda Dungan. "What Were the Effects of the Plastic Bag Environmental Levy on the Litter Problem in Ireland?" http://www.colby.edu/~thtieten/litter.htm/.

Since pollution is a classic externality, markets will generally produce more than the efficient amount of both fund pollutants and stock pollutants. For both pollutants this will imply higher-than-efficient damages and lower-than-efficient control costs. For stock pollutants an excessive amount of pollution would accumulate in the environment, imposing a detrimental externality on future generations as well as on current generations.

The market would not provide any automatic ameliorating response to the accumulation of pollution as it would in the case of natural resource scarcity. Firms attempting to unilaterally control their pollution are placed at a competitive disadvantage. Hence, the case for some sort of government intervention is particularly strong for pollution control.

While policy instruments could in principle be defined to achieve an efficient level of pollution for every emitter, it is very difficult in practice because the amount of information required by the control authorities is unrealistically high.

Cost-effectiveness analysis provides a way out of this dilemma. In the case of uniform mixed-fund pollutants, uniform emission charges or an emission permit system could be used to attain the cost-effective allocation even when the control authority has no information whatsoever on either control costs or damage costs. Uniform emission standards would not, except by coincidence, be cost-effective. In addition, either permits or charges would stimulate more technological progress in pollution control than would emission standards.

Policies to control nonuniformly mixed pollutants must take the location of the emissions into account as well as the amount. This can be accomplished with either an appropriately designed ambient permit system or ambient charge; either one can result in a cost-effective allocation of the control responsibility even when the control authority has no information on control costs. A policy based on emission standards cannot.

Policies ignoring these distinctions are not cost-effective. An excessively narrow focus on local pollution can make the regional pollution problem worse. Similarly, the use of a uniform emission charge or an emission permit system (which are appropriate for uniformly mixed pollutants!) to allocate the responsibility for controlling a local or regional nonuniformly mixed surface pollutant will not be cost-effective whenever transfer coefficients differ.

The fact that auctioned permits or taxes can raise revenue is also an important characteristic. If the revenue from pollution charges or auctioned permits can be used to reduce revenue from other, more distortionary taxes (such as labor or income taxes), greater welfare gains can be achieved from revenue-raising instruments than instruments that raise no revenue. On the other hand, historically at least, transferring some or all of that revenue back to the sources either by granting the permits to them free of charge or including some sort of tax rebate has been an important aspect of securing the political support for implementing the system. Revenue use for this purpose, of course, cannot be used to reduce distortionary taxes.

The permit approach and the charge approach respond differently to growth in the number of sources, to inflation, to technological change, and to uncertainty. As we shall see in the next few chapters, some countries (primarily in Europe) have chosen to rely on emission charges, while others (primarily the United States) have chosen to rely on permits. We can now use this framework to evaluate the rather different policy approaches that have been taken toward the major sources of pollution.

Discussion Questions

1. In his book *What Price Incentives?*, Steven Kelman suggests that from an ethical point of view, the use of economic incentives (such as emission charges or emission permits) in environmental policy is undesirable. He argues that transforming our mental image of the environment from a sanctified preserve to a marketable commodity has detrimental effects not only on our use of the environment but also on our attitude toward it. His point is that applying economic incentives to environmental policy weakens and cheapens our traditional values toward the environment.

   (a) Consider the effects of economic incentive systems on prices paid by the poor, on employment, and on the speed of compliance with pollution control laws—as well as the Kelman arguments. Are economic incentive systems more or less ethically justifiable than the traditional regulatory approach?

   (b) Kelman seems to feel that because emission permits automatically prevent environmental degradation, they are more ethically desirable than emission charges. Do you agree? Why or why not?

Problems

1. Two firms can control emissions at the following marginal costs: $MC_1 = \$200q_1$, $MC_2 = \$100q_2$, where q_1 and q_2 are, respectively, the amount of emissions reduced by the first and second firms. Assume that with no control at all, each firm would be emitting 20 units of emissions or a total of 40 units for both firms.

   (a) Compute the cost-effective allocation of control responsibility if a total reduction of 21 units of emissions is necessary.

   (b) Compute the cost-effective allocation of control responsibility if the ambient standard is 27 ppm, and the transfer coefficients that translate a unit of emissions into a ppm concentration at the receptor are, respectively, $a_1 = 2.0$ and $a_2 = 1.0$.

2. Assume that the control authority wanted to reach its objective in 1(a) by using an emission charge system.

   (a) What per-unit charge should be imposed?

   (b) How much revenue would the control authority collect?

Further Reading

Baumol, W. J., and W. E. Oates. *The Theory of Environmental Policy*, 2nd ed. (Cambridge, UK: Cambridge University Press, 1988). A classic on the economic analysis of externalities. Accessible only to those with a thorough familiarity with multivariable calculus.

Harrington, W., R. D. Morgenstern, and T. Sterner. *Choosing Environmental Policy: Comparing Instruments and Outcomes in the United States and Europe* (Washington, DC: Resources for the Future, 2002). This book uses paired case studies from the United States and Europe to contrast the costs and outcomes of direct regulation on one side of the Atlantic with an incentive-based policy on the other.

OECD. *Economic Instruments for Environmental Protection* (Paris: OECD, 1989). A survey of how economic incentive approaches to pollution control have been used in industrialized nations that belong to the OECD.

OECD. *Environment and Taxation: The Cases of the Netherlands, Sweden, and the United States* (Paris: OECD, 1994). Background case studies for a larger research project seeking to discover the extent to which fiscal and environmental policies could be made not only compatible but mutually reinforcing.

Rock, M. *Pollution Control in East Asia: Lessons from Newly Industrializing Countries* (Washington, DC: Resources for the Future, Inc., 2002). These studies of pollution management in East Asia's newly industrialized economies (NIEs) include successful government responses in Singapore and Taiwan, qualified results in China and Indonesia, and much more limited success in Thailand and Malaysia.

Stavins, R. N. "Experience with Market Based Environmental Policy Instruments," in K. G. Maler and J. R. Vincent, eds. *Handbook of Environmental Economics, Volume 1: Environmental Degradation and Institutional Reponses* (Amsterdam: Elsevier, 2003): 355–435. A review of what we have learned from our experience with market-based instruments.

Sterner, T. *Policy Instruments for Environmental and Natural Resource Management* (Washington, DC: Resources for the Future, Inc., 2003). Intended primarily for audiences in developing and transitional countries, the book compares the accumulated experiences of the use of economic policy instruments in the United States and Europe, as well as in select rich and poor countries in Asia, Africa, and Latin America.

Tietenberg, T., ed. *Emissions Trading Programs: Volume I Implementation and Evolution* and *Volume II Theory and Design*. International Library of Environmental Economics and Policy (Aldershot, UK: Ashgate, 2001). A two-volume collection of the leading published articles on emissions trading, coupled with an editor's introduction that traces the history of our state of knowledge about this policy instrument.

Additional References and Historically Significant References are available on this book's companion Web site www.aw-bc.com/tietenberg.

Appendix

The Simple Mathematics of Cost-Effective Pollution Control

Suppose that each of N polluters would emit u_n units of emission in the absence of any control. Furthermore suppose that the pollutant concentration K_R at some receptor R in the absence of control is:

$$K_R = \sum_{n=1}^{N} a_n u_n + B, \tag{1}$$

where B is the background concentration and a_n is the transfer coefficient. This K_R is assumed to be greater than Φ, the legal concentration level. The regulatory problem therefore is to choose the cost-effective level of control q_n for each of the n sources. Symbolically this can be expressed as minimizing the following Lagrangian with respect to the $N q_n$ control variables:

$$\min \sum_{n=1}^{N} C_n(q_n) + \lambda \left[\sum_{n=1}^{N} a_n(u_n - q_n) - \Phi \right], \tag{2}$$

where $C_n(q_n)$ is the cost of achieving the q_n level of control at the nth source and λ is the Lagrangian multiplier.

The solution is found by partially differentiating (2) with respect to λ and the N q_n's. This yields

$$\frac{\partial C_n(q_n)}{\partial q} - \lambda^* a_n \geq 0, \qquad n = 1, \ldots, N,$$

$$\sum_{n=1}^{N} a_n(u_n - q_n) + B - \Phi = 0.$$

Solving these equations produces the N-dimensional vector q^0 and the scalar λ^*.

Notice that this same formulation can be used to reflect both the uniformly mixed and nonuniformly mixed single-receptor case. In the uniformly mixed case the a_n's all = 1. This immediately implies that the marginal cost of control should be equal for all emitters who are required to engage in some control. (The first N equations would hold as equalities except for any source where the marginal cost of controlling the first unit exceeded the marginal cost necessary to meet the target.) For the nonuniformly mixed single-receptor case, in the cost-effective allocation the control responsibility would be allocated so as to ensure that the ratio of the marginal control costs for two emitters would be equal to the ratio of their transfer coefficients. For J receptors both λ^* and Φ^* would become J-dimensional vectors.

Policy Instruments

A special meaning can be attached to λ. If transferable permits were being used, it would be the market-clearing price of a permit. In the uniformly mixed case, λ would be the price of a permit to emit one unit of emission. In the nonuniformly mixed case, λ would be the price of being allowed to raise the concentration at the receptor location one unit. In the case of taxes, λ represents the value of the cost-effective tax.

Notice how firms choose emissions control when permit price or tax is equal to λ. Each firm wants to minimize its costs. Assume that each firm is given permits of Ω_n, where the regulatory authority ensures that

$$\sum_{n=1}^{N} a_n \Omega_n + B = \Phi$$

for the set of all emitters. Each firm would want to

$$\min c_n(q_n) + P^0 [\Omega_n - a_n(u_n - q_n)].$$

The minimum cost is achieved by choosing the value of q_n (q_n^0) that satisfies

$$\frac{\partial C_n(q_n)}{\partial q_n} - P^* a_n = 0$$

This condition (marginal cost equals the price of a unit of concentration reduction) would hold for each of the N firms. Because P^* would equal λ^* and the number of permits would be chosen to ensure the ambient standard would be met, this allocation would be cost-effective. Exactly the same result is achieved by substituting T^*, the cost-effective tax rate, for P^*.

Stationary-Source Local Air Pollution

*When choosing between two evils, I always like to try
the one I've never tried before.*

—Mae West, Actress

Introduction

Attaining and maintaining clean air is an exceedingly difficult policy task.
In the United States, for example, an estimated 27,000 major stationary
sources of air pollution are subject to control as well as hundreds of thousands of more minor sources. Many distinct production processes emit
many different types of pollutants. The resulting damages range from
minimal effects on plants and vegetation to the possible modification of the
earth's climate.

The policy response to this problem has been continually evolving. The
U.S. experience is not atypical. Congress enacted the first legislation to
grapple with these problems in 1955. Called the Air Pollution Control Act
of 1955, that law mainly subsidized research into air pollution problems.
The following 14 years ushered in a period of vigorous legislative activity.

Yet, the amount of legislation is a misleading indicator of what was actually accomplished. It was not until 1967 that the federal government began
to play much of a role other than subsidizing research, and even the 1967
law was mainly an attempt to cajole the states into action. The common
thread woven by the statutes during this period was a reliance on cooperation from the states.

By 1970 the national government had discovered that this reliance was
misplaced; state cooperation was not forthcoming. Fearing that the imposition of strict controls on industrial sources would place them at a competitive disadvantage in their quest for increases in employment and taxable
industrial property, states were unwilling to take the lead in air pollution
control policy.

In this atmosphere of frustration, the Clean Air Act Amendments of
1970 were passed. They set a bold new direction that has been retained and
refined by subsequent acts. By virtue of that act, the federal government

assumed a much larger and much more vigorous direct role. The U.S. Environmental Protection Agency (EPA) was created to implement and oversee this massive attempt to control the injection of substances into our air. Individually tailored strategies were created to deal with mobile and stationary sources. These strategies depend in part on whether the type of pollutant being controlled is a "conventional" pollutant or a "hazardous" pollutant.

Conventional Pollutants

Conventional pollutants are relatively common substances, found in almost all parts of the country, and are presumed to be dangerous only in high concentrations. In the United States these pollutants are called *criteria pollutants* because the Act requires the EPA to produce "criteria documents" to be used in setting acceptable standards for these pollutants. These documents summarize and evaluate all of the existing research on the various health and environmental effects associated with these pollutants. The central focus of air pollution control during the 1970s was on criteria pollutants.

The Command-and-Control Policy Framework

In Chapter 15 several possible approaches to controlling pollution were described and analyzed in theoretical terms. The historical approach to air pollution control has been based primarily on emission standards. It has been a traditional command-and-control (CAC) approach. In this section we outline the specific nature of this approach, analyze it from an efficiency and cost-effectiveness perspective, and show how a series of recent reforms based on economic incentives has worked to rectify some of these deficiencies.

For each of the conventional pollutants, the typical first step is to establish ambient air-quality standards. These standards set legal ceilings on the allowable concentration of the pollutant in the outdoor air averaged over a specified time period. Many pollutants have the standard defined in terms of a long-term average (defined normally as an annual average) and a short-term average (such as a 3-hour average). These short-term averages can usually be exceeded no more than once a year. These standards have to be met everywhere, though as a practical matter they are monitored at a large number of specific locations. Control costs can be quite sensitive to the level of these short-term averages.

In the United States two ambient standards are defined.[1] The *primary standard*, which is designed to protect human health, was the first standard to be determined, and it had the earliest deadlines for compliance. All pollutants have a primary standard. The *secondary standard* is designed to protect other aspects of human welfare from those pollutants having separate effects. Currently only sulfur oxides have

---

[1]We discuss the U.S. approach in some detail to show how abstract command-and-control concepts can be translated into specific policy. Many industrialized countries have rather similar policies. For more detail on the environmental policies of some European countries and Japan, see Bolotin (1989). The Japanese approach, which is rather different, will be treated in more detail later in this chapter.

separate secondary standards. Protection is afforded by the secondary standard for aesthetics (particularly visibility), physical objects (houses, monuments, and so on), and vegetation. When a separate secondary standard exists, both it and the primary standard must be met. The existing primary and secondary standards are given in Table 16.1.

The ambient standards are required by statute to be determined without any consideration given to the costs of meeting them. They are supposed to be set at a level sufficient to protect even the most sensitive members of the population.

While the EPA is responsible for defining the ambient standards, the primary responsibility for ensuring that the ambient air-quality standards are met falls on the state control agencies. They exercise this responsibility by developing and executing an acceptable state implementation plan (SIP), which must be approved by the EPA. This plan divides the state into separate air-quality-control regions. Special procedures were developed for handling regions that cross state borders, such as metropolitan New York.

The SIP spells out for each control region the procedures and timetables for meeting local ambient standards and for abatement of the effects of locally emitted pollutants on other states. The required degree of control depends on the severity of the pollution problem in each of the control regions. All areas not meeting the original deadlines are designated as *nonattainment regions*.

The areas receiving this designation are subjected to particularly stringent controls. Nonattainment areas were placed within one or seven categories (basic, marginal, moderate, serious, two categories of severe, and extreme), with each having its own criteria for compliance with the standard. In general, the more severe the degree of nonattainment in an area, the more stringent the requirements imposed on it. To prod the states into action, Congress gave the EPA the power to halt the construction of major new or modified pollution sources and to deny federal sewage and transportation grants for any state not submitting a plan showing precisely how and when attainment would be reached.

Recognizing that it is typically much easier and much cheaper to control new sources rather than existing ones, the Clean Air Act established the New Source Review (NSR) Program. This program requires all new major stationary sources (as well as those undergoing major modifications) in both attainment and nonattainment areas to seek a permit for operation. This permit requires compliance with the specified standards (more stringent in nonattainment areas than in attainment areas). The theory was that as old, dirtier plants became obsolete, this program would ensure that their replacements would be significantly less polluting. As Debate 16.1 points out, the New Source Review Program is controversial.

Regions with air quality at least as high as the standards by the original deadline were subject to another set of controls known collectively as the PSD policy. This policy derives its name from its objective, the *prevention of significant deterioration* of the air in cleaner regions. The system of ambient standards prevented the deterioration of the air *beyond* the standard, but air significantly cleaner than the standard would in the absence of the PSD policy have deteriorated until it reached the standard.

The PSD regulations specify the maximum allowable increases or increments in pollution concentration beyond some baseline. To allow some variability in the

TABLE 16.1

National Ambient Air-Quality Standards

Pollutant	Standard Value*	Standard
Carbon Monoxide (CO)		
8-hour Average[1]	9 ppm (10 mg/m³)	Primary
1-hour Average[1]	35 ppm (40 mg/m³)	Primary
Nitrogen Dioxide (NO₂)		
Annual Arithmetic Mean	0.053 ppm (100 µg/m³)	Primary and Secondary
Ozone (O₃)		
1-hour Average[6]	0.12 ppm (235 µg/m³)	Primary and Secondary
8-hour Average[5]	0.08 ppm (157 µg/m³)	Primary and Secondary
Lead (Pb)		
Quarterly Average	1.5 µg/m³	Primary and Secondary
Particulate (PM 10) Particles with diameters of 10 micrometers or less		
Annual Arithmetic Mean[2]	50 µg/m³	Primary and Secondary
24-hour Average[1]	150 µg/m³	Primary and Secondary
Particulate (PM 2.5) Particles with diameters of 2.5 micrometers or less		
Annual Arithmetic Mean[3]	15 µg/m³	Primary and Secondary
24-hour Average[4]	65 µg/m³	Primary and Secondary
Sulfur Dioxide (SO₂)		
Annual Arithmetic Mean	0.03 ppm (80 µg/m³)	Primary
24-hour Average[1]	0.14 ppm (365 µg/m³)	Primary
3-hour Average[1]	0.50 ppm (1,300 µg/m³)	Secondary

Notes: Units of measure for the standards are parts per million (ppm) by volume, milligrams per cubic meter of air (mg/m³), and micrograms per cubic meter of air (µg/m³). Values in parentheses represent approximate equivalent concentrations.

[1] Not to be exceeded more than once per year.

[2] To attain this standard, the expected annual arithmetic mean PM 10 concentration at each monitor within an area must not exceed 50 µg/m³.

[3] To attain this standard, the 3-year average of the annual arithmetic mean PM 2.5 concentrations from single or multiple community-oriented monitors must not exceed 15.0 µg/m³.

[4] To attain this standard, the 3-year average of the 98th percentile of 24-hour concentrations at each population-oriented monitor within an area must not exceed 65 µg/m³.

[5] To attain this standard, the 3-year average of the fourth-highest daily maximum 8-hour average ozone concentrations measured at each monitor within an area over each year must not exceed 0.08 ppm.

[6] (a) The standard is attained when the expected number of days per calendar year with maximum hourly average concentrations above 0.12 ppm is ≤1.

(b) The 1-hour NAAQS will no longer apply to an area 1 year after the effective date of the designation of that area for the 8-hour ozone NAAQS. The effective designation date for most areas is June 15, 2004. (40 CFR 50.9; see Federal Register of April 30, 2004 (69 FR 23996).)

Source: http://www.epa.gov/air/criteria.html.

DEBATE 16.1

Should the New Source Review Program Be Changed?

One of the characteristics of the New Source Review Program is that it requires major stationary sources that are undergoing modifications (not just routine maintenance) to meet the same stringent standards as new sources. Due to this routine-maintenance exemption, a number of older plants were never forced to upgrade their pollution control equipment, and as a result these older plants became responsible for a larger share of the total emissions. For example, the U.S. General Accounting Office (1990) found that at the time of the study, these plants were responsible for 88% of the sulfur oxide emissions and 79% of nitrogen oxide emissions emitted from fossil-fuel electric power plants.

In 1999, under the Clinton administration, EPA began taking enforcement actions against individual companies, including numerous electric utilities that own and operate coal-fired power plants in the Southeast and Midwest. The lawsuits alleged that under the cover of "routine maintenance," plants that should have been retired years earlier were being modified and retained past their normal lives. Using this exemption to prop up these plants was seen as an evasion of the need to retire older plants and replace them with modern plants meeting the more stringent, (and costly) new source control requirements.

When George W. Bush's administration took office, it saw the New Source Review Program as unnecessarily burdensome and moved to modify it. Securing permits under the NSR Program was a time-consuming process—taking on average 18 months to complete. After a comprehensive review of the program, EPA concluded that by making new investments so expensive (in terms of both delay and resources), the cost of the program had impeded or resulted in the cancellation of projects that would have maintained or improved the reliability, efficiency, or safety of existing power plants. Based on these findings, the Bush EPA recommended making it easier for plants to avoid NSR by allowing them to consider expenditures of up to 20% of the replacement cost of the plant annually as routine maintenance. In essence the entire plant could be replaced over a five-year period without triggering the NSR. The Bush EPA also recommended replacing the NSR program with a cap on emissions. Since emitters would have to limit emissions from all plants (new and old) under the cap, they would be free to cut emissions wherever reductions were the cheapest.

An interesting aspect of this approach is that while the EPA can implement the routine-maintenance definition on its own, the cap program intended to replace NSR would have to be passed by Congress. Even if the proposed cap were stringent enough to produce the desired reductions (another source of controversy), implementing only the revised definition without imposing the cap would end up simply loosening air regulations, not reforming them.

size of these increments, Congress specified that PSD regions be subdivided into three types of areas with each type allowed a different increment. Class I areas include national parks and wilderness areas. The increments for these regions are the smallest. Practically any degradation in these areas is considered significant and is disallowed.

All other areas were initially designated as Class II regions, where a modest increment is allowed. States may redesignate any Class II region as a Class I region (thus allowing less future deterioration) or as a Class III region (allowing more). Class III regions are allowed the largest increment. In no case, however, can pollutant concentrations in any PSD region rise above the governing ambient standard.

New sources seeking to locate in PSD regions must secure permits. As a condition of securing their permits, these sources must install the *best available control technology* (BACT). The specific technologies that satisfy their requirement are determined by states on a case-by-case basis. Each new source permitted consumes a portion of the allowable increment. Once the increment has been completely consumed, no further deterioration of the air is allowed in that area even if the air is cleaner than required by the prevailing ambient standard. Thus, where the PSD increments are binding, for all practical purposes they define a tertiary standard varying in magnitude from region to region.

In addition to defining the ambient standards and requiring states to define emission standards, the EPA itself has established national uniform emission standards for new sources of criteria pollutants or major modifications of existing sources, called the New Source Performance Standards (NSPS). They are designed to merely serve as a floor for the emission standards imposed by the states. Congress wanted to ensure that all sources would have to meet a minimum standard regardless of where they were located. This was seen as a way to prevent states from caving in as industry attempted to play one state against another in its attempt to seek the lowest possible emission standards. The state emission standards can be less stringent than the New Source Performance Standards.

Simply stating the regulations is not enough. They must be enforced with appropriate sanctions whenever noncompliance occurs. Congress established the *noncompliance penalty* to promote compliance. Without sanctions, the source benefits from delaying compliance. The equipment purchases necessary to ensure compliance are expensive and add nothing to profits. In addition, court action is slow and sometimes sympathetic toward business. The noncompliance penalty is designed to harmonize these private incentives with the social objectives pursued by the act.

The magnitude of the penalty is determined by the economic value of delay to the source. Any economic gains received by the source as a result of noncompliance are included in the penalty and are transferred to the EPA; this penalty removes any economic incentive for delaying compliance.

One final characteristic of the Clean Air Act is that it rules out tailoring the degree of control to the prevailing meteorological conditions. All strategies must achieve better air quality through emission reductions stringent enough to ensure compliance in adverse conditions.

The Efficiency of the Command-and-Control Approach

Efficiency presumes that the ambient standards are set at efficient levels. To ascertain whether or not the current standards are efficient, it is necessary to inquire into five aspects of the standard-setting process: (1) the threshold concept on which the standards are based, (2) the level of the standard, (3) the choice of uniform standards over standards more tailored to the regions involved, (4) the timing of emission flows, and (5) the failure to incorporate the degree of human exposure in the standard-setting process.

The Threshold Concept.

Some basis is needed for setting the ambient standard. Since the Clean Air Act prohibits the balancing of costs and benefits, some alternative criterion must be used. For the primary (health-related) standard, this criterion is known as the *health threshold*. The standard is to be defined with a margin of safety sufficiently high that no adverse health effects would be suffered by any member of the population as long as the air quality was at least as good as the standards. This approach presumes the existence of a threshold such that concentrations above that level produce adverse health effects, but concentrations below it produce none.

If the threshold concept were valid, the marginal damage function would be zero until the threshold was reached and would be positive at higher concentrations. The belief that the actual damage function has this shape is not consistent with the evidence; adverse health effects can occur at pollution levels lower than the ambient standards. The standard that produces no adverse health effects among the general population (which, of course, includes especially susceptible groups) is probably zero or close to it. It is certainly lower than the established ambient standards. What the standards purport to accomplish and what they actually accomplish are rather different.

The Level of the Ambient Standard.

The absence of a defensible health threshold complicates the analysis (see Debate 16.2). Some other basis must be used for determining the level at which the standard should be established. Efficiency would dictate setting the standard in order to maximize the net benefit, which includes a consideration of costs as well as benefits.

The current policy explicitly excludes costs from consideration in setting the ambient standards. Costs are allowed to enter the process only when the policy instruments used to meet ambient standards are being defined. It is difficult to imagine that the process of setting the ambient standard would yield an efficient outcome when it is prohibited from considering one of the key elements of that outcome!

Unfortunately, for reasons that were discussed in some detail in Chapter 3, our current benefit measurements are not sufficiently reliable as to permit the identification of the efficient level with any confidence. The EPA study of the Clean Air Act, summarized earlier in Chapter 2, found that the total monetized benefits of the Clean Air Act realized during the period from 1970 to 1990 ranges from $5.6 to $49.4 trillion; with a central estimate of $22.2 trillion. That is a very large band of uncertainty.

The study further noted:

> The central estimate of 22.2 trillion dollars in benefits may be a significant underestimate due to the exclusion of large numbers of benefits from the monetized benefit estimate (e.g., all air toxics effects; ecosystem effects; numerous human health effects). (p. ES-8)

These figures suggest that a high degree of confidence can be attached to the belief that government intervention to control air pollution in the United States was justified; but they provide no evidence whatsoever on whether current policy was, or is, efficient.

**DEBATE
16.2**

The Particulate and Smog Ambient Standards Controversy

In proposing more stringent ambient standards for ozone and particulates, the USEPA had concluded that 125 million Americans, including 35 million children, were not adequately protected by the existing standards. The new standards were estimated to prevent one million serious respiratory illnesses each year, and 15,000 premature deaths.

The proposed revisions were controversial because the cost of compliance would be very high. No health threshold existed at the chosen level (some health effects would be noticed at even more stringent levels than those proposed) and the EPA was, by law, prohibited from using a benefit/cost justification. In the face of legal challenge, the EPA found it very difficult to defend the superiority of the chosen standards from slightly more stringent or slightly less stringent standards.

In a decision issued May 14, 1999, the U.S. Court of Appeals for the District of Columbia Circuit overturned the proposed revisions. In a 2–1 ruling the three-judge panel rejected the EPA's approach to setting the level of those standards:

> the construction of the Clean Air Act on which EPA relied in promulgating the NAAQS at issue here effects an unconstitutional delegation of legislative power. . . . Although the factors EPA uses in determining the degree of public health concern associated with different levels of ozone and PM are reasonable, EPA appears to have articulated no "intelligible principle" to channel its application of these factors. . . . EPA's formulation of its policy judgement leaves it free to pick any point between zero and a hair below the concentrations yielding London's Killer Fog.

Though the threat to the EPA's authority was ultimately overturned by the U.S. Supreme Court, the dilemma posed by the absence of a compelling health threshold remains.

Uniformity.   The same primary and secondary standards apply to all parts of the country. No account is taken of the number of people exposed, the sensitivity of the local ecology, or the costs of compliance in various areas. All of these would have some effect on the efficient standard and efficiency would, therefore, dictate different standards for different regions. In general, the evidence suggests that the inefficiencies associated with uniformity are greatest in the rural areas, but we shall leave a full description and interpretation of that evidence for Chapter 21.

The PSD program does introduce some variability by establishing more stringent standards for regions with the cleanest air. If national parks and other Class I areas are especially sensitive to pollution, that portion of the program could represent a move toward efficiency. Since states have some flexibility in choosing which portions of their area would be designated as Class II and Class III regions, it is conceivable, but by no means obvious, that they would make efficient choices.

Timing of Emission Flows.   Because concentrations are important for criteria pollutants, the timing of emissions is an important policy concern. Emissions clustered in time are as troublesome as emissions clustered in space. How do we handle those relatively rare but devastating occasions when thermal inversions prevent the normal dispersion and dilution of the pollutants?

From an economic efficiency point of view, the most obvious approach is to tailor the degree of control to the circumstances. Stringent control would be exercised when meteorological conditions were relatively stagnant, and less control would be applied under normal circumstances. A reliance on a constant degree of control, rather than allowing intermittent controls, raises compliance costs substantially, particularly when the required degree of control is high. The strong stand against intermittent controls in the Clean Air Act, however, rules this out.

Concentration Versus Exposure.   Present ambient standards are defined in terms of pollutant concentrations in the outdoor air. Yet health effects are more closely related to human exposure to pollutants. (Exposure is determined both by the concentrations of air pollutants in each of the places in which people spend time and the amount of time spent in each place.) Since only about 10% of the population's person-hours are spent outdoors, indoor air becomes very important in designing strategies to improve the health risk of pollutants.[2] Some studies have suggested that exposure to pollutants is several times higher indoors than it is outdoors (Smith, 1988). To date very little attention has been focused on controlling indoor air pollution despite its apparent importance.[3]

Cost-Effectiveness of the Command-and-Control Approach

Though the ambient standards are not efficient, determining the magnitude of the inefficiency is plagued by uncertainties. It is not possible to state definitively just how inefficient they are.

Cost-effectiveness is based on somewhat more solid evidence. Though it does not allow us to shed any light on whether a particular ambient standard is efficient or not, cost-effectiveness studies do allow us to see whether the command-and-control policy described above has resulted in the ambient standards being met in the least costly manner possible.

The theory covered in Chapter 15 makes it clear that the CAC strategy will normally not be cost-effective. What it does not make clear, however, is the degree to which this strategy diverges from the least-cost ideal. If the divergence is small, the proponents of reform would not likely be able to overcome the inertia of the status quo. If the divergence is large, the case for reform is stronger.

---

[2]This estimate is for the United States.

[3]The one major policy response to indoor air pollution has been the large number of states that have passed legislation requiring "smoke-free" areas in public places to protect nonsmokers.

The cost-effectiveness of the CAC approach depends on local circumstances such as prevailing meteorology, the locational configuration of sources, stack heights, and how costs vary with the amount controlled. Several simulation models capable of dealing with these complexities have now been constructed for a number of different pollutants in a variety of airsheds (see Table 16.2).

Since for a number of reasons the estimated costs cannot be directly compared across studies, it is appropriate to develop a means of comparing costs that minimizes the comparability problems. One such technique, the one we have chosen, involves calculating the ratio of the CAC allocation costs to the lowest cost of meeting the same objective for each study. A ratio equal to 1.0 implies that the CAC allocation is cost-effective. By subtracting 1.0 from the ratio in the table and multiplying by 100, it is possible to interpret the remainder as the percentage increase in cost from the least-cost ideal due to relying on the CAC system.

Of the nine reported comparisons, eight find that the CAC policy costs at least 78% more than the least-cost allocation. If we omit the Hahn and Noll (1982) study (for reasons discussed in the next two paragraphs), the study involving the *smallest* cost savings (sulfur dioxide control in the Lower Delaware Valley) finds that the CAC allocation results in abatement costs that are 78% higher than necessary to meet the standards. In the Chicago study, the CAC costs are estimated to be 14 times as expensive as necessary, while in the Lower Delaware Valley they are estimated to be 22 times more expensive than necessary.

The Hahn and Noll finding that the CAC strategy was close to being cost-effective was somewhat unique in a couple of respects. Because we can learn something from this study about the conditions under which CAC policies may not be far off the mark, we study it closely.

The city studied by Hahn and Noll, Los Angeles, has a large sulfate problem, necessitating a very high degree of control. In effect, virtually every source is forced to control as much as is economically feasible. As Example 16.1 points out, the command-and-control program to control SO_2 emissions in Germany had a similar outcome (quite cost-effective) for similar reasons (stringent controls resulting in similar marginal control costs). In that case the cost/ineffectiveness resulted mainly from the policy's lack of temporal flexibility.

Air Quality

Each year, the U.S. Environmental Protection Agency derives air-quality trends using measurements from monitors located across the country. Table 16.3 shows the national improvement in air quality (the pollutant concentrations in the ambient air) as well as the reduction in emissions from the criteria pollutants that have occurred over the 20 years from 1983 to 2002.

Though over that 20-year period improvements have occurred for all six pollutants, notice that reductions in air-quality concentrations do not always match reductions in nationwide emissions. The EPA identifies several reasons for this.

- Most monitors are located in urban areas, so air quality is most likely to track changes in *urban* air emissions rather than in the *total* emissions measured in the table.

TABLE 16.2
Empirical Studies of Air Pollution Control

Study and Year	Pollutants Covered	Geographic Area	CAC Benchmark	Assumed Pollutant Type	Ratio of CAC Cost to Least Cost
Atkinson and Lewis (1974)	Particulates	St. Louis Metropolitan Area	SIP regulations	Nonuniformly mixed	6.00
Roach et al. (1981)	Sulfur dioxide	Four Corners in Utah, Colorado, Arizona, and New Mexico	SIP regulations	Nonuniformly mixed	4.25
Hahn and Noll (1982)	Sulfates	Los Angeles	California emission standards	Nonuniformly mixed	1.07
Krupnick (1986)	Nitrogen dioxide	Baltimore	Proposed RACT regulations	Nonuniformly mixed	5.96
Seskin, Anderson, and Reid (1983)	Nitrogen dioxide	Chicago	Proposed RACT regulations	Nonuniformly mixed	14.40
McGartland (1984)	Particulates	Baltimore	SIP regulations	Nonuniformly mixed	4.18
Spofford (1984)	Sulfur dioxide	Lower Delaware Valley	Uniform percentage reduction	Nonuniformly mixed	1.78
	Particulates	Lower Delaware Valley	Uniform percentage reduction	Nonuniformly mixed	22.00
Maloney and Yandle (1984)	Hydrocarbons	All domestic DuPont plants	Uniform percentage reduction	Uniformly mixed	4.15
O'Ryan (1995)	Particulates	Santiago, Chile	Uniform percentage reduction	Nonuniformly mixed	1.31

CAC = command and control, the traditional regulatory approach.
SIP = state implementation plan.
RACT = reasonably available control technologies, a set of standards imposed on existing sources in nonattainment areas.

Example   *16.1*

CONTROLLING SO$_2$ EMISSIONS BY COMMAND-AND-CONTROL IN GERMANY

Germany and the United States took quite different approaches to controlling SO$_2$ emissions. Whereas the United States used a version of emissions trading, Germany used traditional command-and-control regulation. Theory would lead us to believe that the U.S. approach, due to its flexibility, would achieve its goals at a considerably lower expense. The evidence suggests that it did, but the reasons are a bit more complicated than one might suppose.

Due to the large amount of forest death (Waldsterben) in Germany in which SO$_2$ emissions were implicated, the pressure was on to dramatically reduce SO$_2$ emission from large combustion sources in a relatively short period of time. Both the degree of control and the mandated deadlines for compliance were quite stringent.

The stringency of the targets meant that sources had very little control flexibility; only one main technology could meet the requirements, so every covered combustion source had to install that technology. Even if firms would have been allowed to engage in emissions trading once the equipment was installed, the pretrade marginal costs would have been very similar. Since the purpose of trading is to equalize marginal costs, the fact that they were very similar before trading left little room for cost savings from trade.

The main cost disadvantage to the German system was not due to unequal marginal costs but rather to the temporal inflexibility of the command-and-control regulations. As Wätzold (2004) notes:

> The nearly simultaneous installation of desulfurization equipment in LCPs [Large Combustion Plants] all over Germany led to a surge in demand for this equipment with a resulting increase in prices. Furthermore, because Germany had little experience with the necessary technology, no learning effects were achieved; . . . shortcomings that should have come to light before the systems were introduced in the entire fleet of power stations . . . had to be remedied in all power stations. (p. 35)

This was quite different from the U.S. experience. In the U.S. program (described in detail in the next chapter), the ability to bank permits, which provided an incentive for some firms to comply early, and the phased deadline allowed much more flexibility in the timing of the installation of abatement controls; not all firms had to comply at the same time.

Source: F. Frank Wätzold. "SO$_2$ Emissions in Germany: Regulations to Fight Waldsterben," in W. Harrington, R. D. Morgenstern, and T. Sterner, eds. *Choosing Environmental Policy: Comparing Instruments and Outcomes in the United States and Europe* (Washington, DC: Resources for the Future, 2004): 23–40.

TABLE 16.3

Trends in U.S. Emissions and Air Quality

| | Percent Change in Air Quality | |
	1983–2002	1993–2002
NO_2	−21	−11
O_3 1-h	−22	−2[a]
8-h	−14	+4[a]
SO_2	−54	−39
PM_{10}	—	−13
$PM_{2.5}$	—	−8[b]
CO	−65	−42
Pb	−94	−57

| | Percent Change in Emissions | |
	1983–2002	1993–2002
NO_x	−15	−12
VOC	−40	−25
SO_2	−33	−31
PM_{10}[c]	−34[d]	−22
$PM_{2.5}$[c]	—	−17
CO	−41	−21
Pb[e]	−93	−5

—Trend data not available.

[a]Not statistically significant.

[b]Based on percentage change from 1999.

[c]Includes only directly emitted particles.

[d]Based on percentage change from 1985. Emission estimates prior to 1985 are uncertain.

[e]Lead emissions are included in the toxic air pollutant emissions inventory and are presented for 1982–2001.

Negative numbers indicate improvements in air quality or reductions in emissions. Positive numbers show where emissions have increased or air quality has gotten worse.

Source: USEPA http://www.epa.gov/airtrends/sixpoll.html.

- Ozone is formed after directly emitted gases (NO_2 and VOCs) react chemically, so its concentration depends on the chemical reactions as well as on emissions. And those chemical reactions depend on the weather. For example, peak ozone concentrations typically occur during hot, dry, stagnant summertime conditions.

- In these data, some portions of emissions are estimated rather than measured, while the air quality is directly measured.

How typical has the U.S. experience been? Is pollution declining on a world-wide basis? The Global Environmental Monitoring System (GEMS), operating under the auspices of the World Health Organization and the United Nations Environment Program, monitors air quality around the globe. Scrutiny of its reports reveal that the U.S. experience is typical for the industrialized nations, which have generally reduced pollution (both in terms of emissions and ambient outdoor air quality). Some of the reductions achieved in countries such as Japan and Norway have been spectacular. However, the air quality in most developing nations has steadily deteriorated, and the number of people exposed to unhealthy levels of pollution in those countries is frequently very high.[4] Since these countries typically are struggling merely to provide adequate employment and income to their citizens, they cannot afford to waste large sums of money on inefficient environmental policies, especially if the inefficiencies tend to subsidize the rich at the expense of the poor. Some cost-effective, yet fair means of improving air quality must be found.

Innovative Approaches

Fortunately some innovative approaches are available. Since various versions of these approaches have now been implemented around the world, we can learn from the experience gained from their implementation.

The Emissions Trading Program

Stripped to its essentials, the command-and-control approach toward stationary sources involves the specification of emission standards (legal ceilings) on all major emission sources. These standards are imposed on a large number of specific emission points such as stacks, vents, or storage tanks.

The emissions trading program adopted in the United States during the mid-1970s attempted to inject more flexibility into the manner in which the clean air objectives are met. Sources were encouraged to change the mix of control technologies envisioned in the standards as long as air quality was improved or at least not adversely affected by the change. The program was implemented by means of four separate policies, linked by a common element known as the emission reduction credit (ERC). The emission reduction credit is the currency used in trading among emission points, while the offset, bubble, netting, and emissions banking policies govern how the currency can be spent.[5]

The Emission Reduction Credit.
Should any source decide to control any emission point to a higher degree than necessary to fulfill its legal obligations, it can apply to the control authority for certification of the excess control as an emission reduction credit. Certified credits can be banked or used in the bubble, offset, or

---

[4]For sulfur oxides, for example, the GEMS study estimates that only 30 to 35% of the world's population lives in areas where the air is at least as clean as recommended by World Health Organization guidelines.

[5]As described in Chapter 17, modified versions of these policies have also been adopted for controlling acid rain and ozone-depleting chemicals.

netting programs. To receive certification, the emission reduction must be (1) surplus, (2) enforceable, (3) permanent, and (4) quantifiable.

The Offset Policy.   The offset policy was established to resolve a conflict between economic growth and progress toward meeting the ambient standards in nonattainment areas. The dilemma posed by this conflict involved how new or expanded sources could be accommodated while meeting the statutory requirement that the ambient standards be met as expeditiously as possible. Since these sources would add emissions to the region, some means of offsetting them had to be found.

The offset policy allows qualified new or expanding sources to commence operations in a nonattainment area provided they acquire sufficient emission reduction credits from existing sources. Typically they must acquire credits for 20% more reductions in emissions than would be added when the new facility commences operations. By buying the credits, new sources, in effect, finance emission controls undertaken by existing sources, thereby serving as a vehicle for improved air quality. Because regional emissions would be lower after the source began operations (counting the acquired emission reduction credits) than before, economic growth became the means for achieving better air quality rather than the source of further deterioration.

Major new or modified sources are qualified to participate in this program only if they control their own emissions to the degree required by the applicable emission standard and all existing major sources owned or operated by the applicant in the same state as the proposed source are in compliance with their legal control responsibilities.

The Bubble Policy.   The bubble policy allows existing sources to use emission reduction credits to satisfy their SIP control responsibilities. For example, existing sources in nonattainment areas can meet their assigned standards either by adopting the control technology used to define the standard or by adopting some technology that emits the pollutant at a somewhat higher rate, making up the difference with acquired emission reduction credits. The sum of emission reduction credits plus actual reductions must equal the assigned reduction.

This policy derives its unusual name from its treatment of multiple emission points as if they were contained within an imaginary bubble, regulating only the amount leaving the bubble. These bubbles can be extended to include not only emission points within the same plant but emission points in plants owned by other firms as well.

Netting.   Netting allows sources undergoing modification or expansion to escape the burden of new-source review requirements so long as any net increase (counting the emission reduction credits) in plantwide emissions is insignificant. Traditionally, the test of whether a source was subject to the new-source review process or not was applied by calculating the expected increases in emission occurring after modernization or expansion. When these increases passed predetermined thresholds, the source was subject to review. Netting allows emission reduction credits earned elsewhere in the plant to offset the increases expected from the expanded, more modernized portion in order to determine whether the threshold had been exceeded.

By "netting out" of review, the facility may be exempted from the need to acquire preconstruction permits as well as from meeting the associated requirements, such as modeling or monitoring the impact of the new source on air quality, installing the required control technology, or meeting the offset requirement; it may also avoid any applicable bans on new construction. Those facilities satisfying the significant increase threshold must still meet emission limits established by the NSPS. Emission reduction credits cannot be used to avoid this national standard.

Banking.   The banking component of the emissions trading program establishes procedures that allow firms to store emission reduction credits for subsequent use in the bubble, offset, or netting programs. States are authorized to design their own banking programs as long as the rules specify the ownership rights over the banked credits, the sources eligible to bank emission reduction credits, and the conditions governing the certification, holding, and use of these credits.

The Effectiveness of Emissions Trading

Although comprehensive data on the effects of the program do not exist because substantial proportions of it are administered by local areas and no one collects information in a systematic way, some of the major aspects of the experience are clear.

The program has unquestionably and substantially reduced the costs of complying with the requirements of the Clean Air Act. Most estimates place the accumulated capital savings for all component of the program at over $10 billion. This does not include the recurring savings in operating cost. On the other hand, the program has not produced the magnitude of cost savings that was anticipated by most proponents at its inception.

The level of compliance with the basic provisions of the Clean Air Act has increased. The emissions trading program expanded the possible means for compliance and sources have responded.

Thousands of trading transactions have been consummated. Each of these transactions was voluntary and for the participants represented an improvement over the traditional regulatory approach. Several of these transactions involved the introduction of innovative control technologies.

The vast majority of emissions trading transactions involved large pollution sources trading emissions reduction credits either created by excess control of uniformly mixed pollutants (those for which the location of emission is not an important policy concern) or involving facilities in close proximity to one another. Emissions trading seems to work especially well for uniformly mixed pollutants. No diffusion modeling is necessary to establish effects on ambient concentrations, and regulators do not have to worry about trades creating "hot spots" or localized areas of high pollution concentration. Trades can be on a one-to-one basis.

Emissions trading integrates particularly smoothly into any policy structure that is based either directly (through emission standards) or indirectly (through mandated technology or input limitations) on regulating emissions. In this case, emission limitations embedded in the operating licenses can serve as the trading benchmark.

Because emissions trading separates the issue of who will pay for the control from who will install the control, it introduces an additional degree of flexibility. This flexibility is particularly important in nonattainment areas since marginal control costs are so high. Sources that would not normally be controlled because they could not afford to implement the controls without going out of business can be controlled with emissions trading. The revenue derived from the sale of emission reduction credits can be used to finance the controls, effectively preventing bankruptcy.

We have also learned that ERC transactions, where regulators must validate every trade, have higher transactions costs than we previously understood. When nonuniformly mixed pollutants are involved, the transaction costs associated with estimating the air-quality effects are particularly high. Delegating responsibility for trade approval to lower levels of government may in principle speed up the approval process, but unless the bureaucrats in the lower level of government support the program, the gain may be negligible.

One question that always arises about emissions trading is the degree to which market power could undermine its desirable properties. Hahn (1984) has examined the case in which permits are allocated to emitters without charge (as is done in the Emissions Trading Program) rather than allocating them by an auction. His most important finding was that this initial allocation could have an effect on both the final (posttrade) allocation of permits and the permit price in the presence of market power. This finding is in direct contrast to what would happen in purely competitive markets (as described in Chapter 15), where both the final price and the ultimate allocation of permits would be independent of the initial allocation.

It is not hard to obtain an intuitive understanding of why the initial allocation might have an effect on the potential for price-setting behavior. Whenever a single price-setting source receives an initial allocation that is either higher than or lower than its cost-effective allocation, an incentive for trading would be created. When a price-setting source receives in an initial allocation fewer permits than its cost-effective allocation, it would exercise power on the buyer's side of the market. If it received more, it would exercise power on the seller's side of the market. The further the initial allocation diverges from the cost-effective allocation, the greater the potential for the price setter to exercise power over the market.

Is the potential for price manipulation a serious potential flaw in permit markets? Existing simulation studies suggest that it is not. Hahn found in simulating the sulfate market in Los Angeles that the total cost function was rather flat with respect to the initial allocation unless the price-setting firm receives a sufficiently large number of permits to enable it to become virtually a monopoly seller.

In another set of published data from the DuPont Corporation involving some 52 plants and 548 sources of hydrocarbons, Maloney and Yandle (1984) investigated the effects of cartelization of plants on the permit market. Assuming that all sources receive a proportional initial distribution of the permits based on their uncontrolled emissions, they calculate the effects on control costs if plants collude. Their analysis allows collusion to take place separately among buyers and sellers and allows the number of colluding plants to vary from 10 to 90% of the total number of plants buying or selling.

In general, these data support the notion that high degrees of cartelization are necessary before control costs are affected to any appreciable degree and that even high degrees of cartelization do not significantly erode the large savings to be achieved from permit markets. At the 90% credit monopoly (achieved when the cartel controls 90% of all credits sold), for example, yielding a 41% increase in control costs, Maloney and Yandle point out that the cost savings from this severe market power situation, compared with command-and-control regulation, is still 66% (instead of 76%). The presence of market power does not seem to diminish the potential for cost savings very much. Even with market power, transferable permit systems seem to result in lower control costs than the command-and-control allocation.

In summary, the early regulatory reforms embodying transferable permits represented a large, but incomplete step toward cost-effectiveness.

Smog Trading

Whereas the U.S. emissions trading program was initiated and promoted by the federal government, the newest programs have arisen from state initiatives. Faced with the need to reduce ozone concentrations considerably to come into compliance with the ozone ambient standard, states have chosen trading programs as a means of facilitating rather drastic reductions in precursor pollutants.

One of the most ambitious of these programs is California's Regional Clean Air Incentives Market (RECLAIM), established by the South Coast Air Quality Management District, the district responsible for the greater Los Angeles area. Under RECLAIM, each of the almost 400 participating industrial polluters is allocated an annual pollution limit for nitrogen oxides and sulfur, which decrease by 5 to 8% each year for the next decade. Polluters are allowed great flexibility in meeting these limits, including purchasing credits from other firms that have controlled more than their legal requirements.

The RECLAIM program departed from traditional practice in a couple of respects. First, it set a cap on total emissions from this group rather than on emissions from each source; this cap ensures that expansion must be accommodated within the cap (by cutting back a compensating amount somewhere else) rather than by allowing emissions to increase. Second, it changed the nature of the regulatory process. The burden of identifying the appropriate control strategies was shifted from the control authority to the polluter. In part, this shift was a necessity (traditional processes were incapable of identifying enough appropriate technologies to produce sufficiently stringent reductions) and was, in part, motivated by a desire to make the process as flexible as possible.

As a result of this flexibility, many new control strategies can emerge. Instead of the traditional focus on end-of-pipe control technologies, pollution prevention has been given an economic underpinning by this program. All possible pollution reduction strategies can, for the first time, compete on a level playing field.

The RECLAIM program also illustrates a couple of potential problems with permit markets. Compromises designed to gain political feasibility of the system may affect the level of the cap, at least initially. This was certainly the case with

RECLAIM as initial allocations were inflated (Harrison, 2004). An early evaluation of the program by EPA concluded that due to these inflated initial allocations in the earlier years of the program, fewer emissions had been reduced by RECLAIM than would have been reduced by more traditional regulation. The effects over the longer term remain to be seen.

The second problem with RECLAIM arose from a confluence of forces. Due to electric deregulation and a shortage of imported power, power plants in the RECLAIM area were required to run full tilt. These abnormally high production levels generated an abnormally large amount of emissions. Since the supply of permits that determined the level of authorized emissions was fixed by the cap, the price of these permits shot up to politically unsupportable levels.

The very large price increases triggered a "safety valve" mechanism. RECLAIM procedures specified that if permit prices went over some threshold (as it did in this case), the program would be temporarily suspended and an alternative fee per ton would be imposed until the normal operation of the program could resume. This alternative fee, of course, in essence replaced the unacceptably high market price with a somewhat lower, administratively determined price that was politically acceptable. This fee was designed to retain some financial pressure on the plants to reduce emissions without straining the system beyond its tolerance limits and the revenue was used to secure emission reductions from other sources.

This experience provides some insights about both the nature of the problem and a potential solution. When prices rise to levels that jeopardize the integrity of the program, a possibility whenever the fixed supply of permits meets a large, temporary increase in emissions, it is possible to switch to a fee-based system until more normal conditions once again prevail.

Emission Charges

Air pollution emission charges have been implemented by a number of countries, including France and Japan. The French air pollution charge was designed to encourage the early adoption of pollution control equipment, with the revenues returned to those paying the charge as a subsidy for installing the equipment. In Japan, the emission charge is designed to raise revenue to compensate victims of air pollution.

The French charge system has been in effect since 1985. Originally designed to operate until 1990, it was renewed and expanded in that year. The charge is levied on all industrial firms having a power generating capacity of 20 megawatts or more, or industrial firms discharging over 150 metric tons of taxable pollutants. Some 1,400 plants are affected. Some 90% of the charge revenue is recovered by charge payers as a subsidy for pollution control equipment, while the remaining 10% is used for new technological developments.

While data are limited, a few highlights seem clear. The charge level is too low to have any incentive impact. Total revenues are estimated to be about one-tenth of the revenue that would result from a charge sufficient to bring French industries in line with the air pollution control directives of the European Community (Opschoor and Vos, 1989, 34–35).

Economists typically envision two types of effluent or emissions charges. The first, an efficiency charge, is designed to produce an efficient outcome by forcing the polluter to compensate completely for all damage caused. The second, a cost-effective charge, is designed to achieve a predefined ambient standard at the lowest possible control cost. In practice, the French approach fits neither of these designs.

In Japan the charge takes on a different function. As a result of four important legal cases where Japanese industries were forced to compensate victims for pollution damages caused, in 1973 Japan passed the Law for the Compensation of Pollution-Related Health Injury. According to this law, victims of designated diseases, upon certification by a council of medical, legal, and other experts, are eligible for medical expenses, lost earnings, and other expenses; they are not eligible for other losses such as pain and suffering. Two classes of diseases are funded: specific diseases where the specific source is relatively clear and nonspecific respiratory diseases where all polluters are presumed to have some responsibility.

This program is funded by an emissions charge on sulfur dioxides and from an automobile weight tax. The level of the charge/tax is determined by the revenue needs of the compensation fund.

In contrast to emissions trading where ERC prices respond automatically to changing market conditions, emissions charges have to be determined by an administrative process. When the function of the charge is to raise revenue for a particular purpose, charge rates will be determined by the costs of achieving that purpose; when the costs of achieving the purpose rise, the level of the charge must rise to secure the additional revenue.[6]

Sometimes that process produces an unintended dynamic. In Japan, for example, the charge is calculated on the basis of the amount of compensation paid to victims of air pollution in the previous year. While the amount of compensation has been increasing, the amount of emissions (the base to which the charge is applied) has been decreasing. As a result, unexpectedly high charge rates are necessary in order to raise sufficient revenue for the compensation system.

Hazardous Pollutants

Hazardous pollutants are those that pose a localized risk of severe harm to human health. They are distinguished from criteria pollutants both by the degree of harm they pose to those exposed and by the fact that emission usually occurs only at a few key locations. In recognition of these unique characteristics, the Clean Air Act sets up a special process for dealing with hazardous pollutants.

The first step in the control process involves identifying those substances that are designated as hazardous substances and therefore must receive this special treatment. The Act requires the Administrator of the EPA to make and periodically update a list of hazardous pollutants. It allows a great deal of discretion in the choice of criteria to be used in distinguishing hazardous and criteria pollutants and in the length of time necessary to decide whether a substance should be listed.

---

[6]While it is theoretically possible (depending on the elasticity of demand for pollution abatement) for a rise in the tax to produce less revenue, this has typically not been the case.

Once a substance is listed, the EPA must move with great speed (180 days) either to regulate emissions of the substance or to remove it from the list after finding that the evidence failed to support the tentative hazardous-substance designation. The decision to regulate a substance imposes on the EPA a requirement to establish a national emission standard or workplace standard for each regulated substance. These standards must be designed to protect human health with an adequate margin of safety.

The somewhat ambiguous language in this section of the Act has led to a great deal of controversy as well as litigation concerning the meaning of this mandate. It is generally conceded that there is no safe threshold level for airborne carcinogens. Therefore, environmentalists maintain that protecting the public with an adequate margin of safety requires eliminating all exposure to listed substances. Completely eliminating emissions would, at a minimum, be very expensive and may not be possible without shutting down the operation.

In addition to moving very slowly in listing pollutants, the agency began to incorporate risk assessment and benefit/cost analysis into their decisions. The first step in this process is to decide whether the risk posed by the substance is "significant." Substances that are not found to be posing significant risks are not listed. The second step, taken only for listed pollutants, involves identifying the level of control that will be required. This entails comparing the costs of various control possibilities with the damages to health prevented by adopting the controls.

Based on the work of Haigh, Harrison, and Nichols (1983), it is possible to see how this kind of economic analysis can be applied to hazardous pollution regulation. In their study, the authors applied benefit/cost analysis to three hazardous pollutants: benzene, coke oven emissions, and acrylonitrile. Benzene is a major industrial chemical, ranking among the top 15 in terms of production volume. Coke, produced by distilling coal in ovens, is essential to the production of steel. Acrylonitrile is an important industrial chemical used in the manufacture of a wide range of consumer products, including rugs, clothing, plastic pipe, and automobile hoses.

The analysis involved several steps. The amount and location of emissions had to be identified for each substance. The number of people exposed to this risk and the amount of health risk they would experience had to be calculated. Finally a dollar value had to be put on this risk so it could be directly compared with the control costs. All of these steps had to be repeated for each considered regulatory option.

Three regulatory strategies were considered for each pollutant. The first strategy was a rather stringent set of uniformly applied emission standards designed to require the use of the best available technology. (For benzene, the controls were applied to maleic anhydride plants, the largest source of emissions.) The second strategy involved a somewhat more relaxed version of the first strategy. While the standards were still applied uniformly in this second case, the level of required control was lower. The final strategy involved differential controls based on exposure. The notion of uniform controls was dropped in this case in favor of placing heavier controls on those sources posing the greatest health risk.

The authors present their results in two main forms. The first calculates the value of human life that would be needed to justify that particular regulatory option. This form of presentation allows the reader to determine whether the regulatory option is a good idea by supplying his or her own sense of what the value of human

TABLE 16.4

Net Benefits ($Million/Year) of Alternative Strategies for a Value of Life Saved of $1 Million

Regulatory Strategy	Benzene	Coke Oven Emissions	Acrylonitrile
Best Available Technology	−2.2	−8.7	−28.8
Relaxed Uniform	−1.1	−3.2	−8.0
Differential	−0.6	2.3	−4.9

Source: From John A. Haigh, David Harrison, Jr., and Albert L. Nichols. "Benefits Assessment and Environmental Regulation: Case Studies of Hazardous Air Pollutants," John F. Kennedy School of Government Energy and Environment Policy Center Discussion Paper E-83-07 (August 1983). Reprinted by permission.

life should be. The second uses a $1 million value of human life and calculates the net benefits of each option based on that assumption.

Using the $1 million figure for a human life, the results (see Table 16.4) indicate that for all three pollutants, the standard best available technology (BAT) strategy would yield negative net benefits. The combination of uniform standards with a very stringent level of control produces a situation where the costs exceed the benefits. A relaxed uniform standard reduces, but does not eliminate, the negative net benefits. Although lowering the uniform degree of control represents an improvement in the sense that costs are more commensurate with benefits, it still fails to target the reductions in the areas where they result in the most reduction in risk.

By configuring the controls in such a way as to target the costs on those emitters posing the greatest risk to human health (the differential strategy), we achieve a dramatic improvement in net benefits for all three pollutants. For only one, however, coke oven emissions, are the net benefits positive. For the rest, even the differential strategy falls short of being justified by the benefits.

The significance of these data lies less in what they tell us about the correct regulatory option to choose for these specific pollutants than in the clues they provide concerning directions for policy to move in achieving greater efficiency in regulating hazardous pollutants in general. First, tailoring the strategy to specific circumstances can produce significant reductions in cost while achieving the same risk or much larger risk reductions for the same cost. Uniformity, in short, imposes a large cost penalty. Second, the policies being pursued in regulating hazardous pollutants imply values for human life that differ by a factor of more than 100. This finding implies that by allocating more resources to the control of those substances that can be justified with even a lower value of life and less to those that can be justified only with a high value for life, more lives could be saved with the same expenditure of money.

How can these lessons be translated into policy? One answer is to consider the adoption of a charge levied not on emission, but on exposure. By forcing those emitters exposing large numbers of people to a health risk to exert greater cleanup efforts than those emitters exposing fewer people to the same health risk, we can

Example 16.2

TECHNOLOGY DIFFUSION IN THE CHLORINE MANUFACTURING SECTOR

Most of the world's chlorine is produced using one of three types of cells: the mercury cell, the diaphragm cell, and the membrane cell. Generally, the mercury-cell technology poses the highest environmental risk, with the diaphragm-cell technology posing the next highest risk.

Over the last 25 years, the mercury-cell share of the total production has fallen from 22% to 10%; the diaphragm-cell's share has fallen from 73% to 67%, and the membrane-cell's share has risen from less than 1% of the total to 20%.

What role did regulation play? One might normally expect that, prodded by regulation, chlorine manufacturers would have increasingly adopted the more environmentally benign production technique. But that is not what happened. Instead, other regulations made it beneficial for users of chlorine to switch to nonchlorine bleaches, thereby reducing the demand for chlorine. In response to this reduction in demand, a number of producers shut down, and a disproportionate share of the plants that remained open were the ones using the cleaner, membrane-cell production.

Source: L. D. Snyder, N. H. Miller, and R. N. Stavins. "The Effects of Environmental Regulation on Technology Diffusion: The Case of Chlorine Manufacturing," *American Economic Review* Vol. 93, No. 2 (2003): 431–435.

save more lives with the same expenditure of resources. In this context, uniform exposure charges have much to recommend them.

What about the impact of environmental regulation on the diffusion of more environmentally benign technologies? Does the evidence suggest that new technologies with reduced environmental impact are being developed and adopted? As Example 16.2 points out for chlorine manufacturing, the answer is a definite yes, but not quite in the manner expected.

Summary

While air quality has improved in the industrial nations, it has deteriorated in the developing nations. Because the historical approach to air pollution control has been a traditional command-and-control approach, it has been neither efficient nor cost-effective.

The command-and-control policy has not been efficient in part because it has been based on a legal fiction, a threshold below which no health damages are inflicted on any member of the population. In fact, damages occur at levels lower than the ambient standards to especially sensitive members of the population, such as those with respiratory problems. This attempt to formulate standards without reference to control costs has been thwarted by the absence of a scientifically defensible health-based threshold. In addition, the policy fails to adequately consider the timing of emission flows. By failing to target the greatest amount of control on those periods when the greatest damage is inflicted, the current policy encourages too little control in high-damage periods and excessive control during low-damage periods. Current policy has also failed to pay sufficient attention to indoor air pollution, which may well pose larger health risks than outdoor pollution. Unfortunately, because the existing benefit estimates have large confidence intervals, the size of the inefficiency associated with these aspects of the policy has not been measured with any precision.

The policy is not cost-effective either. The allocation of responsibility among emitters for reducing pollution has resulted in control costs that are typically several times higher than necessary to achieve the air-quality objective. This has been shown to be true for a variety of pollutants in a variety of geographic settings.

The EPA has initiated the Emissions Trading Program, based on economic incentives, which was designed to provide more flexibility in meeting the air-quality goals while reducing the cost and the conflict between economic growth and the preservation of air quality. These reforms, known as the bubble, offset, netting, and emissions banking programs, also promised to stimulate more rapid development of new control technologies than was possible under the traditional system. It was an improvement but results fell short of expectations.

France and Japan have both introduced emission charges as part of their approach to pollution control, but neither application fits the textbook model very well. In France the charge level is too low to have the appropriate incentive effects. In Japan the charge is designed mainly to raise revenue for compensating victims of respiratory damage caused by pollution.

The program to control hazardous pollutants is inefficient in both the speed with which the process is operating and quality of the decision being rendered. Faced with unrealistically short deadlines for publishing standards once a hazardous substance is listed, the EPA has reacted by taking an excessively cautious approach to listing hazardous substances. Past decisions have resulted in the application of stringent standards that are uniformly applied to emitters. The evidence suggests that strategies tailored more closely to the risk posed (with emission posing the greatest risk of being reduced more) produce substantially lower risks for the same expenditure as uniformly applied standards. One reform proposal based on this analysis would impose an exposure (as opposed to an emissions) charge on emitters that would take into account not only the concentration of the emission (and the resulting health risk to each exposed person) but also the number of people exposed.

Discussion Questions

1. The efficient regulation of hazardous pollutants should take exposure into account—the more persons exposed to a given pollutant concentration, the larger is the damage caused by it and therefore the smaller is the efficient concentration level, all other things being equal. An alternative point of view would

simply ensure that concentrations would be held below a uniform threshold regardless of the number of people exposed. For this point of view, the public policy goal is to expose any and all people to the same concentration level—exposure is not used to establish different concentrations for different settings. What are the advantages and disadvantages of each approach? Which do you think represents the best approach? Why?

2. European countries have relied to a much greater extent on emission charges than has the United States, which seems to be moving toward a greater reliance on transferable emission permits. From an efficiency point of view, should the United States follow Europe's lead and shift the emphasis toward emission charges? Why or why not?

Problems

1. The marginal control cost curves for two air pollutant sources affecting a single receptor are $MC_1 = \$0.3q_1$ and $MC_2 = \$0.5q_2$, where q_1 and q_2 are controlled emissions. Their respective transfer coefficients are $a_1 = 1.5$ and $a_1 = 1.0$. With no control they would emit 20 units of emission apiece. The ambient standard is 12 ppm.

   (a) If an ambient permit system were established, how many permits would be issued and what price would prevail?

   (b) How much would each source spend on permits if they were auctioned off? How much would each source ultimately spend on permits if each source were initially given, free of charge, half of the permits?

Further Reading

Kosobud, Richard F., William A. Testa, and Donald A. Hanson, eds. *Cost-Effective Control of Urban Smog* (Chicago: Federal Reserve Bank of Chicago, 1993.) The proceedings of a conference providing background information for the Illinois smog trading program.

National Center for Environmental Economics. *The United States Experience with Economic Incentives in Environmental Pollution Control Policy* (Washington, DC: U.S. Environmental Protection Agency, 2001). A survey of what has been tried in the United States and how it has worked. Available on the Web through the portal at http://yosemite.epa.gov/ee/epa/eed.nsf/webpages/homepage

Nichols, Albert L. *Targeting Economic Incentives for Environmental Protection* (Cambridge, MA: MIT Press, 1984). An excellent review of the use of economic incentives to control pollution with a detailed treatment of the use of exposure charges to control air-borne carcinogens.

Opschoor, J. B., and Hans B. Vos. *Economic Instruments for Environmental Protection* (Paris: OECD, 1989). A survey of the use of economic instruments for environmental protection within the OECD countries.

Tietenberg, T. H. "Economic Instruments for Environmental Regulation," *Oxford Review of Economic Policy* Vol. 6 (Spring 1990): 17–33. A detailed examination of the lessons to be learned from early applications of the economic incentives approach to pollution control.

Additional References is available on this book's companion Web site www.aw-bc.com/tietenberg.

Regional and Global Air Pollutants: Acid Rain and Atmospheric Modification

Everything should be made as simple as possible, but not simpler.

—Albert Einstein

Introduction

As the zone of influence of pollutants extends beyond local boundaries, the political difficulties of implementing comprehensive, cost-effective control measures are compounded. Pollutants crossing boundaries impose external costs; neither emitters nor the nations within which they emit have the proper incentives for controlling them.

Compounding the problem of improper incentives is the scientific uncertainty that limits our understanding of most of these problems. Our knowledge about various relationships that form the basis for our understanding of the magnitude of the problems and the effectiveness of various strategies to control them is far from complete. Unfortunately, the problems are so important and the potential consequences of inaction so drastic that procrastination is not usually an optimal strategy. To avoid having to act in the future under emergency conditions when the remaining choices are few in number, strategies with desirable properties must be formulated now on the basis of the available information, as limited as it may be. Options must be preserved.

The costs of inaction are not limited to the damages caused. International cooperation among such traditional allies as the United States, Mexico, and Canada and the countries of Europe has been undermined by disputes over the proper control of acid rain and climate change.

In this chapter we survey the scientific evidence on the severity of global and regional pollution and the potential effectiveness of policy strategies designed to alleviate these problems. We also consider difficulties confronted by the government in implementing solutions and the role of economic analysis in understanding how to circumvent these difficulties.

Regional Pollutants

The primary difference between regional pollutants and local pollutants is the distance they are transported in the air. While the damage caused by local pollutants occurs in the vicinity of emission, for regional pollutants the damage can occur at significant distances from the emission point.

The same substances can be both local pollutants and regional pollutants. Sulfur oxides, nitrogen oxides, and ozone, for example, have already been discussed as local pollutants, but they are regional pollutants as well. For example, sulfur emissions, the focal point for most acid-rain legislation, have been known to travel some 200 to 600 miles from the point of emission before returning to the earth. As the substances are being transported by the winds, they undergo a complex series of chemical reactions. Under the right conditions both sulfur and nitrogen oxides are transformed into sulfuric and nitric acids. Nitrogen oxides and hydrocarbons can combine in the presence of sunlight to produce ozone.

Acid Rain

What Is It?   Acid rain, the popular term for atmospheric deposition of acidic substances, is actually a misnomer. Acidic substances are deposited not only by rain and other forms of moist air but as dry particles as well. In some parts of the world, such as the southwestern United States, dry deposition is a more important source of acidity than wet deposition.

Precipitation is normally mildly acidic, with a global background pH of 5.0 (pH is the common measurement for acidity; the lower the number, the more acidic the substance, with 7.0 being the border between acidity and alkalinity). Industrialized areas commonly receive precipitation well in excess of the global background. Rainfall in eastern North America, for example, has a typical pH of 4.4. Wheeling, West Virginia, once experienced a rainstorm with a pH of 1.5. The fact that battery acid has a pH of 1.0 may help put this event into perspective.

Though natural sources of acid deposition do exist, the evidence is quite clear that anthropogenic (human-made) sources have dominated deposition in recent years. An analysis of ice cores from Greenland, for example, indicates that anthropogenic sulfate has dominated sulfur deposition since the early 20th century, and anthropogenic nitrate has dominated nitrogen deposition since about 1960.

The Effects.   In 1980 the U.S. Congress funded a 10-year study (called the National Acid Rain Precipitation Assessment Program) to determine the causes and effects of acid rain and to make recommendations concerning its control. The report concluded that damage from current and historic levels of acid rain ranged from negligible (on crops) to modest (on aquatic life in some lakes and streams).

The findings from this study were significantly less dire than expected and provided a rather sharp contrast with findings of higher levels of damage in Europe. Studies have documented that Sweden has some 4,000 highly acidified lakes; in southern Norway lakes with a total surface area of 13,000 square kilometers support no fish at all; similar reports have been received from Germany, Scotland, and Canada.

Example	17.1

ADIRONDACK ACIDIFICATION

About 180 lakes in the Adirondack Mountains of New York State, mostly at higher altitudes, which had supported natural or stocked brook trout populations in the 1930s, no longer supported these populations by the 1970s. In some cases entire communities of six or more fish species had disappeared.

The location of these lakes, some distance east of any local emission sources, makes it quite clear that most of the acid deposition is coming from outside of the region. These lakes have relatively little capacity to neutralize deposited acid because they are in areas with little or no limestone or other forms of basic rock that might serve to buffer the acid.

This is a prime recreational area, particularly for fishing. Most of the sites are within the boundary of the 6 million acre Adirondack Park, the last substantially undeveloped area of its size in the northeastern United States. Its remoteness, mountainous terrain, and multitude of lakes provide an accessible outdoor recreation experience for the 55 million people who live within a day's traveling distance.

Once the 1990 amendments to the Clean Air Act (described below) resulted in substantial reductions in acid deposition in response to several new legislative proposals, the policy question became, Would further reduction efforts be justified in terms of net benefits? Using a contingent valuation method that includes both use and nonuse values, Banzhaf, Burtraw, Evans, and Krupnick (2004) estimated the benefits from further reductions in SO_2 and NOx and compared them with the costs of achieving those reductions.

Their preferred estimates of the mean willingness to pay (WTP) for ecological improvements range from $48 to $107 per year per household in New York State. Multiplying these population-weighted estimates by the approximate number of households in the state yields benefits ranging from about $336 million to $1.1 billion per year.

Their estimate of the costs of those reductions attributable to Adirondack improvements range from $86 million in 2010 to $126 million in 2020. Since these cost estimates are significantly less than the benefit estimates, despite the large reductions already achieved, further reductions would be economically justified.

Source: Spencer Banzhaf, Dallas Burtraw, David Evans, and Alan Krupnick. "Valuation of Natural Resource Improvements in the Adirondacks," a Report to the Environmental Protection Agency by Resources for the Future, Inc. (September 2004).

Acid rain has also been implicated in the slower growth, injury, or death not only of European forests, particularly German forests (see Example 16.2), but also of forests in the United States. Acid rain has been found to cause forest and soil degradation in many areas of the eastern United States, with its strongest effect in the high-elevation forests of the Appalachian Mountains from Maine to Georgia, including such high-visibility areas as the Shenandoah and Great Smoky Mountain National Parks.

According to this research, acid rain does not usually kill tress directly. Instead, it is more likely to weaken trees by damaging their leaves, limiting the nutrients available to them, or exposing them to toxic substances slowly released from the soil by the acidic deposition. Quite often, injury or death of trees is a result of the combined effects of acid rain and one or more additional threats such as drought, disease, or exposure to other pollutants.

The Transboundary Problem.   In many countries with a federal form of government, such as the United States, the policy focus in the past has been on treating all pollutants as if they were local pollutants, overlooking the adverse regional consequences in the process. By giving local jurisdictions a large amount of responsibility for achieving the desired air quality and by measuring progress at local monitors, the stage was set for making regional pollution worse rather than better.

In the early days of pollution control, local areas adopted the motto "dilution is the solution." As implemented, this approach suggested that the way to control local pollutants was to emit from tall stacks. By the time the pollutants hit the ground, the concentrations would be diluted, making it easier to meet the ambient standards at nearby monitors.

This approach had several consequences. First, it lowered the amount of emission reduction necessary to achieve ambient standards; with tall stacks any given amount of emission would produce lower ground-level concentrations than an equivalent level of emission from a shorter-stack source. Second, the ambient standards could be met at a lower cost. Using Cleveland, Ohio as a case study, Atkinson (1983) has shown that control costs would be approximately 30% lower, but emissions would be two and one-half times higher if a local, rather than a regional, strategy were followed. In essence, local areas would be able to lower their own cost by exporting emissions to other areas. By focusing its attention on local pollution, the Clean Air Act actually made the regional pollution problem worse.

Crafting a Policy.   Even by the late 1970s it had become painfully clear in the United States that the traditional approach was ill-suited to solve regional pollution problems. Therefore, significant attention was focused on revamping the legislation to do a better job of dealing with regional pollutants such as acid rain.

Politically, that was a tall order. By virtue of the fact that these pollutants are transported long distances, the set of geographic areas receiving the damage is typically not the same as the set of geographic areas responsible for most of the emission causing the damage. In many cases the recipients and the emitters are even in different countries! In this political milieu, it should not be surprising that those bearing damages should call for a large, rapid reduction in emission, while those responsible for bearing the costs of that cleanup should want to proceed more slowly and with greater caution.

Economic analysis has been helpful in finding a feasible path through this political thicket. In particular, a Congressional Budget Office (CBO) study helped to set the parameters of the debate by quantifying the consequences of various courses of action. To analyze the economic and political consequences of various strategies designed to achieve reductions of SO_2 emissions from utilities anywhere from 8 to 12 million tons below the emission levels from those plants in 1980, the CBO (1986) used a computer-based simulation model that relates utility emissions, utility costs, and coal-market supply-and-demand levels to the strategies under consideration.

The results of this modeling exercise will be presented in two segments. In the first segment we examine the basic available strategies including both a traditional command-and-control strategy that simply allocates reductions on the basis of a specific formula and an emissions charge strategy. This analysis demonstrated the sensitivity of costs to various levels of emission reduction and highlighted some of the political consequences of implementing these strategies. The second segment of analysis then considers various strategies designed to mitigate the adverse political effects of the basic strategies as a means of ascertaining what is gained and lost by adopting these compromises.

The first implication of the analysis is that the marginal cost of additional control rises rapidly, particularly after 10 million tons have been reduced (see Table 17.1). The cost of reducing a ton of SO_2 rises from $270 for an 8-million-ton reduction to $360 for a 10-million-ton reduction, while it rises to a rather dramatic $779 per ton for a 12-million-ton reduction. Costs would rise much more steeply as the amount

TABLE 17.1

Costs Associated with Basic Strategies to Reduce Sulfur Emissions

Strategy	Total Program Cost[a] ($ billions)	Annual Cost to Utilities[b] ($ billions)	Key State Employment Change[c] (# of jobs lost)	Cost-Effectiveness[d] ($ per ton)
8-Million-Ton Rollback	$20.4	$1.9	14,100	$270
10-Million-Ton Rollback	$34.5	$3.2	21,900	$360
12-Million-Ton Rollback	$93.6	$8.8	13,400	$779
Emission Charge	$37.5	$7.7	17,900	$327

[a]The present value (in 1985 dollars) of additional discounted utility costs incurred (over a current policy benchmark) from 1986 to 2015, using a real discount rate of 0.03. Any emission charges paid are not included.

[b]The additional cost to utilities of this strategy over the current policy benchmark in 1995 expressed in 1985 dollars. This value includes any emissions charges paid.

[c]The additional coal-mining job losses expected, if this strategy were implemented rather than the current policy benchmark.

[d]The discounted program cost divided by the annual discounted SO_2 reduction measured over the 1986–2015 period.

Source: Congress of the United States, Congressional Budget Office. *Curbing Acid Rain: Cost, Budget, and Coal-Market Effects* (Washington, DC: U.S. Government Printing Office, 1986): xx, xxii, 23, 80.

of required reduction is increased because reliance on more expensive scrubbers would become necessary. (Scrubbers involve a chemical process to extract or "scrub" sulfur gases before they escape into the atmosphere.)

The second insight, one that should be no surprise to readers of this book, is that an emissions charge would be more cost-effective than a comparable command-and-control strategy. Whereas the command-and-control strategy could secure a 10-million-ton reduction at about $360 a ton, the emission charge could do it for $327 a ton. The superiority of the emissions charge is due to the fact that it results in equalized marginal costs, a required condition for cost-effectiveness.[1]

A third insight is that the magnitude of the cost-effectiveness superiority of the emissions charge is not very large, especially when compared with the numbers presented in the previous chapter.

One of the reasons that enacting acid-rain legislation in the United States took until 1990 involved expected coal industry job losses in certain key states. To the extent that coal switching became the utility strategy of choice, those areas producing high-sulfur coal would be hard hit, as they lost business to the low-sulfur coal-producing states. To the extent that scrubbers would be adopted, however, the use of high-sulfur coal could continue with lower employment impacts on employment in those states.

Though the emission charge approach may be the most cost-effective policy, it was not the most popular, particularly in states with many old, heavily polluting power plants. With an emission charge approach, utilities not only have to pay the higher equipment and operating costs associated with the reductions, they also have to pay a charge on all uncontrolled emissions. The additional financial burden associated with controlling acid rain by means of an emission charge would have been significant. Instead of paying the $3.2 billion for reducing 10 million tons under a command-and-control approach, utilities would be saddled with a $7.7 billion financial burden with an emissions charge. The savings achieved from lower equipment and operating costs achieved because the emission charge approach is more cost-effective, would have been more than outweighed by the additional expense of paying the emission charges. What is least-cost to society is not, in this case, least-cost for the utilities.

The Sulfur Allowance Program.

The political dilemma posed by this additional financial burden was resolved by adopting an emissions trading system known as the sulfur allowance program (see Example 17.2). Adopted as part of the Clean Air Act Amendment of 1990, this approach complements, rather than replaces, the traditional approach, which emphasized the attainment of local ambient air-quality standards.

The sulfur allowance program is referred to as a *cap-and-trade* program for good reason. A cap-and-trade program sets an aggregate cap (limit) on emissions from the covered emitters and allocates allowances (emission authorizations) that sum to

---

[1]Why, the alert reader might ask, isn't location of the emissions taken into account? Since the objective was stated as securing a reduction in emissions, not achieving an ambient standard, the cost-effective allocation is achieved when marginal control costs are equalized.

Example 17.2

THE SULFUR ALLOWANCE PROGRAM

Under this innovative approach, allowances to emit sulfur oxides have been allocated to older, sulfur-emitting electricity-generating plants; the number of allowances was restricted to ensure a reduction of 10 million tons in emissions from 1980 levels by the year 2010.

These allowances, which provide a limited authorization to emit one ton of sulfur, are defined for a specific calendar year, but unused allowances can be carried forward into the next year. They are transferable among the affected sources. Any industrial plants reducing emissions more than required by the allowances could transfer the unused allowances to other plants. Emissions in any plant may not legally exceed the levels permitted by the allowances (allocated plus acquired) held by the managers of that plant. An annual year-end audit balances emissions with allowances. Utilities that emit more than authorized by their holdings of allowances must pay a $2,000-a-ton penalty and are required to forfeit an equivalent number of tons in the following year.

An important innovation in this program was ensuring the availability of allowances by instituting an auction market. Each year the EPA withholds 2.24% of the allocated allowances to go into the auction. These withheld permits are allocated to the highest bidders, with successful buyers paying their bid price. The proceeds are refunded to the utilities from whom the allowances were withheld on a proportional basis.

Private allowance holders may also offer allowances for sale at these auctions. Potential sellers specify minimum acceptable prices. Once the withheld allowances have been disbursed, the EPA then matches the highest remaining bids with the lowest minimum acceptable prices on the private offerings and matches buyers and sellers until all remaining bids are less than the remaining minimum acceptable prices.

Sources: Dallas Burtraw. "The SO_2 Emissions Trading Program: Cost Savings without Allowance Trades," *Contemporary Economic Policy* Vol. XIV, No. 2 (1996): 79–94; Nancy Kete. "The U.S. Acid Rain Control Allowance Trading System," in T. Jones and J. Corfee-Morlot, eds. *Climate Change: Designing a Tradeable Permit System* (Paris: Organisation for Economic Co-operation and Development Publication, 1992): 69–93; Renee Rico. "The U. S. Allowance Trading System for Sulfur Dioxide: An Update on Market Experience," *Environmental and Resource Economics* Vol. 5, No. 2 (1995): 115–129.

this cap. The cap feature of this program is important because it represents a substantial change in policy from the old regulatory system. Under the traditional system, emissions from each unit were directly regulated, but not aggregate emissions. Hence as the number of emitters grew, so could aggregate emissions. With a cap that cannot happen. New emitters can only be accommodated within the cap (since total emissions cannot increase) and that can only happen if existing emitters reduce emissions by enough to accommodate the needs of the new emitters. The allowance

Example 17.3

WHY AND HOW DO ENVIRONMENTALISTS BUY POLLUTION?

Among the rather unique features of the sulfur allowance program, two have found particular favor with environmentalists. Not only does the program put a fixed upper limit on total annual sulfur emissions from the utilities sector, but it allows environmental groups to lower that limit by acquiring allowances.

In the auctions run by the Chicago Board of Trade, anyone, including environmental groups, can place a bid. Environmental group bids are typically financed by donations from individuals who want to reduce pollution. Successful bidders acquire allowances for whatever purpose they see fit, including "retiring" them so they cannot be used to legitimize emissions. Every retired ton of sulfur oxide allowances represents an authorized ton of pollution that will not be emitted.

In the 1996 auction, one nonprofit organization known by the acronym INHALE purchased 454 allowances. The Maryland Environmental Law Society (MELS) bought and retired an allowance in the 1994 auction, and became the first student group to do so. Since then, at least 11 law schools have become involved with the retirement of allowances.

Another organization that has raised funds to retire allowances is the Working Assets Funding Source. This nonprofit public-interest company regularly contributes 1% of its revenues to public-service organizations and uses its monthly bills to solicit charitable donations from customers for various featured causes. A summer 1993 campaign asked the 80,000 customers of its long-distance telephone service to add a small donation when paying their bills to support "our goal to reduce SO_2 emissions by 300 tons . . . and spark a movement to do much more." The result was $55,000 in donations, which enabled the group to purchase 289 allowances.

Allowances have also been retired through charitable donations. An agreement between Arizona Public Service Company and Niagara Mohawk Power Corporation, for example, resulted in the donation of 25,000 allowances to the Environmental Defense Fund. In another transaction, Northeast Utilities of Connecticut donated 10,000 allowances to the American Lung Association. The Lung Association has since contacted other utilities through its local chapters in an effort to receive further donations to reduce pollution.

Source: EPA Web page: http://www.epa.gov/docs/acidrain/update3/allws.html (July 1996).

program not only limits aggregate emissions to the level specified by the cap, but it provides an economic incentive (due to the right to sell excess reductions) for those additional reductions to occur.

Under the sulfur allowance program, anyone can purchase allowances. This option is increasingly being chosen by environmental groups as a means of producing fewer sulfur emissions than allowed by law (see Example 17.3).

Results of the Program.   According to official EPA reports, by 2003 the sulfur emission controls on the electric power industry resulted in a reduction in SO_2 emissions of 38% from 1980 levels. Significantly, the electric power industry achieved nearly 100% compliance with program requirements—only one unit had emissions exceeding the SO_2 allowances that it held.

Though a dramatic decline in emissions clearly occurred, how did this decline affect sensitive areas? To find out, EPA investigated sites in New England, New York, Pennsylvania, Virginia, Wisconsin, Michigan, and West Virginia, relying on data from 1990 through 2000. In these states, although they found that approximately one-quarter to one-third of formerly acidic surface waters were no longer acidic, they also found little evidence of a regional change in the acidity status of water in either New England or Virginia. Clearly, reductions in emissions do not immediately produce proportionate increases in water quality.

Was this due to natural conditions or to the geographic pattern of the reductions? Early in the debates about the sulfur allowance program, a number of commentators pointed out that under a trading system only the total emissions are reduced. Due to the flexibility offered by trading, it is theoretically possible for the reductions to be concentrated in a few areas, leaving the rest with unchanged (or possibly even increased) emissions. Did this happen?

Apparently not. Burtraw and Mansur (1999) find that both sulfur depositions and pollutant concentrations decreased, and health benefits actually increased in the East and Northeast due to trading. According to their estimates, national health benefits would be nearly $125 million higher in 2005 than they would have been with the same reduction in emissions achieved without trading.

Has the program resulted in cost savings? According to Ellerman et al. (2000), it has. They find Phase I cost savings of from 33% to 67% over the non-trading alternative. The cost savings apparently resulted from switching to low-sulfur coal, falling prices of low-sulfur coal (due primarily to falling rail rates for transporting that coal), and technical change that reduced the cost of scrubbers. A subsequent study by Ellerman (2003) makes it clear that Phase II costs are estimated to be considerably lower as well. In addition to the above-mentioned factors responsible for lowering costs, additional savings resulted from the banking provisions, which provided plants with great flexibility in timing their reduction investments.

It is easy to understand how tradable emission allowances facilitate achieving the environmental goal at a lower cost. Achieving reductions of the magnitude envisioned by Congress would require some, but not all, utilities to adopt scrubbers. To force all older utilities to adopt scrubbers would be very expensive and unnecessary to achieve the desired reduction target. Yet it is politically and legally difficult under the traditional system to isolate only a few utilities to bear this additional burden for the greater good.

Emission allowance trading solves this problem by allowing some utilities to voluntarily accept greater control and by providing the proper incentive to ensure that some do. The emission standards are stringent enough that some utilities will have to choose scrubbers or another form of overcontrol. While all utilities will face similar, if not identical, allowable emissions standards, some utilities, presumably those for whom adopting scrubbers was the cheapest alternative, will voluntarily choose to install scrubbers. This action will automatically result in their exceeding their legal emission control requirements.

By purchasing sufficient allowances to satisfy their own emission standards when combined with any other additional control, the purchasing firms would eliminate the need to install scrubbers. Sufficient, but not excessive, control will result and market means of selecting those utilities to install scrubbers will have been provided. Significantly, emissions trading also provides a means of sharing the costs of installing scrubbers among all utilities. Those purchasing the emission allowances will, in effect, be subsidizing a portion of the selling firm's installation of the pollution control device. Rather than isolating a few utilities to bear a disproportionate share of the control burden or requiring all utilities to bear the excessive burden of overcontrol in a misguided pursuit of fairness, emission allowance trading promotes voluntary cost sharing. Fairness and efficiency can be compatible goals with the right choice of policy instruments.

Global Pollutants

Ozone Depletion

In the troposphere, the portion of the atmosphere closest to the earth, ozone (O_3) is a pollutant, and its presence has been linked to agricultural damage as well as to some adverse effects on human health. More will be said about this form of tropospheric pollution in the next chapter.

However, in the stratosphere, the portion of the atmosphere lying just above the troposphere, the small amounts of ozone present have a crucial positive role to play in determining the quality of life on the planet. In particular, by absorbing the ultraviolet wavelengths, stratospheric ozone shields people, plants, and animals from harmful radiation, and by absorbing infrared radiation, it is a factor in determining the earth's climate.

Chlorofluorocarbons (CFCs) have been implicated in depleting this stratospheric ozone shield as a result of a complicated series of chemical reactions. These highly stable chemical compounds are used as aerosol propellants and in cushioning foams, packaging and insulating foams, industrial cleaning of metals and electronics components, food freezing, medical instrument sterilization, refrigeration for homes and food stores, and air conditioning of automobiles and commercial buildings.

The major known effect of the increased ultraviolet radiation resulting from ozone depletion is an increase in nonmelanoma skin cancer. Other potential effects, such as an increase in the more serious melanoma form of skin cancer, suppression of human immunological systems, damage to plants, eye cancer in cattle, and an acceleration of degradation in certain polymer materials, are suspected, but are not as well established.

On June 30, 1978, the U.S. Environmental Protection Agency promulgated a regulation banning the manufacture, processing, and distribution of any "fully halogenated chlorofluoroalkane" for those aerosol propellant uses that are subject to the Toxic Substances Control Act (which is almost all aerosol uses) (45 FR 43721). This ban reduced the U.S. share from about one-half to about one-third of worldwide production. Nonetheless, worldwide release of the two principal chlorofluorocarbons—CFC-11 and CFC-12—continued to grow.

Since further progress on this issue was going to require instituting new controls on nonaerosol uses, a group of economists from the Rand Corporation was commissioned by the U.S. EPA to model the regulatory options (Palmer et al., 1980). The resulting study collected detailed information on the costs of controlling nonaerosol applications of these gases in the United States and constructed a 10-year simulation model to capture the effects of various regulatory approaches. Because chlorofluorocarbons accumulate in the atmosphere (they can remain in the atmosphere for approximately a century), the desired reductions were defined in cumulative terms over the 10-year period.

Three specific policies were considered in the analysis: (1) a system of emission standards for producers or users of these gases, which would force them to adopt specific technologies, (2) a constant-emissions charge of $0.50 (in real terms) per pound emitted over the 10 years, and (3) a marketable permit system. In the simulation model all of the approaches were constrained to yield roughly the same cumulative level of emission reduction (see Table 17.2).

Because this is an accumulating pollutant, the permits in this case would be designed to allow a one-time release, not a continuing flow as would be the case with permit systems designed to control more conventional pollutants. The holder of a permit would be entitled to emit a fixed quantity of CFCs any time during the 10-year period. By controlling the number of permits issued, the cumulative emission of CFCs would be controlled.

TABLE 17.2

Comparisons of Alternative Policies Having Similar Cumulative Emissions Reductions

	Emissions Reduction (millions of permit pounds)			Total Compliance Costs (millions of 1976 dollars)		
Policy Design	1980	1990	Cumulative 1980–1990	1980	1990	Cumulative 1980–1990[a]
Mandatory Controls	54.4	102.5	812.3	20.9	37.0	185.3
Economic Incentives						
Constant Charge[b]	54.8	96.9	816.9	12.3	21.8	107.8
Permit System[c]	36.6	119.4	806.1	5.2	35.0	94.7

[a]Present value of annual compliance costs, discounted at 11%.

[b]Based on a constant tax rate of $0.50 from 1980 through 1990 (in 1976 dollars).

[c]Based on permit price or emissions charge rising from $0.25 in 1980 to $0.71 in 1990.

Source: Palmer, Mooz, Quinn, and Wolf (p. 225, Table 4.7).

In this type of system, the price could be expected to rise over time as the remaining number of unused permits declined. Permit use would typically be high in the early years, while substitution options were being worked out, declining to zero at the end of the 10-year period.

Theory tells us that the constant-emission charge modeled in this study would not be fully cost-effective for this problem because the modeled charge does not rise over time. A constant real-emission charge will cause marginal costs to be equated within each period, a part of a cost-effective strategy, but it will fail to signal the increasing scarcity of the allowable CFCs over time, leading to a distorted temporal pattern of permit use. To be specific, since the constant charge has to yield approximately the same cumulative level of emissions reduction as the permit system, the constant-emission charge will be higher than the cost-effective charge in the earlier years and lower than the cost-effective charge in the later years. This, in turn, implies that the constant-charge system will allow too little emission in the earlier years and too much in the later years.

The superiority of the permit system can be seen in Table 17.2. It could produce approximately the same amount of reduction as the mandatory controls at about one-half the cost. The relationship of the constant charge to the permit system is exactly as theory would have us expect. Costs are higher for the charge in the earlier years (since less emission is allowed) and lower in the later years. Over the 10-year period the constant-charge system results in a higher present value of costs due to this intertemporal distortion, though the increase is only about 14%.

Responding to the ozone-depletion threat, 24 nations signed the Montreal Protocol during September 1988. According to this agreement, signatory nations were to restrict their production and consumption of the chief responsible gases to 50% of 1986 levels by June 30, 1998. Soon after the protocol was signed, new evidence suggested that it had not gone far enough; the damage was apparently increasing more rapidly than previously thought. In response, a series of new agreements that generally broadened the number of covered substances and established specific schedules for phasing out their production and use were ratified. Currently some 96-chemicals are presently controlled by these agreements to some degree.

Controlling ozone depletion is generally considered one of the success stories of international environmental agreements. Although industrialized countries recognized the importance of reducing their production and use of harmful chemicals, they also understood that global-scale action was required. To solicit the active participation of developing countries, the agreements included two key provisions: (1) later phase-out deadlines for developing countries and (2) the Multilateral Fund.

In 1990 the parties agreed to establish a Multilateral Fund to help developing countries meet phase-out requirements for chemicals covered by the Montreal Protocol. This Fund was designed to cover the incremental costs that developing countries incur as a result of taking action to eliminate the production and use of ozone-depleting chemicals. Contributions to the Multilateral Fund come from the industrialized countries. The Fund has been replenished five times: U.S. $240 million (1991–1993), U.S. $455 million (1994–1996), U.S. $466 million (1997–1999), and U.S. $440 million (2000–2002), and U.S. $474 million (2003–2005).

The Fund promotes technical change and facilitates the transfer of more environmentally safe products, materials, and equipment to developing countries. It offers developing countries that have ratified the agreement access to technical expertise, information on new replacement technologies, training, and demonstration projects, as well as financial assistance for projects to eliminate the use of ozone-depleting substances.

This particular approach, however, cannot get all the credit. The success of ozone protection has been possible in no small measure because producers were able to develop and commercialize alternatives to ozone-depleting chemicals. Developed countries ended the use of CFCs faster and with less cost than was originally anticipated due to the availability of these substitutes.

Though the agreements specify national phase-down targets, it is up to the countries to design policy measures to reach those targets. The United States has chosen to use a unique combination of product charges and tradable permits to control the production and consumption of ozone-depleting substances (Example 17.4). Most observers believe this combination has been very effective in encouraging the transition away from ozone-depleting substances.

What has been the effect of these agreements on global emissions and the ozone layer? A 2002 assessment panel found that the total combined effective abundance of ozone-depleting compounds in the lower atmosphere has continued to decline slowly from the peak that occurred in 1992–1994. Scientists predict that ozone depletion will reach its worst point during the next few years and then gradually decline until the ozone layer returns to normal around 2050, assuming that the existing agreements are fully implemented.

Climate Change

One class of global pollutants, greenhouse gases, absorb the long-wavelength (infrared) radiation from the earth's surface and atmosphere, trapping heat that would otherwise radiate into space. The mix and distribution of these gases within the atmosphere is in no small part responsible for both the hospitable climate on the earth and the inhospitable climate on other planets. Changing the mix of these gases can modify the climate.

Though carbon dioxide is the most abundant and the most studied of these greenhouse gases, many others have similar thermal radiation properties. These include the chlorofluorocarbons, nitrous oxide, methane, and tropospheric ozone. New evidence suggests that these gases may in the future be even more important in modifying climate than the more abundant CO_2.

The current concern over the effect of this class of pollutants on climate arises because emissions of these gases are increasing over time, changing their mix in the atmosphere. Evidence is mounting that by burning fossil fuels, leveling tropical forests, and injecting more of the other greenhouse gases into the atmosphere, humans are creating a thermal blanket capable of trapping enough heat to raise the temperature of the earth's surface.

The body charged with compiling and assessing the scientific information on climate change, the Intergovernmental Panel on Climate Change, reported its

Example *17.4*

TRADABLE PERMITS FOR OZONE-DEPLETING CHEMICALS

On August 12, 1988, the U.S. Environmental Protection Agency issued its first regulations implementing a tradable permit system to achieve the targeted reductions in ozone-depleting substances. According to these regulations, all major U.S. producers and consumers of the controlled substances were allocated baseline production or consumption allowances using 1986 levels as the basis for the proration. Each producer and consumer was allowed 100% of this baseline allowance initially, with smaller allowances being granted after predefined deadlines. Following the London conference, these percent-of-baseline allocations were reduced to reflect the new, earlier deadlines and lower limits.

These allowances were transferable within producer and consumer categories, and allowances could be transferred across international borders to producers in other signatory nations if the transaction is approved by the EPA and results in the appropriate adjustments in the buyer or seller allowances in their respective countries.

Production allowances can be augmented by demonstrating the safe destruction of an equivalent amount of controlled substances by approved means. Some interpollutant trading is even possible within categories of pollutants. (The categories are defined so as to group pollutants with similar environmental effects.) All information on trades is confidential (known only to the traders and regulators) so it is difficult to know how effective this program has been.

Since the demand for these allowances is quite inelastic, supply restrictions increase revenue. By allocating allowances to the seven major domestic producers of CFCs and halons, the EPA was concerned that its regulation would result in sizable windfall profits (estimated to be in the billions of dollars) for those producers. The EPA handled this problem by imposing a tax on production to soak up the rents created by the regulation-induced scarcity.

This application was unique in two senses. It not only allowed international trading of allowances, but it involved the simultaneous application of permit and tax systems. Taxes on production, when coupled with allowances, have the effect of lowering permit prices. The combined policy, however, is no less cost-effective than permits would be by themselves and it does allow the government to acquire some of the rent that would otherwise go to permit holders.

Source: Tom Tietenberg. "Design Lessons from Existing Air Pollution Control Systems: The United States," in S. Hanna and M. Munasinghe, eds. *Property Rights in a Social and Ecological Context: Case Studies and Design Applications* (Washington, DC: The World Bank, 1995): 15–32.

findings in 2001 on both the sources and likely outcomes of climate change.[2] They found that most of the warming observed over the last 50 years is attributable to human activity. With respect to projected climatic changes they found:

- The globally averaged surface temperature is projected to increase by 1.4° to 5.8°C over the period 1990 to 2100.

- The projected *rate* of warming is much larger than observed changes during the 20th century and is very likely to be without precedent during at least the last 10,000 years.

- Larger year-to-year variations in precipitation are very likely.

- Global mean sea level is projected to rise by 0.09 to 0.88 meter between 1990 and 2100 due primarily to the thermal expansion of the warmer water and the melting of glaciers and ice caps.

Recently scientists have also uncovered evidence to suggest that climate change may occur rather more abruptly than previously thought. Since the rate of temperature increase is a significant determinant of how well ecosystems can adapt to temperature change, this become a matter of some concern. Two examples that raise this concern are the methane trapped in the frozen tundra of the north and the ocean's thermohaline circulation system.

Large quantities of methane gas lie trapped in the frozen tundra. As temperatures warm, the tundra can thaw, releasing the trapped methane. Since methane is a powerful greenhouse gas, this release could accelerate the rate of warming.

Thermohaline circulation, known popularly as the ocean conveyer belt, involves flows of warm water near the surface from the southern hemisphere to the Norwegian Sea and deep-water return flows of cold water. The process that powers this circulation, the sinking of the colder water, is affected by the salinity of the surrounding ocean water. As climate change results in the melting of ice caps and glaciers, adding considerable amounts of freshwater to that part of the ocean, scientists believe that the resulting salinity changes could shut off the thermohaline circulation system. Shutting down this circulation system could result in a prolonged period of intense cold for northern Europe.

What are the likely impacts of this combination of rapidly rising temperatures, rising sea levels, and the potential for more frequent and more intense storms? Another working group of the Panel, tasked with the responsibility to find out, came to several conclusions:[3]

- Recent regional climate changes, particularly temperature increases, have already affected many physical and biological systems.

---

[2]The evidence in this section comes from IPCC. *Climate Change 2001: The Scientific Basis Contribution of Working Group I to the Third Assessment Report of the Intergovernmental Panel on Climate Change.* J. T. Houghton, Y. Ding, D. J. Griggs, M. Noguer, P. J. van der Linden, X. Dai, K. Maskell, and C. A. Johnson, eds. (Cambridge, UK: Cambridge University Press, 2001.)

[3]The evidence in this section comes from IPCC. *Climate Change 2001: Impacts, Adaptation, and Vulnerability. Contribution of Working Group II to the Third Assessment Report of the Intergovernmental Panel on Climate Change.* J. J. McCarthy, O. F. Canziani, N. A. Leary, D. J. Dokken, and K. S. White, eds. (Cambridge, UK: Cambridge University Press, 2001.)

- Natural systems (including coral reefs, mangroves, and tropical forests, among others) are vulnerable to climate change and some will be irreversibly damaged.

- Many human systems are sensitive to climate change and some are quite vulnerable. These systems include water availability, food security, human health, and coastal communities exposed to sea level rise and storm surges.

- Developing countries are expected to feel the most severe effects of climate since they have the fewest resources to commit to adaptation.

These threats pose a significant challenge to our economic and political institutions. Are they up to the challenge? The answer to that is not at all clear because there are significant barriers to any attempt to move toward a solution. Concepts developed earlier in the text can help us understand the nature of these barriers.

Any action taken to moderate climate change provides a global public good, implying the strong possibility of free-rider actions. (Those who do not control greenhouse gases cannot be prevented from reaping the benefits of the actions of those who do.) Free-rider effects not only inhibit participation in the climate-change agreements, they also inhibit the magnitude of corrective actions of participants. And unlike a normal marketed good, the scarcity of a stable, hospitable climate is not reflected in rising prices for that good.

To further complicate matters, the damage caused by greenhouse pollutants is an externality in both space and time. Spatially, the largest emitters (the industrialized nations) have the greatest capacity to reduce emissions, but they are not expected to experience as much damage from insufficient actions as the developing countries. Temporally, the costs of controlling greenhouse gases fall on current generations, while the benefits from controlling greenhouse gases occur well into the future, making it more difficult to convince members of the current generation to join the mitigation effort. The implication of these insights is that decentralized actions by markets and governments are likely to violate both the efficiency and sustainability criteria. International collective action is both necessary and terribly difficult.

What can be done? Four strategies have been considered: (1) climatic engineering, (2) adaptation, (3) mitigation, and (4) prevention. Climate engineering envisions taking actions such as shooting particulate matter into the atmosphere to provide compensating cooling. Adaptation refers to strategies that would allow us to function effectively with changed temperatures. Mitigation would attempt to moderate the temperature rise by strategies designed to increase the planetary capacity to absorb greenhouse gases. Prevention refers to strategies to reduce emissions of greenhouse gases. Since only the last two of these have received serious attention in public policy arenas, we focus on those.

The most significant prevention strategy deals with our use of fossil-fuel energy. Combustion of fossil-fuel energy results in the creation of carbon dioxide. Carbon dioxide emissions can be reduced either by using less energy or by using alternative energy sources (such as wind, photovoltaics, or hydro) that produce no carbon dioxide. Any serious reduction in carbon dioxide emissions would involve dramatic changes in our energy consumption patterns and have a high economic cost. Thus, the debate over how vigorously this strategy is to be followed is a controversial public policy issue.

Should Carbon Sequestration Be Credited?

Both forests and soils sequester (store) a significant amount of carbon. Research suggests that with appropriate changes in practices, they could store much more. Increased carbon sequestration in turn would mean less carbon in the atmosphere. Recognizing this potential has created a strong push in climate-change negotiations to give credit for actions that result in more carbon uptake by soils and forests. Whether that should be allowed and, if so, how it would be done are currently being heavily debated.

Proponents argue that carbon sequestration strategies typically are quite cost-effective. Cost-effectiveness not only implies that the given goal can be achieved at lower cost, but it also may increase the willingness of those who have to pay the costs to accept more stringent goals with closer deadlines. Allowing credit for carbon absorption may also add economic value to sustainable practices (such as limiting deforestation or preventing soil erosion), thereby providing additional incentives for those practices. Proponents further point out that many of the prime beneficiaries of this increase in value would be the poorest people in the poorest countries.

Opponents point out that our knowledge of the science of carbon sequestration is in its infancy, so how much credit should be granted is not at all clear. Obtaining estimates of the amount of carbon sequestered could be both expensive (if done right) and subject to considerable uncertainty. Because carbon absorption could be easily reversed at any time (by cutting down trees or changing agricultural practices), continual monitoring and enforcement would be required, adding even more cost. Even in carefully enforced systems, the sequestration is likely to be temporary (the carbon in completely preserved forests, for example, may ultimately be released to the atmosphere by decay). And finally, the practices that may be encouraged by crediting sequestration will not necessarily be desirable, as when slow-growing old-growth forests are cut down and replaced with fast-growing plantation forests in order to increase the amount of carbon uptake.

Another possible strategy involves encouraging activities that allow more carbon to be absorbed by trees or soils. As Debate 17.1 points out, however, the desirability of this approach is being heavily debated in current climate change negotiations.

Negotiations Over Climate-Change Policy Options.   Early in climate-change negotiations it became clear that cost-effective strategies were a priority. For reasons explained in Chapter 15, the policy choices quickly narrowed down to emissions charges and emissions trading. In general, Europe tended to favor emissions charges, while the United States preferred emissions trading.

Emissions charges could be particularly simple in the climate-change case. Because greenhouse gases are uniformly mixed pollutants, a uniform per-unit charge imposed on all emission sources would be cost-effective. And emissions charges could be expected not only to encourage new, more environmentally benign technologies, but also to raise significant revenue.

Concerns about emissions charges also arose, however, when it became clear that the amount of revenue collected from these taxes would be very large. The concept of taxes imposed by some international authority (who would then have control over all that revenue) was soon replaced by a concept relying on harmonized national taxes where the revenue would stay in the nation that collected it. Nations were not the only ones concerned about the magnitude of tax revenues; firms that would pay them were also concerned about the financial burden those taxes would impose. Simply knowing that the revenue would be kept by their national governments was generally not enough to overcome these concerns.

Concerns over the magnitude and distribution of the revenue were soon joined by concerns over the consequences of participating in a system that taxed only some of the parties. The United States made it clear that it was very reluctant to go along with emission charges. And developing countries would likely not be asked to bear these charges, at least in the early years of control. A system of partial taxation could lead both to leakage (offsetting greenhouse gas emissions from nonparticipating countries) and to significant competitiveness issues.

Leakage can occur when taxed producers try to pass on their additional costs to consumers. If consumers have the choice of importing products from producers in nations with no emissions charges, they are inclined to favor those imports over domestic (taxed) products because they are likely to cost less. Meanwhile, producers in the taxed nations, noticing their market share being eroded by competitors in the untaxed nations, have an incentive to shift their production facilities to the untaxed nations to take advantage of the lower costs. Ultimately, not only could the taxed nations lose production and jobs, but total greenhouse gases could even increase if the reduction in the taxed nations is more than offset by increases in the untaxed nations.

So the emphasis began to shift toward emission trading. In one of the interesting ironies of climate-change policy, the Kyoto Protocol, the main international agreement controlling greenhouse gases, specifically incorporates emission trading, but its prime proponent, the United States, has, by its failure to ratify the agreement, lost its right to participate in the design, evolution, and use of that system.

International Agreements on Climate Change.   The 1992 United Nations Framework Convention on Climate Change (UNFCCC) recognized the principle of global cost-effectiveness of emission reduction and thus opened the way for flexibility. As this early agreement did not fix a binding emission target for any country, however, the need to invest in emission reduction either at home or abroad was not pressing.

In December 1997, though, industrial countries and countries with economies in transition (primarily the former Soviet Republics) agreed to legally binding emission targets at the Kyoto Conference and negotiated a legal framework as a protocol to the UNFCCC-the Kyoto Protocol. This Protocol became effective in February 2005 once at least 55 parties representing at least 55% of the total carbon dioxide (CO_2) emissions had ratified. Russia's ratification put them over the 55% total; the 55-country total had been reached much earlier.

The Kyoto Protocol defines a five-year commitment period (2008–2012) for meeting the individual country emission targets, called "assigned amount obligations," set out in Annex B of the Protocol. Quantified country targets are defined by multiplying the country's 1990 emission level by a reduction factor and multiplying that number by 5 (to cover the five-year commitment period). Collectively, if fulfilled, these targets would represent a 5% reduction in annual average emissions below 1990 levels. The actual compliance target is defined as a weighted average of six greenhouse gases: carbon dioxide, methane, nitrous oxide, HFCs, PFCs, and sulfur hexafluoride. Defining the target in terms of this multigas index, rather than just carbon dioxide, has been estimated to reduce compliance costs by some 22% (Reilly et al., 2002).

The Kyoto Protocol authorizes three cooperative implementation mechanisms that involve tradable permits. These include Emission Trading, Joint Implementation, and the Clean Development Mechanism.

- "Emissions Trading" (ET) allows trading of "assigned amounts" (the national quotas established by the Kyoto Protocol) among countries listed in Annex B of the Kyoto Protocol, primarily the industrialized national and the economics in transition.

- Under "Joint Implementation" (JI) Annex B Parties can receive emissions reduction credit when they help to finance specific projects that reduce net emissions in another Annex B Party country. This "project-based" program is designed to exploit opportunities in Annex B countries that have not yet become fully eligible to engage in the ET program described above.

- The "Clean Development Mechanism" (CDM) enables Annex B Parties to finance emission reduction projects in non-Annex B Parties (primarily developing countries) and receive certified emission reductions (CERs) for doing so. These CERs can be used to fulfill "assigned amount" obligations.

These programs have, in turn, spawned others. Individual companies are even involved. BP, an energy company, has established company-wide goals and an intra-company trading program to help individual units within the company meet those goals. Despite the fact that the United States has not signed the Kyoto Protocol, even American companies, states, and municipalities have accepted voluntary caps on CO_2 and methane emissions and are using trading to facilitate meeting those goals. The Chicago Climate Exchange has been set up to facilitate these trades.

The largest and most important of these is the permit trading system developed by the European Union to facilitate implementation of the Kyoto Protocol (Example 17.5).

While the emissions trading mechanism is the driving force behind the suite of cooperative mechanisms, the CDM provides a means for motivating industrialized countries (or individual companies) to invest in projects in developing countries that result in reductions of greenhouse gases. The incentive to invest is provided by the fact that investors can receive credit for the reductions that are "additional" to reductions that would have been achieved otherwise. Once verified and certified, these credits can then be used as one means of meeting the investor's assigned amount of obligations. The incentive for the host developing countries to participate comes

Example 17.5

THE EUROPEAN EMISSIONS TRADING SYSTEM (EU ETS)

The EU ETS applies to 25 countries, including the 10 "accession" countries, most of which are former members of the Soviet bloc. The first phase, which will run from 2005 through 2007, is considered to be a trial phase. The second phase coincides with the first Kyoto commitment period, beginning in 2008 and continuing through 2012. Subsequent negotiations will specify the details of future phases.

Initially, the program will cover only carbon dioxide (CO_2) emissions from four broad sectors: iron and steel, minerals, energy, and pulp and paper. All installations in these sectors larger than established thresholds are included in the program. More than 12,000 installations are expected to be covered by the program, making it the largest emission trading program ever established.

Individual countries determine the initial allocation by deciding first, how much of the predefined national cap should be allocated to each of these sectors, and second, how much of each sector cap should be allocated to each of the installations in that sector. Making these initial allocations turned out to be a very controversial process because it meant that competitors in different European countries could end up with quite different allocations (and therefore different costs of compliance).

Though this allocation scheme provides installations with the permits free of charge, in the future, permit auctions may be held. Countries will be allowed to choose to auction up to 5% of allowances in the first phase of the program and up to 10% in the second phase.

Countries can use emission reductions acquired from outside the European Union (via the JI or CDM mechanisms) to meet their obligations under the EU ETS. Estimates by Criqui and Kitous (2003) indicate that allowing unrestricted trades should reduce compliance cost by about 24%.

Sources: J. A. Kruger and William A. Pizer. "Greenhouse Gas Trading in Europe: The New Grand Policy Experiment," *Environment* Vol. 46, No. 8 (2004): 8–23 and P. Criqui and A. Kitous. *Kyoto Protocol Implementation: (KPI) Technical Report: Impacts of Linking JI and CDM Credits to the European Emissions Allowance Trading Scheme,* CNRS-IEPE and ENERDATA S.A. for Directorate General Environment, Service Contract No. B4-3040/2001/330760/MAR/E1 (2003) as cited in Kruger and Pizer (2004, Table 2).

from the fact that many of these projects increase productivity while reducing emissions. Projects that replace old coal-burning power plants with facilities based on photovoltaics or natural gas illustrate the point.

Complementary Strategies.   Given the problems associated with identifying promising projects, quantifying the magnitude of the reductions, and monitoring the results, some means of reducing those barriers was clearly called for. In response, the Prototype Carbon Fund (PCF) was established in 1999 by the World Bank to serve as an intermediary for encouraging CDM reductions in greenhouse gases. The PCF, which acts as a kind of greenhouse gas mutual fund, invests contributions made by companies and governments in projects designed to produce emission reductions that are consistent with the Kyoto Protocol. Investors in the PCF receive a pro rata share of the emission reductions. These reductions are verified and certified in accordance with agreements reached with the respective countries hosting the projects.

Another complementary agency, the Global Environmental Facility (GEF), has begun to play an important role in funding deserving projects. Drawing from a Global Environmental Trust Fund, funded by direct contributions from some 26 countries, the GEF provides loans and grants to projects that have a global impact, including projects that reduce climate change. The GEF uses a "marginal external-cost rule" to determine the suitability of projects and the amount of funding provided.

Recognizing that many projects have benefits that flow beyond national borders, and that individual nations are unlikely to consider those global benefits, the GEF picks up the costs that cannot be justified domestically but could be justified internationally. For example, suppose building a coal-fired power plant is the cheapest way for China to provide electricity to its people, but a slightly more expensive wind power plant would result in substantially lower carbon dioxide emissions. Since the benefits from lower carbon dioxide emissions are largely global, not national, China has little incentive to consider them in its decision; the coal-fired plant would be chosen. By picking up the extra cost for the wind facility, the GEF can increase the attractiveness of the alternative facility and thereby ensure that China's decision makes sense globally as well as nationally.

The Case for Emissions Trading.   The case for an emissions trading system is based upon the advantages it would offer compared to other politically feasible alternatives. In the short run, as illustrated by Example 17.5, it offers the possibility of reaching the environmental goals at a lower cost than would be possible if each country were limited to reduction options within its own borders. The Intergovernmental Panel on Climate Change reviewed a host of studies to find out what difference emissions trading would make on costs. They concluded:

> In the absence of emissions trading between Annex B countries, the majority of global studies show reductions in projected GDP of about 0.2% to 2% in 2010 for different . . . regions. With full emissions trading between Annex B countries, the estimated reductions in 2010 are between 0.1% and 1.1% of projected GDP. (p. 10)

It is worth noting that these studies predict that the effect of controlling climate change is to slow growth, not to stop or reverse it. As Azar and Schnieder (2002) point out, one way to contextualize the cost of stabilizing emissions in the 350–550 ppm range is to recognize that it involves a delay of from one to three years in reaching the new, higher-wealth level.

In the long run, the cost of control will depend crucially on the extent to which innovative approaches to climate-change control are developed and implemented. By providing each nation with an economic incentive to go beyond its assigned reduction (thereby creating a demand for additional cost-effective strategies), emission trading facilitates technological change. By offering greater flexibility in how the emission reductions are achieved (as well as by providing economic incentives for the adoption and use of unconventional approaches), emission trading can significantly lower the long-run cost. Lower long-run cost may be an important element in gaining greater international acceptance of the idea of limits and reducing the difficulties associated with ensuring compliance.

Because it separates the issue of who pays for control from who implements control, emission trading facilitates transboundary cost sharing (an item of particular importance to both the developing countries and the transition economies of Eastern Europe) and facilitates the mobilization of private capital for controlling climate change. Private capital is likely to be a critically important component of any effective climate-change strategy as long as public capital remains insufficient to do it alone.

Controversies.
However, emission trading is not without its problems. In Debate 17.1 we explored the issues associated with allowing carbon sequestration credits to be certified as tradable allowances. Other controversies range from such fundamental issues as the morality of global emissions trading (Debate 17.2) to concerns about weaknesses in the implementation details.

Perceived implementation deficiencies also come in for their share of concern. First, greenhouse gas emission trading will only achieve the goals of the Protocol if monitoring and enforcement is adequate. Monitoring and enforcing international agreements is much more difficult than enforcing domestic laws and regulations. Effective monitoring and enforcement in this international context is far from a foregone conclusion. Second, due to the way the goals of the Protocol were specified, some countries (specifically Russia and the Ukraine) find themselves with a considerable number of "unearned" surplus allowances to sell. (Since Protocol requirements are defined in terms of 1990 emissions levels and emissions in these countries have fallen below those levels due to the depressed state of their economies, the difference, known popularly as "hot air," can be traded to other countries.) The presence of these surplus allowances naturally lowers prices and allows countries to undertake less domestic abatement than would otherwise have been necessary.

The Timing of Policy.
How large should current investments in greenhouse gas reduction be? In order to answer this question, we must first discover just how serious the problem is and then ascertain the costs of being wrong, either by acting too hastily or by procrastinating. Because rampant uncertainties attend virtually every link in the logical chain from human activities to subsequent consequences, we cannot at this juncture state unequivocally how serious the damage will be.

Is Global Greenhouse Gas Trading Immoral?

In a December 1997 editorial in the *New York Times,* Michael Sandel, a Harvard government professor, suggested that greenhouse gas trading is immoral. The crux of his argument is that treating pollution as a commodity to be bought and sold not only removes the moral stigma that is appropriately associated with it, but trading reductions undermines an important sense of shared responsibilities that global cooperation requires. He illustrated the point by suggesting that legitimizing further emission by offsetting it with a credit acquired from a project in a poorer nation would be very different from penalizing the firm for emitting, even if the cost of the permit were equal to the penalty. Not only would the now-authorized emission become inappropriately "socially acceptable," but the wealthier nation would have met its moral obligation by paying a poorer nation to fulfill a responsibility that should have been fulfilled by a domestic emission reduction.

Published responses to this editorial countered with several points. First, it was pointed out that since it is voluntary, international emissions trading typically benefits both nations; one nation is not imposing its will on another. Second, the historical use of these programs has resulted in much cleaner air at a much lower cost than would otherwise have been possible, so the ends would seem to justify the means. Third, with few exceptions, virtually all pollution control regulations allow some emission that is not penalized; this is simply a recognition that zero pollution is rarely either efficient or politically feasible.

Source: Michael J. Sandel. "It's Immoral to Buy the Right to Pollute" with replies by Steven Shavell, Robert Stavins, Sanford Gaines, and Eric Maskin from the December 17, 1997, *New York Times,* excerpts reprinted in Robert N. Stavins, ed. *Economics of the Environment: Selected Readings,* 4th ed. (New York: W. W. Norton & Company, 2000): 449–452.

We can, however, begin to elaborate the range of possibilities and see how sensitive the outcomes are to the choices before us.

Benefit/cost studies of options for controlling climate change that ignore uncertainties in the state of our knowledge typically suggest a "go slow" or "wait-and-see" policy. The reasons for these results are instructive. First, the benefits from current control are experienced well into the future, while the costs occur now. The present-value criterion in benefit/cost analysis discounts future values more than current values. Second, both energy-using and energy-producing capital are long-lived. Replacing them all at an accelerated pace now would be more expensive than replacing them over time closer to the end of their useful lives. Third, the models anticipate that the number of new emissions reducing technologies would be larger in the future and, due to this larger menu of options, the costs of reduction would be lower with delay.

The use of benefit/cost analysis based upon the present-value criterion in climate-change discussion is controversial. Though this approach is not inherently biased against future generations, their interests will only be adequately protected if they are adequately compensated for the damage inflicted on them. Because it is not obvious that any material compensation supplied by growth would be adequate, the long lead times associated with this particular problem place the interests of future generations in maintaining a stable climate in jeopardy, raising an important ethical concern (Portney and Weyant, 1999).

The other reasons have economic merit, but they do not imply a "wait-and-see" policy. Spreading the capital investment decisions over time assumes that some of them take place now as current capital is replaced. Further, the expectation that future technical change can reduce costs will only be fulfilled if the incentives for producing the technical change are in place now. In both cases, waiting simply postpones their start.

Another powerful consideration in the debate over the timing of control investments involves uncertainty about both the costs and the benefits of climate change. Governments must act without complete knowledge. How can they respond reasonably to this uncertainty?

The risks of being wrong are clearly asymmetric. If it turns out that we controlled more than we must, current generations would bear a larger-than-necessary cost. On the other hand, if the problem turns out to be as serious as the worst predictions indicate, catastrophic and largely irreversible damage to the planet could be inflicted on future generations.

Yohe, Andronova, and Schlesinger (2004) investigate both consequences of being wrong using a standard, well-respected global climate model. Their model assumes that decision-makers choose global mitigation policies in 2005 that will be in effect for 30 years, but that in 2035 policy-makers would be able to modify the policies to take into account the better understanding of climate change consequences that would have afforded by the intervening 30 years. The specific source of uncertainty in their model results from our imperfect knowledge about the relationship between the atmospheric greenhouse gas concentrations and the resulting increase in temperature. The specific question they examine is, "What is the best strategy now?"

They find that a hedging strategy that involves modest reductions now dominates a "wait-and-see" strategy. Not only does current action initiate the capital turnover process and provide incentives for technical change, but it allows the avoidance of very costly and potentially irreversible mistakes later. Since emissions from the "wait-and-see" strategy would be much higher by 2035, the reductions necessary to meet a given concentration target would have to be larger and concentrated within a smaller period of time. If in 2035, for example, scientists discover the need to stabilize the greenhouse gas concentration target at a specific level to avoid exceeding important thresholds (such as the thermohaline circulation or methane examples discussed above), that may not only be much more difficult and much more expensive to do later, but it may be impossible.

Creating Incentives for Participation in Climate-Change Agreements.
Since ratifying the climate-change agreement is a voluntary act, the branch of economics known as game theory has been used to study what mechanisms can be used to encourage participation in light of the serious public-good problems created by the fact that free riders cannot be excluded from the benefits of those who join the agreement (Barrett, 1990). This is important work because it suggests that the

free-rider problem is not necessarily a fatal flaw in the search for solutions to the climate-change problem (Carraro, 2002).

One strategy that we have already discussed relies upon the use of cost-effective policies. Since cost-effective policies reduce the cost, but not the benefits, of participation, those policies should make participation more likely by increasing the net benefits from participation.

Another strategy involves "issue linkage" in which countries simultaneously negotiate a climate-change agreement and a linked economic agreement. Typical candidates for linkage are agreements on trade liberalization, cooperation on research and development (R&D), or international debt. The intuition behind this approach is that some countries gain from resolving the first issue, while others gain from the second. Linking the two issues increases the chances that cooperation may result in profitable participation in both and, hence, increases the incentives to join the coalition of those ratifying the climate-change agreement.

To understand how this works, consider a research-and-development example from Cararro (2002). To counteract the incentive to free ride on the benefits from climate change, suppose only ratifiers of both agreements share in the insights gained from research and development in the ratifying countries. The fact that this benefit can only be obtained by ratifying the climate-change agreement as well as the R&D agreement provides an incentive to ratify both. Since those nations choosing not to ratify can be excluded from the research-and-development benefits, to obtain those benefits, they would have to join the agreement.

Another strategy for encouraging participation involves transfers from the gainers to the losers. Some countries have more to gain from an effective agreement than others. If the gainers were willing to share some of those gains with reluctant nations who have more to lose, the reluctant nations could be encouraged to join. Some interesting work (Chandler and Tulkens, 1997) has shown that it is possible to define a specific set of transfers such that each country is better off participating than not participating. That is a powerful, comforting result.

Summary

Regional pollutants differ from local pollutants chiefly in the distance they are transported in the air. Whereas local pollutants damage the environment near the emission site, regional pollutants can cause damage far from the site of emission. Some substances, such as sulfur oxides, nitrogen oxides, and ozone, are both local and regional pollutants.

As the zone of influence of pollutants extends beyond local boundaries, the political difficulties of implementing comprehensive, cost-effective control measures increase. Pollutants crossing political boundaries impose external costs; neither the emitters nor the nations within which they emit have the proper incentives to institute efficient control measures.

Acid rain is a case in point. Sulfate and nitrate deposition has caused problems both between regions within countries and between countries. In the United States, until 1990 the Clean Air Act had had a distinctly local focus. To control local pollution problems, state governments required the installation of tall stacks to dilute the pollution before it hit the ground level. In the process, a high proportion of the emissions were exported to other areas, reaching the ground hundreds of miles from the point of injection. A focus on local control made the regional problem worse.

Finding solutions to the acid-rain problem has been very difficult because those bearing the costs of further control are not those who will benefit from the control. In the United States, for example, opposition from the Midwestern and Appalachian states had delayed action on acid-rain legislation. Stumbling blocks included the higher electricity prices that would result from the control and the employment impacts on those states that would suffer losses of jobs in the high-sulfur coal-mining industry.

These barriers were overcome by the 1990 Clean Air Act Amendments, which instituted the sulfur allowance program. This program placed a cap on total emissions from the utility sector for the first time and implemented a cost-effective way of reducing emissions to the level specified by the cap.

Ozone-depleting gases, the first of the discussed global pollutants, are a problem because they have been implicated in the destruction of the stratospheric ozone shield that protects the earth's surface from harmful ultraviolet radiation. Because this is an accumulating pollutant, an efficient response to this problem would involve reducing use over time. In principle, this could be accomplished by either an emission charge that rises over time or a permit system that allows a fixed amount of emissions.

Preimplementation studies of nonaerosol uses of CFCs, the primary ozone-depleting gases, found that economic incentive approaches such as these could achieve the emission target at about one-half the cost of regulatory standards. These studies also indicated, however, that emission charges would impose large additional financial burdens on the emitters. (The emission charge payments on uncontrolled emissions would be 15 times as large as the payments for controlling the pollution.) To restrict their accumulation in the atmosphere, the international agreements on ozone-depleting substances created a system of limits on their production and consumption. As part of its obligation under the agreements, the United States has adopted a transferable allowance system, coupled with a tax on the additional profits generated by restricting the supply of allowances. Internationally, this agreement is considered a success in no small part because the Multilateral Fund and other incentives, such as delayed compliance deadlines, facilitated the participation of developing countries.

Climate change is appropriately considered a more difficult problem to solve. In addition to the features it shares with ozone depletion, such as the free-rider problem and the fact that the current generation bears the costs while the benefits accrue in the future, climate change presents some unique challenges. Some countries, for example, may be benefited, not harmed, by climate change, diminishing even further their incentive to control. And in contrast to ozone-depleting substances, which had readily available substitutes, controlling greenhouse gases means controlling energy use from fossil fuels, the lynchpin of modern society.

Fortunately, economic analysis of the climate-change problem not only defines the need for action, but also sheds light on effective forms that action might take. The empirical studies suggest that it makes sense to take action now to reduce emissions of greenhouse gases in order to provide insurance against the adverse, possibly irreversible consequences if the damage turns out to be higher than anticipated. Though policies in the Kyoto Protocol such as the emissions trading program, joint implementation, and the clean development mechanism use basic economic concepts to forge practical, cost-effective means of controlling climate change, we have also seen that the implementation details matter.

Economics also sheds light on both the barriers to effective participation in climate-change agreements and some potential solutions as well. The free-rider effect is a significant barrier to participation, but strategies that flow from game theory (such as international transfers and issue linkage) can be used to build incentives for participation. Some international cost sharing is likely to be as necessary an ingredient in a successful attack on the climate problem as it was in the ozone-depletion case.

During the next few decades, options must not only be preserved, they must be enhanced. Responding in a timely and effective fashion to global and regional pollution problems will not be easy. Our political institutions are not configured in such a way as to make decision-making on a global scale simple. International organizations exist at the pleasure of the nations they serve. Only time will tell if the mechanisms of international agreements described in this chapter will prove equal to the task.

Problems

1. Explain why an acid rain policy using emissions charge revenue to provide capital and operating subsidies for scrubbers is less cost-effective than an emission charge policy alone.

2. The transfer costs associated with an emissions charge approach to controlling chlorofluorocarbon pollution are unusually large in comparison to other pollutants. What circumstances would lead to high transfer costs?

Further Reading

OECD. *Climate Change: Designing a Practical Tax System* (Paris: OECD, 1992). Fourteen essays grappling with the practical issues associated with designing a tax-based approach for controlling global warming.

OECD. *Climate Change: Designing a Tradeable Permit System* (Paris: OECD, 1992). Eleven essays grappling with the practical issues associated with designing a permit-based approach for controlling global warming.

Tietenberg, T., ed. *The Economics of Global Warming.* The International Library of Critical Writings in Economics (Cheltenham, UK: Edward Elgar Publishing Limited, 1997). A collection of 31 essays dealing with all economic aspects of policies to control climate change.

Van Ierland, Ekko, ed. *International Environmental Economics* (Amsterdam: Elsevier, 1994). Contains five essays on the economics of climate change.

Additional References is available on this book's companion Web site www.aw-bc.com/tietenberg.

Chapter 18

Mobile-Source Air Pollution

*There are two things you shouldn't watch being made,
sausage and law.*

—Anonymous

Introduction

Though they emit many of the same pollutants as stationary sources, mobile sources require a different policy approach. These differences arise from the mobility of the source, the number of vehicles involved, and the role of the automobile in the modern lifestyle.

Mobility has two major impacts on policy. On the one hand, pollution is partly caused by the temporary location of the source—a case of being in the wrong place at the wrong time. This occurs, for example, during rush hour in metropolitan areas. Since the cars have to be where the people are, relocating them—as might be done with electric power plants—is not a viable strategy. On the other hand, it is more difficult to tailor vehicle emission rates to local pollution patterns, since any particular vehicle may end up in many different urban and rural areas during the course of its useful life.

Mobile sources are also more numerous than stationary sources. In the United States, for example, while there are approximately 27,000 major stationary sources, well over 100 million vehicles travel on American roadways. Enforcement is obviously more difficult as the number of sources being controlled increases.

Where stationary sources generally are large and run by professional managers, automobiles are small and run by amateurs. Their small size makes it more difficult to control emissions without affecting performance, while amateur ownership makes it more likely that emission control will deteriorate over time due to a lack of dependable maintenance and care.

These complications might lead us to conclude that perhaps we should ignore mobile sources and concentrate our control efforts solely on stationary sources. Unfortunately, that is not possible. Though each individual vehicle represents a miniscule part of the problem, mobile sources collectively represent a significant proportion of three criteria pollutants—ozone, carbon monoxide, and nitrogen dioxide as well as a significant source of greenhouse gases.

For two of these—ozone and nitrogen dioxide—the process of reaching attainment has been particularly slow. With the increased use of diesel engines, mobile sources are becoming responsible for a rising proportion of particulate emissions, and vehicles that burn leaded gasoline were, until legislation changed the situation, a major source of airborne lead.

Since it is necessary to control mobile sources, what policy options exist? What points of control are possible and what are the advantages or disadvantages of each? In exercising control over these sources, the government must first specify the agent charged with the responsibility for the reduction. The obvious candidates are the manufacturer and the owner-driver. The balancing of this responsibility should depend on a comparative analysis of costs and benefits, with particular reference to such factors as (1) the number of agents to be regulated; (2) the rate of deterioration while in use; (3) the life expectancy of automobiles; and (4) the availability, effectiveness, and cost of programs to reduce emissions at the point of production and at the point of use.

Although automobiles are numerous and ubiquitous, they are manufactured by a small number of firms. Since it is easier and less expensive to administer a system that controls relatively few sources, regulation at the point of production has considerable appeal.

Some problems are associated with limiting controls solely to the point of production, however. If the factory-controlled emission rate deteriorates during normal usage, control at the point of production may buy only temporary emission reduction. Though the deterioration of emission control can be combated with warranty and recall provisions, the costs of these supporting programs have to be balanced against the costs of local control.

Since automobiles are durable, new vehicles make up only a relatively small percentage of the total fleet of vehicles. Therefore, control at the point of production, which affects only new equipment, takes longer to produce a given reduction in aggregate emissions since newer, controlled cars replace old vehicles very slowly. Control at the point of production produces emission reductions more slowly than a program securing emission reductions from used as well as new vehicles.

Some possible means of reducing mobile-source pollution cannot be accomplished by regulating emissions at the point of production because they involve choices made by the owner-driver. The point of production strategy is oriented toward reducing the amount of emissions per mile driven in a particular type of car, but only the owner can decide what kind of car to drive, as well as when and where to drive it.

These are not trivial concerns. Diesel and hybrid automobiles, buses, trucks, and motorcycles emit rather different amounts of pollutants than do standard gasoline-powered automobiles. Changing the mix of vehicles on the road affects the amount and type of emissions even if passenger miles are not changed.

Where and when the car is driven is also important. Since clustered emissions cause higher concentration levels than dispersed emissions, driving in urban areas causes more environmental damage than driving in rural areas. Local control strategies could internalize these location costs, while a uniform national strategy focusing solely on the point of production could not.

Timing of emissions is particularly important because conventional commuting patterns lead to a clustering of emissions during the morning and evening rush hours. Indeed, plots of pollutant concentrations in urban areas during an average day typically produce a graph with two peaks corresponding to the two rush hours.[1] Since high concentrations are more dangerous than low concentrations, some spreading over the 24-hour period could also prove beneficial.

The Economics of Mobile-Source Pollution

Vehicles emit an inefficiently high level of pollution because their owner-drivers are not bearing the full cost of that pollution. This inefficiently low cost, in turn, has two sources: (1) implicit subsidies for road transport and (2) a failure to internalize external costs.

Implicit Subsidies

Several categories of the social costs associated with transporting goods and people over roads are related to mileage driven, but the private costs do not reflect that relationship. For example:

- Road construction and maintenance costs, which are largely determined by vehicle miles, are mostly funded out of tax dollars; the marginal private cost of an extra mile driven on road construction and maintenance is zero, though the social cost is not.

- Despite the fact that building and maintaining parking space is expensive, parking is frequently supplied by employers at no marginal cost to the employee. The ability to park a car for free creates a bias toward private auto travel since other modes receive no comparable subsidy.

Externalities

Road users also fail to bear the full cost of their choices because many of the costs associated with those choices are actually borne by others. For example:

- The social costs associated with accidents are a function of vehicle miles. The number of accidents rises as the number of miles driven rises. Generally the costs associated with these accidents are paid for by insurance, but the premiums for these insurance policies rarely reflect the mileage-accident relationship. As a result the additional private cost of insurance for additional miles driven is typically zero, though the social cost is certainly not zero.

- Road congestion creates externalities by increasing the amount of time required to travel a given distance.

- Recent studies have indicated high levels of pollution inside vehicles, caused mainly by the exhaust of cars in front.

---

[1]The exception is ozone formed by a chemical reaction involving hydrocarbons and nitrogen oxides in the presence of sunlight. Since, for the evening rush-hour emissions, too few hours of sunlight remain for the chemical reactions to be completed, graphs of daily ozone concentrations frequently exhibit a single peak.

FIGURE 18.1

Congestion Inefficiency

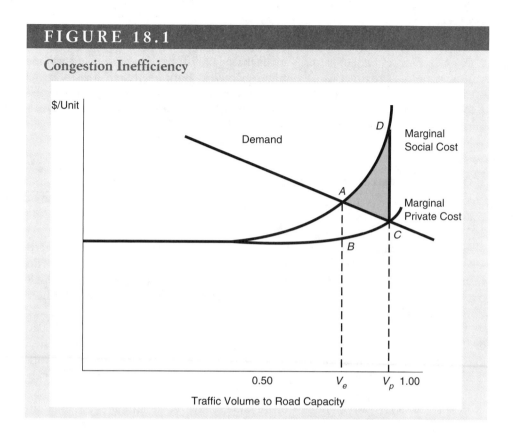

To elaborate on the congestion point, consider Figure 18.1. As traffic volumes get closer to the design capacity of the roadway, traffic flow decreases; it takes more time to travel between two points. At this point, the marginal and private social costs begin to diverge. While the driver entering a congested roadway will certainly consider the extra time it will take her to travel that route, she will not consider the extra time that her presence imposes on everyone else; it is an externality.

The efficient ratio of traffic volume to road capacity (V_e) occurs where the marginal benefits (as revealed by the demand curve) equal the marginal social cost. Because individual drivers do not internalize the external costs of their presence on this roadway, too many drivers will use the roadway and traffic volume will be too high (V_p). The resulting efficiency losses would be measured by the triangle ACD (the shaded area).

Consequences

Understated road transport costs create a number of perverse incentives. Too many vehicles use the roads. Too many miles are driven. Too many trips are taken. Transport energy use is too high. Pollution from transportation is excessive. Competitive modes, including mass transit, bicycles, and walking, all suffer from an inefficiently low demand.

Perhaps the most pernicious effect of understated transport cost, however, is its effect on land use. Low transport cost encourages dispersed settlement patterns.

Residences can be located far from work and shopping because the costs of travel are so low. Unfortunately, this pattern of dispersal creates a path dependence that is hard to reverse. Once settlement patterns are dispersed, it is difficult to justify high-volume transportation alternatives (such as trains or buses). Both need high-density travel corridors in order to generate the ridership necessary to pay the high fixed cost associated with building and running these systems. With dispersed settlement patterns, sufficiently high travel densities are difficult, if not impossible, to generate.

Policy Toward Mobile Sources

History

Concern about mobile-source pollution originated in Southern California in the early 1950s following a path-breaking study by Dr. A. J. Haagen-Smit of the California Institute of Technology. The study by Dr. Haagen-Smit identified motor vehicle emissions as a key culprit in forming the photochemical smog for which Southern California was becoming infamous.

In the United States, the Clean Air Act Amendments of 1965 set national standards for hydrocarbon and carbon monoxide emissions from automobiles to take effect during 1968. Interestingly, the impetus for this act came not only from the scientific data on the effects of automobile pollution, but also from the automobile industry itself. The industry saw uniform federal standards as a way to avoid a situation in which every state passed its own unique set of emission standards, something the auto industry wanted to avoid. This pressure was successful in that the law prohibits all states except California from setting their own standards.

By 1970 the slow progress being made on air pollution control in general and automobile pollution in particular created the political will to act. In a "get tough" mood as it developed the Clean Air Act amendments of 1970, Congress required new emissions standards that would reduce emissions by 90% below their uncontrolled levels. This reduction was to have been achieved by 1975 for hydrocarbon and carbon monoxide emissions and by 1976 for nitrogen dioxide. It was generally agreed at the time the Act was passed that the technology to meet the standards did not exist. By passing this tough act, Congress hoped to force the development of an appropriate technology.

It did not work out that way. The following years ushered in a series of deadline extensions. In 1972 the automobile manufacturers requested a one-year delay in the implementation of the standards. The administrator of the EPA denied the request and was taken to court. At the conclusion of the litigation in April 1973, the administrator granted a one-year delay in the 1975 deadline for the hydrocarbon and carbon monoxide standards. Subsequently, in July 1973, a one-year delay was granted for nitrogen oxides as well.[2] It was the first of many deferred deadlines.

---

[2]The only legal basis for granting an extension was technological infeasibility. Only shortly before the extension was granted, the Japanese Honda CVCC engine was certified as meeting the original standards. It is interesting to speculate on what the outcome would have been if the company meeting the standards was American rather than Japanese.

Structure of the U.S. Approach

The current U.S. approach to mobile-source air pollution has served as a model for mobile-source control in many other countries (particularly in Europe). We therefore examine this approach in some detail.

The U.S. approach represents a blend of controlling emissions at the point of manufacture with controlling emissions from vehicles in use. New-car emission standards are administered through a certification program and an associated enforcement program.

Certification Program.

The certification program tests prototypes of car models for conformity to federal standards. During the test a prototype vehicle from each engine family is driven 50,000 miles on a test track or a dynamometer, following a mandated, strict pattern of fast and slow driving, idling, and hot-and-cold starts. The manufacturers run the tests and record emission levels at 5,000-mile intervals. If the vehicle satisfies the standards over the entire 50,000 miles, it passes the deterioration portion of the certification test.

The second step in the certification process is to apply less demanding (and less expensive) tests to three additional prototypes in the same engine family. Emission readings are taken at the 0 and 4,000-mile points and then, using the deterioration rate established in the first portion of the test, are projected to the 50,000-mile point. If those projected emission levels meet the standards, then that engine family is given a certificate of conformity. Only engine families with a certificate of conformity are allowed to be sold.

Associated Enforcement Program.

The certification program is complemented by an associated enforcement program that contains assembly-line testing, as well as recall and antitampering procedures and warranty provisions. To ensure that the prototype vehicles are representative, the EPA tests a statistically representative sample of assembly-line vehicles. If these tests reveal that more than 40% of the cars do not conform with federal standards, the certificate may be suspended or revoked.

The EPA has also been given the power to require manufacturers to recall and remedy manufacturing defects that cause emissions to exceed federal standards. If the EPA uncovers a defect, it usually requests the manufacturer to recall vehicles for corrective action. If the manufacturer refuses, the EPA can order a recall.

The Clean Air Act also requires two separate types of warranty provisions. These warranty provisions are designed to ensure that a manufacturer will have an incentive to produce a vehicle that, if properly maintained, will meet emission standards over its useful life. The first of these provisions requires the vehicle to be free of defects that could cause the vehicle to fail to meet the standards. Any defects discovered by consumers would be fixed at the manufacturer's expense under this provision.

The second warranty provision requires the manufacturer to bring any car that fails an inspection and maintenance test (described below) during its first 24 months or 24,000 miles (whichever occurs first) into conformance with the standards. After the 24 months or 24,000 miles, the warranty is limited solely to the replacement of devices specifically designed for emission control, such as catalytic converters. This further protection lasts 60 months.

The earliest control devices used to control pollution had two characteristics that rendered them susceptible to tampering: they adversely affected vehicle performance, and they were relatively easy to circumvent. As a result, the Clean Air Act Amendments of 1970 prohibited anyone from tampering with an emission control system prior to the sale of an automobile, but, curiously, prohibited only dealers and manufacturers from tampering after the sale. The 1977 amendments extended the coverage of the postsale tampering prohibition to motor vehicle repair facilities and fleet operators.

Lead.   Section 211 of the U.S. Clean Air Act provides the EPA with the authority to regulate lead and any other fuel additives used in gasoline. Under this provision gasoline suppliers are required to make unleaded gasoline available. By ensuring the availability of unleaded gasoline, this regulation sought to reduce the amount of airborne lead, as well as to protect the effectiveness of the catalytic converter, which was poisoned by lead.[3]

On March 7, 1985, the EPA issued regulations imposing strict new standards on the allowable lead content in refined gasoline. The primary phaseout of lead was completed by 1986. These actions followed a highly publicized series of medical research findings on the severe health and developmental consequences, particularly to small children, of even low levels of atmospheric lead. The actions worked. A 1994 study showed that U.S. blood-lead levels declined 78% from 1978 to 1991.

Local Responsibilities.   The Clean Air Act Amendments of 1977 recognized the existence of nonattainment areas. Special requirements were placed on control authorities to bring nonattainment areas into attainment. Since many of the nonattainment areas received that designation for pollutants generated by mobile sources, local authorities in those areas were required to take further actions to reduce emissions from mobile sources.

Measures that local authorities are authorized to use include requiring new cars registered in that area to satisfy the more stringent California standard (with EPA approval) and the development of comprehensive transportation plans. These plans could include measures such as on-street parking controls, road charges, and measures to reduce the number of vehicle miles traveled.

In nonattainment regions that could not meet the primary standard for photochemical oxidants, carbon monoxide, or both by December 31, 1982, control authorities could delay attainments until December 31, 1987, provided they agreed to a number of additional restrictions. For the purposes of this chapter, the most important of these is the requirement that each region gaining this extension must establish a vehicle inspection and maintenance (I&M) program for emissions.

The objective of the I&M program is to identify vehicles that are violating the standards and to bring them into compliance, to deter tampering, and to encourage regular routine maintenance. Because the federal test procedure used in the certification process is much too expensive to use on a large number of vehicles, shorter, less expensive tests were developed specifically for the I&M programs. Because of the

---

[3]Three tankfuls of leaded gas used in a car equipped with a catalytic converter would produce a 50% reduction in the effectiveness of the catalytic converter.

expense and questionable effectiveness of these programs, they are one of the most controversial components of the policy package used to control mobile-source emissions.

Alternative Fuels and Vehicles

In an attempt to foster the development of alternative vehicles and alternative fuels that would be less damaging to the environment, Congress and some states have passed legislation requiring their increased use. Title II of the Clean Air Act Amendments of 1990 mandates the sale of cleaner burning reformulated gasoline in certain CO and severe ozone nonattainment regions. In the Energy Policy Act, passed in 1992, Congress requires the federal government (and some private fleet owners) to purchase alternative-fueled vehicles. The government has also attempted to introduce some regulatory flexibility designed to provide even further incentives for fleet owners (see Example 18.1). California has pushed the envelope even further. In September 1990, the California Air Resources Board (CARB) passed its Low Emission Vehicle (LEV) and Zero Emission Vehicle (ZEV) regulations. The former requires increasingly stringent emissions standards over time for conventionally fueled vehicles. The latter mandated that a certain percentage of new cars and light trucks sold in the state must be zero emission vehicles (defined as vehicles that directly emit no VOCs, NOx, or CO; any indirect emissions from producing the electricity are not counted).

When these ZEV regulations were written, the focus was on electric vehicles, but over time the emphasis has come to include hybrids (vehicles powered by a combination of gasoline and electric power) and fuel-cell vehicles. In response to this trend, the California regulations were modified in 2004. Under the new regulations auto manufacturers can meet their ZEV obligations in one of two ways.

To fulfill the first option, manufacturers must sell a vehicle mix of 2% pure ZEVs, 2% AT-PZEVs (vehicles earning advanced technology partial ZEV credits), and 6% PZEVs (extremely clean conventional vehicles). The ZEV obligation is based on the number of passenger cars and small trucks a manufacturer sells in California.

Or, manufacturers may choose a new alternative ZEV compliance strategy, meeting part of their ZEV requirement by producing their sales-weighted market share of approximately 250 fuel-cell vehicles by 2008. The remainder of their ZEV requirements could be achieved by producing 4% AT-PZEVs and 6% PZEVs. The required number of fuel-cell vehicles (to which the market share is applied) will increase to 2,500 from 2009 to 2011, 25,000 from 2012 to 2014, and 50,000 from 2015 to 2017. Automakers are allowed to substitute battery-electric vehicles for up to 50% of their fuel-cell vehicles requirements.

Clearly this is an attempt to force automotive technology using a rather innovative method—mandated sales quotas for clean vehicles. Notice that selling this number of clean vehicles depends not only on how many are manufactured, but also on whether demand for those vehicles is sufficient. If the demand is not sufficient, manufacturers will have to rely on factory rebates or other strategies to promote sufficient demand. Inadequate demand is not a legal defense for failing to meet the deadlines.

How well this strategy works in forcing the development and market penetration of new automotive technologies remains to be seen. Other states, particularly in the northeast, have now followed suit, so the size of the potential market is growing.

Example 18.1

PROJECT XL—THE QUEST FOR EFFECTIVE, FLEXIBLE REGULATION

Project XL is a U.S. pilot program that allows state and local governments, businesses, and federal facilities to develop with USEPA innovative strategies to test better or more cost-effective ways of achieving environmental and public health protection. In exchange, the EPA authorizes sufficient regulatory flexibility to conduct the experiment. The objective is to produce both better environmental quality and lower compliance costs than would otherwise be possible with traditional, "one-size-fits-all" regulation.

One example of a project involves the United States Postal Service (USPS), the State of Colorado, and the USEPA. The USPS wanted to replace some of its aging, high-polluting vehicles in the Denver area. Denver is a nonattainment area for carbon monoxide. Colorado rules required that in the Denver area, 50% of all new fleet vehicles purchased must be certified as low emitting vehicles (LEVs). Due to the special requirements for USPS vehicles, the only bid that met the other USPS specifications was for Transitional Low-Emitting Vehicles (TLEVs), which could not meet the LEV requirement.

Rather than continue operating its aging fleet, the USPS applied for, and received, permission from both Colorado and USEPA to replace 512 aging postal vehicles in Denver with TLEVs. The new vehicles are able to use up to 85% ethanol fuel. In addition, USPS would relocate 282 1987–1991 vintage vehicles to areas with less need to reduce emissions.

The USPS proposal will result in lower emissions of carbon monoxide than would have been achieved even if compliance with the original Colorado rules were possible and will become part of Denver's state implementation plan to reach attainment.

Source: http://www.epa.gov/projectxl/usps/index.htm.

European Approaches

By the late 1980s emission standards patterned after the 1983 American standards were required for all new cars in Austria, Sweden, Switzerland, Norway, and Finland. West Germany, Denmark, and the Netherlands have introduced tax incentives and lower registration fees for cleaner cars.

On October 1, 1989, the European Community's 12 member nations imposed U.S.-style emission standards on all new cars, starting with cars equipped with engines over two liters. Similar emission controls were extended to all engine sizes by 1993. The European Union banned leaded gasoline in 2000.

The Soviet Union has, in principle, agreed to follow the example of Western Europe in introducing more stringent emission controls. Since unleaded gasoline is not widely available in the Soviet Union, rapid change to catalytic converters is not expected.

The Netherlands, Norway, and Sweden are using differential tax rates to encourage consumers to purchase (and manufacturers to produce) low emitting cars before regulations take effect requiring all cars to be low emitting. Tax differentiation confers a tax advantage (and, hence, after-tax price advantage) on cleaner cars. The amount of the tax usually depends on (1) the emission characteristics of the car (heavier taxes being levied on heavily polluting cars), (2) the size of the car (in Germany heavier cars qualify for larger tax advantages to offset the relatively high control requirements placed upon them), and (3) the year of purchase (the tax differential is declining since all cars will eventually have to meet the standards). It apparently works. In Sweden, 87% of the new cars sold qualified for the tax advantage, while in Germany the comparable percentage was over 90% (Opschoor and Vos, 1989, 69–71).

Europe not only has much higher gasoline prices, but it has also developed strategies to make better use of transportation capital. Its intercity rail system is better developed than in the United States, and public transit ridership is typically higher within cities. Europe has also been a pioneer in the use of car-sharing arrangements (Example 18.2).

An Economic and Political Assessment

The difficulties of controlling mobile sources are illustrated by the U.S. experience. An infeasible compliance schedule for meeting the ambient standards was established for mobile-source pollutants by the 1970 amendments to the Clean Air Act. The chief instruments to be used by local areas in meeting these standards were the new-car emission standards. Because these applied only to new cars, and because new cars made up such a small proportion of the total fleet, significant emission reductions were not experienced until well after the deadline for meeting the ambient standards. This created a very difficult situation for local areas, since they were forced to meet the ambient standards prior to the time that the emission standards (the chief sources of reduction) were having much of an impact.

The only strategy open to them was the development of local strategies to make up the difference. Recognizing the difficulties the states faced, the EPA granted an extension of the deadline for submitting the transportation plans that would spell out the manner in which the standards would be reached. This extension was challenged in court by the Natural Resource Defense Council, which successfully argued that the EPA did not have the authority to grant the extension. Faced with the court's decision, the EPA was forced to reject the state implementation plans submitted by most states as inadequate, because those plans could not ensure attainment by the deadlines. Because the law clearly states that the EPA must substitute its own plan for an inadequate plan, the EPA found itself thrust into the unfamiliar and unpleasant role of defining transportation control plans for states with rejected SIPs.

Two main problems with this development surfaced: the EPA was not administratively equipped either in terms of staff or resources to design and implement these

Example 18.2

CAR-SHARING: BETTER USE OF AUTOMOTIVE CAPITAL?

One of the threats to sustainable development is the growing number of vehicles on the road. Though great progress has been made since the 1970s in limiting the pollution each vehicle emits per mile of travel, as the number of vehicles and the number of miles increase, the resulting increases in pollution offset much of the gains from the cleaner vehicles.

How to limit the number of vehicles? One strategy that has become rather widespread in Europe and is just beginning to make a dent in America is car-sharing. Car-sharing recognizes that the typical automobile sits idle most of the time, a classic case of excess capacity. (Studies in Germany suggest the average vehicle use per day is one hour.) Therefore the car-sharing strategy tries to spread ownership of a vehicle over several owners who share both the cost and the use.

The charges imposed by car-sharing clubs typically involve an upfront access fee plus fees based both on time of actual use and mileage. (Use during the peak periods usually costs more.) Some car-sharing clubs offer touch-tone automated booking, 24-hour dispatchers, and such amenities as child-safety seats, bike racks, and roof carriers.

Swiss and German clubs started in the late 1980s. As of 1998, an estimated 25,000 Germans and 20,000 Swiss belonged to car-sharing groups.

What could the contribution of car-sharing be to air pollution control in those areas where it catches on? It probably does lower the number of vehicles and the resulting congestion. In addition, peak-hour pricing probably encourages use at the less polluted periods. On the other hand, it does not necessarily lower the number of miles driven, which is one of the keys to lowering pollution. The contribution of this particular innovation remains to be clarified by some solid empirical research.

Source: Mary Williams Walsh. "Car-Sharing Holds the Road in Germany," *Los Angeles Times* (July 23, 1998): A1.

plans and, because of the severity of the mismatch between deadline and implementation, the EPA could have done very little, even if the staff and resources had been available.

The EPA made a valiant but futile attempt to meet its statutory responsibilities. It concluded that the best way to resolve its dilemma was to work backward from the needs to the transportation plans and, once the plans were defined, to require states to implement and enforce them. To ensure state cooperation, they set up a system of civil penalties to be applied against states that failed to cooperate.

The resulting plans were virtually unenforceable because they were so severe. For example, in order to meet the ambient standard in Los Angeles by the deadline, the plan designed by the EPA called for an 82% reduction in gasoline consumption in the Los Angeles basin. The reduction was to be achieved through gasoline rationing during the six months of the year when the smog problem was most severe. In publishing the plan, the EPA Administrator William Ruckelshaus acknowledged that it was infeasible and would effectively destroy the economy of the state if implemented, but argued that he had no other choice under the law.

The states raised a number of legal challenges to this approach, which were never really resolved in the courts by the time Congress revised the act in 1977. The Clean Air Act Amendments of 1977 remedied the situation by extending the deadlines.

The lesson from this episode seems to be that tougher laws do not necessarily result in more rapid compliance. By creating a statutory requirement that could not be met, virtually nothing was accomplished as the various parties attempted to fashion a resolution through the courts.

Technology Forcing and Sanctions

This lesson was underscored by the EPA's experience in gaining compliance with the national emission standards by the automobile manufacturers. The industry was able to obtain a number of delays in meeting those standards. The law was so tough that it was difficult to enforce within the time schedule envisioned by Congress.

This problem was intensified by the sanctions established by the Act to ensure compliance. They were so brutal that the EPA was unwilling to use them; they did not represent a credible threat. For example, when an engine family failed the certification test, the law is quite specific in stating that vehicle classes not certified as conforming with the standards cannot be sold! Given the importance of the automobile industry in the American economy, this sanction was not likely to be applied. As a result there were considerable pressures on the EPA to avoid the sanctions by defining more easily satisfied procedures for certification and by setting sufficiently flexible deadlines that no manufacturer would fail to meet them.

Differentiated Regulation

In controlling the emissions of both mobile sources and stationary sources, the brunt of the reduction effort is borne by new sources. This raises the cost of new sources, and from the purchaser's point of view, increases the attractiveness of used cars relative to new ones. The benefit from increased control (cleaner air) is a public good and therefore cannot be appropriated exclusively by the new-car purchasers. One result of a strategy focusing on new sources would be to depress the demand for new cars while enhancing that for used cars.

Apparently this is precisely what happened in the United States (Gruenspecht, 1982). In response to the higher cost of new cars, people held onto old automobiles longer. This has produced several unfortunate side effects. Since new cars are substantially cleaner than older cars, emission reductions have been delayed. In effect, this shift in fleet composition is equivalent to a setback of three to four years in the timetable for reducing emissions (Crandall et al., 1986, 96). Also, since older cars get worse gas mileage, gasoline consumption is higher than it would otherwise be. The focus on new sources is, to some extent, inevitable; the lesson to be drawn is that by ignoring these behavioral responses to differentiated regulation, the policy-maker is likely to expect results sooner than is feasible.

Uniformity of Control

With the exception of the California standards, which are more stringent, the Clean Air Act requires the same emission standards on all cars. The calculations were designed to ensure that required levels of control would be sufficient to meet the ambient standards in Los Angeles or in high-altitude cities such as Denver. As a result, many of the costs borne by people in other parts of the country—particularly rural areas—do not yield much in the way of benefits.

This sounds like an inefficient policy since the severity of control is not tailored to the geographic need, and, indeed, most of the studies that have been accomplished indicate that this is so.

It is generally shared conclusion that the costs of control exceed the benefits for automobile pollution control (Crandall et al., 1986, 109–16). Large uncertainties in the benefit estimations, a theme we have explored in several previous chapters, and the failure of any of these studies to consider the role of auto emissions of carbon in climate change force us to take these results with a grain of salt. It is nonetheless interesting that because the current policy forces manufacturers to operate on a very steep portion of the marginal control cost function, benefit uncertainty does not seem to affect the conclusion that the current standards are inefficiently strict with current technology. New technologies and the need to control CO_2 may change that conclusion.

The Deterioration of New-Car Emission Rates

As part of its investigation of the Clean Air Act, the National Commission on Air Quality investigated the emissions of vehicles in use and compared these emission levels to the standards. Their estimates were a blend of actual measured emissions for model years already in the fleet plus forecasts for future model years based on a knowledge of the technologies to be used. Particularly for hydrocarbons and carbon monoxide, the deterioration of emission rates in use was pronounced.

The Commission also investigated the factors contributing to poor in-use emissions performance. It found that the principal reason for the poor performance was improper maintenance. Carburetor and ignition-timing misadjustment were key factors. Component failure and tampering were also found to affect emission levels, though to a lesser degree.

Inspection and Maintenance (I&M) Programs.   One policy response to emission rate deterioration (along with requiring manufacturers to grant extended warranties for emission control systems) was to require I&M programs in non-attainment areas. How successful was this approach?

These programs have met with mixed success at best over the past decade. Motorists have little incentive to comply with the requirements unless forced to do so, since repair costs can be high and the benefits of repair are mostly externalities. This means that enforcement is the key component, but due to the sheer number of vehicles involved, it is also very difficult.

What is the evidence? One review of the evidence (Harrington et al., 2000) found these programs to be relatively cost-effective, although significant opportunities for targeting the programs remain unexploited. In addition to targeting programs at the areas where vehicle air pollution problems are severe, programs could also do a better job of targeting the problem vehicles. A relatively few vehicles typically turn out to be responsible for a disproportionate share of the mobile-source pollution. This implies that for most vehicles, the test is expensive, but it produces little private or social benefit. To the extent that these programs could identify the few high-emitting vehicles (through remote sensing, for example) and bring them into conformance at a reasonable cost, these programs could be much more cost-effective.

A few states have adopted I&M programs that assign a supplementary role to on-road emissions testing by using remote-sensing technology. In some states (for example, Texas), roadside enforcement officers use remote sensors to identify vehicles that have malfunctioning emission control systems (similar to the way radar is used to identify speeders). Using the recorded license numbers, the owners of the vehicles can then be contacted and required to take appropriate corrective actions. Other states, such as Colorado and Missouri, use a "clean screening" program, in which roadside remote sensing is used to exempt vehicles from central testing requirements.

Challenges remain for expanded use of remote sensing, however. Further controlled testing of remote-sensing devices is necessary to improve quality control, and the technology must be further developed to be able to measure the full range of automotive pollutants (especially particular matter).

Alternative Fuels.

In addition to controlling in-use emissions by means of I&M programs, the Clean Air Act Amendments of 1990 required nonattainment areas to use cleaner-burning automotive fuels (oxygenated fuels) during the winter months in some cases and year-round (reformulated gasoline) in the worst cases. Ethanol and methyl tertiary butyl ether (MTBE) were the two additives most widely used to meet the oxygen content standard.

Largely due to cost, most non-Midwestern states opted for gasoline with the additive MTBE rather than ethanol. MTBE is designed to make gasoline burn cleaner and more efficiently. Unfortunately, once it entered into widespread use, it was discovered that it spreads rapidly as gasoline escapes from leaky underground storage tanks, thereby contaminating sources of groundwater and drinking water. Once in soil or water, MTBE breaks down very slowly while accelerating the spread of other contaminants in gasoline, such as benzene, a known carcinogen. Once these properties became known, several states passed measures to ban or significantly limit the use of MTBE in gasoline.

The MTBE story provides an interesting case study of the problems that can occur with a strategy that relies on a "technical fix" to solve air pollution problems. Sometimes the effects of the "solution" can, in retrospect, turn out to be worse than the original problem.

Even before the MTBE water contamination issue surfaced, questions were being raised about the cost-effectiveness of using oxygenated fuels. For example, when Rask (2004) compared the oxyfuel smog test results to emissions' improvements resulting from emissions system repairs, he found increased maintenance and repairs to be a much more cost-effective strategy for lowering CO and HC emissions than oxyfuels.

In 1989 the South Coast Air Quality Management District identified 120 options for reducing volatile hydrocarbons. The average cost-effectiveness of the 68 measures proposed was $12,250 per ton. While early estimates such as these should not determine the outcome of the search for alternatives, they certainly do suggest that caution in proceeding too rapidly down this path would be in appropriate.

Lead Phaseout Program

Following the path broken by the Emissions Trading Program, the government began applying the transferable permit approach more widely. In the mid-1980s, prior to the issuance of new, more stringent regulations on lead in gasoline, the EPA announced the results of a benefit/cost analysis of their expected impact. The analysis concluded that the proposed 0.01 gram per leaded gallon (gplg) standard would result in $36 billion ($1983) in benefits (from reduced adverse health effects) at an estimated cost to the refining industry of $2.6 billion.

Although the regulation was unquestionably justified on efficiency grounds, the EPA wanted to allow flexibility in how the deadlines were met without increasing the amount of lead used. While some refiners could meet early deadlines with ease, others could do so only with a significant increase in cost. Recognizing that meeting the goal did not require every refiner to meet every deadline, the EPA initiated an innovative program to provide additional flexibility in meeting the regulations (see Example 18.3). The program was successful in reducing both lead emissions and the concentration of lead in the ambient air. From 1981 to 2001, emissions of lead fell by 93% and concentrations of lead in the air fell by 94%.

Possible Reforms

We have seen that the current approach has some salient weaknesses. Reliance on controlling emissions at the point of production has produced major improvements in cars leaving the assembly line, but emission rates deteriorate with use. The use of uniform standards has resulted in more control than necessary in rural areas and perhaps less than necessary in the most heavily polluted areas. Manufacturers have been able to delay implementation deadlines because the sanctions for noncompliance are so severe that the EPA is reluctant to deny a certificate of conformity.

Fuel Taxes

As controls on manufacturers have become more common and vehicles have become cleaner, attention is increasingly, turning to the user. Drivers have little incentive to drive or maintain their cars in a manner that minimizes emissions because the full social costs of road transport have not been internalized by current policy. How far from a full internalization of cost are we? Table 18.1 looks at this issue from the point of view

Example   *18.3*

GETTING THE LEAD OUT: THE LEAD PHASEOUT PROGRAM

Under the Lead Phaseout Program, a fixed number of lead rights (authorizing the use of a fixed amount of lead in gasoline produced during the period) were allocated to the 195 or so refineries. (Due to a loophole in the regulations, some new "alcohol blender" refineries were created to take advantage of the program, but their impact was very small). The number of issued rights declined over time. Refiners who did not need their full share of authorized rights could sell their rights to other refiners.

Initially no banking of rights was allowed (rights had to be created and used in the same quarter), but the EPA subsequently allowed banking. Once banking was initiated, created rights could be used in that period or any subsequent period up to the end of the program in 1987. Prices of rights, which were initially about 0.75 cent per gram of lead, rose to 4 cents after banking was allowed.

Refiners had an incentive to eliminate the lead quickly because early reductions freed up rights for sale. Acquiring these credits made it possible for other refiners to comply with the deadlines, even in the face of equipment failures or acts of God; fighting the deadlines in court, the traditional response, was unnecessary. Designed purely as a means of facilitating the transition to this new regime, the lead banking program ended as scheduled on December 31, 1987.

Sources: Barry D. Nussbaum. "Phasing Down Lead in Gasoline in the U.S.: Mandates, Incentives, Trading and Banking," in T. Jones and J. Corfee-Morlot, eds. *Climate Change: Designing a Tradeable Permit System* (Paris: Organisation for Economic Co-operation and Development Publication, 1992): 21–34; and Robert W. Hahn and Gordon L. Hester. "Marketable Permits: Lessons from Theory and Practice," *Ecology Law Quarterly* Vol. 16 (1989): 361–406.

of fuel taxes. It estimates how much higher current fuel taxes would have to be in selected countries in order to internalize the full social cost of road transport. The amount of increase would be quite large. Though it was not included in this study, its unusually low gasoline taxes would support a conjecture that especially large increases would be required in the United States as well.

But fuel taxes are not the only way to begin to internalize costs, and, by themselves, they would be a blunt instrument anyway because they would typically not take into account when and where the emissions occurred. One way to focus on these temporal and spatial concerns is through congestion pricing.

Congestion Pricing

Several Far East cities have undertaken some innovative approaches. Perhaps the most innovative can be found in Singapore, where the price system is used to reduce

TABLE 18.1

Current Fuel Taxes as a Percentage of the Level Needed to Internalize the Social Costs of Road Transport (1992)

Country	Gasoline	Diesel
Austria	25	23
Denmark	40	30
France	39	23
Germany	50	33
Italy	59	44
Netherlands	59	29
Norway[a]	52	—
Spain	52	39
Sweden[b]	60	40
Switzerland	27	31
United Kingdom	47	45

[a]In the midst of raising diesel tax.

[b]1993.

Source: Adapted from Table 10.4 in Per Kågeson. *Getting the Prices Right: A European Scheme for Making Transport Pay Its True Costs* (Stockholm: European Federation for Transport and Environment, 1993): 170.

congestion (see Example 18.4). Bangkok prohibits vehicles transporting goods from parts of the metropolitan area during various peak hours, leaving the roads to buses, cars, and motorized tricycles.

Toll rings have existed for some time in Oslo, Norway, and Milan, Italy. In the United States, electronic toll collection systems are currently in place on the Santa Monica freeway (California), the Oklahoma turnpike, the Dallas North Tollway (Texas), and the Lake Pontchartrain Causeway (Louisiana). Reserved express bus lanes are also common in the United States. (Reserved lanes for express buses lower the relative travel time for bus commuters, thereby providing an incentive for passengers to switch from cars to buses.)

Private Toll Roads

New policies are also being considered to ensure that road users pay all the costs of maintaining the highways, rather than transferring that burden to taxpayers. One strategy, which has been implemented in Mexico and in Orange County, California, is to allow construction of new private toll roads. The tolls are set high enough to recover all construction and maintenance costs and in some cases may include congestion pricing.

CAFE Standards

The Corporate Average Fuel Economy (CAFE) program, established in 1975, was designed to reduce American dependence on foreign oil by producing more

Example   18.4

INNOVATIVE MOBILE-SOURCE POLLUTION CONTROL STRATEGIES: SINGAPORE

Singapore has one of the most comprehensive strategies to control vehicle pollution in the world. In addition to imposing very high vehicle registration fees, this approach also includes:

- Central Business District parking fees that are higher during normal business hours than during the evenings and on weekends.
- An area-licensing scheme that requires the display of a specific purchased vehicle license in order to gain entry to restricted downtown zones during restricted hours. These licenses are expensive and penalties for not having them displayed when required are very steep.
- Electronic peak-hour pricing on roadways. These charges, which are deducted automatically using a "smart card" technology, vary by roadway and by time of day. Conditions are reviewed and charges are adjusted every three months.
- An option for people to purchase an "off-peak" car. Identified by a distinctive red license plate that is welded to the vehicle, these vehicles can only be used during off-peak periods. Owners of these vehicles pay much lower registration fees and road taxes for them.
- Limiting the number of new vehicles that can be registered each year. In order to ensure that they can register a new car, potential buyers must first secure one of the fixed number of licenses by submitting a winning financial bid.
- An excellent mass-transit system that provides a viable alternative to automobile travel.

Has the program been effective? Apparently it has been quite effective in two rather different ways. First, it has provided a significant amount of revenue for the government, which the government can use to reduce more burdensome taxes. (The revenues go into the General Treasury; they are not earmarked for the transport sector.) Second, it has caused a large reduction in traffic-related pollution in the affected areas. The overall levels of carbon monoxide, lead, sulfur dioxide, and nitrogen dioxide are now all within the human health guidelines established by both the World Health Organization and the United States Environmental Protection Agency.

Source: N. C. Chia and S. Y. Phang. "Motor Vehicle Taxes as an Environmental Management Instrument: The Case of Singapore," *Environmental Economics and Policy Studies* Vol. 4, No. 2 (2001): 67–93.

fuel-efficient vehicles. Though it is not an emission control program, fuel efficiency does affect emissions.

The program requires each automaker to meet government-set miles-per-gallon targets (CAFE standards) for all its car and light truck fleets sold in the United States each year. The unique feature is that the standard is a *fleet average*, not a standard for each vehicle. As a result, automakers can sell some poor-mileage vehicles as long as they sell enough high-mileage vehicles to raise the average to the standard. The CAFE standards took effect in 1978, mandating a fleet average of 18 miles per gallon (mpg) for cars. The standard increased each year until 1985 when it reached 27.5 mpg.

Most, but not all, observers believe that the CAFE standards did in fact reduce imports. During the 1977–1986 period, oil imports fell from 47% to 27% of total oil consumption.

CAFE standards, however, have had their share of problems. When Congress instituted the CAFE standards, light trucks were allowed to meet a lower fuel-economy standard because they constituted only 20% of the vehicle market and were used primarily as work vehicles. Light truck standards were set at 17.2 mpg for the 1979 model year and went up to 20.7 mpg in 1985. With the burgeoning popularity of SUVs, which are counted as light trucks, trucks now comprise nearly half the market. In addition, intense lobbying by the auto industry resulted in an inability of Congress to raise the standards from 1985 until 2004. The ultimate result of the lower standards for trucks and SUVs and the increasing importance of trucks and SUVs in the fleet of on-road vehicles was that average miles per gallon for all vehicles declined, rather than improved.

A more fundamental debate about CAFE standards involves its effectiveness relative to fuel taxes (Debate 18.1).

DEBATE 18.1

CAFE Standards or Fuel Taxes?

Increasing the fuel efficiency of oil consumption could in principle be accomplished by increasing either fuel taxes or fuel-efficiency standards. By raising the cost of driving, the former would encourage auto purchasers to seek more fuel-efficient vehicles, while the later would ensure that the average new vehicle sold was fuel efficient. Does it make a difference which strategy is followed?

It turns out that it does, and economics can help explain why. Think about what each strategy does to the marginal cost of driving an extra mile. Increased fuel taxes raise the marginal cost per mile driven, but fuel-economy standards lower it. In the first case, each mile consumes more fuel and that fuel costs more. In the second case, the more fuel-efficient car uses less fuel per mile so the cost has gone down.

Following economic logic leads immediately to the conclusion that even if both strategies resulted in the same fuel economy, the tax would reduce oil consumption by more because it would promote fewer miles driven. On these grounds, a tax is better than a fuel-economy standard.

Supporters of fuel-economy standards, however, counter with a political feasibility argument. They point out that in the United States, sufficiently high gasoline taxes to produce that level of reduction could never have passed Congress, so the fuel-economy standards were better, indeed much better, than no policy at all.

Parking Cash-Outs

Providing parking spaces for employees costs employers money, yet most of them provide this benefit free of charge. This employer-financed subsidy reduces one significant cost of driving to work. Since this subsidy only benefits those who drive to work, it lowers the relative cost of driving vis à vis all other transport choices, such as walking, biking, public transport, and so on. Since most of those choices create much less air pollution, the resulting bias toward driving creates an inefficiently high level of pollution.

One way to rectify this bias is for employers to compensate employees who do not use a parking space with an equivalent increase in income. This would transfer the employer's savings in not having to provide a parking spot to the employee and remove the bias toward driving to work.

Feebates

Another strategy is targeted at consumers purchasing new vehicles. Feebates combine taxes on purchases of new high-emitting vehicles with subsidies for purchases of new low-emitting vehicles. By raising the relative cost of high-emitting vehicles, it encourages consumers to take the environmental effects of those vehicles into account. The revenue from the taxes can serve as the financing for the subsidies, but previous experience indicates that policies such as this are rarely revenue-neutral.

Pay-As-You-Drive (PAYD) Insurance

Another possibility for internalizing an environmental externality associated with automobile travel, thereby reducing both accidents and pollution, involves changing the way car insurance is financed. As Example 18.5 illustrates, small changes could potentially make a big difference.

Accelerated Retirement Strategies

A final reform possibility involves strategies to accelerate the retirement of older, polluting vehicles. This could be accomplished either by raising the cost of holding onto older vehicles (as with higher registration fees for vehicles that pollute more) or by providing a bounty of some sort to those retiring heavily polluting vehicles early.

One version of the bounty program has become known as "cash for clunkers." Under this program, stationary sources are allowed to claim emission reduction credits for heavily polluting vehicles that are removed from service. In one version of the program, heavily polluting vehicles are identified either by inspection and maintenance programs or remote sensing. Vehicle owners can bring their vehicle up to code, usually an expensive proposition, or they can sell it to the company running the cash-for-clunker program. Purchased vehicles are usually disassembled for parts and the remainder is recycled. The number of emission reduction credits earned by the company running the program depends on such factors as the remaining useful life of the car and the estimated number of miles it would be driven and is generally controlled so that the transaction results in a net increase in air quality.

Example 18.5

MODIFYING CAR INSURANCE AS AN ENVIRONMENTAL STRATEGY

Although improvements in automobile technology (such as air bags and antilock brakes) have made driving much safer than in the past, the number of road deaths and injuries is still inefficiently high. Since people do not consider the full societal cost of accident risk when deciding how much and how often to drive, the number of vehicle miles traveled is excessive. Although drivers may take into account the risk of injury to themselves and family members, other risks are likely to be externalized. They include the risk of injury their driving poses for other drivers and pedestrians, the costs of vehicular damage that is covered through insurance claims, and the costs to other motorists held up in traffic congestion caused by accidents. Externalizing these costs artificially lowers the marginal cost of driving, thereby inefficiently increasing the pollution from the resulting high number of vehicle miles.

Implementing PAYD insurance could reduce those inefficiencies. With PAYD insurance, existing rating factors (such as age, gender, and previous driving experience) would be used by insurance companies to determine a driver's per-mile rate, and this rate would be multiplied by annual miles driven to calculate the annual insurance premium. This approach has the effect of drastically increasing the marginal cost of driving an extra mile without raising the amount people spend annually on insurance. Estimates by Harrington and Parry (2004) suggest that calculating these insurance costs on a per-mile basis would have the same effect as raising the federal gasoline tax from $0.184 to $1.50 per gallon for a vehicle that gets 20 miles per gallon. This is a substantial increase and could likely have a dramatic effect on people's transport choices (and, therefore, the pollution they emit) despite the fact that it imposes no additional financial burden on them.

Source: Winston Harrington and Ian Parry. "Pay-As-You-Drive for Car Insurance," in R. Morgenstern and P. Portney, eds. *New Approaches on Energy and the Environment: Policy Advice for the President* (Washington, DC: Resources of the Future, 2004): 53–56.

Retirement strategies would tend to counteract the tendency for vehicles to be used longer as a result of the new source focus of current automotive regulations. By eliminating these heavily polluting vehicles from the fleet earlier than would otherwise be the case, greater emission reductions could be achieved at an earlier date. This approach could be applied selectively in those local areas for which it could make a significant difference.

We also have learned some things about what doesn't work very well. One increasingly common strategy involves limiting the days any particular vehicle can be used, as a means of limiting miles traveled. As Example 18.6 indicates, this strategy can backfire!

Example 18.6

COUNTERPRODUCTIVE POLICY DESIGN

As one response to unacceptably high levels of traffic congestion and air pollution, the Mexico City administration imposed a regulation that banned each car from driving on a specific day of the week. The specific day when the car could not be driven was determined by the last digit of the license plate.

This approach appeared to offer the opportunity for considerable reductions in congestion and air pollution at a relatively low cost. In this case, however, the appearance was deceptive because of the way in which the population reacted to the ban.

An evaluation of the program by the World Bank found that in the short run the regulation was effective. Both pollution and congestion were reduced. However, in the long run the regulation not only was ineffective, it was counterproductive (it paradoxically increased the level of congestion and pollution). This paradox occurred because a large number of residents reacted by buying an additional car (which would have a different banned day), and once the additional cars became available, total driving increased. Policies that fail to anticipate and incorporate behavior reactions run the risk that actual and expected outcomes may diverge considerably.

Source: Gunnar S. Eskeland and Tarhan Feyzioglu. "Rationing Can Backfire: The 'Day Without a Car Program' in Mexico City," World Bank Policy Research Working Paper 1554 (December 1995).

Summary

The current policy toward motor vehicle emissions blends point-of-production control with point-of-use control. It began with uniform emissions standards.

Grams-per-mile emissions standards, the core of the current approach in both the United States and Europe, have, in practice, had many deficiencies. While they have achieved lower emissions per mile, they have been less effective in lowering aggregate emissions and in ensuring cost-effective reductions.

Aggregate mobile-source emissions have been reduced by less than expected because of the large offsetting increase in the number of miles traveled. Unlike sulfur emissions from power plants, aggregate mobile-source emissions are not capped, so as miles increase, emissions increase.

The efficiency of the emissions standards has been diminished by their geographic uniformity. Too little control has been exercised in highly polluted areas, and too much control has been exercised in areas with air quality that exceeds the ambient standards.

Local approaches, such as targeted inspection and maintenance strategies and accelerated retirement strategies, have had mixed success in redressing this imbalance. Since a relatively small number of vehicles is typically responsible for a disproportionately large share of the emissions, a growing reliance on remote sensing to identify the most polluting vehicles is allowing the policy to target resources where they will produce the largest net benefit.

The historic low cost of auto travel has led to a dispersed pattern of development. Since dispersed patterns of development make mass transit a less-viable alternative, a downward spiral of population dispersal and low mass-transit ridership occurs. In the long run, part of the strategy for meeting ambient standards will necessarily involve changing land-use patterns to create the kind of high-density travel corridors that are compatible with effective mass-transit use. Though these conditions already exist in much of Europe, it is likely to evolve in the United States over a long period of time. Ensuring that the true social costs of transportation are borne by those making residential and mode-of-travel choices will start the process moving in the right direction.

A couple of important insights about the conventional environmental policy wisdom can be derived from the history of mobile-source control. Contrary to the traditional belief that tougher laws produce more environmental results, the sanctions associated with meeting the grams-per-mile emissions standards were so severe that, when push came to shove, authorities were unwilling to impose them. Threatened sanctions will only promote the desired outcome if the threat is credible. The largest "club" is not necessarily the best "club."

The second insight confronts the traditional belief that simply applying the right technical fix can solve environmental problems. The gasoline additive MTBE was advanced as a way to improve the nation's air. With the advantage of hindsight, we now know that its pollution effects on groundwater have dwarfed its positive effects on air quality. Though technical fixes can and do have a role to play in environmental policy, they also can have large, adverse, unintended consequences.

Looking toward the future of mobile-source air pollution control, two new emphases are emerging. The first involves encouraging the development and commercialization of new, cleaner automotive technologies ranging from gas-electric hybrids to fuel-cell vehicles powered by hydrogen. Policies such as fuel-economy standards, gasoline taxes, feebates, and sales quotas imposed on auto manufacturers for low-emitting vehicles are designed to accelerate their entry into the vehicle fleet.

The second new emphasis focuses on influencing driver choices. The range of available policies is impressive. One set of strategies focuses on bringing the private marginal cost of driving closer to the social marginal cost through such measures as congestion pricing and Pay-As-You-Drive auto insurance. Others, such as parking cash-outs, attempt to create a more level playing field for choices involving the mode of travel for the journey to work.

Appropriate regulation of emissions from mobile sources requires a great deal more than simply controlling the emissions from vehicles as they leave the factory. Vehicle purchases, driving behavior, fuel choice, and even residential and employment choices must eventually be affected by the need to reduce mobile-source emissions. Affecting the choices facing automobile owners can only transpire if the economic incentives associated with those choices are structured correctly.

Discussion Questions

1. When a threshold concentration is used as the basis for pollution control as it is for air pollution, one possibility for meeting the threshold at minimum cost is to spread the emissions out over time. One way to accomplish this is to establish a peak-hour pricing system in which more is charged for emissions during peak periods.
   (a) Would this represent a movement toward efficiency? Why or why not?
   (b) What effects should this policy have on mass-transit usage, gasoline sales, downtown shopping, and travel patterns?

2. What are the advantages and disadvantages of using an increase in the gasoline tax to move road transport decisions toward both efficiency and sustainability?

Further Reading

Button, Kenneth J. *Market and Government Failures in Environmental Management: The Case of Transport* (Paris: OECD, 1992). Analyzes and documents the types of government interventions such as pricing, taxation, and regulations that often result in environmental degradation.

Crandall, Robert W., Howard K. Gruenspecht, Theodore E. Keeler, and Lester B. Lave. *Regulating the Automobile* (Washington, DC: Brookings Institution, 1986). An examination of the effectiveness and efficiency of the federal regulation of automobile safety, emissions, and fuel economy in the United States.

Harrington, W., and V. McConnell. "Motor Vehicles and the Environment," in H. Folmer and T. Tietenberg, eds. *International Yearbook of Environmental and Resource Economics 2003/2004* (Cheltenham, UK: Edward Elgar, 2003): 190–268. A comprehensive survey of what we have learned from economic analysis about cost-effective ways to control pollution from motor vehicles.

MacKenzie, James J. *The Keys to the Car: Electric and Hydrogen Vehicles for the 21st Century* (Washington, DC: World Resources Institute, 1994). Surveys the environmental and economic costs and benefits of alternative fuels and alternative vehicles.

Mackenzie, James J., Roger C. Dower, and Donald D. T. Chen. *The Going Rate: What It Really Costs to Drive* (Washington, DC: World Resources Institute, 1992). Explores the full cost of a transportation system dominated by the automobile.

OECD. *Cars and Climate Change* (Paris: OECD, 1993). Examines the possibilities, principally from enhanced energy efficiency and alternative fuels, for reducing greenhouse emissions from the transport sector.

Additional References is available on this book's companion Web site www.aw-bc.com/tietenberg.

Chapter 19

Water Pollution

*It was the best of times, it was the worst of times, it was
the age of wisdom, it was the age of foolishness, it was
the epoch of belief, it was the epoch of incredulity . . .*
—Charles Dickens, *A Tale of Two Cities* (1859)

Introduction

While various types of pollution share common attributes, important differences are apparent as well. These differences form the basis for the elements of policy unique to each pollutant. We have seen, for example, that although the types of pollutants emitted by mobile and stationary sources are often identical, the policy approaches differ considerably.

Water pollution control has its own unique characteristics as well. Three stand out as having particular relevance for policy:

1. Recreation benefits are much more important for water pollution control than for air pollution control.
2. Large economies of scale in treating sewage and other wastes create the possibility for large, centralized treatment plants as one control strategy, while for air pollution, on-site control is the standard approach.
3. Many causes of water pollution are difficult to trace to a particular source as in smokestacks or cars for air pollution. Runoff from streets and agriculture as well as atmospheric deposition of pollutants are major *nonpoint* sources of water pollution. (Nonpoint sources are diffuse and not associated with specific discharge points.) Control of these sources adds additional complexities for water pollution control.

These characteristics create a need for yet another policy approach. In this chapter we explore the problems and prospects for controlling this unique and important form of pollution.

Nature of Water Pollution Problems

Types of Waste-Receiving Water

Two primary types of water are susceptible to contamination. The first, *surface water*, consists of the rivers, lakes, and oceans covering most of the earth's surface. Historically, policy-makers have focused almost exclusively on preventing and cleaning up lake and river water pollution. Only recently has ocean pollution received the attention it deserves.

Groundwater, once considered a pristine resource, has been shown to be subject to considerable contamination from toxic chemicals. *Groundwater* is subsurface water that occurs beneath a water table in soils or rocks, or in geological formations that are fully saturated.

Groundwater is a vast natural resource. It has been estimated that the reserves of groundwater are approximately 88 times the annual flow of surface water. Groundwater is used primarily for irrigation and as a source of drinking water.

While surface water serves as a significant source of drinking water, it has many other uses as well. Recreational benefits such as swimming, fishing, and boating are important determinants of surface water policy in areas where the water is not used for drinking.

Sources of Contamination

Whereas some contamination has been accidental, the product of unintended and unexpected waste migration to water supplies, a portion of the contamination was deliberate. Watercourses were simply a convenient place to dump municipal or private sewage and industrial wastes. Along the shoreline of many lakes or rivers, pipes dumping human or industrial wastes directly into the water were a common occurrence before laws limiting this activity were enacted and enforced.

Contamination of groundwater occurs when polluting substances leach into a water-saturated region. Many potential contaminants are removed by filtration and adsorption as the water moves slowly through the layers of rock and soil. Toxic organic chemicals are one major example of a pollutant that may not be filtered out during migration. Once these substances enter groundwater, very little, if any, further cleansing takes place. Moreover, since the rate of replenishment for many groundwater sources, relative to the stock, is small, very little mixing and dilution of the contaminants occur (see Example 19.1).

For lake and river pollution policy purposes, it is useful to distinguish between two sources of contamination—point and nonpoint sources—even though the distinction is not always crystal clear. *Point sources* generally discharge into surface waters at a specific location through a pipe, outfall, or ditch, while *nonpoint sources* usually affect the water in a more indirect and diffuse way. From the policy point of view, nonpoint sources are more difficult to control and have received little legislative attention until recently. As a result of the gains made in controlling point sources, nonpoint sources now compose over half of the waste load borne by the nation's waters.

Example 19.1

INCIDENTS OF GROUNDWATER POLLUTION

Traditional policies have paid little attention to groundwater, partly because of the high cost of testing and monitoring. Accumulating evidence, however, suggests that groundwater in many locations is contaminated by toxic chemicals. This may be posing unacceptable health risks for the public, since groundwater is widely used for drinking. Many of the chemicals now being discovered in drinking water are either known or suspected carcinogens or mutagens.

Examples of groundwater contamination by toxic organic substances include the following:

1. A Massachusetts Legislative Commission on Water Supply found that at least one-third of the 351 communities in the Commonwealth were affected by chemical contamination of drinking water, and wells were restricted or closed in 22 towns.
2. All wells in Groveland and Rowley (Massachusetts) were closed because of trichloroethylene (TCE) contamination, a known carcinogen in animals.
3. California public health officials closed 37 public wells that supplied water to 400,000 people in the San Gabriel Valley because of TCE contamination.
4. The 11-acre Ossineke Groundwater Contamination site in Michigan resulted from a series of unrelated spills and incidents that contaminated the groundwater of local residents within the LaBell subdivision. Incidents included leaking underground storage tanks, accidental spills of fuel onto the ground, and suspected releases of fuel and other organic compounds into the ground. A second potential source was a laundry/dry cleaning facility and its washwater pond.
5. Arsenic was discovered in a city well serving Murray City, Utah. The city blames a former mining site.

Source: EPA Web site at http://www.epa.gov/superfund/index.htm/.

Rivers and Lakes. The most important nonpoint sources of pollution for rivers and lakes are agricultural activity, urban storm-water runoff, silviculture, and individual disposal systems. Contamination from agriculture includes eroded topsoil, pesticides, and fertilizer. Urban storm-water runoff contains a number of pollutants, including, typically, high quantities of lead. Forestry, if not carefully managed, can contribute to soil erosion and, by removing shade cover, could have a large impact on the temperature of normally shaded streams. In some developing countries more than 95% of urban sewage is discharged into surface waters without treatment.

The contamination of groundwater supplies usually results from the migration of harmful substances from sites where high concentrations of chemicals can be found. These include industrial waste storage sites, landfills, and farms.

FIGURE 19.1

Economic Efficiency When Return Flows Are Contaminated

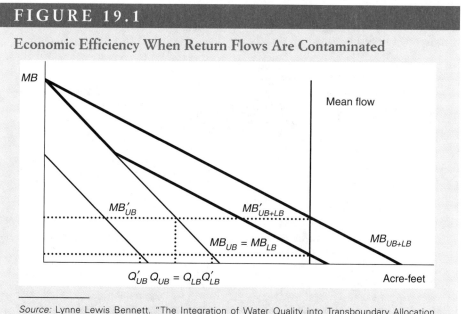

Source: Lynne Lewis Bennett. "The Integration of Water Quality into Transboundary Allocation Agreements: Lessons from the Southwestern United States," *Agricultural Economics* Vol. 24 (2000): 113–125.

The primary point sources are industries and municipalities. The primary non-point sources involve agricultural activity of one form or another.

Recall that the efficient allocation of uncontaminated water requires marginal benefits to be equalized across all uses (see Figure 10.3). However, if return flows are contaminated, this can alter the efficient allocation.[1] Figure 19.1 shows the efficient allocation when return flows are contaminated in the case of two users: an upper basin (*UB*) user and a downstream lower basin (*LB*) user. If they had identical marginal benefits for uncontaminated water, the two users should receive equal amounts of water (recall Figure 10.3). However, subtracting the effect of contaminated return flows from the upper basin marginal benefit function (MB'_{UB}) changes the efficient allocation to one with unequal sharing. In particular, more water would be allocated to the lower basin user (Q'_{LB}) and less to the upper basin user (Q'_{UB}). (See Bennett, 2000, for a more detailed discussion.) Accounting for water quality can be an important and often-overlooked factor in allocation decisions.

Ocean Pollution.
The two primary sources of ocean pollution that we will discuss are oil spills and ocean dumping. Since a great deal of oil is transported over

---

[1]Return flow is a measure of the unused portion of water. For example, in agriculture, water withdrawal is the amount of water taken from a source and applied to a field. Consumptive use is the amount actually used by the plant. Return flow is the unconsumed portion that will eventually return to the watercourse and is usually owned by a downstream user. Return flows will bring with them leached contaminants, pesticides, fertilizers, and salts from the soil.

TABLE 19.1

Notable Oil Spills

Rank	Spill Size (tonnes)	Ship Name	Year	Location
1	287,000	*Atlantic Empress*	1979	Off Tobago, West Indies
2	260,000	*ABT Summer*	1991	700 nautical miles off Angola
3	252,000	*Castillo de Bellver*	1983	Off Saldanha Bay, South Africa
4	223,000	*Amoco Cadiz*	1978	Off Brittany, France
5	144,000	*Haven*	1991	Genoa, Italy
6	132,000	*Odyssey*	1988	700 nautical miles off Nova Scotia, Canada
7	119,000	*Torrey Canyon*	1967	Scilly Isles, U.K.
8	115,000	*Sea Star*	1972	Gulf of Oman
9	100,000	*Irenes Serenade*	1980	Navarino Bay, Greece
10	100,000	*Urquiola*	1976	La Coruna, Spain
11	95,000	*Hawaiian Patriot*	1977	300 nautical miles off Honolulu
12	95,000	*Independenta*	1979	Bosphorus, Turkey
13	88,000	*Jakob Maersk*	1975	Oporto, Portugal
14	85,000	*Braer*	1993	Shetland Islands, U.K.
15	80,000	*Khark 5*	1989	120 nautical miles off Atlantic coast of Morocco
16	77,000	*Prestige*	2002	Off the Spanish coast
17	74,000	*Aegean Sea*	1992	La Coruna, Spain
18	72,000	*Sea Empress*	1996	Milford Haven, U.K.
19	72,000	*Katina P*	1992	Off Maputo, Mozambique
35	37,000	*Exxon Valdez*	1989	Prince William Sound, Alaska, U.S.

Source: International Tanker Owners Pollution Federation Limited Web site: http://www.itopf.com/stats.html (accessed 1/17/05).

the oceans and is produced from platforms exploiting fields under the ocean, oil spills have become a more common occurrence (see Table 19.1). Various unwanted by-products of modern life have also been dumped into ocean waters based upon the mistaken belief that the vastness of the oceans allowed them to absorb large quantities of waste without suffering noticeable damage. Dumped materials have included sewage and sewage sludge, unwanted chemicals, trace metals, and even radioactive materials.

Types of Pollutants

For our purposes, the large number of water pollutants can be usefully classified by means of the taxonomy developed in Chapter 15.

Fund Pollutants.   Fund pollutants are those for which the environment has some assimilative capacity. If the absorptive capacity is high enough relative to the rate of injection, they may not accumulate at all. One type of fund water pollutant is called *degradable* because it degrades, or breaks into its component parts, within the water. Degradable wastes are normally organic residuals that are attacked and broken down by bacteria in the stream.

The process by which organic wastes are broken down into component parts consumes oxygen. The amount of oxygen consumed depends upon the magnitude of the waste load. All of the higher life-forms in watercourses are *aerobic;* they require oxygen for survival. As a stream's oxygen levels fall, fish mortality increases, with the less tolerant fish becoming the first to succumb. The oxygen level can become low enough that even the aerobic bacteria die. When this happens, the stream becomes *anaerobic* and the ecology changes drastically. This is an extremely unpleasant circumstance because the stream takes on a dark hue, and the stream water stinks!

To control these waste loads, two different types of monitoring are needed: (1) monitoring the ambient conditions in the watercourse; and (2) monitoring the magnitude of emissions. One measure commonly used to keep track of ambient conditions for these conventional fund pollutants is dissolved oxygen (DO). The amount of *dissolved oxygen* in a body of water is a function of ambient conditions, such as temperature, stream flow, and the waste load.[2] The measure of the oxygen demand placed on a stream by any particular volume of effluent is called the *biochemical oxygen demand* (BOD).

Using modeling techniques, emissions (measured as BOD) at a certain point can be translated into DO measures at various receptor locations along a stream. This step is necessary in order to implement an ambient permit system or an ambient emission charge.

If we were to develop a profile of dissolved oxygen readings on a stream where organic effluent is being injected, that profile would typically exhibit one or more minimum points called oxygen sags. These *oxygen sags* represent locations along the stream where the dissolved oxygen content is lower than at other points. An ambient permit or ambient charge system would be designed to reach a desired DO level at those sag points, while an emission permit or emission charge system would simply try to hit a particular BOD reduction target. The former would take the location of the emitter into account, while the latter would not. Later in this chapter we examine studies that model these systems on particular watercourses.

A second type of fund pollutant, thermal pollution, is caused by the injection of heat into a watercourse. Typically, *thermal pollution* is caused when an industrial plant or electric utility uses surface water as a coolant, returning the heated water to the watercourse. This heat is dissipated in the receiving waters by evaporation. By raising the temperature of the water near the outfall, thermal pollution lowers the dissolved oxygen content and can result in dramatic ecological changes in that area.

Yet another example is provided by a class of pollutants, such as nitrogen and phosphorus, that are plant nutrients. These pollutants stimulate the growth of

---

[2]The danger of anaerobic conditions is highest in the late summer and early fall, when temperatures are high and the stream flow is low.

aquatic plant life, such as algae and water weeds. In excess, these plants can produce odor, taste, and aesthetic problems. A lake with an excessive supply of nutrients is called *eutrophic*.

The various types of fund pollutants could be ordered on a spectrum. On one end of the spectrum would be pollutants for which the environment has a very large absorptive capacity and on the other end pollutants for which the absorptive capacity is virtually nil. The limiting case, with no absorptive capacity, are stock pollutants.

Near the end of that spectrum is a class of inorganic synthetic chemicals called *persistent* pollutants. These substances are called persistent because their complex molecular structures are not effectively broken down in the stream. Some degradation takes place, but so slowly that these pollutants can travel long distances in water in a virtually unchanged form.

These persistent pollutants accumulate, not only in the watercourses, but in the food chain as well. The concentration levels in the tissues of living organisms rise with the order of the species. Concentrations in lower life-forms such as plankton may be relatively small, but, because small fish eat a lot of plankton and do not excrete the chemical, the concentrations in small fish would be higher. The magnification continues as large fish consume small fish; concentration levels in the larger fish would be even higher.

Because they accumulate in the food chains, persistent pollutants present an interesting monitoring challenge. The traditional approach would involve measurements of pollutant concentration in the water, but that is not the only variable of interest. The damage is related not only to its concentration in the water, but its concentration in the food chain as well. Although monitoring the environmental effects of these pollutants may be more compelling than monitoring other pollutants, it is also more difficult.

A final type of fund pollutant, infectious organisms such as bacteria and viruses, is carried into surface water and groundwater by domestic and animal wastes and by wastes from such industries as tanning and meat packing. These live organisms may either thrive and multiply in water or their population may decline over time, depending upon how hospitable or hostile the watercourse is for continued growth.

Stock Pollutants.

The most troublesome cases of pollution result from stock pollutants, which merely accumulate in the environment. No natural process removes or transforms stock pollutants; the watercourse cannot cleanse itself of them.

Inorganic chemicals and minerals comprise the main examples of stock pollutants. Perhaps the most notorious members of this group are the heavy metals, such as lead, cadmium, and mercury. Extreme examples of poisoning by these metals have occurred in Japan. One ocean-dumping case was responsible for *Minamata disease*, named for the location where it occurred. Some 52 people died and 150 others suffered serious brain and nerve damage. Scientists puzzled for years over the source of the ailments until tracing them to an organic form of mercury that had accumulated in the tissues of fish eaten three times a day by local residents.

In the United States, mercury contamination of fish has led to consumption advisories for many freshwater and migratory fish. Women of childbearing age and children especially are cautioned against eating large amounts of certain species.

In another case in Japan, known as the *itai itai* (literally, ouch-ouch) *disease*, scientists traced the source of a previously undiagnosed, extremely painful bone disease to the ingestion of cadmium. Nearby mines were the source of the cadmium, which apparently was ingested by eating contaminated rice and soybeans.

Most recently, medicinal waste has been found in watercourses and in fish tissue. In 2002 the USGS tested 139 rivers in 30 states and found that 80% of the streams sampled resulted in evidence of residuals from drugs such as birth control pills and antidepressants. Residuals from soaps and perfumes were also found. While the damage that will ultimately be caused by these substances is not yet clear, it is certainly a new twist in water pollution control policy.

As is typical with persistent pollutants, some of the stock pollutants are difficult to monitor. Those accumulated in the food chains give rise to the same problem as is presented by persistent pollutants. Ambient sampling must be supplemented by sampling tissues from members of the food chain. To further complicate matters, the heavy metals may sink rapidly to the bottom, remaining in the sediment. While these could be detected in sediment samples, merely drawing samples from the water itself would allow these pollutants to escape detection.

Traditional Water Pollution Control Policy

Water pollution control policies vary around the world. In this section we begin with a somewhat detailed discussion of U.S. policy, which provides a rather rich example of a typical legal approach to regulation. This is followed by a discussion of the European approach, which depends more heavily on economic incentives.

U.S. policy for water pollution control predates federal air pollution control. We might suppose that the policy for water pollution control would, therefore, be superior, since authorities had more time to profit from early mistakes. Unfortunately, that is not the case.

Early Legislation

The first federal legislation dealing with discharge into the nation's waterways occurred when Congress passed the 1899 Refuse Act. Designed primarily to protect navigation, this act focused on preventing any discharge that would interfere with using rivers as transport links. All discharges into a river were prohibited unless approved by a permit from the Chief of the U.S. Engineers. Most permits were issued to contractors dredging the rivers, and they dealt mainly with the disposal of the removed material. This act was virtually unenforced for other pollutants until 1970, when this permit program was rediscovered and used briefly (with little success) as the basis for federal enforcement actions.

The Water Pollution Control Act of 1948 represented the first attempt by the federal government to exercise some direct influence over what previously had been a state and local function. A hesitant move, since it reaffirmed that the primary responsibility for water pollution control rested with the states, it did initiate the authority of the federal government to conduct investigations, research, and surveys.

The first hints of the current approach are found in the amendments to the Water Pollution Control Act, which were passed in 1956. Two provisions of this act were especially important: (1) federal financial support for the construction of waste treatment plants and (2) direct federal regulation of waste discharges via a mechanism known as the *enforcement conference*.

The first of these provisions envisioned a control strategy based on subsidizing the construction of a particular control activity—waste treatment plants. Municipalities could receive federal grants to cover up to 55% of the construction of municipal sewage treatment plants. This approach not only lowered the cost to the local governments of constructing these facilities, it also lowered the cost to users. Since the federal government contribution was a grant, rather than a loan, the fees charged users did not reflect the federally subsidized construction portion of the cost. The user fees were set at a lower rate that was high enough to cover merely the unsubsidized portion of construction cost, as well as operating and maintenance cost.

The 1956 amendments envisioned a relatively narrow federal role in the regulation of discharges. Initially, only polluters contributing to interstate pollution were included, but subsequent laws have broadened the coverage. By 1961 discharges into all navigable water were covered.

The mechanism created by the amendments of 1956 to enforce the regulation of discharges was the enforcement conference. Under this approach the designated federal control authority could call for a conference to deal with any interstate water pollution problem, or it could be requested to do so by the governor of an affected state. The fact that this authority was discretionary and not mandatory and that the control authority had very few means of enforcing any decisions reached meant that the conferences simply did not achieve the intended results.

The Water Quality Act of 1965 attempted to improve the process by establishing ambient water-quality standards for interstate watercourses and by requiring states to file implementation plans. This sounds like the approach currently being used in air pollution control, but there are important differences. The plans forthcoming from states in response to the 1965 Act were vague and did not attempt to link specific effluent standards on discharges to the ambient standards. They generally took the easy way out and called for secondary treatment, which removes 80–90% of BOD and 85% of suspended solids. The fact that these standards bore no particular relationship to ambient quality made them difficult to enforce in the courts, since the legal authority for them was based on this relationship.

Subsequent Legislation

Point Sources.   As discussed in the preceding chapters, an air of frustration regarding pollution control pervaded Washington in the 1970s. As with air pollution legislation, this frustration led to the enactment of a very tough water control law. The tone of the act is established immediately in the preamble, which calls for the achievement of two goals: (1) "... that the discharge of pollutants into the navigable waters be eliminated by 1985"; and (2) "... that wherever attainable, an interim goal of water quality which provides for the protection and propagation of fish, shellfish, and wildlife and provides for recreation in and on the water be achieved by June 1, 1983." The stringency of these goals represented a major departure from past policy.

This act also introduced new procedures for implementing the law. Permits were required of all dischargers (replacing the 1899 Refuse Act, which, because of its navigation focus, was difficult to enforce). The permits would be granted only when the dischargers met certain technology-based effluent standards. The ambient standards were completely bypassed as these effluent standards were uniformly imposed and, hence, could not depend on local water conditions.[3]

According to the 1972 amendments, the effluent standards were to be implemented in two stages. By 1977 industrial dischargers, as a condition of their permit, were required to meet effluent limitations based on the "best practicable control technology currently available" (BPT). In setting these national standards, the EPA was required to consider the total costs of these technologies and their relation to the benefits received, but not to consider the conditions of the individual source or the particular waters into which it was discharged. In addition, all publicly owned treatment plants were to have achieved secondary treatment by 1977. By 1983 industrial discharges were required to meet effluent limitations based on the presumably more stringent "best available technology economically achievable" (BAT) while publicly owned treatment plants were required to meet effluent limitations that depended on the "best practicable waste treatment technology."

The program of subsidizing municipal water treatment plants, begun in 1956, was continued in a slightly modified form by the 1972 Act. Whereas the 1965 Act allowed the federal government to subsidize up to 55% of the cost of construction of waste treatment plants, the 1972 Act raised the ceiling to 75%. The 1972 Act also increased the funds available for this program. In 1981 the federal share was reduced to 55%.

The 1977 amendments continued this regulatory approach, but with some major modifications. This legislation drew a more careful distinction between conventional and toxic pollutants, with more stringent requirements placed on the latter, and it extended virtually all of the deadlines in the 1972 Act.

For conventional pollutants, a new treatment standard was created to replace the BAT standards. The effluent limitations for these pollutants were to be based on the "best conventional technology," and the deadline for these standards was set at July 1, 1984. In setting these standards, the EPA was required to consider whether the costs of adding the pollution control equipment were reasonable when compared with the improvement in water quality. For unconventional pollutants and toxics (any pollutant not specifically included on the list of conventional pollutants), the BAT requirement was retained but the deadline was shifted to 1984.

Other deadlines were also extended. The date for municipalities to meet the secondary treatment deadline moved from 1977 to 1983. Industrial compliance with the BPT standards was delayed until 1983 whenever the contemplated system had the potential for application throughout the industry.

---

[3]Actually, the ambient standards were not completely bypassed. If the uniform controls were not sufficient to meet the desired standard, the effluent limitation would have to be tightened accordingly.

The final modification made by the 1977 amendments involved the introduction of pretreatment standards for waste being sent to a publicly owned treatment system. These standards were designed to prevent the discharges that could inhibit the treatment process and to prevent the introduction of toxic pollutants that would not be treated by the waste treatment facility. Existing facilities were required to meet the standards three years after the date they were published, while facilities constructed later would be required to meet the pretreatment regulations upon commencement of operations.

Nonpoint Sources.   In contrast to the control of point sources, the EPA was given no specific authority to regulate nonpoint sources. This type of pollution was seen by Congress as a state responsibility.

Section 208 of the act authorized federal grants for state-initiated planning that would provide implementable plans for areawide waste treatment management. Section 208 further specified that this areawide plan must identify significant nonpoint sources of pollution, as well as procedures and methods for controlling them. The reauthorization of the Clean Water Act, passed over President Reagan's veto during February 1987, authorized an additional $400 million for a new program to help states control runoff, but it still left the chief responsibility for controlling nonpoint sources to the states.

The main federal role for controlling nonpoint sources has been the Conservation Reserve Program. Designed to remove some 40 to 45 million acres of highly erodible land from cultivation, this act provides subsidies to farmers for planting grass or trees. These subsidies are designed to result in reduced erosion and to reduce loadings of nitrogen, phosphorus, and total suspended solids.

Since the late 1980s, efforts focused on nonpoint sources have increased dramatically. Voluntary programs and cost-sharing programs with landowners have been the most common tools. Regulatory approaches for storm sewers are also utilized. Section 319 of the Clean Water Act specifies guidelines for state implementation of nonpoint source management plans. In 2003, the EPA devoted a large portion of its Section 319 funds ($100 million) to address areas where nonpoint source pollution has significantly impaired water quality.[4]

The Safe Drinking Water Act

The 1972 policy focused on achieving water quality sufficiently high for fishing and swimming. Because that quality is not high enough for drinking water, the Safe Drinking Water Act of 1974 issued more stringent standards for community water systems. The primary drinking water regulations set maximum allowable concentration levels for bacteria, turbidity (muddiness), and chemical-radiological contaminants. National secondary drinking water regulations were also established to protect "public welfare" from odor and aesthetic problems that may cause a substantial number of people to stop using the affected water system. The secondary standards are advisory for the states; they cannot be enforced by the EPA.

---

[4]*U.S. Federal Register* Vol. 68, No. 205 (October 2003).

The 1986 amendments required the EPA to issue primary standards within three years for 83 contaminants and at least 25 more by 1991, to set standards based on best available technology, and to monitor public water systems for both regulated and unregulated chemical contaminants. Approximately 60,000 public water systems are subject to these regulations. Civil and criminal penalties for any violations of the standards were also increased by the amendments.

Ocean Pollution

Oil Spills.   The Clean Water Act prohibits discharges of "harmful quantities" of oil into navigable waters. Since the EPA regulations define "harmful" to include all discharges that "violate applicable water quality standards or cause a film or sheen upon the surface of the water," virtually all discharges are prohibited.

Industry responsibilities include complying with Coast Guard regulations (which deal with contingency planning in case of a spill and various accident avoidance requirements) and assuming the financial liability for any accident. If a spill does occur, it must be immediately reported to the Coast Guard or the EPA. Failure to report a spill can result in a fine up to $10,000 and/or imprisonment for up to one year.

In addition to giving notice, the discharger must either contain the spill or pay the cost of cleanup by a responsible government agency. The discharger's liability for the government's actual removal cost is limited to $50 million unless willful negligence or willful misconduct can be proved. Successful proof of willful negligence or willful misconduct eliminates the liability limit. In addition to cleanup costs, removal costs also include compensation for damages to natural resources. (Natural resource damages are defined as "any costs or expenses incurred by the federal government or any state government in the restoration or replacement of natural resources damaged or destroyed as a result of a discharge of oil . . .".)

Ocean Dumping.   Except for oil spills, which are covered by the Clean Water Act and the Oil Pollution Act of 1990, discharges to the ocean are covered by the Marine Protection Research and Sanctuaries Act of 1972. This act governs all discharges of wastes to ocean waters within U.S. territorial limits and discharges of wastes in ocean waters by U.S. vessels or persons regardless of where the dumping occurs. With only a few exceptions, no ocean dumping of industrial wastes or sewer sludge is now permitted. Radiological, chemical, and biological warfare agents and high-level radioactive wastes are specifically prohibited by the statute. Under the amended statute, the only ocean-dumping activities permitted are the disposal of dredged soil, fish wastes, human remains, and submerged vessels. This dumping is subject to specific regulations and is approved on a case-by-case basis.

Citizen Suits

The degree to which environmental quality is improved by public policy depends not only on the types of policies, but also on how well those policies are enforced. Policies that initially seem to offer promise may, in the glare of hindsight, prove unsuitable if enforcement is difficult or lax.

The enforcement of the environmental statutes has long been the responsibility of state and federal environmental agencies. Enforcement at the state and federal level occurs through administrative proceedings or through civil and criminal judicial action. Since limited staff and resources do not enable these government agencies to fully enforce all of the environmental statutes, however, these methods alone do not provide the necessary level of enforcement.

During the early 1970s, a pervasive recognition that the government had neither the time nor the resources to provide sufficient enforcement led Congress to create a private alternative—citizen suits. Though citizen suits are now authorized by a number of different environmental statutes, the program has been particularly successful in enforcing the Clean Water Act.

Empowered as private attorney generals, citizens are authorized to exercise oversight over government actions and to initiate civil proceedings against any private or public polluter violating the terms of its effluent standard. Environmental groups such as the Natural Resources Defense Council and the Sierra Club have become active participants in the process. Citizens may sue for an injunction (a court order requiring the illegal discharge to cease), but in addition are also given the power to "... apply any appropriate civil penalties." The amount of penalty can vary between $10,000 and $25,000 per day, per violation.

Efficiency and Cost-Effectiveness

Ambient Standards and the Zero-Discharge Goal

The 1956 amendments defined ambient standards as a means of quantifying the objectives being sought. A system of ambient standards allows the control authority to tailor the quality of a particular body of water to its use. Water used for drinking would be subject to the highest standards, swimming the next highest, and so on. Once the ambient standards are defined, the control responsibility could be allocated among sources. Greater efforts to control pollution would be expended where the gap between desired and actual water quality was the largest.

Unfortunately, the early experience with ambient standards for water was not reassuring. Rather than strengthening the legal basis for the effluent standards, while retaining their connection to the ambient standards, Congress chose to downgrade the importance of ambient standards by specifying a zero-discharge goal. Additionally, the effluent standards were given their own legal status apart from any connection with ambient standards. The wrong inference was drawn from the early lack of legislative success.

In his own inimitable style, Mark Twain (1893) put the essential point rather well:

> We should be careful to get out of an experience only the wisdom that is in it—and stop there; lest we be like the cat that sits down on a hot stove lid. She will never sit down on a hot stove lid again—and that is well; but also she will never sit down on a cold one anymore. [p. 125]

The most fundamental problem with the current approach is that it rests on the faulty assumption that the tougher the law, the more that is accomplished. The zero-discharge goal provides one example of a case in which passing a tough standard, in the hopes of actually achieving a weaker one, can backfire. Kneese and Schultze (1975) point out that in the late 1960s, the French experimented with a law that required zero discharge and imposed severe penalties for violations. The result was that the law was never enforced because it was universally viewed as unreasonable. Less control was accomplished under this unenforceable law than would have been accomplished with a less stringent but enforceable one.

Is the U.S. case comparable? It appears to be. In 1972 the EPA published an estimate of the costs of meeting a zero-discharge goal, assuming that it is feasible. They concluded that over the decade from 1971 to 1981, removing 85 to 90% of the pollutants from all industrial and municipal effluents would cost $62 billion. Removing all of the pollutants would cost $317 billion, more than five times as much, and this figure probably understates the true cost (Kneese and Schultze, 1975, 78).

Is this cost justified? Probably not for all pollutants, though for some it may be. Unfortunately, the zero-discharge goal makes no distinction among pollutant types. For some fund pollutants it seems extreme. Perhaps the legislators realized this because when the legislation was drafted, no specific timetables or procedures were established to ensure that the zero-discharge goal would be met by 1985 or, for that matter, anytime.

National Effluent Standards

The first prong in the two-pronged congressional attack on water pollution was the national effluent standards (the other being subsidies for the construction of publicly owned waste treatment facilities). Deciding on the appropriate levels for these standards for each of the estimated 60,000 sources is not a trivial task. Not surprisingly, difficulties arose.

Enforcement Problems.   Soon after passage of the 1972 amendments, the EPA geared up to assume its awesome responsibility. Relying on a battery of consultants, it began to study the technologies of pollution control available to each industry in order to establish reasonable effluent limits. In establishing the guidelines, the EPA is required to take into account "the age of the equipment and facilities involved, the process employed, the engineering aspects of the application of various types of control techniques, process changes, nonwater quality environmental impact (including energy requirements) and such factors as the Administrator deems appropriate. . . ."

It is not clear whether this provision means that individual standards should be specified for each source, or general standards for broad categories of sources. Cost-effectiveness would require the former, but in a system relying on effluent standards, the transaction costs associated with that approach would be prohibitively high and the delay unacceptably long. Therefore, the EPA chose the only feasible interpretation available and established general standards for broad categories of sources. While the standards could differ among categories, they were uniformly applied to the large number of sources within each category.

The EPA inevitably fell behind the congressional deadlines. In fact, not one effluent standard was published within the year deadline. As the standards were published, they were immediately challenged in the courts. By 1977 some 250 cases had been mounted, challenging the published standards (Freeman, 1978, 46). Some of the challenges were successful, requiring the EPA to revise the standards. All of this took time.

By 1977 the EPA was having so much trouble defining the BPT standards that the deadlines for the BAT standards were completely unreasonable. Furthermore, for conventional pollutants, not only the deadlines but the standards themselves were irrational. Many bodies of water would have met the ambient standards without the BAT standard, while for others, the effluent standards were not sufficient, particularly in areas with large nonpoint pollution problems. In addition, in some cases the technologies required by BPT would not be compatible (or even necessary) once the BAT standards were in effect. The situation was in a shambles.

The 1977 amendments changed both the timing of the BAT standards (delaying the deadlines) and their focus (toward toxic pollutants and away from conventional pollutants). As a result of these amendments, the EPA was required to develop industry effluent standards based on the BAT guidelines for control of 65 classes of toxic priority pollutants. In a 1979 survey, the EPA discovered that all primary industries regularly discharge one or more of these toxic pollutants. As of 1980 the EPA had proposed BAT effluent limitations for control of toxic priority pollutants for nine primary industries.

The 1977 amendments certainly improved the situation. Because toxics represent a more serious problem, it makes sense to set stricter standards for those pollutants. Extension of the deadlines was absolutely necessary; there was no alternative.

These amendments have not, however, resulted in a cost-effective strategy. In particular, they tend to retard technological progress and to assign the responsibility for control in an unnecessarily expensive manner.

Allocating Control Responsibility.   Because the effluent standards established by the EPA are based upon specific technologies, these technologies are known to the industries. Therefore, in spite of the fact that the industry can choose any technology that keeps emissions under the limitation stated in the standard, in practice industries tend to choose the specific equipment cited by the EPA when it established the standard. This, they reason, minimizes their risk. If anything goes wrong and they are hauled into court, they can simply argue that they did precisely what the EPA had in mind when it set the standard.

The problem with this reaction is that it focuses too narrowly on a particular technology rather than on the real objective, emission reduction. The focus should be less on the purchase of a specific technology and more on doing what is necessary to hold emissions down, such as maintenance, process changes, and so on. In a field undergoing rapid technological change, tying all control efforts to a particular technology (which may become obsolete well before the standards are revised) is a poor strategy. Unfortunately, technological stagnation has become a routine side effect of the current policy, to the detriment of securing clean water.

In allocating the control responsibility among various sources, the EPA was constrained by the inherent difficulty of making unique determinations for each source and by limitations in the Act itself, such as the need to apply relatively uniform standards. We know from Chapter 15 that uniform effluent standards are not cost-effective, but it remains an open question whether or not the resulting increases in cost are sufficiently large to recommend an alternative approach, such as effluent charges or permits. The fact that the cost increases are large in the control of stationary-source air pollution does not automatically imply that they are large for water pollution control as well.

A number of empirical studies have investigated how closely the national effluent standards approximate the least-cost allocation (see Table 19.2). These studies support the contention that EPA standards are not cost-effective, though the degree of cost-ineffectiveness is typically smaller than that associated with the standards used to control air pollution.

Perhaps the most famous study examining the cost-effectiveness of uniform standards in contrast with emission and ambient charges and permits was conducted on the Delaware Estuary (Kneese and Bower, 1968). This river basin, though small by the standards of the Mississippi or other major basins, drains an area serving a population in excess of 6 million people. It is a highly industrial, densely populated area.

In this study, a simulation model was constructed to capture the effect on ambient dissolved oxygen content of a variety of pollutants discharged by a large number of polluters into the river at numerous locations. In addition, this model was capable of simulating the cost consequences of various methods used to allocate the responsibility for controlling effluent to meet dissolved oxygen standards.

Four specific methods of allocating responsibility were considered. The first was the *least-cost* (LC) method, which would correspond to an ambient charge or ambient permit system. This method takes both locations of the emissions and control costs into account.

The second method was a *uniform treatment* (UT) strategy in which all discharges were faced with an effluent standard requiring them to remove a given percentage of their waste before discharging the remainder into the river. This method mirrors, in a crude way, the current EPA strategy.

The third method simulated the allocation attained from the use of a *uniform emission charge* (UEC) or an emissions permit system. This method takes control costs, but not emission locations, into account. The final case simulates a *zoned effluent charge* (ZEC). For this case the river basin was subdivided into a series of zones. All dischargers within a zone would face the same emission charges, while dischargers in different zones could face different emission charges. This fourth simulation was an intermediate step between the first and third strategies. It allowed location to be more of a factor than in the third method but less of a factor than in the first method. The first simulation would be identical to the fourth if the zones were sufficiently small that each discharger was in its own unique zone; it would be identical to the third if one zone contained all sources (see Table 19.3).

For control of water pollution, the UT strategy does increase the cost substantially. For either dissolved oxygen objective, the costs are roughly three times higher.

TABLE 19.2

Empirical Studies of Water Pollution Control

Study and Year	Pollutants Covered	Geographic Area	CAC Benchmark	DO Target (mg/liter)	Ratio of CAC Cost to Least-Cost
Johnson (1967)	Biochemical oxygen demand	Delaware Estuary-86-mile reach	Equal proportional treatment	2.0	3.13
				3.0	1.62
				4.0	1.43
O'Neil (1980)	Biochemical oxygen demand	20-mile segment of Lower Fox River in Wisconsin	Equal proportional treatment	2.0	2.29
				4.0	1.71
				6.2	1.45
				7.9	1.38
Eheart, Brill, and Lyon (1983)	Biochemical oxygen demand	Willamette River in Oregon	Equal proportional treatment	4.8	1.12
				7.4	1.19
		Delaware Estuary in PA, DE, and NJ	Equal proportional treatment	3.0	3.00
				3.6	2.92
		Upper Hudson River in New York	Equal proportional treatment	5.1	1.54
				5.9	1.62
		Mohawk River in New York	Equal proportional treatment	6.8	1.22

CAC = command and control, the traditional regulatory approach.

DO = dissolved oxygen: higher DO targets indicate higher water quality.

Source: T. H. Tietenberg. *Emmissions Trading: An Exercise in Reforming Pollution Policy* (Washington, DC: Resources for the Future, 1985): 46, Table 5.

TABLE 19.3

Cost of Treatment under Alternative Programs: The Delaware Estuary

DO Objective (ppm)	Program			
	LC	UT	UEC	ZEC
		(million dollars per year)		
2	1.6	5.0	2.4	2.4
3-4	7.0	20.0	12.0	8.6

Source: Table 16 Cost of Treatment under Alternative Programs (p.164) from *Economics and the Environment* by Allen V. Kneese (Penguin Books, 1977). Copyright © Allen V. Kneese, 1977. Reproduced by permission of Penguin Books Ltd.

Also of interest is the fact that the zonal system results in costs that are quite close to the minimum for the higher DO objective, while the UEC does not. Even rudimentary attempts to take location into account may make a big difference for water pollution just as it does for air pollution.

Despite this evidence, the regulatory reform movement that played such an important role for air pollution control has been much slower to emerge for water pollution control. An early attempt at trading was implemented for the Fox River in Wisconsin, but only one trade was made in the first ten years after implementation.

More recently, however, watershed-based trading programs are gaining attention and are being explored by the USEPA. In 1996, the USEPA issued a "Draft Framework for Watershed Based Trading" and began exploring trading programs for the Tar-Pamlico River in North Carolina, Long Island Sound, Chesapeake Bay, and the Snake and Lower Boise Rivers in Idaho. Most of the markets currently in place focus on either nitrogen or phosphorous trading and are too new to evaluate. Ex-ante studies, however, suggest that the economic benefits can be large as illustrated in Example 19.2. Tradable permit cost savings were explored for treating hypoxic conditions in Long Island Sound. Allowing firms the flexibility to exploit economies of scale in pollution control technology can provide for large savings.

In 2003 the USEPA issued a "Water Quality Trading Policy." This policy supports market-based programs for certain pollutants if they can help meet Clean Water Act Goals (USEPA, 2004).

The European Experience.   Economic incentives have been important in water pollution control in Europe, where effluent charges play a prominent role in a number of countries.[5] These charge systems take a number of forms. One common approach is illustrated by Czechoslovakia, which uses charges to achieve predetermined ambient standards. Others, such as the former West Germany, use

---

[5]For a summary of this experience, see Opschoor and Vos (1989).

Example 19.2

EFFLUENT TRADING AND THE COST OF REDUCING WASTE TREATMENT DISCHARGES INTO LONG ISLAND SOUND

Long Island Sound experiences severe hypoxia (low levels of dissolved oxygen) during the summer months. This *eutrophication* is caused primarily by excess nitrogen discharges from municipal sewage treatment plants. As discussed elsewhere in this chapter, most past policies for water pollution control focused on technology standards to control discharges. Economic theory suggests that lower costs can be achieved by providing flexibility to the plants via a permit trading program. In the late 1990s, Connecticut, New York, and the USEPA began exploring this possibility for sewage treatment plants with discharges reaching Long Island Sound. The plan targeted trading to certain management zones. The plan was aimed at meeting the management goals of Phase III of the Management Plan adopted in 1994 to control hypoxia. The overall goal of this management plan was a 58.5% reduction in nitrogen over 15 years, beginning in 1999.

Bennett et al. (2000) estimate the costs associated with the proposed scheme whereby trading is restricted to the 11 management zones designated by the *Long Island Sound Study*. They then estimate the cost savings of alternative programs that expand the zone of trading to (1) trading among sources and across zones, but within state boundaries and (2) trading across all sources. For each trading scenario, polluting sources are grouped into trading "bubbles" that are based on geographic location. Trading is allowed to take place within each bubble, but not among bubbles. The first scenario consists of 11 bubbles (the management zones). The second scenario has two bubbles, one for Connecticut and one for New York. The third scenario consists of one large bubble.

Bennett et al. find what economic theory would predict, that cost savings rise (and rise substantially) as the scope of trading expands (meaning, fewer bubbles). Expanding trading across the two state bubbles could save up to 20% or $156 million based on their estimates. The table below is reproduced from their results.

Number of Trading Bubbles	Present Value of Total Costs ($ million)	Cost Savings Relative to 11 Bubbles ($ million)	Percentage Savings
11	781.44	—	—
2	740.55	40.89	5.23
1	625.14	156.30	20.00

Not all discharges have the same impact on the problem. It turns out that discharges from zones in the eastern portion of Long Island Sound and the northern parts of Connecticut do not have as detrimental effects as those closer to New York City.

Continued

Despite differences in abatement cost, the proposed management plan recommends that each management zone be responsible for an equal percentage of nitrogen reduction.

While marginal abatement costs vary widely across management zones (suggesting that trades could reduce costs), the marginal contributions to damages also vary widely, thus ruling out a simple system of ton-for-ton effluent trades. (As Chapter 15 pointed out, more complicated ambient trades would be required to achieve cost-effectiveness for this nonuniformly mixed pollutant.) Currently, in recognition of this complexity, trading is not being considered across the boundaries of the 11 management zones despite the apparent potential cost savings.

Source: Bennett, Lynne Lewis, Steven G. Thorpe, and A. Joseph Guse. "Cost-Effective Control of Nitrogen Loadings in Long Island Sound," *Water Resources Research* Vol. 36, No. 12 (December 2000): 3711–3720.

charges mainly to encourage firms to control more than their legal requirements. A third group, illustrated by Hungary and the former East Germany, shows how charge systems have been combined with effluent standards.

Czechoslovakia has used effluent charges to maintain water quality at predetermined levels for several decades. A basic charge is placed on BOD and suspended solids and complemented by a surcharge ranging from 10 to 100%, depending upon the contribution of the individual discharge to ambient pollutant concentrations. The basic rates can be adjusted to reflect the quality of the receiving water. This system is conceptually very close to the ambient emission charge system known to be cost-effective.

The charge system in the former West Germany was announced in 1976 and implemented in 1981. The level of charge is related to the degree of compliance with the standards. Firms failing to meet their required standards pay a charge on all actual emissions. If, according to the issued permit, federal emission standards (which are separately defined for each industrial sector) are met, the charge is lowered to 50% of the base rate and is applied to the level of discharge implied by the minimum standard. If the firm can prove the discharge to be lower than 75% of minimum standards, one-half of the base rate is applied to the (lower) actual discharge level. The charge is waived for three years prior to the installation of new pollution control equipment promising further reductions of at least 20%. Revenues from the charges can be used by the administering authorities for administrative costs and financial assistance to public and private pollution abatement activities.

The final approach, used in Hungary and the former East Germany, combines effluent charges with effluent standards. The charge is levied on discharges in excess of fixed effluent limits. In the Hungarian system, the level of the charge is based on the condition of the receiving waters, among other factors. Initially, the Hungarian charges had little effect, but when the charge levels were raised, a flurry of waste treatment activity resulted.

Though these European approaches differ from one another and are not all cost-effective, their existence suggests that effluent charge systems are possible and practical. The German Council of Experts on Environmental Questions estimated the German effluent charge policy to be about one-third cheaper for the polluters as a group than an otherwise comparable uniform treatment policy. Furthermore, it encouraged firms to go beyond the uniform standards when such effort was cost-justified.

In a very different approach, Bystrom (1998) examines reducing nonpoint source nitrogen pollution by constructing wetlands in Sweden, where reducing nitrogen loads to the Baltic Sea is an important policy goal. Though it is well known that wetlands can help reduce nitrogen concentrations through the uptake of biomass, how cost-effective is this approach when it is compared to alternative, more traditional methods of control?

To answer this question, Bystrom estimates nonpoint source abatement costs for constructed wetlands and compares them to the costs of reducing nitrogen by means of land-use changes such as the planting of fuel woods. This study finds that marginal abatement costs for wetlands are lower than transitioning to different crops, but still higher than the marginal costs of simply reducing the use of nitrogen fertilizer.

Municipal Waste Treatment Subsidies

The second phase of the two-pronged water pollution control program involves subsidies for waste treatment plants. This program has run into problems as well, ranging from deficiencies in the allocation of the subsidies to the incentives created by the program.

The Allocation of Funds.   Since the available funds were initially allocated on a first-come, first-served basis, it is not surprising that the funds were not spent in areas having the greatest impact. It was not uncommon, for example, for completed treatment plants to dump effluent that was significantly cleaner than the receiving water. Also, federal funds have traditionally been concentrated on smaller, largely suburban communities rather than on the larger cities with the most serious pollution problems.

The 1977 amendments attempted to deal with this problem by requiring states to set priorities for funding treatment works while giving the EPA the right, after holding public hearings, to not only veto a state's priority list but also to request a revised list. This tendency to ensure that the funds are allocated to the highest-priority projects was reinforced with the passage of the Municipal Wastewater Treatment Construction Grant Amendments of 1981. Under this act, states are required to establish project priorities for targeting funds to projects with the most significant water quality and public health consequences.

Operation and Maintenance.   This approach subsidized the *construction* of treatment facilities but provided no incentive to *operate* them effectively. The existence of a municipal waste treatment plant does not by itself guarantee cleaner water. The EPA's annual inspection surveys of operating plants in 1976 and 1977 found only about half of the plants performing satisfactorily. More recent surveys have found that the general level of waste treatment performance has remained substantially unchanged from previous years.

When sewage treatment plants chronically or critically malfunction, the EPA may take a city to court to force compliance with either a direct order or a fine. Because of various constitutional legal barriers, it is very difficult to force a city to pay a fine to the federal treasury. Without an effective and credible sanction, the EPA is in a difficult position to deal with municipalities. Therefore, the end of the treatment plant malfunction problem cannot yet be pronounced with any assurance.

Capital Costs.   Due to the federal subsidies, local areas ended up paying only a fraction of the true cost of constructing these facilities. Since much of the money came from federal taxpayers, local communities had less incentive to hold construction costs down. The Congressional Budget Office (1985) estimated that substantially increasing the local share could reduce capital costs by as much as 30%. Local areas are more careful with their own money.

Pretreatment Standards

To deal with untreatable hazardous wastes entering municipal waste treatment plants, the EPA has defined pretreatment standards regulating the quality of the wastewater flowing into the plants. These standards suffer the same deficiencies as other effluent standards; they are not cost-effective (see Example 19.3). The control over wastewater flows into treatment plants provides one more aspect of environmental policy where economic incentive approaches offer yet another opportunity to achieve equivalent results at a lower cost.

Nonpoint Pollution

The current law does little to control nonpoint pollution, which in many areas is a significant part of the total problem. In some ways, the government has tried to compensate for this uneven coverage by placing more intensive controls on point sources. Is this emphasis efficient?

It could conceivably be justified on two grounds. If the marginal damages caused by nonpoint sources are significantly smaller than those of point sources, then a lower level of control could well be justified. Since in many cases nonpoint source pollutants are not the same as point source pollutants, this is a logical possibility.

Or, if the costs of controlling nonpoint sources even to a small degree are very high, this could justify benign neglect as well. Are either of these conditions met in practice?

Costs.   Research on economic incentives for nonpoint source pollution control is relatively new as cost information is relatively scarce. Some of the case-specific studies available, however, can give us a sense of the economic analysis. Most of the available studies focus on nonpoint source pollution from agriculture.

McCann and Easter (1999) measured the size of transaction costs associated with various agricultural nonpoint source pollution control policies. Transaction costs (the administrative costs associated with implementing a policy) are an

Example 19.3

COST-EFFECTIVE PRETREATMENT STANDARDS

The electroplating operations of the Rhode Island jewelry industry produce high concentrations of cyanide, copper, nickel, and zinc, which are routinely discharged into municipal sewer systems. Since the treatment plants are not designed to remove these hazardous substances, the EPA has defined pretreatment standards to prohibit excessive concentrations of these metals from entering the plants. These standards are financially burdensome, with some estimates suggesting that some 30 to 60% of the small firms could go out of business if the standards were imposed.

An economic analysis by Opaluch and Kashmanian (1985) of the alternatives for meeting EPA concentration objectives concludes that EPA pretreatment standards achieve the objective at a cost almost 50% greater than the least-cost means of achieving the same concentration objectives. An emission permit system with a permit price of $40 per pound would, after trading, achieve the target at a cost of $12.5 million. Compared to the $19.3 million the EPA proposal would cost, this represents a considerable savings.

If the permits were auctioned, the government would collect some $5.0 million from the sale. Although the financial burden of this auction system for allocating permits would be lower on the jewelry industry as a whole than complying with the EPA proposal, even considering this $5.0 million transfer, not every segment of the industry would be better off with the auction. In particular, the permit fees paid by large firms would be sufficiently high that they would bear more financial burden under the auction scheme than with the EPA proposal. If the permits were grandfathered (allocated free of charge) rather than auctioned, however, all existing firms would be better off under the permit system than under the EPA proposal.

Source: James J. Opaluch and Richard M. Kashmanian. "Assessing the Viability of Marketable Permit Systems: An Application in Hazardous Waste Management," *Land Economics* Vol. 61 (August 1985): 263–271.

important consideration for nonpoint source pollution control, because monitoring costs tend to be much higher than for point sources. The net gain from implementing a policy is the abatement cost savings minus the transaction costs; if the transaction costs are too high, they can offset all or a major part of the abatement cost gains from implementing the policy.

McCann and Easter looked specifically at the Minnesota River, where severe water-quality problems made the river "unswimmable, unfishable and uncanoeable" near the Twin Cities. Four policies aimed at reducing agricultural sources of phosphorous were considered: education about best management practices, a conservation tillage requirement, expansion of a program that obtained permanent development rights, and a tax on phosphorous fertilizers. They found that a tax on phosphorous fertilizers had the lowest transaction costs ($0.94 million). Educational programs had the second lowest transaction costs at $3.11 million. Conservation tillage and expansion of the conservation easement program had the highest transaction costs at $7.85 million and $9.37 million, respectively. In terms of transaction costs, their results suggest a comparative advantage for input taxes relative to the other approaches. However, since the price elasticity of demand for phosphorous fertilizers has been estimated at between –$0.25 and –$0.29, a considerable tax increase would be needed to guarantee the desired level of water-quality improvements.

Schwabe (2001) examines various policy options for nonpoint source pollution control for the Neuse River in North Carolina. He compares cost-effectiveness of both the initial and final proposed rules considered by the State of North Carolina. In 1998, nutrient loads in the Neuse River basin were so high that the basin received a *Nutrient Sensitive Waters* classification. In the two years prior to his study, two large swine waste spills caused major algal blooms and 11 million fish kills. The State of North Carolina initially proposed a rule requiring all farms with land adjacent to a stream to install vegetative filter strips. This was compared to a uniform rollback that measured loadings by county with the objective of a 30% reduction in total nitrogen loadings. Using a least-cost mathematical programming model, Schwabe finds that the uniform rollback is the more cost-effective strategy, especially since the 30% reduction target would be unlikely to be met using the initial rule. However, the author notes that the dominance of the uniform strategy is specific to this particular setting and should not be taken as a general proposition.

The fact that point and nonpoint sources have received such different treatment from the EPA suggests the possibility that costs could be lowered by a more careful balancing of these control options. One study of phosphorous control in the Dillon reservoir in Colorado by Industrial Economics, Inc. (1984) supports the validity of this suspicion.

In this reservoir, four municipalities constitute the only point sources of phosphorous, while there are numerous uncontrolled nonpoint sources in the area. The combined phosphorous load on the reservoir from point and nonpoint sources was projected to exceed its assimilative capacity.

The traditional way to rescue the projected phosphorous load would be to impose even more stringent controls on the point sources. The study found, however, that by following a balanced program controlling both point and nonpoint sources, the desired phosphorous target could be achieved at a cost of approximately $1 million a year less than would be spent if only point sources were controlled more stringently. The more general point to be carried away from this study is that as point sources are controlled to higher and higher degrees, rising marginal control costs will begin to make controlling nonpoint sources increasingly attractive.

Oil Spills

One of the chief characteristics of the current approach to oil spills is that it depends heavily on the ability of the legal system to internalize the costs of a spill through liability law. In principle, the approach is straightforward. Forcing the owner of a vessel to pay for the costs of cleaning up the spill, including compensation for natural resource damages, creates a powerful incentive to exercise care. But is the outcome likely to be efficient in practice?

FIGURE 19.2

Oil Spill Liability

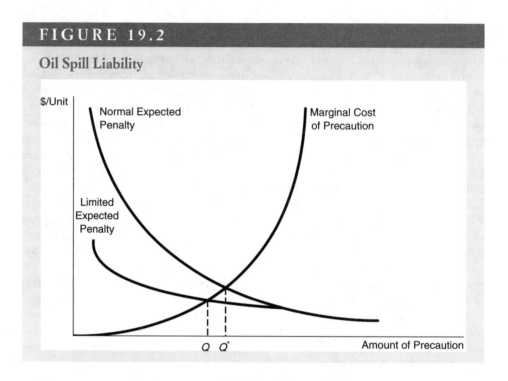

One problem with legal remedies is their high administrative cost; assigning the appropriate penalties is no trivial matter. Even if the court were able to act expeditiously, the doctrines it imposes are not necessarily efficient since the financial liability for cleaning up spills is limited by statute. This point is demonstrated in Figure 19.2, which depicts the incentives of a vessel owner to take precautions. The owner will minimize costs by choosing the level of precaution that equates the marginal cost of additional precaution with the resulting reduction in the marginal expected penalty. The marginal reduction in expected penalty is a function of two factors: the likelihood of a spill and the magnitude of financial obligation it would trigger. This function slopes downward because larger amounts of precaution are presumed to yield smaller marginal reductions in both the likelihood and magnitude of resulting accidents.

The vessel owner's cost-minimizing choice with unlimited liability is depicted as Q^*. As long as the imposed penalty equaled the actual damage and the probability of having to pay the damage once an accident occurred was 1.0, this outcome would normally be efficient. The external costs would be internalized. The owner's private costs would be minimized by taking all possible cost-justified precaution measures to reduce both the likelihood and the seriousness of any resulting spill; taking precautions would simply be cheaper than paying for the cleanup.

Limited liability, however, produces a different outcome. With limited liability, the expected penalty function rotates inward for levels of precaution lower than that level that would produce an accident resulting in damages exactly equal to the limit.[6] Lower levels of precaution imply damages that exceed the limit, but the vessel owner would not have to pay anything above the limit. (The only benefit to the vessel owner faced with limited liability of increasing precaution at lower levels of precaution is the reduction in the likelihood of a spill; in this range, increasing precaution does not reduce the magnitude of the financial payment should a spill occur.) The deviation in the magnitude of the limited expected penalty function from the normal expected penalty function is greatest at lower levels of precaution; it declines to zero at that precaution level where the expected magnitude of an accident is equal to the liability limit.

What is the effect of limited liability on the vessel owner's choice of precaution levels? As long as the liability limit is binding (which appears to routinely be the case with recent spills), the owner will choose too little precaution. (The owner's choice is depicted as Q in Figure 19.2.) Both the number and magnitude of resulting spills would be inefficiently large.[7]

Citizen Suits.[8]   Initiated during the 1970s, citizen suits add a private enforcement alternative to public enforcement in correcting environmental market failures. Public and private enforcement are partial substitutes. If government enforcement were complete, all polluters would be in compliance and citizen suits would have no role to play. Noncompliance is a necessary condition for a successful suit. In the early 1980s when public enforcement decreased, private enforcement—citizen suits—increased to take up the slack. Lax public enforcement appears to have played a significant role in the rise of citizen suits.

All attorney's fees incurred by the citizen group in any successful action under the Clean Water Act must be reimbursed by the defendants. Reimbursement of attorney's fees has affected both the level and focus of litigation activity. By lowering the costs of bringing citizen suits, attorney fee reimbursement has allowed citizen groups to participate far more often in the enforcement process than otherwise would have been possible. Since courts only reimburse for appropriate claims (noncompliance claims that are upheld by the court), citizen groups are encouraged to litigate only appropriate cases.

The existence of citizen suits should affect the decision-making process of the polluting firm. Adding citizen suits to the enforcement arena increases the expected penalty to the noncomplying firm by increasing the likelihood that the firm will face an enforcement action. While this can be expected to increase the amount of precaution taken by the firm, the unavailability of compliance data makes it impossible to confirm this expectation, though participants believe compliance has increased.

While citizen suits probably do lead to greater compliance, greater compliance is not necessarily efficient, especially if the defendant polluters face inefficiently harsh standards. If the standards are excessively high, citizen suits have the potential

---

[6]To avoid confusion, note that the marginal expected penalty for additional precaution when the damage would exceed the liability limit is not zero. While further precaution does not lower the ultimate penalty in this range, it does lower the likelihood of an accident and, hence, the expected penalty.

[7]Suppose at the efficient level of precaution, the magnitude of a resulting spill was less than the liability limit. How would this be depicted graphically? Would you expect the vessel owner's choice to be efficient?

[8]This section is based on Naysnerski and Tietenberg (1992).

to promote inefficiency by forcing firms to meet standards where the marginal benefits are significantly lower than the marginal costs. However, if the effluent standards are either inefficiently low or efficient, the existence of citizen suits will necessarily create a more efficient outcome. In these cases, increasing compliance is perfectly compatible with efficiency.

An Overall Assessment

Though the benefit estimates from water pollution control are subject to much uncertainty, they do exist. While being careful not to place too much reliance on them, we can see what information can be gleaned from the studies in existence.

Freeman (1990) has summarized these studies, focusing on 1985 as a target year. His survey of the field suggests that the 1985 benefit (in 1984 dollars) from conventional water pollution control policy could be as low as $5.7 billion or as high as $27.7 billion with a most likely point estimate of $14.0 billion. This compares to estimated 1985 annual costs (in 1978 dollars) ranging from a low of $25 billion to a high of $30 billion. Thus Freeman estimates that the net benefit from conventional control is probably negative.

A more recent study, using a different methodology, concludes that the current net benefits are positive but are likely to become negative as costs escalate in the future. Relying on benefits estimates derived from contingent valuation, Carson and Mitchell (1993) estimate that aggregate benefits in 1990 exceeded aggregate costs by $6.4 billion. They also found, however, that projected aggregate costs would exceed aggregate benefits because of the high marginal costs and the low marginal benefits associated with bringing the remaining bodies of water up to swimmable quality.

Using cost-effective policies rather than the current approach, it would be possible to reduce costs substantially without affecting the benefits. Cost-effectiveness would require the development of better strategies for point source control and for achieving a better balance between point and nonpoint source control. The resulting reduction in costs probably would allow net benefits to remain positive in the future. That result would not necessarily make the policy efficient, however, because the level of control might still be too high or too low. Unfortunately, the evidence is not rich enough to prove whether the overall level of control maximizes the net benefit.

In addition to promoting current cost-effectiveness, economic incentive approaches would stimulate and facilitate change better than a system of rigid, technology-based standards. Russell (1981) has attempted to assess the importance of the facilitating role by simulating the effects on the allocation of pollution control responsibility in response to regional economic growth, changing technology, and changing product mix. Focusing on the steel, paper, and petroleum refining industries in the 11-county Delaware Estuary Region, his study estimated the change in permit use for three water pollutants (BOD, total suspended solids, and ammonia) that would have resulted if a marketable permit system were in place over the 1940–1978 period. The calculations assume that the plants existing in 1940 would have been allocated permits to legitimize their emissions at that time, that new sources would have had to purchase permits, and that plant shutdowns or contractions would free up permits for others to purchase.

This study found that for almost every decade and pollutant, a substantial number of permits would have been made available by plant closing, capacity contractions, product-mix changes, and/or by the availability of new technologies. In the absence of a marketable permit program, a control authority would not only have to keep abreast of all technological developments so emission standards could be adjusted accordingly, but it would also have to ensure an overall balance between effluent increases and decreases so as to preserve water quality. This tough assignment is handled completely by the market in a marketable permit system, thereby facilitating the evolution of the economy by responding flexibly and predictably to change.

Marketable permits encourage, as well as facilitate, this evolution. Since permits have value, in order to minimize costs, firms must continually be looking for new opportunities to control emissions at lower cost. This search eventually results in the adoption of new technologies and in the initiation of changes in the product mix that result in lower amounts of emissions. The pressure on sources to continually search for better ways to control pollution is a distinct advantage that economic incentive systems have over bureaucratically defined standards.

Summary

Historically, policies for controlling water pollution have been concerned with conventional pollutants discharged into surface waters. More recently, concerns have shifted toward toxic pollutants, which apparently are more prevalent than previously believed; toward groundwater, which traditionally was thought to be an invulnerable pristine resource; and toward the oceans, which were mistakenly considered immune from most pollution problems because of their vast size.

Early attempts at controlling water pollution followed a path similar to that of air pollution control. Legislation prior to the 1970s had little impact on the problem. Frustration then led to the enactment of a tough federal law that was so ambitious and unrealistic that little progress resulted.

There the similarity ends. Whereas in air pollution a wave of recent reforms have improved the process by making it more cost-effective, no parallel exists for control of water pollution. Current policy toward cleaning up rivers and lakes is based upon the subsidization of municipal waste treatment facilities and national effluent standards imposed on industrial sources.

The former approach has been hampered by delays, by problems in allocating funds, and by the fact that about half of the constructed plants are not performing satisfactorily. The latter approach has given rise to delays and to the need to define the standards in a series of court suits. In addition, effluent standards have assigned the control responsibility among point sources in a way that excessively raises cost. Nonpoint pollution sources have, until recently, been virtually ignored. Technological progress is inhibited rather than stimulated by the current approach.

This lack of progress could have been avoided. It did not result from a lack of toughness. Rather, it has resulted from a reliance on direct regulation rather than on emission charges or emission permits, which are more flexible and cost-effective in both the dynamic and static sense. In this respect, the United States can perhaps take some lessons from the European experience.

The court system has assumed most of the responsibility for controlling oil spills. Those responsible for the spills are assessed the financial liability for cleaning up the site and compensating for any resulting damages to natural resources. While in principle this approach can be efficient, in practice it has been hampered by liability limitations and the huge administrative burden an oil spill trial entails.

Enforcement is always a key to successful environmental and natural resource policy. One recent innovation in enforcement involves giving private citizen groups the power to bring noncomplying firms into court. By raising the likelihood that noncomplying firms would be brought before the court and assessed penalties for noncompliance, this new system can be expected to increase compliance.

Discussion Questions

1. "The only permanent solution to water pollution control will occur when all production by-products are routinely recycled. The zero-discharge goal recognizes this reality and forces all dischargers to work steadily toward this solution. Less stringent policies are at best temporary palliatives." Discuss.
2. "In exercising its responsibility to protect the nation's drinking water, the government needs to intervene only in the case of public water supplies. Private water supplies will be adequately protected without any government intervention." Discuss.

Problem

1. Consider the situation posed in Problem 1(a) in Chapter 15.
   (a) Compute the allocation that would result if 10 emission permits were given to the second source and 9 were given to the first source. What would be the market permit price? How many permits would each source end up with after trading? What would the net permit expenditure be for each source after trading?
   (b) Suppose a new source entered the area with a constant marginal cost of control equal to $1,600 per unit of emission reduced. Assume further that it would add 10 units in the absence of any control. What would be the resulting allocation of control responsibility? How much would each firm clean up? What would happen to the permit price? What trades would take place?

Further Reading

Letson, D. "Point/Nonpoint Source Pollution Reduction Trading: An Interpretive Survey," *Natural Resources Journal* Vol. 32 (1992): 219–232. Considers a host of implementation details that must be resolved if point/nonpoint source trading is to live up to its potential.

Russell, Clifford, and Jason Shogren, ed. *Theory, Modeling and Experience in the Management of Nonpoint-Source Pollution* (Hingham, MA: Kluwer Academic Publishers, 1993). A collection of 12 essays providing a state-of-the-art review of the economic perspective on nonpoint source pollution.

Additional References and Historically Significant References are available on this book's companion Web site www.aw-bc.com/tietenberg.

Toxic Substances

The fact that a problem will certainly take a long time to solve, and that it will demand the attention of many minds for several generations, is no justification for postponing the study. . . . Our difficulties of the moment must always be dealt with somehow, but our permanent difficulties are difficulties of every moment.

—T. S. Eliot, *Christianity and Culture* (1949)

Introduction

It is one of the ironies of history that the place that focused public attention in the United States on toxic substances is called the Love Canal. *Love* is not a word any impartial observer would choose to describe the relationships among the parties to that incident.

The Love Canal typifies in many ways the dilemma posed by toxic substances. Until 1953, Hooker Electrochemical (now Hooker Chemical, a subsidiary of Occidental Petroleum Corporation) dumped waste chemicals into an old abandoned waterway known as the Love Canal, near Niagara Falls, New York. (Hooker was acquired by Occidental Petroleum in 1968.) At the time it seemed a reasonable solution, since the chemicals were buried in what was then considered to be impermeable clay.

In 1953 Hooker deeded the Love Canal property for $1 to the Niagara Falls Board of Education, which then built an elementary school on the site. The deed specifically excused Hooker from any damages that might be caused by the chemicals. Residential development of the area around the school soon followed.

The site became the center of controversy when, in 1978, residents complained of chemicals leaking to the surface. News reports emanating from the area included stories of spontaneous fires and vapors in basements. Medical reports suggested that the residents had experienced abnormally high rates of miscarriage, birth defects, and diseases of the liver.

Similar contamination experiences befell Europe and Asia. In 1976 an accident at an F. Hoffmann-La Roche & Co. plant in Sevesco spewed dioxin over the Italian countryside. Subsequently, explosions in a Union Carbide plant in Bhopal, India, spread deadly gases over nearby residential neighborhoods with significant loss of life, and water used to quell a warehouse fire at a Sandoz warehouse near Basel, Switzerland, carried an estimated 30 tons of toxic chemicals into the Rhine River, a source of drinking water for a number of towns in Germany.

In previous chapters we touched on a few of the policy instruments used to combat toxic substance problems. Emission standards govern the types and amounts of substances that can be injected into the air. Effluent standards regulate what can be discharged directly into water sources, and pretreatment standards control the flow of toxics into waste treatment plants. Maximum concentration levels have been established for many substances in drinking water.

This impressive array of policies is not sufficient to resolve the Love Canal problem or others having similar characteristics. When violations of the standards for drinking water are detected, for example, the water is already contaminated. Specifying maximum contaminant levels helps to identify when a problem exists, but it does nothing to prevent or contain the problem. The various standards for air and water emission that do protect against *point* sources do little to prevent contamination by *nonpoint* sources. Furthermore, most waterborne toxic pollutants are stock pollutants, not fund pollutants; they cannot be absorbed by the receiving waters. Therefore, temporally constant controls on emissions (a traditional method used for fund pollutants) are inappropriate for these toxic substances since they would allow a steady rise in the concentration over time. Some additional form of control is necessary.

In this chapter we describe and evaluate the policies that deal specifically with the creation, use, transportation and disposal of toxic substances. Many dimensions will be considered: What are appropriate ways to dispose of toxic substances? How can the government ensure that all waste is appropriately disposed of? How do we prevent surreptitious dumping? Who should clean up old sites? Should victims be compensated for damages caused by toxic substances under the control of someone else? If so, by whom? What are the appropriate roles for the legislature and the judiciary in creating the proper set of incentives?

Nature of Toxic Substance Pollution

The main objective of the current legal system for controlling toxic substances is to protect human health, though protecting other forms of life is a secondary objective. The potential health danger depends upon the toxicity of a substance to humans and their exposure to the substance. *Toxicity* occurs when a living organism experiences detrimental effects following exposure to a substance. In normal concentrations, most chemicals are not toxic. Others, such as pesticides, are toxic by design. Yet, in excess concentrations, even a benign substance such as table salt can be toxic.

A degree of risk is involved when using any chemical substance. There are benefits as well. The task for public policy is to define an acceptable risk by balancing the costs and benefits of controlling the use of chemical substances.

Health Effects

The two main health concerns associated with toxic substances are risk of cancer and effects on reproduction.

Cancer.   Since the 1900s, mortality rates have fallen for most of the major causes of death. The most conspicuous exception is cancer. Cancer incidence rates for all types of cancers combined increased from the mid-1970s through 1992, subsequently declined from 1992 to 1995, and then stabilized from 1995 to 2000.

While many suspect the mortality rate for cancer may be related to increased exposure to carcinogens, proving or disproving this link is very difficult due to the latency of the disease. *Latency* refers to the state of being concealed during the period between exposure to the carcinogen and the detection of cancer. Latency periods for cancer run from 15 to 40 years in length, but have been known to run as long as 75 years.

In the United States, part of the increase in cancer has been convincingly linked to smoking, particularly among women. The proportion of women who smoke has increased, and the incidence of lung cancer has increased as well. Smoking does not account for all of the increase in cancer, however.

Though it is not entirely clear what other agents may be responsible, one suggested cause is the rise in the manufacture and use of synthetic chemicals since World War II. A number of these chemicals have been shown in the laboratory to be carcinogenic. That does not necessarily implicate them in the rise of cancer, however, because it does not take exposure into account. The laboratory can reveal, through animal tests, the relationship between dosage and resulting effects. To track down the significance of any chemical in causing cancer in the general population would require an estimate of how large a segment of the population was exposed to various doses. Currently, our data are not extensive enough to allow these kinds of calculations to be done with any confidence.

Reproductive Effects.   Tracing the influence of environmental effects on human reproduction is still a new science. A growing body of scientific evidence, however, suggests that exposure to smoking, alcohol, and chemicals may contribute to infertility, may affect the viability of the fetus and the health of the infant after birth, and may cause genetic defects that can be passed on for generations.

Problems exist for both men and women. In men, exposure to toxic substances has resulted in lower sperm counts, malformed sperm, and genetic damage. In women, exposure can also result in sterility or birth defects in their children.

Policy Issues

Many aspects of the toxic substance problem make it difficult to resolve. Three important aspects are the number of substances involved, latency, and uncertainty.

Number of Substances.   Of the 2 million or so known chemical compounds, approximately 70,000 are actively used in commerce. More than 30,000 of these are in substantial use. Many exhibit little or no toxicity, and even a very toxic substance represents little risk as long as it is isolated. The trick is to identify problem substances and to design appropriate policies as responses. The massive number of substances involved makes that a difficult assignment.

Latency.   The period of latency exhibited by many of these relationships compounds the problem. Two kinds of toxicity are exhibited: acute and chronic. *Acute toxicity* is present when a short-term exposure to the substance produces a detrimental effect on the exposed organisms. *Chronic toxicity* is present when the detrimental effect arises from exposure of a continued or prolonged nature.

The process of screening chemicals as potentially serious causes of chronic illness is even more complicated than that of screening for acute illness. The traditional technique for determining acute toxicity is the lethal-dose determination, a relatively quick test performed on animals that calculates the dose that results in the death of 50% of the animal population. This test is less well suited for screening substances that exhibit chronic toxicity.

The appropriate tests for discovering chronic toxicity have typically involved subjecting animal populations to sustained low-level doses of the substance over an extended period of time. These tests are very expensive and time-consuming. A two-year bioassay for carcinogenic effects of a single chemical would cost around $1.25 million. If the EPA were to do the tests, given its limited resources, it could only test a few of the estimated 500 new chemicals introduced each year. If the industries were to do the tests, the expense could preclude the introduction of many potentially valuable new chemicals that have limited, specialized markets.

The EPA has attempted to respond by developing a series of screening tests that can be accomplished in a shorter period of time and at less expense. The chemicals identified by those screening tests as posing an unacceptable risk can be subjected to more expensive tests. As long as the short tests are sufficiently reliable for screening, the testing problem can be reduced to manageable proportions.

One particularly promising class of screening tests involves adding a chemical substance to a bacteria culture no longer capable of growth. If the substance is a mutagen, and therefore a likely carcinogen, the bacteria resume growth. While these tests are considerably cheaper to perform, the correlation between mutagens and carcinogens is not perfect. Benzene, a known carcinogen, is not a mutagen. Some carcinogens could slip through the mutagen screening process undetected.

Uncertainty.   Another dilemma inhibiting policy-makers is the uncertainty surrounding the scientific evidence on which regulation is based. Effects uncovered by laboratory studies on animals are not perfectly correlated with effects on humans. Large doses administered over a 3-year period may not produce the same effects as an equivalent amount spread over a 20-year period. Some of the effects are *synergistic*—that is, their effects are compounded by other variable factors. They are either more serious or less serious in the presence of other substances or conditions than they would be in the absence of those substances or conditions. (Asbestos workers are 30 times more likely than their nonsmoking fellow workers to get lung cancer if they smoke, for example). Once cancer is detected, in most cases it does not bear the imprint of a particular source. Policy-makers have to act in the face of limited information.

From an economic point of view, how the policy process reacts to this dilemma should depend on how well the market handles toxic substance problems. To the extent that the market generates the correct information and provides the appropriate incentives, policy may not be needed. On the other hand, when the government can best generate information or create the appropriate incentive, intervention may be called for. As the following pages demonstrate, the nature of the most appropriate policy response may depend crucially on the type of relationship existing between the toxic source and the affected party or parties.

Market Allocations and Toxic Substances

Toxic substance contamination can arise in a variety of settings. In order to define the efficient policy response, we must examine what responses would be forthcoming in the normal operation of the market. Let's look at three possible relationships between the source of the contamination and the victim: employer-employee, producer-consumer, and producer-third party. The first two involve normal contractual relations among the parties, while the latter involves noncontracting parties whose connection is defined solely by the contamination.

Occupational Hazards

Many occupations involve risk, including, for some people, exposure to toxic substances. Do employers and employees have sufficient incentives to act in concert toward achieving safety in the workplace?

The caricature of the market used by the most ardent proponents of regulation suggests not. In this view, the employer's desire to maximize profits precludes spending money on safety. Sick workers can simply be replaced. Therefore, the workers are powerless to do anything about it; if they complain, they are fired and replaced with others who are less vocal.

The most ardent opponents of regulation respond that this caricature omits significant market pressures and is not a particularly accurate guide. They argue that it fails to take into account employee incentives and the feedback effects of those incentives on employers.

If employees are to accept work in a potentially hazardous environment, they will do so only if appropriately compensated. Riskier occupations should call forth higher wages. The increase in wages should be sufficient to compensate them for the increased risk. These higher wages represent a real cost of the hazardous situation to the employer. They also produce an incentive to create a safer work environment, since greater safety would result in lower wages. One cost could be balanced against the other. What was spent on safety could be recovered in lower wages (see Figure 20.1).

The first type of cost, the marginal increase in wages, is drawn to reflect the fact that the lower the level of precaution, the higher the wage bill. Two such curves are drawn to reflect high-exposure and low-exposure situations. The high-exposure case refers to a situation in which larger numbers of workers are exposed, while in the low-exposure case, few are exposed. The low-exposure cost curve rises more slowly because the situation is less dangerous at the margin. In the high-exposure case, the

FIGURE 20.1

Market Provision of Occupational Safety

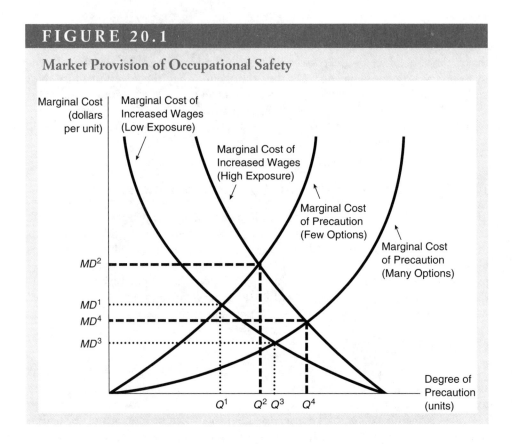

sensitivity of wages to precaution is much higher because the damage caused at the margin is much larger.

The second type of curve, the marginal cost of providing precaution, is drawn to reflect increasing marginal cost. The two different curves depict different production situations. A firm with a few expensive precautionary options will face a steeply sloped marginal cost curve, while a firm with many cheaper options will face a lower marginal cost at every comparable degree of precaution chosen.

The graph depicts four possible outcomes—one for each possible combination of these four marginal cost curves. Notice that very different choices will be made, depending on the circumstances. Also notice that the level of risk chosen (as indicated by the marginal damage, labeled MD) and the degree of precaution are not perfectly correlated. The highest marginal risk is MD^2, but the associated level of precaution (Q^2) is not the largest. The reason, of course, is that the cost of taking precautions matters, and sometimes it is cheaper to accept the risk and compensate for it than it is to prevent it.

Because the marginal increased wages curve accurately reflects marginal damages (since the higher wages are demanded by workers to compensate them for damages), these market equilibria are also efficient. Thus, the efficient resolution of the occupational hazards problem varies not only from substance to substance, but from plant to plant as well. As long as this stylized view of the world is correct, the market will tailor the appropriate degree of precaution to the situation.

Proponents point out that this allocation would also allow more choices for workers than would, for example, a system requiring all workplaces to be equally safe. With varying occupational risk, those occupations with more risk (such as working with radioactive materials) would attract people who were less averse to risk. These workers would receive higher-than-average wages (to compensate them for the increased risk), but paying these higher wages would be cheaper to the firm (and hence, consumers) than producing a workplace safe enough for the average worker. The risk-averse workers would be free to choose less risky occupations.

Existing empirical studies make clear that wages in risky occupations do contain a risk premium (Viscusi and Aldy, 2003). Two conclusions about these risk premiums seem clear from these studies: (1) the willingness to pay for apparently similar risk reductions varies significantly across individuals; and (2) the revealed willingness to pay for risk reduction is substantial.

What is the appropriate role for the public sector in controlling contamination in the workplace? One point raised by the court system is whether market solutions always satisfy ethical norms. For example, if the employee is a pregnant woman and the occupational hazard involves potential damage to the fetus, does the expectant mother have the right to risk the unborn child, or is some added protection for the fetus needed? Furthermore, if the lowest-cost solution is to ban pregnant, or even fertile, women from a workplace that poses a risk to a fetus, is that an acceptable solution, or is it unfair discrimination against women? As Example 20.1 suggests, these are not idle concerns.

Ethical concerns are not the only challenges for market solutions. The ability of the worker to respond to a hazardous situation depends on his or her knowledge of the seriousness of the danger. With toxic substances, that knowledge is likely to be incomplete. Consequently, the marginal increased wages function may be artificially rotated toward the origin; the employer would choose too little precaution. By having access to the health records of all employees, the employer may be in the best position to assess the degree of risk posed, but the employer also has an incentive to suppress that information. To publicize risk would mean demands for higher compensatory wages and possible lawsuits.

Information on the dangers posed by exposure to a particular toxic substance is a public good to employees; each employee has an incentive to be a free rider on the discoveries of others. Individual employees do not have an incentive to bear the cost of doing the necessary research to uncover the degree of risk. Thus, it seems neither employers nor employees can be expected to produce the efficient amount of information on the magnitude of risk.[1]

As a result, the government may play a substantial role in setting the boundaries on ethical responses, in stimulating research on the nature of hazards, and in providing for the dissemination of information to affected parties. It does not

---

[1]Unions would be expected to produce more efficient information flows since they represent many workers and can take advantage of economies of scale in the collection, interpretation, and dissemination of risk information. Available evidence suggests that the preponderance of wage premiums for risk have been derived from unionized workers.

Example 20.1

SUSCEPTIBLE POPULATIONS IN THE HAZARDOUS WORKPLACE

Some employees are especially susceptible to occupational hazards. Pregnant women and women in the childbearing years are particularly vulnerable. When an employer attempts to manage a work situation that poses a hazardous threat, either the susceptible population can be separated from the hazard or the hazard can be controlled to a sufficient level that its risk is acceptable to even the most susceptible employees.

The economic aspects of this choice are easily deduced from Figure 20.1. Suppose that the firm has few control options and is on the uppermost of the two marginal cost-of-precaution curves. By removing the susceptible population, it could face the low-exposure curve. Removal of the susceptible population results in lower marginal risk to the workers, lower costs to the firm, and less precaution taken. But is it fair to those who are removed from their jobs?

This issue came to a head in 1978 when American Cyanamid decided to respond to an occupational risk by banning all fertile women from jobs in the section manufacturing lead chromate pigment at Willow Island, West Virginia. After reviewing the decision, the Occupational Safety and Health Administration (OSHA) cited the company under the general duty clause of the Occupational Safety and Health Act, which requires an employer to provide a workplace free of hazards, and fined it $10,000. That was not the last of it. In early 1980, the Oil, Chemical, and Atomic Workers Union sued the company under the 1964 Civil Rights Act on the grounds that the company had discriminated unfairly against women. In March of 1991 the Supreme Court ruled that banning fertile women from any workplace posing a risk to a fetus was not an acceptable way to control risk. The hazards must be reduced.

Source: International Union v. Johnson Controls, 499 U.S. 187 (1991).

---

necessarily follow, however, that the government should be responsible for determining the level of safety in the workplace once this information is available and the ethical boundaries are determined.

Our analysis suggesting that the market will not provide an efficient level of information on occupational risk is consistent with the enactment of "right-to-know" laws in several states. These laws require businesses to disclose to their employees and to the public any potential health hazards associated with toxic substances used on the job. Generally employers are required to (1) label toxic substance containers, (2) inventory all toxic substances used in the workplace, and (3) provide adequate training on the handling of these substances to all affected employees. Significantly, proponents of these laws suggest that the targets are not the large chemical companies, which generally have excellent disclosure programs, but the smaller, largely nonunion plants.

Product Safety

Exposure to a hazardous or potentially hazardous substance can also occur as a result of using a product, as when eating food containing chemical additives or when using pesticides. Does the market efficiently supply safe products?

One view holds that the market pressures on both parties are sufficient to yield an efficient level of safety. Safer products are generally more expensive to produce and carry a higher price tag. If consumers feel that the additional safety justifies the cost, they will purchase the safer product. Otherwise they won't. Producers supplying excessively risky products will find their market drying up, because consumers will switch to competing brands that are more expensive but safer. Similarly, producers selling excessively safe products (meaning they eliminate, at great cost, risks consumers are perfectly willing to take in return for a lower purchase price) find their markets drying up as well. Consumers will choose the cheaper, riskier product.

This theory also suggests that the market will not (and should not) yield a uniform level of safety for all products. Different consumers will have different degrees of risk aversion. While some consumers might purchase riskier, but cheaper, products, others might prefer safer, but more expensive, products.[2]

Thus, it would be common to find products with various safety levels supplied simultaneously, reflecting and satisfying different consumer preferences for risk. Forcing all similar products to conform to a single level of risk would not be efficient. Uniform product safety is no more efficient than uniform occupational safety.

If this view of the market were completely accurate, government intervention to protect consumers would not be necessary to ensure the efficient level of risk. By the force of their collective buying habits, consumers would protect themselves.

The problem with the market's ability to provide such self-regulation is the availability of information on product safety. The consumer acquires his or her information on a product generally from personal experience. With toxic substances the latency period may be so long as to preclude any effective market reaction. Even when some damage results, it is difficult for the consumer to associate it with a particular source. While an examination of the relationships between purchasing patterns of a large number of consumers and their subsequent health might well reveal some suggestive correlations, it would be difficult for any individual consumer to deduce this correlation.

While the government may need to ensure that consumers receive adequate information on product risks, the need to dictate a prevailing level of safety is much less clear, particularly if the dictated level is uniformly applied. In situations where adequate information is available on the risks, consumers should have a substantial role in choosing the acceptable level of risk through their purchases.

---

[2]A classic example is provided by the manner in which Americans choose their automobiles. It is quite clear that some larger cars are safer and more expensive than smaller, cheaper cars. Some consumers are willing to pay for the safety, and others are not.

Third Parties

The final case involves *third parties*, victims who have no contractual relationship to the source. When groundwater is contaminated by a neighboring waste treatment facility, by surreptitious dumping of toxic wastes, or by the improper applications of a pesticide, the victims would be third parties. In any of these situations, the affected party cannot bring any direct market pressure to bear on the source. Since these non-point sources are generally not controlled by the air and water regulations, the case for additional government intervention is strongest for third-party situations.

This does not necessarily imply, however, that executive or legislative remedies are appropriate. The most appropriate response may well come from simply requiring better information on the risk or, as discussed in Chapter 4, from using the judicial system to impose liability.

Liability law provides one judicial avenue for internalizing the external costs in third-party situations. If the court finds that damage occurred, that it was caused by a toxic substance, and that a particular source was responsible for the presence of the substance, the source can be forced to compensate the victim for the damages caused. Unlike regulations that are uniformly (and, hence, inefficiently) applied, a court decision can be tailored to the exact circumstances involved in the suit. Furthermore, the impact of any particular liability assignment can go well beyond the parties to that case. A decision for one plaintiff can remind other sources that they should take the efficient level of precaution now to avoid paying future damages.

In principle, liability law can force sources, including nonpoint sources, to choose efficient levels of precaution. Unlike regulation, liability law can provide compensation to the victims. How well it functions in practice remains to be seen in the rest of the chapter. Example 20.2 shows how a judicial response to one spill transformed the way one company handled its environmental responsibilities.

Current Policy

Common Law

The common-law system is an extremely complicated approach to controlling risks. When a victim seeks recourse through the court system, a number of legal grounds can be used to pursue a claim. Not all of these may be available to every plaintiff (the person initiating the suit), since the appropriate doctrine depends partially on the legal tradition in the jurisdiction where the suit is filed. Not all jurisdictions allow a plaintiff to file on all grounds. Two of the more common legal grounds are negligence and strict liability.

Negligence.
Negligence is probably the most common legal theory used by plaintiffs to pursue claims. This body of law suggests that the defendant (the party allegedly responsible for the contamination) owes a duty to the plaintiff (the affect-ed party) to exercise due care. If that duty has been breached, the defendant is found negligent and is forced to compensate the victim for damages caused. If the defendant

Example   20.2

JUDICIAL REMEDIES IN TOXIC SUBSTANCE CONTROL: THE KEPONE CASE

Kepone is a highly toxic substance used in the manufacture of pesticides. Kepone was produced at Hopewell, Virginia, by Life Science Products Company, a company started by former employees of Allied Chemical Corporation. The kepone produced by Life Science was sold to Allied Chemical.

Conditions at the plant and spills into the James River resulted in high contamination levels that affected workers and people eating fish taken from the river. Allied Chemical Corporation was indicted by a grand jury on criminal charges during May 1976, and was subsequently sued by various injured parties. Eventually, it paid more than $20 million in compensation, penalties, and legal fees.

As a result of the suit, Allied and a number of other companies have begun to dramatically increase expenditures on prevention. In 1977 Allied hired Arthur D. Little, a consulting firm, to develop a broad program to anticipate and prevent further accidents. By 1981 Allied had over 400 employees concerned with environmental control.

Interestingly, the staff has discovered that pollution control sometimes yields unexpected benefits. In the past, Allied treated its waste, including calcium chloride, from its Baton Rouge plant and discharged it into the river. New regulations from the EPA would have raised the costs of treating the waste. Allied decided to look for a market for the calcium chloride and found one, turning a liability into an asset.

The kepone suit changed this corporation's behavior, as well as the behavior of other chemical companies. They have found that anticipating can be much less costly than reacting.

Source: This example is based upon Georgette Jasen. "Like Other New-Breed Environmental Managers, Hillman of Allied Isn't Merely a Trouble Shooter," *The Wall Street Journal* (July 30, 1981): 50.

is found to have exercised due care and to have performed that duty to the plaintiff, no liability is assessed. Under negligence law, the victim bears the liability unless it can be proved that the defendant was negligent.

Interestingly, the test conventionally applied by the courts in deciding whether the defendant has exercised due care, the Learned Hand formula, is fundamentally an economic one. Named after the judge (yes, Learned Hand!) who initially formulated it, this test suggests that the defendant is guilty of negligence if the marginal loss caused by the contamination, multiplied by the probability of contamination, exceeds the marginal cost of preventing the contamination. This is simply a version of the expected net benefit formula developed in Chapter 3. The maximization of expected net benefits is efficient as long as society is risk-neutral. Therefore, the common-law approach embodied in negligence law in principle is compatible with efficiency.

Sometimes the plaintiff can prove negligence on the part of the defendant by showing that the defendant violated a statute. In many states, any related statutory violation is taken as sufficient proof of negligence.

Strict Liability.   Strict liability can be used by plaintiffs in some states and in some circumstances. Under this doctrine, the plaintiff does not have to prove negligence. As long as the defendant's activity causes damage, the defendant is declared liable even if the activity is completely legal and complies with all relevant laws.

Strict liability is usually applied in circumstances where the activity in question is inherently hazardous. Since the disposal of toxic substances is frequently considered such an activity, states are increasingly allowing toxic substance suits to be brought under this doctrine. In contrast to negligence, this doctrine transfers liability for damages to the source whether or not the source has exercised much care.

Strict liability can also be compatible with efficiency.[3] The agent dealing with toxic wastes must balance the costs of taking precautions with the likelihood of and expected costs of lawsuits. In cases where the precautionary expenditures are particularly high and the damages low, only limited precaution is likely to be taken. However, for truly dangerous substances it is advantageous to take extraordinary precautions and avoid large damages.

Criminal Law

Strict liability and negligence are civil law doctrines in which one private party sues another. Increasingly in environmental policy, the civil law approach is being complemented by the use of criminal law in which the government serves as prosecutor, presumably acting as an agent of the people. The kepone case, described in Example 20.2, involved both civil and criminal law.

Criminal law affords regulators a different menu of remedies than available from civil law. Financial penalties imposed under criminal law cannot be covered by insurance as civil penalties can. Jail sentences may be handed out to those found breaking the law. Corporate executives, for example, could spend up to five years in jail for particularly onerous violations of the law. Fines could also be levied against guilty parties.

Several important aspects other than remedies also differentiate the civil and criminal judicial approaches to pollution control. Criminal charges can be brought against only those charged with breaking one or more specific laws, while civil suits can be brought against those causing damage, whether or not a law has been violated. The burden of proof is higher in a criminal trial. To convict a person, the state must prove the defendant is guilty "beyond a reasonable doubt," whereas in civil trials, the decision is based merely upon the "preponderance of evidence." The presumption of innocence, an important part of criminal trials, has no counterpart in civil trials. Civil trials create no presumption in favor of either party.

---

[3]One well-known case where strict liability will not be efficient is when the victims can influence the likelihood of contamination and the magnitude of the damage caused. With full compensation, the victim's incentive to take precautions is undermined. In most toxic substance cases, the role of the victim is minimal, so this potential source of inefficiency is not important.

The final major difference between civil liability law and criminal law is that *civil liability law compensates victims directly while criminal law does not.* Criminal law focuses on punishing the perpetrator rather than on compensating the victim.[4] Though the severity of punishment can be tailored to the amount of damage caused, the correspondence between the length of a jail sentence and the damage caused is much less indirect than forcing the defendant to pay exact monetary damages. By breaking the link between the monetary damage caused and the punishment received—the cornerstone of liability law—criminal law would be less likely to result in efficient resolutions of toxic chemical contamination problems than civil law. Efficiency could result, but it would be more of a coincidence than an inherent characteristic of the process.

Statutory Law

These civil and criminal common-law remedies have been accompanied by a host of legislative remedies. The statutes have evolved over time in response to particular toxic substance problems. Each time a new problem surfaced and people were able to get legislators aroused, a new law was passed to deal with it. The result is a collage of laws on the books, each with its own unique focus. We cover only the main ones here.

Federal Food, Drug, and Cosmetic Act.   The first concerns with toxic substances arose with *food additives*, since these are ingested and potentially pose a serious and immediate threat to health. Food and drug additives are regulated under the Federal Food, Drug, and Cosmetic Act. The organization administering this act is the Food and Drug Administration (FDA).

This act contained a general safety provision authorizing the FDA to prohibit the sale of any food that "contains any poisonous or deleterious substance which may render it injurious to health." This provision was complemented in 1958 by a provision known as the Delaney Clause after its legislative sponsor. This provision states that no additive should be deemed safe if it was found to induce cancer in humans or animals. Coupled with the first provision, this addition prohibits any food additive determined by the FDA to be a carcinogen in any dosage.

For decades, EPA and the Food and Drug Administration attempted to evade the complete lack of flexibility in the Delaney Clause by applying various exceptions and limitations. Once the courts upheld the zero-risk standards imposed by the Delaney Clause and that was seen as imposing an unacceptable burden on society, Congress stepped in to amend the food safety laws. The Food Quality Protection Act of 1996 established a "reasonable certainty" standard for evaluating additive and pesticide levels in food instead of the Delaney Clause's zero-tolerance policy.

Manufacturers wishing to introduce new food additives or drugs must demonstrate the safety of their products through premarket testing. No premarket testing is required for cosmetics. For the FDA to take any action on cosmetics, it must bear the burden of proof to demonstrate the product is unsafe. The burden is on the manufacturer to prove the safety of food additives and drugs.

---

[4]Criminal law remedies forcing restitution do compensate the victim, but they are the exception rather than the rule. With restitution, the guilty party is forced to pay a stipulated amount of money to the victim as part of the punishment.

Occupational Safety and Health Act.   The Occupational Safety and Health Act created the Occupational Safety and Health Administration (OSHA) and charged the agency with the regulatory responsibility for protecting workers from hazards in the workplace. The Act also created the National Institute for Occupational Safety and Health (NIOSH), which, among other responsibilities, must make recommendations for the OSHA regulatory standards.

In 1974, OSHA promulgated the first regulation establishing levels of pollutants that would be acceptable in the workplace atmosphere. The statute required the standards to be established at a level sufficiently stringent so that no employee would suffer material impairment of health, even if that employee were exposed to the substance on a regular basis throughout his or her working life. In addition, occupational standards requiring special precautions and/or protective devices have been adopted or proposed for a number of workplace contaminants.

Carcinogens are handled more severely. Once any substance is confirmed as a carcinogen, ambient workplace standards are set, rapidly followed by the imposition of special handling requirements, protective devices, and minimum contact regulations.

The approach taken by OSHA was to specify, often in excruciating detail, acceptable contaminant levels, as well as the approaches to be taken by employers to ensure the attainment of those containment levels.[5] In response to adverse public opinion about silly regulations, OSHA has streamlined its regulations.

Federal Environmental Pesticide Control Act.   The Environmental Pesticide Control Act provides for the registration of all pesticides, the certification of individuals applying these pesticides, and the premarket testing of all new pesticides.

All pesticide registrations automatically expire every five years. To secure a new registration, the manufacturer must prove that the benefits derived from that pesticide outweigh its social costs. When the evidence permits, the EPA has the power to prohibit the sale of a pesticide or to restrict its use to specific applications. The EPA has used this power to dramatically decrease the use of a number of pesticides, with DDT being the earliest and most publicized example.

Certification procedures for individuals applying the pesticides represent a recognition that the danger posed is to a large extent dependent on how the substances are applied. With this procedure, the EPA can ensure proper training for commercial applicators, and by threatening the withdrawal of certification (and the livelihood of the applicators), the EPA can influence their behavior.

Resource Conservation and Recovery Act.   To counteract the unsafe dumping of toxic wastes, Congress passed Subtitle C of the Resource Conservation and Recovery Act. This act imposes standards for handling, shipping, and disposing of toxic wastes.

The regulations implementing this act define hazardous waste and establish a cradle-to-grave management system, including standards for generators of

---

[5]The humor in the situation was nicely illustrated by an ad for a political candidate opposed to OSHA. A cowboy is pictured riding off to the prairie. On the back of his horse is strapped a plastic toilet required by an OSHA regulation setting the maximum distance any employee could be from a comfort station.

hazardous wastes, standards for transporters, and standards and permit requirements for owners and operators of facilities that treat, store, or dispose of hazardous wastes.

The centerpiece of this rather large regulatory system is a manifest system for keeping track of the fate of the substances from their creation to their disposal. Waste generators are required to prepare a manifest for all controlled substances. If the substance is on the EPA list, it must be properly packaged and labeled, and must be delivered only to a permitted waste disposal site. Through this recording system, the EPA hopes to monitor all hazardous substances and detect any surreptitious dumping. Failure to comply with the act is punishable by civil penalties and, in certain cases, by fines and imprisonment.

This Act was amended by the Hazardous and Solid Waste Amendments of 1984. The 1984 Amendments contain three major categories of changes: (1) they expanded the amount of waste covered by the regulations; (2) they limited or, in some cases, banned the use of land disposal for certain kinds of waste; and (3) they brought under regulation some activities not previously controlled, such as underground storage tanks for certain chemicals.

Toxic Substances Control Act.   The Toxic Substances Control Act was passed as a complement to the Resource Conservation and Recovery Act. Whereas the Resource Conservation and Recovery Act was designed to ensure safe handling and disposal of existing substances, the Toxic Substances Control Act was designed to provide a firmer basis for deciding which of the chemical substances not controlled by the above acts should be allowed to be commercially produced.

This Act requires the EPA to inventory the approximately 55,000 chemical substances in commerce; to require premanufacture notice to the EPA of all new chemical substances; and to enforce record keeping, testing, and reporting requirements so that the EPA can assess and regulate the relative risks of chemicals. At least 90 days before manufacturing or importing a new chemical, a firm must submit test results or other information to the EPA showing that the chemical will not present "an unreasonable risk" to human health or the environment.

On the basis of the information in the premanufacture notification, the EPA may limit the manufacture, use, or disposal of the substance. The act is significant in that it represents one of the few instances where the burden of proof is on the manufacturer to prove that the product should be marketed, rather than forcing the EPA to show why it should not be marketed.

Comprehensive Environmental Response, Compensation, and Liability Act.   Known popularly as the "Superfund Act," the Comprehensive Environmental Response, Compensation, and Liability Act created a fund to be used for the cleanup of existing toxic waste sites. The revenue was derived mainly from taxes on chemical industries. It offers compensation for the loss or destruction of natural resources controlled by the state or federal government, but it does not provide any compensation for injured individuals.

This act, as amended, authorized federal and state governments to respond quickly to incidents such as occurred in Times Beach, Missouri. Times Beach, a town of 2,800 residents located about 30 miles southwest of St. Louis, had been contaminated by dioxin. Dioxin is a waste by-product created during the production of certain chemicals. One such chemical is Agent Orange, the defoliant used during the Vietnam War. The contamination occurred when a state oil hauler bought about 55 pounds of dioxin in 1971 from a now-defunct manufacturer, mixed it with oil, and under contract with the local government, spread it on unpaved roads as a dust control measure. On December 23, 1982, after soil tests revealed dangerous levels of dioxin, the Centers for Disease Control recommended total evacuation of the town.

By February 22, 1983, the federal government had authorized a transfer of some $33 million from the Superfund to cover the cost of buying out all businesses and residents and relocating them. For its part, the State of Missouri agreed to pay 10% of the $33 million cost into the Superfund, and fund representatives were free to attempt to recover damages from the responsible parties. By June 1983, all but 40 families had been relocated. Federal and state agencies then burned more than 265,000 tons of contaminated soil. In 1999, the State of Missouri opened Route 66 State Park on the site, and it has now been removed from the Superfund list.

The existence of the Superfund allows the governments involved to move rapidly. They are not forced to wait until the outcome of court suits against those responsible to raise the money or to face the uncertainty associated with whether the suits would ultimately be successful.

In addition to programs that focus on setting standards, another set of policies focus on the strategic use of information both to inform and to motivate change.

The Toxic Release Inventory Program

The Toxic Release Inventory (TRI) was enacted by the U.S. Congress in January 1986 as a part of the Environmental Protection and Community Right to Know Act (EPCRA). It is designed to provide information to the public on releases of toxic substances into the environment. Most of the substances involved are not themselves subject to release standards.

TRI states that firms that *use* 10,000 or more pounds of a listed chemical in a given calendar year, or firms that *import, process, or manufacture* 25,000 or more pounds of a listed chemical must file a report on each of the chemicals in existence within the plant if they also have ten or more full-time employees.

Reporting of emissions or use of listed chemicals is accomplished annually. (For the data, see http://www.epa.gov/tri/.) The reports include such information as the name of the company, the name of the parent company if it exists, the toxic released and frequency of release, and the medium in which the chemical is released. The information is available to the public. Firms must also separately report emissions to their state and local authorities as well as to fire and emergency officials.

Has TRI reduced toxic emissions into the environment? EPA's annual reports reveal that substantial reductions have occurred. Though careful examination of the filings (for example, Natan and Miller, 1998) has found that some of these reductions merely reflect a change in definition, other reductions have been found to be genuine. Apparently, the reported magnitude of the reductions is overstated, but real reductions have occurred.

The 33/50 Program

To complement and reinforce the TRI Program, the EPA initiated the 33/50 Program in February 1991. This program set national goals of 33% reduction in 17 priority toxic chemicals by 1992, and 50% reduction by 1995. The reductions were to be achieved voluntarily by program participants, and compliance with the guidelines was measured using the TRI reports.

The program emphasized pollution prevention rather than end-of-pipe control. The initial invitation list, which contained the names of 555 companies with substantial chemical releases, was subsequently expanded to 5,000. Some 1,300 corporations ultimately signed up to participate. Participants collectively reduced their emissions by more than 50%, a total of 757 million pounds of pollutants, by 1994—a year ahead of schedule.

Can we learn anything about what kinds of firms would join a program like this and what motivated them to do so? Arora and Cason (1996) attempted to isolate the factors that influence a firm's decision to participate. The study found: (1) the largest firms with the greatest toxic releases were the most likely to participate in this voluntary program; (2) firms apparently do not free ride on emission reductions prior to the program's initiation or participate to divert attention away from poor compliance with other regulations; and (3) firms in industries with more contact with final consumers were more likely to participate in the program than firms that only sell to other firms.

Proposition 65

Proposition 65 was established in the State of California by popular vote in November 1986, after the inception of the Toxic Release Inventory by the EPA. Prop 65 requires companies producing, using, or transporting one or more of the listed chemicals to notify those who are potentially impacted. Chemicals are listed as carcinogenic or as causing reproductive harm. When their use or potential exposure levels exceed "safe harbor numbers" established by a group of approved scientists, the impacted people must be notified. The "safe harbor" threshold is uniquely determined for each chemical and depends upon its intrinsic potency or the potency of a released mixture.

The program involved three forms of notification: (1) warning labels must be placed on all products that will cause adverse health effects when used for a prolonged period of time; (2) a company whose toxic emissions to air, ground, or water exceed levels deemed safe for prolonged exposure must provide public notification; and (3) workers must be warned of the potential danger if toxic chemicals defined by Prop 65 are used in manufacturing a product or are created as a by-product of manufacturing.

Only companies with ten or more full-time workers are required to notify endangered people of exposure. Nonprofit organizations like hospitals, recycling plants, and government organizations, which account for over 65% of California's pollution, are not required to comply with Prop 65.

Under the Proposition, private citizens, other industry members, and environmental groups can sue companies that fail to notify people of exposure in an appropriate fashion. Plaintiffs who make a successful legal claim get to keep a substantial portion of the settlement; this encourages private enforcement of the law and reduces government monitoring. Industry members also have a strong incentive to monitor each other, so that one company does not cheat and look greener than its rivals.

International Agreements

One of the issues erupting during the 1990s concerned the efficiency and morality of exporting hazardous waste to areas that are willing to accept it in return for suitably large compensation. A number of areas, particularly poor countries, appear ready to accept hazardous waste under the "right conditions." The right conditions usually involve alleviating safety concerns and providing adequate compensation (in employment opportunities, money, and public services) so as to make acceptance of the wastes desirable from the receiving community's point of view. Generally, the compensation required is less than the costs of dealing in other ways with the hazardous waste, so the exporting nations find these agreements attractive as well.

A strong backlash against these arrangements arose when opponents argued that communities receiving hazardous waste were poorly informed about the risks they faced and were not equipped to handle safely the volumes of material that could be expected to cross international boundaries. In extreme cases, the communities were completely uninformed as sites were secretly located by individuals with no public participation in the process at all.

The Basel Convention on the Control of Transboundary Movements of Hazardous Wastes and Their Disposal was developed in 1989 to provide a satisfactory response to these concerns. Under this Convention, the 24 nations that belong to the Organisation for Economic Co-operation and Development (OECD) were required to obtain written permission from the government of any developing country before exporting toxic waste there for disposal or recycling. This was followed in 1994 by an additional agreement on the part of most, but not all, industrialized nations to completely prohibit the export of toxic wastes from any OECD country to any non-OECD country.

An Assessment of the Legal Remedies

The Common Law

Judicial-Legislative Complementarity. Common law provides a potentially useful complement to statutory law for occupational, consumer product, and third-party hazards. For all three types of toxic substance problems, the market may create pressures preventing the flow of information about the dangers of these substances. The parties in the best position to transmit the information (employers or producers) are not always willing to seek or relay the information to parties who can best assess the risk (employees, consumers, or third parties). In a market where damages are not placed on the source, sources have little incentive to uncover potential problems. Uncovering health problems will only lower sales or increase wages.

Legislative remedies such as the "right-to-know" laws described earlier are insufficient if there is too little information to be shared. Because court actions that subject sources to liability for their damages make health damage information useful to the firm, they create incentives to keep good records and to analyze the results. The failure to accurately perceive a health risk could cause an enormous financial burden on the company. It is cheaper to anticipate and prevent damages before the cost becomes prohibitive.

Even premarket testing of consumer products by the government is an inadequate substitute for the judicial approach. Government has neither the staff nor the financial resources to serve as the sole source of health damage information. Some substances inevitably slip through the safety net provided by government testing. It is essential that the prime responsibility for testing fall on the producer, with the costs being passed on to the consumer as part of the price of the product. The government would then bear the responsibility for ensuring the validity of the testing process.

Judicial remedies are especially important in handling third-party contamination. Without liability, the incentive to exercise due care by the manufacturers, transporters, users, and disposers of these substances would be inefficiently low. The use of the court system to control the third-party problem was enhanced by the passage of the Resource Conservation and Recovery Act.

Because of the manifest system created by this Act, good information is available to the courts on the types and quantities of substances that are sold or transported. It also assists in tracing responsibility so that the sources can be identified and confronted with the evidence. This record-keeping system is immensely costly, however, and may turn out, in the glare of hindsight, to be excessively ambitious. Furthermore, hazardous wastes that never leave the generating facility comprise an overwhelming percentage of the total hazardous wastes, but these are not covered by the manifest system.

Two additional features of judicial remedies make them a useful complement to legislative remedies. First, liability law may provide the only means of compensating the victim of a toxic substance accident. Even the "Superfund" bill does not compensate individuals for health-related damages. It only compensates for property damage.

The second attractive feature of judicial remedies is the degree to which they can be tailored to individual circumstances. We have seen in the chapters on air and water pollution the strong tendency for legislative remedies to be applied uniformly. We have also seen that uniform remedies are rarely efficient and that often the resulting loss of net benefits is substantial. When the courts impose liability remedies correctly, an efficient allocation of precaution would automatically be tailored to the specific circumstances involved.

Limitations of Judicial Remedies.   The common law is far from a panacea, however. It does not cope with the largest or most complex problems, such as the emission of hazardous substances by large numbers of sources affecting large numbers of people. This was illustrated nicely in *Roger J. Diamond v. General Motors*, a California case in which the judge ruled that the court system was not the appropriate forum to resolve the Los Angeles problem of air pollution. The problem was so complex and involved so many parties that it had to be resolved by the legislature.

Court remedies are administratively expensive and can be used efficiently only when they are used sparingly.

The common law also currently places a large, difficult-to-meet burden of proof on the plaintiff. Generally, a plaintiff must be able to (1) identify the harmful substances; (2) demonstrate that the defendant was the source of this substance; and (3) prove that identifiable damages occurred as a result of the presence of that substance. The last two steps may be difficult to establish in practice.

Suppose, for example, that a well owner who discovered a harmful substance in the well simultaneously experienced a series of illnesses for which he or she had no medical history. The owner might have discovered a source emitting the same chemical nearby, but that is not enough evidence to win a lawsuit. The court would have to be convinced not only that the substance had traveled from that specific source to that specific well, but also that any documented illnesses were caused by the substance and not by unrelated causes. The frequent failure to establish these links can undermine the incentive properties of common law.

Japan's court system has reacted to this problem by shifting the burden of proof from the injured plaintiff to the industry. The plaintiffs in those cases have to establish the nature and cause of their diseases and the mechanism by which they were affected. To establish the link to the defendant, they must be able to introduce a high statistical correlation between the defendant's activity and the incidence of the disease. Once these elements have been established, a rebuttable presumption is created that shifts the burden of proof to the defendant. The defendant is then liable unless it can be proved that its activities are not responsible for the damage.

If the American court system were to move in this direction, it would represent a radical departure from current practice.[6] The statistical approach lacks the rigor usually required by American courts because establishing a positive correlation between activity levels and the incidence of the disease does not establish causation. Other factors correlated with the activities of the defendant may be responsible.

The Japanese system does, however, effectively raise the question of who should bear the burden of proof. If the source were to bear it, nuisance suits could arise. Nuisance suits are filed mainly to harass defendants by making them spend a lot of money on defense. Such suits are without merit. As we have seen, however, if the plaintiff bears the burden of proof, the burden is particularly difficult, because the defendant generally knows so much more about the contaminating activities.

The Japanese approach gets around this problem by placing a sequential burden of proof on each party. The plaintiff is required to bear a burden sufficiently large that nuisance cases are eliminated. On the other hand, for serious cases where the plaintiff has been able to bear this initial burden of proof, the defendant (who presumably is the most knowledgeable about the subject) must then gather the information at his or her disposal.

Although we can quibble about whether the initial burden on the plaintiff is too low or too high under the Japanese system, with its inherent shared responsibility,

---

[6]Some movement in this direction is now evident. A plaintiff with asbestosis, for example, may be required to prove only that the disease is more probably than not caused by any of several asbestos manufacturers. Having met this burden of proof, the plaintiff shifts the burden to the individual manufacturer to prove, if it can, that it did not cause the plaintiff's disease. See *Abel v. Eli Lilly & Co.*, 343 N.W. 2d 164 (1984).

this system reduces the likelihood of nuisance suits while providing incentive for the most knowledgeable party to supply the necessary information to reach a decision.

One final concern should be noted about judicial remedies. Sometimes the source of the toxic substance problem is "judgment proof" in the sense that it has no assets (or too few assets) to pay the damages. The marginal cost of additional damages to the source is zero, and profit-maximizing behavior leads the source to exercise too little precaution.

This problem is more serious for toxic substances than for conventional pollutants, because the latency of the effects means the suits must be filed much later than other kinds of suits. By this time, the source may have gone out of business or have been transformed into a different corporate entity somewhat immune from past transgressions.

Joint and Several Liability Doctrine.

In interpreting the "Superfund" Act, the courts have allowed the government to sue "potentially responsible parties" (that is, disposal site owners and operators, waste generators, and transporters) for damages and site recovery costs under the joint and several liability doctrine.[7] Reduced to its essence, the joint and several liability doctrine makes each successfully sued defendant potentially liable for an amount up to the entire damage caused, regardless of the magnitude of its individual contribution. Because of this doctrine, the government can elect to sue only a few of the wealthiest responsible parties, thereby reducing litigation costs. In one case, the EPA elected to sue only 10% of the responsible parties, letting the others off the hook.

Successfully sued defendants retain the right of contribution, which allows parties that have made payments (either by settling out of court or in response to a court decision) to seek reimbursement from other potentially responsible parties that have not. This right of contribution can be exercised by those settling out of court as well as those assessed damages following a trial. Once a party signs a consent decree of either type, however, they cannot be sued for contribution by other parties.

The government enforces this act by seeking to encourage potentially responsible parties (PRPs) to initiate cleaning up the site on their own, but is prepared to initiate the investigation and even to clean up identified hazardous waste sites on its own, if necessary financing the effort from the several-billion-dollar Hazardous Substance Response Trust Fund created by the Act. It then seeks reimbursement from parties who are potentially responsible for the conditions at each particular site. The PRPs are liable for any costs of restoring the site to a safe status as well as "damages for injury to, destruction of, or loss of natural resources, including the reasonable costs of assessing such injury, destruction, or loss resulting from such a release."

If any liable party "fails without sufficient cause to properly provide removal or remedial action," they may be assessed punitive damages of "three times the amount of any costs incurred by the Fund as a result of such failure to take proper action."

Designed primarily as a means of raising private funds to clean up hazardous waste sites, joint and several liability has not exactly worked as smoothly as expected,

---

[7]Hooker Chemical, for example, was found liable for response costs at the Love Canal under the joint and several liability doctrine. See *U.S. v. Hooker Chemical and Plastics Corporation* 18 ELR 20580.

even as a means of collecting revenue. At least one study (Dower, 1990) has put the administrative cost of litigation under Superfund at 55% of actual cleanup costs. Between 1981 and 1992 only 4% of the receipts used from cleanup were recovered from potentially responsible parties (Congressional Budget Office, 1994, 5).

Joint and several liability has also created some perverse incentives.[8] Under the joint and several liability doctrine the expected liability a potentially responsible party faces is very uncertain; it could range anywhere from 0% to 100% of the cleanup costs regardless of the degree of precaution undertaken. Since larger firms are usually targeted by the EPA for Superfund suits, they have an incentive to take more than the efficient amount of precaution. Meanwhile, smaller firms, who may expect to get off the hook because the legal expenses of suing them exceeds the potential recovery, have little or no incentive to take appropriate precautions.

The uncertainty associated with expected damage payments has also wreaked havoc with the insurance market. Insurance companies have no idea how to set premiums and many have left the market for environmental risks entirely. Without insurance, the probability of bankruptcy increases. Bankrupt firms contribute very little to the cleanup.

The Statutory Law

A commendable virtue of common law is that remedies can be tailored to the unique circumstances the parties find themselves in. But common law remedies are also expensive to impose, and they are ill-suited to solving widespread problems affecting large numbers of people. Thus, statutory law has a complementary role to play as well.

Balancing the Costs.   Statutory law, as currently structured, does not efficiently fulfill its potential as a complement to the common law due to the failure of current law to balance compliance costs with the damages being protected against.

As discussed previously, the Delaney Clause, the most flagrant example, precludes any balancing of costs whatsoever in food additives. A substance that has been known to be carcinogenic in any dose cannot be used as a food additive even if the risk is counterbalanced by a considerable compensating benefit.[9] A rule this stringent can lead to considerable political mischief as attempts are made to circumvent it.

The Delaney Clause is not the only culprit; other laws also fail to balance costs. The Resource Conservation and Recovery Act requires the standards imposed on waste generators, transporters, and disposal site operators to be high enough to protect human health and the environment. No mention is made of costs.

These are extreme examples, but even in less extreme cases, policy-makers must face the question of how to balance costs. The Occupational Safety and Health Act, for example, requires standards that ensure "to the extent feasible that no employee will suffer material impairment of health or functional capacity. . . ." In changing the standard for the occupational exposure to benzene from 10 to 1 ppm, the EPA

---

[8] A formal analysis of these incentives can be found in Tietenberg (1989).

[9] Interestingly, a number of common foods contain natural substances that in large enough doses are carcinogenic. Radishes, for example, could probably not be licensed as a food additive because of the Delaney Clause.

had presented no data to show that even a 10-ppm standard causes leukemia. The EPA based its decision on a series of assumptions indicating that some leukemia might result from 10 ppm, so even fewer cases might result from 1 ppm.

In a case receiving a great deal of attention, the Supreme Court set aside a benzene standard largely on the grounds that it was based on inadequate evidence. In rendering their opinion the justices stated:

> The Secretary must make a finding that the workplaces in question are not safe. But "safe" is not the equivalent of "risk-free." A workplace can hardly be considered "unsafe" unless it threatens the workers with a significant risk of harm (100 S. Ct. 2847).

In a concurring opinion that did not bind future decisions because it did not have sufficient support among the remaining justices, Justice Powell went even further:

> . . . the statute also requires the agency to determine that the economic effects of its standard bear a reasonable relationship to the expected benefits (100 S. Ct. 2848).

It seems clear that the notion of a risk-free environment has been repudiated by the high court, as it should have been. But what is meant by an *acceptable risk*? Efficiency clearly dictates that an acceptable risk is one that maximizes the net benefit. Thus the efficiency criterion would support Justice Powell in his approach to the benzene standard.

It is important to allay a possible source of confusion. The fact that it is difficult to set a precise standard using benefit/cost analysis because of the imprecision of the underlying data does not imply that some balancing of benefit and cost cannot, and should not, take place. It can and it should. While benefit/cost analysis may not be sufficiently precise and reliable to suggest, for example, that a standard of 8 ppm is efficient, it usually is reliable enough to indicate clearly that 1 ppm and 15 ppm are inefficient. By failing to consider compliance cost in defining acceptable risk, statutes are probably attempting more and achieving less than we might hope for.

Degree and Form of Intervention.   The second criticism of the current statutory approach concerns both the degree of intervention and the form that intervention should take. The former issue relates to how deeply the government controls go, while the latter relates to the manner in which the regulations work.

The analysis in the second section of this chapter suggested that consumer products and labor markets require less government intervention than third-party cases. The main problem in those two areas was seen as the lack of sufficient information to allow producers, consumers, employees, and employers to make informed choices. With the Delaney Clause as an obvious exception, most consumer-product safety statutes deal mainly with research and labeling. They are broadly consistent with the results of our analysis.

This is not, however, the case with occupational exposure. Government regulations have had a major and not always beneficial effect on the workplace. By covering such a large number of potential problems, OSHA has spread itself too thin and has had too little impact on problems that really count. Selective intervention, targeted at those areas where OSHA efforts could really make a difference, would get more results.

The form the OSHA regulations have taken also causes inflexibility. Not content merely to specify exposure limits, the regulations also specify the exact precautions to be taken. The contrast between this approach and the marketable permit approach in air pollution is striking.

Under emissions trading, the EPA specifies the emission cap but allows the source great flexibility in meeting that cap. OSHA regulations, by dictating the specific activities to be engaged in or to be avoided, deny this kind of flexibility. In the face of rapid technological change, inflexibility can lead to inefficiency even if the specified activities were efficient when first required. Furthermore, having so many detailed regulations makes enforcement more difficult and probably less effective.

A serious flaw in the current approach to controlling hazardous wastes is in the insufficient emphasis placed on reducing the generation and recycling of these wastes. The imposition of variable unit taxes (called waste-end taxes) on waste generated or disposed of would not only spur industry to switch to less toxic substances and would provide the needed incentives to reduce the quantity of these substances used, it would also encourage consumers to switch away from products using large amounts of hazardous materials in the production process because higher production costs would be translated into higher product prices. Although a number of states have adopted waste-end taxation, unfortunately the Superfund has not.

Scale.   The size of the hazardous waste problem dwarfs the size of the EPA staff and budget assigned to control it. The Superfund process for cleaning up existing hazardous waste sites is a good case in point. During its first 12 years, the Superfund program placed 1,275 sites on the National Priorities List for extensive remedial cleanup. Despite public and private spending of more than $13 billion through 1992, only 149 of the 1,275 sites had completed all construction work related to cleanup and just 40 had been fully cleaned up (CBO, 1994). According to the USEPA (2004), although substantial progress has been made over the past quarter century, a considerable amount of cleanup work remains. At current levels of site cleanup activity in the United States (about $6–8 billion annually), it would take 30 to 35 years to complete most of the work needed. Under current regulations and practices an estimated 294,000 sites will need to be cleaned up. These cleanups are estimated to cost in the neighborhood of $209 billion.

The huge scale of controlling toxic substances has important implications for both the bureaucracy and the citizens it serves. Priorities must be established and the most serious problems attacked first. It is a fact of life that an exclusive reliance on the bureaucracy to provide complete safety is infeasible. Citizens should not abdicate their own responsibilities after being lulled into a false sense of security by the mistaken impression that the bureaucracy can and should provide adequate protection.

Performance Bonds: An Innovative Proposal

The current control system must cope with a great deal of uncertainty about magnitude of future environmental costs associated with the use and disposal of potentially toxic substances. The costs associated with collecting funds from responsible parties through litigation are very high. Many potentially responsible parties declare bankruptcy when it is time to collect cleanup costs, thereby isolating them from their normal responsibility. One proposed solution (Russell, 1988; Costanza and Perrings, 1990) would require the posting of a dated performance bond as a necessary condition for disposing of hazardous waste. The amount of the required bond would be equal to the present value of anticipated damages. Any restoration of the site resulting from a hazardous waste leak could be funded directly and immediately from the accumulated funds; no costly and time-consuming legal process would precede receipt of the funds necessary for cleanup. Any unused proceeds would be redeemable at specified dates if the environmental costs turned out to be lower than anticipated. As Example 20.3 points out, performance bonds may also be applied to producers of potentially toxic substances.

Summary

The potential for contamination of the environmental asset by toxic substances is one of the most complex environmental problems. The number of potential substances that could prove toxic number literally in the millions. Some 55,000 of these are in active use.

The market provides a considerable amount of pressure toward resolving toxic substance problems as they affect employees and consumers. With reliable information at their disposal, all parties have an incentive to reduce hazards to acceptable levels. This pressure is absent, however, in cases involving third parties. Here the problem frequently takes the form of an external cost imposed on innocent bystanders.

The efficient role of government can range from ensuring the provision of sufficient information (so that participants in the market can make informed choices) to setting exposure limits on hazardous substances. Unfortunately, the scientific basis for decision-making is weak. Only limited information on the effects of these substances is available, and the cost of acquiring complete information is prohibitive. Therefore, priorities must be established and tests developed to screen substances so that efforts can be concentrated on those substances that seem most dangerous.

In contrast to air and water pollution, the toxic substance problem is one in which the courts may play a particularly important role. Although screening tests will probably never be foolproof, and therefore some substances may slip through, they do provide a reasonable means for setting priorities. Liability law not only creates a market pressure for more and better information on potential damages associated with chemical substances, it also provides some incentives to manufacturers of substances, the generators of waste, the transporters of waste, and those who dispose of it to exercise precaution. Judicial remedies also allow the level of precaution to vary with the occupational circumstances and provide a means of compensating victims.

Judicial remedies, however, are insufficient. They are expensive and ill-suited for dealing with problems affecting large numbers of people. The burden of proof under the current American system is difficult to surmount, though in Japan some radical new approaches have been developed to deal with this problem. The joint

Example 20.3

PERFORMANCE BONDS FOR BROMINATED FLAME RETARDANTS

Brominated flame retardants (BFRs) are organic compounds used as additives to reduce the flammability of plastics and textiles. Their use was stimulated not only by government regulations attempting to reduce the risk posed by flammability, but also by the lower bromine prices that resulted from banning bromine (thereby lowering demand) in a few uses such as fumigants for agriculture. (Lower bromine prices made BFRs cheaper to make, thereby increasing their attractiveness to plastics producers.) Though a large and growing number of BFRs exist, considerable uncertainty also exists about the environmental fate and long-run toxicity of many of the compounds.

Traditional remedies such as banning particular compounds seem insufficient, since some of the substitutes for banned substances may turn out to be worse than the original substances. The government is not in a position to pick winners and losers at this early stage, and the very real risk posed by flammability suggests that some BFR compounds should be used, at least until demonstrably safer compounds are developed.

Performance bonds have been suggested as one way to resolve this dilemma. Producers of flame retardants would be required to put up a pool of deposits sufficient to cover possible future damages. To the extent that those damages would not materialize, the deposits (plus accumulated interest) would be refunded.

The performance-bond approach shifts the financial risk of damage from the victims to the producers and, in so doing, provides incentives to ensure product safety. Internalizing the costs of toxicity would sensitize producers not only to the risks posed by particular BFRs (or substitutes) but also to the amounts used. Performance bonds also provide incentives for the firms to monitor the consequences of their choices because they bear the ex post burden of proving that the product was safe (in order to support claims for unused funds). Though similar to liability law in their ability to internalize damage costs, performance bonds are different in that they require that the money for damages be available up front.

Performance bonds are not without their problems, however. Calculating the right pool of deposits requires some understanding of the magnitude of potential damages. Furthermore, establishing causality between BFRs and any resulting damages is still necessary in order to make payments to victims as well as to establish the amount of the pool that should be returned.

Sources: Molly K. Macauley, Michael D. Bowes, and Karen L. Palmer. *Using Economic Incentives to Regulate Toxic Substances* (Washington, DC: Resources for the Future, Inc., 1992); J. F. Shogren, J. A. Herriges, and R. Govindasamy. "Limits to Environmental Bonds," *Ecological Economics* Vol. 8, No. 2 (1993): 109–133.

and several liability doctrine has created some perverse incentives and has wreaked havoc on the market for environmental insurance.

The statutory responses, though clearly a positive step, seem to have gone too far in regulating behavior. The exposure standards in many cases fail to balance the costs against the benefits. Furthermore, OSHA and the EPA have gone well beyond the setting of exposure limits by dictating specific activities that should be engaged in or avoided. The enforcement of these standards has proved difficult and has probably spread the available resources too thin.

The theologian Reinhold Niebuhr once said, "Democracy is finding proximate solutions to insoluble problems." That seems an apt description of the institutional response to the toxic substance problem. Our political institutions have created a staggering array of legislative and judicial responses to this problem that are neither efficient nor complete. They do, however, represent a positive first step in what must be an evolutionary process.

Discussion Questions

1. How should the courts resolve the dilemma posed in Example 20.1? Why?
2. Over the last several decades in product liability law, there has been a movement in the court system from caveat emptor ("buyer beware") to caveat venditor ("seller beware"). The liability for using and consuming risky products has been shifted from buyers to sellers. Does this shift represent a movement toward or away from an efficient allocation of risk? Why?
3. Would the export of hazardous waste to developing countries be efficient? Sometimes? Always? Never? Would it be moral? Sometimes? Always? Never? Make clear the specific bases for your judgments.

Further Reading

Crandall, Robert W., and Lester B. Lave. *The Scientific Basis of Health and Safety Regulation* (Washington, DC: Brookings Institution, 1981). For each of five health and safety regulatory actions, this book juxtaposes the views of a scientist, an economist, and a regulator on the scientific basis for the regulation and the desirability of the resulting decision. Cases considered are passive restraints in automobiles, cotton dust, saccharin, waterborne carcinogens, and sulfur dioxide.

Dower, Roger C. "Hazardous Waste," in Paul R. Portney, ed. *Public Policies for Environmental Protection* (Washington, DC: Resources for the Future, 1990): 151–194. Examines policies related to the disposal of hazardous waste.

Graham, John D., Laura C. Green, and Marc J. Roberts. *In Search of Safety: Chemicals and Cancer Risk* (Cambridge, MA: Harvard University Press, 1988). A detailed examination of the attempts to regulate two suspected carcinogens, benzene and formaldehyde.

Macauley, Molly K., Michael D. Bowes, and Karen Palmer. *Using Economic Incentives to Regulate Toxic Substances* (Baltimore, MD: Johns Hopkins University Press for Resources for the Future, Inc., 1992). Using case studies, the authors evaluate the attractiveness of incentive-based policies for the regulation of four specific substances: chlorinated solvents, formaldehyde, cadmium, and brominated flame retardants.

Magat, Wesley A., and W. Kip Viscusi. *Information Approaches to Regulation* (Cambridge, MA: The MIT Press, 1992). Draws from several empirical studies to assess the effectiveness of information strategies for controlling environmental risk.

Shapiro, Michael. "Toxic Substances Policy," in Paul R. Portney, ed. *Public Policies for Environmental Protection* (Washington, DC: Resources for the Future, 1990): 195–242. A comprehensive analysis of the U.S. statutes and implementation procedures used to combat environmental risks posed by toxic substances.

Viscusi, W. Kip. *Risk by Choice: Regulating Health and Safety in the Workplace* (Cambridge, MA: Harvard University Press, 1983). Examines the proper role for regulation of occupational risks in the market context where these policies must operate.

Additional References is available on this book's companion Web site www.aw-bc.com/tietenberg.

Environmental Justice

There are many in this old world of ours who hold that things break about even for all of us. I have observed for example that we all get the same amount of ice. The rich get it in the summertime and the poor get it in the winter.

—Bat Masterson, Gunfighter/Newspaper Reporter

Introduction

Are environmental risks distributed fairly? Are the costs of attempting to control those environmental risks distributed fairly? Previous chapters have suggested that, though existing policies have not been efficient, the net benefits have, in general, been positive. While positive net benefits imply that the gains from environmental policy have exceeded the losses for society as a whole, this may not be true for all members of society. Some segments of society may bear a disproportionate share of the costs.

Paying attention to environmental justice makes sense for two reasons, one ethical and the other pragmatic. The ethical dimension concerns whether the distribution of risks, benefits, and costs is in accordance with the norms of social justice. The desire for just policies is a conventional complement to the desire for efficient policies. The pragmatic dimension emphasizes the relationship between the distributional burden and both the likelihood that environmental legislation will pass and its ultimate form. Policies and programs that are perceived as unfair will stand little prospect of passage even if they enhance the prospects for efficiency and sustainability. Identifying the sources of unfairness and restructuring programs to eliminate them increases the likelihood that otherwise desirable programs can proceed.

In economics, as in other disciplines, the norms of social justice are not sufficiently well defined such that no norm is beyond reproach. Nonetheless, some conventional approaches have arisen that can serve to guide our inquiry. These involve two concepts known as horizontal and vertical equity.

503

Horizontal equity occurs when people with equal income are treated equally. (The conventional definition of "equals" in economics is based upon income levels.) With respect to pollution control, the principle of horizontal equity is satisfied if all persons with the same income level receive the same net benefit. This principle can be used to assess the geographic and the racial fairness of policy. If people with comparable income levels in different parts of the country or from different ethnic backgrounds receive different net benefits, then the horizontal equity principle is violated.

Vertical equity deals with the treatment of unequals, or, using income as a basis, with the treatment of those with different income levels. The first step in assessing whether a particular policy satisfies vertical equity is to calculate how the net benefit is distributed among income groups: *progressively, regressively, or proportionally.*

The distribution is said to be proportional if the net benefits received by various income groups are proportional to income. It is said to be regressive if the net benefits represent a larger proportion of the income of the rich than of the poor; it is progressive if, as a proportion of their income, the poor receive a larger share than the rich.[1] One implication of this definition is that a policy that confers a larger net benefit on the rich than the poor is not necessarily regressive. A regressive allocation occurs only if the ratio of net benefit to income is larger for the rich than the poor. According to conventional practice, regressive policies violate the vertical equity principle. This practice is in line with the evident societal concern for the poor that is manifested in the health, housing, and income transfer programs that exist solely to improve their economic status. Both regressive policies and those that violate the horizontal equity criterion are, according to these criteria, considered unfair. We now turn to the evidence.

The Incidence of Hazardous Waste Siting Decisions

History

In 1979, Robert Bullard, then a sociologist at Texas Southern University, completed a report describing a futile attempt by an affluent African-American neighborhood in Houston, Texas, to block the location of a hazardous waste site within their community. His analysis suggested that race, not just income status, was a probable factor in this local land-use decision.

Environmental justice became a national issue in 1982 when some 500 demonstrators protested against the location of a proposed PCB landfill in a predominantly low-income community in North Carolina. On returning from the protests, Walter Fauntroy, the District of Columbia congressional delegate, asked the General Accounting Office (GAO) to study the characteristics of hazardous waste sites in the

---

[1]It is also possible to use these concepts to refer to the distribution of benefits or costs. Benefits are regressive if the *rich get* a larger proportional share, while costs are said to be regressive if the *poor* get a larger proportional share. The easiest way to keep these straight is to remember that progressive means beneficial to the poor.

EPA's Region 4 (Georgia, Florida, Mississippi, Alabama, Kentucky, Tennessee, North Carolina, and South Carolina). The 1983 study found that three of the four commercial hazardous waste facilities were in predominantly African-American communities, and the fourth was in a low-income community.

In 1987 the United Church of Christ Commission for Racial Justice examined the issue of hazardous waste siting for the nation as a whole. According to their statistical analysis of communities with commercial hazardous waste facilities:

- "Race proved to be the most significant among the variables tested . . ."

- "Communities with the greatest number of commercial hazardous waste facilities had the highest composition of racial and ethnic residents. In communities with two or more facilities or one of the nation's five largest landfills, the minority population was more than three times that of communities without such facilities (38 percent vs. 12 percent)."

In communities with uncontrolled toxic waste sites, they found:

- "Three out of every five Black and Hispanic Americans lived in communities with uncontrolled toxic waste sites.

- Approximately half of all Asian/Pacific Islanders and American Indians lived in communities with uncontrolled toxic waste sites."

In 1994, the Center for Policy Alternatives issued "Toxic Wastes and Race Revisited: An Update of the 1987 Report." That study found that commercial toxic waste facilities were even more likely to be located in minority communities in recent years than in 1980, despite growing national attention to the issue.

Not all studies have reached this conclusion, but in a detailed review of the literature, Hamilton (2003) finds that for most U.S. studies, low-income and minority residents do indeed face higher risks from hazardous waste facilities. Less detailed information exists on the exposure of residents, by income, to hazardous waste risks in other industrialized countries.

Recent Research and the Emerging Role of Analysis Using GIS

The application of geographic information systems (GIS) technology has allowed studies of hazardous waste citing via census tract data to become more sophisticated. Most regional offices of the EPA, for example, now use demographic data from the U.S. Census Bureau combined with GIS mapping. This technique allows for the overlay of census data onto concentric rings around a hazardous waste facility or a Superfund site, for example, to find out who lives in close proximity to the site. What have these most recent studies found?

The results from these studies are quite varied. Using only one measure of equity, such as low income, could prove misleading. Hamilton and Viscusi (1999), for example, consider multiple measures of equity, including racial distribution, mean household income, and potential cancer risks and their work demonstrates how sensitive the results are to the measure that is used.

Other studies have utilized the EPA's Toxic Release Inventory (TRI) data. This data set contains self-reported information on the toxic releases from all reporting plants. Using an air pollution index by zip code, Brooks and Sethi (1997) find that demographic groups most likely to face the threat of exposure to toxic air emissions include minorities, renters, people with incomes below the poverty line, and individuals with fewer years of schooling. Similar results were found by Sadd et al. (1999) for metropolitan Los Angeles. Using both GIS and Census Tract data, they find that TRI tracts (census tracts with an emitting facility in the data set) had higher percentages of minorities including Latino residents, lower incomes (both per capita and household), higher percentages of industrial land, lower property values, and higher percentages of persons employed in manufacturing. Similar results were found for Hillsborough County in Florida (Chakraborty, 2001). What explains these findings? What do these findings imply for policy?

The Economics of Site Location

One point of departure is to attempt to understand the dynamics of site location and how both income and race might play a role. Our analysis begins by recognizing that hazardous waste facilities are generally unpopular neighbors. Even if the treatment of hazardous waste makes sense for society as a whole, all potential recipient communities must face the NIMBY (Not in My Backyard) opposition.

Understanding the economics of site location requires consideration of the incentives facing both the owners of the proposed facility and the incentives of the recipient community. Since the owners want to maximize net benefits, they will look for a site that will be able to process the wastes at a low cost. Being located near the sources of the waste would be attractive as a means of holding transport costs down. Low land costs would also be attractive since these facilities are frequently land-intensive. Finally, the site should pose as few risks as possible in order to limit future liability.

The recipient community has its own agenda in order to ensure that it reaps benefits that outweigh costs. They would want to ensure, insofar as possible, that the site was safe for both employees and the inhabitants of the surrounding community. They would also want adequate compensation for assuming the risk. This compensation could take many forms (employment, enhanced tax revenues, new public services, and so on).

What does efficiency suggest about the characteristics of recipient communities? Low-income communities become attractive as disposal sites not only because land prices are relatively low in those communities, but also because those communities will typically require less compensation in order to accept the risk. Targeting low-income communities would be the expected, not the exceptional, outcome. Furthermore, once hazardous waste facilities are located in a community, the composition of that community is likely to become even more low income due to migration and the negative effects on surrounding property values. Assuming that the willingness to pay for risk-avoidance is higher for higher-income families, more lower-income families may be attracted by the unusually low land prices (or rents), while higher-income families may depart for less risky neighborhoods. Even if the community were not low income at the time of the siting, it is likely to become more so over time.

While even an efficient siting process might target a disproportionate share of these facilities in low-income communities, it is much more difficult to develop an efficient explanation for why race is a more important predictor than income. Explaining that finding requires greater attention to market failures.

Efficient location requires both full information and adequate enforcement of agreements. In the absence of full information, recipient communities can fail to fully understand the risk and therefore are likely to undervalue it. One hypothesis to explain the importance of race is that minority communities have a less adequate flow of information than comparably situated white communities. This means they are likely to be subject to flawed agreements. Another hypothesis is that they lack the resources to enforce community will, perhaps because of underrepresentation on governing boards. This hypothesis implies that even potentially efficient agreements may be inefficiently implemented (Bullard, 1990). Taken as a whole, this evidence on the prominence of race as an independent predictor variable (over and above income) suggests not only that the current siting process violates the horizontal equity criterion, but also that it is not efficient. Until such time as recipient communities can be guaranteed both full information and the capability to enforce the community's will, the hazardous waste siting process will remain seriously flawed.

The Policy Response

In recognition of these circumstances, the Office of Environmental Equity was officially established within the U.S. Environmental Protection Agency on November 6, 1992. Its mandate is to deal with environmental impacts affecting people of color and low-income communities. Though the concern that was responsible for the creation of this office was largely focused on the siting of hazardous waste facilities, the concerns of this office go well beyond that. Initial efforts are focused on gathering more information about the problem and strengthening enforcement inspections and compliance monitoring in impacted communities.

In 1994, President Clinton issued Executive Order 12898, "Federal Action to Address Environmental Justice in Minority Populations and Low-Income Populations." The goal of this order was to make sure that minority groups and low-income populations are not subjected to an unequal or disproportionately high level of environmental risks.

How effective has the order been? In 2004 the EPA issued an evaluation report of this Executive Order and did not give it a good grade. In fact, the report suggests that Executive Order 12898 has not been fully implemented and that the EPA has "not consistently integrated environmental justice into its day-to-day operations." The report also states that the "EPA has not . . . identified populations addressed in the Executive Order, and has neither defined nor developed criteria for determining the disproportionately impacted."[2]

Interestingly, while computing technology has allowed for more sophisticated and detailed analyses, such sophistication may have contributed to a lack of

---

[2]Report of the Office of the Inspector General, March 1, 2004.

consistency in environmental justice measurements and, therefore, the conclusions that depend upon them. In the 2004 evaluation report on environmental justice (mentioned above), the Office of the Inspector General finds that the "EPA's decision not to provide a definition for identifying communities that are minority, low-income and disproportionately impacted by environmental risk has resulted in inconsistent approaches by the regional offices."[3] Faced with the lack of a uniform national definition, regional offices came up with their own and, as a result, are now using different (and inconsistent) definitional thresholds for factors such as "low-income." This implies that otherwise identical tracts could be labeled as low income according to one regional definition, but not low income according to another. Any systematic comparison of tracts in different regions is impossible with inconsistent definitions.

Does it matter empirically? Apparently it does. The report presents findings from a test in Worcester, Massachusetts, which has a population of 172,648. Using EPA Region 6's protocol, 102,885 residents would be identified as potential environmental justice individuals,[4] but using Region 5's protocol, only 59,731 individuals would be so identified. This is a difference of 43,154 persons! Region 1, the region in which Worcester is actually located, found 72,416 potential environmental justice individuals. Apparently with the current state of the art, the number of "disproportionately impacted" individuals depends on whom you ask and on what particular definitions they are using.

Environmental Justice in Canada and Europe.

Though the number of empirical studies outside the United States is rather limited, some case studies have been accomplished, particularly in Canada and Europe. These case studies are useful in helping to discern what kinds of strategies can be effective in the quest to achieve environmental justice in the siting of hazardous waste facilities.

Public participation has been cited as an important factor in the successful siting of hazardous waste facilities in the Canadian provinces of Alberta and Manitoba. ("Successful" in this case means not only that the facility was able to find a home, but also that no environmental justice concerns have arisen after the fact in the host communities.) The siting process in these provinces is not only voluntary, but it provides multiple stages at which the community can exercise veto power over the project.

Interestingly, the resulting locations are not always in low-income neighborhoods. In fact, one such location, the town of Swan Hills, has an average household income significantly higher than the average in the province and one of the lowest levels of unemployment (Rabe, 1994).

Why would any community accept such a facility? Potential jobs at the facilities were apparently one large factor leading to acceptance of these projects. How universal might that finding be?

---

[3]Office of the Inspector General, 2004, 19.

[4]An environmental justice individual is one who is "disproportionately impacted," a term the EPA defines as "the adverse effects of environmental actions that burden minority and/or low-income populations at a higher rate than the general population" (Office of the Inspector General, 2004, i).

One corollary of the jobs hypothesis might be that we would expect the presence of local high unemployment to increase the likelihood a community would accept a hazardous waste facility. That seems to be the case. In a survey of successful sitings in France, Hungary, Italy, the Netherlands, and Spain, for example, Dente et al. (1998) find that areas with higher unemployment are, as expected, more likely to accept facilities. They also find, however, that communities are more likely to accept waste if it is seen as "local" since, in that case, the residents of the host community will also be reaping the benefits from employment in the plants generating the waste.

The Role of Risk Perception.   The "not in my backyard," or NIMBY, attitude has been explored in both the economics and cognitive psychology literatures. Some studies suggest that differences between perceived and actual risks cause the NIMBY phenomenon even though many regulatory policies are based on perceived risks (Hamilton, 2003).

Delving into the psychology of risk perception, Messer et al. (2004) summarize the results of a study that evaluated the benefits of hazardous waste cleanup under the Comprehensive Environmental Response, Compensation, and Liability Act (CERCLA), more commonly known as Superfund. Although this legislation was passed in 1980, legal complexities in the Act have delayed the cleanup of many Superfund sites. In particular, they wanted to know if the length of delay affected the ultimate recovery of property values after the cleanup.

The authors examined four Superfund sites: Operating Industries, a landfill in Los Angeles; Montclair, West Orange, and Glen Ridge Townships in New Jersey, formerly the site of U.S. Radium Corporation; and Indistriplex and Water Wells G&H in Woburn, Massachusetts and Eagle Mine, Colorado, respectively. Cleanup was significantly delayed and/or hampered at all of these sites.

They found that the designation of the site as a Superfund site, the cleanup itself, and the associated news items all negatively affected the property values. Media announcements can affect public perceptions of risk so profoundly that a "shunning" of the property may result. Current owners may not be willing to stay in their homes if their perceived costs of remaining are greater than the value of their homes and potential buyers are likely to be few and far between. In this study, property values continued to fall over time as cleanup was delayed. If cleanup was delayed for 20 years, for example, benefits of cleanup (measured by the recovery of property values) would be negligible, since it would take another 5–10 years for property values to recover (Messer et al., 2004).

Compensation as a Policy Instrument.   One policy device for attempting to achieve environmental justice is paying compensation or host fees to communities accepting hazardous waste facilities. In principle, this would serve to make sure that benefits, not merely the costs, accrue to the local community and paying the compensation would internalize the cost of the environmental risk to those whose waste was being treated.

While compensation frequently is an effective device for finding common ground, as Debate 21.1 suggests, that is not always the case!

DEBATE 21.1

DOES OFFERING COMPENSATION FOR ACCEPTING AN ENVIRONMENTAL RISK ALWAYS INCREASE THE WILLINGNESS TO ACCEPT THE RISK?

One week before a referendum in Switzerland on the siting of a nuclear waste repository, a survey was conducted in the community where the repository was to be located. Researchers found that an offer of compensation to accept the facility reduced willingness to accept it! Specifically, Frey and Oberholzer-Gee (1997) and Frey et al. (1996) found that when asked whether they would accept a nuclear waste repository without compensation, 50.8% of the respondents said "yes." This rate dropped to 24.6% when compensation was offered! The researchers suggest that acceptance rates drop with compensation because offering the compensation crowds out a feeling of civic duty. If respondents feel that accepting a facility is part of his/her civic duty, he/she will be less likely to feel this sense of responsibility once a payment is introduced. In this context, the authors believe that the compensation was viewed as a morally unacceptable bribe and, hence, should be rejected.

An alternative explanation might suggest that compensation could play a signaling role. Perhaps the perceived risks are small until such time as compensation is offered. At that moment, introducing compensation into the mix might be taken by the community as a signal that the risks are much higher than previously thought—indeed, so high that compensation must be paid!

How common is this outcome? In a very different setting (Japan), Lesbirel (1998) examined the siting of energy plants. In this context, the author found that compensation did, as expected, actually facilitate the siting of these plants. He interprets his findings as consistent with the belief that in Japan, institutional structures facilitate participatory negotiations on risk-management strategies that result in productive bargaining between the plants and host communities. This process effectively removes the moral stigma and eliminates the signaling role of compensation.

What is the moral to the story? This evidence suggests that compensation does not automatically increase the likelihood of a community accepting a hazardous facility, but it might. The context matters.

Sources: Bruno S. Frey and Felix Oberholzer-Gee. "The Cost of Price Incentives: An Empirical Analysis of Motivation Crowding Out," *American Economic Review* Vol. 87, No. 4 (1997): 746–755; Bruno S. Frey, Felix Oberholzer-Gee, and Reiner Eichenberger. "The Old Lady Visits Your Backyard: A Tale of Morals and Markets," *Journal of Political Economy* Vol. 104, No. 6 (1996): 1297–1313; S. Hayden Lesbriel. *NIMBY Politics in Japan: Energy Siting and the Management of Environmental Conflict* (New York: Cornell University Press, 1998).

The Incidence of Pollution Control Costs: Individual Industries

How about traditional air and water pollutants? What does the evidence show about the distribution of risk and the distribution of policy benefits and costs? The initial incidence of much of the current policy falls on industry. In order to comply with air, water, and solid waste regulations, industries have had to invest a considerable amount of capital in equipment.

The proportion of new plant and equipment expenditures allocated to pollution control in the average industry is large, though it has diminished since the mid-1970s. The distribution of the cost burden among industries is quite uneven.

The fact that the costs of pollution control may fall initially on the source of pollution does not mean that the entire burden ultimately resides there, however. In general, the ultimate incidence of pollution control costs is determined by the nature of the market. Depending on such factors as barriers to entry and elasticity of demand, these costs can be passed forward to consumers in the form of higher prices, backward to laborers in the form of lower employment and/or wages, or directly to the owners in the form of lower returns on their capital investment (or any combination of the three).

A Competitive Industry

Incidence.   In order to understand the conditions under which the costs can be passed forward or backward, it is necessary to be fairly specific about how an industry reacts to a change in its cost structure. To get at the essence of the problem without unnecessary detail, consider a perfectly competitive industry that is composed of identical firms. Assume that this industry is initially in long-run equilibrium (see Figure 21.1). Faced with the market determined price of p^0, the representative firm maximizes its profits by producing q^0, where marginal cost equals price. Since the

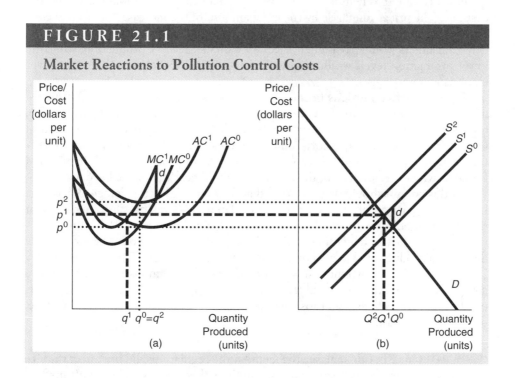

FIGURE 21.1

Market Reactions to Pollution Control Costs

(a)

(b)

price is also equal to average cost at q^0, economic profits are zero. Firms have no incentive to enter or exit the industry.

Suppose now that this equilibrium is disturbed by an EPA regulation forcing each firm to reduce its pollution. Assume that the effect of this regulation on the industry can be reflected as a uniform upward shift in the marginal and average cost curves by a vertical distance d. Because the market supply curve is the sum of the marginal cost curves of the individual firms (all of which have shifted up by d), it will shift up by d as well. Therefore, the market price will rise from p^0 to p^1, an increase less than d. In the short run, price does not rise the full amount of the increase in marginal cost.

The effect on the individual firm can now be seen. The firm would maximize profits by producing the smaller amount q^1 because that is where the new marginal cost curve (MC^1) equals the new price (p^1). Notice, however, that p^1 is lower than AC^1 when q^1 is produced so that economic profits would be negative. Therefore, firms would exit the industry until zero economic profits were restored.

This departure is reflected in market supply as a further shift leftward. The magnitude of the shift is determined by the amount of exit needed to restore the equality of price and average cost. This occurs at price p^2, which is exactly d greater than p^0. The market would produce the smaller amount Q^2, but each remaining firm would produce the same amount it had before the increase in cost.

In the short run, in response to a uniform increase in marginal cost of d, price would rise by less than d, all firms would reduce production, and negative profits would be earned. In the long run, zero profits would be restored by firms leaving the industry, but all remaining firms would produce the same amount as before the cost rise. The price would rise by the exact amount of the increase in marginal cost. Notice that in this case, consumers and laborers would both bear a part of the burden. Consumers would pay higher prices for a smaller level of production, while the lower production levels would imply a lower demand for labor and, hence, lower employment and wages.

The respective burdens borne by these two segments of the population are determined to a large extent by the elasticity of demand for the product. Imagine, for example, that the demand curve for the product was perfectly inelastic (a vertical line) at Q^0. In this case, the short-run price increase would be equal to d and short-run economic profits would be zero. Since the level of production and the demand for labor would be unaffected, the consumer would bear the entire burden.

At this point it should be easy to see that the more elastic the demand curve, the larger the impact on production and, hence, labor. This relationship suggests that the impact of pollution control depends not only on the degree of labor intensiveness of the industry, which determines how severely labor would be affected by declines in production, but also by the elasticity of demand, which determines how large the declines in production would be. For example, industries facing severe competition from imports not subject to the same controls would face greater threats of employment declines than those producing products with no effective substitute, domestic or foreign.

Scale Effects.   In our analysis, the fact that the regulations did not affect the size distribution of firms arises from our assumptions that the cost curves shift upward uniformly by d, that all firms in the industry were identical, and that the regulations affected the cost structure of every firm in the industry in exactly the same way. If the cost curves were not uniformly shifted upward, the firm would not produce the same amount after the regulation as before, because economies of scale would have been affected. In addition, because industries are not really populated by identical firms and the regulations have not been uniformly applied, both the number of firms in an industry and the size of the average firm can be affected by the regulations.

Some recent empirical studies have suggested that the air and water pollution control regulations have not been neutral with respect to the size distribution of firms, but the evidence is incomplete and not conclusive. With respect to the uniform application of regulations, Evans (1986) has found that pollution abatement costs per employee are typically smaller for small firms operated by single-plant companies than for large plants operated by multiplant companies. He attributes this to "regulatory tiering," a strategy designed in part to offer special protection to small business. Under regulatory tiering, small firms face less stringent standards and/or less rigorous enforcement.

Based on this evidence alone, it would be reasonable to expect that the regulatory structure might have reduced the market shares of larger firms by raising costs more for them than their smaller competitors, but that does not appear to have been the case. Pashigian (1984), for example, found that after controlling for changes in fuel costs, market size, and other regulatory programs, industries with relatively high environmental regulatory burdens had become more capital-intensive, had larger increases in mean plant size, and had larger decreases in the number of plants in the industry during the regulatory period than industries with low regulatory burdens. Pittman (1981) also found for water pollution control that the regulations tended to increase the economies of scale in complying plants, resulting in an increase in the operating capacity of the optimally sized plant.

On the surface, the Evans evidence seems to contradict the Pashigian and Pittman evidence, but that need not be the case. First, the Pittman results deal with scale effects on complying plants, not the relationships among large and small plants per se. Second, while the regulations may well favor *existing* small plants, they may discourage potential new small plants from entering an industry. Finally, although the movement of market shares may well coincide with the peak of regulatory activity, correlation does not necessarily imply causation; the changes in the size distribution of firms could have occurred for reasons other than environmental regulations. More research may shed more light on these relationships and help us to clear away the remaining ambiguity.

Monopoly

The effect of pollution control expenditures on any industry also depends on the market structure of that industry. In a monopoly, the entry of new firms would not occur with or without environmental controls. The absence of this pressure changes the way in which a typical firm would react to regulations.

The effect of an increase in control costs on a monopoly is shown in Figure 21.2. Initially, the monopoly is shown in a profit-maximizing equilibrium, where it produces at Q^0 and charges price P^0. If an environmental regulation forced its marginal

FIGURE 21.2

Effect of Pollution Control Costs on a Monopoly

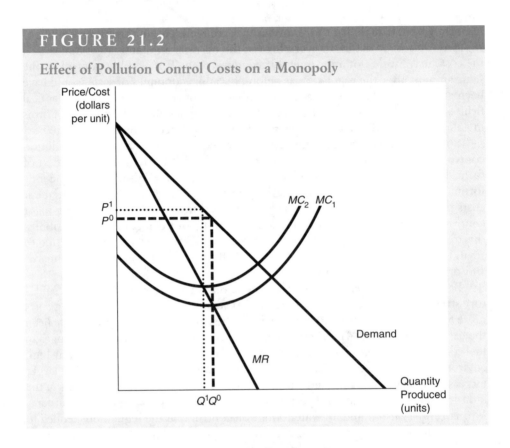

cost to rise uniformly from MC^1 to MC^2, the firm would no longer maximize output by producing at Q^0. It must adjust its output level. At Q^0, marginal cost exceeds marginal revenue, so profits would be increased by reducing output until marginal cost once again was equal to marginal revenue. That would occur at output level Q^1. The price corresponding to this is P^1.

Some interesting differences are evident between the effect of a similar rise in control cost on a monopoly and on a competitive firm. The price, for example, does not rise as much in a monopolized industry as it would in a competitive industry. In the competitive industry, if the marginal cost curve shifts up by an amount d, the price eventually shifts up by the same amount. In a monopoly, the price shifts up by less than d. This result runs contrary to a commonly preconceived notion that a monopoly would automatically pass on all costs. It would not, because it would lose profits if it did. The monopoly would not pass on all costs, because to do so would cause demand to be reduced excessively. It pays the monopolist to absorb part of the cost.

As long as the competitive industry and the monopoly face identical market demand curves, the monopoly would reduce production by a smaller amount than would the competitive industry. The effect on employment would be smaller in a monopoly than in a comparable competitive industry. To some extent, a monopolist insulates its workers from cost shocks.

New-Source Bias.   The current system of controls has another feature we have not yet considered in the analysis. Under the current regulatory approach, new sources face more stringent control requirements than existing sources, resulting in higher compliance costs. Under conditions of stable demand, no new firms would be entering, so no firms would be bearing the higher new-source costs.

Differentiated regulation would not make any difference when demand is stable. However, if demand were increasing over time, then new firms would enter the market. When an industry is growing, the imposition of higher control costs on new firms, but not on old ones, would delay the entrance of new firms and would reduce their market share relative to what their share would be with regulations affecting old and new plants to the same degree.

In a study of capital turnover in the electric power industry, Maloney and Brady (1988) and Nelson et al. (1993) found that the new-source bias embodied in the regulatory system has had a significant independent effect on increasing the amount of time existing facilities are operated before retirement. By imposing a disproportionate share of the pollution control burden on new facilities, the desirability of investing in new plants has been diminished. Since the older plants pollute more, this reduction in the rate of capital turnover results in a delay in the amount of emission reduction achieved by any particular date.

Old plants can actually benefit from this new-source bias in the regulation and could end up making positive profits. These profits would not generally be bid to zero because the normal mechanism for accomplishing that result (competition from new low-cost firms) is not allowed to work.

Since the new firms are higher-cost producers, because of higher control costs, their profits would be bid to zero. Meanwhile, existing firms receive a form of Ricardian rent.

Other studies have confirmed the fact that existing regulations have increased, rather than reduced, the value of existing firms by limiting competition from potential entrants. Maloney and McCormick (1982), for example, found evidence of this in several different industries.[5]

When OSHA imposed a standard limiting the amount of cotton dust exposure for workers in textile plants, new and old firms faced very different compliance costs. An examination of stock prices revealed that a number of textile firms affected by the standard registered an increase in value at the same time that OSHA announced its proposed standards. Moreover, the value increases were positively related to the fraction of cotton used by the firms in their production.

This finding suggests that the value of existing plants was increased, not reduced, by the regulation.

Maloney and McCormick also found that an increase in stock prices of companies owning smelters occurred immediately following a 1973 Supreme Court decision to uphold the Prevention of Significant Deterioration program. This decision had the effect of limiting competition from new smelters that otherwise would have located in PSD regions, increasing the value of existing firms. Clearly, environmental

---

[5]A portion of this evidence has been challenged in Hughes, Magat, and Ricks (1986).

DEBATE 21.2

Jobs Versus the Environment: Which Side Is Right?

Debates over environmental regulations frequently boil down to whether or not companies having to install abatement technologies will have to cut jobs in order to pay for the cleanup. Anticipated job losses can sway voters and legislators toward imposing more lenient standards.

Morgenstern et al. (2002) examine the jobs-versus-the-environment argument for four industries: pulp and paper mills, plastic manufacturers, petroleum refiners, and iron and steel mills. They find that increased stringency of environmental policies does not cause significant job loss.

Key to this study is the measurement of job loss. Environmental regulations can cause displacement of workers from their current jobs, but they also can create jobs in pollution abatement. Some industries may lose while others gain. Thus gross job loss figures for the nation as a whole, which net out the gains and losses across industries, may camouflage the fact that some industries have been hit particularly hard. Gross job changes for the nation as a whole and net job loss within the industry are both relevant, but they have different social implications.

Using the Longitudinal Research Database collected by the U.S. Census Bureau, the Pollution Abatement Cost and Expenditure Survey, and the Manufacturing Energy Consumption Survey, Morgenstern et al. (2002) estimate the net job effect from regulation as between 2.8 jobs lost and 5.9 jobs gained per $1 million of regulatory expense. Nationally, the average gross job effect is a net gain of 1.5 jobs per $1 million in additional abatement spending (across the four industries).

Assessing the results, the authors suggest that, however measured, only a small portion (2%) of job decreases in manufacturing can be attributed to environmental regulation (14,000 of the 632,000 jobs lost between 1984 and 1994). Additionally, environmental spending may have created 29,000 jobs during the same time period.

While this study does not solve the entire debate, it certainly sheds some light on the issue. Policy-makers should not only examine potential job losses, but also potential job shifts and gains from environmental spending.

Source: Richard D. Morgenstern, William Pizer, and Jhih-Shyang Shih. "Jobs Versus the Environment: An Industry-Level Perspective," *Journal of Environmental Economics and Management* Vol. 43 (2002): 412–436.

regulations have rather complicated effects on industries, but the notion that these regulations force many firms out of business seems clearly overstated.

The employment impacts of environmental policy are complex. Some evidence suggests that environmental spending costs jobs, while other analysis suggests that environmental spending may actually promote jobs. As Debate 21.2 points out, both may be right depending on how the employment effects of environmental policy are measured.

The Generation of Pollutants

Firms generate pollutants in the process of producing products to satisfy domestic household demand, export markets, and the government. In this sense, households bear some responsibility for the generation of pollutants; the number and types of products households demand will have an effect on the amounts and types of pollutants emitted. Following this logic, it should be possible not only to discover the amounts and types of products that households in various income groups purchase, on average, but also to use this information to derive the resulting pattern of emissions. With this information in hand, it is possible to estimate how the distribution of pollution generation varies by income class.

Using a large input-output model as the basis for their calculations, Bingham et al. (1987) found that pollution generation per household increases as household income increases. Although this study found that, on average, a dollar spent in a low-income household produces as much pollution as a dollar spent in a high-income household, high-income households spent much more.

The Incidence on Households

An increase in environmental cost affects households in a number of ways. Increases in the prices of products purchased by households cause a decline in the purchasing power of a fixed income. Declines in wages or employment lead to lower incomes, as do the reduced dividends being derived from the lower earnings of industries with some market power.

These are not the only channels, however, by which households end up bearing the costs of pollution control. The money paid to municipalities to subsidize the construction of waste treatment plants is derived from tax revenues. The ultimate incidence of control costs depends not only on the nature of demand and market structure of the industries, it depends on the tax structure as well.

A number of studies have been accomplished within the last few decades that trace the expenditures back through these channels of influence for the purpose of estimating the ultimate incidence of control expenditures. Because of the complexity of these relationships, the estimates are necessarily crude, but some clear insights do emerge.

Air Pollution

Households receive rather different net benefits from stationary source and mobile air pollution control because of the rather different ways in which their respective cost burdens are shared. Therefore, we need to consider each of these separately in order to assess the effects as a whole.

Automobile Control.
In the early 1970s, the EPA released a study suggesting that the costs of automobile air pollution control were probably progressively distributed. In essence, the argument was that since the poor had lower rates of auto

ownership, and the control policy was focused on new cars, the largest burdens would fall on the middle- and upper-income groups.

Subsequent studies have not supported that conclusion. Rather, they suggest that the problem is more complex than realized by the early EPA study. In particular, the increase in the cost of emission controls on new cars affects used-car prices.

These secondary effects create a fairly complicated incidence pattern. While new-car buyers clearly face higher prices, the owners of used cars receive a gain in the form of a higher resale value for their cars. This gain, however, is transitory. All future purchasers of automobiles will pay higher prices regardless of whether they buy new cars or used cars.

Some studies have attempted to trace these effects. Only Freeman (1977) attempts to capture the short-term effects. He derives two rather interesting results: (1) the gain to used-car owners within each income group (caused by the increased resale value of the used car) is, on balance, larger than the loss (caused by the cost of the emission controls) to new-car owners in that same income group, and (2) the gains are progressively distributed. Thus, in the short run, the automobile pollution control costs are more than offset by used-car capital gains, and the largest capital gains are received by lower-income groups.

As interesting as this result is, we should not make too much of it. The offsetting capital gain is a one-time benefit, not to be repeated. Furthermore, it can only be realized when the automobile is sold. And as soon as another car is purchased, the higher cost associated with the emission controls would have to be paid regardless of whether a new or used car were purchased.

For these reasons, the most interesting aspect of automobile air pollution control cost incidence concerns the long run when all cars cost more. Once again, several factors should be considered: (1) the increase in cost to new-car purchasers, (2) the increase in cost to used-car purchasers, and (3) the number of new-car and used-car purchasers in each income group.

All studies have found that in the long run automobile pollution control costs are regressively distributed. Harrison (1975) has the most complete description of the incidence. He finds, for example, that costs are higher in the suburbs than in the central city, and are higher in smaller cities than in larger cities. He also finds the degree of regressivity higher in the suburbs and generally in smaller cities. (Los Angeles is an exception, being a large city with a highly regressive incidence.)

This evidence addresses only part of the story. In order to determine the ultimate incidence, it is necessary to complement these estimates of cost incidence with some estimate of the benefits. To complement his analysis of the distribution of the cost burden, Harrison also conducted a detailed study of the incidence of the benefits of automobile pollution control policy. Because of the difficulties of estimating a generally accepted monetary value for benefits, he measured benefits solely in terms of improvements in the concentrations of three automobile pollutants (carbon monoxide, nitrogen oxides, and ozone). These improvements were calculated for each geographic area and, using data on the income levels of people in those areas, he calculated the degree of reduced exposure experienced by each of these groups.

He found that the benefits from improvement in air quality were progressive *for those living in urban areas*. Furthermore, they were most progressively distributed in the very largest cities. This results from the disproportionate representation of the poor in the most heavily polluted areas in our largest cities.

When he combines his cost and benefit estimates for other parts of the country, Harrison concludes:

> Households living in suburban areas, small urban areas, and nonurban areas—which make up two-thirds of the United States households—do poorly under the current scheme. Households in these areas gain quite modest air-quality benefits while paying large costs. Lower income groups in these areas fare particularly poorly since the costs fall quite heavily upon them under the current scheme. (p. 109)

In a general sense, the Harrison study suggests that the automobile air pollution control policy, so carefully designed to be uniformly applied, has led to a highly unbalanced distribution of the benefits. The imbalance appears both in the distribution of net benefits among geographic areas and the distribution among socioeconomic groups. Those living in rural areas, particularly the poor, seem to be relatively more burdened than other segments of society.

Stationary-Source Control.   Are these results unique to automobile control? Because the programs are quite different, we cannot assume similarity without performing the analysis. Stationary-source controls also result in higher prices, but the commodities affected are not the same. Furthermore, while rates of automobile ownership are quite low among the poor, particularly the urban poor, the exposure to increases in other commodity prices might well reach more of the poor.

Most studies assume that increased costs of stationary-source controls are passed forward to consumers in the form of higher prices. Therefore, they affect households in proportion to what each household spends on that commodity. In general, the poor spend a higher proportion of their income on these commodities, meaning they save less. Therefore, it is not surprising that those who have derived estimates have found them to be regressively distributed (Dorfman, 1977; Gianessi et al., 1979).

Studies of the benefits of air pollution control tell a rather different story. A study by Asch and Seneca (1978) examined how the exposure to air pollution was distributed in the United States. They wanted to know if exposure was systematically related to the economic and social characteristics of the population.

To answer this question, they constructed two different samples of data. The first sample consisted of observations on the annual geometric mean concentrations of particulates taken from 284 cities. Socioeconomic variables, such as income levels, age composition, and education levels, were collected for these cities. Performing separate computations for each state, the particulate pollution levels were correlated with these socioeconomic characteristics. In virtually all states they found high pollutant concentrations in cities with higher percentages of lower-income people, higher percentages of the aged, and higher percentages of nonwhites.

They complemented this analysis with another sample that examined the intracity variation in air quality. For this second sample, the exposure to three air pollutants—sulfur dioxide, nitrogen dioxides, and particulates—was correlated with socioeconomic characteristics within three cities: Chicago, Cleveland, and Nashville. Measuring pollution levels and socioeconomic characteristics at a number of sites within each city allowed for a much more precise link between local pollution levels and the immediately affected population to be established.

The income-distribution measures consistently confirmed that the poorest residents of these cities experienced higher pollution levels. Higher pollution levels were generally found in neighborhoods with lower property values. The results for racial exposure were mixed. In Chicago, higher pollution levels were found in neighborhoods with a high percentage of nonwhites, but in Cleveland, the opposite was true—higher concentrations of nitrogen dioxide were found in neighborhoods containing relatively high proportions of whites. Subsequent analysis by Brajer and Hall (1992) for the South Coast Air Basin of California unambiguously found that ethnic minorities (and children) received the greatest exposure to pollution.

Asch and Seneca also examined whether the improvements in air quality achieved in the early 1970s were progressively, proportionally, or regressively distributed. They found that the physical improvements were progressively distributed—the lower-income portions of the cities received the greatest reductions in pollutant concentrations. They found that many high-income areas actually became more polluted during the period. Similar results were obtained for the New York region (Zupan, 1973).

A Combined Assessment.   The Asch-Seneca and Zupan studies deal with exposure rather than economic benefits. The two are not the same because the concept of economic benefits deals with the worth of reducing exposure, not merely the exposure reduction. Gianessi, Peskin, and Wolff (1979) attempted to bridge this gap by distributing to local areas the national damage estimates computed by the EPA and then prorating the benefits among socioeconomic groups on the basis of exposure.

Their first finding was that the variability of benefit per family estimates across regions and income groups was several times larger than the variability in costs. While the average family in large urban areas received many times the benefits from the program than did the average suburban or rural family, their costs differed by a much smaller amount. Therefore, it is not surprising that the heavily industrialized, highly populated areas of the eastern United States lead the list of the largest gainers, while the rural and agricultural areas are at the bottom of the list.

Gianessi, Peskin, and Wolff also considered the specific areas in which net benefits are positive or negative. For automobile air pollution, they found only 4 areas of the country (Jersey City, New York, Patterson, and Newark) enjoyed positive net benefits. For stationary-source pollution, they found 61 (out of 274) areas receiving positive net benefits. When the mobile and stationary-source net benefits were combined, they found 24 areas experiencing positive net benefits. These 24 areas contain approximately 28% of the population. The majority of the areas (and population) are paying costs for air pollution control that are higher than the benefits received.

Analyzing the distribution of net benefits among income classes, the Gianessi, Peskin, and Wolff study found the net benefit from stationary-source pollution to be progressively distributed, and the net benefit from mobile-source control to be regressively distributed. The combination of policies yields ambiguous results with no clear pattern emerging. Generally, the poor and lower-middle class seem somewhat harder hit, although the poorest of the poor end up with the smallest net burden.

We probably should not make too much of any listing of areas that are net beneficiaries or net losers, such as the one described above, because the magnitude of the net benefit is subject to a great deal of uncertainty, particularly in the calculation of benefits. It does seem clear, however, that automobile air pollution control policy and, to a lesser extent, stationary-source air pollution control policy, violate both the horizontal and vertical equity dimensions. Equals in different parts of the country are not treated equally, and the net benefits of air pollution control policy are distributed in a mildly regressive manner.

Greenhouse Gas Control.   What are the distributional effects of climate-change policy? Dinan and Rogers (2002) examined the distributional implications of using various approaches to reduce U.S. carbon emissions 15% below 1998 levels. Their results demonstrate that distributional effects hinge crucially not only on whether permits are grandfathered or auctioned, but also on how any collected revenues would be used.

In general they find that households in the lowest income quintile would be worse off when grandfathered emission permits are used while, due to large increases in the value of their stockholdings, households in the top income quintile would be better off. Furthermore, they find auctioned emission permits to be regressive if revenues are used to cut payroll taxes, and highly regressive if they are used to cut corporate taxes. However, if the revenue from auctioned permits or taxes was distributed equally to each household or in some pro-poor fashion, the lowest income quintile would be better off and the highest income quintile worse off.

Parry (2004) examines the incidence of emissions permits, among other control instruments, to control power plant emissions of SO_2, carbon, and NOx. His results suggest that using grandfathered emissions permits to reduce carbon emissions by 10% and NOx emissions by 30% can be highly regressive. He also finds that the SO_2 cap imposed by the 1990 Clean Air Act Amendments is also regressive but much less so than the carbon and NOx policies. Using a revenue-raising instrument and equal per-household distribution of the revenues would make all of these programs progressive.

These results not only suggest that it is possible to design policies that are both effective and fair, but also point out that achieving that goal would require some fairly large changes in how policies are currently implemented.

Water Pollution

Water pollution presents an interesting contrast. The program of control erected to combat water pollution includes not only industrial effluent standards similar to the industrial emission standards used to combat air pollution, but it also includes federal subsidies to waste treatment plants. Since these subsidies are financed through the tax system, their impact could conceivably be quite different from measures financed chiefly by higher product prices.

Point Sources.   Three separate studies (Dorfman, 1977; Gianessi et al., 1979; and Lake et al., 1979) sought the distribution of costs of federal water pollution control policy for point sources. All three studies came to similar conclusions.

In general, they found that the distribution of the costs was regressive. The industrial effluent standards imposed a large regressive burden, while the burden of subsidies for municipal treatment plants was progressive. Industrial standards were found to be regressive because they result in higher consumer prices. Because the poor spend a larger percentage of their income and save less, they are affected proportionately more. Progressiveness of the municipal waste treatment subsidies results from their major source of financing—the progressive tax system.

To place these results into perspective, Gianessi and Peskin (1981) compared the incidence of water pollution costs to the incidence of air pollution costs. They found the cost of water pollution control incidence less regressive, partly because of the manner in which municipal treatment plant subsidies are financed and partly because of the lack of any component in the water pollution policy resembling the highly regressive automobile policy.

The conclusion that the municipal waste treatment subsidies are progressive has not gone unchallenged. In an examination of the incidence of these subsidies in EPA region VII (Iowa, Missouri, Kansas, and Nebraska), Collins (1977) found that they tended to redistribute income from the middle-income classes primarily to the very rich. This conclusion depends critically on one particular assumption in the analysis and characteristics that may be somewhat unique to the region studied.

This study assumes that the subsidies received by industrial users of the waste treatment plants are not passed forward to consumers in lower prices, but rather are retained by the owners. Since the owners of capital, in general, tend to be in the upper portion of the income distribution, this assumption results in a major gain by that group. If this assumption were changed to distribute the subsidy to industrial customers rather than owners, the burden of the municipal waste treatment subsidy would be quite progressive.

Assuming that the owners of capital retain the subsidy turns out to be particularly important in the Collins study, because over one-half of the subsidies in the region studied accrue to industrial users. Using exactly the same methodology as Collins to estimate the distributional burden of waste treatment subsidies within the Boston metropolitan area, Ostro (1981) found the burden to be quite progressively distributed. This rather different finding results from the fact that in Boston, the industrial share of the subsidy was only 7.85%, making the results less sensitive to the assumption about the incidence of the industrial subsidy.

The literature on the distribution of the benefits of water pollution control is very thin. In one study, Winston Harrington (1981) investigated the distribution of water-based recreation benefits resulting from the implementation of the BPT portion of the 1972 Water Pollution Control Amendments. Using the RFF Water Network Model to simulate the effects of the policy on water quality and an econometric model to estimate the change in recreational demand resulting from the improvement in water quality, Harrington found the benefits to be very unequally distributed. In particular, he found whites favored relative to nonwhites, middle-income families favored relative to the poor, city dwellers favored relative to those living in the country, and northeast residents favored relative to those residing in other regions.

Implications for Policy

These observations suggest that neither the efficiency nor the sustainability criterion is sufficient to ensure environmental justice. While efficiency maximizes the net benefits, it says nothing about who will receive them. While sustainability protects the interests of future generations, it remains silent on the distribution of the costs and benefits among the current generation.

Since most of the environmental risks are disproportionately borne by the poor and minorities, it is tempting to simply assume that reducing those risks would also disproportionately benefit the same groups. While there is an element of truth in that statement, it is far from the whole truth.

Consider the components of the net benefits associated with any policy that lowers environmental risk. On the benefits side, the improvements in environmental quality from a particular policy would not necessarily occur in those geographic areas where the poor or minorities are most exposed. On the cost side, we have learned that both the size of the cost burden and its distribution are affected by the choice of policy instruments. With revenue-raising policy instruments, the primary determinant of the progressiveness of the burden is how the revenue is distributed.

These insights provide both a basis for optimism and a sense of the difficulty of the task that lies ahead. The optimism comes from the fact that neither efficiency nor sustainability is fundamentally incompatible with the achievement of social justice. Policies can be designed to be just, as well as efficient and sustainable. The sense of the difficulty comes not only from the realization that just outcomes are not the normal outcomes from efficient and sustainable policy, but also that achieving them will require policy reform.

As Example 21.1 points out, for example, emissions trading with "grandfathered" initial allocations can result in more just outcomes than the traditional command-and-control policy.[6] Other studies reviewed in this chapter have pointed out that the use of revenue-raising instruments (such as auctioned permits or emissions charges) can result in even more just outcomes than grandfathered emissions trading *provided that the revenue is distributed in a particular way*. If the revenue is not distributed in that prescribed way, the burden can be even less just. Historically, at least in the United States, it has been difficult to get revenue-raising instruments implemented at all. Even if they become politically feasible, there would be no guarantees that the revenue would be distributed in the required manner.

The siting of hazardous waste facilities also raises important policy questions. The appropriate policy responses fall into two different categories.

First, governments must use consistent definitions of affected parties in order not only to understand the magnitude of the problem, but also to be able to target

---

[6]This is not universally true. Parry (2004) shows that if all the permit rent is passed forward to consumers in the form of higher product prices, emissions trading could actually be more regressive than the command-and-control allocation.

Example 21.1

DISTRIBUTIONAL IMPACTS OF RECLAIM

As discussed in Chapter 16, the Regional Clean Air Incentives Market (RECLAIM) is an emissions trading program established by the California South Coast Air Quality Management District (SCAQMD) to control smog. While the desire to implement a more cost-effective policy was a main motivating force behind its implementation, how RECLAIM would affect the poor, small businesses, and jobs was also a prime concern. To inform the policy process, SCAQMD hired a consulting firm to conduct a detailed analysis of the likely distributional impacts of moving from a command-and-control approach to RECLAIM. The analysis predicted:

- Emissions trading would reduce overall control costs by about 40% compared to the equivalent command-and-control regulations.
- These cost reductions would tend to benefit low-income households most.
- Small businesses would likely gain substantially from emissions trading, assuming their initial allocations of permits were the same as under command-and-control.
- How individual industries fared would largely be determined by initial permit allocation.
- RECLAIM would generally enhance employment by lowering costs and allowing an expanded output.

The basic message is that although the distributional impacts are to a large extent determined by the initial allocation of permits, an initial allocation based on the command-and-control allocation can simultaneously achieve both equity and cost-effectiveness objectives.

Source: David Harrison, Jr. *The Distributive Effects of Economic Instruments for Environmental Protection* (Paris: Organisation of Economic Co-operation and Development, 1994).

resources where they are most needed. Inconsistent definitions are likely to promulgate ineffective responses.

Second, the achievement of environmental justice depends on the empowerment of the minority and low-income populations most likely to be adversely affected. As long as they remain ignorant of the risks they face from proximate facilities and are excluded from decision-making processes, they will continue to bear a disproportionate burden. As we have seen from the examples in this chapter from Canada and Europe, it is possible not only to provide adequate information, but also to design inclusive processes that result in the willing acceptance of these facilities by host communities.

Summary

Are environmental risks and the policies used to reduce them fair? Apparently not. The siting of hazardous waste facilities, for example, seems to have resulted in a distribution of risks that violates the horizontal equity criterion. Among low-income populations, minority communities seem to bear a disproportionate burden. This outcome suggests that current siting policies are neither efficient nor fair. The responsibility for this policy failure seems to lie mainly with the failure to ensure informed consent of residents in recipient communities and very uneven enforcement of existing legal protections.

Examining the fairness of pollution control policy requires a knowledge of how the costs and benefits are initially distributed and how these burdens can be shifted by market reactions. Beginning with the initial incidence of control costs on industries, we discovered a high degree of variability among industries. The ability of these industries to shift this burden to consumers or employees depends upon such factors as the market demand for the product, labor intensiveness of the production process, and market structure. Some industries are hit much harder than others.

The empirical evidence on the ultimate incidence suggests that the costs are regressively distributed in general for air pollution, while the benefits are progressively distributed. Low-income groups and minorities generally face higher pollutant exposure levels. The evidence further suggests that net benefits are progressively distributed for stationary-source controls but regressively distributed for mobile sources.

For air pollution control as a whole, net benefits are mildly regressively distributed because of the dominance of automobile pollution control. Environmental policy does not live up to the vertical equity criterion, though the degree by which it fails is small.

Current pollution control policy violates the horizontal equity principle as well. Net benefits are substantially higher for residents of large urban areas than they are for suburban or rural residents.

Less evidence is available on the distribution of water pollution control net benefits, though the evidence we have suggests they violate both the horizontal and vertical equity criteria as well. Though the costs of water pollution control are less regressive than their air pollution control counterparts, the benefits seem to be regressively distributed with a high degree of geographic variability.

While the air and water pollution control policy results strongly suggest that current distribution of benefits is not as equitable as it might be, they provide little evidence of any intentional exploitation of the poor. Many parts of the control policy involve progressively distributed net benefits, particularly for the urban poor. The regressive nature of the entire package is milder than would be the case if the rich were out to exploit the poor.

The lack of fairness in current pollution control policy has apparently not diminished the popular support for environmental policy to any appreciable degree. According to polls, public support remains high. Regional self-interest has been a factor, however, in determining the form of environmental legislation.

Though previous policies have generally not gotten it right, as least in the United States, it is possible to achieve more effective policy while promoting environmental justice. More targeted policies and an increased reliance on cost-effective policies in controlling stationary sources are a step in the right direction. Empowering low-income and minority communities with better information and more inclusive decision-making processes would certainly make the largest difference.

Discussion Questions

1. "The goals of environmental policy and our concern for the poor inevitably conflict. The burden of any attempt to improve the environment necessarily falls disproportionately on the poor." Discuss.
2. "Environmental policy in the United States has been extremely fair in that it has been uniformly applied. This is evident, for example, in the uniform ambient air-quality standards, uniform new-source performance standards, uniform hazardous pollutant standards, uniform new-car emission standards, and uniform discharge standards for water pollution." Does uniformity in these policies guarantee "fairness"? Defining "fairness," explain why or why not.

Further Reading

Christiansen, G. B., and T. H. Tietenberg. "Distributional and Macroeconomic Aspects of Environmental Policy," in Allen V. Kneese and James L. Sweeney, eds. *Handbook of Natural Resource and Energy Economics* (Amsterdam: North-Holland, 1985). A more detailed and more technical survey of the material covered in this chapter.

Elliott, Donald, Bruce A. Ackerman, and John C. Millian. "Toward a Theory of Statutory Evolution: The Federalization of Environmental Law," *Journal of Law, Economics, and Organization* (Fall 1985): 313–340. An attempt to explain the economic and political forces that led to very strong U.S. environmental legislation in a period when environmental special interest groups played only a small lobbying role.

Gordon, David, ed. "Environment," in *Problems in Political Economy: An Urban Perspective* (Lexington, MA: DC Heath, 1981). An interesting treatment of the radical, conservative, and liberal points of view on the distribution of benefits from pollution control policy. Unfortunately, this discussion was dropped in the second edition.

Harrison, David, Jr. *The Distributive Effects of Economic Instruments for Environmental Policy* (Paris: OECD, 1994). Reviews the available evidence on the effects of various environmental policy instruments on low-income groups as well as measures to alleviate possible adverse impacts.

Peskin, Henry. "Environmental Policy and the Distribution of Benefits and Costs," in Paul R. Portney, ed. *Current Issues in U.S. Environmental Policy* (Baltimore: Johns Hopkins University Press for Resources for the Future, 1978). A more policy-oriented discussion of the distribution of the benefits and costs of the Clean Air Act Amendments of 1970 than the readings discussed in this text.

Additional References is available on this book's companion Web site www.aw-bc.com/tietenberg.

Development, Poverty, and the Environment

*If there is any period one would desire to be born in,
is it not the age of revolution when the old and the
new stand side by side and admit of being compared?
When the energies of all men are searched by fear,
and by hope? When the historic glories of the old can
be compensated by the rich possibilities of the new
era? This time, like all times, is a very good one, if
we but know what to do with it.*

—Ralph Waldo Emerson, *The American Scholar* (1873)

Introduction

In previous chapters we invested a considerable amount of time and effort
in investigating individual environmental and natural resource problems
and the policy responses that have been, and could have been, taken to solve
them. In general, solutions are possible, and our economic and political
institutions, with some exceptions, seem to be muddling through.

Our next step must be a consideration of the global economic system
and the scale of the challenge it faces in this century. Perhaps the major
challenge is finding a way to deal effectively with global poverty without
jeopardizing the environment or degrading the resource base passed on to
future generations.

Poverty has emerged as one significant cause of environmental problems. The worst recorded air pollution is not found, as might be expected,
in the highly industrialized cities of the high-income countries, but rather
in the major cities of lower-income countries. Deforestation is caused in
part by the migration of landless peasants into the forests, seeking a plot of
land to work. Soil erosion is caused, in part, when the poor are driven to
farm highly erodible land in an attempt to survive. Dealing effectively with
these environmental problems, and the human suffering that lies behind
them, will require raising living standards.

527

Traditionally this has been accomplished through economic development.[1] One model for the development of the less industrialized countries is the path of rapid economic growth followed by the industrialized countries. How appropriate a model is this?

Examining the appropriateness of the traditional economic growth approach to development should start by studying that model and its success or lack of success as a means of eliminating poverty. We will begin by defining how economic growth takes place and how the growth process is affected by increasing resource scarcity and rising environmental costs. This understanding will then be used to characterize what changes in the growth process of industrialized nations can be expected in the future.

Next, we explore the relationship between growth and development in the industrialized countries. Has growth increased the well-being of the average citizen in the developed countries? Or has the evident elevated consumption of material goods made possible by economic growth merely masked large offsetting problems that would cause an appropriately measured standard of living to go down, not up?

The fate of the average citizen, of course, does not always shed light on the fate of the poor. How have the poor fared in periods of rapid economic growth? Is John Kennedy's metaphor "A rising tide lifts all ships" apt, or does a rising tide leave more people stranded?

While the historical experience in the industrialized countries is revealing, the transferability of this experience into a context for the developing world is by no means obvious. To what extent can economic growth provide an answer to the crushing problems of poverty that infect developing countries? What are the barriers to achieving increased standards of living for the poor in developing countries in a finite world?

The Growth Process

Nature of the Process

How does economic growth occur? It occurs in two main ways: through increases in inputs such as capital, labor, energy, and other resources, or through increases in the productivity of those resources as a result of technological progress. The former source of growth involves increasingly greater outputs, given the state of the art in production, while the latter source involves improvements in the state of the art.

Increases in Inputs. The amount of growth occurring from increases in inputs is governed by two important economic concepts: economies of scale and the law of

---

[1]Herman Daly's useful distinction between growth and development is employed here. Development refers to a qualitative increase in well-being, while growth refers to an expansion in physical output of goods and services. They are related, but by no means synonymous, concepts. It is conceptually possible to have growth without development and development without growth, but historically the two have been inextricably entwined. See Daly and Cobb (1989).

diminishing returns. *Economies of scale* refers to the amount of increase in output obtained when all inputs are increased in the same proportion. The *law of diminishing returns* governs the relationship between inputs and output when some inputs are increased and others are held fixed.

If an increase in all inputs would lead to the same percentage increase in output, the process is said to exhibit *constant returns to scale. Increasing (decreasing) returns to scale* refers to a situation when the percentage increase in output is larger (smaller) than the percentage increase in all inputs.

The law of diminishing returns governs what happens when some, but not all, of the inputs are increased. Suppose, for example, that all the inputs are held fixed, except for capital, which increases. As constant and successive increments of capital are added to the other fixed resources, the law of diminishing returns implies that eventually a point will be reached where each increment of input will produce smaller and smaller increments of output.

Technological Progress.   The final source of growth, technological progress, involves the implementation of better, less wasteful ways of doing things. With technological progress, growth can occur even in the absence of increases in inputs simply because the available inputs are used more effectively. For example, with a new production technique, less energy might be wasted or fewer resources used to make a product.

Potential Sources of Reduced Growth

Historically, increases in factor inputs and technological progress were both important sources of growth. This does not automatically mean that in the future, they will continue to provide growth at historic levels, however. A number of reasons suggest caution in extrapolating historically valid arguments into the future.

Reduced Input Flows.   Not all input flows are continuing at historic levels. Population growth has slowed considerably in most countries, which causes the growth in the labor force to slow and possibly stop. The growth fed by increasing labor is diminishing and will continue to diminish in the future.

The cost of energy and raw materials seems to be rising, even in real terms. Producers respond to higher relative prices by cutting back on the use of these inputs, which diminishes their contribution to the growth process.

Capital formation has played a pivotal role in the past and is likely to continue doing so (Jorgenson et al., 1988). As workers were given more sophisticated capital equipment to work with, their productivity increased.

Capital has broken down the barriers imposed by human limitations. Earth moving, once limited by the strength and endurance of workers, with the advent of bulldozers is limited no more. Size of the market, once limited by the time and effort required to transport commodities in a horse and buggy, expanded with the advent of the railroad, the truck, and the airplane. Limits on corporate controllability imposed by the size and competence of record-keeping staffs—as they attempted to stay on top of the information and paper flows—have fallen in the face of computers providing instant access to important information compiled in the most useful format.

Although capital is a reproducible asset, some indirect limits may diminish its role in the future. These include limitations on substitutability for other factors, on the productivity of future investment, and on the incentive to invest. We consider each of these in turn.

The ability of capital to sustain historical growth rates lies in part in its ability to substitute for those factor inputs that are experiencing limits. In Chapter 14 we introduced the concept known as the elasticity of substitution and noted that when this concept takes on a value of one or greater, substitution is easy and growth should not be inhibited.

The first substitution possibility we consider is between capital and labor. As population growth dwindles, the growth rate in the supply of labor diminishes as well. Historically, the economic growth rate has exceeded the growth rate of labor supply, as capital was continually substituted for labor. Most studies of production have found capital and labor to be quite strong substitutes. When we think about the modern manufacturing sector, this seems quite reasonable. Therefore, dwindling population, by itself, doesn't seem a particularly large barrier.

Describing the substitution possibilities for other resources, however, becomes more complex. No general consensus has emerged from empirical work concerning the degree of substitutability existing between capital and resources. The degree of substitutability seems to depend upon the industry being considered.

The relationship between capital and energy is even more puzzling. Studies of the capital-energy relationship over time in the United States find that capital and energy are complements, rather than substitutes. Thus, capital and energy have together substituted for labor and other resources but not for each other. If one thinks of the tractor, the bulldozer, and the airplane, this seems like a natural finding.

The question of interest is whether capital and energy will remain complements in the future or whether substitution of capital for energy might be possible. This is an especially important question in light of the links between fossil-fuel energy use and climate change. If the attack on climate change includes a reduction in the use of fossil-fuel energy and capital is a complement with energy, climate change strategies would have the side effect of reducing the rate of capital formation.

In some energy uses, substitution is clearly feasible because energy-saving equipment, such as computer-controlled heating and cooling, already exists. Furthermore, some capital investments will clearly hasten the transition to passive solar energy, which conserves energy by making better use of what is available.

In other sectors such as transportation, the substitution possibilities are not quite as obvious, but that does not mean they do not exist. Bicycles are used in many European countries as a substitute for automobile transportation. To some extent, communication can even substitute for transportation, as more people use home-based computer terminals and phone lines to do their jobs without leaving home. While our historical experience would suggest limited substitution possibilities, it is not at all clear that experience is relevant for the future. Nonetheless, it would be premature to feel confident that the future elasticity of substitution between capital and energy will be uniformly greater than 1.0. Though it is likely that the elasticity of substitution between energy and labor is quite high, this does not offer much promise for growth in an era of declining growth in the labor force. Some drag on economic growth from higher energy prices appears likely.

The second possible source of growth drag relates to the future productivity of capital. As pollution rises, the amount of resources committed to combating it also rises. A substantial proportion of new plant and equipment expenditures is being allocated to pollution control. Unlike conventional investments, however, these investments do not cause more goods to be produced; they produce a cleaner environment. Because the value of this cleaner environment is not usually recorded in the conventional measures of economic output, conventionally measured output should rise more slowly as a larger proportion of inputs is diverted from productivity enhancement to environmental enhancement.

The final source of drag concerns the incentive to invest. The amount of capital investment should depend upon the rate of return on that investment. The more profitable the investment is, the larger the amount undertaken. Yet we have already identified two related factors that reduce the rate of return on investments: the regulatory bias against new sources and the composition of investment. By focusing on new sources, the regulatory system diminishes the relative profitability of new investment while enhancing the profitability of existing capital stock. This new-source bias diminishes the incentive to invest in new capital. Meanwhile, the large proportion of new plant and equipment expenditures going for pollution control tends to diminish the profitability of those expenditures, since improvements in the environment do not, in general, add to profits.

In sum, it appears that expecting increases in capital to completely compensate for reduced flows of other inputs would be risky. Some important transitions are occurring. While they do not imply a cessation of growth catastrophically or otherwise in the near future, these transitions certainly suggest some diminution in the rate of economic growth resulting from reduced factor input flows.

Limits on Technological Progress

Can technological progress take up the slack? If technological progress is to compensate for declining input flows, an increase in the rate of technological progress must occur. Is that likely?

Some observers are beginning to suggest that the degree to which technological progress can continue to play its historic role as a growth stimulant may be limited. Some of these limits are perceived as institutional and a matter of choice, while others are perceived as natural and inexorable.

The new-source regulatory bias in pollution control policy provides an example of an institutional limit. Because most technological progress bears fruit when it is embodied in new or modified production facilities, this new-source bias inhibits technological progress by reducing the number of these facilities.

Another institutional barrier is the decreasing commitment of resources to basic research, particularly by the public sector. Since basic research is frequently a precursor for technological progress, this trend could also diminish the rate of technological progress.

The Natural Resource Curse

A final, especially intriguing possible source of growth drag might pose special problems for resource-abundant nations. Common sense suggests that those countries blessed with abundant resource endowments would be more likely to prosper. In fact, the evidence suggests the opposite—resource-abundant countries are less likely to experience rapid development (see Example 22.1).

Example 22.1

THE "NATURAL RESOURCE CURSE" HYPOTHESIS

Perhaps surprisingly, there is robust evidence that countries endowed with an abundance of natural resources are likely to develop less rapidly. And it is not merely because resource-rich countries are subject to volatile commodity prices.

Why might a large resource endowment exert a drag on growth? Several possibilities have been suggested. Most share the characteristic that resource-rich sectors are thought to "crowd out" investment in other sectors that might be more likely to support development.

- One popular explanation, known as the "Dutch Disease," is usually triggered by a significant increase in revenues from raw material exports. The resulting boom draws both labor and capital out of traditional manufacturing and causes it to decline.
- Another explanation focuses on how the increase in domestic prices that typically accompanies the resource boom impedes the international competitiveness of manufactured exports and therefore export-led development.
- A third explanation suggests that the large rents to be gained from the resource sectors in resource-abundant countries would cause entrepreneurial talent and innovation to be siphoned away from other sectors. Thus resource-rich countries could be expected to have lower rates of innovation, which, in turn, results in lower rates of development.

While countries with large resource endowments may not have the significant opportunities for development that might have been expected, it is encouraging to note that lots of countries without large resource endowments have not been precluded from achieving significant levels of development.

Sources: J. D. Sachs and A. M. Warner. "The Curse of Natural Resources," *European Economic Review* Vol. 45, No. 4–6 (2001): 827–838; R. M. Auty. *Sustaining Development in Mineral Economies: The Resource Curse Thesis* (London: Routledge, Inc.); and T. Kromenberg. "The Curse of Natural Resources in the Transition Economies," *Economics of Transition* Vol. 12, No. 3 (2004): 399–426.

Environmental Policy

We have seen that pollution control laws impose large compliance costs on industry. These should have some effect on inflation (by boosting output prices), employment, and growth. The question of interest is how large those impacts have been, and could be expected to be, in the future.

In general, the impact of traditional environmental policy on the rate of inflation (measured using the urban consumer price index) is very small. Pollution control expenditures are a relatively small percentage of production costs.

The effect on employment is particularly interesting. We suggested in the previous chapter that one effect of the new-source bias would be to diminish the adverse employment impacts on existing pollution sources. Any adverse employment impacts that occur are further offset to some degree by the gains in employment experienced by firms producing the pollution control equipment. The sales and employment in these industries would have increased as a direct result of the environmental regulations. Are these effects large enough to offset the negative effects on employment resulting from the price increases triggered by increasing costs of pollution control?

At least in the Los Angeles area, the evidence seems to suggest that strict environmental policy has not triggered increases in unemployment (see Example 22.2).

However, this generally positive prognosis for the impact of environmental policy on employment should not obscure the problems. Gains in employment generally benefit a different set of workers than losses do. New jobs are rarely in the same location as those lost and rarely involve the same skill levels. Even when overall employment effects are positive, the rising costs of environmental control could cause severe localized problems.

How much responsibility for the slowdown in productivity in the 1970s can be attributed to environmental policy? Using comparative data from the United States, Canada, and West Germany, Conrad and Morrison (1989) found that only a small part was the result of diverting investments toward environmental control. In fact, some government requirements to install cleaner equipment may have raised productivity by forcing firms to invest in newer and more efficient equipment. For industries in the United States, attributing somewhere in the neighborhood of 12% of the responsibility of the productivity slowdown to environmental regulations seems a common finding (Barbera and McConnell, 1990; Gray, 1987; Christainsen and Haveman, 1981; Norsworthy, Harper, and Kunze, 1979). If these simulations are at all accurate, environmental policy does not bear responsibility for much of the decline in the economic growth rate in the late 1970s.

Energy

A second possible source of growth drag considered in the previous section was energy. Since large price increases occurred during 1973–1974, this period provides a unique opportunity to study the magnitude of the growth-inhibiting effects of energy.

What should we expect to find? Since energy and capital historically have been complements, we should find that price increases would slow down capital formation. At the same time, the fact that energy and labor are substitutes would suggest that

Example **22.2**

JOBS VERSUS THE ENVIRONMENT: WHAT IS THE EVIDENCE?

The employment effects of environmental regulation are a hot political topic. Public opinion surveys show strong support for measures intended to produce a cleaner environment, but workers often feel that these measures threaten their jobs.

Is their anxiety justified? Theory tells us that regulation can reduce employment by raising marginal costs and decreasing sales; it also tells us that regulation can increase employment by creating a demand for workers to monitor and maintain pollution control equipment. Empirical studies have produced conflicting results.

One particularly interesting way to gather evidence on this subject would be to examine the employment consequences of regulation in a geographic area that has experienced particularly stringent regulation. One study that did precisely that focused on the regulation of air pollution in manufacturing plants in the Los Angeles region. Because this area has some of the worst air quality in the nation, the South Coast Air Quality Management District has been forced to adopt regulations of unprecedented stringency to comply with national air-quality standards. The study examines employment growth in the Los Angeles region in plants subject to these regulations, and compares growth at these plants to employment growth at similar plants in Texas and Louisiana, areas that had no significant increase in local air-quality regulation.

The results indicate that in the 1979 to 1991 period in the Los Angeles Basin, increases in air-quality regulation involving substantial increases in cost did not appreciably affect employment. In fact, the study found very small *increases* in employment. Although the increases were not statistically significant, they were sufficient to rule out the possibility that the regulation had led to large decreases in employment.

Source: E. Berman and L. T. M. Bui. "Environmental Regulation and Labor Demand: Evidence from the South Coast Air Basin," *Journal of Public Economics* Vol. 79 (February 2001): 265–295.

the use of labor should be rising, which, in turn, would cause the average productivity of labor to fall.

On a general level the evidence is consistent with this set of expectations. Investment was lower and the average productivity of labor fell. Work by Jorgenson (1981) and Uri and Hassanein (1982) confirms this impression.

Focusing on 1973–1976, a period characterized by rapidly increasing energy prices, Jorgenson first examined the question of whether the decline in growth was due to declines in input growth or to declines in productivity. He found that input declines were much less significant than declines in productivity. He then attempted to discover the sources of this productivity decline by looking at the specific experience of 35 different industries.

Though a decline in economy-wide productivity could conceivably be caused either by a shift in resources from high-productivity industries to low-productivity industries or by a decline in productivity within each industry, Jorgenson found the latter to be far more important than the former. His analysis of the causes of these declines revealed that in 29 of the 35 sectors examined, technical change was biased toward the use of energy. This result suggests that in 1973–1976, productivity growth resulting from technical progress declined as energy prices rose. If this is an accurate depiction of the future, as well as the past, then this evidence provides some, albeit weak, empirical confirmation that higher energy prices might depress the rate of technological progress.

One puzzle to be explained by those who believe energy prices have already played a significant role in productivity declines is how that could be so when the energy cost share is so small. Factors with small cost shares should in general have small effects on output.

Some work by Berndt and Wood (1987) suggests a resolution to this puzzle that seems consistent with the evidence. They suggest that in the short run, the capital services provided by the capital stock are largely fixed, as are its operating characteristics. Once the capital stock is in place, the ratio of energy to capital services actually utilized is therefore fixed. Dramatic changes in energy prices therefore affect the degree to which this capital is used, with the most energy-inefficient vintages being used least. By lowering the utilization of the existing capital stock, higher energy prices reduce total factor productivity.

In this story, the lower productivity does not necessarily persist. As long as new capital that uses less energy can be purchased, utilization rates rise and productivity is restored as these new machines are installed. Once the stock of capital adjusts to the new regime of higher energy prices, productivity growth rebounds.

The key to thinking about the long run is to keep straight the differences between *ex post* and *ex ante* substitution possibilities. Ex ante refers to the time period prior to investment, while ex post refers to the time period after the equipment is installed. Limited ex post substitution possibilities, which seem to have played a significant role in the slowdown of productivity growth after the major energy price increases in the 1970s and early in the 1980s, do not automatically indicate that ex ante substitution possibilities will be small. It is the ex ante substitution possibilities that will determine the future of economic growth over the long run.

During the relatively robust U.S. economy of the 1990s, the surge of technical change in the form of the digital revolution was apparently very important in increasing labor productivity (Jorgenson et al., 2002). Was this surge in technical change promoted by the relatively low energy prices at the time, or independent of them? The energy price spikes in the early part of the first decade of the 21st century will provide a new source of variation to be analyzed once sufficient time has elapsed to assess their impact. Stay tuned!

Most visions of sustainable development suggest the need for increasing the efficiency with which energy is used. In practice, this means investing in energy conservation in order to make better use of a smaller fossil-fuel energy flow. What employment and income effects can be expected from investments in energy conservation?

Geller et al. (1992) have investigated this question by constructing two quantitative scenarios—a business-as-usual scenario and a high-energy-efficiency scenario. The high-energy-efficiency scenario involves an additional annual investment of about $49 billion in energy efficiency. They conclude that in addition to producing some rather dramatic reductions in pollutants (a 24% reduction in carbon dioxide, for example), the energy-efficiency scenario results in both a rise in personal income (0.5% by 2010) and a net increase in jobs (1.1 million by 2010). The largest increases in jobs were estimated to occur in the construction, retail trade, and service industries, while the largest decreases were in the traditional energy supply sectors. Other studies have found that transitioning from depletable to renewable energy sources is also likely to increase, rather than decrease, employment (Renner, 1991, 25).

Outlook for the Near Future

Some of what the future portends for the United States and other developed countries is becoming clear. Because we are in a period of transition, some striking differences are emerging between our experiences in the recent past and what we will encounter in the near future. Though a detailed examination would be beyond the scope of our study, we will highlight some of the emerging changes.

Population Impacts

The dramatic fall in fertility rates experienced by most countries of the world will have a profound impact. Inevitably, the average age of the population will rise, putting pressure on social security systems. Since the United States relies on an unfunded social security system, current payments to retirees are financed out of current payments by workers.

The importance of this point was underscored when U.S. President George W. Bush identified social security reform as a main priority for his second term in office. As long as the population is growing, the ratio of workers to retirees remains high enough to provide adequate benefit levels for retirees without putting excessive strain on current workers. When population growth declines, however, as is now happening, the ratio of workers to retirees declines as well. To keep the system solvent, benefit growth has to decline and/or worker payments have to increase. Neither is a politically attractive option. Demographic change can be painful.

Studies by economists suggest that other labor market implications of declining population growth may also be significant. One very positive effect may well be a reduction in the unemployment rates of young adults. The labor market will more easily absorb the smaller number of inexperienced workers.

As population growth declines, the labor force should grow more slowly as well, creating some upward pressure on wages. Higher wages should reinforce and support the rising labor participation rates for women and should entice older workers to stay in the labor force longer. Enhanced job opportunities for women should help to keep the fertility rate low, reinforcing the tendency toward low population growth rates. A period of tight labor markets should also have an equalizing effect on the income distribution unless the economy responds by outsourcing the jobs or replacing labor with capital (computers, for example).

The Information Economy

The importance of capital and resources in the American economy is a product of the Industrial Revolution. The Industrial Revolution ushered in an era of mass production where manufacturing replaced agriculture as the dominant source of employment and earnings. This transformation depended upon massive amounts of capital investment and the scale of operations it brought about consumed large amounts of resources.

It now seems clear that the economy is in the midst of an equally important transformation from an industrial society to an economy based on information. The key elements of this transformation are a change from a goods-producing to a service economy, a rise in the importance of theoretical knowledge as a source of growth, and an increasing reliance on information processing.

This transformation has profound implications for our society. Computer-controlled robots will step in to fill the slots vacated by lower population growth in a direct substitution of capital for labor. Working at home has already become possible for larger numbers of people as computer communication provides a substitute for transportation. Such changes will boost productivity while reducing pollution and our dependence on raw materials and energy. Intelligence will eventually replace oil as the prime mover of the system. Education is, therefore, growing in importance, not only as the means of providing that skilled labor, but as the wellspring of ideas that fuel the new growth.

Other effects of the information economy will directly affect environmental policy. The lower cost of gathering, storing, and structuring information as well as the lower cost of providing more universal access to it will enable a host of new disclosure strategies. These can serve to promote both efficient policy and environmental justice. New possibilities for quick and effective information sharing streamline cooperation among governments and nongovernmental organizations as they jointly seek sustainable outcomes. Better information technology also enhances monitoring and enforcement of environmental policies, historically one of the weak links. The new analytical techniques that are part and parcel of the information economy (such as geographic information systems) will be able to provide a better foundation for policy.

Better information technology is, however, a two-edged sword. Following the events of 9/11, it has became clear that better information technology has also made coordination easier for those seeking to destroy, rather than to build. In response to that threat, governments have allowed measures that significantly change the privacy border, a different, but nonetheless troubling threat. Information technology, it seems, is a mixed bag.

The Growth-Development Relationship

Has economic growth historically served as a vehicle for development? Has growth really made the average person better off? Would the lowest-income members of the United States and the world fare better with economic growth or without it?

These turn out to be difficult questions to answer in a way that satisfies everyone, but we must start somewhere. One appropriate point of departure is clarifying what we mean by growth. Some of the disenchantment with growth can be traced to the way that growth is measured. It is not so much that all growth is bad, but that increases in conventional indicators of growth are not always good. Some of the enthusiasm for zero economic growth stems from the fact that economic growth, as currently measured, can be shown to have several undesirable characteristics.

Conventional Measures

A true measure of development would increase whenever we, as a nation or as a world, were better off and decrease whenever we were worse off. Such a measure is called a *welfare measure* and no conventional existing measure is designed to be a welfare measure.

What we currently have are *output measures*, which attempt to indicate how many goods and services have been produced, not how well off we are. Measuring output sounds fairly simple, but it is not. The measure of economic growth with which most are familiar is based upon the GDP, or gross domestic product. This number represents the sum of the outputs of goods and services produced by the economy in any year. Prices are used to weight the importance of these goods and services in GDP. Conceptually, this is accomplished by adding up the value added by each sector of the production process until the product is sold.

Why weight by prices? Some means of comparing the value of extremely dissimilar commodities is needed. Prices provide a readily available system of weights that takes into account the value of those commodities to consumers. From early chapters we know that prices should reflect both the marginal benefit to the consumer and the marginal cost to the producer.

GDP is not a measure of welfare and was never meant to be one. One limitation of this indicator as a measure of welfare is that it includes the value of new machines that are replacing worn-out ones rather than increasing the size of the capital stock. To compensate for the fact that some investment merely replaces old machines and does not add to the size of capital stock, a new concept known as net domestic product (NDP) was introduced. NDP is defined as the gross domestic product minus depreciation.

NDP and GDP share the deficiency that they are both influenced by inflation. If the flow of all goods and services were to remain the same while prices doubled, both NDP and GDP would also double. Since neither welfare nor output would have increased, an accurate indicator should reflect that fact.

To resolve this problem, national income accountants present data on *constant-dollar* GDP and *constant-dollar* NDP. These numbers are derived by "cleansing" the actual GDP and NDP data to take out the effects of price rises. Conceptually, this is accomplished by defining a market basket of goods that stays the same over time. Each year this same basket is repriced. If the cost of the goods in the basket went up 10%, then because the quantities are held constant, we know that prices went up by 10%. This information is used to remove the effects of prices on the indicators; remaining increases should be due to an increased production of goods and services.

This correction does not solve all problems. For one thing, not all components of GDP contribute equally to welfare. Probably the closest component we could use in the existing system of accounts would be consumption, the amount of goods and services consumed by households. It leaves out government expenditures, investments, exports, and imports.

The final correction that could easily be made to the existing accounts would involve dividing real consumption by the population to get *real consumption per capita*. This correction allows us to differentiate between rises in output needed to maintain the standard of living for an increasing population and rises indicating more goods and services consumed by the average member of that population.

Real consumption per capita is about as close as we can get to a welfare-oriented output measure using readily available data. Yet it is a far cry from being an ideal welfare indicator.

In particular, changes in real consumption per capita fail to distinguish between economic growth resulting from a true increase in income, and economic growth resulting from a depreciation in what economists have come to call "natural capital," the stock of environmentally provided assets such as the soil, the atmosphere, the forests, wildlife, and water.

The traditional definition of income was articulated by Sir John Hicks (1947):

> The purpose of income calculations in practical affairs is to give people an indication of the amount they can consume without impoverishing themselves. Following out this idea, it would seem that we ought to define a man's income as the maximum value which he can consume during a week, and still expect to be as well off at the end of the week as he was at the beginning. [p. 172]

While human-created capital (such as buildings, bridges, and so forth) is treated in a manner consistent with this definition, natural capital is not. As human-created capital wears out, the accounts set aside an amount called depreciation to compensate for the decline in value as the equipment wears out. No increase in economic activity is recorded as an increase in income until depreciation has been subtracted from gross returns. That portion of the gains that merely serves to replace worn-out capital is not appropriately considered income.

No such adjustment is made for natural capital in the standard national income accounting system. Depreciation of the stock of natural capital is incorrectly counted as income. Development strategies that "cash in" the endowment of natural resources are in these accounts indistinguishable from development strategies that do not depreciate the natural capital stock; the returns from both are treated as income.

Consider an analogy. Many high-quality private educational institutions in the United States have large financial endowments. When considering their budgets for the year, these institutions take the revenue from tuition and other fees and add in some proportion of the interest and capital gains earned from the endowment. Except in extraordinary circumstances, standard financial practice, however, does not allow the institution to attack the principal. Drawing down the endowment and treating this increase in financial resources as income is not allowed.

Yet that is precisely what the traditional national accounts allow us to do in terms of natural resources. We can deplete our soils, cut down our forests, and douse ocean coves with oil, and the resulting economic activity is treated as income, not as a decline in the endowment of natural capital.

Because the Hicksian definition is violated for natural capital, policy-makers are misled. By relying upon misleading information, policy-makers are more likely to undertake unsustainable development strategies.

Adjusting the national income accounts to apply the Hicksian definition uniformly to human-made and natural capital could, in resource-dependent countries, make quite a difference. For example, Robert Repetto (1989) and colleagues of the World Resources Institute studied the growth rates of gross national product in Indonesia using both conventional unadjusted figures and figures adjusted to account for the depreciation of natural capital. Their study found that while the unadjusted gross national product increased at an average annual rate of 7.1% from 1971 to 1984, the adjusted estimates rose by only 4.0% per year.

Motivated by a recognition of these serious flaws in the current system of accounts, a number of other industrial countries have now proposed (or in a few cases have already set up) systems of adjusted accounts including Norway, France, Canada, Japan, the Netherlands, and Germany. Significant differences of opinion on such issues as whether the changes should be incorporated into a complementary system of accounts or into a complete revision of the standard accounts remain to be resolved.

In the United States, the Bureau of Economic Analysis (1994) published some initial estimates of the value of the U.S. stock of minerals—oil, gas, coal, and non-fuel minerals—and how the value of that stock (in constant dollars) has changed over time. The objective was to determine whether current use patterns are consistent with the constant-value version of the sustainability criterion. Declining values would indicate a violation of the criterion while constant or increasing values would be compatible with it. In general they found that the value of additions just about offset the value of the depletion; for the period 1958–1991, their estimates suggest that the criterion was not violated. It is not possible to examine what has happened over time since these estimates fell victim to budget cutting and were discontinued.

Alternative Measures

Are we fulfilling the sustainability criterion or not? Although that turns out to be a difficult question to answer, a number of indicators have now been designed to allow us to make some headway. These indicators differ in both their construction and the insights that can be derived from them.

Adjusted Net Savings.   We begin with an indicator that attempts to provide an empirical method for judging whether or not we are fulfilling the weak sustainability criterion. Recall from Chapter 5 that a decline in total capital indicates unsustainability according to the weak sustainability criterion. This implies that net savings, which is the addition to the value of total capital, must be positive. Negative net savings implies that the total capital stock has gone down, a violation of the criterion.

Adjusted net savings (formerly called "genuine savings") is the sustainability indicator that examines a net savings concept that explicitly considers natural capital. Constructed by the Environmental Economics group of the World Bank, adjusted net savings estimates are derived by making four types of adjustments to standard national accounting measures of gross national savings. First, estimates of capital consumption of produced assets are deducted to obtain net national savings.

Second, current expenditures on education are added to net domestic savings as an appropriate value of investments in human capital (in standard national accounting, these expenditures are treated as consumption). Third, estimates of the depletion of a variety of natural resources are subtracted to reflect the decline in asset values associated with their extraction and harvest. Estimates of resource depletion are based on the calculation of resource rents. Rents are derived by taking the difference between world prices and the average unit extraction or harvest costs (including a "normal" return on capital). Finally, pollution damages are deducted. Because many pollution damages are local in their effects, and therefore difficult to estimate without location-specific data, the World Bank estimates include only global climate change damages from carbon dioxide emissions.

What do these estimates show? Generally, adjusted savings indicate that the countries violating the weak sustainability criterion are some of the former Soviet Republics and countries in Sub-Saharan Africa and the Middle East.[2] Higher-income countries are generally estimated to be weakly sustainable because their savings and expenditures on education are large enough to offset declines in the value of natural capital.

Genuine Progress Indicator.

The Genuine Progress Indicator (GPI), developed and maintained by an organization called Redefining Progress in San Francisco, differs from adjusted savings in two main ways: (1) it focuses on an adjusted measure of consumption, rather than savings, and (2) it includes many more categories of adjustments.[3]

The GPI adjusts national personal consumption expenditures in several ways. The most unique (and the most controversial) adjusts personal consumption expenditures for income distribution; more equal income distributions increase the GPI, while less equal income distributions reduce it.[4] Using personal-consumption expenditures adjusted for income inequality as its base, the GPI then adds or subtracts categories of spending based on whether they enhance or detract from national well-being. Examples of additions include: the value of time spent on household work, parenting, and volunteer work; and the value of both services of consumer durables (such as cars and refrigerators) and services of highways and streets. Examples of subtractions include: defensive expenditures, defined as money spent to maintain the household's level of comfort, security, or satisfaction such as personal water filters, locks or security systems, hospital bills from auto accidents, or the cost of repainting houses damaged by air pollution; social costs such as the cost of divorce, crime, or loss of leisure time; and the depreciation of environmental assets and natural resources (due to the loss of farmland, wetlands, and old-growth forests; the reduction of stocks of energy and other natural resources; and damaging effects of wastes and pollution).

---

[2]Up-to-date data can be found on the World Bank's Environmental Economics and Indicators Web site: http://lnweb18.worldbank.org/ESSD/envext.nsf/44ByDocName/GreenAccountingAdjustedNetSavings/.

[3]Details about this indicator, including the data and its calculation, can be found on the Redefining Progress Web site at http://www.redefiningprogress.org/.

[4]This step relies on the measure of inequality known as the Gini coefficient, which is defined in the Glossary to this text.

According to this indicator, not only do traditional accounting measures such as the Gross Domestic Product considerably overstate the health of the economy, but in several years since the 1970s, per capita well-being has actually declined. In those years, declines in income inequality and leisure time, coupled with increases in the costs of crime, pollution, and other social ills, have more than offset the increases due to larger levels of economic activity and increases in socially productive activities such as volunteerism.

Ecological Footprint.   Another example of an indicator, the Ecological Footprint, differs considerably from the other two in that it is based upon a physical measure rather than an economic measure. The Ecological Footprint indicator attempts to measure the amount of renewable and nonrenewable ecologically productive land area that is required to support the resource demands and absorb the wastes of a given population or specific activities.[5] The footprint is expressed in "global acres." Each unit corresponds to one acre of biologically productive space with "world average productivity." Every year has its own set of equivalence factors since land-use productivities change over time. By comparing this "footprint" to the amount of ecologically available land, deficits or surpluses can be uncovered.

This indicator, like the others, departs from a calculation of national consumption, which is calculated by adding imports to, and subtracting exports from, domestic production. This balance is computed for 72 categories such as cereals, timber, fishmeal, coal, and cotton. The footprint (in terms of acres) for each category of resource uses is calculated by dividing the total amount consumed in each category by its ecological productivity (or yield per unit area). In the case of carbon dioxide (CO_2) emissions, the footprint is calculated by dividing the emissions by the average assimilative capacity of forests to find the number of acres necessary to absorb the pollutants.

According to this indicator, the industrialized nations have the most unsustainable consumption levels (meaning that their consumption requires more ecologically productive land than is domestically available). This analysis also suggests that current global consumption levels cannot be sustained indefinitely by the current amount of ecologically productive land—we are in a deficit situation.

The Human Development Index.   One dissatisfaction with all of these measures of well-being is their focus on an average citizen. To the extent that the most serious problems of deprivation are not experienced by the average member of society, this focus may leave a highly misleading impression about well-being. To rectify this problem, in 1990 the United Nations Development Program (UNDP) constructed an alternative measure, the Human Development Index (HDI). This index has three major components: longevity, knowledge, and income.

Though highly controversial because both the measures to be included in this index and the weights assigned to each component are rather arbitrary, the

---

[5]The details about this indicator can also be found on the Redefining Progress Web site at http://www.redefiningprogress.org/footprint/. Anyone can have his/her own ecological footprint calculated by answering a few questions at http://www.myfootprint.org/.

UNDP (2004) has drawn some interesting conclusions from the results of comparing HDIs among countries:

- The link between per capita national income and human development is not automatic; it depends on how the income is spent. Some relatively high-income countries (such as South Africa and the Persian Gulf states) do not fare as well as expected in human development terms, while some low-income countries (such as Sri Lanka and Cuba) were able to achieve a higher level of human development than would be expected given their income levels.
- Nonetheless, income is a major determinant of the capacity to improve human development. It is not a coincidence that the top five countries in terms of the human development index (Norway, Sweden, Australia, Canada, and the Netherlands) are all very-high-income countries.

Growth and Poverty: The Industrialized Nations

Conceiving of the growth-development relationship only in terms of the effects on the average citizen obscures a great deal of what may be happening in a society. Two societies may have the same per capita growth in average well-being, but if the fruits of this growth are shared uniformly in one and unequally in the second, it seems overly simplistic to argue that the increase in welfare levels would be the same in the two countries.

While the evidence suggests that economic growth has improved the lot of the average citizen in the developed world, it tells us little about how the poorest members of society have fared. To determine whether the poorest citizens also benefit from growth, we must dig deeper into the nature of the growth process.

History is one source of information about this relationship. To exploit that source, we shall examine the data for a period of particularly high economic growth in the United States. Did it benefit the poor, or were they left behind?

The Effects on Income Inequality

Growth can help the poor in two main ways. First it can provide more opportunity to earn income either by increasing the number of available jobs, by increasing the wages paid, or some combination of the two. Second, it is generally believed that income transfers are politically easier when the amount to be shared is growing. The donors can give up some of their gains and still be better off, whereas in a no-growth situation, any sharing must come from a reduction in the real income of the donor.

The experience from the United States suggests that periods of economic growth have reduced the degree of poverty. While growth itself has been a factor, government transfers have made the most difference. Economic growth, in the absence of transfers, would not have lifted many persons from below to above the poverty threshold. The linkage between growth and the poor depends more upon its effect on the willingness to transfer than on direct market effects. Although growth cannot be seen as a vehicle that inevitably creates equality of income among the rich and poor, the evidence shows that, in the United States at least, the quality of life experienced by the poor has been improved by it. This improvement has come both from a general rising standard of living and a rise in transfers from the rich to the poor.

Poverty in the Less Industrialized Nations

Economic growth can be a vehicle for development and this form of development can benefit the poor as well as the rich according to the historical experience in the industrialized nations. Though the relationship between economic growth and poverty is neither inevitable nor universally effective, it does provide one possible path for dealing with poverty.

How relevant is this experience for developing countries? Is economic development solving the poverty problem?

In September 2000 the member states of the United Nations unanimously adopted the Millennium Declaration, which set a number of Millennium Development Goals. Among others, these goals call for

- Reducing the proportion of people living on less than $1 a day to half the 1990 level by 2015—from 27.9% of all people in low- and middle-income economies to 14.0%

- Halving the proportion of people who suffer from hunger between 1990 and 2015

- Ensuring that, by 2015, children everywhere, boys and girls alike, will be able to complete a full course of primary schooling

- Reducing by two-thirds, between 1990 and 2015, the under-five mortality rate

- Halting and reversing the spread of HIV/AIDS by 2015

These goals serve as useful benchmarks for judging progress. What is the evidence?

According to the World Bank (2004), the proportion of people living on less than $1 a day dropped by almost half between 1981 and 2001, from 40 to 21% of the global population, but that is not yet near the goal of 14%. But the progress that has been achieved has been uneven. While rapid economic growth in East and South Asia pulled over 500 million people out of poverty in those two regions alone, the proportion of poor grew, or fell only slightly, in many countries in Africa, Latin America, Eastern Europe, and Central Asia.

Uneven regional progress is accompanied by uneven progress across the various hazards poor people face. Worldwide, for example, an estimated 840 million people, most of them in low-income countries, are chronically undernourished, and economic growth by itself does not seem to resolve this problem. Despite impressive economic growth in South Asia, for example, that region still registers malnutrition among children reaching almost 50%, along with chronically low school enrollment and completion rates. The World Bank reports that if current trends persist, by 2015 children in more than half of developing countries will still not be on track to complete their primary education.

Public services in health, nutrition, and education often fail poor people. For example, in 20 developing countries where sufficient data for analysis were available, child mortality rates fell only half as fast for the poorest 20% of the population as for the population as a whole. In addition, HIV/AIDS has infected more than 60 million people worldwide, with more than 95% of them in developing countries, and 70% in Sub-Saharan Africa.

Appropriateness of the Traditional Model

How appropriate is the traditional economic growth model for these countries? Does it point the way out of poverty?

Scale.   One of the first indicators that traditional models may be inappropriate derives from the ecological effects of the proposed global scale of economic activity necessary to eradicate poverty if the model of development followed by the industrialized nations of Asia, Europe, and Africa were adopted by the rest of the world. As Jim MacNeill, the former director of the World Commission on Environment and Development, has stated, "If current forms of development were employed, a five to ten-fold increase in economic activity would be required over the next fifty years to meet the needs and aspirations of a population twice the size of today's 5.2 billion, as well as to begin to reduce mass poverty." Whether increases of this magnitude could be accomplished while still respecting the atmospheric and ecological systems on which all economic activity ultimately depends is not at all obvious.

Increased energy consumption to support new industry would add greenhouse gases. Increased refrigeration would add more of the gases depleting the stratospheric ozone level. The industrialized nations have freely used the very large capacity of the atmosphere to absorb these gases. Little absorptive capacity is left. Most observers seem to believe that to meet the challenge, we need to take an activist stance by controlling population, severely reducing emissions of these gases in the industrialized world, and discovering new forms of development that are sustainable.

Forms of Development.   Economics can assist in the process of characterizing forms of development. Appropriate development should capitalize on local strengths and stay away from weaknesses; it should be sensitive to factor prices.

Many, if not most, of the developing nations are labor-surplus economies. It follows that their strategy for development, at least in the beginning stages, should be labor intensive. Labor-intensive processes serve the twin purposes of capitalizing on an abundant resource and providing a source of income to large numbers of people.[6]

While the forms of development in the industrialized nations are increasingly going to rely on a highly skilled labor force, that is inappropriate for countries where the educational systems may not currently be able to supply sufficient numbers of skilled workers to fill the need. By effectively utilizing the low-skilled workforce, developing countries can increase their incomes, decrease population growth, and ultimately create the wealth needed to support a strong educational system.

---

[6]Contrast this with capital-intensive processes that use much less labor and distribute more of the returns to the owners of capital, who are typically well-off.

Development in the industrialized countries has also been very fossil-fuel dependant. While this may be appropriate when supplies of fossil fuels are plentiful and the remaining capacity of the environment to accept the by-product gases is unlimited, it is certainly less appropriate for a future plagued by diminishing supplies and climate change.

Barriers to Development

What are the barriers to raising standards of living in developing countries? Rising populations face increasingly limited access to land, health services, education, and financial resources. Many of these problems are intensified by the current international economy. Heavy debt burdens, falling prices for their exports, and the flight of capital that could be used to create jobs and income are all significant barriers to sustainable development.

Population Growth.   Poverty begets poverty. The positive feedback loop between population growth and poverty is one powerful example. Population growth rates are typically higher, substantially higher, in low-income populations. High infant mortality causes parents to compensate with large numbers of births. Children provide one of the few available means of old-age security. Knowledge about birth control techniques is sparse and the availability of contraceptives is limited. Women frequently have low levels of education and in some cultures large families are the only possible way for women to achieve status. Larger populations in turn tend to increase the degree of poverty by lowering wages and by spreading the family resources allocated to children over a larger number.

Population growth also puts increased pressure on the natural resource base. Pushing larger numbers of people onto marginal land increases soil erosion and deforestation. Increasing population density can cause the carrying capacity of the land to be exceeded. In parts of Africa where nomadic tribes have coexisted for centuries with a fragile ecosystem, larger populations and reduced mobility have resulted in such a serious deterioration of the ecosystem that it is no longer able to satisfy basic human needs.

Land-Ownership Patterns.   Pressures on the land arising from population growth are exacerbated by patterns of land ownership in many of the lower-income countries. In agricultural economies, access to land is a key ingredient in any attempt to eradicate poverty, but land ownership is frequently highly concentrated among a few extremely wealthy owners. Improvements in agricultural techniques can do little to raise living standards if peasants do not have access to their own land.

One common measure of the degree of inequality in land ownership is the Gini coefficient. The Gini coefficient can take on values of 0.0 (which would indicate perfect equality) to 1.0 (which would indicate perfect inequality). Perfect equality would occur if every farmer owned exactly the same amount of land. Perfect inequality would imply that all land was owned by a single farmer.

In Latin America, Gini coefficients in excess of 0.75 are common. This region has the most skewed land-ownership patterns on the globe, a legacy of colonial times when colonial rulers accumulated vast amounts of land. Asian nations are somewhat better with Gini coefficients ranging from 0.51 to 0.64, while in Africa, where collective tribal land ownership is common, the coefficients fall between 0.36 and 0.55.

Trade Policies.   Some of the barriers faced by developing countries as they attempt to raise living standards have been erected by the industrialized nations. Trade policies are one example. The terms of trade for many developing countries have deteriorated in the recent past. When the terms of trade deteriorate, exports from developing countries can purchase fewer imports.

Some of the reasons for this deterioration are rather natural effects of markets rather than misguided policies. Included in this category are the import substitutions in the industrialized world (such as when optical fibers are substituted for copper in phone lines) and lower demand for developing-country exports triggered by lower economic growth in the industrialized countries.

But political factors are also important. When political forces in the developed countries conspire to eliminate or substantially reduce natural markets for the developing countries, these policies not only exacerbate the poverty in the developing nations, but they have a direct degrading effect on the environment.

The Multi-Fiber Arrangement, originally implemented in 1974, is a case in point. Its effect has been to severely reduce developing-country exports of textiles and other products made from fibers. In developing countries, fiber products are produced by labor-intensive techniques, causing the employment impact to be high. The opportunity to provide the fiber raw materials is another source of employment for local sustainable agriculture. By artificially reducing the markets for these products and the fibers from which these products are manufactured, the agreement has forced some nations to substitute resource-intensive economic activities, such as timber exports, for the more environmentally congenial fiber-based manufacturing in order to earn foreign exchange.

Agricultural trade flows not only demonstrate how price distortions can be translated into unsustainable development, but also show how they can exacerbate poverty. In general, price distortions and artificially supported exchange rates have resulted in a pattern of trade that involves excessive agricultural production in the developed world and too little in the developing world. Agriculture in the developed world is supported by a number of different subsidies. In the developing world, the bias operates to promote underproduction rather than overproduction. Overvalued exchange rates increase the attractiveness of importing food and decrease the attractiveness of exporting food.

By discouraging small-scale agriculture in developing countries, an activity that would provide income to a segment of the population faced with the most severe forms of poverty, biased trade flows exacerbate the poverty problem. Furthermore, since income increases targeted on this particular group typically lead to slower population growth, even some of the population pressures on the environment could ultimately be related to biases in current trade patterns.

One common stereotype of the difference between developed and less developed countries involves their respective supplies of minerals. According to this stereotype, less developed countries control most of the world's mineral resources, while the developed world creates the demand for them. If accurate, this view would suggest that rising mineral prices would eventually create favorable terms of trade for most developing countries.

Unfortunately, upon closer inspection this stereotype represents at best an oversimplification. While exports of minerals have increased from less developed to developed countries, not all less developed countries share these higher export levels. A few have large reserves of petroleum or nonfuel minerals, but most do not. The benefits from increasing mineral prices tend to bypass most less developed countries.

Debt.   Many developing countries have staggering levels of debt to service. Unfortunately, even private capital is flowing out of the capital-poor countries where it is desperately needed and into the capital-rich countries. The World Bank estimates that the stock of "flight" capital held abroad by citizens of severely indebted countries equals a significant fraction of their countries' external debt.

In periods of high real interest rates, servicing these debts puts a significant drain on foreign exchange earnings. Using these foreign exchange earnings to service the debt eliminates the possibility of using them to finance imports for sustainable activities to alleviate poverty. According to *The Economist* ("Debtors',"1989, 73), in all but one of the most indebted countries, the ratio of investment to gross domestic product was substantially lower in the 1982–1988 period (when the debt burden was heaviest) than in the previous six years. In Argentina, the ratio fell from 25% to 15%, while comparable figures for Venezuela indicate a fall from 33% to 18%. This fall in investment has, in turn, reduced the growth of output and exports in debtor nations and thereby further undermined their ability to repay their debts.

With the notable exception of a relatively few oil-rich nations, most developing countries import a great deal of energy. Because this demand is relatively price-inelastic, their expenditures on imports have risen tremendously without similar compensating increases in receipts from the sale of exports.

The situation is reversed in many of the oil-exporting countries, which are commanding abnormally high prices for their oil. Their favorable terms of trade, however, have not always insulated them from development difficulties. Nigeria is a classic example. Buoyed by oil exports, the local wage structure and exchange rates ended up severely harming agricultural production. Resources flowed out of agricultural production and into oil production. Even the income distribution was adversely affected, becoming much more unequally distributed (Hogendorn, 1997).

In recognition of the threat to development posed by debt, in 1996 the Heavily Indebted Poor Countries (HIPC) Initiative was established as a joint collaboration between the World Bank and the International Monetary Fund. It stated aim is to reduce the excessive debt burdens faced by the world's poorest nations.

As of September 2004, 27 countries were receiving debt relief under the Initiative. HIPC relief committed to the 27 countries, together with other debt relief initiatives, represents a two-thirds reduction in the overall debt stock of these countries. Debt service-to-exports ratios have also been substantially reduced to an average of 10%, allowing more resources to be committed to public expenditures. As a result, poverty-reducing government spending is projected to rise from less than twice that of debt-service payments to almost four times. Poverty-reducing expenditures in the 27 countries that receive HIPC assistance are projected to have increased from 6.4% of GDP in 1999 to 7.9% of GDP in 2003.[7]

The HIPC Initiative is not a panacea. Even if all of the external debts of these countries were forgiven, most would still depend on significant levels of external assistance. As a group, their receipts from external assistance have exceeded their debt-service payment for many years.

The evidence suggests that while growth is no panacea for the problems of the developing world, it is probably better than no growth. However, the traditional form of growth experienced in the industrialized countries is not likely to be the most appropriate form for the less developed countries in the future. Circumstances have changed since the Industrial Revolution. Furthermore, the factor endowments in developing countries are not the same as those in the industrialized countries. Changing circumstances call for changing approaches.

Natural Disasters.   As the Asian tsunami in December 2004 demonstrated, natural disasters can deal a devastating blow to development. Not only were hundreds of thousands of people killed, but the economic infrastructure (tourism, fishing, agriculture, and so on) on which the livelihoods of survivors depends was badly damaged or destroyed.

While natural disasters cannot be controlled in the same way pollution is controlled, we are not powerless. For a given risk, warning systems and disaster planning can help reduce the damage. The magnitude of the risk may be controlled as well by reducing the vulnerability of populations. As the number of people to be accommodated grows and the amount of available land does not, the tendency to exploit land with a higher vulnerability to natural disaster increases as well. Whether this is manifested as building on highly erodable hillsides in California that are susceptible to wild fires or farming the deltas in Bangladesh that are vulnerable to storm surge, human choices affect the magnitude of the risk. Population pressure makes risky choices more likely.

Summary

Historically, increases in inputs and technological progress were important sources of economic growth in the industrialized nations. In the future some factors of production, such as labor, will not increase as rapidly as they have in the past. The effect of this decline on growth depends on the interplay among the law of diminishing marginal productivity, substitution possibilities, and technological progress. The law of diminishing marginal productivity suggests slower growth rates, while technological progress and the availability of substitution possibilities counteract this drag. One view foresees limits to technological progress imposed by the second law of thermodynamics, implying that the growth process must culminate in a steady or stationary state where growth ultimately diminishes to zero.

---

[7]Up-to-date information on this program is available from the informational Web site http://www.imf.org/external/np/exr/facts/hipc.htm/.

Our examination of empirical evidence suggests that increased environmental control has not currently had a large impact on the economy as a whole, although certain industries have been hit quite hard. Environmental policy has triggered only a small rise in the rate of inflation and a mild reduction in growth. Environmental policy has apparently contributed more jobs than it has cost.

The situation is similar for energy. Though rather large increases in energy prices have occurred, the portion of the slowdown in economic growth during the 1970s attributed to these increases is not large. Some diminution of growth has certainly occurred, but it seems premature to suggest that rising energy prices have already forced a transition to a period of substantially lower growth rates.

This is not to say, however, that the economy is not being transformed. It is. Two particularly important aspects of this transformation are the decline in population growth and the rise in importance of information as a driving economic force. Both aspects tend to reduce the degree that physical limits constrain economic growth and increase the degree to which current welfare levels are sustainable.

We have examined a series of indicators that attempt to shed light on the degree to which current national practices are sustainable. Though all of these indicators are both incomplete and flawed, they all convey some important insights.

Because it is based on the weak sustainability criterion, which is limited in scope, the adjusted net savings indicator is not particularly helpful in validating the practices in countries that are identified by this indicator as being sustainable. Yet it can be helpful identifying countries that are not sustainable (as well as the sources of their unsustainability), since any failure to pass this weak test sends a powerful signal of serious problems. The fact that many of the countries that fail this test are low-income countries reminds us that poverty can be both a cause and an effect of unsustainability.

The Genuine Progress Indicator provides a helpful reminder that increases in traditional accounting measures, which are uniformly trumpeted in the press as evidence of "progress," may not represent an increase in well-being at all. Traditional accounting techniques measure economic activity, not well-being.

The Ecological Footprint provides helpful reminders that scale does matter and that the earth on which we all depend is ultimately limited in its ability to fulfill our unlimited wants. Though the Ecological Footprint finding that we have already exceeded the earth's carrying capacity is not definitive, it does usefully lay to rest the naïve view that our ability to consume is limitless and emphasize that we had better start thinking about how to stay within those limits. The Ecological Footprint also is helpful in pointing out that affluence is fully as big a challenge to sustainability as poverty.

The Human Development Index reminds us that the relationship between income growth and the well-being of the poorest citizens of the world is far from a sure thing, in contrast to what some would have us believe. While income growth can provide the means for empowerment of the poor, it can only do so when accompanied by appropriate policy measures such as ensuring universal health care and education and limiting the perverse effects of corruption. The Index also identifies a number of low-income countries that have made great strides in ensuring that the fruits of development do reach the poor.

The outlook for the developing nations is mixed at best. Solving many of their future environmental problems will require raising standards of living. However, following the path of development pioneered by the industrialized nations is probably not possible without triggering severe global environmental problems; the solution would become the problem. New forms of development will be necessary.

The less industrialized countries must overcome a number of significant barriers if development is to become a reality. At the local level, rising populations face increasingly limited access to land or productive assets. At the national level, corruption and development policies discriminate against the poor. Globally, their situation is worsened by rising debt burdens, falling export prices for the products they sell, and the flight of capital that could be used to create jobs and income.

How can the barriers be overcome? What new forms of development can be introduced? By what means can they be introduced? We deal with these questions in the next chapter.

Discussion Questions

1. "Economic growth has historically provided a valuable vehicle for raising the standard of living. Now that the standard of living is so high, however, further economic growth is unnecessary. When the undesirable side effects are considered, it is probably counterproductive. Economic growth is a process that has outlived its usefulness." Discuss.
2. Is affluence part of the problem or part of the solution when it comes to environmental problems? Why?

Further Reading

Dasgupta, Partha. *An Inquiry into Well-Being and Destitution* (Oxford: Oxford University Press, 1993). A seminal work that deals comprehensively with the forces that create and accentuate poverty and their interaction with economic growth.

Durning, Alan B. "Poverty and the Environment: Reversing the Downward Spiral," Paper No. 92 (Washington, DC: Worldwatch Institute, 1989). A very thorough examination of the degree of developing-country poverty, the sources of that poverty, the resulting effects on the environment, and some strategies to deal with these problems.

Neumayer, E. "Indicators of Sustainability," in T. Tietenberg and H. Folmer, eds. *The International Yearbook of Environmental and Resource Economics: 2004/2005* (Cheltenham, UK: Edward Elgar, (2004): 139–188. This survey essay reviews empirical methods for judging sustainability and provides solid critiques of their strengths and weaknesses.

Renner, Michael. "Jobs in a Sustainable Economy," Paper No. 104 (Washington, DC: Worldwatch Institute, 1991). Reviews both the evidence on how a transition to sustainable development would affect the availability of jobs and the policy options that could ease any negative employment consequences.

Additional References and Historically Significant References are available on this book's companion Web site www.aw-bc.com/tietenberg.

Chapter 23

The Quest for Sustainable Development

The challenge of finding sustainable development paths ought to provide the impetus—indeed the imperative—for a renewed search for multilateral solutions and a restructured international economic system of co-operation. These challenges cut across the divides of national sovereignty, of limited strategies for economic gain, and of separated disciplines of science.

—Gro Harlem Brundtland, Prime Minister of Norway,
Our Common Future (1987)

Introduction

Delegations from 178 countries met in Rio de Janeiro during the first two weeks of June 1992 to begin the process of charting a sustainable development course for the future global economy. Billed by its organizers as the largest summit ever held, the United Nations Conference on Environment and Development (known popularly as the Earth Summit) sought to lay the groundwork for solving global environmental problems. The central focus for this meeting was sustainable development.

What is sustainable development? According to the Brundtland Report, which is widely credited with raising the concept to its current level of importance, "Sustainable development is development that meets the needs of the present without compromising the ability of future generations to meet their own needs" (World Commission on Environment and Development, 1987). But that is far from the only possible definition.[1] A nascent concept, sustainable development is still in the process of being refined and clarified.

---

[1]One search for definitions produced 61, though many were very similar. See Pezzey (1992).

Part of the widespread appeal of the concept, according to critics, is due to its vagueness. Being all things to all people can build a large following, but it also has a substantial disadvantage; close inspection may reveal the concept to be vacuous. As the emperor discovered about his new clothes, things are not always what they seem.

In this chapter we look hard at the concept of sustainable development and whether or not it is useful as a guide to the future. What are the basic principles of sustainable development? What does sustainable development imply about changes in the way our system operates? How could the transition to sustainable development be managed? Will the global economic system automatically produce sustainable development or will policy changes be needed? What policy changes?

Sustainability of Development

Suppose we were to map out possible future trends in the long-term welfare of the average citizen. Using a time scale measured in centuries on the horizontal axis (see Figure 23.1), four basic culture trends emerge, labeled A, B, C, and D, with t^0 representing the present. D portrays continued exponential growth in which the future becomes a simple repetition of the past. Although this scenario is generally considered to be infeasible, it is worth thinking about its implications if it were feasible.

FIGURE 23.1

Possible Alternative Futures

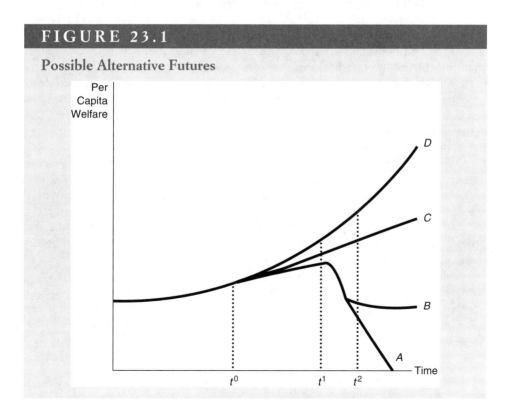

In this scenario not only would current welfare levels be sustainable, but growth in welfare would be sustainable. Our concern for intergenerational justice would lead us to favor current generations, since they would be the poorest. Worrying about future generations would be unnecessary if unlimited growth were possible.

The second scenario (C) envisions slowly diminished growth culminating in a steady state where growth diminishes to zero. The welfare of each future generation is at least as well-off as all previous generations. Current welfare levels are sustainable, though current levels of welfare growth would not be. Since the level of welfare of each generation is sustainable, artificial constraints on the process would be unnecessary. To constrain growth would injure all subsequent generations.

The third scenario (B) is similar in that it envisions initial growth followed by a steady state, but with an important difference—those generations between t^1 and t^2 are worse off than the generations preceding them. Neither growth nor welfare levels are sustainable at current levels, and the sustainability criterion would call for an immediate transition to sustainable welfare levels.

The final scenario (A) denies the existence of sustainable per capita welfare levels, suggesting that the only possible sustainable level is zero. All consumption by the current generation serves simply to hasten the end of civilization.

These scenarios suggest three important dimensions of the sustainability issue: (1) the existence of a positive sustainable level of welfare; (2) the magnitude of the ultimate sustainable level of welfare vis à vis current welfare levels; and (3) the sensitivity of the future level of welfare to actions by previous generations. The first dimension is important because if positive sustainable levels of welfare are possible, scenario A, which in some ways is the most philosophically difficult, is ruled out. The second is important because, if the ultimately sustainable welfare level is higher than the current level, radical surgery to cut current living standards is not necessary. The final dimension raises the issue of whether the ultimate sustainable level of welfare can be increased or reduced by the actions of current generations. If so, the sustainability criterion would suggest taking these impacts into account, lest future generations be unnecessarily impoverished by involuntary wealth transfers to previous generations.

The first dimension is relatively easy to dispense with. The existence of positive sustainable welfare levels is guaranteed by the existence of renewable resources, particularly solar energy, as well as by nature's ability to assimilate a certain amount of waste.[2] Therefore we can rule out scenario A.

No one knows exactly what level of economic activity can ultimately be sustained, but the prediction of early societal collapse certainly seems grossly exaggerated. Since growth is slowing as a natural process, the most serious excesses of unregulated growth (such as pollution) are being mitigated, and solar energy is abundant, scenario C seems likely, though with current levels of information no one can completely rule out B.

Current generations can affect the sustainable welfare levels of future generations both positively and negatively. We could use our resources to accumulate a

---

[2]One study has estimated that humans are currently using approximately 19% to 25% of the renewable energy available from photosynthesis. On land the estimate is more like 40% (Vitousek et al., 1986).

capital stock, providing future generations with shelter, productivity, and transportation, but our decaying inner cities illustrate that machines and buildings do not last forever. Even capital that physically stands the test of time may become economically obsolete by being ill suited to the needs of subsequent generations.

Our most lasting contribution to future generations would probably come from what economists call human capital—investments in people. Though the people who receive education and training are mortal, the ideas they bring forth are not. Knowledge endures.[3]

Current actions could also reduce future welfare levels, however. Fossil-fuel combustion could modify the climate to the detriment of future agriculture. Current chlorofluorocarbon emissions might, by depleting the atmosphere's ozone, raise the incidence of skin cancer. The storage of radioactive wastes could increase the likelihood of genetic damage in the future. The reduction of genetic diversity in the stock of plants and animals could well reduce future medical discoveries.

Suppose that high levels of sustainable welfare are feasible. Would our economic system automatically choose a growth path that produces sustainable welfare levels, or could it choose one that enriches current generations at the expense of future generations?

Market Allocations

Market imperfections, including intertemporal externalities, open-access resources, and market power create incentives that can interfere in important ways with the quest for sustainable development.

Allowing open access to resources promotes unsustainable allocations. Because open-access resources are overexploited by current generations, diminished stocks are left for the future. In the extreme, it is even possible that some harvested species would become extinct.

Intertemporal externalities also undermine the ability of the market to produce sustainable outcomes. Emissions of greenhouse gases impose a cost on future generations that is external to current generations. Current actions to reduce the gases will impose costs on this generation, but the benefits would not be felt until significantly later. Economic theory clearly forecasts that too many greenhouse gas emissions would be forthcoming for the sustainability criterion to be satisfied.

The general conclusion that market imperfections exacerbate the problem of unsustainability, however, would not be correct. For example, the existence of an oil cartel holding up prices serves to retard demand and conserve more for future generations than would otherwise be the case.

Markets can sometimes provide a safety valve to ensure sustainability when the supply of a renewable resource is threatened. Fish farming is one example where declining supplies of a renewable resource trigger the availability of an alternative renewable substitute. Even when the government intervenes detrimentally in a way

---

[3]While it is true that ideas can last forever, the value of those ideas may decline with time as they are supplanted by new ideas. The person who conceived of horseshoes made an enormous contribution to society at the time, but the value of that insight to society has diminished along with our reliance on horses for transportation.

that benefits current generations at the expense of future generations, as it did with natural gas, the market can limit the damage. The market for renewable forms of energy provides a substitute for natural gas, so the effect of government regulation made the transition significantly less smooth than it might have been, rather than preventing the transition altogether.

The notion that left to their own devices markets would automatically provide for the future is naïve, despite their apparent success in providing for generations in the past.

Efficiency and Sustainability

Suppose future governments were able to eliminate all market imperfections, restoring efficiency to the global economic system. In this idealized world, intertemporal and contemporaneous externalities would be reduced to efficient levels. Access to common resources would be restricted to efficient levels and harvesting excess capacity would be eliminated. Competition would be restored to previously cartelized natural resource markets. Would this package of policies be sufficient to achieve sustainability, or is something more required?

One way to examine this question is to examine a number of different models that capture the essence of intertemporal resource allocation. For each model the question becomes, "Will efficient markets automatically produce sustainable development?" The conclusion to be drawn from these models is very clear; restoring efficiency is *not* sufficient to produce sustainability.

Take the allocation of depletable resources over time. Imagine a simple economy where the only activity is the extraction and consumption of a single depletable resource. Even when the population is constant and demand curves are stable, the efficient quantity profiles show declining consumption over time. In this hypothetical world, later generations would be unambiguously worse off unless current generations transferred some of the net benefits into the future. Even an efficient market allocation would not be sustainable in the absence of transfers.

The existence of an abundant renewable backstop resource would not solve the problem; even in this more congenial set of circumstances, the quantity profile of the depletable resource would still involve declining consumption until the backstop was reached. In the absence of compensating transfers, even efficient markets would use depletable resources to support a higher current standard of living than could ultimately be supported.

In a historically important article, Dasgupta and Heal (1979) find a similar result for a slightly more realistic model. They assume an economy in which a single consumption good is produced by combining capital with a depletable resource. The finite supply of the depletable resource can be used to produce capital as well as be used in combination with capital to produce the consumption good. The more capital produced, the higher is the marginal product of the remaining depletable resource.

They prove that a sustainable constant consumption level exists in this model. The rising capital stock (implying a rising marginal product for the depletable resource) would compensate for the declining availability of the depletable resource.

They also prove, however, that the use of any positive discount rate would necessarily result in declining consumption levels, a violation of the sustainability criterion. Discounting, of course, is an inherent component of dynamically efficient allocations.

In all of these models, sustainable development is possible, but it is not the choice made by markets, even efficient markets. Why not? What would it take to ensure sustainable allocations? Hartwick (1977) shows that the achievement of a constant per capita consumption path (which would satisfy our definition of sustainability) results when all scarcity rent is invested in capital. None of it should be consumed by current generations.

Would this be the normal outcome? No, it would not. With a positive discount rate, some of the scarcity rent is consumed, violating the Hartwick rule. The point is profound. Restoring efficiency will typically represent a move toward sustainability, but it will not, by itself, always be sufficient. Further policies must be implemented to guarantee sustainable outcomes.

In Chapter 5 we pointed out that maintaining a nondeclining value of the capital stock (both physical and natural) provided an observable means of checking on the sustainability of current activity. If the value of the capital stock is declining, the activity is unsustainable (see Example 23.1). Can we automatically conclude that a nondeclining value of the capital stock implies the sustainability of current consumption levels? According to work by Asheim (1994) and elaborated on by Pezzey (1994), we cannot. Rising net wealth can coincide with unsustainability when the capital stock is being valued at the wrong (that is, unsustainable) prices. When nonrenewable resources are being used up too rapidly, this drives prices down. Using these prices can create the false impression that the value of the depletion is less than the value of the additional investment and, therefore, that the value of the capital stock is rising. In fact, at the correct prices, it may be falling.

Another study by Howarth and Norgard (1990) comes to a similar conclusion from a different perspective. They derive competitive resource allocations across generations assuming that each generation is assigned a specific share of the available depletable resources. This share is then varied and a new allocation calculated for each to reveal the effect of this intertemporal assignment of property rights to resources among generations. For our purposes, two of their conclusions are relevant: (1) the resulting allocations are sensitive to the initial allocation of the resource rights across generations; and (2) assigning all of the rights to the first generation would not produce a sustainable outcome. Efficient allocations of depletable resources do not necessarily produce sustainable development.

How about with renewable resources? At least renewable resource flows could, in principle, endure forever. Are efficient market allocations of renewable resources compatible with sustainable development? John Pezzey (1992) has examined the sustainability of an allocation of a single renewable resource (such as corn) over time. Sustained growth of welfare can occur in this model, but only if two conditions both hold: (1) the resource growth rate exceeds the sum of the discount rate and the population growth rate; (2) and the initial food supply is sufficient for the existing population. The first condition is sometimes difficult to meet, particularly with rapid population growth and slow-growing biological resources. Sustainable development

Example 23.1

RESOURCE DEPLETION AND ECONOMIC SUSTAINABILITY: MALAYSIA

The historical record suggests, oddly enough, that countries with abundant natural resources tend to suffer a disadvantage in economic development. Why? One possible explanation for the apparent curse of natural resources is that resource-rich countries have not invested enough in reproducible capital to offset resource depletion. Natural resources are a form of capital that, if depleted, must be either replenished or substituted if countries are to expand their asset base and sustain their consumption levels.

Malaysia is a particularly interesting country for examining this issue. Although it is one of the most resource-rich countries in the world, its per capita GDP growth rate during the last three decades has been among the highest in the world. But the very extraordinariness of Malaysia's resource-richness raises a troubling question: Is the country indeed on a sustainable growth path, or has it managed to keep growing simply by developing new resources?

In the Vincent (1997) study, net investment (gross investment minus depreciation of physical and natural capital) and net domestic product (NDP-GDP minus depreciation of the two types of capital) were estimated for Malaysia and its three constituent regions (Peninsular Malaysia, Sabah, Sarawak) for all years from 1970 to 1990. The estimates reflected depreciation of two categories of natural resources, mineral and timber, that were the most important ones in the country.

At the national level, per capita net investment was found to be positive in all years but one. Hence, per capita total capital stocks increased in Malaysia during the 1970s and 1980s, despite the depletion of the country's mineral and timber resources. This was not the case in all three regions, however. Per capita net investment was positive in Peninsular Malaysia in all years, but it was negative in every year after 1975 in Sabah and in every year but one after 1983 in Sarawak.

The lesson for other resource-rich countries is to emulate Peninsular Malaysia's example by adopting economic policies that result in the productive reinvestment of a substantial portion of resource rents. Sabah and Sarawak have instead grown by simply raising their natural resource output and consuming much of the rents thus generated. Although Malaysia's development appears to be sustainable at the national level, it might not be so in all subnational regions.

Source: Jeffrey R. Vincent. "Resource Depletion and Sustainability in Malaysia," *Environment and Development Economics* Vol. 2, Part 1 (February 1997):19–37.

of renewable resources is much harder in the presence of rapid population growth rates because the pressure to exceed sustainable harvest rates becomes irresistible.

The second condition raises a more general and a more difficult concern. It implies the distinct possibility that if the starting conditions are sufficiently far from a sustainable path, sustainable outcomes may not be achievable without outside intervention. The simplest way to see this point is to note that a country that is so poor that it is reduced to eating all the seed corn sacrifices its future in order to survive in the present. The double message that can be derived from these results is that: (1) it is important to ensure that conditions do not deteriorate to this extent by acting quickly and (2) foreign aid is probably an essential part of sustainability policies for the poorest nations.

Global climate change presents a different example where efficiency may not be sufficient for sustainability. Since the present-value component of dynamic efficiency emphasizes short-term over long-term consequences, the current costs of controlling emissions would be weighed more heavily than the distant future damages caused by climate change. Though this approach is not inherently biased against future generations, their interests would only be adequately protected if they would be willing to accept monetary compensation for a modified climate and if current generations were willing to set aside sufficient proceeds to provide this compensation. Since it is not obvious that either condition would be satisfied in practice, the long lead times associated with this particular problem jeopardize the interests of future generations in maintaining a stable climate.

Efficient allocations can also violate the notion of sustainability in a deeper sense. Because our definition of weak sustainability is based on nondeclining aggregate welfare levels, it does not require the preservation of individual resources. Harvesting fish stocks to extinction, for example, would be compatible with our definition of weak sustainability as long as future generations were sufficiently compensated.

But we don't really know how much they would value the continued existence of those fish stocks. Not only is our knowledge extremely limited in regard to the ultimate ecosystem effects of the extinction of any species, we have no idea how valuable those fish would be to future generations. It is possible that they would value the continued existence of the population substantially more than we. Not only would the appropriate amount of the compensation be difficult to determine (since we don't know their preferences), but compensating future generations would be silly if they value the continued existence of the population more than any compensation (including accrued interest) we could reasonably pay.

One straightforward way to deal with this uncertainty is to include in the definition of sustainability some protection of the resources themselves. According to this logic, since it is impossible to know the value future generations will place on specific renewable resources, we can only preserve their options by guaranteeing access to the resources. Efficiency would certainly not guarantee this outcome.

We must be careful to distinguish between what has been said and what has not been said. Restoring efficiency will generally result in an improvement in sustainability, but it may not be either necessary or sufficient. Three different cases can emerge. In the first case the private inefficient outcome is sustainable and the efficient outcome is also sustainable. In this case, restoring efficiency will raise well-being, but it is not necessary for sustainability. This case might prevail when resources are extraordinarily abundant relative to their use. In the second case the private inefficient equilibrium is unsustainable, but the efficient outcome is sustainable. In this case, restoring efficiency not only increases current well-being, but it is also sufficient to ensure sustainability. In the final case neither the private inefficient outcome nor the efficient outcome is sustainable. In this case, restoring efficiency will not be enough to produce a sustainable outcome. Some sacrifice by current generations would be necessary to ensure adequate protection for the well-being of future generations.

While efficient markets cannot always achieve sustainable development paths, this does not mean that they would never, or even normally, result in sustainable allocations! Indeed, the historical record reviewed in the previous chapter suggests that the incompatibility of the efficiency criterion and the sustainability criterion has been the exception, not the rule. Capital accumulation and technological progress have expanded the ways in which resources could be used and have increased subsequent welfare levels in spite of a declining resource base. Nonetheless, the two criteria are not inevitably compatible. As resource bases diminish and global externalities increase, the conflict between these criteria can be expected to become more important.

Trade and the Environment

One of the traditional paths to development involves opening up the economy to trade. Freer international markets provide lower prices for consumer goods (due to the availability of and competition from imported products) and the opportunity for domestic producers to serve foreign markets. As we have seen, the law of comparative advantage suggests that trade can benefit both parties. One might suspect (correctly) that as one moves from theory to practice, the story would become a bit more complicated.

The Role of Property Rights.
From our previous studies in this book, it should be clear that trade can certainly inflict detrimental (and inefficient) effects on the environment when some nations (presumably those in the less developed South) have poorly defined property rights or have not internalized their externalities (such as pollution). Chichilnisky (1994) has shown that in this kind of situation, the tragedy of the commons can become greatly intensified by freer trade. Poorly defined property rights in the exporting nations encourage the importing nations (by artificially lowering prices) to greatly expand their consumption of the underpriced resources. In this scenario, trade intensifies environmental problems by increasing the pressure on open-access resources and hastening their degradation.

Pollution Havens and the Race to the Bottom.
The failure to control externalities such as pollution provides another possible route, known as the "pollution havens" hypothesis, for trade to induce environmental degradation. According to this hypothesis, producers affected by stricter environmental regulations in one country will either move their dirtiest production facilities to countries with less stringent environmental regulations (presumed to be lower-income countries) or face a loss of market share. Consumers in the country with the strict regulation have an incentive to prefer the cheaper goods produced in the pollution havens.

Pollution levels can change in the pollution havens for three different reasons: (1) the composition effect, (2) the technique effect, or (3) the scale effect. According to the *composition effect*, emissions change as the mix of dirty and clean industries changes; as the ratio of dirty to clean industries increases, emissions increase, even if total output remains the same. (Notice that this is the expected outcome from the pollution havens hypothesis.) The *technique effect* involves the ratio of emissions per unit output in each industry. Emissions could increase in pollution havens if each firm in the pollution haven became dirtier as a result of openness to trade. And finally the *scale effect* looks at the role of output level on emissions; even if the composition and technique effects were zero, emissions could increase in pollution havens simply because output levels increased.

In addition to suggesting a channel for degradation, this hypothesis, if correct, provides a justification for developing countries to accept lower environmental standards. In this view, lower environmental standards protect against job loss. In other words, it suggests a "race to the bottom" feedback mechanism where competitive incentives among nations force developing countries to keep environmental standards weak in order to attract jobs, and jobs move to those locations in search of the lower costs resulting from lower standards.

What is the evidence on the empirical validity of the pollution havens hypothesis and its race to the bottom implication? Earlier surveys of the empirical work, such as Dean (1992), found absolutely no support for the effect of environmental regulation on either trade or capital flows. Jaffe et al. (1995) reach the same conclusion in their survey of the effect of environmental regulations on U.S. competitiveness. Several recent studies reviewed by Copeland and Taylor (2004), however, have begun to find that environmental regulation can influence trade flows and plant location, all other things being equal, though the effects are small.

Some of this work focuses on the effect of environmental regulations on the movement of production among states within the United States rather than to developing countries. Studies by Kahn (1997), Greenstone (2002), and Becker and Henderson (2000), for example, find that growth in such indicators as manufacturing activity and employment as well as new plant start-ups for polluting industries were higher in attainment areas than in the more stringently regulated nonattainment areas.

Has there been a discernable exodus of dirty industries to developing countries? Apparently not. Studies that attempt to isolate composition, technique, and scale effects generally find that the composition effect (the most important effect for confirming the pollution havens hypothesis) is small relative to scale effects. Furthermore, technique effects normally result in less, not more, pollution (Hettige, Mani, and Wheeler, 2000). Though trade can increase pollution through the scale effect, these findings are quite different from what we would expect from a race to the bottom.

Actually, these results should not be surprising. Because pollution control costs comprise a relatively small part of the costs of production, it would be surprising if lowering environmental standards could become a major determinant of either firm location decisions or the direction of trade.

The Porter "Induced Innovation" Hypothesis.   The story does not end there. Michael Porter (1991), a Harvard Business School professor, has argued that more environmental protection can, under the right circumstances, promote jobs, not cause them to be lost. Now known as the "Porter induced innovation hypothesis," this view suggests that firms in nations with the most stringent regulations experience a competitive advantage rather than a competitive disadvantage. Under this nontraditional view, strict environmental regulations force firms to innovate, and innovative firms tend to be more competitive. This advantage is particularly pronounced for firms producing pollution control equipment (which can then be exported to firms in countries subsequently raising their environmental standards), but it might also be present for firms that when forced to change their production processes for environmental reasons, find that their production costs are lower, not higher. Some instances of regulation-induced lower production costs have been recorded in the literature (Barbera and McConnell, 1990), but few studies have attempted to examine the Porter hypothesis in its entirety.

While it seems clear that innovation induced by environmental regulation could simultaneously increase productivity (lower costs) and lower emissions, it is less clear why this would necessarily always or even normally be the case. And if it were universally true, it is not clear why all firms would fail to adopt these techniques even in the absence of regulations.

The Porter hypothesis is valuable because it reminds us that a particularly ingrained piece of conventional wisdom ("environmental regulation reduces firm competitiveness") is frequently wrong. It would be a mistake, however, to use it as confirmation of the much stronger proposition that environmental regulation is universally good for competitiveness.

The Environmental Kuznets Curve.   Though proponents of free trade have come to recognize the potential problems for the environment posed by free trade, particularly in the face of externalities or poor property right regimes in the exporting countries, they tend to suggest that these problems will be self-correcting. Specifically, they argue that as freer trade increases incomes, the higher incomes will promote more environmental protection.

The specific functional relationship underlying this view comes from some earlier work by Simon Kuznets, a Harvard professor, and so has become known as the Environmental Kuznets Curve. According to this relationship, environmental degradation increases with higher incomes up to some income level (the turning point). After the turning point, however, higher incomes result in reductions in environmental degradation. Some apparent confirmation of this view came from early studies that plotted variables such as SO_2 concentrations against per capita incomes using countries as the unit of observation (data points).

Since those early studies, the existence of this relationship and its use to suggest the self-correcting nature of trade-induced environment problems have little empirical support (Neumayer, 2001). The early studies used different nations as data points, but the interpretation that was put on the relationship was that an individual country would eventually increase environmental protection as its income increased. Subsequent studies that looked at how environmental protection varied over time within an individual country as income increased frequently did not find the expected relationship (Vincent, 1997). Other studies found that it seemed to apply to some pollutants (such as SO_2) but not to others (such as CO_2) (World Bank, 1992; and List and Gallet, 1999). And finally, as Example 23.2 illustrates, some case

Example 23.2

HAS NAFTA IMPROVED THE ENVIRONMENT IN MEXICO?

The North American Free Trade Agreement (NAFTA) took effect in 1994. By lowering tariff barriers and promoting the freer flow of goods and capital, NAFTA integrated the United States, Canada, and Mexico into a single, giant market. The agreement has apparently been successful in promoting trade and investment. Has it also been successful in promoting environmental protection in Mexico?

According to a study by Kevin Gallagher (2004), it has not, though not necessarily due to the forces identified by the pollution havens hypothesis. Some effects clearly resulted in less pollution and others more, though on balance, air quality has deteriorated.

The pollution havens hypothesis might lead us to expect a relocation of heavily polluting firms from the United States to Mexico, but that apparently did not happen. None of the numerous statistical tests performed by the author supported the hypothesis.

In terms of positive effects on air quality from trade, Gallagher found significant shifts in Mexican industry away from pollution-intensive sectors; the post trade Mexican industrial mix was less polluting than the pretrade industrial mix (the opposite of what would be expected from the pollution havens hypothesis). He even found that some Mexican industries (specifically steel and cement) were cleaner than their counterparts in the United States, a fact he attributes to their success in securing new investment for more modern plants with cleaner technologies.

The largest trade-related source of air-quality degradation was the scale effect. Though the posttrade industrial mix generally shifted away from the most polluting sectors (meaning fewer average emissions per unit output), the promotion of exports increased output levels considerably. Increased output meant more emissions (in this case, almost a doubling).

One expectation emanating from the Environmental Kuznets Curve is that the increased incomes from trade would result in more environmental regulation, which, in turn, would curb emissions. That expectation was not met either. Gallagher found that both real government spending on environmental policy and the number of Mexican plant-level environmental compliance inspections fell by 45% after NAFTA, despite the fact that income levels reached the turning point expected by the pretrade studies.

Source: K. P. Gallagher. *Free Trade and the Environment: Mexico, NAFTA and Beyond* (Palo Alto, CA: Stanford University Press, 2004).

studies in countries that have experienced considerably freer trade regimes have generally experienced intensified, not reduced, environmental degradation.

What are we to make of this evidence? Apparently environmental regulations are not a major determinant of either firm location decisions or the direction of trade. This implies that reasonable environmental regulations should not be held hostage to threats that polluters will leave the area and take their jobs with them; with few exceptions, firms that are going to move will move anyway, while firms that are not going to move will tend to stay whatever the regulatory environment.

When deterioration is caused by inadequate local property right regimes or inadequate internalization of externalities, it may not be necessary or desirable to prevent trade, but rather to correct these sources of market failure. These inefficiencies associated with trade could be solved with adequate property regimes and appropriate pollution control mechanisms. On the other hand, if establishing appropriate property regimes or pollution control mechanisms is not politically feasible, other means of protecting the resources must be found, including possibly restricting trade. However, caution must be used in imposing these trade restrictions, since they are a second-best policy instrument in this case and can even be counterproductive.[4]

While the foregoing argument suggests that the starkest claims against the environmental effects of free trade do not bear up under close scrutiny, it would be equally wrong to suggest that opening borders to freer trade inevitably results in a gain in efficiency and/or sustainability. The truth, it seems, depends on the circumstances, so pure ideology does not get us very far. The context matters.

Since new trade institutions are now emerging, new issues with enormous implications for the environment are emerging with them. Among these issues are the environmental consequences of (1) protections for companies investing in foreign countries that are adversely affected by environmental regulations and (2) international trade rules under the General Agreement on Tariffs and Trade (GATT) and the World Trade Organization.

Investor Protections: NAFTA's Chapter 11.   The North American Free Trade Agreement (NAFTA) includes an array of new corporate investment rights and protections that are unprecedented in scope and power. NAFTA allows corporations to sue the national government of a NAFTA country in secret arbitration tribunals if they feel that a regulation or government decision adversely affects their investment in a way that violates these new NAFTA rights. If the corporation wins, the taxpayers of the "losing" NAFTA nation must foot the bill.

The environmental concern raised by this provision is that it could be used to require governments to compensate companies that are financially damaged by legitimate environmental regulations, something that has historically not been the case. Requiring companies to be compensated could in turn put a significant damper on efforts to enact environmental legislation.

---

[4]Barbier and Schulz (1997) note a case in which a trade restriction designed to protect against deforestation from excessive export logging can sufficiently lower the value of the forest that the land is deforested to facilitate its conversion to agriculture.

How strong this effect will be remains to be seen, but several cases involving environmental legislation have already arisen. For example, consider the effect of this rule on the movement away from the gasoline additive MTBE discussed in Chapter 18. In 1999, the State of California decided to phase out MTBE. Suspected by the World Health Organization of being carcinogenic, MTBE had been found to have contaminated at least 10,000 groundwater wells in the state. The MTBE ban went into effect January 1, 2004.

A Canadian company, Methanex Corporation, which has a subsidiary in the United States, filed a NAFTA Chapter 11 claim against the United States. The company produces methanol, a component of MTBE, and alleges that California's ban of MTBE constitutes an expropriation of their investment, by interfering with their ability to do business. The company is seeking $970 million in compensation. As of June 2004, the case was still being adjudicated.

Many observers, including many proponents of freer trade, believe this rule has gone too far. It is hard to imagine how secret proceedings could be justified. They are an anachronism in a society that places so much emphasis on freedom of information. In addition, plaintiffs in Chapter 11 actions should have to show that the government agency was discriminating against the foreign firm; a finding that a uniformly applied action had a differentially large impact on them should not be sufficient to justify compensation.

Trade Rules Under GATT and the WTO

The General Agreement on Tariffs and Trade (GATT), the international agreement that laid the groundwork for the World Trade Organization (WTO) was first signed in 1947. That agreement provided an international forum for encouraging free trade between member states by regulating and reducing tariffs on traded goods and by providing a common mechanism for resolving trade disputes. Having now replaced the GATT forum, the WTO is the sole global international organization dealing with the rules of trade between nations.

As an organization devoted to freer trade, the WTO adjudicates disputes among trading nations through the lens of its effect on trade. Domestic restrictions on trade of any kind (including environment restrictions) are suspect unless they pass muster. To decide whether they pass muster or not, the WTO has evolved a set of rules to define the border between acceptable actions and unacceptable actions.

These rules examine, for example, such things as differential treatment. A disputed environmental action that discriminates against goods from another country (rather than holding imports and domestically produced goods to the same standard) is unacceptable. Disputed actions that are not the lowest-cost (and least injurious to trade) action that could have been taken to address the particular environmental problem are also unacceptable.

One of the most controversial rules involves a distinction between "product" concerns and "process" concerns (Debate 23.1). At the risk of oversimplification, regulations that address product concerns (such as mandating the highest acceptable residual pesticide levels in foods) are acceptable, but regulations addressing the process by which the product was made or harvested (such as banning steel from a

DEBATE 23.1

SHOULD AN IMPORTING COUNTRY BE ABLE TO USE TRADE RESTRICTIONS TO INFLUENCE HARMFUL FISHING PRACTICES IN AN EXPORTING NATION?

Yellowfin tuna in the Eastern Tropical Pacific often travel in the company of dolphins. Recognizing that this connection could be exploited to more readily locate tuna, tuna fishermen used it to increase their catch with deadly effects for dolphins. Having located dolphins, tuna vessels would use giant purse seines to encircle and trap the tuna, capturing (and frequently killing) dolphins at the same time.

In response to public outrage at this technique, the United States enacted the Marine Mammal Protection Act (MMPA). This act prohibited the importation of fish caught with commercial fishing technology that results in the incidental kill or serious injury of ocean mammals in excess of U.S. standards.

In 1991, a GATT panel ruled on an action brought by Mexico asserting that U.S. law violated GATT rules because it treated physically identical goods (tuna) differently. According to this ruling, countries could regulate products that were harmful (as long as they treated domestic and imported products the same), but not the processes by which the products were harvested or produced in foreign countries. Using domestic regulations to selectively ban products as a means of securing change in the production or harvesting decisions of other countries was ruled a violation of the international trade rules.

The United States responded by mandating an ecolabeling program. Under this law, tuna caught in ways that killed dolphins could be imported, but exporters were not allowed to use the "dolphin-safe" label. Tuna caught with purse seines nets could only use the "dolphin-safe" label if special on board observers witnessed no dolphin deaths. Mexico has since argued that this situation did not satisfy the GATT ruling of 1991 and continues to hold the threat of a WTO case over the head of the United States.

Sources: The official GATT history of the case can be found at http://www.wto.org/english/tratop_e/envir_e/envir_backgrnd_e/c8s1_e.htm#united_states_tuna_mexico and an environmental take on it can be found on the Public citizen Web site at http://www.citizen.org/trade/wto/ENVIRONMENT/articles.cfm?ID=9298/.

---

particular country because it is made in coal-burning plants) are not acceptable. In the latter case, the steel from coal-burning plants is indistinguishable from steel made by other processes, so the product is considered to be homogeneous and treating it as different is unacceptable.

The inability of any country to address process concerns in its imports clearly limits its ability to internalize externalities. In light of this interpretation, one way to internalize externalities in other countries would be to use means other than trade (international agreements to limit carbon emissions, for example). Another, as Debate 23.1 points out, is to use ecolabeling as a means of putting as least some market pressure on the disputed practices. How far that labeling can go without triggering a negative WTO ruling remains to be seen.

A Menu of Opportunities

Is sustainable development just an unrealistic attempt to provide unsupported optimism in the face of a bleak future? Human nature being what it is, we need to have hope. When the situation is hopeless, the natural human tendency is to create scenarios that offer the illusion of hope. Is sustainable development one of those illusions? Or can reasonable, skeptical people find grounds for believing in the existence of new forms of development that can raise living standards while respecting both the environment and the rights of future generations?

While it is not possible in the space we have to go into detail about the various techniques that fulfill this vision, it is possible to convey a flavor. Hopefully this flavor will be sufficient to demonstrate that sustainable development is a pragmatic possibility, not merely an illusion.

Agriculture

Most experts believe that food supply can be expanded to meet the forecasted increases in population, but sustainable development requires this expansion to take place in a way that does not destroy the natural environment (Crosson and Rosenberg, 1989). What are the prospects?

Multiple cropping, which includes crop rotations, intercropping (sometimes with trees and annual crops sharing the same fields), overseeding legumes into cereals, and double cropping, is one technique that offers the potential for reduced agricultural chemicals, increased productivity, less erosion, and more effective use of water. The concept is not new. A system employed in Central America since pre-Columbian times intermixes maize, beans, and squash. The maize provides a trellis for the beans; the beans enrich the soil with nitrogen; and the squash provides ground cover, reducing erosion, soil compaction, and weed growth.

Trees can be used in multiple cropping. In West Africa, leaf litter from the *Acacia alba* enriches the soil for the benefit of various grain and vegetable crops grown between them. In the American Midwest, farmers are experimenting with growing corn with other, low-growing plants. In one experiment in Nebraska, two-row corn windbreaks were spaced every 15 rows through a field of sugar beets. The wind shelter provided by the corn increased sugar production by 11%. The greater access to sunlight and carbon dioxide increased corn yields by 150%.

In Montana, tall wheatgrass, a perennial, has been used to protect winter wheat. In winter, wheatgrass barriers capture snow, forming a uniform layer that insulates dormant plants from the effects of extremely low temperatures. In spring, the snow melts, providing the moisture winter wheat needs for early growth. Once the winter wheat begins to grow, the wheatgrass serves as a wind barrier.

Multiple cropping can reduce the need for pesticides. In fields where crops are rotated regularly, pests (weeds, insects, and pathogens) cannot adapt themselves to a single set of environmental conditions and therefore do not increase as quickly.

Biotechnology and new irrigation techniques also offer prospects for reduced fertilizer and water use. Developing plants that "fix" nitrogen in the soil would lessen the demand for nitrogen fertilizer, while incorporating genes from pest-resistant plants into commercial crops could reduce the need for pesticides. Trickle (or drip) irrigation systems would reduce the amount of water needed by increasing the efficiency of the water used. Already widely used in Israel and part of the United States, trickle irrigation can also reduce the problems associated with salt buildup.

Energy

Prior to the 1970s, increases in the GNP were always accompanied by proportionate increases in energy consumption. This relationship proved so stable that it was used for forecasting energy consumption. Some observers at the time took this relationship as evidence that proportionate increases in energy would be a necessary condition for growth.

Following the oil embargo and the accompanying increases in prices during the 1970s, it became clear that growth and energy consumption did not have to move in lockstep. The industrialized world's energy intensity—the amount of energy used to produce one unit of gross national product—fell by one-fifth between 1973 and 1985. In the United States, the GNP grew 40% while energy consumption remained constant during this period.

Energy efficiency (getting the same energy services out of a smaller input of energy) and energy conservation (using fewer energy services) are the short-run keys to energy sustainability by making the depletable sources of energy last longer. We are already witnessing energy conservation as communication is substituted for transportation (consider, for example, online shopping leading to fewer trips to the mall or working at home via computer leading to fewer commutes to the office). Examples of energy efficiency are easy to find as well. New lightbubs use much less electricity per lumen of output. Modern refrigerators and air conditioners provide a comfortable environment with much less electricity than historic models. The emerging field of green architecture is designing buildings that make much smaller demands of all sorts on the environment. And studies of future possibilities suggest that we have only scratched the surface.

In the long run, we can turn to fuel substitution. A host of renewable fuel possibilities exist from passive and active solar, wind, photovoltaics, hydro, hydrogen fuel cells, and tidal power from the ocean, to mention some possibilities currently receiving attention. Stimulated by both diminishing fossil-fuel energy supplies and accumulating pollution from their combustion, many more possibilities will presumably emerge as human ingenuity responds to the realization that our energy future must be quite different from our energy past.

Waste Reduction

Sustainable development involves a more integrated approach to production than traditionally practiced in order to reduce raw material demands and waste discharge. In such an integrated system, the consumption of energy and materials is optimized; waste generation is minimized; and the effluents of one process—whether they are spent catalysts from petroleum refining, fly and bottom ash from electric-power generators, or discarded plastic containers from consumer products—serve as raw materials for another process.

As the costs of waste disposal rise and the regulations dealing with hazardous waste disposal become more strict, examples of industries adopting this type of integrated approach become more prevalent (Frosch and Gallopoulos, 1989). Meridian National, a Midwestern steel processing company, now reprocesses the sulfuric acid with which it removes scale from steel sheets and slabs, reuses the acid, and sells ferrous sulfate compounds to magnetic tape manufacturers.

At the Atlantic Richfield Company's Los Angeles refinery complex, a series of relatively low-cost changes have reduced waste volumes from about 12,000 tons a year during the early 1980s to about 3,400 tons by the end of the decade. Since disposal costs were about $300 a ton, the company saved over $2 million a year in disposal costs alone.

Markets have been found for much of Atlantic Richfield's former waste, adding further revenue. The company sells its spent alumina catalysts to Allied Chemical and its spent silica catalysts to cement makers. Alkaline carbonate sludge from a water-softening operation at the refinery goes to a sulfuric acid manufacturer a few miles away, where it neutralizes acidic wastewater.

Sustainable development frequently requires changes in the way economic activities are conducted. Some of those changes are already occurring (see Example 23.3). Others await additional policy changes.

Managing the Transition

If, in fact, sustainable development is possible and unfettered markets are not capable, by themselves, of managing the transition, what can be done? How can the transition to sustainable development be accomplished?

Our situation is similar to that of the thoroughly disoriented tourist, a central character in Maine folklore. Enticed by unusually brilliant fall foliage, a tourist forsook the security of the well-marked main highways for some less-traveled country roads. After an hour of driving, he was no longer sure he was even headed in the right direction. Seeing a Maine native mending a fence, he pulled over to the side of the road to seek assistance. After hearing the tourist's destination, the native sadly shook his head and in his best Maine accent responded, "If I was goin' they-uh, I sure wouldn't start from he-uh!"

Had we known long ago that human activities could seriously impact environmental life-support systems and could deny future generations the quality of life to which our generation has become accustomed, we might have chosen a different, more sustainable path for improving human welfare. The fact that we did not have that knowledge and therefore did not make that choice years ago means that current generations are faced with making more difficult choices with fewer options. These choices will test the creativity of our solutions and the resilience of our social institutions.

The task of managing the transition to sustainable development is made all the more difficult by the fact that some entrenched development paths are not only themselves unsustainable, but they have so dominated sustainable strategies that switching from one to the other has become very difficult.

Example *23.3*

SUSTAINABLE DEVELOPMENT: THREE SUCCESS STORIES

In Kenya, 83% of the urban population and 17% of rural households use charcoal stoves known as jikos. A household in Nairobi with one wage earner typically spends more than one-fifth of its income on charcoal. The typical jiko is very energy inefficient; it represents an unnecessary drain on both income and the forests that supply the wood for charcoal.

In 1981 the government of Kenya and a local nongovernmental organization began a project disseminating a new, more energy-efficient stove. By 1985 the new stove had captured 10% of the market. Nationwide, savings on fuel were in the neighborhood of $2 million annually.

Much of Central America is faced with declining soil fertility due to soil erosion and monocropping. Guinope, Honduras, was not an exception. Farmers were migrating out of the area, and those remaining were plagued by low incomes.

In 1981, World Neighbors, a private voluntary organization, introduced a sustainable agriculture program that relied on soil conservation practices in use elsewhere in Central America. The program included constructing drainage ditches, planting grass barriers, erecting rock walls, training farmers in fertilization methods using chicken manure, intercropping leguminous plants, and using some chemical fertilizers. Significantly, no subsidies were involved at all. All costs were borne by the farmers.

In the first year, the yields tripled, in some cases quadrupled. Nearby villages have requested training, and the program is spreading rapidly.

In Brazil, some 500,000 rubber tappers (seringueiros) have made their living from the Amazon since the late 1800s. Recently their livelihood was threatened by the migration of large numbers of people to the forests seeking land. Encouraged by government subsidies, these migrants ultimately discovered the land to be unsuited for agriculture once the forest canopy has been removed. One sustainable form of land use was being jeopardized by another unsustainable land use.

On June 30, 1987, the Brazilian government created an extractive reserve for the rubber tappers and in the process provided protection for the countless genetic species found in the forest. The extractive reserve allows continued extraction of rubber (as well as nuts and other renewable products), but protects the forest and its people from the ravages of deforestation.

Source: Walter V. C. Reid. "Sustainable Development: Lessons from Success," *Environment* Vol. 31 (May 1989): 7–9, 29–35.

Southern California represents a case in point. In the Los Angeles air basin, the ambient air-quality standards, designed to protect human health, were being violated on the order of 150 out of the 365 days a year. Due to the way the city has developed, regulators in Los Angeles face a very difficult problem. As a prime example of an automobile city, population growth in Los Angeles has spawned land-use patterns that accommodate the automobile and are, in turn, accommodated by the automobile. Responding to a massive program of highway construction and low gasoline prices, the city has become very spread out with highly dispersed residential and employment locations. Since the efficient use of mass transit requires the existence of high-density travel corridors, an effective public transit alternative is now difficult to implement, though it could have been quite possible before the highly dispersed land-use patterns became so firmly entrenched. The options left open to these regulators have steadily diminished over time. The entire fabric of life in the Los Angeles area is so interwoven with automobile access that the problem cannot be solved without envisioning fairly radical changes in lifestyle.

In addition to the difficulty of reversing historic land-use patterns that seem inconsistent with the goal of sustainable development, we face the problem of how to prevent more inefficient development from occurring in the future. Local officials across the country are pushing a variety of measures to preserve open space. Here too the market may be enlisted as part of the preservation strategy. (see Example 23.4).

To meet the challenges of the next century, it will be necessary to foster and to support institutional change by being somewhat more creative in the way that we deal with environmental policy. One key to exploiting these opportunities involves harnessing the power of the marketplace and focusing that power on the reduction, or hopefully even eradication, of poverty in an environmentally sound manner.

Opportunities for Cooperation

While the list of barriers to international cooperation is certainly imposing, the new global environmental problems also offer new opportunities for cooperation, opportunities that in some ways are unprecedented. Although the degree to which various nations are affected by these problems differs, a point made above, it is also true that some potential common ground exists.

One important foundation for this common ground is the inefficiency of many current economic activities. In many cases, these inefficiencies are very large indeed; resources are being wasted. Whenever resources are wasted, much more environmental improvement could be obtained for current expenditures or the same improvement could be realized with a much smaller commitment of resources. By definition, moving from an inefficient policy to an efficient one creates gains to be shared. Agreements on how these gains should be shared among the cooperating parties can be used to build coalitions for change.

The level and form of any such cost-sharing arrangements, however, are usually not clearly specified. With the appropriate choice of policy instruments, much of this cost sharing could be handled by normal market forces.

The natural reluctance of nations to impose increasingly stringent environmental policies within their borders can be diminished by ensuring that the policies imposed are cost-effective. We live in an age when the call for tighter environmental controls intensifies with each new discovery of yet another injury modern society is inflicting on the planet. But resistance to additional controls is also growing with the recognition that the cost of compliance is growing as all the easy techniques

Example 23.4

CONTROLLING LAND DEVELOPMENT WITH TDRS

How can unique environmental sites be preserved from the threat of development? One way, of course, is for them to be purchased as a preserve either by the government or by a private group committed to preservation, such as The Nature Conservancy. The considerable amount of financial resources needed to implement this approach, however, has limited its impact.

An alternative approach, which mobilizes private funds for preservation, involves the use of transferable development rights (TDRs). Pioneered by New York City in the 1970s as a means of protecting historic buildings, this approach severs, for some particularly unique land, the historic connection between the ownership of land and the right to develop it.

Owners of land that should be preserved are typically opposed to preservation because they bear all the costs while society as a whole bears the benefits. Transferable development rights changes that dynamic by allowing the owners of preserved land to sell their development rights to developers. The revenue from selling these rights compensates the owners for their inability to develop their land.

How it works can be illustrated with an example. The New Jersey Pinelands is a largely undeveloped, marshy area in the southeastern part of the state encompassing approximately one million acres. It provides habitat for several endangered species. In an effort to direct development to the least environmentally sensitive areas, the Pinelands Development Commission created Pineland Development Credits (PDCs), a form of transferable development rights.

Landowners in environmentally sensitive areas receive PDCs in exchange for limiting development at the rate of 1 PDC for every 39 acres of existing farmland, 1 PDC for every 39 acres of preserved upland, and 0.2 PDC for every 39 acres of wetlands. To create a demand for these credits, developers seeking to increase the standard density on land zoned for development are required to acquire one PDC for every four units of increase.

The commission also established a Pinelands Development Credit Bank to act as a purchaser of last resort for PDCs at the statutory price of $10,000 per credit. In 1990 the bank auctioned its inventory at the price of $20,200 per PDC. By 1997, developers had used well over 100 PDCs.

Source: Robert C. Anderson and Andrew Q. Lohof. *The United States Experience with Economic Incentives in Environmental Pollution Control Policy* (Washington, DC: Environmental Law Institute, 1997).

are used up. By choosing cost-effective and flexible policy instruments, the potential for backlash can be reduced.

Policy instrument choice can also affect enforceability. In developing countries, local communities typically have the greatest accessibility to and knowledge about local biological resources. As these countries have undergone a centralization of political power, including the power to control these resources, some of the local commitment to them has been lost. Policy instruments that reestablish this commitment by offering these local communities a stake in the preservation of the resource can enhance enforceability. Subsequent sections present some specific examples of how this can be accomplished.

By being creative in the design of policy instruments, the incentives of local and global communities can become compatible. In some cases, being creative requires the use of conventional economic instruments in unconventional ways, but in others it requires the use of unconventional instruments in unconventional ways.

Unconventional approaches are not pipe dreams. Most of them have been successfully employed in one form or another in local communities around the globe. The experience with these instruments in their current setting provides a model for their use on an international level. How well this model fits remains an open question, but it is better to sit down for a dinner with a full menu offering some novel, but interesting choices rather than one offering only a limited selection of familiar, unappetizing fare.

Restructuring Incentives

How can economic incentives be used to provide the kinds of signals that will make sustainable development possible? Perhaps the best way to begin to answer this question is to recall a few examples of how this approach has worked in practice.

Consider just a few specific examples drawn from earlier chapters:

- establishing an individual transferable quota system for managing a fishery can raise incomes while protecting the fish stock. Changing the incentives for over fishing can lead to outcomes that are both ecologically and economically desirable.

- introducing forest certification can enable conscientious buyers to purchase only sustainably harvested wood, while debt nature swaps can make debt work for preservation rather than against it.

- removing the subsidies from water use and eliminating "use it or lose it" regulations can promote water conservation, making the available supplies last longer.

- requiring new emitters entering a nonattainment area to purchase "offsets" makes economic growth a vehicle for improving air quality, not for degrading it.

- using volume-based pricing for trash and imposing expanded producer responsibility on manufacturers provides both consumers and producers with incentives to recycle more and dispose of less.

- imposing renewable portfolio standards provides incentives for utilities to increase their reliance on renewable sources of energy, while transferable energy certificates lower the cost of the transition.

It now remains only to show how the entire menu of economic incentive policies can be woven together in a manner that facilitates international cooperation in the resolution of international environmental problems. Economic analysis suggests five principles that can provide the foundation for this approach.

The Full-Cost Principle.

According to the full-cost principle, all users of environmental resources should pay their full cost. Those using the environment as a waste repository, for example, would be presumed responsible not only for controlling pollution to the full extent required by the law, but also for restoring environmental resources damaged beyond some de minimus amount and for compensating those suffering damage.

This principle is based upon the presumption that humanity has a right to a reasonably safe and healthy environment. Since this right has been held in common for the stratosphere and the international sections of the oceans, no administrative body has either the responsibility or the authority for protecting that right. As a result it has been involuntarily surrendered on a first-come, first-served basis without compensation.

Although climate change imposes both an international and intergenerational environmental cost, currently that cost is not being borne, or even recognized, by those who are not part of the Kyoto Protocol. Furthermore, those choosing unilaterally to reduce their emissions expose themselves to the higher costs associated with mitigating strategies. Applying the full-cost principle would send a strong signal to all users of the environment that the atmosphere is a scarce, precious resource and should be treated accordingly. Products produced by manufacturing processes that are environmentally destructive would become relatively more expensive; those produced by environmentally benign production processes would become relatively cheaper. Implementing the full-cost principle would end the implicit subsidy that all polluting activities have received since the beginning of time. When the level of economic activity was small, the corresponding subsidy was also small and therefore probably not worthy of political attention. Since the scale of economic activity has grown, however, the subsidy has become very large indeed; ignoring it leads to significant resource distortion.

The transition to a more sustainable economic system will depend on the development of new technologies and upon much greater levels of energy efficiency than are currently being achieved. Those transitions will not occur unless the prevailing economic incentives support and encourage them. Once the full-cost principle was in effect, the incentives would be changed; greater energy efficiency and the development of new technologies would become top-priority objectives.

Implications for the legal system would flow from the full-cost principle as well. For example, international laws should permit full recovery for damage caused by oil spills or other environmental incidents. Not only should the contaminated site be restored insofar as possible, but those suffering demonstrable losses should be fully compensated.

Making explicit environmental costs that have previously been hidden is only one side of the coin; the other is eliminating inappropriate subsidies. Subsidies that are incompatible with the full-cost principle should be eliminated. Implicit subsidies should be targeted as well as explicit subsidies. For example, when the pricing of environmental resources is subject to government regulation (such as water in the

American Southwest), prices should not simply be determined by historic average cost; they should reflect the scarcity of the resource.

For one way to accomplish this, recall our discussion of incremental block pricing. Incremental block pricing provides a practical means of implementing this recommendation without jeopardizing the traditional legal constraint that water distribution utilities can earn no more than a fair rate of return. With incremental block pricing, the price of additional water consumed rises with the amount consumed per unit time. While the first units consumed per month up to some predetermined threshold would be relatively cheap, units consumed beyond the threshold would face a much higher price that truly reflects the scarcity of the resource. By ensuring that the marginal units consumed are priced at full cost, adequate incentives to conserve would be introduced.

The transition to the full-cost principle could proceed gradually, beginning in certain sectors, moving to others as greater familiarity with the approach was gained. A complete, immediate transition is not an essential ingredient of a rational approach.

The Cost-Effectiveness Principle.

A policy is cost-effective if it achieves the policy objective at the lowest possible cost. Cost-effectiveness is an important characteristic because it can diminish political backlash by limiting wasteful expenditures.

Appropriate implementation of the full-cost principle would automatically produce cost-effectiveness as a side benefit. Should acceptance of the full-cost principle falter, however, cost-effectiveness could be elevated to a primary policy goal, worthy in its own right. It provides a desirable, if less than perfect, fallback position.

Since political acceptance of the full-cost principle is by no means a foregone conclusion, tradable permits offer a practical way to implement the cost-effectiveness principle for pollution control and other policy venues. The case for tradable permits is based on the advantages that it would offer compared to other politically feasible alternatives.

Consider how it is playing out for climate change. In the short run, the three Kyoto trading mechanisms (emissions trading, joint implementation, and the clean development mechanism) offer the possibility of reaching the stipulated goals at a lower cost than would be possible if each country were limited to reduction options within its own borders. Making it easier to reach the goals usually increases compliance and may provide the means for more countries to join the Protocol. That certainly seemed to be the case for convincing Russia to join.

Because they separate the issue of who pays for control from who implements control, these mechanisms facilitate transboundary cost sharing (an item of particular importance to both the developing countries and the transition economies of Eastern Europe). Tradable permits also facilitate the mobilization of private capital for controlling climate change; private capital is likely to be a critically important component of any effective climate-change strategy as long as public capital remains insufficient to do it alone.

Finally, and perhaps most importantly, emissions trading mechanisms facilitate the development and implementation of novel approaches to climate-change control. By offering greater flexibility in how the emission reductions are achieved (as well as by providing economic incentives for the adoption and use of unconventional approaches), tradable entitlements can significantly lower the long-run cost. Lower long-run cost may be an important element in gaining greater international acceptance of the idea of tighter limits and reducing the difficulties associated with ensuring compliance.

And the tradable entitlement concept is increasingly being used in other environmental policy arenas such as managing fisheries and controlling water and land use.[5] In general, this approach can be used any time a cap should be placed on resource use and it is appropriate to formalize the rights held by users. As scarcity deepens, caps may become a much more important part of the policy mix.

The Property Rights Principle.

Part of the evident loss of efficiency in modern environmental problems involves perverse incentives resulting from misspecified property rights. According to the property right principle, local communities should have a property right over flora and fauna within their border. This property right would entitle the local community to share in any benefits created by preserving the species. Ensuring that local property rights over genetic resources are defined and respected would give local communities a much larger stake in some of the global benefits to be derived from the use of those resources and would enhance the prospects for effective enforcement.

Consider the problem of stemming the decline in the elephant population as an example. Insofar as permitted by the migratory nature of the herd, the property rights principle would confer the right to harvest a fixed number of elephants to the indigenous peoples who live in the elephants' native habitat. Ownership of harvesting rights in addition to the possibility of continued employment as long as the herd was preserved would ensure an income to the local community, giving it a stake in preserving the herd. Preventing poaching would become easier because poachers would become a threat to the local community, not merely a threat to a distant national government that inspires little allegiance.

A somewhat related application of the property rights principle could provide an additional means of resolving the diminishing supply of biologically rich tropical rain forests. One of the arguments for preserving biodiversity is that it offers a valuable gene pool for the development of future products such as medicines or food crops. Typically, however, the nations that govern the forestland containing this biologically rich gene pool have not shared in the wealth created by the products derived from it. One solution to this problem is universal acceptance of the principle that the nations that contain these biologically rich resources within their borders be entitled to a stipulated royalty on any and all products developed from the genes obtained from these preserves.

In the absence of royalty arrangements, nations cutting down their tropical forests have little incentive to protect the gene pool harbored within those forests because they are unlikely to reap any of the rewards that will ultimately result.

---

[5]For a list of studies examining the range of uses of tradable entitlements in environmental policy, see the extensive bibliography compiled by the author of this text at http://www.colby.edu/~thtieten/trade.html/.

Exploitation of the gene pool and the economic rewards that result from it typically accrue only to those nations and to those companies that can afford the extensive research. By establishing the principle that stipulated royalty payments would accrue to the nation from which the original genes were extracted, local incentives would become more compatible with global incentives.

Implementing this recommendation would not be trivial. Though it is not hard to envision licenses being required of all those conducting research or collecting specimens of local flora or fauna, it is more difficult to imagine a process that would guarantee royalty payments on every new derivative genetic discovery. For developing countries to be aware of new discoveries would be difficult enough, but the need to enforce the terms of the license on a company that is physically located in another country could prove inordinately time-consuming and expensive.

An often overlooked aspect of the property rights principle is the way in which it can promote human rights. Often the historic use of resources by indigenous peoples results in an informal set of access rights. Informal rights work fine as long as the pressure from competing rights is not too strong. However, when users with access to modern technology begin to expand their usage (think trawlers in fisheries or huge water bottling plants), informal rights can go by the boards. One way to protect indigenous rights is to formalize them, thereby increasing their security by making them enforceable.

The Sustainability Principle.

According to the sustainability principle, all resources should be used in a manner that respects the needs of future generations. Adopting the foregoing three principles would go a long way toward restoring efficiency. And restoring efficiency would set in motion the transition toward producing sustainable outcomes. As we have seen, however, restoring efficiency would not be sufficient. Other policies would be needed to satisfy the sustainability principle.

Restoring intergenerational fairness in the use of depletable resources might be an appropriate place to start. As the economic models have made clear, current incentives for sharing the wealth from the use of depletable resources are biased toward the present, even in efficient markets. Clearly this could be rectified by transferring some of the created wealth into the future, but how much?

Salah El Serafy (1981) has developed an ingenious, practical way to answer this question. Calculate the present value of the net benefits received from the extraction of a depletable resource over its useful life. This becomes the wealth to be shared. Using standard annuity tables, calculate the constant annual payments that could be made from this fund forever. (In essence, these payments represent the dividends and interest derived from the wealth; the principal would be left intact.) This constant annual payment is what can be consumed from the wealth created from the depletable resources. Receipts in excess of this amount (in the years the resource is being extracted and sold) must be paid into the fund. All succeeding generations receive the same annual payment; the payments continue forever.

The payments could be invested in research rather than in instruments producing a financial return. Such a strategy might envision, for example, setting aside through taxation a certain proportion of all proceeds from depletable resources for funding research on substitutes likely to be used by future generations. In the case of fossil fuels, for example, one might subsidize research into fuel cells or wind energy so that as fossil fuels are depleted, future generations would have the ability to switch to alternative sources easily without diminishing living standards in the process.

Another adjustment would confront the possibility of species extinction. Compensating future generations for extinct species (the implicit strategy in an efficient allocation) is not an adequate response. Not only do we not know the appropriate level of compensation, but it is possible that the preferences of future generations would be such that the value of the preserved species would exceed any possible compensation our generation would be willing to offer. Given this uncertainty about their preferences, one strategy would be to incorporate species preservation into our definition of sustainability to allow future generations to make their own valuations. With this approach, strategies that lead to species extinction would simply be infeasible, regardless of the net benefit calculations; they would never be chosen. The interests of future generations would be protected by preserving their options rather than by attempting to second-guess their preferences.

Adjusting the national income accounts would be another immediate implication of the sustainability principle. The income accounts must conform with the Hicksian definition of income. All of the costs, including the depreciation of natural capital, should be subtracted from the gross receipts in producing a national income figure. Failure to do this, as is the current practice, provides very misleading signals to the public sector. These misleading signals provide powerful incentives for public figures to engage in economic activities that violate the sustainability principle.

The Information Principle.

Polls generally show that regardless of their social circumstances, people care about the environment and are willing to commit resources to its preservation. To energize and focus that reservoir of goodwill, however, it is necessary to ensure that the citizens are informed. Recognizing the wisdom of this simple observation has paved the way for a new set of strategies designed to improve citizen participation in environmental policy.

Implementing the information principle can take a number of forms. In some countries it has meant increasing the freedom of the press to report on environmental matters. In others, it means providing better access to government records that reveal the quantities and types of pollutants being injected into the air and water. Computerized records have certainly facilitated this access.

It can also mean labeling green products to allow environmentally conscious consumers to use that as one element of their choice. "Dolphin-safe tuna" provides a classic example of how this approach has been used quite successfully.

One of the appeals of information strategies is their ability to achieve results when more traditional approaches prove inadequate. In many developing countries, for example, human and financial resources are so scarce as to preclude traditional regulatory approaches to pollution control. Fortunately, that does not necessarily mean that pollution goes uncontrolled. Appropriately designed information strategies may result in significant pollution control even in the absence of traditional monitoring and enforcement (see Example 23.5).

Example **23.5**

REPUTATIONAL STRATEGIES FOR POLLUTION CONTROL IN INDONESIA

Inhibited by a regulatory structure that was not able to produce widespread compliance with water pollution control laws due to a lack of resources, in 1993 the government of Indonesia instituted a unique complementary program to increase compliance. Known by its acronym PROPER (Program for Pollution Control, Evaluation and Rating), this system evaluated 187 factories. Depending upon their pollution output, these factories were assigned to one of five color-coded categories. The categories ranged from black (no effort to control pollution) to gold (polluter exceeds legal limits by at least 50% for air, water, and hazardous waste and makes extensive use of clean technology, pollution prevention, and so on).

The key to the system was not only that the names of the factories and their ratings would be made public, but that the ratings would be conducted periodically, allowing factories to gain public acknowledgment for improving their ratings. The hope was that firms would be sufficiently motivated by possible damage to their reputations by adverse publicity that they would improve their environmental performance.

The early results were encouraging. In the first six months following the announcement of the ratings, the number of firms in the black category fell by half (from 6 to 3), while the number of factories meeting or exceeding legal requirements went from 66 to 76.

Though the program was dropped in 1997, a victim of the Asian economic crisis, in light of its value, it was reinstated in 2002 when economic conditions improved.

Sources: S. Afsah and D. Wheeler. "Indonesia's New Pollution Control Program: Using Public Pressure to Get Compliance," *East Asian Executive Reports* Vol. 18, No. 5 (May 1996): 11–13; and Shakeb Afsah et al. "What Is PROPER? Reputational Incentives for Pollution Control in Indonesia," World Bank Working Paper (November 1995).

Forced Transition

Suppose that current levels of welfare were shown to be unsustainable and that an immediate transition to a new, lower standard of living were necessary to protect future generations. Suppose further that a "guided forced transition" would be less painful than a laissez-faire forced transition. How could that more abrupt transition be negotiated?

The most concrete proposals for a forced transition to the steady state come from Herman Daly (1991), an economist formerly with the World Bank. Daly is very sympathetic with the goal of a rapid transition to sustainable development and has spent a good deal of his professional life looking into the best way to achieve that objective. We will focus on his proposals in examining how an economy might be forced to this new sustainable path more rapidly than would normally be the case.

Defining the Target

Daly begins by attempting to define the steady state, the target of his approach, and how we know when it is achieved. His definition is couched in physical, rather than value, terms. For Daly the *steady-state economy* is characterized by constant stocks of people and physical wealth maintained at some chosen, desirable level by a low rate of *throughput*. This throughput—flow of resources and energy—provides direct consumption benefits (such as food and shelter) and investment, insofar as necessary to counteract depreciation of the capital stock.

Conceiving of the steady state in physical rather than value terms is significant because it forms an important difference between Daly and others who see the steady state as simply the absence of any development. Daly recognizes that some development would and should occur even in the steady state in spite of a constant stock of people and physical wealth. For example, as society learned more efficient ways to use energy, the value derived from the flow of energy may increase, even when the flow itself does not. Due to technological progress, the value of the services received can grow, even if the physical stocks and flows are unchanging. *The steady state and zero economic growth are not necessarily the same thing.*

Institutional Structure

Daly sees three institutional modifications as necessary for the rapid attainment of the steady state:

1. An institution for stabilizing population
2. An institution for stabilizing the stock of physical wealth and throughput
3. An institution to ensure that the stocks and flows are distributed fairly among the population

Allocation among alternative uses is handled by the market. Collective decisions are made on scale and distribution, but allocation remains with the market. Daly argues that the questions of scale, distribution, and allocation involve three separate policy goals and cannot all be served by the single instrument of prices. Market prices achieve the goal of efficient allocation; other institutions are necessary to achieve an optimal (sustainable) scale and an optimal (fair) distribution.

Population Stabilization.
According to the Daly proposals, population would be stabilized over the long run using an idea first put forth by Kenneth Boulding (1964). In this scheme each individual would be given the right to produce one (and only one!) child. Because this scheme over a generation allows each member of the current population to replace himself or herself, births would necessarily equal deaths and population stability would be achieved.

This scheme would award each person a certificate entitling the holder to have one child. Couples could pool their certificates to have two. Every time a child was born, a certificate would be surrendered. Failure to produce a certificate would cause the child to be put up for adoption.

Certificates would be fully transferable. Families who placed a particularly high value on children could purchase extra certificates, while those who viewed parenting with something less than enthusiasm could sell certificates. As one of its virtues, this system would ensure that the overall objective of population stability would be achieved, but no family would be required to maintain a particular family size. Though every couple would be guaranteed the right to have two children, they could choose to have fewer or more than two.

Stock and Throughput Stabilization.

Daly suggests that throughput should be held at some minimum level using depletion quotas for all depletable resources. These quotas would define the amount of the resource that could be extracted and used. Any extraction and use in excess of this quota would be illegal.

The size of these quotas would be determined by bureaucrats, but according to Daly, these bureaucrats would follow a specific rule. The quotas would be set at a level sufficiently stringent that the price of the resource in question would equal the price of the closest renewable substitute. When no close renewable substitute was available, the bureaucrats would be empowered to decide the most ethical level. Because the quotas would be auctioned off by the government, the government would extract all of the scarcity rent associated with the depletable resources. The quota prices would equal the scarcity rent of the covered resources.

Ensuring Distributional Fairness.

Daly also sees a need to override the normal channels for distributing income in the steady-state economy. In a growth economy, tensions between the rich and poor can be ameliorated by the opportunities for social and economic mobility that a growth economy provides. In a steady-state economy, those opportunities are diminished as the number of new jobs created is smaller.

To alleviate these tensions, Daly proposes the establishment of a maximum and minimum income level, as well as a maximum limit on wealth. The minimum income level would be financed in part by progressive taxes with 100% marginal rates above the maximum income and wealth limits. Since these 100% tax rates would presumably yield very little revenue (the incentive to earn more having been eliminated), most of the revenue would come from the sale of depletion quotas and from lower tax rates on income levels between the minimum and maximum.

Administration

The Daly system would be expensive to implement. Large bureaucratic staffs would be needed to define the quotas, run the auctions, and ensure compliance. In an age where public sentiment seems to be for decreasing rather than increasing bureaucracy, this proposal would buck the trend. A universal quota system for depletable and renewable resources, in addition to being bureaucratically cumbersome, holds the potential to disrupt a smoothly operating institutional structure. Historically, the only time a system such as this has been acceptable is during a war.[6]

Child certificates would also be administratively cumbersome and, in most of the industrialized world, unnecessary. In addition, child certificates raise moral questions. For example, this system tends to preserve the existing racial status quo. To minority groups with above-average birth rates and below-average incomes, this looks like a policy to limit their proportion in the population. Even though that is clearly not the intended result, the suspicions raised create unnecessary tensions.

Summary

Sustainable development refers to a process for providing for the needs of the present generation (particularly those in poverty) without compromising the ability of future generations to meet their own needs.

Market imperfections frequently make sustainable development less likely. Intergenerational externalities such as climate modification impose excessive costs on future generations. Free access to biological common-property resources can lead to excessive exploitation and even extinction of the species.

Even efficient markets do not necessarily produce sustainable development. Restoring efficiency is desirable and helpful but insufficient as a means for producing sustainable welfare levels. While in principle dynamically efficient allocations produce extraction profiles for depletable resources that are compatible with the interests of future generations, in practice this is not necessarily the case. Guaranteeing sustainability frequently requires compensation from the present to future generations, but profit-maximizing behavior produces compensation levels that are too low. Furthermore, adequate compensation levels may be difficult to define at best, and it is not clear that financial payments can adequately compensate future generations for all of the options they might be asked to forego.

When trade is used as part of the development strategy, it must be used carefully. The effects of trade on the environment are neither universally benign nor universally detrimental. Context matters.

The empirical evidence on trade and the environments has two strong messages for developing countries:

1. Lowering environmental standards to compete internationally for jobs is a self-defeating strategy.
2. Waiting for higher incomes from development to solve environmental problems will substantially raise the cost of dealing with them.

New sustainable forms of development are possible, but they will not automatically be adopted. Economic incentive policies can facilitate the transition from

---

[6]In a personal communication honoring my request that he review this chapter and the one that precedes it, Herman Daly responded, "In my view the real threat to freedom and stimulus to bureaucratic control is *crisis* and avoidance of crisis with a bit of collective action now seems a good strategy for maximizing freedom over the long run."

unsustainable to sustainable activities. Five principles provide a framework for using economic incentives to manage this transition:

1. All users of environmental resources should pay their full cost to ensure a level playing field between those resources that damage the environment and those that don't (the full-cost principle).
2. All environmental policies should be implemented in a cost-effective manner to ensure that the maximum environmental quality is received for the expenditure (the cost-effectiveness principle).
3. Rights over environmental resources should be designed in such a manner as to promote equitable stewardship (the property rights principle).
4. All current uses of resources should be compatible with the needs of future generations, and the present-value criterion should be used only to choose among allocations that meet this sustainability test (the sustainability principle).
5. All citizens should be kept as informed as is practical about the environmental consequences of current decisions to allow citizens to participate as fully as possible in the transition to sustainable development (the information principle).

If it turns out that universally higher standards of living are not possible without exceeding the carrying capacity of the planet, a rapid transition to a new steady state involving levels of welfare lower than current levels would be needed. To examine how this might occur, we considered the proposals of economist Herman Daly. He sees three institutional modifications as necessary: (1) a new mechanism to control the distribution of income and wealth; (2) a system of annual quotas to govern the rate of consumption of both depletable and renewable resources; and (3) a plan to control population. The institutional modifications suggested by Daly would be implemented at a very high cost.

The search for solutions must recognize that market forces are extremely powerful. Attempts to negotiate agreements that seek to block those forces or to meet them head-on are probably doomed to failure. Nonetheless, it is possible to negotiate agreements that harness those forces and channel them in directions that enhance the possibilities of international cooperation. To take these steps will require thinking and acting in somewhat unconventional ways. Whether the world community is equal to the task remains to be seen.

Discussion Questions

1. Discuss the mechanism favored by Daly to control population growth. What are its advantages and disadvantages? Would it be appropriate to implement this policy now in the United States? For those who believe that it would, what are the crucial reasons? For those who believe it is not appropriate, are there any circumstances in any countries where it might be appropriate? Why or why not?
2. "Every molecule of a nonrenewable resource used today precludes its use by future generations. Therefore, the only morally defensible policy for any generation is to use only renewable resources." Discuss.

3. "Future generations can cast neither votes in current elections nor dollars in current market decisions. Therefore, it should not come as a surprise to anyone that the interests in future generations are ignored in a market economy." Discuss.

4. "Trade simply represents economic imperialism where one country exploits another. The environment is the inevitable victim." Discuss.

Further Reading

Battie, Sandra S. "Sustainable Development: Challenges to the Agricultural Economics Profession," *American Journal of Agricultural Economics* Vol. 71 (December 1989): 1083–1101. Contrasts the viewpoints of "deep ecology" sustainable development advocates with those of traditional economists and suggests some things each can learn from the other.

Copeland, B. R., and M. S. Taylor. "Trade, Growth, and the Environment," *Journal of Economic Literature* Vol. 42 (March 2004): 7–71. An excellent survey of the lessons to be derived from the theory and empirical work focusing on the relationship between trade and the environment.

Jansson, Ann Mari, et al., eds. *Investing in Natural Capital: The Ecological Economics Approach to Sustainability* (Washington, DC: Island Press, 1994). Proceedings of an international workshop involving ecologists and economists in a joint search for new approaches to sustainable development.

OECD. *The Environmental Effects of Trade* (Paris: OECD, 1994). Contains background documents for OECD discussions on the environmental effects of trade, including sector studies on agriculture, forestry, fisheries, endangered species, and transport.

Pearce, David, Anil Markandya, and Edward B. Barbier. *Blueprint for a Green Economy* (London: Earthscan, 2000). Seeks to answer the question, "If we accept sustainable development as a working idea, what does it mean for the way we manage a modern economy?"

Pezzey, J. C. V., and M. A. Toman. "Progress and Problems in the Economics of Sustainability," in T. Tietenberg and H. Folmer, eds. *The International Yearbook of Environmental and Resource Economics: A Survey of Current Issues* (Cheltenham, UK: Edward Elgar, 2002). A comprehensive review of what we have learned from economic analysis about the nature and consequences of sustainability by two major contributors to the literature.

Sterner, Thomas, ed. *Economic Policies for Sustainable Development* (Norwell, MA: Kluwer Academic Publishers, 1994). A collection of 17 essays that describe the state of the art in the use of new economic instruments to achieve sustainable development.

Stewart, Richard B. "Environmental Regulation and International Competitiveness," *Yale Law Journal* Vol. 102 (June 1993): 2039–2106. A comprehensive survey of the trade and environment literatures.

Additional References and Historically Significant References are available on this book's companion Web site www.aw-bc.com/tietenberg.

Visions of the Future Revisited

Mankind was destined to live on the edge of perpetual disaster. We are mankind because we survive. We do it in a half-assed way, but we do it.
—Paul Adamson, a fictional character in James A. Michener's *Chesapeake*

We have now come full circle. Having begun our study with two lofty visions of the future, we proceeded to dissect the details of the various components of these visions—population, the management of depletable and renewable resources, pollution, and the growth process itself. During these inquiries we gained a number of useful insights about individual environmental and natural resource problems. Now it is time to step back and coalesce those insights into a systematic assessment of the two visions.

Addressing the Issues

In Chapter 1 we posed a number of questions to serve as our focus for the overarching issue of growth in a finite environment. Those questions addressed three major issues: (1) How is the problem correctly conceptualized? (2) Can our economic and political institutions respond in a timely and democratic fashion to the challenges presented? (3) Can the needs of the present generation be met without compromising the ability of future generations to meet their own needs? Can short-term and long-term goals be harmonized? The next three segments of this section summarize and interpret the evidence uncovered.

Conceptualizing the Problem

At the beginning of this book we suggested that if the problem is characterized as an exponential growth in demand coupled with a finite supply of resources, the resources must eventually be exhausted. If those resources are essential, society will collapse when the resources are exhausted.

We have seen that this is an excessively harsh characterization. The growth in the demand for resources is not insensitive to their scarcity. Though the rise in energy prices was triggered more by cartel actions than by scarcity, it is possible to use higher energy prices as an example of how the economic system reacts.

The growth in demand following the increase in prices in the 1970s fell dramatically, with petroleum experiencing the largest reductions. In the United States, for example, total energy consumption in 1981 (73.8 quadrillion BTUs) was lower than it was in 1973 (74.6 quadrillion BTUs), despite increases in income and population. Petroleum consumption went from 34.8 quadrillion BTUs in 1973 to 32.0 quadrillion BTUs in 1981. Though some of this reduction was caused by sluggishness of the economy, price certainly played a major role.

Price is not the only factor that retards demand growth. Declines in population growth also play a significant role. Since the developed nations appropriate a disproportionate share of the world's resources, the dramatic declines in population growth in those countries has had a disproportionate effect on slowing the demand for resources.

Characterizing the resource base as finite—the second aspect of the model—is also excessively harsh: (1) this characterization ignores the existence of a substantial renewable resource base; (2) it focuses attention on the wrong issue; and (3) it supports ill-conceived attempts to measure the size of the resource base. We consider each problem in turn.

In a very real sense, the resource base is not finite. Plentiful supplies of renewable resources including, significantly, energy are available. The normal reaction to increasing scarcity of depletable resources is to switch to renewable resources. That is clearly happening. The most dramatic examples can be found in the transition to wind, solar, and hydrogen fuel cells.

Labeling the resource base as finite is also misleading because it suggests that our concern should be "running out." In fact, for most resources we shall never run out. Millions of years of finite resources are left at current consumption rates. The rising cost of extracting and using those resources including environmental costs is the chief threat to future standards of living, not the potential for exhausting them. The limits on our uses of these resources are not determined by their scarcity in the crust of the earth, but rather by what we would have to sacrifice to extract and process the ores. The work by Skinner and others suggests that we may not be willing to pay the price required to extract some of the lower-grade sources of those minerals.

Ignorance of this basic point has led to a number of ill-fated attempts to measure the size of this finite resource base. Conventional physical indicators, such as the static and the exponential reserve indices, are excessively pessimistic because they fail to take into account possibilities for expanding current reserves. Historically, no forecast based on these techniques has stood the test of time. There is no reason to expect any similar forecast to do so in the future. They are convenient since they can be readily calculated and easily interpreted, but they are also usually dead wrong.

Current reserves can be expanded in many ways. These include finding new sources of conventional materials, as well as discovering new uses for unconventional materials, including what was previously considered waste. We can also stretch the useful life of these reserves by reducing the amount of materials needed to produce the products. Striking examples include the diminishing size of a typical computer system needed to process a given amount of information and the substantially diminished amount of energy needed to heat a well-designed home.

Although our ability to assess what is happening to cost is far from perfect, two things seem clear. Historically, very little, if any, evidence supports a fear of impending scarcity of minerals. Our ability to develop lower-cost technologies for processing resources dominated the necessity to extract lower-grade sources. As a result, in real terms, extraction costs typically have fallen, rather than risen, over time. How long that will continue remains an open question.

Not all errors in resource-base measurement have been committed by those having a tendency to understate the adequacy of the resource base. Errors in the other direction are committed by those who point to the abundance in the earth's crust and atmosphere of almost all substances on which we depend. While the abundance of those substances may not be in doubt, the amounts we actually use will no doubt fall far short of the amounts available.

Paradoxically, some of the most obvious cases in which limits are being approached and the carrying capacity concept has the most validity involve renewable resources rather than depletable resources. Population growth is a key contributor to this phenomenon. Expanding populations force the cultivation of marginal lands and the deforestation of large biologically rich tracts. The erosion of overworked soils diminishes their fertility and ultimately their productivity. Biological resources such as fisheries can be overexploited, even to the point of extinction. Trade can intensify these processes, especially when property regimes do not adequately protect the resources. The problem with these resources is not their finiteness, but the way in which they have been managed.

Correct conceptualization of the resource scarcity problem suggests that both extremely pessimistic and extremely optimistic views are wrong. Impenetrable proximate physical limits on resource availability are typically not the problem; improper incentives and inadequate information are frequently much more serious. But believing in unlimited amounts of all resources that could support continued economic growth at current rates forever is equally naïve. Plenty of resources are available if we are willing to pay the price, but that price is now rising. Transitions to renewable resources, recycled resources, and less costly depletable resources have already begun.

Institutional Responses

One of the keys to understanding how society will cope with increasing resource scarcity and environmental damage lies in understanding how social institutions will react. Are market systems, with their emphasis on decentralized decision-making, and democratic political systems, with their commitment to public participation and majority rule, equal to the challenge?

Our examination of the record seems to suggest that while our economic and political systems are far from infallible and some rather glaring deficiencies have become evident, no fatal flaws have become evident.

On the positive side, markets have responded swiftly and automatically to deal with those resources experiencing higher prices. Demand has been reduced and substitution encouraged. Markets for recycling are growing and consumer habits are changing. No one has had to oversee these responses to make sure they occur. As long as property rights are well defined, the market system provides incentives for consumers and producers to respond to scarcity in a variety of useful ways (see Example 24.1).

Example   24.1

PRIVATE INCENTIVES FOR SUSTAINABLE DEVELOPMENT: CAN ADOPTING SUSTAINABLE PRACTICES BE PROFITABLE?

Motivated by what it perceived to be great inefficiencies associated with its industry, the Interface Corporation, a carpet manufacturer, has totally transformed the nature of its business.

First, the company recognized that unworn carpet, usually under furniture, did not need to be replaced. Thus, the traditional wall-to-wall carpet was replaced with a carpet tile system. Whereas in traditional practice, wear in any part of the carpet meant that the entire carpet had to be replaced, with carpet tiles only those specific tiles showing wear are replaced. As an added benefit, the reduction in carpet replacement simultaneously reduces the amount of potentially harmful glue fumes being released into the indoor air.

Next, Interface totally changed its relationship with its customers. Rather than selling carpet, Interface leases it. In effect, it has become a seller of carpet services rather than a seller of carpets. Carpet tiles can be easily replaced or cleaned overnight by Interface employees, eliminating the loss of productivity that could occur from halting company activities during the day. The cost to consumers is substantially lower not only because less carpet is replaced, but also because leasing allows tax advantages. Leased carpet is treated by the tax code as an expense, not an asset.

The environment has also benefited. In traditional industry practice, most used carpet was transported to a landfill. Much of the rest was remanufactured into much-lower-valued uses. Seeing that as a waste of resources, Interface created an entirely new product, Solarium, that, when recycled at the end of its useful life, could be remanufactured back into new Solarium. Not only is this production process 99.7% less wasteful in terms of its drain on energy and raw materials, the product is reportedly highly stain-resistant, four times as durable as regular carpet material, and easily cleaned with water.

These moves toward more sustainable manufacturing did not result from government mandates. Rather, an innovative company found that it could benefit itself and the environment at the same time.

Source: Paul Hawken, Amory Lovins, and L. Hunter Lovins. *Natural Capitalism: Creating the Next Industrial Revolution* (Boston: Little, Brown and Company, 1999).

As compelling as the evidence is for this point of view, it does not support the conclusion that, left to itself, the market would automatically choose a dynamically efficient or a sustainable path for the future. Market imperfections frequently make sustainable development less likely. The most serious limitations of the market become evident in how it treats free-access resources, such as the fish we eat, the air we breathe, and the water we drink. Left to its own devices, a market will overexploit free-access resources, substantially lowering the net benefits received by future generations. If not compensated for by sufficient increases in net benefits elsewhere in the economy, such exploitation could result in a violation of the sustainability criterion.

Even efficient markets do not necessarily produce sustainable development. Restoring efficiency is a desirable, but insufficient means for producing sustainable welfare levels. While in principle dynamically efficient allocations produce extraction profiles for depletable resources that are compatible with the interests of future generations, in practice this is not necessarily or even normally the case. Guaranteeing sustainability in the face of declining supplies of depletable resources requires compensation from present to future generations, but profit-maximizing behavior produces compensation levels that are too low. Furthermore, adequate compensation levels may be difficult to define at best, and it is not clear that financial payments could adequately compensate future generations for the options they might be asked to forgo.

The market has some capacity for self-correction. The decline of free-access fish catches, for example, has led to the rise of private-property fish farming. The artificial scarcity created by imperfectly defined property rights gives rise to incentives for the development of a private-property substitute.

This capacity of the market for self-healing, while comforting, is not always adequate. In some cases cheaper, more effective solutions (such as preventing the deterioration of the original natural resource base) are available. Preventive medicine is frequently superior to corrective surgery. In other cases, such as when our air is polluted, no good private substitutes are available. To provide an adequate response, it is sometimes necessary to complement market decisions with political ones.

The need for government intervention is particularly acute in controlling pollution. Uncontrolled markets not only produce too much pollution, but they also tend to underprice commodities that contribute to pollution either when produced or consumed. Firms that unilaterally attempt to control their pollution run the risk of pricing themselves out of the market. Government intervention is needed to ensure that firms that neglect environmental damage in their operating decisions do not thereby gain a competitive edge.

Significant progress has been made in reducing the amount of pollution, particularly conventional air pollution. Recently, regulatory innovations such as the sulfur allowance program and the Swedish NOx charge represent major steps toward the development of a flexible but potential framework for controlling air pollutants. By making it less costly to achieve environmental goals, these reforms have limited the potential for a backlash against the policy. They have brought perceived costs more in line with perceived benefits.

It would be a great mistake, however, to assume that government intervention has been uniformly benign. The acid-rain problem was almost certainly made worse by a policy structure that focused on local rather than regional pollution problems. Requiring scrubbers for all new coal-fired electrical generating stations was done for purely political reasons and served to raise the cost of compliance unnecessarily.

One aspect of the policy process that does not seem to have been handled well is the speed with which improvement has been sought. Public opinion polls have unambiguously shown that the general public supports environmental protection even when it raises costs and lowers employment. Policy-makers have reacted to this resolve by writing very tough legislation designed to force rapid technological development.

Common sense suggests that tough legislation with early deadlines can achieve environmental goals more rapidly than weaker legislation with less tight deadlines. Common sense is frequently wrong. Writing tough legislation with early deadlines can have the opposite effect. Unreasonably tough regulations are virtually impossible to enforce. Recognizing this, polluters have repeatedly sought (and received) delays in compliance. It has frequently been better, from the polluter's point of view, to spend resources to change the regulations than to comply with them. This would not have been the case with less stringent regulations, since the firms would have had no legally supportable grounds for delay.

Perhaps the most flagrant examples of counterproductive government intervention are to be found in treatment of energy and water resources. By imposing price ceilings on natural gas and oil, the government removed much of the normal resiliency of the economic system. With price controls, the incentives for expanding the supply are reduced and the time profile of consumption is tilted toward the present. As was the case with natural gas, these controls can even cause biases that interfere with the transition to renewable resources. By holding water prices below the marginal cost of supply, water authorities have subsidized excess use. Resources that in a normal market would have been conserved for future generations are, with price controls, consumed by the current generation. When price controls are placed on normal market transactions. The smooth transition to renewable resources that characterizes the normal market allocation is eliminated; shortages can arise.

Price controls are also playing a key role in the world hunger problem. By controlling the price of food, many developing countries have undervalued domestic agriculture. The long-run effect of these controls has been to increase the developing countries reliance on food imports at a time when foreign exchange to pay for those imports is becoming increasingly scarce. Whereas developed countries have gone substantially down the road to price decontrol, less developed countries have not yet been able to extricate themselves to a similar degree.

In summary, the record compiled by our economic and political institutions has been mixed. It seems clear that simple prescriptions such as "leave it to the market" or "more government intervention" simply do not bear up under a close scrutiny of the record. The relationship between the economic and political sectors has to be one of selective engagement, complemented in some areas by selective disengagement. Each problem has to be treated on a case-by-case basis. As we have seen in our examination of a variety of environmental and natural resource problems, the efficiency and sustainability criteria allow such distinctions to be drawn, and they can serve as a basis for policy reform.

Sustainable Development

Historically, increases in inputs and technological progress have been important sources of economic growth in the industrialized nations. In the future, some factors of production, such as labor, will not increase as rapidly as they have in the past. The effect of this decline on growth depends on the interplay among the law of diminishing marginal productivity, substitution possibilities, and technological progress. The law of diminishing marginal productivity suggests slower growth rates, while technological progress and the availability of substitutes counteract this drag. One view foresees limits to technological progress imposed by the second law of thermodynamics, implying that the growth process must culminate in a steady or stationary state where growth ultimately diminishes to zero.

Our examination of empirical evidence suggests that increased environmental control has not currently had a large impact on the economy as a whole, although certain industries have been hit quite hard. Environmental policy has triggered only a small rise in the rate of inflation and a mild reduction in growth. Environmental policy has apparently contributed more jobs than it has cost. The notion that respecting the environment is incompatible with a healthy economy is demonstrably wrong.

The situation is similar for energy. Though rather large increases in energy prices occurred during the 1970s, the portion of the slowdown in productivity growth during this period that is attributed to these increases is not large. Some diminution of growth has certainly occurred, but it seems premature to suggest that rising energy prices have already forced a transition to a period of substantially lower productivity growth.

The economy is being transformed, however. It is not business as usual. Two particularly important aspects of this transformation are the decline in population growth and the rise in importance of information as a driving economic force. Both aspects tend to reduce the degree that physical limits constrain economic growth and increase the degree to which current welfare levels would be sustainable.

Recognizing that conventional measures of economic growth shed little light on the question, some crude attempts have been made to estimate whether or not growth in the industrialized countries has historically made the citizens of those countries better off. Results of these studies suggest that because growth has ultimately generated more leisure, longer life expectancy, and more goods and services, it has been beneficial. Yet other measures, such as the ecological footprint, convey a more cautionary story. They remind us that our inability to measure precisely the carrying capacity for humans in no way diminishes the existence and importance of those limits.

Our examination of the evidence suggests that the notion that all of the world's people are automatically benefited by economic growth is naïve. Growth has demonstrably benefited the poor in the developed countries, but that is certainly not inevitable. The most successful countries use development to find better access to education and health care.

The future outlook for the less industrialized nations is mixed at best. Solving many of their future environmental problems will require raising standards of living. However, following the path of development pioneered by the industrialized nations is probably not possible without triggering severe global environmental problems; the solution would become the problem. New forms of development will be necessary.

The less industrialized countries must overcome a number of significant barriers if development is to become a reality. At the local level, rising populations face increasingly limited access to land or productive assets. At the national level, corruption and development policies discriminate against the poor. Globally, their situation is worsened by rising debt burdens, falling prices for exports, and the flight of capital that could be used to create jobs and income.

New sustainable forms of development are possible and desirable, but they will not automatically be adopted in either the high-income or the low-income nations. Are cooperative solutions possible? Can any common ground be established?

The experience in the United States suggests that cooperative solutions may be possible even among traditional adversaries. Environmental regulators and lobbying groups with a special interest in environmental protection in the United States have traditionally looked upon the market system as a powerful and potentially dangerous adversary. It was widely recognized that the market unleashed powerful forces and was widely lamented that those forces clearly acted to degrade the environment. Meanwhile, development proponents have traditionally seen environmental concerns as blocking projects that had the potential to raise living standards significantly. Conflict and confrontation became the modus operandi for dealing with this clash of objectives.

The climate for dealing effectively with both concerns has improved dramatically within the last few years. Not only have development proponents learned that in many cases short-term wealth enhancement projects that degrade the environment are ultimately counterproductive, but environmental groups have come to realize that poverty itself is a major threat to environmental protection. No longer are economic development and environmental protection seen as an "either-or" proposition. Rather, the focus has shifted toward the identification of policies or policy instruments that can promote the alleviation of poverty while protecting the environment.

The economic incentives approach to environmental and natural resource regulation has, in the last decade or so, become a significant component of environmental and natural resource policy. Instead of mandating prescribed actions, such as requiring the installation of a particular piece of pollution control equipment, this approach achieves environmental objectives by changing the economic incentives of those doing the polluting. Incentives can be changed by fees or charges, transferable permits, or even liability law. By changing the incentives an individual agent faces, that agent can use his or her typically superior information to select the best means of meeting his or her assigned responsibility. When it is in the interest of individuals to change to new forms of development, the transformation can be amazingly rapid.

Public policy and sustainable development must proceed in a mutually supportive relationship (see Example 24.2). The government must ensure that the

Example 24.2

PUBLIC/PRIVATE PARTNERSHIPS: THE KALUNDBORG EXPERIENCE

Located on an island 75 miles off the coast of Copenhagen, the city of Kalundborg has achieved a remarkable symbiosis among the various industries that provide the employment base for the city. The four main industries, along with small businesses and the municipal government, began developing cooperative relationships in the 1970s designed to lower disposal costs, attain less expensive input materials, and receive income from their waste products.

A coal-fired power plant (Asnaes) transports its residual steam to a refinery (Statoil). In exchange, Statoil gives Asnaes refinery gas that Asnaes burns to generate electricity. Asnaes sells excess steam to a local fish farm, to a heating system for the city, and to a pharmaceuticals and enzyme producer (Novo Nordisk). Continuing the cycle, the fish farm and Novo Nordisk send their sludge to farms to be used as fertilizer. Produced fly ash is sold to a cement plant and gypsum produced by its desulfurization process is sold to a wallboard manufacturer. Statoil, the refinery, sells the sulfur removed from its natural gas to a sulfuric acid manufacturer, Kemira.

This entire process resulted not from centralized planning, but simply because it was in the individual best interests of the public and private entities involved. Although the motives were purely financial, this synergetic situation has clear environmental benefits. It is therefore likely to be economically, as well as environmentally, sustainable.

Source: Pierre Desroches. "Eco-Industrial Parks: The Case for Private Planning," *Report # RS 00-1,* Political Economy Research Center, Bozeman, MT 59718.

market is sending the right signals to all participants so that the sustainable outcome is compatible with other business objectives. Economic incentive approaches are a means of establishing that kind of compatibility. The experience with the various versions of this approach used in the United States, Europe, and Asia suggests that economic approaches in general are both feasible and effective.

How about global environmental problems?

By being creative in the design of policy instruments, the incentives of local and global communities can become compatible. Whenever resources are wasted, much more environmental improvement could be obtained for current expenditures, or the same improvement could be realized with a much smaller commitment of resources. By definition, moving from an inefficient policy to an efficient one creates gains to be shared. Agreements on how these gains should be shared among the cooperating parties can be used to build coalitions.

Economic incentives approaches could be helpful here as well. Emissions trading facilitates cost sharing among participants while ensuring cost-effective responses to the need for additional control. By separating the question of what control is undertaken from the question of who ultimately pays for it, the government significantly widens the control possibilities. Conferring property rights for biological populations on local communities provides an incentive for those communities to protect the populations. Strategies for reducing debt can diminish the pressure on forests and other natural resources that may be "cashed in" to pay off the debt.

The courts are beginning to use economic incentives as well; judicial remedies for environmental problems are beginning to take their place alongside regulatory remedies. Take, for example, the problem of cleaning up already-closed toxic waste sites. Allowing the government to sue all potentially responsible parties accomplishes a double purpose: (1) it ensures that the financial responsibility for contaminated sites is borne by those who directly caused the problem, and (2) it encourages those who are currently using those sites to exercise great care, lest they be forced to bear a large financial burden in the event of an incident. The alternative remedy of putting the burden on taxpayers would have resulted in less revenue raised, fewer sites restored, and less adequate incentives for users to exercise care.

Europe has tended to depend more on the effluent or emission charge. This approach places a per-unit fee on each unit of pollution discharged. Faced with the responsibility for paying for the damage caused by their pollution, firms recognize it as a controllable cost of doing business. This recognition triggers a search for possible ways to reduce the damage, including changing inputs, changing the production process, transforming the residuals to less-harmful substances, and recycling by-products. The experience in the Netherlands, a country where the fees are higher than in most other countries, suggests that the effects can be dramatic.

Fees also raise revenue. Successful development, particularly sustainable development, requires a symbiotic partnership between the public and private sectors. To function as an equal partner, the public sector must be adequately funded. If it fails to raise adequate revenue, the public sector becomes a drag on the growth process, but if it raises revenue in ways that distort incentives that, too, can act as a drag on development. Effluent or emission charges offer the realistic opportunity to raise revenue for the public sector while reducing the drag from more distortionary taxes. Whereas other types of taxation discourage growth by penalizing legitimate development incentives, emission or effluent charges provide incentives for sustainable development. Some work from the United States suggests that the drag on development avoided by substituting effluent or emission charges for more traditional revenue-raising devices such as capital gains, income, and sales taxes could be significant.

Incentives for forward-looking public action are as important as those for private action. The current national income accounting system provides an example of a perverse economic signal. Though national income accounts were never intended to function as a device for measuring the welfare of a nation, in practice that is how they are used. National income per capita is a common metric for evaluating how well-off a nation's people are. Yet the current construction of those accounts sends the wrong signals.

Rather than recognizing oil spills for what they are, namely a source of decline in the value of the endowment of natural resources in the area, they increase the national income; spills boost GNP! All the cleanup expenditures serve to increase national income, but no account is taken of the consequent depreciation of the natural environment. Under the current system, the accounts make no distinction between growth that is occurring because a country is damaging its natural resource endowment with a consequent irreversible decline in its value, and sustainable growth where the value of the endowment remains. Only when suitable corrections are made to these accounts will governments be judged by the appropriate standards.

The power of economic incentives is certainly not inevitably channeled toward the achievement of sustainable growth. They can be misapplied as well as appropriately applied. Tax subsidies to promote cattle ranching on the fragile soil in the Brazilian rain forest stimulated an unsustainable activity, which has done irreparable damage to an ecologically significant area. They must be used with care.

A Concluding Comment

A complementary relationship that holds promise is currently evolving among the economic system, the court system, and the legislative and executive branches of government. We are, however, not yet out of the woods. Significantly, we the public must learn that part of the responsibility is ours. The government cannot solve all problems without our significant participation.

Not all behavior can be regulated. It costs too much to catch every offender. Our law enforcement system works because most people obey the law, whether anyone is watching or not. A high degree of voluntary compliance is essential for the system to work smoothly.

The best resolution of the toxic substance problem, for example, is undoubtedly for all makers of potentially toxic substances to be genuinely concerned about the safety of their products and to bite the bullet whenever their research raises questions. The ultimate responsibility for developing an acceptable level of risk must rest on the integrity of those who make, use, transport, and dispose of the substances. The government can assist by penalizing and controlling those few who fail to exhibit this integrity, but it can never substitute for integrity on a large scale. We cannot and should not depend purely upon altruism to solve these problems, but we should not underestimate its importance either.

We also need to recognize that markets serve our preferences as consumers. Making sure our purchases reflect environmental values will help markets move in the right direction. Fuel-efficient automobiles will enter the market much faster if many consumers demand them.

The notion that we are at the end of an era may well be true. But we are also at the beginning of a new one. What the future holds is not the decline of civilization but its transformation. As the opening quote to this chapter suggests, the road may be strewn with obstacles and our social institutions may deal with those obstacles with less grace and less finesse than we might hope for, but we are unquestionably making progress.

Problem Set Answers

CHAPTER 2

1. a. Net benefits are maximized where the demand curve intersects the marginal-cost curve. Therefore, the efficient q would occur when $80 - 1q = 1q$. Thus the efficient $q = 40$ units.

   b. Draw the diagram. Draw a horizontal line from the place where the demand curve intersects the marginal-cost curve to the vertical axis. This intersection will take place at a price of $40. The net benefits can now be computed as the sum of the upper right triangle (the area under the demand curve and over this line) and the lower right triangle (the area under the price line and over the marginal-cost curve). The area of a right triangle is $1/2 \times$ base $\times$ height. Therefore, the net benefits are $1/2 \times \$40 \times 40 + 1/2 \times \$40 \times 40 = \$1,600$.

CHAPTER 3

1. In order to maximize net benefits, Coast Guard oil spill prevention enforcement activity should be increased until the marginal benefit of the last unit equals the marginal cost of providing that unit. Efficiency requires that the level of the activity be chosen so as to equate marginal benefit with marginal cost. When marginal benefits exceed marginal cost (as in this example), the activity should be expanded.

2. a. According to the figures given, the per-life cost of the standard for unvented space heaters lies well under the implied value of life estimates given in the chapter, while per-life cost implied by the proposed standard for formaldehyde lies well over those estimates. In benefit/cost terms the allocation of resources to fixing unvented space heaters should be increased, while the formaldehyde standard should be relaxed somewhat to bring the costs back into line with the benefits.

   b. Efficiency requires that the marginal benefit of a life saved in government programs (as determined by the implied value of a human life in that context) should be equal to the marginal cost of saving that life. Marginal costs should be equal only if the marginal benefits are equal and, as we saw in the chapter, risk valuations (and hence the implied value of human life) depend on the risk context, so it is unlikely they are equal across all government programs.

597

CHAPTER 4

1. a. This is a public good, so add the 100 demand curves vertically. This yields $P = 1,000 - 100q$. This demand curve would intersect the marginal-cost curve when $P = 500$, which occurs when $q = 5$ miles.
    b. The net benefits are represented by a right triangle where the height of the triangle is $500 ($1,000, the point where the demand curve crosses the vertical axis, minus $500, the marginal cost) and the base is five miles. The area of a right triangle is $1/2 \times \text{base} \times \text{height} = 1/2 \times \$500 \times 5 = \$1,250$.
2. a. Consumer surplus = $800. Producer surplus = $800. Consumer surplus plus producer surplus = $1,600 = net benefits.
    b. The marginal revenue curve has twice the slope of the demand curve, so $MR = 80 - 2q$. Setting $MR = MC$ yields $q = 80/3$ and $P = 160/3$. Using Figure 4.7, producer surplus is the area under the price line (FE) and over the marginal-cost line (DH). This can be computed as the sum of a rectangle (formed by FED and a horizontal line drawn from D to the vertical axis) and a triangle (formed by DH and the point created by the intersection of the horizontal line drawn from D with the vertical axis).

    The area of any rectangle is base × height. The base = 80/3 and the

$$\text{Height} = P - MC = \frac{160}{3} - \frac{80}{3} = \frac{80}{3}.$$

Therefore, the area of the rectangle is 6,400/9. The area of the right triangle is

$$\frac{1}{2} \times \frac{80}{3} \times \frac{80}{3} = \frac{3,200}{9}.$$

$$\text{Producer surplus} = \frac{3,200}{9} + \frac{6,400}{9} = \frac{\$9,600}{9}.$$

$$\text{Consumer surplus} = \frac{1}{2} \times \frac{80}{3} \times \frac{80}{3} = \frac{\$32,000}{9}.$$

    c.   1. $\dfrac{\$9,600}{9} > \$800$ 2. $\dfrac{\$3,200}{9} < \$800$ 3. $\dfrac{\$12,800}{9} < \$1,600$

3. The policy would not be consistent with efficiency. As the firm considers measures to reduce the magnitude of any spill, it would compare the marginal costs of those measures with the expected marginal reduction in its liability from reducing the magnitude of the spill. Yet the expected marginal reduction in liability would be zero. Firms would pay $X regardless of the size of the spill. Since the amount paid cannot be reduced by controlling the size of the spill, the incentive to take precautions that reduce the size of the spill will be inefficiently low.

4. If "better" means efficient, this common belief is not necessarily true. Damage awards are efficient when they equal the damage caused. Ensuring that the award reflects the actual damage will appropriately internalize the external cost. Larger damage awards are more efficient only to the extent they more closely approximate the actual damage. Because they promote an excessive level of precaution that cannot be justified by the damages, awards that exceed actual cost are inefficient.

CHAPTER 5

1. a. Ten units would be allocated to each period.
    b. $P = \$8 - 0.4q = \$8 - \$4 = \$4$
    c. User cost $= P - MC = \$4 - 2 = \$2$
2. Because in this example the static allocations to the two periods (those that ignore the effects on the other period) are feasible within the 20 units available, the marginal user cost would be zero. With a marginal cost of $4.00, the net benefits in each period would independently be maximized by allocating 10 units to each period. In this example no intertemporal scarcity is present, so price would equal $4.00 marginal cost.
3. Refer to Figure 5.2. In the second version of the model, the lower marginal extraction cost in the second period would raise the marginal net benefit curve in that period (since marginal net benefit is the difference between the unchanged demand curve and the lower MC curve). This would be reflected in Figure 5.2 as a parallel leftward shift out of the curve labeled "present value of marginal net benefits in period 2." This shift would immediately have two consequences: it would move the intersection to the left (implying relatively more would be extracted in the second period), and the intersection would take place at a higher vertical distance from the horizontal axis (implying that the marginal user cost would have risen).

CHAPTER 6

1. According to the microeconomic theory of fertility, the impact would be greater for tuition-funded education. With tuition funding, the cost of education for an additional child would be the present value of all tuitions paid. With property tax funding, the cost of education for an additional child would be miniscule; the amount the family would pay would depend on the value of their property, not on the number of children in the family. Hence, the marginal cost of an additional child is higher with tuition funding, so the impact on the desired number of children would be larger.
2. Industrialization does lower population growth in the third stage (when birthrates fall), but it increases population growth in the second stage (when death rates fall but birthrates remain high). Therefore the statement provides an accurate description of the long run but not the short run.

CHAPTER 7

1. From the hint, $MNB_1/MNB_2 = (1 + k)/(1 + r)$. Notice that when $k = 0$, this reduces to $MNB_2 = MNB_1(1 + r)$, the case we have already considered. When $k = r$, then $MNB_1 = MNB_2$; the effect of stock growth exactly offsets the effect of discounting, and both periods extract the same amount. If $r > k$, then $MNB_2 > MNB_1$. If $r < k$, then $MNB_2 < MNB_1$.

2. a. With a demand curve shifting out over time, the marginal net benefits from a given future allocation increase over time. This raises the marginal user cost (since it is the opportunity cost of using the resource now) and, hence, the total marginal cost. Thus, the initial user cost would be higher.
    b. Less of the resource would be consumed in the present; more would be saved for the future.

3. a. This turns out to have the same effect as the environmental cost pictured in Figures 7.6a and 7.6b. The tax serves to raise the total marginal cost and, hence, the price. This tends to lower the amount consumed in all periods compared to a competitive allocation.
    b. The tax also serves to reduce the cumulative amount extracted because it raises the marginal cost of each unit extracted. Some resources that would have been extracted without the tax would not be extracted with the tax; their after-tax cost to the producer exceeds the cost of the substitute. The price would be higher with the tax in all periods prior to the without-tax switch point. After that time the price would be equal to the price of the substitute with or without the tax.

4. The cumulative amount ultimately taken out of the ground is determined by the point at which the marginal extraction cost equals the maximum price consumers will pay for the depletable resource. In this model the maximum price is the price of the substitute. Neither the monopoly nor the discount rate affects either the marginal extraction cost or the price of the substitute, so they will have no effect on the amount ultimately extracted. The subsidy, however, has the effect of lowering the net price (price minus subsidy) of the substitute. The intersection of marginal extraction cost and the net price will therefore occur when a smaller cumulative amount has been extracted than would be the case in the absence of the subsidy.

CHAPTER 8

1. During a recession, the demand curve shifts inward. If price is held constant, then the quantity demanded is reduced. Since the burden of holding the price up falls on the cartel, while the competitive fringe can keep on producing, the demand reduction causes production to fall most heavily in OPEC nations. This causes the cartel market share to fall. To protect their individual market shares, members start cutting prices. In growing markets, cartel market shares can be protected without cutting prices.

2. a. $$\text{Producer surplus} = \frac{\$3,200}{9}, \qquad P = MC = \frac{\$80}{3}.$$

$$\text{Consumer surplus} = \frac{\$9,600}{9}, \qquad q = \frac{\$80}{3}.$$

   b. This is the mirror image of the monopoly allocation. The net benefits are identical in the two allocations, but they are distributed among producers and consumers rather differently. With this form of price control, the consumer surplus is larger and the producer surplus is smaller than the corresponding concepts when the allocation is governed by a monopoly. Essentially, the rectangle discussed in the answer to part (b) of the second problem in Chapter 4 goes to consumers with price ceilings and to producers in a monopoly.

3. The paper company. The high-cost energy is appropriately assigned to the five paper machines because that is the energy cost that would be eliminated if the machines were shut down. The company would not shut down all energy sources in proportion; it would shut down the most expensive sources. In making a shutdown decision, therefore, it is essential that the machines in question cover the cost of the energy that would be saved if the machines were shut down; otherwise the company is losing money.

4. Peaking plants run only a small percentage of the time, so the capital expenditures remain unused most of the time. Operating costs are incurred only when they are needed. It makes sense, therefore, for utilities to design peaking plants so as to keep capital costs as low as possible, even if it means incurring higher operating cost. Base-load plants, on the other hand, run almost continuously, so the capital costs are prorated over a very large number of kilowatt-hours and therefore are less of a burden.

CHAPTER 9

1. a. Assume that only virgin ores are used. In this case $P = MC_1$, so $10 - 0.5q_1 = 0.5q_1$ or $q_1 = 10$. This implies $MC_1 = 5$. The marginal cost of producing any units using recycled products is clearly higher than 5, so none will be used. Therefore, 10 units would be produced, and all of them would be produced using virgin ores.

   b. With the higher demand curve the price will be high enough to stimulate the producer to make some of the product with recycled materials. The key to solving this problem is recognizing that the producer will equate the marginal costs of products made with recycled materials and those made with virgin ores. Using this fact, we can set $0.5q_1 = 5 + 0.1q_2$ or $q_1 = 10 + 0.2q_2$. Substituting this into the demand function yields

$$P = 20 - 0.5(10 + 0.2q_2 + q_2) \quad \text{or} \quad P = 15 - 0.6q_2.$$

   Solving for $P = MC$ yields

$$15 - 0.6q_2 = 5 + 0.1q_2 \quad \text{or} \quad q_2 = \frac{100}{7}$$

and

$$q_1 = 10 + 0.2\left(\frac{100}{7}\right) = \frac{90}{7}.$$

The solution can be verified by showing $P = MC_1 = MC_2 = \frac{45}{7}$.

2. a. They will not have the same effect. Because the royalty is a per-ton fee, it raises the marginal cost of extraction to the firm, but the bonus bid, which does not affect the marginal cost of extraction, does not. If the mineral has an increasing marginal cost of extraction, less will be extracted with a royalty system than with a bonus bid system because the marginal cost of extraction (including the royalty payment) will hit the backstop price at a smaller cumulative amount extracted.

    b. The bonus bid is consistent with efficiency because it does not distort the allocation over time. The allocation that maximized firm profits before the bonus bid will still maximize it after the bonus bid. While the government shares the profits, it does so without distorting incentives. By raising the marginal cost of extraction, royalty schemes distort incentives.

    c. With a bonus bid scheme, the firm bears the risk. The government gets a fixed payment. The firm can either win big or lose big, depending on how valuable the deposit turns out to be. With the royalty scheme, the risk is shared. If the mine turns out to be very valuable, profits and government fees both go up. If the deposit turns out not to be very valuable, the firm gains little but so does the government.

3. Rising societal disposal cost is certainly one of the factors that should stimulate higher recycling rates, but it is by no means the only one. And as long it is not the only factor, recycling rates will not automatically increase in response. First, this higher social cost must be reflected in increasing marginal disposal costs facing individuals in order to provide the incentive to recycle; rising social costs do not automatically result in rising individual marginal costs. Second, markets must exist for the recycled materials. Collecting them does no good if they can't be put to good use.

CHAPTER 10

1. Since the amount of capacity needed would depend on the maximum flow during the year, the extra cost of expanding capacity during this high-flow period should be reflected in higher prices charged to users during these periods.

2. Assuming the rate was correct, the flat rate would be more efficient because it would confront the user with a positive marginal cost of further consumption. The marginal cost of further consumption with a flat fee is zero.

CHAPTER 11

1. Norland has the comparative advantage in producing A. For every unit of A it produces, Norland gives up two units of B. This is a lower opportunity cost than incurred by Souland, which gives up three units of B for each unit of A produced. Souland has a comparative advantage in producing B.

2. Food stamp programs give the poor more money to spend on food, thus shifting their demand curve for food to the right. Only if supply is perfectly inelastic would this shift in demand increase prices without increasing quantity sold. On the other hand, prices would normally rise somewhat unless the supply curve was perfectly elastic. In general, the more elastic the supply curve, the larger would be the increase in quantity sold and the smaller would be the increase in prices for a given shift in demand.

3. Soil erosion diminishes future productivity, but its prevention requires current outlays. If the renter has a long-term lease, and hence would be able to recoup the investment, he or she might well take efforts to prevent soil erosion. If, however, the renter has a short-term lease, he or she would not be likely to prevent soil erosion. The losses would accrue to the absentee landlord, who would be less knowledgeable about the extent of the problem.

CHAPTER 12

1. The plot being turned into a housing development would have the shortest rotation period because the cost of delaying the harvest would be greatest in this case. It would include an additional cost—the cost of delaying the construction of the housing development—that would have to be factored in, causing net benefits to be maximized at an earlier harvest age.

2. The cost trend is the result of two offsetting trends. Harvesting cost is a function of the volume of wood, so it increases as the volume of wood increases. Since these costs are discounted, however, costs further in the future are discounted more. When the tree growth gets small enough, the discounting effect dominates the growth effect and the present values of the costs decline.

CHAPTER 13

1. a. The maximum sustainable yield is obtained when the marginal benefit of an additional reduction in the population size is zero: $20P - 400 = 0$ or $P = 20,000$ tons. The maximum sustainable yield can then be calculated using the g equation: $g = 4(20) - 0.1(20)^2 = 40$ tons.

    b. The efficient sustained yield can be found by setting marginal cost equal to marginal benefit: $20P - 400 - 2(160 - P)$; therefore, $P = 32.7$, which is a larger population than the one that would produce the maximum sustainable yield.

2. a. No, despite the fact that this approach yields the efficient sustainable yield, this is not an efficient solution. Net benefits would not be maximized because costs would be too high. Everyone would have an incentive to capture as large a share of the quota for him or herself as quickly as possible. This would lead to excessively large boats and would not guarantee that the fishermen who could catch the fish most cheaply would do the harvesting. The net benefits would be smaller than possible.

    b. Yes, this would be efficient. This quota system creates exclusive property rights and, therefore, eliminates the need to catch as much as possible as soon as possible. Each fisherman can proceed on the most individually appropriate schedule because his or her share of the catch is guaranteed. Since the need to rush harvesting is eliminated, the need for excessively large boats is also eliminated. Fishermen with high harvesting costs would find it in their interest to sell their quotas to fishermen with low harvesting costs in order to maximize their return from their quota. These transfers guarantee that the fish are caught by those with the lowest harvesting costs, so net benefits are maximized.

3. The increase in the license fee is represented as a parallel upward shift of the total cost line, whereas the per-unit tax on effort is represented as a leftward rotation of the total cost curve around the zero effort point. The latter increases the marginal cost of fishing effort, while the former has no effect on the marginal cost.

    In the private-property fishery, the license fee will have no effect on effort (unless it is so high as to make fishing unprofitable, in which case the effort will drop to zero), while the tax on effort will unambiguously reduce effort.

    In the free-access fishery, both will reduce effort by exactly the same amount. (Remember, in the free-access fishery the equilibrium occurs where total cost equals total benefit. Since these two policy instruments raise the same revenue, both affect total cost by the same amount.)

CHAPTER 15

1. a. In a cost-effective allocation of emission reduction, the marginal control costs should be equal. So $\$200q_1 = \$100q_2$. Furthermore, the total reduction is 21 units, so $q_1 + q_2 = 21$. Solving the first of these equations for q_1 yields $q_1 - 0.5q_2$. Substituting this into the second yields $0.5q_2 + q_2 = 21$. Solving this for q_2 results in $q_2 = 14$ and $q_1 = 7$.

    b. From the text we know that in a cost-effective allocation with a single receptor

    $$MC_1 = MC_2.$$

    Therefore,

    $$\frac{\$200q_1}{2} = \frac{\$100q_2}{1}$$

Furthermore,

$$a_1(20 - q_1) + a_2(20 - q_2) = 27 \quad \text{or} \quad 2(20 - q_1) + (20 - q_2) = 27.$$

From the first equation it is clear that in a cost-effective allocation, $q_1 = q_2$. It remains to derive the total amount of control using the second equation: $2(20 - q_1) + (20 - q_1) = 27$ so $q_1 = 11$ and $q_2 = 11$.

2. a. From the text we know $T = MC_1 = MC_2$. From Problem 1(a) we know $MC_1 = MC_2 = \$1,400$. Therefore $T = \$1,400$.

   b. Revenue $= T(20 - q_1) + T(20 - q_2) = \$1,400(13) + \$1,400(6) = \$26,600$.

CHAPTER 16

1. a. There would be 12 permits issued, each worth 1 ppm. The price of the permit will be that price that will clear the market; that is

$$MC_1 = MC_2 = P.$$

We know that in equilibrium, $\dfrac{0.3q_1}{1.5} = \dfrac{0.5q_2}{1.0}$, or $q_1 = 2.5q_2$

Further,

$$a_1(20 - q_1)a_2(20 - q_2)12 \quad \text{or} \quad 1.5(20 - 2.5q_2) + 1.0(20 - q_2)12.$$

Solving this equation yields $q_2 = 9$ and $q_1 = 20$. So,

$$P = \frac{0.3(20)}{1.5} = \frac{0.5(8)}{1.0} = \$4 \text{ per ppm.}$$

   b. Permits auctioned off

First source $= P(20 - q_1)a_1 = \$4(20 - 20)1.5 = \$0$,

Second source $= P(20 - q_2)a_2 = \$4(20 - 8)1.0 = \$48$.

The six permits are worth \$24, so the first source would sell all its permits for a gain of \$24. The second source would keep its initial allocation of six permits and would buy six more at a cost of \$24. The cost to the second source exactly balances the gain to the first.

CHAPTER 17

1. The emission charge equalizes marginal cost, a required condition for cost-effectiveness. The subsidies induce utilities to choose options with a higher marginal cost. By equalizing their after-subsidy marginal costs, utilities will minimize their outlays. This will not minimize total costs of control, since a greater reliance on scrubbers will result than would be cost-effective.

2. High transfer costs in this context arise from a combination of high charges and large amounts of uncontrolled emissions. This circumstance arises when the marginal cost of control function rises steeply at relatively low levels of control. Since the charge is equal to the marginal cost of control, high marginal control costs imply a high charge rate. Furthermore, if the function rises steeply at relatively low levels of control, then there are large amounts of emissions to which this high rate of charge is applied. Multiplying a high charge times a large amount of uncontrolled emissions yields high transfer costs.

CHAPTER 19

1. a. This allocation would be similar to that in Problem 2(a) in Chapter 15. The price would be $1,400. In the final allocation, the first source would control 7 units and would hold 13 permits, whereas the second source would control 14 units and hold 6 permits. The first source would have to purchase 4 permits—the 13 it needs to minimize cost minus the 9 it was initially given—at a total cost of $5,600. The second source would sell 4 permits, thereby moving from the 10 held initially to the 6 it needs to minimize costs, so it would gain $5,600 from the sale.

    b. We know that in the final equilibrium, the marginal control cost will be equal. Since for the third source the marginal control cost is constant at $1,600, this will determine the final marginal control cost. The final permit price will be $1,600. The control allocation can be found for the first and second sources by choosing the level of control that yields a marginal control cost equal to $1,600. Thus $1,600 = $200q_1$, so $q_1 = 8$ and $1,600 = $100q_2$, so $q_2 = 16$.

      The third source will have to clean up sufficient additional emissions to meet the target. Uncontrolled emissions were stated to be equal to 50. The first two sources would clean up 24 units, leaving 26 units uncontrolled. Since the target emission level is stated as 19 units, the third source would have to clean up the remaining 7 units ($q_3 = 7$). The third source would have to purchase three permits since it received no initial allocation. Two would be purchased from the second source, and one would be purchased from the first.

Glossary

Acid Rain—The atmospheric deposition of acidic substances.

Acute Toxicity—The degree of harm caused to living organisms as a result of short-term exposure to a substance.

Aerobic—Water containing sufficient dissolved oxygen concentrations to sustain organisms requiring oxygen.

Age Structure Effect—Changes in the age distribution induced by the rate of population growth.

Alternative Fuels—Unconventional fuels such as ethanol and methanol.

Ambient Permit System—A type of transferable permit system in which permits are defined in terms of the right to affect the concentration at a receptor site by a given amount. This design can achieve a cost-effective allocation of control responsibility when the objective is to achieve a prespecified concentration objective at a specific number of receptor locations.

Ambient Standards—Legal ceilings placed on the concentration level of specific pollutants in the air, soil, or water.

Anaerobic—Water containing insufficient dissolved oxygen concentrations to sustain life.

Anthropocentric—Human-centered.

Aquaculture—The controlled raising and harvesting of fish. (Called "mariculture" when, as is the case with some salmon fisheries, the facilities are in the ocean.) Aquaculture can provide the opportunity to create a private-property regime for affected fisheries.

Asset—An entity that has value and forms part of the wealth of the owner.

Assigned Amount Obligations—The level of greenhouse gas emissions that ratifying nations are authorized under the Kyoto Protocol.

Automobile Certification Program—The testing of automobiles at the factory for conformity to federal emissions standards.

Average-Cost Pricing—When prices charged for resource use are based on average costs. (Sometimes used by regulatory agencies to ensure that regulated firms make zero economic profits, but it is not normally efficient.)

Backstop Resource—A substitute resource available in sufficiently large quantities that its marginal user cost is zero.

Base-Load Plants—Electric generators that produce virtually all the time. (They generally have high fixed costs, but low variable costs.)

Benefit/Cost Analysis—An analysis of the quantified gains (benefits) and losses (costs) of an action.

Best Available Technology Economically Achievable—A more stringent effluent standard than best practicable control technology, which has been defined by the EPA as "the very best control and treatment measures that have been or are capable of being achieved."

Best Practicable Control Technology—An effluent standard that considers the cost of the pollution control technology in relation to the benefits received from its use.

Biochemical Oxygen Demand—The measure of the oxygen demand placed on a stream by any particular volume of effluent.

Block Pricing—A form of pricing in which the charge per unit consumption is held fixed until a threshold is reached where a new per-unit charge is imposed for all consumption beyond the threshold. For increasing block pricing, the per-unit charge after the threshold is higher.

Boserup Hypothesis—A negative feedback loop in which increasing population triggers an increasing demand for agricultural products, which in turn stimulates innovations that allow more intensive, but still sustainable agriculture.

Bubble Policy—Specific transferable permit program for controlling air pollution. Allows existing sources to use emission reduction credits to partially or completely satisfy state implementation plan emissions standards.

Bycatch—Untargeted fish that are unintentionally caught as part of the harvest of targeted species.

Cap-and-Trade System—A form of emissions trading where the government specifies a cap on emissions and allocates allowances to emission sources based upon this cap. These allowances are freely transferable among sources. Distinguished from the credit form of emission trading.

Carbon Tax—A policy that would control climate modification by placing a per-unit emissions tax on all carbon-emitting sources.

Carrying Capacity—The level of population a given habitat can sustain indefinitely.

Cartel—A collusive agreement among producers to restrict production and raise prices. In this case the group tends to act like a monopolist and to share the gains from collusive behavior.

Cash Crop—An agricultural commodity that can be directly sold for money (as opposed, for example, to a crop raised purely for consumption by the family).

Cash for Clunkers—Under this transferable permit program, emission reduction credits can be earned by removing high-polluting vehicles from service and recycling them. Usually owners of these vehicles are offered a cash payment to surrender their vehicles.

Chapter 11—A provision in the North American Free Trade Agreement that protects investors from government regulations that decrease the value of their investments.

Choke Price—The maximum price anyone would be willing to pay for a unit of the resource. At higher prices, the demand for that resource would be zero.

Chronic Toxicity—The degree of harm caused to living organisms as a result of continued or prolonged exposure to a substance.

Clawson-Knetsch Method—One method for using travel costs to estimate the recreational value of a resource.

Clean Development Mechanism—An emissions trading mechanism set up under the Kyoto Protocol that allows industrialized countries to invest in greenhouse gas reducing strategies in developing countries and to use the resulting certified reductions to meet their assigned amount obligations.

Closed System—No inputs enter the system, and no inputs leave the system.

Coase Theorem—A remarkable proposition, named after Nobel Laureate Ronald Coase, that suggests that in the absence of transaction costs, an efficient allocation will result regardless of the property rule chosen by the court.

Cobweb Model—A theory in which long lags between planting decisions and harvest can influence farmer's production decisions in such a way as to intensify or dampen price fluctuations.

Command and Control—Controlling pollution by means of a system of government-mandated legal restrictions. Under this approach the government has the responsibility not only for setting the environmental targets, but also for allocating the source-specific responsibilities for meeting those targets.

Common-Pool Resource—A resource that is shared among several users.

Common-Property Regimes—A property rights system in which resources are managed collectively by a group.

Comparative Advantage—In trade theory a comparative advantage prevails for products that have the lowest opportunity cost of production.

Competitive Equilibrium—The resource allocation at which supply and demand are equal when all agents are price takers.

Composite Asset—An asset made up of many interrelated parts.

Composition of Demand Effect—Shifts in demand brought about by changes in the relative cost of inputs. (For example, rising costs of ores coupled with stable prices for recycled inputs could make the products of firms relying more heavily on recycled inputs relatively less expensive and hence more attractive to consumers.)

Congestion Externalities—Higher costs imposed on others resulting from an attempt to use resources at a higher-than-optimal capacity.

Congestion Pricing—Charging higher tolls during peak hours to discourage vehicle traffic (and the resulting air pollution) and encourage public transit ridership.

Conjoint Analysis—A survey-based technique that derives willingness to pay by having respondents choose between alternate states of the world where each state of the world has a specified set of attributes and a price.

Conjunctive Use—The combined management of surface and groundwater to optimize their joint use and to minimize the adverse effects of excessive reliance on a single source.

Conservation Easements—Legal agreements between landowners and land trusts or government agencies that permanently limit uses of land in specifically defined ways in order to protect its conservation value.

Constant Dollar—Purging increases in output measures that are due to price increases.

Consumer Surplus—The value of a good or service to consumers above the price they have to pay for it. Calculated as the area under the demand curve that lies above the price.

Consumption—The amount of goods and services consumed by households.

Contingent Ranking—A valuation technique that asks respondents to rank alternative situations involving different levels of environmental amenity (or risk). These rankings can then be used to establish trade-offs between more of the environmental amenity (or risk) and less (or more) of other goods that can be expressed in monetary terms.

Contingent Valuation—A survey method used to ascertain willingness to pay for services or environmental amenities.

Conventional Pollutants—Relatively common substances found in most parts of the country, and presumed to be dangerous only in high concentrations.

Corporate Average Fuel Economy (CAFE) Standards—Minimum average miles-per-gallon standards imposed on each auto manufacturer for new vehicles sold in a specific vehicle class. Autos are in one class and SUVs and light trucks in another.

Cost-Benefit Ratio Criterion—No activity where the present value of net benefits is less than zero should be undertaken.

Credit Trading—A form of emissions trading where the government specifies source-specific baselines for authorized emissions. Firms that control more than required by this baseline are allowed to have the excess certified as an emissions reduction credit. This credit can then be transferred to another source to use in meeting its baseline. Distinguished from the cap-and-trade approach.

Criteria Pollutants—Conventional air pollutants with ambient standards set by the Environmental Protection Agency (includes sulfur oxides, particulate matter, carbon monoxide, ozone, nitrogen dioxide, and lead).

Current Reserves—Known resources that can profitably be extracted at current prices.

Dampened Oscillation—In the absence of further supply shocks, the amplitude of price and quantity fluctuations decreases to the point of equilibrium.

Debt-Nature Swap—The purchase and cancellation of developing-country debt in exchange for environmentally related action on the part of the debtor nation.

Deep Ecology—The view that the environment has an intrinsic value, a value that is independent of human interests.

Degradable—Pollutants that degrade, or break into component parts, within water.

Delaney Clause—A provision in U.S. law that states that no food additive should be deemed safe if it is found to induce cancer in humans or animals.

Demand Curve—A function that relates the quantity of a commodity or service consumers wish to purchase to the price of that commodity.

Descriptive Economics—The branch of economics that is concerned with describing alternative resource allocations without forming a judgment as to their desirability. Concerned with "what is."

Differentiated Regulation—Imposing more stringent regulations on one class of sources (such as new vehicles) than on others (such as used vehicles).

Discount Rate—The rate used to convert a stream of benefits and/or costs into its present value.

Dissolved Oxygen—Oxygen that naturally occurs in water and is usable by living organisms.

Divisible Consumption—One person's consumption of a good diminishes the amount available for others. (For example, if I use some timber to build my house, you receive no benefits from that timber.)

Double Dividend—A second welfare advantage that accrues to revenue-raising pollution control policy instruments (over and above the welfare gain due to pollution reduction) when the revenue is used to reduce distortionary taxes (thereby reducing the welfare losses associated with those taxes).

Downward Spiral Hypothesis—A positive feedback loop in which increasing population triggers a cycle of sustained, reinforced environmental degradation.

Durability Obsolescence—A depreciation in the value of a current product when its usefulness declines due to wear and tear.

Dynamic Efficiency—The chief normative economic criterion for choosing among various allocations occurring at different points in time. An allocation satisfies the dynamic efficiency criterion if it maximizes the present value of net benefits that could be received from all possible ways of allocating those resources over time.

Dynamic Efficient Sustained Yield—The sustained yield that produces the highest present value of net benefits.

Ecological Footprint—A sustainability indicator that attempts to measure the amount of ecologically productive land that is required to support the resource demands and absorb the wastes of a given population and their economic activities.

Economies of Scale—The percentage increase in output exceeds the percentage increase in all inputs. Equivalently, average cost falls as output expands.

Efficient Level of Durability—The level of durability that maximizes the present value of net benefits society receives from the product.

Efficient Pricing—A system of prices that supports an efficient allocation of resources. Generally, efficient pricing is achieved when prices are equal to total marginal cost.

Elasticity of Substitution—A measure of the degree to which two factor inputs complement or substitute for one another in production.

Emission Charge—A charge levied on emitters for each unit of a pollutant emitted into the air or water.

Emission Permit System—A type of transferable permit system in which the permits are defined in terms of the right to emit a stipulated amount of emissions. This design can be used to achieve a cost-effective allocation of control responsibility for uniformly mixed pollutants.

Emissions Banking—Firms are allowed to store emissions reduction credits or allowances for subsequent use or sale.

Emissions Reduction Credit (ERC)—Part of a transferable permits system. Any source reducing emissions beyond required levels can receive a credit for excess reductions. These can be banked for future use or sold to other sources.

Emission Standard—A legal limit placed on the amount of a pollutant an individual source may emit.

Emissions Trading—An economic incentive based alternative to the command-and-control approach to pollution control. Under emissions trading, a regulatory agency specifies an allowable level of pollution that will be tolerated and allocates emission authorizations among sources of pollution. Total emissions authorized by these allowances cannot exceed the allowable level. Pollution sources are free to buy, sell, or otherwise trade allowances. The two specific forms of emissions trading are the cap-and-trade system and credit trading. In addition to its use to describe this generic form of pollution control policy, this term also has been used to describe some specific programs such as the Kyoto Protocol's greenhouse gas trading program, the earliest U.S. trading program for criteria pollutants, and the current CO_2 program in the European Union.

Enforceability—Property rights should be secure from involuntary seizure or encroachment from others.

Entropy—Amount of energy not available for work.

Environmental Kuznets Curve—An empirical relationship that shows environmental degradation first increasing, then decreasing, as per capita income increases.

Environmental Sustainability—This definition of sustainability is fulfilled if the physical stocks of designated resources do not decline.

Eutrophic—A body of water containing an excess of nutrients.

Exclusivity—All benefits and costs accrued as a result of owning and using the resources should accrue to the owner, and only the owner, either directly or indirectly by sale to others.

Expanded Producer Responsibility—The belief that manufacturers of products should have the responsibility to take the packaging and the products back at the end of their useful lives in order to promote efficient packaging and recycling. (Also called the "take-back" principle.)

Expected Present Value of Net Benefits—The sum over possible outcomes of the present value of net benefits for a policy, where each outcome is weighted by its probability of occurrence.

Expected Value—In situations where the value of a resource depends on which of several outcomes might prevail, the expected value of a resource is the sum over all outcomes of the likelihood of each outcome multiplied by the value that would prevail in that outcome.

External Diseconomy—The affected party is damaged by an externality. (For example, my well is polluted by chemicals from a factory next door.)

External Economy—The affected party is benefited by an externality. (For example, my neighbor decides not to develop a wetland that serves as a recharge area for my water supply.)

Externality—The welfare of some agent, either a firm or household, depends on the activities of some other agent. The externality can take the form of either an external economy or external diseconomy.

Fashion Obsolescence—A depreciation in the value of current products when consumers prefer new products for reasons of taste.

Feebates—A system that combines taxes on purchases of new high-emitting vehicles with subsidies for new purchases of low-emitting vehicles. The revenue from the taxes is supposed to serve as the primary source of funding for the subsidies.

Feedback Loop—A closed path that connects an action to its effect on the surrounding conditions that, in turn, can influence further action.

Female Availability Effect—A reduction (or increase) in the labor force participation of women due to an increase (or reduction) in the rate of population growth.

First Law of Thermodynamics—Neither energy nor matter can be created or destroyed.

Fixed Cost—Production costs that do not vary with output.

Free-Rider Effect—When a good exhibits both the consumptive indivisibility and nonexcludability properties, consumers may enjoy the benefits of goods purchased by others without paying anything themselves. (For example, countries that decide not to take any steps to control global warming can "free ride" on the steps taken by others.)

Functional Obsolescence—A depreciation in the value of a current product caused by the arrival of a new product that can perform the function in a superior manner.

Fund Pollutants—Pollutants for which the environment has some absorptive capacity; if the rate of emission exceeds this capacity, then fund pollutants accumulate.

Gaia Hypothesis—An example of a negative feedback loop suggesting that, within limits, the world is a living organism with a complex feedback system that seeks an optimal physical and chemical environment.

Genetically Modified Organisms—A term that designates crops that carry new traits that have been inserted through advanced genetic engineering methods involving the manipulation of DNA.

Genuine Progress Indicator—A sustainability indicator that attempts to establish the trend of well-being over time by taking into account the effects of development on resource depletion, pollution damage, and distribution of income.

Gini Coefficient—One measure of the degree of inequality in income or owned assets such as land or financial wealth. Values can range from 0.0 (perfect equality—every household is the same) to 1.0 (perfect inequality—one household owns everything).

Global Environmental Facility—An international organization, loosely connected to the World Bank, that provides loans and grants to developing countries to facilitate projects that contribute to solving such global problems as protecting the oceans, preserving biodiversity, protecting the ozone layer, and controlling climate modification. The fund uses the "marginal external cost" rule to allocate funds.

Global Pollutant—A pollutant that travels to the upper atmosphere and causes damage. (Examples include ozone-depleting and greenhouse gases.)

Government Failure—An inefficiency produced by some government action.

Greenhouse Gases—Global pollutants that contribute to climate modification by absorbing the long-wave (infrared) radiation, thereby trapping heat that would otherwise radiate into space. (Includes carbon dioxide, methane, and chlorofluorocarbons, among others.)

Groundwater—Subsurface water that occurs beneath a water table in soils, rocks, or fully saturated geological formations.

Groundwater Contamination—Pollution that leaches into a water-saturated region.

Hartwick Rule—The weak sustainability criterion can be fulfilled if all scarcity rent from depletable resources is invested in capital.

Health Threshold—A standard to be defined with a margin of safety sufficiently high that no adverse health effects would be suffered by any member of the population as long as the pollutant concentration is at least the minimum standard level.

Hedonic Property Studies—A valuation technique that allows the value of an environmental amenity (or risk) to be determined from differences in the values of property exposed to different levels of the amenity (or risk).

Hedonic Wage Studies—A valuation technique that allows the value of an environmental amenity (or risk) to be determined from differences in the values of wages paid to workers exposed to different levels of the amenity (or risk).

High-Grading—Discarding low-value fish in favor of high-value fish in order to increase the income derived from a harvest quota.

Horizontal Equity—Treating people with equal incomes equally.

Host Fees—Fees collected from disposers that are used to compensate a community hosting a regional landfill. Designed to increase the willingness of communities to host these facilities.

Human Development Index—A socioeconomic indicator constructed by the United Nations Development Program that is based upon longevity, knowledge, and income.

Hypothetical Bias—Ill-considered responses that may arise in surveys based on contrived rather than actual situations or choices.

Impact Analysis—An analysis that attempts to make explicit, to the extent possible, the consequences of proposed actions. May mix quantitative with qualitative information and monetized with nonmonetized information.

Income Elasticity—Measures the percentage change in demand for commodities or services in response to a 1% change in income.

Individual Transferable Quotas (ITQs)—A means of protecting a fishery and the income derived from it by limiting the number of fish caught. Individual fishermen are allocated quotas that entitle them to portions of the authorized total allowable catch. These quotas can be transferred to other fishermen or used to legalize their harvest.

Indivisible Consumption—One person's consumption of a good does not diminish the amount available for others. (For example, the benefits I receive from controlling greenhouse gases do not diminish the benefits you receive.)

Information Bias—Arises when contingent valuation survey respondents are forced to value attributes with which they have little or no experience.

Information Worker—A person whose income originates primarily in the manipulation of symbols or information.

Intangible Benefits—Benefits that cannot be easily assigned a monetary value.

Interactive Resources—The size of the resource stock is determined jointly by biological considerations and actions taken by humans.

Joint and Several Liability—A common-law doctrine used to assign the cost of cleaning up Superfund sites that states that any subset of parties responsible for the contamination can be assessed the entire cost regardless of the magnitude of their individual contribution.

Joint Implementation—A project-based emission trading mechanism set up under the Kyoto Protocol in which an investor from one industrialized country can get emission reduction credits for certified greenhouse gas reductions resulting from investments in a project in another industrialized country.

Kyoto Protocol—An international agreement to control greenhouse gases that went into effect in February 2005.

Land Trust—An organization specifically established to hold conservation easements and to ensure that the use of land conforms to the terms of the easements.

Latency—The period between exposure to a toxic substance and the detection of harm caused by that substance.

Law of Comparative Advantage—A country or region should specialize in the production of those commodities for which it has a comparative advantage.

Law of Diminishing Marginal Productivity—In the presence of a fixed factor, successively larger additions of variable factors will eventually lead to a decline in the marginal productivity of the variable factors.

Law of Diminishing Returns—The relationship between inputs and outputs when some inputs are increased and others are fixed, eventually leading to the decreased productivity of the variable inputs.

Lead Phaseout Program—A transferable permit program designed to lower the costs of phasing out lead in gasoline as well as to eliminate lead earlier than otherwise would have been possible. It allocated transferable rights to use lead in refining gasoline to refiners. The number of rights declined over time until at the end of the program they expired.

Liability Rules—Rules that award monetary compensation from an injurer to an injured party after damage has occurred. Valuation must be accomplished by the courts.

Low-Emission Vehicles—A class of vehicles that can satisfy much more stringent emissions standards than currently imposed on conventional vehicles.

Marginal Cost of Exploration—The marginal cost of finding additional units of the resource.

Marginal Cost Pricing—Basing the prices charged for resource use upon marginal costs. (This pricing scheme is generally consistent with efficiency.)

Marginal External Cost Rule—Used by the Global Environmental Facility to disperse funds. According to this rule, the facility will fund additional expenses associated with investments that contribute to the global environment (produce positive global net benefits), but cannot be justified domestically (since the domestic marginal costs exceed domestic marginal benefits). Countries are expected to pick up that portion of the expenses that can be justified domestically (where the domestic marginal benefits exceed domestic marginal costs).

Marginal Extraction Cost—The cost of mining an additional unit of resource.

Marginal Opportunity Cost—The additional cost of providing the last unit of a good as measured by what is given up.

Marginal User Cost—Present value of forgone future opportunity costs at the margin.

Marginal Willingness to Pay—The amount of money an individual is willing to pay for the last unit of a good or service.

Marine Reserve—A specific geographic area that prohibits harvesting of fish and enjoys a very high level of protection from other threats such as pollution.

Market Economy—An economic system in which resource allocation decisions are guided by prices that result from the voluntary production and purchasing decisions by private consumers and producers.

Market Failure—An inefficient allocation produced by a market economy.

Maximum Net Present Value Criterion—Resources should be allocated to those uses that maximize the present value of the net benefits received from all possible uses of those resources.

Maximum Sustainable Yield—The maximum harvest that could be sustained forever.

Mean Annual Increment—The cumulative volume of a forest stand at the end of each decade divided by the number of years the stand has been in existence.

Microeconomic Theory of Fertility—A theory that attempts to attribute differences in fertility to the economic environment within which childbearing decisions are made.

Mineralogical Threshold—A sharp discontinuity in the manner in which minerals are extracted; the existence of this threshold implies a sharp discontinuity in the marginal extraction cost.

Minimum Viable Population—The level of population below which regeneration is negative, leading ultimately to extinction.

Model—Formal or informal framework for analysis that highlights some areas of the problem in order to better understand complex relationships.

Monopoly—A situation in which the seller side of the market is dominated by a single producer.

Montreal Protocol—An international agreement to control ozone-depleting gases.

Multilateral Fund—A fund set up by the parties to the Montreal Protocol to help developing countries meet the phaseout requirements for ozone-depleting gases.

Myopia—Nearsightedness; excessive concern for the present.

Natural Capital—The endowment of environmental and natural resources.

Natural Equilibrium—Stock levels that persist in the absence of outside influences.

Natural Resource Curse Hypothesis—Suggests that countries with abundant natural resources are likely to grow more slowly than their less-endowed counterparts.

Negative Feedback Loop—A closed path of action and reaction that is self-limiting rather than self-reinforcing.

Negligence—A doctrine in tort law suggesting that the party responsible for a tortious act owes a duty to the affected party to exercise due care. Failure to fulfill that duty can lead to a requirement for the injurer to pay compensation to the victim.

Net Adjusted Savings—An indicator that attempts to measure whether an economy is acting sustainably when judged by the weak sustainability criterion. (Formerly called genuine savings.)

Net Benefit—The excess of benefits over costs resulting from some allocation.

Netting—A transferable permit program for air pollution control in which firms undergoing modifications or expansion may avoid New Source Review requirements if the resulting increase in emissions falls under a prespecified threshold.

New Scrap—Waste composed of the residual materials generated during production. (Also called preconsumer scrap.)

New Source Bias—A bias in investment choices related to the decision whether to build a new source versus keeping an old source running longer. The bias results when new sources of pollution face more stringent control requirements than existing sources, resulting in higher compliance costs.

New Source Performance Standard—A legally specified amount of emission control required of new market entrants regardless of production location. States can require more, but not less, than this degree of control.

New Source Review Process—All large new or expanding sources are subject to preconstruction review and permitting. These firms are typically subjected to more stringent requirements. The specific requirements depend on whether the source is attempting to locate in an attainment or a nonattainment area.

Nonattainment Region—A region in which the pollution concentrations exceed the ambient standards, so more stringent environmental regulations are in effect.

Noncompliance Penalty—A charge used to reduce the profitability of noncompliance with pollution control requirements. It is designed to eliminate all the economic advantage gained from noncompliance.

Nonexcludability—No individual or group can be excluded from enjoying the benefits a resource may confer, whether they contribute to its provision or not.

Nonpoint Sources—Diffuse sources such as runoff from agricultural or developed land.

Nonrenewable Resources—Resources that cannot be reproduced during a human time scale, so their supply is finite and limited.

Nonuniformly Mixed Pollutants—For these pollutants, the damage they cause is a function not only of the amount of emissions, but also the location of the emissions sources. (Examples include particulates and lead.)

Nonuse (Passive Use) Values—Resource values that arise from motivations other than personal use.

Normative Economics—The branch of economics that is concerned with evaluating the desirability of alternative resource allocations. It is concerned with "what ought to be."

Occupational Hazards—Risks undertaken during the course of a job.

Offset Policy—One specific transferable permit program. New emitters attempting to enter a nonattainment area must secure sufficient emissions reduction credits from existing sources to cover 120% of their emissions.

Old Scrap—Waste recovered from products used by consumers. (Also called post-consumer scrap.)

Open-Access Resources—Common-pool resources with unrestricted access.

Open System—A system that imports and exports matter or energy.

Opportunity Cost—The net benefit forgone because the resource providing the service can no longer be used in its next-most-beneficial use.

Optimal—Best or most favorable option.

Optimization Procedure—A systematic method for finding the optimal means of accomplishing an objective.

Option Value—The value people place on having the option to use a resource in the future.

Output Measure—A measure currently used in national income accounting to indicate how many goods and services have been produced.

Overallocation—More than the optimal level of a resource is dedicated to a given use or time period.

Overshoot and Collapse—A forecast that involves exceeding the natural carrying capacity of the environment, with the consequence that society collapses.

Oxygen Sag—A point of low dissolved oxygen concentration generally located around effluent injection points.

Ozone-Depleting Gases—Global pollutants that destroy the stratospheric ozone layer. (Includes chlorofluorocarbons and halons, among others.)

Pareto Optimality—An allocation such that no reallocation of resources could benefit any person without lowering the net benefits for at least one other person. (Named after economist Vilfredo Pareto.)

Pay-As-You-Drive (PAYD) Insurance—A system in which an individual's annual premium for automobile insurance is calculated by multiplying a rating factor times the number of miles driven. It is designed to reduce inefficiency by internalizing those costs of accidents that are related to the amount of driving.

Peaking Units—Those electricity-producing facilities used only during peak periods. (They generally have low fixed costs, but high variable costs.)

Peak-Load Pricing—Charging resource users during the peak period the higher cost of supplying resources during that period. The surcharge during the peak period is designed to cover the cost of expansion since the need to expand is triggered by increased demands during the peak period.

Peak Periods—Times of especially high resource demand. (For example, the demand for electricity during the hottest part of the summer when air-conditioning is in heavy use.)

Pecuniary Externalities—External effects that are transmitted through higher prices. (For example, the value of my land increases because surrounding employers expand their operations, thereby creating a scarcity of housing in the immediate area.) Unlike most externalities, pecuniary externalities do not generally result in inefficient allocations.

Performance Bond—An amount of money required to be placed into a trust fund by those initiating risky projects to cover the costs of any anticipated damages.

Persistent Pollutants—Inorganic synthetic pollutants with complex molecular structures that are not effectively broken down in water.

Planned Obsolescence—Attempts by producers to increase production by selling products with a shorter life span.

Planning Horizon—The time period over which the benefits and costs are considered in time-related decisions. For a specific investment such as a power plant, for example, the planning horizon might correspond to the useful life of the project. For forestry, it could either correspond to the age of the stand of trees when harvested (the finite planning horizon) or extend forever (the infinite planning horizon). In addition to considering the age at which to harvest the stock (the focus of the finite planning horizon model), the infinite horizon model must also take into account a perpetual sequence of forestry decisions (such as restocking, harvesting, preservation, and so on).

Point Sources—Sources of pollution that discharge effluent through a readily identifiable emission point such as an outfall or discharge pipe. (Most industrial and municipal sources are point sources.)

Pollution Absorptive Capacity—The ability of the environment to absorb pollutants without incurring damage.

Pollution Haven Hypothesis—Stricter environmental regulations in one country either encourage domestic production facilities to locate in countries with less stringent regulations or encourage increased imports from those countries.

Porter Hypothesis—Firms facing stringent environmental regulations derive a competitive advantage because they are forced to innovate. Innovation typically increases productivity.

Positive Feedback Loop—A closed path of action and reaction that is self-reinforcing rather than self-limiting.

Positive Net Present Value Criterion—This criterion requires the present value of benefits to be larger than the present value of costs for any project that is to be undertaken.

Potential Reserves—The amount of resource reserves potentially available at different price levels.

Present Value—The current discounted value of a stream of benefits and/or costs over time.

Prevention of Significant Deterioration Policy—A U.S. policy designed to prevent the degradation of air quality in attainment regions.

Price Controls—The establishment of maximum or minimum prices by the government.

Primary Effects—The direct, measurable effects of an action.

Primary Standard—An ambient air pollution standard designed to protect human health.

Prior Appropriation Doctrine—Entitlements for water are allocated to the agent who diverts and first puts water to a beneficial use.

Private Marginal Cost—The cost of producing an additional unit of the resource that is born by the producer.

Producer Surplus—The value of a good or service to producers above the cost to them of producing it. Calculated as the area below the price line that is above marginal cost.

Product Charges—A charge imposed on a product that is associated with emissions (such as a gasoline tax). This indirect form of controlling emissions is used when is it difficult to place the charge directly on emissions.

Production Function—A mathematically expressed relationship between inputs and outputs.

Property Rights—A bundle of entitlements defining the owner's rights, privileges, and limitations for use of the resource.

Property Rules—Legal rules that govern the initial allocation of entitlements. Valuation of the entitlements is left to the market.

Proportional Distribution—The net benefits from a policy received by various income groups are proportional to income.

Proposition 65—A California law that requires companies producing, using, or transporting one or more of the specified substances in amounts over the "safe harbor" threshold to notify those who are potentially impacted.

Prototype Carbon Fund—An intermediary set up to encourage developing-country reductions in greenhouse gases. It acts as a kind of mutual fund by picking promising investment opportunities under the clean development mechanism for donor countries and transferring the resulting emission reduction credits to the donors for use in meeting their assigned amount obligations.

Public Good—A resource characterized by nonexclusivity and indivisibility.

Real Consumption Per Capita—Constant-dollar consumption divided by population.

Real-Resource Costs—As opposed to transfer costs, these are costs borne by both private parties and society as a whole because they involve the loss of net benefits, not merely their transfer.

Recycling Surcharge—Imposed at the time of commodity purchase, this charge attempts to recover from the consumer the cost of recycling and/or disposal of the commodity after its useful life.

Regional Pollutants—Pollutants that can cause damage some distance from the emission source. (Examples include the precursors for acid rain and tropospheric ozone.)

Regressive Distribution—Net benefits from a policy received by various income groups represent a larger portion of the income of the rich than of the poor.

Renewable Portfolio Standards—These standards specify enforceable targets and deadlines for producing specific proportions of electricity from renewable resources.

Renewable Resources—Resources that can be naturally regenerated over time on a human time scale.

Rent Seeking—The use of resources in lobbying and other activities directed at securing increased profits through protective regulation or legislation.

Replacement Rate—The level of the total fertility rate that is compatible with a stationary population.

Res Nullius **Regime**—A property rights system in which no one owns or exercises control over resources. Resources covered by this regime can usually be exploited on a first-come, first-served basis.

Resource Endowment—The natural occurrence of resources in the earth's crust and atmosphere.

Resource Taxonomy—A classification system used to characterize the nature of natural resource stocks in terms of the certainty of the stock estimates and the economic likelihood of their recovery.

Retirement Effect—The increase (or decrease) of the percentage of the population composed of individuals over 65 years of age induced by a low (or high) population growth rate.

Return Flow—A term used in water management that refers to the unconsumed portion from an upstream user's water allocation that will eventually return to the watercourse (and, hence, be available to a downstream user).

Riparian Rights—Allocates the right to use water to the owner of the land adjacent to the water, as long as no adverse effects are imposed on other rights holders.

Risk-Free Cost of Capital—Rate of return earned on an investment when the risk of earning more or less than expected returns is zero.

Risk-Neutrality—An agent who has no preference between options that produce the same expected value.

Risk Premium—Additional rate of return required to compensate the owners of the capital when the expected and actual returns may differ. It represents compensation for a willingness to undertake some risk.

Scale Effects—How the size of an operation affects average costs.

Scarcity Rent—Producer's surplus that persists in long-run equilibrium due to fixed supply or increasing costs.

Secondary Effects—Indirect consequences of an action; beyond primary effects.

Secondary Standard—An ambient standard designed to protect those aspects of human welfare other than health.

Second Law of Thermodynamics—Entropy, the energy not available for work, increases.

Severance Tax—A tax levied on minerals as they are extracted.

Socialist Economy—A centrally planned economy where the means of production are controlled by the government.

Social Marginal Cost—The cost of producing an additional unit of the resource that is borne by society at large. Generally includes private marginal costs plus external marginal costs.

Stable Equilibrium—A level of stock that will be restored following temporary shocks.

Starting-Point Bias—Arises when a contingent valuation survey respondent is asked to check off his or her answer from a predetermined range of possibilities and the answers depend on the range specified by the survey instrument.

Static Efficiency—The chief normative economic criterion for choosing among various allocations when time is not an important consideration. An allocation satisfies the static efficiency criterion if it maximizes the net benefits from all possible uses of the resource.

Static Efficient Sustained Yield—The sustained catch level in a fishery that produces the largest annual recurring net benefit.

Stationary Population—A population in which age- and sex-specific fertility rates yield a birthrate that is constant and equal to the death rate, so the population growth rate is zero.

Stationary Source—An immobile pollution source. (Industrial sources, for example, as opposed to automobiles.)

Statistically Significant—Observed differences are unlikely to result from pure chance.

Steady-State Economy—Characterized by constant stocks of people and physical wealth maintained at some chosen, desirable level by a low rate of throughput.

Stock Pollutants—Pollutants that accumulate in the environment because the environment has little or no absorptive capacity for them.

Strategic Bias—A respondent provides a biased answer to a contingent valuation survey in order to influence a particular outcome.

Strategic Petroleum Reserve—A petroleum stockpile established by an importing nation to minimize the damage that could be done by an embargo imposed by a foreign supplier. It would serve as an alternative source of supply for a short period.

Stratosphere—The atmosphere that lies above the troposphere. It extends to about 31 miles above the earth's surface.

Strict Liability—A tort law doctrine requiring that the party responsible for pollution contamination compensate victims for damage caused. Differs from negligence in that the victim does not have to prove negligence by the injurer.

Strong Global Scarcity Hypothesis—According to this hypothesis, scarcity becomes sufficiently deep that the output of food is not able to keep pace with population growth; per capita food production declines.

Strong Sustainability—This definition of sustainability is fulfilled if the natural capital stock does not decline.

Suboptimal Allocation—An allocation that could be rearranged so that one or more people could be made better off while no one was made worse off. Also called an inefficient allocation.

Subsidies—Payments or tax breaks from the government that make the cost to the buyer lower than the marginal cost of production.

Substitution—Replacing one resource with another. May occur, for example, when the original resource is no longer cost-effective or is diminishing in quantity or quality.

Sulfur Allowance Auction—Run by the Chicago Board of Trade, this annual auction requires utilities to place a proportion of these allowances up for sale each year. The proceeds are returned to the utilities. (This is called a "zero revenue auction" since the government derives no revenue from it.) It ensures the continual availability of permits and provides good public information on prices.

Sulfur Allowance Program—A transferable permit program targeted at electric utilities that is designed to reduce sulfur emissions from 1980 levels by 10 million tons. Involves an auction and an emissions cap.

Surface Pollutants—Pollutants that can cause damage mainly on the earth's surface or lower atmosphere. (Examples include industrial particulates and lead.)

Surface Water—The freshwater in rivers, lakes, and reservoirs that collects and flows on the earth's surface.

Sustainability Criterion—A criterion for judging the fairness of allocations of resources among generations. Generally requires that resource use by any generation should not exceed a level that would prevent future generations from achieving a level of well-being at least as great.

Sustainable Forestry—Forestry practices that are consistent with one of the definitions of sustainability, though most commonly this term refers to compatibility with the environmental sustainability criterion.

Sustainable Yield—Harvest levels that can be maintained indefinitely; achieved by setting the annual harvest equal to the annual net growth of the population.

Synergistic—The dose-response relationship is dependent upon several interrelated factors.

System Dynamics—A computer technique developed by Professor Jay Foster and colleagues at MIT that depicts likely future outcomes of the world economy; this technique specifically incorporates positive and negative feedback loops.

"Take-Back" Principle—The belief that manufacturers of products should have the responsibility to take the packaging and the products back at the end of their useful lives in order to promote efficient packaging and recycling. (Also called expanded producer responsibility.)

Tangible Benefits—Benefits that can reasonably be assigned a monetary value.

Technological Progress—An innovation in process or technique that allows more output or services to be derived from a given set of inputs.

Theory of Demographic Transition—A theory that shows how population growth is related to the stages of industrial development.

Thermal Pollution—Pollution caused by the injection of heat into a watercourse.

Third Parties—Victims who have no contractual relationship to a pollution source. (They are neither consumers of the product produced by the source nor employed by the source.)

The 33/50 Program—A voluntary U.S. program designed to complement the Toxic Release Inventory in which participants agreed to reduce toxic emissions by 33% in 17 priority pollutants by 1992 and 50% by 1995.

Throughput—Flow of resources and energy.

Tortious Act—An action whereby one party injures another, thereby entitling the injured party to sue for compensation.

Total Cost—The sum of fixed and variable costs.

Total Fertility Rate—The number of live births an average woman has in her lifetime if, at each year of age, she experiences the average birthrate occurring in the general population of similarly aged women.

Toxicity—The degree of harm caused to living organisms as a result of exposure to the substance.

Toxic Release Inventory—A system for reporting toxic emissions releases from individual facilities in the United States. By making the data public, it was designed to warn communities of the risks they face and to encourage reductions prior to regulation.

Tradable Energy Certificates—An official record granted to producers of qualified renewable energy that can be sold separately from the power to allow the recovery of the extra costs associated with renewable power.

Transactions Costs—Costs incurred in attempting to complete transactions. (For example, in buying a home, these might include payments to the broker for arranging the sale, to the bank for one-time special fees, and to the government for the required forms. The value of the time expended in negotiating would also be a transactions cost.)

Transferability—Property rights can be exchanged among owners on a voluntary basis.

Transferable Emission Permit—A pollution control policy requiring each emitter of a pollutant to possess permits for the amount of pollution it releases. The total number of permits (and, hence, the total amount of emissions) is typically limited. Permits are transferable and may be bought or sold.

Transfer Coefficient—A coefficient used in simulating pollutant flows. It relates the degree to which pollution concentrations at a specific receptor site are increased by a one-unit increase in emissions from a specific source.

Transfer Cost—A cost to a private party that is not a cost to society as a whole, because it involves a transfer of net benefits from one component of society to another.

Troposphere—The atmosphere that is closest to the earth. Its depth ranges from about 10 miles over the equator to about five miles over the poles.

Two-Part Charge—As used in water management, this type of charge combines volume pricing with a monthly fee that doesn't vary with the amount used. The monthly fee is designed to help cover fixed costs.

Underallocation—Less-than-optimal levels of a resource are dedicated to a given use or time period.

Uniform Emission Charge—A charge on effluent that applies the same per-unit rate to all sources regardless of their size or location.

Uniformly Mixed Pollutants—For these pollutants, the damage done to the environment depends on the amount of emissions that enters the atmosphere. The location of emissions is not a matter of policy concern. (Examples include ozone-depleting gases and greenhouse gases.)

Uniform Treatment—A strategy to reduce effluent levels by a specified percentage at each emissions level.

User Cost—Opportunity cost created by scarcity. It represents the value of an opportunity forgone when the resource can no longer be used in its next-best use. (For example, for a unit of a depletable resource used now, the user cost is the net benefits that would have been received by saving it and using it during the next time period.)

Usufruct Right—Holders of this right may use a resource (normally subject to restrictions), but do not have full ownership rights.

Variable Cost—Production costs that vary with output.

Vertical Equity—Treating people with different incomes differently. Criterion requires treating the poor more favorably.

Volume Pricing—Making the cost of the service a function of the volume used. Used both in trash disposal and water distribution.

Weak Global Scarcity Hypothesis—According to this hypothesis, production is able to keep pace with population growth, but the supply curve is sufficiently steeply sloped that food prices increase faster than other prices in general; the relative price of food increases over time, and the problem is affordability rather than physical availability.

Weak Sustainability—Resource use by previous generations should not exceed a level that would prevent future generations from achieving a level of well-being as least as great. This definition of sustainability is fulfilled if the total capital stock (natural capital plus physical capital) does not decline.

Welfare Measure—A measure of development that increases or decreases in relation to how well-off society is.

Youth Effect—The increase (or decrease) of the percentage of the population composed of individuals under 15 years of age induced by a high (or low) population growth rate.

Zero Discharge—No emissions of the targeted pollutant are allowed.

Zero-Emissions Vehicle—Automobiles that directly emit no air pollutants. (Examples include vehicles powered by solar energy and fuel cells. Electric automobiles are also normally included despite the fact that producing the electricity typically results in pollution.)

Zoned Effluent Charge—A charge on effluent that applies different per-unit rates to sources depending on their location. Generally sources closer to, and upstream from, locations with more serious pollution problems face higher rates.

Name Index

Subject Index